Emotion Science

To my father
Bill Fox (1915–2004)
who would have loved this

Elaine Fox

Emotion Science

COGNITIVE AND NEUROSCIENTIFIC APPROACHES TO UNDERSTANDING HUMAN EMOTIONS

palgrave
macmillan

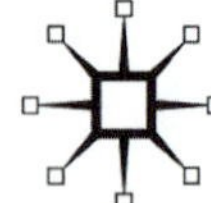

First published 2008 by
PALGRAVE MACMILLAN

Palgrave Macmillan in the UK is an imprint of Macmillan Publishers Limited, registered in England, company number 785998, of Houndmills, Basingstoke, Hampshire RG21 6XS.

Palgrave Macmillan in the US is a division of St Martin's Press LLC, 175 Fifth Avenue, New York, NY 10010.

Palgrave Macmillan is the global academic imprint of the above companies and has companies and representatives throughout the world.

Palgrave® and Macmillan® are registered trademarks in the United States, the United Kingdom, Europe and other countries.

ISBN-13: 978–0–230–00517–4 hardback
ISBN-10: 0–230–00517–9 hardback
ISBN-13: 978–0–230–00518–1 paperback
ISBN-10: 0–230–00518–7 paperback

This book is printed on paper suitable for recycling and made from fully managed and sustained forest sources. Logging, pulping and manufacturing processes are expected to conform to the environmental regulations of the country of origin.

A catalogue record for this book is available from the British Library.

Library of Congress cataloguing-in-publication data
Fox, Elaine.
Emotion Science: an integration of cognitive and neuroscientific Approaches/Elaine Fox.
p. cm.
Includes index.
ISBN 0–230–00517–9 (alk-paper)
1. Emotions. I. Title.
BF531.F69 2008
152.4—dc22 2008016411

10 9 8 7 6 5 4 3 2 1
17 16 15 14 13 12 11 10 09 08

Printed in China

CONTENTS

LIST OF FIGURES

LIST OF TABLES

LIST OF BOXES

PREFACE

Emotions are at the heart of what it means to be human. Indeed, emotions are at the heart of what it means to be alive. At a minimum, every living creature must be able to avoid danger (e.g., predators) and approach rewards (e.g., food) and it is emotions that enable these behaviours. Thus, scientists have studied emotions across a wide range of species, using many different levels of analysis from molecules and single cells, to genes, to brain circuits, to actual behaviours to feelings. When surveying this field, it is clear that scientists studying different levels of analysis often use widely different methods and it is difficult to integrate their research findings. This is apparent even in limited areas of research. To illustrate, I have been interested for several years in how a number of cognitive and neural processes relating to selective attention and memory can influence emotions. From the early days of this research, two things were immediately apparent. First, the relations among cognitive and emotional processes appear to be bi-directional. In other words, while cognitive processes do have a strong effect on emotions it is also the case that emotions have a strong effect on many aspects of cognition. Moreover, these interactions can occur at a number of different levels (e.g., feelings, facial expressions, motor actions, neural responses). Second, there are clear individual differences in the strength and persistence of emotion–cognition interactions. At the extreme, people with emotional disorders such as depression and anxiety show stronger cognitive biases and brain responses towards certain types of emotional stimuli. Thus, a depressed individual is likely to selectively remember only negative experiences and may quickly forget more happy occasions. These cognitive biases are likely to play an important role in the development and maintenance of emotional disorders. However, these biases also operate across the spectrum of anxiety and depression and have a profound effect on how people experience their everyday world, even those who do not suffer from any particular disorder. Thus, I wanted to write a book that would cover the broad span of emotion science from the highs and lows of our everyday experiences to the destructiveness of the emotional disorders. There is no doubt in my mind that the study of 'normal' emotions can be informed by the study of the emotional disorders. Likewise, studying people with anxiety and depression is likely to teach us much about our everyday experience of emotions and moods. The relative lack of books that introduce research from both the basic and the clinical science of emotions was one of my major motivations to write this book.

Another major motivating factor was the absence of a book that provided an introduction to emotion science that included the work from the burgeoning field of cognitive and affective neuroscience. I have taught undergraduate courses in Cognition and Emotion at the University of Essex for many years and always struggled to find a single book that would introduce students to the core topics of cognition and emotion, as well as providing coverage of the neural circuitry involved in emotions and emotional disorders. In recent years, there have been rapid advances in technology that allow us to investigate the human brain as it is thinking, remembering, making decisions, and even feeling. The development of functional magnetic resonance imaging (fMRI), for example, has allowed unprecedented images of the human brain in action. These developments are crucial to emotion science and are leading to exciting new developments in which the traditional methods of cognitive and social psychology are being integrated with neuroscientific and genetic techniques. There are many advanced books that cover neuroscience. However, there is a need for a book that covers the more traditional topics that occur in Cognition and Emotion, as well as the topics and methodologies being developed in neuroscience.

As I began reading for this book, I also became aware that the traditional discipline of cognition and emotion often restricted itself to a small set of research methods, with researchers ignoring large research areas such as investigations of emotional responses in animals. However, in terms of understanding how we respond to different affective situations, it seems that animal work can be very illuminating. To give just one illustration, it is clear that the development of the typical symptoms of post-traumatic stress disorder (PTSD) can be understood by studying how animals (e.g., rats) respond to severe stress. The brain circuits involved are similar across many species, including humans, and much of the scientific work on the development of treatments for emotional disorders is based on animal research. Thus, there was a further need for a book that drew upon evidence from across many disciplines and specialities.

Emotion science is a thriving scientific discipline involving scientists across a range of different areas (e.g., genetics, neuroscience, psychology, biology, psychiatry). There is a gradual acceptance that it is necessary to incorporate research from across all of these disciplines and levels of analysis in order to develop a complete understanding of human emotions, mood states and subjective feelings. I hope that this book can provide an introduction to this exciting field. I have done my best to be fair-minded in the treatment of evidence, but my own research interests and views are clearly likely to lead to some biases in interpretation. Each chapter is followed by a brief summary and I have also included recommendations for further reading at the end of each chapter. I hope that by presenting a sufficient range of evidence in each chapter along with the recommended reading there should be more than enough to allow you to develop and draw your own conclusions.

Writing this book was a significant challenge and I am grateful to many people who provided support and advice along the way. Kevin Dutton has shared most of the emotions with me and has been a constant and loving companion throughout. The initial inspiration to write this book came from many detailed discussions about the nature of emotions with George Ellis (University of Cape Town) to whom I am grateful. Jaime Marshall of Palgrave Macmillan persuaded me that writing this book was a good idea and provided help and guidance with the publication process. Much of this book was written while I was a Visiting Scientist at the MRC Cognition and Brain Sciences Unit in Cambridge, which provided a stimulating intellectual environment. In particular, I am grateful to former and current members of the CBU emotion group especially Phil Barnard, Andy Calder, Tim Dalgleish, Barney Dunn, Emily Holmes, Bundy Mackintosh, Andrew Lawrence, and Fionnuala Murphy for providing feedback and advice on many aspects of the book. I was also lucky to spend several months working with Colin MacLeod in the fantastic environs of the University of Western Australia and I am grateful for several discussions about the book with Colin, as well as Andrew Mathews, Valerie Ridgeway, and Colette Hirsh during this period. I also thank Naz Derakshan who provided much feedback and encouragement throughout the writing of the book. Several anonymous reviewers provided constructive feedback and criticism on earlier drafts of chapters. Last but not least I am grateful to my laboratory group at the University of Essex who put up with long periods of absence while I was away writing: Chris Ashwin, Stacy Eltiti, Anna Ridgewell, Denise Wallace, Kelly Garner, Helen Standage, Alan Yates and Konstantina Zoughou. Chris Ashwin in particular provided much-needed help in preparing illustrations and Caroline Henderson at Essex helped with preparing references.

ACKNOWLEDGMENTS

The authors and publishers wish to thank the following for permission to use copyright material:

American Association for the Advancement of Science for Figure 1 from T. Canli et al., 'Amygdala response to happy faces as a function of extraversion',*Science,* 296, 2191, AAAS. **American Medical Association** for one table from R.C. Kessler et al., 'Lifetime and 12-month prevalence of DSM-III-R psychiatric disorders in the US', *Archives of General Psychiatry,* 51, 8–19.

American Psychological Association for Figures 1 and 5 in P.J. Lang, 'The emotion probe: Studies of motivation and attention', *American Psychologist,* 50, 371–85 © 1995; Figure 1 from G.H. Bower, 'Mood and Memory', *American Psychologist,* 36(2) 129–48 © 1981; Figure 2 from E. Diener et al., 'Beyond the hedonic treadmill: Revising the adaptation theory of well-being', *American Psychologist,* 61, 305–14 © 2006; one table from M. Seligman et al., 'Positive psychology progress', *American Psychologist,* 60, 410–21; one table from M.E. McCullough, R.A. Emmons and J. Tang, 'The grateful disposition: A conceptual and empirical topography', *Journal of Personality and Social Psychology,* 82, 112–27 © 2002; one figure from J.A. Russell, 'A circumplex model of affect', *Journal of Personality and Social Psychology,* 39, 1161–78 © 1980; Figure 2 from G. Rogers and W. Revelle, 'Personality, mood, and the evaluation of affective and neutral word pairs', *Journal of Personality and Social Psychology,* 74, 1592–605 © 1998; Figure 1(b) from D.G. Dillon and K.S. LaBar, 'Startle modulation during conscious emotion regulation is arousal dependent', *Behavioral Neuroscience,* 119, 1118–24 © 2005; Figure 1 from T. Canli et al., 'A double dissociation between mood states and personality traits in the anterior cingulate', *Behavioral Neuroscience,* 118(5), 897–904 © 2004; one figure from Adolphs et al., 'The amygdala's role in long-term declarative memory for gist and detail', *Behavioral Neuroscience,* 115(5), 983–92 © 2001; one figure from J.P. Forgas, 'Mood and judgment: The affect infusion model', *Psychological Bulletin,* 117, 1–28 © 1995; Experiment 4 from E. Fox, R. Russo, R.J. Bowles and K. Dutton, 'Do threatening stimuli draw or hold visual attention in sub-clinical anxiety?', *Journal of Experimental Psychology: General,* 130, 681–700 © 2001; two figures from E. Fox, A. Mathews, A.J. Calder and J. Yiend, 'Anxiety and sensitivity to gaze direction in emotionally expressive faces', *Emotion,* 7(3), 478–86 © 2007; Figure 1 from J. Joormann and I.H. Gotlib, 'Selective attention to emotional faces following recovery from depression', *Journal of Abnormal Psychology,* 116, 80–5, © 2007.

Blackwell Publishing for two figures from E. Phelps, S. Ling and M. Carrasco, 'Emotion facilitates perception and boosts the perceptual benefits of attention', *Psychological Science,* 17(4), 292–9 © 2006; one figure from A.R. Hariri and D.R. Weinberger, 'Functional neuroimaging of genetic variation in serotonergic neurotransmission,' *Genes, Brain and Behavior,* 2, 341–9; two figures from J.M.G. Williams et al., *Cognitive Psychology and Emotional Disorders* © 1988.

Elsevier Limited for one figure from J. Gray, 'The psychophysiological basis of introversion-extraversion', *Behavior Research & Therapy,* 8, 249–66 © 1970; one figure from J. Panksepp, 'Emotional endophenotypes in evolutionary psychiatry', *Progress in Neuro-psychopharmacology & Biological Psychiatry,* 30, 774–84 © 2006, Figure 1 from K.C. Berridge and T.E. Robinson, 'Parsing reward', *Trends in Neurosciences,* 26(9), 507–13 © 2003; Figures 1, 2a, 2c, 4a and 4b from *Neuron,* 30(3), P. Vuilleumier, J.L. Armony, J. Driver and R.J. Dolan, 'Effects of attention and emotion on face processing in the human brain: An event-related fMRI study', 829–41 © 2001; Figure 4 from P. Vuilleumier and G. Pourtois, 'Distributed and interactive brain mechanisms during emotion face perception: Evidence from functional neuroimaging',

Neuropsychologia, 45(1), 174–94 © 2007; one figure from P. Vuilleumier et al., 'Neural response to emotional faces with and without awareness: Event-related fMRI in a parietal patient with visual extinction and spatial neglect', *Neuropsychologia* 40 (12), 2156 © 2002, Figure 1 from S. Hamann, *Trends in Cognitive Sciences,* 5, 394–400 ©2001, one figure from G.H. Bower, K.P. Monteiro and S.G. Gilligan, 'Emotional mood as a context of learning and recall', *Journal of Verbal Learning and Verbal Behavior,* 17, 573–85 © 1978; Figures 4 and 5 from M.X. Cohen, J. Young, J.M. Baek, C. Kessler and C. Ranganath, 'Individual differences in extraversion and dopamine genetics predict neural reward responses', *Cognitive Brain Research,* 25 (3), 851–61 © 2005, Figure 1 from K. Mogg, K. and B.P. Bradley, 'Time course of attentional bias for fear-relevant stimuli in spider-fearful individuals', *Behavior Research & Therapy,* 44 (9), 1241–50 © 2006, with permission from Elsevier.

Guilford Press: New York for Table 1 (p. 543) from L.J. Levine and D.A. Pizarro, 'Emotion and memory research: A grumpy overview', *Social Cognition,* 22, 530–54; Figures 1.4 and 1.5 from J.J. Gross and R.A. Thompson, 'Emotion regulation: Conceptual foundations', in J.J. Gross (ed.), *Handbook of Emotion Regulation* (pp. 3–24) © 2007.

International Universities Press for one table from A.T. Beck, *Cognitive Therapy and the Emotional Disorders* © 1979.

Institute for Personality and Ability Testing Inc. for '"The sixteen personality factors" derived by Cattell and measured on the 16-PF Questionnaire' from S.R. Conn, S. and M.L. Rieke © 1994.

John Wiley & Sons for four figures from P.J. Lang et al., 'Looking at pictures: Affective, facial, visceral, and behavioral reactions', *Psychophysiology,* 30, 261–73.

Lippincott Williams and Wilkins for two figures from M.F. Bear, B.W. Connors and M.A. Pradiso (2001) *Neuroscience: Exploring the Brain.* 2nd edn; one table from W.C. Sanderson and D.H. Barlow (1990) 'A description of patients diagnosed with DSM-III-R Generalized Anxety Disorder', *Journal of Nervous and Mental Disease,* 178, 588–91; one figure from R.J. Davidson et al., 'Alterations in brain and immune function produced by mindfulness meditation', *Psychosomatic Medicine,* 65, 564–70. American Psychosomatic Society.

MIT Press Journals for one figure from C.M. van Reekum et al., 'Individual differences in amygdala and ventomedial prefrontal cortex activity are associated with evaluation speed and psychological well-being', *Journal of Cognitive Neuroscience,* 19, 237–48 © 2007.

National Academy of Sciences, USA for Figure 3 from L. Cahill, R.J. Haier, J. Fallon, M. Akire, C. Tang, D. Keator, J. Wu and J. McGaugh, 'Amygdala activity at encoding correlated with long-term, free recall of emotional information', *Proceedings of the National Academy of Sciences,* 93, 8016–321, 1996; Figure 2 from M.T. Alkire, R.J. Haier, J.H. Fallon and L. Cahill, 'Hippocampal, but not amygdala, activity at encoding correlates with long-term, free recall of nonemotional information', *Proceedings of the National Academy of Sciences,* 95, 14506–10, 1998; Figure 4 from E.A. Kensinger and S. Corkin, 'Two routes to emotional memory: Distinct processes for valence and arousal', *Proceedings of the National Academy of Sciences,* 101, 3310–15, 2004.

Nature Publishing Group for Figures 1 and 3b from D. Grandjean et al., 'The voices of wrath: Brain responses to angry prosody in meaningless speech', *Nature Neuroscience,* 8(2), 145–6 © 2005; Figure 1a from P. Vuilleumier, 'Staring fear in the face', *Nature,* 433, 22–3 © 2005; one figure from A. Caspi and T.E. Moffitt, 'Gene-environment interactions in psychiatry: Joining forces with neuroscience', *Nature Reviews Neuroscience,* 7, 583–90 © 2006.

Oxford University Press for Table 5 from K.R. Scherer, 'Appraisal considered as a process of multi-level sequential checking', in K.R. Scherer, A. Schorr and T. Johnstone (eds), *Appraisal Processes in Emotion: Theory, Methods Research* (pp. 92–120) (2001); two figures in J. Gray, *The Neuropsychology of Anxiety: An Enquiry into the Functions of the Septo-hippocampal System* (1982); Figure 5.1 in J.A. Gray and N. McNaughton, *The Neuropsychology of Anxiety: An Enquiry into the Functions of the Septo-hippocampal System* (2000); one figure from I.B. Levitan and L.K. Kaczmarek, *The Neuron: Cell and Molecular Biology* (1997); Figure 2.1 in E.T. Rolls, *Emotion Explained* (2005); Figure 11.9 and Table 11.2 in M.M. Bradley and P.J. Lang,

'Measuring emotion: Behavior, feeling and physiology', in R. Lane and R. Nadel, *Cognitive Neuroscience of Emotion*, pp. 242–76. (2000); Figure 1 in P.A. Lewis, H.D. Critchley, P. Rothstein and R.J. Dolan, 'Neural correlates of processing valence and arousal in affective words', *Cerebral Cortex*, 17, 742–8 (2006); Figure 9.2 from P.C. Watkins, 'Gratitude and subjective well-being' in R.A. Emmons and M.E. McCullough, *The Psychology of Gratitude* (2004).

Psychology Press for one figure from E. Fox, V. Lester, R. Russo, R.J. Bowles, A. Pichler and K. Dutton, 'Facial expressions of emotion: Are angry faces detected more efficiently?', *Cognition & Emotion,* 14, 61–92; one figure from S.A. Christianson and E.F. Loftus, 'Remembering emotional events: The fate of detailed information', *Cognition & Emotion,* 5, 81–108.

Psychonomic Society Publications for data from Figure 3b of F.C. Murphy, I. Nimmo-Smith and A.D. Lawrence, 'Functional neuroanatomy of emotions: A meta-analysis', *Cognitive, Affective & Behavioral Neuroscience*, 3, 207–33 (2003); two figures from E. Fox, R. Russo and G.A. Georgiou, 'Anxiety modulates the degree of attentive resources required to process emotional faces', *Cognitive, Affective & Behavioral Neuroscience*, 5, 396–404 (2005).

Sage Publications for Figure 1 from R. Cools, A.J. Calder, A.D. Lawrence, L. Clark, E. Bullmore and T.W. Robbins, 'Individual differences in threat sensitivity predict serotonergic modulation of amygdala response to fearful faces', *Psychopharmacology,* 180(4), 670–9 © 2005; Table 5 from C.L. Rusting and R.J. Larsen, 'Personality and cognitive processing of affective information', *Personality and Social Psychology Bulletin,* 24, 200–13 © 1998; one figure from E.W. Dunn, T.D. Wilson and D.T. Gilbert, 'Location, Location, Location: The misprediction of satisfaction in housing lotteries', *Personality and Social Psychology Bulletin,* 29, 1421–32 (2003).

Taylor & Francis Group for Table 4 from C.J. Beedie, P.C. Terry and A.M. Lane, 'Distinctions between emotion and mood', *Cognition & Emotion,* 19(6), 847–78.

University of Washington for images from 'The Digital Anatomist: Interactive Atlases', © 1994–2005 University of Washington. All rights reserved. The Atlases are a project of the Structural Informatics Group, Department of Biological Structure, University of Washington and developed by Professor John Sundsten.

Every effort has been made to trace all the copyright-holders, but if any have been inadvertently overlooked the publishers will be pleased to make the necessary arrangement at the first opportunity.

1 INTRODUCTION TO EMOTION SCIENCE

What are emotions? Why do we have them? Do emotions change our thoughts and memories? Do our memories affect our emotions? Are emotions the same as feelings? Are some people more susceptible to developing emotional disorders? All of these questions are important and have been addressed by research in a variety of scientific disciplines as well as by many subjects in the humanities. *Emotion Science* reviews evidence from psychological science (especially cognitive psychology) and neurobiology in an attempt to develop a deeper understanding of emotion and, in particular, the nature of the links between processes that have traditionally been considered 'cognitive' and those that have traditionally been considered 'emotional' or 'affective'.

DIFFERENT FRAMEWORKS TO STUDY EMOTION

When we think about our lives, it is frequently the *affective* qualities of different situations that most readily come to mind. Think of some moments of joy and despair that you have experienced. Chances are that these events will seem to have an enduring quality quite different from more mundane events. What are the fundamental characteristics of emotional experiences? Imagine the situation where you are waiting to receive news of important exam results. If the results are good you might leap in the air shouting for joy. Your heart might beat faster with excitement and you might even start dancing. In contrast, if the results are not good you may feel depressed, a lump may form in your throat, and you may begin to think of all the things that you will now not be able to do. Emotional episodes like this typically contain a number of different components such as actions, thoughts, feelings, bodily changes and so on.

In the *scientific* investigation of emotions, different research traditions have tended to focus on different components of emotion. However, it is important to remember that most of the components that make up an emotion are almost always present. In terms of our everyday understanding of emotions, many people would argue that *feelings* are the most important and salient aspects of emotions. It is how things *feel* that influences our thoughts and memories and determines our enjoyment (or otherwise) of different situations. Some research traditions reflect this commonsense view and emphasize the role of feelings or subjective experience as a crucial part of emotion science. Other research traditions, however, argue that, while feelings are important, they may not be central to the understanding of emotions. Instead, these traditions consider that a range of physiological, neural and behavioural responses to a specific stimulus are more fundamental and often take place before feelings develop. This perspective suggests that an analysis of feelings is not likely to tell us very much about the core emotional responses that may occur before we experience any feelings.

A recurring problem in emotion science is that different research traditions often focus on different aspects of emotions and therefore tend to ask very different questions. Moreover, the different research traditions differ with respect to how they define emotion, and how they conceptualize the temporal and causal relationships among the various emotional components. On top of this, different traditions use quite different techniques and research methodologies in their investigations. In this book I attempt to examine emotion science by drawing on research from a range of different traditions. The primary focus, however, is on research from a number of disciplines within psychological science (especially cognitive psychology, social psychology and clinical psychology) and neuroscience (especially cognitive neuroscience and affective neuroscience). These approaches, and why they are important for understanding emotions, will be considered in detail. First some broad frameworks that have been influential in the scientific study of emotions are presented.

Emotions are biologically given

Many researchers in emotion science assume that emotions have evolved as a result of biological evolution. This perspective proposes that emotions or *affect programs* were selected by nature because they provided good solutions to ancient and recurring problems that faced our ancestors (e.g., Ekman, 1992a; Öhman and Birbaumer, 1993; Tomkins, 1984; Tooby and Cosmides, 1990). An evolutionary perspective inevitably leads to questions about the *functions* of the processes under investigation as well as consideration of some of the broader problems facing our species. If our ancestors were to successfully pass their genes on to the next generation, they had to overcome a series of critical ecological problems. At the very least, the following achievements were essential:

(a) The ability to find adequate food, drink and shelter.
(b) The ability to get access to sexual partners.
(c) The ability to provide adequate protection and nurturing for offspring.
(d) The ability to avoid danger.
(e) The ability to escape from life-threatening events.

If we think about these situations in a bit more detail, it becomes clear that all of these problems are structured to a large extent by emotions (Tooby and Cosmides, 1990, 2000).

This biological perspective assumes that emotions are best understood as solutions selected by nature to make us want to do what our ancestors had to do in order to pass their genes on to the next generation. It is important to note that this perspective shifts the emphasis in emotion science from an examination of human feelings to the range of action tendencies and response patterns that we share with many other species (Öhman and Birbaumer, 1993). Emotions are viewed as complex responses to a meaningful event (e.g., presence of a mate or a predator). Furthermore, these complex responses contain a number of different components (behavioural, physiological etc) that can often act independently of each other. The degree of coupling or coherence between the different components is an important issue. While the evidence on this is somewhat mixed (e.g., Feldman Barrett, 2006a; Mauss et al., 2005), many biological theories assume that tight coherence helps to ensure that emotions are able to serve particular functions (e.g., Scherer, 2001). Because emotions involve many different action tendencies (e.g., rapid escape) they often require extensive metabolic support from bodily mechanisms that relate to arousal processes. For instance, when rapid escape is required the body releases large quantities of the hormone *adrenaline* (also know as *epinephrine*), which provides the individual with a significant boost in energy and physical ability. Thus, emotions are viewed as *embodied* processes that will generally have physiological as well as cognitive and behavioural implications for the organism.

Many theories of emotion are predicated on the idea that emotions and affective experiences are biologically given. Investigators do not necessarily believe that emotions are hard-wired into our brain in an inflexible way. Instead, most researchers assume that a core set of primary emotional systems are given to us by nature, but that these systems can be modified by learning and their expression can be shaped by culture (e.g., Ekman, 1999). A fundamental assumption, however, is that emotions are seen as genetically coded systems of response that can be triggered by objects or situations that are relevant in a biological or evolutionary sense. Evidence for this perspective comes from animal research showing that certain stimuli do seem to elicit emotions in a fairly automatic way. Thus, rats do not have to learn to fear cats. They will respond to the odour of a cat with a classic fear response even when they have been raised under laboratory conditions and have had no prior exposure to cats (Panksepp, 1998). Similarly, young monkeys will learn to fear snakes after just one experience of seeing an adult display fear of a snake. However, watching an adult demonstrate the same fear display to a bunch of flowers does not result in a learned fear response (Mineka et al., 1984). This classic experiment demonstrates that this is a *selective* learning process, with fear responses being learned much more easily for biologically relevant stimuli (snakes) than for less relevant stimuli (flowers). Further evidence for an evolutionary approach comes from the fact that the most common fears and phobias that occur in people relate to spiders, open spaces, sudden loud noises, snakes etc. These stimuli generally do not represent frequently encountered dangers in most contemporary societies. Nevertheless, phobias for these types of situations occur far more frequently than for guns, knives or electrical sockets which almost certainly represent a more probable danger for most of us.

These results taken together suggest that evolution has provided us with a variety of fairly automatic responses to stimuli that were either dangerous or advantageous to our ancestors. These same stimuli are considered to remain to this day as important antecedents to our emotional responses (e.g., Öhman, 1986; Öhman and Mineka, 2001). Further evidence consistent with a biological approach is that a core set of emotions – *anger*, *fear*, *happiness*, *sadness*, *disgust* – appear to be associated with specific facial expressions that are recognized across cultures (Ekman, 1992a). We do not need to speak someone's language to know when that person is feeling angry. Moreover, across many different species, including humans, the behavioural and facial

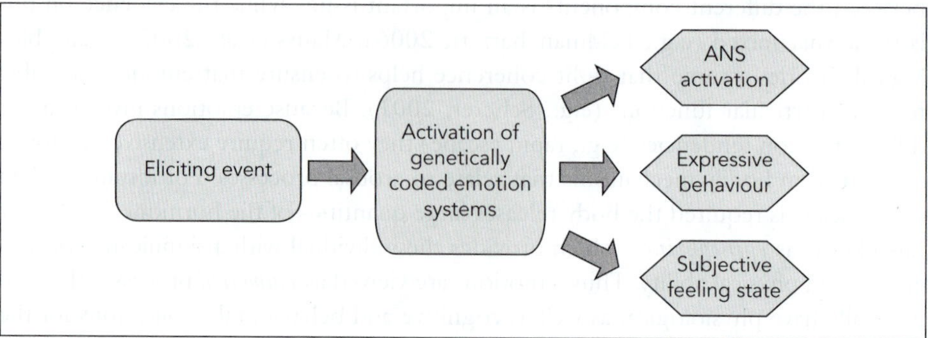

FIGURE 1.1 A schematic overview of the evolutionary view of emotion

displays indicating that something is disgusting or pleasant appear to be very similar (Berridge, 1999).

The biological approach assumes that emotional systems have evolved to help an organism to navigate the complexities of the physical and social world. The *function* of emotions in this view is to facilitate the rapid coordination of the body's various processes including motor systems, energy levels, physiological reactions and cognitive processes. Thus, if an animal detects the presence of a predator it might stop what it is doing and scan the environment for signs of threat, as well as work out potential escape routes. At the same time, the body might mobilize resources to provide sufficient energy for rapid escape, while shutting down irrelevant physiological processes such as digestion. The emotion of fear in this example serves to *interrupt* ongoing processes to allow a fast shift of attention towards potential danger. Individuals who can rapidly notice and respond to potential dangers or opportunities are far more likely to survive and pass on their genes compared with individuals who miss these significant events. In this perspective, therefore, emotions are viewed as adaptations to significant problems, especially problems that were common for our ancestors. In other words, emotions allow a range of different processes to be coordinated in order to solve an immediate and urgent problem (Cosmides and Tooby, 2000). A schematic diagram of the evolutionary perspective is shown in Figure 1.1.

Emotions are socially constructed

A very different approach suggests that emotions are not biological entities at all, but rather are socially constructed narratives that give shape and meaning to our social world. The idea here is that emotions are the products of a particular culture and they are produced by that culture in order to help define its values and assist members of a society to negotiate particular social roles (e.g., Averill, 1985; Harré, 1986; Kitayama and Markus, 1994; Mesquita, 2003; Mesquita et al., 1997; Wierzbicka, 1994). Much like languages, this perspective assumes that emotions are learned behaviours that can only be acquired if people are exposed to them within a particular culture. Culturally-based theories of emotion have traditionally been heavily influenced by the disciplines of sociology and especially anthropology. For example, in one anthropological study of how different cultures can be interpreted it was argued that both ideas and emotions are 'cultural artefacts' in human societies (Geertz, 1973). The suggestion is that different cultures will value emotions in different ways, and these different value systems will, in turn, play an important role in how people experience emotions. A clear prediction of these models, therefore, is that different cultures will experience emotions to different degrees. Rather than there being a set of universal emotions, there will be a set of different emotions that are determined by cultural values rather than by biological imperatives. This view is supported by the discovery that different emotions are expressed in different languages in quite different ways (Wierzbicka, 1994).

Research examining emotional expression among Japanese and American samples illustrates this framework (Kitayama et al., 2000; Markus and Kitayama, 1991). How individuals interpret or construe their main goals in life is heavily determined by their culture. In particular, two kinds of self-construal that differ across different cultures have been identified: the *independent self* and the *interdependent self* (Markus and Kitayama, 1991; Triandis, 1989). The 'independent self' is essentially a form of individualism in which independence from others is valued and the self-concept is seen as being unique and stable across different situations. Moreover, the assumption is that behaviour is caused by *internal* factors such as personal motivations. In contrast, the 'interdependent self' is identified where more collectivist notions are valued. The assumption here is that the concept of self is derived primarily by means of connections to other people. Thus, one's identity and status is determined by connections within important groups (family, society etc) rather than by individual endeavour. This view places great value on fulfilling one's social roles and duties, and considers that behaviour is caused by *external* factors such as the social context. An interesting outcome of this form of self-construal is that identity is not seen as stable, but rather can vary across different contexts (Markus and Kitayama, 1991). The independent or individualist self is widespread across Northern Europe and Northern America, while the interdependent self is more common in much of Asia, Africa, Mediterranean Europe and South America.

Kitayama et al. (2000) set out to test the hypothesis that these differences in how the self is construed would result in different emotions being prevalent in different cultures. Groups of Japanese and North American adults were asked to rate how often they experienced a range of different emotions. These results were analyzed by breaking all the emotions down into the general dimensions of pleasant–unpleasant and engaged–disengaged. Consistent with their concern for maintaining harmony and balance the Japanese reported a much greater frequency of interpersonally engaged emotions, both positive or negative. In contrast, the Americans reported a much higher frequency of positive emotions – consistent with their concern for a positive self-esteem (the pursuit of happiness etc). A particularly interesting finding within this study was that the experience of positive and negative emotions *was* negatively correlated in the American sample. This means that if people experienced more positive emotions (e.g., joy) they were *less* likely to experience negative emotions (e.g., sadness) and vice versa. This is consistent with the cultural view prevalent in many Western societies that positive emotions should be emphasized and that negative emotions should be minimized. In contrast, the experience of positive and negative emotions was positively correlated in the Japanese sample, indicating that people tended to experience the same amount of positive and negative feelings. This is consistent with the cultural view, important in Japan, that maintaining balance and harmony is more important than experiencing pleasant feelings.

Kitayama et al.'s (2000) results also reflect cultural differences in determining how an individual might learn to cope with his or her environment. In North America, people are expected to cope with difficult situations by imposing their will and trying to change the environment to make it better. In marked contrast, in Japan, people are expected to cope with difficult situations by fitting in and adjusting to the situation rather than trying to change it (Weisz et al., 1984). These deeply ingrained cultural norms mean that different emotions may be valued in very different ways across different cultures. Anger, for example, is often acceptable in Western societies because it indicates that people are asserting their will over a perceived slight. However, in many Asian societies, the expression of anger is frowned upon because it indicates social disharmony and suggests that the person is not conforming to the social rule of maintaining balance and fitting in with the social group.

A further prediction of a cultural approach to emotions is that some emotions may be unique to particular cultures. A number of such emotions have been identified. One example is the emotion of *amae*, which is considered to be a basic emotion in Japan. There is no precise word in English for *amae* but it refers to the pleasant feeling that arises from a sense of togetherness, especially when this emerges from complete dependence on another person. It is the emotion that is experienced when people feel that they are completely accepted by either another person or a social group. *Amae* is clearly an emotion that fits with the cultural imperative in Japan of fitting in with others and living in harmony. People in Western countries can easily understand the notion of *amae* even though they do not have a specific word for it and probably do not experience it. The cultural perspective argues that Westerners do not experience this emotion because it is not consistent with their cultural imperative of asserting independence and autonomy.

Another emotion that appears to be unique and probably not as easy to understand in different cultures is the 'state of being a wild pig' that is experienced in the Gururumba people of New Guinea. This emotion is common among men between the ages of about 25 and 35 years. Men experiencing this emotion tend to run wild, often attacking people at random and stealing items from friends and strangers alike. This 'state of being a wild pig' is tolerated in Gururumban society and men in the grip of this emotion are given a lot of leeway in terms of their financial and social responsibilities (Evans, 2001; Newman, 1964). This is very handy, of course, since this is precisely the age at which men will have considerable marital and financial responsibilities! Thus, the emotion of 'being a wild pig' can greatly help young men to cope with their increasing social responsibilities. This is consistent with the cultural view that emotions serve the function of allowing people to cope efficiently with the demands of their social roles within a given culture (Averill, 1985). A schematic diagram of the social constructionist perspective is shown in Figure 1.2.

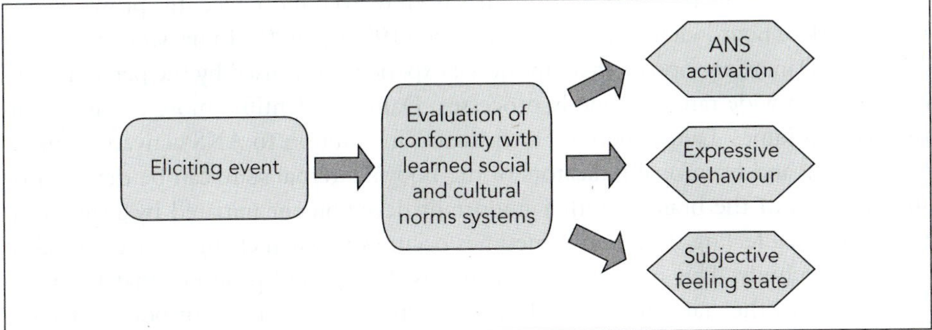

FIGURE 1.2 Schematic overview of the social constructionist or cultural view of emotion

Emotions are the result of perception of bodily changes

In addition to the broad evolutionary and culturally-based frameworks within which emotions have been investigated, there are two main empirical approaches to the scientific investigation of emotions. The first makes the assumption that emotions arise because of our perceptions of bodily states. In commonsense terms, we might think that we first experience an emotion (e.g., fear) and then we experience a range of bodily changes (e.g., heart beating more rapidly, sweating palms etc). However, William James, who was one of the pioneers of scientific psychology in the United States, argued for the directly opposite view. He proposed that once we noticed a particular object (a bear in the woods was his favourite example) a variety of physiological changes took place (e.g. activation of the brain's autonomic system), and it was the perception of these bodily changes that was the emotion (James, 1884). A Danish physiologist, Carl Lange, also independently arrived at the same conclusion around the same time (Lange, 1885), so it is often called the *James–Lange theory of emotions.* A famous implication of this view, as proposed by James, is that you do not run because you are afraid, rather you are afraid because you run! This ordering of events is shown schematically in Figure 1.3.

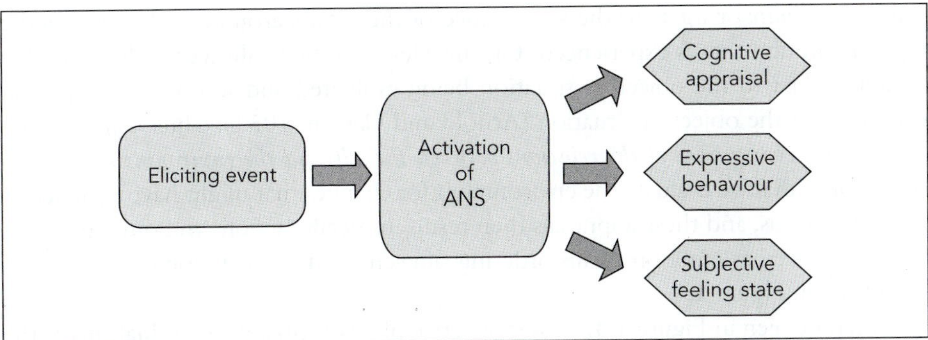

FIGURE 1.3 Schematic overview of the 'emotions as perceptions of bodily changes' view

The James–Lange theory of emotion has been revived more recently, primarily due to the work of neuroscientist Antonio Damasio (1994b, 1999). In his *somatic-marker hypothesis,* Damasio proposes that emotional experience is caused by the perception of changes in a wide range of bodily processes. Damasio identifies more changes than the original James–Lange theory. For instance, in addition to ANS activation, many biochemical and hormonal indicators of the body's internal state can be detected by specific parts of the brain. Another important development initiated by Damasio is that emotional feeling states can sometimes occur even when changes have not taken place in the body. This has been called the 'as-if loop' and proposes that the brain can enter into the state that it would have been in had a variety of bodily changes actually taken place. Just as we can have a visual experience of a bright red balloon by imagining this event in the absence of the actual object, Damasio argues that we can experience a feeling state in the absence of the actual bodily changes. Another difference between Damasio's theory and the original James–Lange view is that the brain can detect changes in internal bodily state that are not necessarily made available to conscious awareness. This means that emotions are not necessarily conscious, which is quite different from the view of James who equated *emotions* with conscious *feeling states.* In summary then, one empirical tradition in the scientific study of emotion is the view that our emotions are essentially caused by a perception of changes in our internal bodily states (see Figure 1.3).

Emotions are the result of cognitive appraisals

Another common tradition in the scientific study of emotion is the assumption that a cognitive appraisal of the significance of an object is a precursor to an emotional response. This is a very ancient philosophical view, as reviewed by Lyons (1999). For example, the Greek philosopher Aristotle wrote around 330 BC that feelings were caused by our beliefs about the world and our relations to the people around us. Thus, he considered that anger was an 'impulse' that resulted from the evaluation that either you or your friends had been insulted in some way. Contemporary models based on the idea that emotions are elicited by an evaluation of the meaning or significance of events began in the 1950s and 1960s with the work of Magda Arnold and others (Arnold, 1960; Arnold and Gasson, 1954). The central idea is that the way we *evaluate* or *appraise* the significance of the events around us determines the type of emotion that is experienced. On this view, emotions always involve a double reference; first to the object or situation being evaluated and second to the person experiencing the object or situation (Arnold and Gasson, 1954). Thus, *cognitive appraisals are evaluations of the relations between the self and the environment.* The assumption is that we evaluate the environment for changes that might have a particular relevance for us, and these appraisals then result in specific actions and outcomes that are experienced as emotions. This ordering of events in the elicitation of emotions is illustrated in Figure 1.4.

As can be seen in Figure 1.4, this perspective places appraisals or evaluations at the very heart of the emotional response. Cognitive appraisal models were developed to

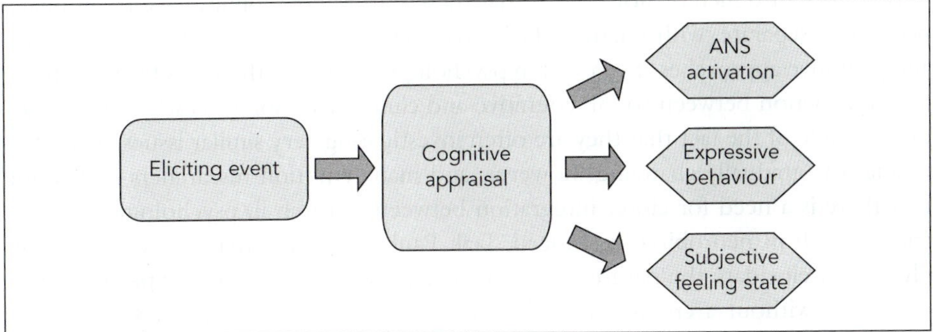

FIGURE 1.4 Schematic overview of the 'emotions as the result of cognitive appraisals' view

better understand how one emotion could be differentiated from another. For example, it has often been observed that different people can experience quite different emotions in response to the same eliciting event. This fact is not well explained by strict evolutionary-based accounts of emotion. While the evolutionary approach assumes that emotions are related to biological adaptations in our distant ancestral past, cognitive appraisal models link emotions to the more immediate processes of evaluation of meaning and the assessment of coping capabilities (e.g., Lazarus, 1966). Thus, if a person's actions are interpreted as being insulting to you the emotion of anger will be elicited, whereas if the person's actions are interpreted as being threatening then the emotion of fear will be experienced. Thus, appraisal-based models can provide an explanation as to why the same situation can lead to different emotions in different people and at different times. From this perspective, it is not the situation itself that produces an emotion, but rather it is how that situation is *evaluated* in reference to current goals that produces an emotion.

NEUROSCIENCE AND COGNITIVE APPROACHES

The focus of this book is on the scientific investigation of emotions by means of *cognitive* and *neuroscientific* approaches. There are good scientific grounds to argue that cognitive psychology and cognitive neuroscience have the potential to deepen our understanding of emotions. The notion that cognition is important for emotions and the idea that emotions are implemented in some way in the brain are both very ancient ideas. Recent years have seen startling advances in our understanding of the neuroanatomy and the neural circuitry underlying emotions as well as in the development of techniques to elucidate the nature of emotion–cognition interactions. The neurobiology of emotions has traditionally been conducted with animals (e.g., rodents) but the relatively recent improvements in brain imaging technologies have led to an explosion of research with human participants. In parallel streams of research, cognitive, social and clinical psychologists have developed a range of behavioural tasks to uncover many of the ways in which cognitive processes can modulate affective responses and vice versa. Thus, the time seems ripe to forge closer links between cognitive and neuroscientific approaches to emotion science.

A consistent difficulty, however, is that these research disciplines have traditionally been quite separate, with relatively little cross-referencing between the neuroscience and cognitive approaches. Even within psychological science, there has been relatively little interaction between social, cognitive and clinical psychologists who study emotion, in spite of the fact that they are often investigating very similar issues. This state of affairs is gradually changing, however, and many emotion researchers now argue that there is a need for closer integration between research in psychological science and research in neurobiology. Indeed, Jaak Panksepp warns that, 'psychology simply cannot elucidate the nature of primal affective processes (or other primary brain processes) without a credible neural analysis' (Panksepp, 1992, p. 558). Likewise, neuroscience is unlikely to get very far without addressing the range of psychological processes involved in our mental lives. A more explicit integration of neural and psychological approaches to emotion is likely to lead to a fuller and deeper understanding of how emotions influence cognitive processes and, in turn, how cognition influences emotional processes. Historically, cognition and emotion have frequently been considered as separate entities. Contemporary research, however, suggests that the two concepts are actually closely intertwined and interdependent at both neural and psychological levels. Even the basic anatomy of the brain itself suggests a close interdependence between *cognitive* and *emotional* or *affective* processes.

Is there an emotion centre in the brain?

Historically, it has been assumed that the brain contained a region or centre that was dedicated to emotion. This is illustrated in Paul MacLean's (1973) theory in which he argued that emotions are implemented in a range of mid-brain areas called the *limbic system* (see Box 1.1 for details). The notion of a limbic system that controls emotional responsiveness is attractive and plausible. However, on the basis of subsequent evidence it seems that this idea is incorrect (LeDoux, 1987). For example, extensive neurobiological research has now shown that no single region of the brain seems to be dedicated to emotion. Rather, the evidence suggests that different brain circuits control different aspects of emotion processing. Thus, the idea that *emotions* are limbic and subcortical while *cognitions* are cortical is far too simplistic. Indeed, Richard Davidson (2003) has identified this notion as one of the seven 'sins' of emotion science (see Table 11.1 (p. 349) for a sneak preview of the other six sins). More subtle and sophisticated models are now being developed which suggest that the brain circuits underlying emotion and cognition overlap to a considerable extent. As pointed out in the introduction to the *Handbook of Affective Sciences*:

> It is simply not possible to identify regions of the brain devoted exclusively to affect or exclusively to cognition. This fact should dispel claims about their independence and help to foster a more nuanced appreciation of the ways in which affect and cognition interact. (Davidson et al., 2003, p. 5)

While there is no *emotion centre* in the brain, there are particular regions of the brain that do seem to play a particularly important role in emotions. However, it is of interest to note that researchers who study emotions in animals and researchers who study emotions in humans and other primates identify different areas of the brain as being important. Emotion research with non-primate animals such as rats has generally focused on the behavioural and physiological reactions (e.g., freezing or fleeing from danger) that occur in response to emotion-inducing stimuli, and this research tends to concentrate on *subcortical* structures (i.e., those lying underneath the cortex in mid-brain regions) (e.g., Gray, 1987; LeDoux, 1996; Panksepp, 1998). In contrast, investigators who study emotions in humans and other primates tend to emphasize *cortical* areas (e.g., Damasio, 1994b; Davidson et al., 1999; Rolls, 1999). In an excellent overview, Kent Berridge (2003) acknowledges this distinction. The *human–cortical* and *animal–subcortical* view of emotions is probably a 'sin' (Davidson, 2003), which has arisen from methodological differences between different research traditions, and it does tend to exaggerate the perceived difference between humans and other animals.

An extensive survey of the literature indicates that there are actually surprisingly few qualitative differences between primates (including humans) and non-primate animals in terms of the brain structures involved in emotions (Berridge, 2003). Nevertheless, there clearly are some differences and it is important not to assume that the implementation of emotions is identical across different species. In terms of the human brain a key difference from other species is the relative expansion of the neocortex relative to other brain areas. The physical expansion of the human neocortex and forebrain has been called *encephalization* (Jerison, 1977) and means that there are clear quantitative differences in the anatomy of the human brain when compared to other mammals (Berridge, 2003). In particular, the relative amount of information processing given over to the neocortex in humans is very large and this relative explosion of *cognition* during evolution is likely to have had a profound influence on emotional processing in the human brain. In particular, many psychologists have pointed out that cognitive elaboration plays an important role in human emotion, leading to a rich emotional life laden with symbolism and culture (e.g., Ellsworth, 1994a). In addition to this, human emotion is influenced to a large extent by the development of language, which enables us to elaborate emotions both to ourselves and to others. This involvement of symbolism and language in emotion processing implicates a range of cortical structures and is likely to strengthen the links between cortical and subcortical areas in humans to a much greater extent than in other animals. Thus, while the processing of emotion has clearly not 'moved' from subcortical to cortical regions of the brain in humans, it is possible that the 'centre of gravity' of emotion processing may have shifted slightly upward (Berridge, 2003). In other words, while the core processes of emotion remain grounded in subcortical structures, it is likely that *feelings* in humans may have spread upwards into cortical regions.

Empirical evidence hinting at the possibility of a subtle reorganization of the neural basis of emotions in humans comes from the fact that damage to the cortex is far more disruptive to emotional processing in humans than in rats. For example, the entire neocortex of a rat can be removed without any apparent changes to normal emotional responses (Panksepp et al., 1994). In marked contrast, however, damage to

BOX 1.1

The triune brain theory

In 1937, the neurologist James Papez wrote a classic paper entitled 'A proposed mechanism for emotion'. This speculative paper was one of the earliest attempts to consider how emotion might be implemented in the brain. Papez argued that sensory information from both the external world and inside the body would enter the brain through the various *sensory systems* and would reach the *thalamus*, which is a bit like the brain's sensory relay station. From the thalamus, information was then split into three main pathways: one to the *striatal* region (movement), one to the *neocortex* (thoughts), and one to the *limbic system* (feelings).

This analysis inspired Paul MacLean to develop a more comprehensive theory suggesting that the human brain consists of three distinct systems, each of which developed during a distinct phase of evolution. According to MacLean, the *striatal* region of the brain is the most basic part of the forebrain and became enlarged with the evolution of reptiles. It is involved with a range of basic survival behaviours such as defending a territory, hunting, foraging for food, forming social groups, grooming, mating, flocking and migrating, and was called the *reptilian brain*. As mammals gradually began to diverge from reptiles in the course of evolution, the next layer of brain developed, which MacLean called the *paleomammalian* brain or what has become more widely known as the *limbic system*.

The main difference between mammals and reptiles, according to MacLean, is that mammals are much more social creatures who are generally born in a fairly helpless state and require maternal care to develop. Thus, the more sophisticated aspects of social functioning, such as maternal care, were controlled by structures within the limbic system. This system in particular enabled the development of a range of emotions which were important for cohesive social development.

The final major phase in the evolution of the human brain was the development of the *neocortex*, which MacLean argued was distinctive to higher mammals.

the neocortex in humans generally results in profound deficits in emotional processing (e.g., Damasio, 1994b). Thus, while a range of distributed brain regions are undoubtedly involved in emotional processing in all non-primate and primate (including humans) animals, the *relative* importance of cortical regions is probably greater in humans.

Some basic neuroanatomy

While there are no brain regions that are *unique* to emotion there are areas of the brain that are crucial for normal emotions to develop. The assumption underlying much neuroscience research is that if the parts of the brain that are involved in the generation and maintenance of emotion are identified, then it will be easier to investigate generalities across different species as well as addressing questions about what goes wrong in emotional disorders. Throughout this book we will come across many

The frontal lobes of the neocortex, or just *cortex*, takes up about 80% of the human brain, and represents the greatest increase in size relative to other brain areas during evolution. The cortex is the part of the brain that accommodates many 'higher' functions such as the development of language, more sophisticated problem solving and reasoning etc. In addition, many scientists assume that the cortex plays a role in inhibiting the behaviours controlled by the *limbic* and *reptilian* regions. MacLean's stages of the evolution of the human brain are shown in Figure 1.5. It is important to note that each brain area is assumed to have developed from the lower brain area and so there are rich interconnections between each of these regions.

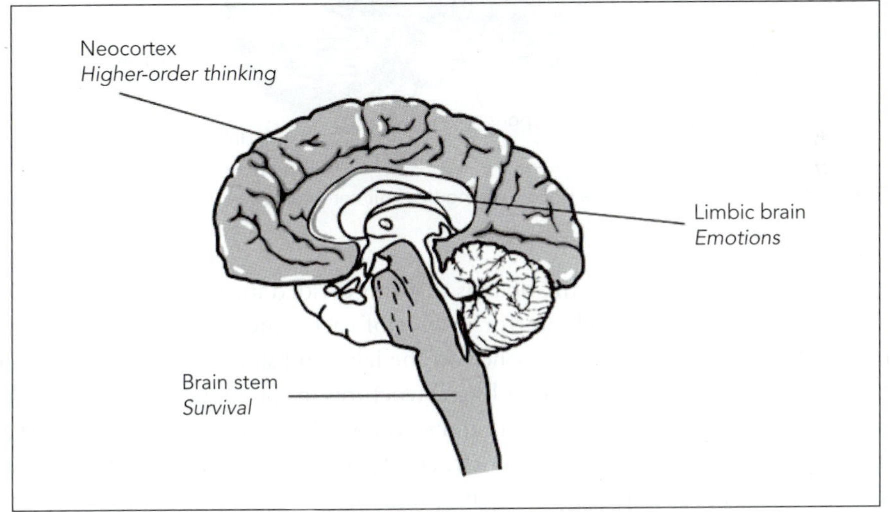

FIGURE 1.5 Maclean's stages of the evolution of the human brain

different brain areas, some with complicated Latin names. It is important, therefore, to have some basic understanding of the overall structure of the brain and where the different brain regions are situated. The human brain can be divided from top to bottom into three broad regions:

1 the cerebrum
2 the mid-brain region
3 the brain stem.

This division more or less follows from the structure outlined by MacLean (1990). The cerebrum consists of the *neocortex,* which is seen as the crumpled folds of tissue on the outside of the brain and is particularly well developed in humans compared with other species. The cerebrum is divided into four lobes, the frontal, temporal, parietal and occipital as shown in Figure 1.6.

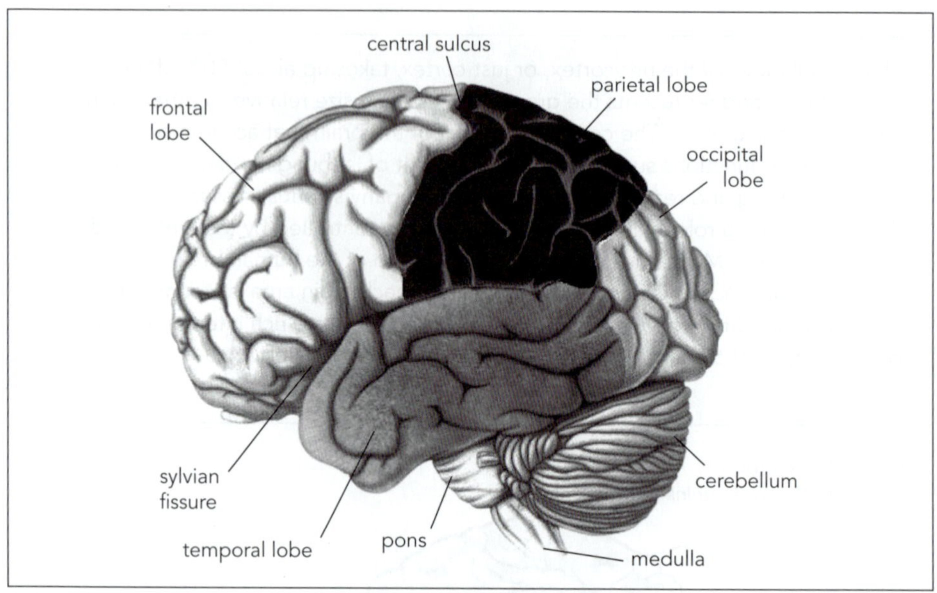

FIGURE 1.6 Schematic view of the brain showing the four cerebral lobes
Source: Adapted from Bear et al. (2001).

Another obvious feature of the brain is that it is divided into two hemispheres, left and right, which are essentially mirror images of each other. Thus, all of the many structures in the brain occur twice, once on the left-hand side and once on the right-hand side. While we often talk about brain structures in the singular, e.g., *the* frontal cortex, *the* hippocampus, *the* amygdala and so on we should remember that there are actually two frontal *cortices*, right and left, and two *amygdalae*, right and left. In addition to dividing the brain into two hemispheres we also need some way of agreeing on particular locations within these hemispheres. Neuroanatomy – the study of the structure of the brain and spinal cord – has developed a number of terms which will help us to understand what part of the brain we are dealing with. Figure 1.7 shows a diagram of the left hemisphere of a human brain with the area where the face would be towards the left and the back of the head towards the right. Technically, the direction pointing towards the front is called *anterior* or *rostral* or *frontal*, whereas the direction pointing towards the back of the head is called *posterior* or *caudal* (see Figure 1.7). As well as the front–back direction we can also think of the brain in terms of the up–down direction. The upper direction (towards the sky) of each brain area is called *dorsal*, while the lower direction (towards the ground) is called *ventral*.

The brain is also traditionally divided into what are called *lateral* and *medial* views. Imagine that the brain is cut straight down through the middle, right between the eyes and the middle of the nose from top to bottom. Figure 1.8 shows the view we would now see if we are looking directly at this mid-point. This is known as a *medial* view, because it is close to the *mid-line* of the brain between the two hemispheres. On the other hand, Figure 1.7 shows the *lateral* view of the left hemisphere, i.e. that part which is far away from the middle of the brain. Thus, a medial view of a structure

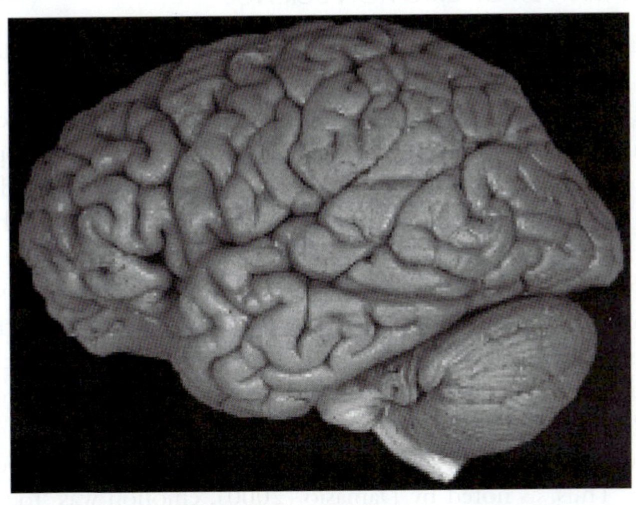

FIGURE 1.7 A lateral view of the left hemisphere of the human brain
The front (anterior) of the brain is towards the left and the back (posterior) is towards the right of the picture.

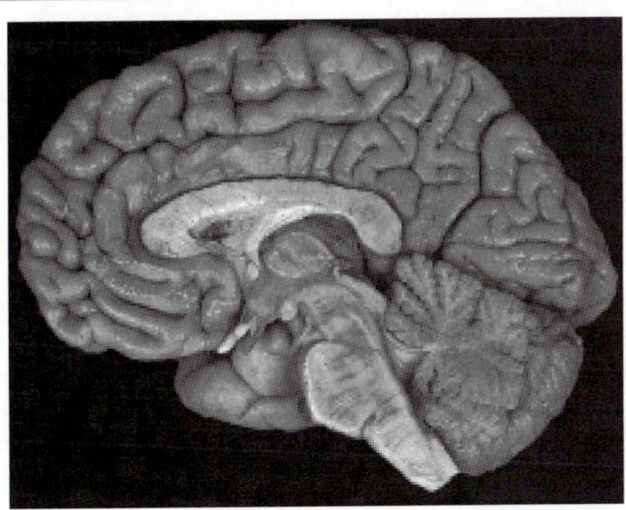

FIGURE 1.8 A medial view of the human brain
The front (anterior) of the brain is towards the left and the back (posterior) is towards the right of the picture.

is close to the mid-line, whereas a lateral view is further away from the mid-line. It is worth spending some time learning these different terms because they will help you to understand much of the terminology that will be used throughout this book. Good introductions to the structure of the central nervous system can be found in many introductory neuroscience textbooks. Particularly excellent discussions and graphic illustrations can be found in Posner and Raichle (1995) and Bear et al. (2001).

THE SUBJECT MATTER OF EMOTION SCIENCE

Affective processes and emotions are fundamentally important in our lives. Affective processes are important in regulating our relationships and social interactions, they are important in helping us to communicate effectively with one another, and almost certainly are important in maintaining good health and in the development of disease (Davidson, Scherer and Goldsmith, 2003; henceforth referenced as Davidson et al., 2003). The study of emotion has had a long history in both philosophy and psychology. However, for a number of reasons emotion research has taken a back seat in scientific research until recently. In psychology, for example, the study of emotion was suppressed during the behaviourist era, primarily because of the absence of objective ways in which to measure emotions and their associated feelings without resort to introspection. In addition to this, an historic trend deriving from the Greek philosopher Plato (375 BC) tended to set emotions or 'passions' against reason, and assumed that emotions were in some way inferior to cognition and impeded thinking and reasoning. Thus, as noted by Damasio (2000), emotion was 'too subjective; it was too elusive and vague; it was too much at the opposite end of the finest human ability, reason' (p. 12).

The relative neglect of emotion is changing and the study of emotion has become something of a 'hot topic' in both psychology and the burgeoning field of cognitive neuroscience (e.g., Lane and Nadel, 2000; LeDoux, 1996; Niedenthal and Kitayama, 1994). Moreover, a new multidisciplinary field of *affective neuroscience* has been defined (Davidson and Sutton, 1995; Davidson et al., 2003; Panksepp, 1998). Also, the American Psychological Association introduced a new scientific journal called *Emotion* in 2000 to provide an outlet for the increasing number of scientific studies in emotion science. An emerging theme in much contemporary work in emotion science relates to the nature of emotion–cognition interactions. It has been shown that many fundamental cognitive operations such as selective attention, memory, and decision-making are susceptible to the influence of emotions. Thus, *emotions influence cognitions.* Conversely, biases in cognitive processes can themselves have profound and long lasting effects on emotional responses. Thus, *cognitions influence emotions.* These bi-directional influences have led to suggestions that dynamic systems approaches are required in order to understand the nature of emotion–cognition interactions (e.g., Lewis, 2005).

DEFINING AFFECT: EMOTIONS, MOODS AND FEELINGS

While there is no general agreement about how emotions should be defined, it is proposed here that useful distinctions can be made between *emotions*, *feelings*, *moods* and *affect*. *Emotions* are often considered to be discrete and consistent responses to an internal or an external event which has a particular *significance* for the organism. Thus, *sensing significance* or *evaluating* an object or situation is a key component of emotions. Emotions are also rather brief in duration and consist of a coordinated set of responses to a significant event. These responses may be verbal, physiological, behavioural and neural. *Feelings* are probably best understood as the subjective representation of emotions. In other words, while emotions are public affairs, the feelings associated with these emotions are private to the individual experiencing them. *Moods* refer to a more diffuse affective state that generally lasts for a much longer duration than emotions and are usually less intense. The term *affect* is probably best reserved for the entire topic of emotions, feelings and moods together, even though it is often used interchangeably with *emotion*. Table 1.1 outlines the six major affective phenomena that are incorporated within the developing discipline of *Affective Science* (Davidson et al., 2003).

This book will deal with many of the components that make up affective science (especially emotions, moods, affective style and temperament) and will examine how these affective processes influence and are influenced by cognitive processes (especially attention, memory and decision making). One difficulty is that emotions and moods may be studied at many different levels. Thus, some investigators focus on the neural mechanisms that are correlated with particular mood states, and they may further focus on the actions of specific small groups or neurons or on the actions of larger brain circuits. Other researchers may focus on cognitive processes that correlate with particular mood states as assessed by behavioural tasks, while still others may concentrate on how people say they feel in different situations. Neural response, behavioural and motor outputs and subjective feelings are all important aspects of affect. Much of the research discussed in this book comes from investigations of a single level of analysis. However, it is important to remember that at some stage we should step back and examine affect at multiple levels of analysis (Teasdale and Barnard, 1993). An important focus for research is to address the question of how different levels relate to each other and this is especially important in facilitating the integration of cognitive and neuroscience research (Lewis, 2005).

TABLE 1.1 Phenomena included under the rubric of 'affective science' as outlined by Davidson et al. (2003)

Affective phenomena	*Definition*
Emotion	A relatively brief episode of coordinated brain, autonomic and behavioural changes that facilitate a response to an external or internal event of significance for the organism
Feelings	The subjective representation of emotions
Mood	A diffuse affective state that is often of lower intensity than emotion, but considerably longer in duration
Attitudes	Relatively enduring, affectively coloured beliefs, preferences and predispositions toward objects or persons
Affective style	Refers to relatively stable dispositions that bias an individual toward perceiving and responding to people and objects with a particular emotional quality, emotional dimension or mood
Temperament	Affective styles that are apparent early in life, and thus may be determined by genetic factors

AFFECT–COGNITION INTERACTIONS

Cognition refers to a person's mental processes and assumes that the mind has internal mental states (e.g., beliefs, desires, intentions) which can be understood in terms of information processing. A cognitive process is generally assumed to have taken place when information coming in through the senses is transformed in some way. In a classic text outlining the field of cognitive psychology, cognition was defined as 'all processes by which the sensory input is transformed, reduced, elaborated, stored, recovered and used' (Neisser, 1967). The scientific strategy used in cognitive psychology has been to break down cognition into many component parts, such as perception, attention, memory, decision-making and problem solving, in addition to language. In considering how affect might influence cognition, it might also be useful to break down each construct into its component parts and ask how emotions, moods and feelings might influence specific cognitive components (e.g., attention, decision-making).

The focus of this book will be the examination of how emotions, moods and feelings influence cognitive processes and how cognitive processes influence emotions, moods and feelings. A particular aim is to consider how these affect–cognition interactions are implemented at a neural level. Affect and cognition are interdependent processes that interact with each other in a highly dynamic way. Our memories of the past; our decisions and plans for the future; what we attend to on a moment to moment basis; what we think about as we day-dream; all of these cognitive operations are coloured by emotions and moods, just as emotions and moods are themselves influenced by cognitive processes. The logic is that in order to gain a more complete understanding of the richness of our mental life we need to more fully understand the role of affect and the general 'sensing of significance', and how these processes interact with the traditionally defined 'cognitive' processes.

Oatley and Johnson-Laird (1987) made this explicit in their 'cognitive theory of emotions' when they suggested that a primary function of certain *basic* emotions is to coordinate a complex cognitive system. They point out that the world we inhabit is fairly unpredictable and therefore a complex cognitive system needs to be highly flexible in order to adapt to a dynamic environment. A primary function of emotions on this view is to reorganize the cognitive system in a way that facilitates the priorities of a given emotion. In other words, one of the consequences of experiencing an emotion is a reordering of processing priorities so that goals that are relevant to the specific emotion become more salient (Simon, 1967). For example, a student may be studying in a library with the intention of spending a least two hours working on a class assignment. The primary goal in this case is to complete the class assignment in a relatively short period of time. However, if the fire alarm goes off after 20 minutes, a new goal of survival needs to be prioritized and the sensible action is to defer the current goal, stop working, and leave the library as soon as possible. The activation of the emotion of fear essentially achieves this aim by reordering the priorities of different goals.

How emotions and moods influence cognition will be discussed throughout this book. On the other hand, it is also clear that cognitive processes themselves can and do influence our emotions as well as our ongoing moods. Thus, how we think can have a profound influence on how we feel. In a very real sense, how we process information can determine our general happiness and sense of well-being. A positive outlook and ability to 'see the best' of a difficult situation is often an important determinant of happiness. Conversely, a tendency to look upon the negative side of life can result in a downward negative spiral. Individual variations in fundamental biases in processing positive and negative information have even been implicated in the development of serious affective disorders such as anxiety and depression (e.g., Williams et al., 1988).

CONTROVERSIES IN EMOTION SCIENCE

Emotion science incorporates a vast range of research across different disciplines all using very different definitions and very different techniques. For example, a researcher studying the fear system in rats might surgically implant an electrode deep inside the brain of the rat and then measure the activity of neurons in this area when the animal notices a predator. Other studies might present humans with fear-related images (e.g., photographs of threatening scenes) and measure the degree of changes occurring in their brains by means of a brain scanner. Some studies require people to evaluate complex stimuli such as pictures or stories and then assess how their feelings change by means of a questionnaire. Others might study people with clinical anxiety disorders and investigate the effectiveness of drugs known to modify levels of particular brain chemicals in alleviating feelings of fearfulness. Obviously, all of these research strategies are telling us something about the emotion of fear, and all are important in their own right. However, it comes as no great surprise to find that the types of questions addressed by different researchers might be very different and, more importantly, the conclusions reached about the nature of fear might also be very different. Thus, a real challenge in emotion science is to somehow integrate the many facts we know about emotion from across these many different disciplines and research strategies.

This book attempts to integrate research from different paradigms while at the same time addressing each issue in a reasonable degree of detail. In particular, the aim is to try and bring together neuroscientific and cognitive research on affect. This approach should help to distil knowledge accruing from a wide range of research disciplines and facilitate the understanding of emotions and moods from the actions of a single cell to the most complex of our subjective affective experiences. Indeed, it is argued in this book that much of what might seem like inconsistencies and confusion in emotion science may be due to different researchers using the same terminology to study quite different phenomena. By being careful to define what different terms refer to (e.g., affect, emotions, feelings, moods) and by acknowledging that affect can be studied at many different levels (e.g., neuronal groups, neurochemicals, physiological responses, subjective experience) we hopefully will come closer to an understanding of the nature of emotions and the role they play in our lives.

PLAN OF THIS BOOK

The aim of this book is to provide an overview of the scientific study of emotions and moods. Research from a variety of perspectives will be considered, and, while greater emphasis will be given to studies on humans, studies on other animals will also be discussed. Chapter 2 will flesh out what is meant by the terms *emotions, moods* and *feelings*, and will point out that much of the apparent confusion in emotion science may well be due to these terms being used interchangeably in different studies. This chapter also provides a brief historical overview and considers a range of research methodologies that are used in emotion science. Chapter 3 addresses the research literature on temperament and personality. These are enduring personal structures and processes that have a profound impact on the affective aspects of our lives. A number of influential theories relating to how people (and animals) differ in *temperament* are presented. The primary focus of this chapter concerns variations of *emotional reactivity* in a number of response systems (physiological, neural, cognitive) in both stressful and positive situations. Recent work in this area, for example, indicates that genetic variations may play an important role in how responsive people are to a variety of positive and negative stimuli. While there is abundant evidence examining the *production* and *perception* of different emotions in different situations and how this relates to individual differences in appraisal and biological make-up, less attention has been paid to how emotions are *regulated*. However, it is clear that the regulation of emotions is of fundamental importance to our ability to detect emotions in others, and to the intensity of the emotions that we might experience. Emotion regulation and research on how these processes may differ among individuals is also discussed in Chapter 3.

Chapters 4 and 5 address a fundamental disagreement between different research traditions in terms of the *nature* or the *structure* of affect. One tradition assumes that at least some emotions are given to us by nature, and represent what might be called 'natural kinds' (Panksepp, 2000). This view that there is a core set of discrete emotions – fear, anger, happiness, sadness, disgust – that have fairly separate neural structures and physiological response patterns is discussed in Chapter 4. A contrasting *dimensional approach* proposes that emotions are better understood as representing variations along two broad dimensions of experience, such as valence (good versus bad) and activation (active versus passive). Research in this tradition has tended to concentrate on the subjective experience of emotional *feelings* in humans and is discussed in Chapter 5.

Chapter 6 reviews research addressing the nature of the relations between affect and cognition. Following an overview of some historical landmarks in the history of affective science, empirical evidence investigating how affect may influence some fundamental mechanisms of perception and attention is addressed. The large literature demonstrating how affect can influence how we make judgments and decisions about everyday objects and events is also discussed. Chapter 7 goes on to overview the large body of work investigating the role of affect in memory. For example, are emotional events better remembered than non-emotional events? If so, does affect play a role during the *encoding* of information, during the *consolidation* of information in memory, or at the point of *retrieval*? The role of current mood state in influencing memory is also reviewed in this chapter. Chapter 8 directly addresses the question of how people react differently to affective information. In particular, individual differences in genetic make-up, neuroanatomy and function, and cognitive biases are examined in relation to differences in how people respond to both negative and positive life events. Chapter 9 asks what factors might render some people more vulnerable to the development of emotional disorders. Much of the research in emotion science has focused on the development of emotional *disorders*, which is understandable given the high personal and financial costs associated with clinical anxiety and depression. However, many people go through what seem like horrendous trauma and yet emerge apparently unscathed. It is important to ask what it is that makes some people better able to withstand stress and hardship than others. This *resilience* in the face of adversity is discussed in Chapter 10 and the determinants of human *happiness* and *well-being* are also considered. Finally, Chapter 11 provides a theoretical overview of emotion science and identifies important research priorities in order to facilitate progress in our understanding of emotions, emotional disorders and emotional well-being. To anticipate, the conclusion is drawn that many of the controversies in emotion science are due to investigators examining different aspects or levels of affect (e.g., subjective experience versus cognitive operation versus neural activation) and then developing theories that are claimed to explain all levels. The case is put for a *multi-level* approach that allows for the integration of neurobiological, cognitive and subjective levels of affect (Lewis, 2005; Teasdale and Barnard, 1993).

Emotion Science aims to provide a clear introduction to the scientific study of emotion, with a particular emphasis on integrating research in the cognitive psychology of emotion with research on emotion from a neuroscientific perspective. These approaches complement each other and together should give us a deeper understanding of emotions and affective life. The primary aims of this book are:

- To provide an overview of scientific research on emotions, moods and feelings from a range of disciplines within psychology and neuroscience.
- To highlight some of the main theoretical issues and questions that should be addressed in order for progress to be made in our understanding of affect.
- To address the question of why some people are more or less vulnerable to the development of emotional problems and why some people are happier than others.
- To attempt to integrate research and theory from neurobiological and psychological perspectives.

This is a tall order and it is hoped that, at the very least, this book will give you something of a flavour of the excitement of contemporary research in emotion science.

RECOMMENDED READING

Charles Darwin's (1872/1998) *The Expression of Emotions in Man and Animals* provides an interesting introduction to Darwin's thoughts and experiments on emotion with a contemporary commentary by Paul Ekman. New York: Oxford University Press (3rd edn).

Excellent introductions to neuroscientific approaches to emotions with a personal perspective are provided by:

Joseph LeDoux (1996) *The Emotional Brain: The Mysterious Underpinnings of Emotional Life.* New York: Simon & Schuster.

Jaak Panksepp (1998) *Affective Neuroscience: The Foundations of Human and Animal Emotions.* New York: Oxford University Press.

Edmund T. Rolls (2005) *Emotions Explained.* Oxford: Oxford University Press.

Highly readable and more general introductions to emotions are provided by:

Paula M. Niedenthal, Silvia Krauth-Gruber and Francois Ric (2006) *Psychology of Emotion: Interpersonal, Experiential, and Cognitive Approaches.* Hove: Psychology Press.

Keith Oatley, Dacher Keltner and Jennifer M. Jenkins (2006) *Understanding Emotions.* Malden, MA: Blackwell Publishing (2nd edn).

There are a number of comprehensive edited books containing chapters by many different experts in emotion science:

Richard J. Davidson, Klaus R. Scherer and H. Hill Goldsmith (2003) *Handbook of Affective Sciences.* New York: Oxford University Press.

James J. Gross. (2007) *Handbook of Emotion Regulation.* New York: Guilford Press.

Richard D. Lane and Lynn Nadel (2000) *Cognitive Neuroscience of Emotion.* New York: Oxford University Press.

Michael Lewis and Jeannette M. Haviland-Jones (2000) *Handbook of Emotions.* New York: Guilford Press (2nd edn).

2 THE NATURE AND MEASUREMENT OF EMOTIONS, MOODS AND FEELINGS

There is little doubt that emotions, moods and feelings play a central role in our lives. Consider the overwhelming joy of a parent upon seeing his infant take her first step; the ongoing sadness we feel when one of our parents dies; the intense fear we might feel when approached by a large growling dog. Emotions, moods and their associated feelings are constant companions to our everyday life. This chapter presents a brief history of scientific research on *affect* in order to determine what is generally meant by the terms *emotions*, *feelings* and *moods*. A particular aim is to describe the various methods that have been used to measure the different aspects of affect. Since the success of any scientific endeavour can stand or fall on the quality of the measurement techniques available it is important to evaluate those that emotion scientists commonly use.

DEFINING EMOTIONS AND MOODS

Emotion

There is no general agreement in emotion science on how emotion should be defined. However, many theorists agree that each emotion consists of a number of different components – subjective report, physiological response, cognitive appraisal and so on. It is generally assumed that each component fulfils a specific *function* in coping with the situation that has triggered the emotion. An important question concerns whether *cognitive appraisals* should be considered as *causes* of emotions (which is implied by most appraisal-based models – Arnold, 1960; Lazarus, 1966), or whether they should be thought of as *components* of emotion. The *component process model* (Scherer, 1979, 1984, 2001) proposes that appraisals are important components of emotion and that emotions are only experienced when several different subsystems are coordinated in order to produce *an adaptive reaction to an event that is appraised as significant for the person's well-being*. The component process model breaks down emotions in terms of their *functions* and identifies the main 'organismic subsystems' that have evolved to achieve these functions. The key point is that the *components* of an emotion episode are the particular states of the five subsystems at any given point in time. The *process* refers to the coordinated changes that take place over time, hence the name *component process* model. From this perspective, an emotion is considered to be an 'episode of interrelated, synchronized changes in the states of all or most of the five organismic subsystems in response to the evaluation of an external or internal stimulus event as relevant to major concerns of the organism' (Scherer, 2005, p. 697). In other words, all components including the appraisal of the situation are considered

TABLE 2.1 The relationship between the components of emotion and the organismic subsystems and functions of emotion

Emotion component	*Organismic subsystem*	*Emotion function*
Cognitive component (appraisal)	Information processing	Evaluation of events and objects
Neurophysiological component (bodily symptoms)	Support	System regulation
Motivational component (action tendencies)	Executive	Preparation and direction of action
Motor expression component (facial and vocal expression)	Action	Communication of reaction and behavioural intention
Subjective feeling component (emotional experience)	Monitor	Monitoring of internal state and organism–environment interaction

Source: Adapted from Scherer (2001).

to be an integral part of the emotion episode. The five components and their respective subsystems are outlined in Table 2.1.

Three of the components of emotion outlined in Table 2.1 – bodily symptoms, behavioural expression and subjective experience – have long been considered to be crucial elements of emotion. The induction of *action-tendencies* has also been widely assumed to be related to emotional arousal (e.g., flight–fight tendencies) as well as being important in differentiating among different emotions (e.g., Frijda, 1986). Scherer (2005) acknowledges that the inclusion of the cognitive component is controversial, since some theorists make the assumption that emotion and cognition are separate but interacting systems. For example, Izard (1977) has argued that a distinction should be made between an *emotion* and an *emotion schema*. On this view, 'emotion' refers to a coordinated response to an environmental event and does not require any prior appraisal. In contrast, 'emotion schema' refers to a mental representation that integrates these emotional responses with complex cognitive appraisals. Izard suggests that researchers' tendency not to distinguish between emotions and emotion schemas has resulted in much confusion in emotion science (Izard, 1977; 2007).

The component process view argues that all five components – cognitive, bodily symptoms, action tendencies, expression and feelings – probably operate independently of each other most of the time. The special nature of emotion, from this perspective, requires that all of these systems become coordinated and synchronized for a short period of time, and that this synchronization is driven by appraisal processes (Scherer, 2005). For example, someone might wonder whether the new person he has just met might be a potential romantic partner. Is the cab driver's speeding putting my life in danger? Is it safe to take an ecstasy pill offered at a party? Emotions can therefore be seen as reactions to events and situations that seem to be important to our welfare (Ekman, 2004). It is commonly assumed that emotions begin very quickly and that we are usually not aware of the processes in our mind that trigger them. While there is still some controversy regarding the extent of cognitive appraisal required to elicit an emotion there is fairly general agreement that emotions prepare us to deal with significant events (either good or bad) without having to think too much about them (e.g., LeDoux, 1996; Öhman, 2000).

Emotions can be understood then as coordinated reactions to a number of different objects and situations which are often called *emotionally competent stimuli*. An important question, of course, concerns what constitutes an 'emotionally competent stimulus'? Is any stimulus that is appraised as significant in some way emotionally competent? Or are some stimuli more likely to be always appraised as significant because of their biological or social significance? One possibility is that the stimuli that elicit emotions can be broken down into the broad categories of *rewards* and *punishers* (e.g., Rolls, 1999, 2005). A *reward* is anything for which an animal (or human) will work, while a *punisher* is anything that an animal or human will work to escape or avoid. Thus, emotions can be defined as 'states elicited by rewards and punishers, that is, by instrumental reinforcers' (Rolls, 2005, p. 11). Take happiness as an example. Imagine that you receive a prize for writing the best essay in your class. This reward produces a state of pleasure or happiness. In contrast, a punisher such as failing an examination might produce a state of fear and apprehension. The reduction of emotionally competent stimuli to rewards and punishments is an elegant way of describing the induction of emotions. However, this reduction does seem to lose something of the complexity of the stimuli and the appraisals that can elicit specific emotions.

Some investigators have suggested that emotions are best understood as *action tendencies* which prepare the organism to *act* in some ways rather than others (e.g., Frijda, 1986). From an evolutionary perspective, emotions are the means by which nature regulates behaviour in relation to the agendas set by the demands of biological evolution (Tooby and Cosmides, 1990). From a cultural or social constructionist perspective emotions are the means by which our relationships with others in a group or society are regulated (Mesquita, 2003). Whatever perspective one takes, it is clear that emotions have important biological, psychological and social functions. Ray Dolan (2002) has suggested that, as psychological experiences, emotions have three unique qualities:

1 Unlike most psychological states, emotions are *embodied* and manifest in clearly recognizable and stereotyped, behavioural patterns of facial expression, comportment and autonomic arousal.
2 They are less susceptible to our *intentions* than other psychological states.
3 They are less *encapsulated* than other psychological states, as evident in their global effects. When we are sad, the whole world looks grey, we find it difficult to concentrate and we become highly selective in what we can remember.

MOOD

In psychiatry, the word 'mood' is used to denote states of happiness and sadness and their extremes (mania and depression). In everyday usage, however, the term 'mood' is often used to cover a much wider range of feelings. For example, we might describe a 'moody' person as one who experiences a range of emotions in fairly unpredictable ways. Morris defines mood in a broad way as being a cue to the person about the resources available to meet environmental demands (Morris, 1989, 1992). Lazarus (1991) presents a similar notion in suggesting that 'moods are concerned with larger, longer lasting, existential issues about the person's life and how it is going ... moods are transcendentally important ... in how we judge our adaptational status' (p. 49). Thus, in a general sense moods are seen as appraisals of our general well-being.

Prinz (2004) has also argued that mood reflects one's general position in life, which can explain why some situations can elicit very strong emotions without necessarily inducing moods. Take road rage as an example. Being cut up on the highway can produce intense anger and aggression but does not tend to lead to ongoing mood changes since being cut up on a motorway is not typically construed as evidence that one is not faring well in life (Prinz, 2004). In contrast, losing one's job marks a potential reduction in financial security and therefore is likely to induce an intense emotion as well as an enduring mood state. Prinz concludes that the functions of moods and emotions are different: moods are set up to detect global changes in organism–environment relations, while emotions are set up to detect more localized changes.

Damasio (1999) defines moods as 'states of emotion' that tend to become frequent or even continuous over long periods of time. Since moods are essentially emotions that are dragged out over time, according to this view, the collections of responses that characterize emotions (bodily changes, feelings etc) are also experienced over longer durations. The assumption that moods are a subset of emotions is also reflected by Prinz (2004) who argues that moods are a special case of emotion and do not represent an independent category. It is clear that, in order to arrive at a definition of mood, most researchers have contrasted moods with emotions. Therefore, let us have a closer look at the distinctions that have been made between these two terms.

DISTINGUISHING MOODS AND EMOTIONS

As shown in Table 2.2, emotions are considered to be of short duration, to occur in response to sudden specific events, to be relatively intense with accompanying physiological arousal and to tend to bias actions. This fits with the notion that a major function of emotions is to facilitate adaptation to important events. In contrast, moods are seen as more enduring and less intense affective states. They have a more diffuse physiological arousal and tend to bias cognitions rather than actions. Moreover moods may actually be induced by emotions. This pattern fits with the possible function of moods as signals of how we are doing in life in a general way. We should note at this point that there is not universal agreement on these distinctions and good discussions are available in, for example, Ekman and Davidson, 1994, pp. 51–96; Ketter et al., 2003).

Emotions are often elicited by specific events that can occur very suddenly, whereas moods tend to occur in response to events that are more general and develop over time (Davidson, 1994b). Thus, the weather can often induce different mood states

TABLE 2.2 Distinctions between emotions and moods

Distinctions	*Emotions*	*Moods*
Duration	Seconds to minutes	Hours to days
Function	Biasing actions	Biasing cognitions
Nature of antecedent event	Sudden events Specific events Object focused	General non-specific events Emotions Diffuse
Relative intensity	High	Low
Autonomic arousal	Acute Perhaps specific	Variable Diffuse
Neural substrates	Predominance of subcortical activation (?) Rapid neurochemical changes	Predominance of cortical activation (?) Long lasting neurochemical changes

(e.g., Schwarz and Clore, 1983), but is unlikely to induce specific emotions (unless of course there are violent storms or tornados!). In general, it seems that the coordinated reactions we call emotions are related to specific objects, whereas moods lack such an obvious focus (Clore et al., 1994; Frijda, 1994c; Morris, 1989). If one is experiencing the *emotion* of happiness, for example, one is probably happy about a very specific event such as being offered a new job. However, if one is experiencing a happy *mood*, one is not happy about anything in particular, but rather happy in a more general way. In evaluating the literature on the neurobiology of emotion, Edmund Rolls (2005) has come to a very similar conclusion. He distinguishes moods and emotions as follows:

> An emotion consists of cognitive processing that results in a decoded signal that an environmental event (or remembered event) is reinforcing, together with the mood state produced as a result. If the mood state is produced in the absence of the external sensory input and the cognitive decoding … then this is described only as a mood state, and is different from an emotion in that there is no object in the environment towards which the mood state is directed. (Rolls, 2005, p. 13)

On this view, a mood is normally elicited by a reinforcer (just like an emotion) but does not involve the decoding of a stimulus in terms of whether it is a reward or a punisher. Thus, a mood is considered to be an emotion without the cognitive appraisal of the reinforcing properties of a given stimulus. It is therefore easy to see why mood states are not necessarily associated with an object, while emotions are always related to a specific object. In agreement with this, Jerome Kagan has argued that emotions refer to a 'temporary change in psychological and biological processes to particular classes of incentives', while mood refers to 'a salient, enduring emotional quality displayed in a variety of situations' (Kagan, 1994, p. 74). For this reason, emotions tend to be tied to particular situations whereas moods can transcend contexts.

Davidson (1994b) captures a widely accepted view when he suggests that moods are always present in that they provide the emotional colour or background to our everyday life. An interesting implication of this is that, if moods are continually present, then our cognitive processes will always be biased or modulated to some extent. Perhaps moods can be thought of as the *affective background* while emotions can be seen as perturbations or disruptions that are superimposed upon this background (Davidson, 1994b). In general, then, it seems that an *emotion* is best regarded as a reaction to a particular situation or object that can be quite intense, and represents a temporary coordination of various components. In contrast, *mood* can be seen as a generally less intense experience that lasts for a longer time than an emotion, and is often more general or non-specific (e.g., Ekman, 1992a; Ellis and Moore, 1999; Forgas, 1995).

Beedie et al. (2005) have developed the distinction further and pointed out that moods and emotions are likely to differ from each other according to more than one criterion. For example, a difference between moods and emotions at a physiological level will almost certainly result in differences in phenomenal experience, which in turn are likely to lead to differences in the expressions, behaviours and linguistic descriptions linked with the two states. They propose that *folk psychology* (or common sense) theories of mood and emotion might offer the potential for further study of both constructs. Folk theories are based on 'the assumptions, hypotheses and beliefs of ordinary people about behaviour and mental experience' (Colman, 2001, p. 283). Emotion researchers have emphasized the value of folk theories for scientific enquiry (e.g., Lazarus, 1999; Levenson, 1994). For example, Lazarus (1999) argues that, as long as hypotheses are formulated appropriately, folk theories can be evaluated by controlled observation – which is the hallmark of science – as readily as any other theory. Beedie et al. (2005) adopted such an approach by asking 106 people from many different walks of life what they believed to be the difference between an emotion and

TABLE 2.3 A summary of the distinctions between emotions and moods

Criterion	*Emotion*	*Mood*
Anatomy	Related to the heart	Related to the mind
Awareness of cause	Individual is aware	Individual may not be aware
Cause	Specific event	Cause less well defined
Clarity	Clear	Nebulous
Consequences	Behavioural and expressive	Cognitive
Control	Uncontrollable	Controllable
Display	Displayed	Not displayed
Duration	Brief	Enduring
Experience	Felt	Thought
Intensity	High	Low
Intentionality	Related to specific object	Objectless
Physiology	Distinct responses	No distinct responses
Stability	Fleeting and volatile	Stable
Timing	Rises and dissipates rapidly	Rises and dissipates slowly

Source: Adapted from Beedie et al. (2005).

a mood. The resulting responses were analyzed by means of standardized qualitative procedures. In addition, they conducted a content analysis of 65 articles published in the scientific literature, all of which included criteria to distinguish moods and emotions. The eight key themes that emerged were: intensity, duration, physiology, cause, awareness of cause, consequences, function and intentionality. Interestingly, all of these criteria also emerged in the answers given by the respondents in the study. A summary of these results is presented in Table 2.3.

Beedie et al.'s study has provided a fascinating insight into the distinctions people make in everyday life between moods and emotions. The authors are careful, however, to point out the potential limitations of this kind of qualitative analysis. For example, if people represent emotional reality accurately then it makes sense to use these representations when trying to understand the underlying phenomena. However, if it turns out that people's representations are distorted in some way then a reliance on self-report measures means that we are 'in danger of developing theories based on emotional ideology instead of emotional reality' (Parkinson, 1995, p. 347). This brings us to the important question of how we can adequately *measure* the various components of emotions and moods.

THE MEASUREMENT OF AFFECT

There are clearly a number of components involved in both emotions and mood states. It comes as no surprise, then, that a wide range of measurement instruments is available. Some of these focus on subjective self-report (how someone feels), others focus on physiological and behavioural indicators, while others provide direct measures of brain activity. Another issue concerns how emotions and moods can be elicited under laboratory conditions. If we look carefully at specific studies, we will see that it is sometimes unclear whether a mood state or an emotion is being investigated, and it is likely that a mixture of moods and emotions might be activated in many of these studies. To illustrate, moods are often induced by asking people to recall a traumatic (or exciting) event that happened to them. In other studies, they are given lists of negative or positive statements to read. For example, a common method used is a *mood induction procedure* developed by Velten (1968). This technique requires a person to read a list of either sad (e.g., 'I am less successful than other people') or happy (e.g., 'I can feel a smile on my face') self-statements. Subjective report generally indicates that positive and negative moods can be reliably induced by these methods. However, it is not always clear whether it is a mood or an emotion that is being induced. If we give someone a long list of negative statements (e.g., I am a failure; the world is a bad place etc), for example, we might just as easily induce the emotion of sadness as the mood of sadness.

Inducing emotions might be somewhat easier in animals. For example, the smell of a cat seems to induce an instant fear response in rats (Panksepp, 1998). Thus, cat odour is presumably a strong emotionally competent stimulus for rats. Emotionally competent stimuli, such as angry facial expressions, are often used to induce emotions in humans. More cognitive tasks (e.g., remember a traumatic event) are also widely used, but these may be less effective in eliciting genuine emotions over and above changes in mood state. A further complication relates to the fact that the neurophysiological bases of moods and emotions are likely to be shared. This is particularly the case if moods are a subset of emotions as many investigators have argued (e.g., Damasio, 1999; Izard, 1977; Prinz, 2004; Rolls, 2005). Coan and Allen (2007) provide an excellent overview of how affective responses can be elicited and measured under laboratory conditions. The following sections provide a brief overview of the more common techniques used to measure emotions, moods and feelings.

MEASURING EMOTIONS

An obvious feature of an emotion is that it is accompanied by a *subjective experience*, or what we would normally call a *feeling*. We can generally tell somebody else how it *feels* to be angry, sad, in love and so on. Many theorists argue that such conscious states can only be reported from a first-person point of view. In other words, no matter how many other components or correlates of emotion we measure, we cannot replace the direct report of the person experiencing the feeling (e.g., Feldman Barrett, Mesquita et al., 2007). Nevertheless, many emotion scientists argue that emotions cannot be described completely by relying solely on subjective report. While it is important to know how somebody feels and the range of emotions they experience, the problem is that emotions also involve a host of physiological changes (e.g., your heart might beat faster if you are feeling afraid etc) as well as behavioural changes (e.g., a smoker might smoke more when feeling anxious), and we may not always be aware of these changes. Thus, relying on a purely subjective account of what it feels like to be fearful, or angry, or happy can be highly informative but is likely to fall short of giving us an understanding of the complexity of emotions.

Many investigators assume that emotions evolved from rather simple reflexive actions, and that many of these action tendencies and their physiological correlates are still part of the human response repertoire (e.g., Frijda, 1986). Obtaining a measure of these behavioural and physiological outputs can therefore provide an alternative window into the processes and mechanisms involved in emotions. To illustrate, the primitive response of moving towards positive things and moving away from negative things is the basis for all behaviour (Schneirla, 1959). When confronted by the species appropriate stimuli of *appetite* or *aversion*, insects, birds, fishes, reptiles, and mammals all show similar stimulus-driven *approach* and *avoidance* behaviour. Thus, measures of simple approach and avoidance behaviour can be easily designed and are likely to be informative in terms of investigating emotions. In complex organisms, including humans, however, the development of extensive neural mechanisms allows for a greater variety and complexity of responses. It is clear that humans can do more than approach or avoid and this greater flexibility facilitates adaptation to a range of different environments. Many behavioural, physiological, neural and subjective responses have been utilized to measure these more complex aspects of the different components of emotion.

Measurement of the behavioural correlates of emotion

A range of useful behavioural responses are shared by most living organisms. For example, the behaviours associated with aggressive attack and defence (e.g., increasing apparent size, biting, kicking etc) are highly developed survival tools that vary only in detail across a range of species. For humans, some of the more obvious behaviours associated with emotions are facial expressions. Think of the wide grin a person might have when finding out that he has passed an important exam, or the drooping lips and downcast aspect of a sad face when someone finds out that she has not got the job she really wanted. Other behaviours include screaming when afraid, or shouting loudly when angry. A problem for researchers is that people are, of course, able to suppress many of these behavioural indicators of emotion. Someone may feel very sad and depressed, but nevertheless may make a big effort to appear happy to others by smiling and joking. Thus, relying only on the observation of behaviours as indicators of emotion can be problematic. In addition, there are varying cultural rules about which emotions it is acceptable to express. For example, in Japan it is not socially acceptable to display anger or aggression. Thus, when studying emotion on the basis of behavioural responses we need to be careful that we are aware of possible cultural differences in expression. What we observe on the outside may not always accurately reflect the emotion being experienced on the inside.

Observational techniques are also used in both animal and human research. By observing children or animals in naturalistic environments, for example, a number of different behavioural responses (e.g., fear displays) can be examined in relation to the presence of particular stimuli. Many animal species exhibit a range of behaviours that indicate emotional states, especially distress. For instance, newborn rats emit ultrasonic vocalizations if they fall out of their nest, and these calls lead the mother to retrieve the infant instantly. Rodents are also highly sensitive to odours, which can often act as strong signals of danger eliciting specific behaviours which might be interpreted as *fear* responses. A common behavioural measure in animal studies is the amount of locomotion engaged in. For example, introducing cat fur into a rat's cage can have a dramatic effect on the rats' behaviour. Even when rats have had no experience with cats, the percentage of time spent in exploring their environment decreases by almost 100% when a cat smell is introduced (Panksepp, 1998).

Mice have also been shown to avoid mice who have received strong electric shocks more than non-stressed mice by smell alone, indicating that there is likely to be a chemical alarm signal to which the mice are reacting (Carr et al., 1970). Field work has also found that one species of small African monkeys, called vervets, has developed an extensive range of alarm calls, each of which seems to indicate a different type of predator. For example, one alarm call relates to aerial predators such as eagles, another to ground predators such as snakes, and one relates specifically to leopards. When these calls are taped and played back to the monkeys in the wild they react to the different vocal signals as if the appropriate predator was actually present. In response to the call indicating the presence of eagles they might look up into the sky and attempt to take cover, whereas in response to the 'snake' alarm call they might look frantically around the grass and perhaps run up a tree (Seyfarth et al., 1980a).

Charles Darwin was one of the first scientists to explicitly link behavioural expressions of emotions between humans and other animals in his classic book *The Expression of Emotions in Man and Animals.* Among the most common behaviours associated with human emotions are, of course, facial expressions. Darwin (1872/1998) conducted one of the first studies of facial expression and concluded that similar facial expressions indicated similar emotions throughout the world. Paul Ekman has been one of the most prolific contemporary researchers on the nature of facial expressions, and has been a strong advocate of the idea that facial expressions of emotion are universal rather than culture-specific (Ekman, 1992a, 1999). Ekman noted that wherever he travelled in the world he had little difficulty in recognizing people's emotional expressions in spite of language barriers. To study this more systematically, he investigated an isolated non-literate group of people in Papua New Guinea (Ekman et al., 1969). He showed them photographs of common emotional expressions, which had been posed by Caucasian (American) actors and asked them to indicate what emotion the faces expressed. The success rate for these people, who had little experience with Caucasian faces, was well above chance. For the emotions of happiness, surprise, anger, fear, sadness and disgust there was very high agreement. He then asked the New Guineans to show him what their face would look like if they were happy, sad, fearful and so on. The videotapes of these posed expressions were then presented to American students, along with the (translated) labels to which the New Guineans had been responding, and it was found that there was very high agreement in associating particular emotions with particular facial expressions. These results strongly suggest that facial expressions of emotion might occur cross-culturally, and this work will be discussed in more detail in Chapter 4.

This brief overview indicates that there are clear behavioural indicators of what emotion an animal or a person is experiencing. This should not surprise us, of course, given the important role that emotions are likely to play in social communication. The fact that there are clear behavioural indicators of emotion is consistent with both biological and cultural accounts of emotion. Investigating the behavioural correlates of emotion can be highly informative in helping us to understand the role of emotions in everyday life.

Measurement of the physiological correlates of emotion

In addition to behavioural responses, emotions are also associated with a range of physiological reactions such as your heart racing when you feel very excited or very frightened. Likewise, when you are anxious or nervous you may notice the palm of your hand sweating. Less obvious are a range of internal changes, such as various hormones that may be released into the bloodstream during emotional episodes. To illustrate, under conditions of extreme danger (e.g., being attacked by a predator), blood will be diverted towards the muscles and the brain to allow for fast reactions, and away from less vital functions such as digestion. Meanwhile, extra adrenaline is produced

TABLE 2.4 The sympathetic and parasympathetic sections of the ANS and physiological responses associated with emotions

Sympathetic ANS (dominant during arousal)	*Parasympathetic ANS (dominant during rest)*
Pupil dilation	Pupil constriction
Inhibition of saliva production	Flow of saliva stimulated
Acceleration of heart rate	Heart rate slowed
Bronchi dilated	Bronchi constricted
Digestion inhibited	Digestion stimulated
Adrenaline and noradrenaline released	–
Conversion of glycogen to bile increased	Release of bile stimulated
Bladder contraction inhibited	Bladder contracted

by the adrenal gland causing accelerated heart rate, constriction of the blood vessels (vasoconstriction), increased breathing rate and reduced activity in the gut. Many scientists assume that these responses are selected by evolution to prepare the body for 'flight' or 'fight'. These physiological changes are controlled by the *autonomic nervous system* (ANS), which is a complex network of fibres that extends throughout the body and sends signals to the various body organs, muscles and glands. The ANS is concerned with regulating the functioning of the body's internal environment, and, as we shall see, this is very important for emotion. There are two main sections of the ANS (see Table 2.4): the *sympathetic ANS* controls the effects associated with arousal, while the *parasympathetic ANS* controls the effects that occur when we are resting.

A number of techniques have been developed to measure the physiological correlates of emotion, and these methods usually measure arousal in one way or the other (see Coan and Allen, 2007, for further details). A brief description of some typical techniques is outlined in Table 2.5.

Measurement of the neural correlates of emotion

In recent years, there have been significant advances in uncovering how emotions are represented within the brain. Historically, a group of brain areas known as the *limbic system* was hypothesized to be associated with the experience and expression of emotions (see Box 1.1). While some of the structures that make up the *limbic system* (e.g., cingulate cortex, hippocampus, thalamus, hypothalamus, amygdala) are important for emotions, recent research indicates that different brain circuits control different aspects of emotion and many brain areas involved in emotion are also involved in a range of other functions (e.g., Lane and Nadel, 2000; LeDoux, 1987).

Much of what we know about the brain and emotion comes from research with animals (see LeDoux, 1996; Panksepp, 1998; Rolls, 1999). For example, the surgical removal of specific brain structures has led to success in increasing the understanding of the functions of particular brain regions in relation to certain tasks. Another common technique used in animal research is *single cell recording*. This involves the surgical implantation of an electrode deep within the brain which can directly measure

TABLE 2.5 Common techniques for measuring physiological responses in emotion science

Technique	*Description*
Skin conductance response (SCR)	By applying a small electric current across the fingers the electrical resistance of the skin can be measured. Even very small differences in the amount of sweat can be detected. These changes are usually measured in units called micro siemens (μS). The SCR is sometimes called the *galvanic skin response* (GSR) and is a very sensitive measure of physiological arousal.
Heart rate (HR)	The number of heart beats that occur per minute (bpm) can be measured by a simple transducer which converts the movement produced by the pulse into electrical energy. Changes in HR provide a good index of changes in arousal.
Blood pressure (BP)	Systolic blood pressure (SBP) is the pressure in the arteries when blood has been pumped out of the heart, whereas diastolic blood pressure (DBP) is the lower pressure when blood is being drawn back into the heart. BP is measured in millimetres of mercury (mmHg) and normal BP is expressed as SBP over DBP.
Cortisol level	The steroid hormone cortisol can be measured in the blood, urine or saliva and is a good indicator of ANS arousal.
Electromyography (EMG)	Small electrodes can be placed on the skin (usually over the muscles beneath the eyes) and the level of muscle tension and activity can be measured. The *startle reflex* is measured by EMG and is the sudden muscle contraction that occurs when you blink or are surprised. This is another a good measure of arousal.
Respiration rate	Changes in respiration rate can be measured in terms of breaths per minute and also provides a good measure of physiological arousal.

the activity of a single neuron or a small group of neurons. Electrodes are sometimes implanted within the brain of a person in order to control epileptic seizures and this provides an opportunity to measure the response of small groups of neurons while that person is engaging in some emotion-related task (e.g., looking at emotional pictures).

The major advance in uncovering the neural basis of human emotions has come about by the dramatic technological developments in the *functional* imaging of the brain. The techniques in widespread use are *positron emission tomography (PET)*, *functional magnetic resonance imaging (fMRI)*, *electroencephalography (EEG)*, and *magnetoencephalography (MEG)*. Both PET and fMRI work by detecting changes in regional blood flow and metabolism within the brain. For example, neurons in the brain that are more active use more glucose and oxygen. When this happens, more blood is sent to the active areas. PET involves a person being injected with a mildly radioactive substance that emits positrons (positively charged electrons), and these can then be detected by the PET scanner, thus revealing those areas within the brain where most metabolic activity is taking place. fMRI works by taking advantage of the fact that blood containing a lot of oxygen has a different magnetic resonance from blood with less oxygen. More active regions of the brain use more oxygen, and this activity can be detected by using an 11-ton magnet which surrounds the person's head. fMRI is now the method of choice since it is completely non-invasive (e.g., it

TABLE 2.6 Techniques used to measure brain activity

Technique	*Advantages*	*Disadvantages*
Single cell recording	Can measure single neurons Excellent temporal resolution Excellent spatial resolution Direct measure of activity	Invasive
PET	Good spatial resolution	Poor temporal resolution Invasive Indirect measure of activity
fMRI	Excellent spatial resolution Non-invasive	Poor temporal resolution Indirect measure of activity
EEG and ERPs	Excellent temporal resolution Non-invasive	Poor spatial resolution
MEG	Excellent temporal resolution Fairly direct measure of neural activity	Poor spatial resolution Other sources of magnetism may interfere with measurement

does not require any injections of radioactive substances) and also the scans can be made much more rapidly (around 50 msec) than PET (around 1000 msec). Thus, by detecting changes in blood flow, both PET and fMRI can reveal the areas of the brain that are most active during a given task.

EEG works by measuring the electrical activity of the brain. This is also a non-invasive technique involving the placement of several small electrodes around the person's head. These electrodes are taped to the head, along with conductive paste to allow for a low-resistance connection. They are then connected to a series of amplifiers and recording devices which give a continuous read-out of the electrical activity occurring in the cortex. From this EEG reading, we can obtain a measure called an *event-related potential*, or ERP, which is a specific electrical signal occurring in response to a specific stimulus. The ERP has proved very useful in emotion research.

Finally, the newer MEG technique involves the use of a super-conducting quantum interference device (SQUID), which can measure the magnetic fields produced by the brain's electrical activity. All of these methods have been used in emotion research and each has its own advantages and disadvantages as shown in Table 2.6.

Measurement of the subjective correlates of emotion

Many people consider that the subjective component of emotion is the most important because what an emotion feels like is often what is most salient to us. However, whether it is possible to obtain an accurate account of our own inner experience is a question that has had a chequered history in psychology. The founding fathers of experimental psychology in both Europe (Wilhelm Wundt) and the USA (William James) were both strong advocates of *introspection* as an important method for the fledgling science. As argued by William James, 'Introspective observation is what we have to rely on first and foremost and always. The word introspection need hardly be defined – it means, of course, looking into our own minds' (James, 1890/1950).

For a variety of historical and methodological reasons introspection is now rarely used in cognitive psychology or cognitive neuroscience. Nevertheless, there have been recent calls to reconsider the potential of introspective report in contemporary cognitive research (Hurlburt and Heavey, 2001; Jack and Roepstorff, 2002). One reason why introspection is often not trusted by cognitive psychologists or neuroscientists arises from evidence that we are not particularly good at looking into our own minds. For example, people generally have a very poor understanding of the causes of their own behaviour. Nisbett and Wilson (1977) reviewed situations in which it had been shown that external factors could predict which objects people would choose (e.g., they might always choose the object in a particular location on a display). However, when asked *why* they chose a particular item people usually provided very elaborate reasons (e.g., it looked nicer, it seemed to be a better quality etc) rather than the real reason which was manipulated by the experimenter. We all have a natural tendency to provide a reasonable explanation for our behaviour but this is often wrong. This has led some to conclude:

> the accuracy of subjective reports is so poor as to suggest that any introspective access that may exist is not sufficient to produce generally correct or reliable reports. (Nisbett and Wilson, 1977, p. 233)

Related to this, there is also a deeper problem in relying solely on a subjective account of emotions because we are often unaware of the triggers that elicit our emotions in the first place. Thus, in addition to being poor at knowing *why* we do certain things (Nisbett and Wilson, 1977), we may also not have much knowledge of what triggers our emotions. There is substantial evidence from cognitive psychology that stimuli which are presented outside our conscious awareness can still affect our behaviour. A good example is the *mere exposure effect*, which is the finding that we tend to like stimuli that have been repeatedly presented even though we may not be aware of the repeated presentation (Zajonc, 1968). This preference for familiar items is the basis for successful advertising. In a classic demonstration of a subliminal mere exposure effect, a number of Chinese ideographs were presented to people who could not speak Chinese for just 1 ms at a time. Not surprisingly, people were unable to select which particular ideographs had been presented from among similar shapes. Thus, when asked to recognize which items had been presented and which had not, people responded at a chance level (i.e., 50% correct). However, when the question was changed and people were asked to say which shapes they *preferred*, stimuli that had previously been presented were selected well above the level that would be expected by chance (around 65%). Thus, even though there was no explicit recognition of the items, those items that had been presented subliminally were preferred over those that had not been presented. People preferred stimuli that they were not aware they had seen. Subjective report would clearly be useless in a situation like this, as we cannot report what we are not aware of! Box 2.1 presents further evidence that emotions can be activated by stimuli that are presented outside conscious awareness (LeDoux, 1996; Morris et al., 1999, 2001; Öhman and Mineka, 2001).

BOX 2.1

Can an emotional response be elicited without conscious recognition of the eliciting stimulus?

This fundamental question concerns whether we need to consciously perceive a stimulus in order for an emotion to occur, or whether an emotion can be elicited by the presence of 'hidden' stimuli of which we are not consciously aware. This question has been addressed experimentally by the use of the '*visual backward masking*' paradigm which can render a briefly presented stimulus invisible. The extent to which a target stimulus is perceived is dependent on the time interval between the onset of the target (let's say a photograph of a face) and the onset of the masking stimulus (which might be a photograph composed of face parts). This interval is usually called the *stimulus onset asynchrony* (SOA). When the SOA is short (less than 30 ms), the masking stimulus tends to completely block any recognition of the target stimulus. When asked to say what they saw, people generally report seeing the second stimulus (the mask) but not the first. Nevertheless, even though the target stimulus is blocked from awareness several experiments show that masked stimuli can influence a person's behaviour and judgment (see Bornstein and Pittman, 1992).

Öhman and Soares (1994) used the backward masking paradigm to investigate the automatic activation of a fear response. They selected two groups of highly fearful people, one group were afraid of snakes but not spiders, while the other group were afraid of spiders but not snakes. A (non-fearful) control group was also tested. Pictures of snakes, spiders, flowers and mushrooms were presented on a screen for 30 ms and then followed by a masking stimulus (pictures of similar objects cut into pieces and randomly re-assembled) for 100 ms. When the feared objects were viewed under conditions of full awareness there was a distinct psychophysiological response consisting of a large skin conductance response (SCR – sweaty palms), heart-rate acceleration, blood pressure increases, and an enhanced startle reflex. Snake-fearful participants showed enhanced SCRs to pictures of masked snakes, while spider-fearful participants showed enhanced SCRs to spiders, even though they were not aware of what was being presented. The non-fearful control participants showed no difference in SCRs to the fear-related or control stimuli.

Morris et al. (1998) also used backward masking in an experiment measuring brain activity by means of fMRI. They found that the presentation of fearful facial expressions led to an activation of the amygdala, even though participants were not aware of what was being presented. Thus, both functional neuroimaging and psychophysiological research demonstrate that the physiological and neural components of emotion can be activated without any conscious recognition of the eliciting stimulus. Unfortunately, people were not asked if they experienced any emotion in these experiments and so we have no index of the subjective component of emotion.

The evidence that emotional responses can be activated by stimuli of which we are not aware has led many researchers to suggest that we need indices of emotion other than self-report. However, cognitive scientists have probably gone too far and have tended to abandon the attempt to measure subjective report altogether (Jack and Roepstorff, 2002).

While traditional introspective measures of subjective experience have been problematic, better methods of investigating people's subjective experience are being developed. One such method, for example, involves interrupting the flow of consciousness by means of a bleeper (Hurlburt and Heavey, 2002; Hurlburt, 1997). This method is called *descriptive experience sampling* (DES), and uses a beeper that goes off at random times to cue people to report their ongoing inner experience at that moment. They are asked immediately, 'What was occurring in your inner experience at the moment of the beep?' With practice, people can get quite good at this technique and can answer the question with ease. Given that introspective report is the only type of evidence that can bear directly on our consciousness and subjective states (Feldman Barrett, Mesquita et al., 2007; Jack and Roepstorff, 2002), it is clearly important to develop more accurate methods of accessing subjective experience. Methods such as DES or simply keeping a diary record (Bolger et al., 2003) have tremendous potential in emotion science, although they have not yet been used very extensively. Far more common is the use of questionnaire measures, which are designed to enable people to report subjective feeling states.

Questionnaire-based measures of emotion

When assessing the subjective experience of emotion it is important to ask whether we are interested in fairly transient states or whether we want to index more stable feelings of emotion. For example, on a particular day I might feel very irritable and angry, whereas on most days I might feel very calm and happy. When filling out a questionnaire we need to be sure that we are assessing how people feel at the particular time they are been assessed and not reporting their more general feelings. This distinction between *state* and *trait* aspects of emotion is important for all emotion components, of course, but has been addressed primarily in relation to the subjective assessment of emotions and moods. Charles Spielberger (1966) was one of the first to argue that emotional phenomena can be described as having two forms: *state* and *trait*. This distinction is often made in terms of the *duration* of an emotional experience. To say that somebody is high in self-reported trait-anxiety or depression, for example, means that this is a relatively enduring ongoing state of affairs. As described by Lazarus (1994), an emotion *trait* refers to a tendency to react in a particular way to what he calls an 'adaptational encounter'. In contrast, an emotion *state* refers to a transient reaction to specific situations. Thus, the level of state emotion reported provides an index of how someone feels at a particular moment. It is no surprise then that state emotion often has a greater range of intensity than trait emotion. It should be noted, however, that state and trait aspects of emotion do not imply that there are necessarily differences in the quality of the experience. The idea is that the emotional state (e.g., anger) often

TABLE 2.7 Some common questionnaire-based measures of felt emotion and the feeling states that they are designed to measure

Instrument	*Description*
Beck Depression Inventory (BDI)	A 21-item questionnaire designed to measure *depression*. Each item (e.g., 'I am useless') is rated on a 0–3 scale (completely disagree to completely agree). Thus the range of possible scores is 0–63.
Beck Anxiety Inventory (BAI)	Similar to the BDI except that items relate to *anxiety* rather than depression.
Spielberger Trait-State Anxiety Inventory (STAI)	This consists of two 20-item sections. One asks people to report how they 'generally feel' and this indicates *trait anxiety*, while the other asks people to report how they feel 'right now' and this indicates *state anxiety*. The range for both measures is 20–80.
Profile of Mood States (POMS)	This consists of 65 scales that provide a measure of six different mood states. These are: Tension–Anxiety; Depression–Dejection; Anger–Hostility; Fatigue; Vigour; Confusion–Bewilderment; and Total Mood Disturbance.
Positive and Negative Affect Scales (PANAS)	Consists of 20 adjectives (e.g., determined, upset) which people rate on a scale of 1 (very slightly or not at all) to 5 (extremely) according to how they feel 'right now'. Two separate indices are provided for *positive affect* (PA: range = 5–50) and *negative affect* (NA: range = 5–50).
Multiple Affect Adjective Checklist (MAACL)	Consists of a number of adjectives, which people can select according to how they feel at a given moment.

refers to a particular episode of limited duration, while an emotional trait refers to the tendency of the individual to experience a particular emotion with increased frequency. Therefore, if we talk of someone as being an angry person, we do not mean that that person is angry all of the time, rather, we mean that he becomes angry more easily and more frequently than most people. Likewise, people who differ on trait-anxiety, for example, differ in the number of times that they experience elevations in state-anxiety, and do not necessarily differ permanently in the level of felt anxiety. Some of the more common questionnaire measures of felt emotion (or mood) are presented in Table 2.7. These questionnaires are widely used in emotion science and we will come across many of these in future chapters.

Measurement of the cognitive correlates of emotion

In emotion science (and indeed psychology generally) the term *cognition* is used in a number of different ways. When we talk about the cognitive correlates of emotion, many scientists assume that we are talking about the fundamental biases in perception, attention and memory that seem to be a feature of different emotional states. Many of these biases have been uncovered by means of behavioural techniques for deriving objective measures of internal processes. These techniques originating in cognitive psychology have proved to be very useful in emotion research.

Probably the most widely used behavioural measure is the simple *reaction time*, or RT. This is a precise measure (usually in milliseconds, ms) of how quickly people can make a motor or verbal response to a particular stimulus. For instance, we might ask someone to press one button (A) when a noun with a positive valence (e.g., holiday, prize) is presented on a computer screen but to press another button (B) when a noun with a negative valence (e.g., cancer, failure) is presented. The computer measures the time that elapsed from the onset of the word on the screen to the time that the person pressed the correct button (e.g., 520 ms). We can also get a measure of errors in this type of task by calculating how many times across a large number of trials the person made the correct and incorrect responses. In a typical experiment, several hundred individual trials may be presented in a random order (e.g., 100 positively valenced word trials and 100 negatively valenced word trials) and the average RT can then be calculated for each condition in the experiment. Researchers are usually careful to ensure that only RTs for the correct trials (i.e., those trials in which the participant made the right response) are included in the average, and then the mean error-rate can also be calculated and compared for each condition. In the above example, we might find that the RT to positive words was 785 ms on average, while the mean RT for negative words was 620 ms. Likewise, we might find that the mean error-rate for positive and negative words was 7% and 5%, respectively. This pattern of results would suggest to us that negative words are processed more quickly and more accurately than positive words. Thus, RT can provide us with an indirect measure of mental activity and has been used in a wide variety of behavioural tasks in emotion research (as well as in other areas of psychology).

In addition to investigating how quickly people can respond to emotionally valenced information, we can also ask whether our memory is better or worse for information that differs in valence. Are we more likely to remember an exciting or frightening event than an event that is fairly neutral? There are different ways in which we can assess memory and a number of different tasks have been used in emotion science. For example, one technique would be to show people lists of 20 positive and 20 negative words and ask them to simply look at each word for 1 second. Then half an hour later, after doing a variety of other tasks, we could unexpectedly ask people to recall as many of the words as they can. The key comparison would be to see whether people are more likely to recall the negative or the positive words. We might find, for instance, that people recalled an average of 8 of the negative words (40%), but only 5 of the positive words (25%) and this 15% difference might suggest to us that negative information is more likely to be remembered. There are many variations of this type of simple *recall* task, and there are also a number of different tasks which use RT as the main dependent (or outcome) variable. The more common behavioural tasks used in emotion research are briefly described in Table 2.8.

Summary

It seems that a complete account of emotion must take into account many different aspects or components of emotion. The components that are agreed upon by most emotion researchers are *behavioural, physiological and neural*, while there is more controversy about whether *cognitive factors* (e.g., appraisals and biases) are components of emotion, or, rather, are causes of emotion. Finally, most agree that the *subjective*

TABLE 2.8 Some common behavioural tasks used to index internal cognitive processes in emotion research

Type of task	*Description*
Emotional Stroop	Emotional (e.g., hate) and neutral (e.g., hand) words are presented in different colours and the RT to indicate the ink colour is measured.
Visual search	An array of negative (e.g., pictures of snakes) and neutral or positive (e.g., pictures of flowers) stimuli is rapidly presented (every 300 ms) on a computer screen, and the RT to determine whether a particular target is presented in the display is measured.
Dot-probe	Pairs of pictures (e.g., a happy and an angry facial expression) are displayed side by side for about 500 ms. When the pictures disappear a probe appears in one of the two locations. Faster RTs are often observed when the probe replaces the negative picture.
Attentional cueing	A cue (flash of light, or object which can be negative or positive) is briefly presented (usually around 50 ms) in a particular location on a computer screen. RTs to detect a neutral target such as the letter X are usually faster when the image appears in the cued location.
Simple recall	Lists of words or pictures are presented for about 5 seconds each during an *encoding phase*. Some time later people are asked to recall as many items as they can. This is often called a *retrieval phase*. The valence of the stimuli can be varied.
Recognition memory	List of words or pictures are presented during an *encoding* phase just as with simple recall. However, during retrieval people are given cues (e.g., lists of words that have been presented as well as similar words that have not been presented). The task is to identify or *recognize* the items that were previously presented. Performance on recognition tasks is usually much better than with simple recall (e.g., remembering someone's name is much easier if you are given a choice of four names to choose from).
Implicit memory	Several tasks measure memory at an implicit level (i.e., indirectly). For example, during the encoding phase a list of words may be presented for about 5 seconds each. Then, after several other unrelated tasks, a person might be asked to complete word fragments for which there are a number of different solutions (e.g., D_E, could be DIE or DYE). People tend to complete word fragments by using words that were presented in the original list. This is evidence of *implicit* memory, the important point being that people have no explicit knowledge of the fact that the item was presented previously.

component is important, although some scientists are sceptical that feelings can be accurately measured. There is a general sense that feelings are different in some way from the other components of emotion. For this reason, we will devote an entire section of this chapter to *feelings* because they are effectively the mental representations of both emotions and moods.

MEASURING MOODS

The terms 'emotions' and 'moods' have often been used interchangeably and a failure to keep a clear separation between the two concepts may have hampered the development of research in emotion science. Indeed, most of the measures discussed in the previous section can also be used to measure mood states and it is not always clear whether moods or emotions are being measured.

Measurement of the physiological and neural correlates of mood

As we saw when discussing the different components of emotions, a variety of physiological (e.g., HR, SCR, cortisol) and brain imaging (e.g., EEG, PET, fMRI) measures are available to emotion scientists. All of these techniques are equally applicable to the study of mood states. Indeed, investigating the psychophysiological correlates of mood has less practical problems given the different time frames involved. For example, if emotions only last a couple of seconds this does not give much time to assess the changes in regional blood flow when emotions are elicited. However, since moods are thought to last for longer periods the investigation of mood states should be easier than investigating emotions. These practical issues raise the important question of just what is being measured in brain imaging studies of emotions. A further complication is that most of what we know about the neurophysiology of mood states comes from the investigation of abnormal mood states. Mood disorders (depression and mania) are common and are thought to reflect the altered functioning of many parts of the brain at the same time. This is not surprising when one considers the range of symptoms that are typical of major depression, as shown in Table 2.9. Major depression is diagnosed when these behavioural and subjective symptoms occur every day for at least two weeks and are not related to any obvious reason (e.g., death of a loved one). Clinical or major depression affects about 5% of the population in developed countries.

Given the range of symptoms associated with depressed mood, brain measures have tended to focus on variations in the level of diffuse neuromodulatory systems in regulating mood. The first indication that problems with modulatory systems might be involved in depression came with the discovery of the drug *reserpine* in the 1960s. This drug was designed to reduce high blood pressure, but it was discovered by accident that the drug produced psychotic depression in about 20% of patients. It is now known that reserpine lowers the levels of some neurotransmitters such as *dopamine (DA)* and *serotonin (5-HT)*. It has therefore been hypothesized that a reduction of these neurotransmitters in the brain might be important in inducing depression. This idea was supported by another accidental discovery. A group of drugs designed to treat tuberculosis were found to lead to a marked elevation in mood. These drugs inhibit *monoamine oxidase (MAO)*, the enzyme that destroys the monoamine neurotransmitters, and therefore produce increased levels of these neurotransmitters in the brain. There are four monoamine neurotransmitters: dopamine, serotonin, adrenaline

TABLE 2.9 Symptoms associated with major depression

Lowered mood
Decreased interest or pleasure in all activities
Loss of appetite or increased appetite
Insomnia or hypersomnia
Fatigue
Feelings of worthlessness and guilt
Diminished ability to concentrate
Recurrent thoughts of death

(also known as epinephrine), and noradrenaline (also known as norepinephrine). These observations led to the *monoamine hypothesis of mood disorders*, which proposes that depressed mood (as measured by subjective report or behavioural observations) is related to a depletion of monoamine neurotransmitters (particularly serotonin and noradrenaline) in the brain, whereas elevated mood is related to an increase in the amount of monoamine activity.

There is support for this hypothesis in that most of the drugs that are effective in treating depression lead to an increase in neurotransmission at what are called *serotonergic* and/or *noradrenergic* synapses. However, things are not so straightforward because some drugs that increase activity in the same neurotransmitter systems do not have the effect of raising depressed mood. For example, cocaine increases the levels of these neurotransmitters in the brain but it does not have an anti-depressant effect in depressed patients. In addition, while anti-depressant drugs increase neurotransmission almost immediately, it usually takes several weeks for their anti-depressant effects to emerge clinically. This implies that some other action of these drugs is important in changing mood. One possibility is that anti-depressant drugs might promote long-term adaptive changes in the brain (e.g., modification of receptor systems) and it is these changes that alleviate the depressed mood. One such adaptation occurs in what is known as the *hypothalamic–pituitary–adrenal (HPA) axis.* The activity of the HPA is critical in helping an individual respond to stress and is closely involved with anxiety disorders. However, this system is now thought to be intimately involved in mood disorders as well (Nemeroff, 1998).

The HPA system regulates the secretion of cortisol from the adrenal gland in response to stress. The hypothalamus releases a chemical called *corticotropin-releasing hormone (CRH)*, which is a chemical messenger that travels to the pituitary gland positioned just below the hypothalamus. The pituitary gland then releases a hormone called *adrenocorticotropic hormone (ACTH)*, which travels in the blood stream to the adrenal glands situated on top of the kidneys. The presence of ACTH at the adrenal gland stimulates the release of *cortisol*, which is important in coordinating the body's physiological response to stress.

According to Charles Nemeroff (1998), the HPA axis is the main site where genetic and environmental influences converge to cause mood disorders. It is known that increased activity of the HPA axis is associated with anxiety disorders and it is also known that there is a high degree of co-morbidity between anxiety and depression. In other words, people with clinical depression are also highly anxious, while people with anxiety disorders are often also depressed. As with anxiety, research has shown that overactivity of the HPA axis is also common in major depression (Heuser, 1998). It is of interest to note that the HPA system is itself regulated by the amygdala and the hippocampus, two brain areas that are known to be critical to affect. Activation of the amygdala *stimulates* the HPA system while the hippocampus *suppresses* the HPA system. The hippocampus contains receptors that are sensitive to circulating cortisol and this sensitivity is critical in the feedback regulation of the HPA axis in order to prevent excessive cortisol release. A graphic representation of this system is shown in Figure 2.1.

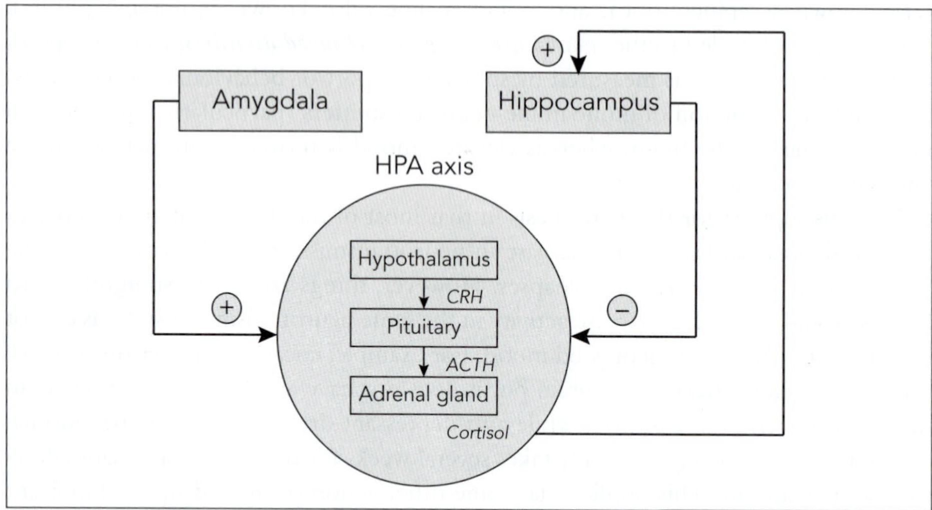

FIGURE 2.1 Regulation of the hypothalamic–pituitary–adrenal (HPA) axis

The receptors in the hippocampus that are sensitive to circulating cortisol are called *glucocorticoid receptors*, and the number of these receptors has been found to be reduced in depression (Plotsky et al., 1995). A reduction of glucocorticoid receptors would disrupt the feedback mechanism of the HPA, which would explain why the HPA is overactive in depression and anxiety. Evidence for this overactivity comes from the finding that the concentration of CRH in the cerebrospinal fluid is increased in untreated depressed patients relative to healthy controls (Catalan et al., 1998; Nemeroff et al., 1984). In the Catalan et al. study, for example, a strong correlation was found between concentration of CRH and depressive mood, with the highest levels occurring in the most severely depressed patients.

In a fascinating series of studies, it has been found that the number of glucocorticoid receptors present in the brain is regulated to a large extent by the nature of life experience. For example, rats receiving abundant maternal care when they are pups have a greater number of glucocorticoid receptors in their hippocampus, have less CRH in their hypothalamus, and show less anxiety when they are adults compared to rats receiving inadequate care as pups (Liu et al., 1997). An interesting finding, however, is that an increase in tactile stimulation seems to make up for a lack of maternal care. For example, young rats who were patted and stroked very frequently had an increased number of glucocorticoid receptors compared to those who received minimal tactile stimulation. Unfortunately, however, the beneficial effects of experience, which allow the animal to handle stress better in later life seem to be restricted to a critical period of early postnatal life (Liu et al., 1997). Similar findings have been reported in human research, and it is known that childhood neglect and abuse can significantly increase the risk of the development of mood and anxiety disorders in later life (see Chapter 9). The animal experiments showing reduced glucocorticoid receptors, elevations in CRH and decreased feedback inhibition of the HPA axis suggest that the brain might be particularly vulnerable to mood disorders in these individuals. Ryff and Singer (2003) support this notion by pointing out that the linkage of affective experience to health outcomes seems to be more closely related to mood states than to emotions. The factors that have most consequences for health are 'those features of the affective experience of long duration: prolonged mood states and emotional dispositions, and more important, chronic recurrent emotions and their cumulation over time' (p. 1093). Chronic overactivity of systems such as the HPA axis is strongly associated with the development of cardiac disease and general physical decline, but the good news is that these effects can be offset to some extent by positive mood states, such as optimism and hope (see Ryff and Singer, 2003, for review).

In addition to research examining the role of neuromodulatory systems in mood states, research has also been conducted on the neural structures and mechanisms underlying mood (see Ketter et al., 2003, for review). Studies using fMRI have shown that emotions may be mediated primarily by phylogenetically old anatomical structures including the amygdala, and the anterior cingulate cortex (ACC). These structures are closely linked to motor circuits and could therefore provide action-oriented responses which are triggered by perceptual inputs. In contrast, moods may be related to a more refined cognitively-oriented response which is triggered by more complex cognitive processing. This cognitive response is likely to be mediated by more recent (in evolutionary terms) regions within the prefrontal cortex (PFC) areas (Ketter et al., 2003).

Measurement of the cognitive correlates of mood

The most common research strategy in this field is to investigate the effects of mood on memory or social judgment. In a typical experiment, a particular mood state is induced (usually happy or sad) by means of reading valenced sentences, hypnosis, or the recall of autobiographical events relating to the relevant mood. The induction of the appropriate mood state is usually confirmed by means of a self-report measure such as the POMS or the MAACL (see Table 2.7). Participants are then asked to perform some task such as learning a list of words, which generally relate to both positive (e.g., joy, holiday) and negative (e.g., death, cancer) valence. Later, when people are once again in a neutral mood, they are asked to recall as many of the words as they can. A typical finding is that people who were in a happy mood when they learned the material are more likely to recall positive words, whereas people who were in a sad mood when learning the material are more likely to recall the negative words (Bower et al., 1981). This is an example of *mood congruent encoding*, which is discussed in Chapter 7, and demonstrates that people who are in a particular mood state are more likely to encode and remember information that is consistent with that mood state.

In addition to memory, studies have also found that current mood state can be an important determinant of the type of judgments people make about their future. For instance, when people were asked general questions about how healthy and happy they are likely to be in the future, it was found that their current mood state predicted whether they were likely to make positive or negative judgments (Schwarz and Clore, 1983). Current mood as determined by the weather also influences how we judge our current well-being and satisfaction with life. In an interesting study, Schwarz and Clore (1983) telephoned people in Illinois on either a cloudy overcast day or on a bright sunny day. One group of people were asked 'How's the weather down there today?' and then were asked to rate their general life satisfaction on a scale of 0 to 8. Another group were simply asked to rate their satisfaction with life and no mention was made of the weather. The interesting finding was that people were much less satisfied with their life on a cloudy day compared to a sunny day, but *only* if they had not been asked about the weather. In other words, when people could attribute their current mood state to the weather this did not seem to influence their general sense of well-being. However, when they did not attribute their current mood to the weather then this mood state seemed to have an important influence on their judgment of general satisfaction with life.

It also seems to be the case that different mood states can bias our perceptions so that we tend to notice information which is consistent with our current mood state. An experiment reported by Niedenthal and Setterlund (1994) demonstrates this nicely. They induced either a sad or a happy mood in people by playing them different types of music. Music is known to be a powerful modulator of mood state and has been widely used in mood induction research. Once the different mood states were induced, people were asked to make *lexical decisions* to words presented on a computer screen as quickly as they could. Thus, if a real word in English was presented they had to press one button, whereas if a non-word (e.g., Chaer) was presented they had to press the other button. Reaction time (RT) was the main dependent measure used. The results clearly showed that when people were in a happy mood they were quicker to identify happy words than sad ones. However, when they were in a sad mood their RTs for sad words were faster than their RTs for happy words.

Summary

It is clear that mood states, just like emotions, have a range of behavioural, neural, physiological and cognitive components. Much of the focus in measuring the neural components of mood has been on assessing levels of different neurotransmitters in the brain. Mood states also have clear subjective components in that we 'know' what it feels like to be sad as opposed to happy, or irritable, or apprehensive. An interesting question concerns whether feelings are related to emotions or moods, or both. Feelings may not differ between emotions and moods. For example, the emotion of sadness may feel very similar to a sad mood. Alternatively, an emotion may feel different from a mood.

THE EXPERIENCE OF EMOTIONS AND MOODS

As discussed in previous sections, emotion scientists have identified a number of different components of emotions and mood states, and developed a variety of methods to measure these states. One component is the conscious experience of affect – the feeling states that many would argue are the essential ingredients of human emotion and represent what we most notice and remember about our emotional lives. When we talk about emotions and moods in everyday life, we almost invariably talk about how we *felt* in various situations (sad, angry, happy etc). As Ray Dolan (2002) rather nicely put it 'what we notice and remember is not the mundane but events that evoke feelings of joy, sorrow, pleasure, and pain' (p. 1191). Indeed many of the important events in our lives are probably characterized mainly on the basis of the intensity of our feelings in the situation at the time. This idea has been supported by a study in which Jaak Panksepp (2000) asked people from different walks of life to rank various components of emotion (e.g., feelings, physiological changes, thoughts etc) in order of importance. Almost all of the groups he tested rated feelings as being the most important. The only group who did not concur was a group of philosophy majors, who claimed that thoughts were more important than feelings!

Some emotion theorists have even argued that affective responses (emotions and moods) and feelings are so closely related in everyday life that it makes little sense to distinguish them. It is not difficult, however, to see that feelings can be quite separate from the other components. Imagine the following scenario: you are deep in thought about an essay you have to write by the end of the week and step out onto the road without seeing an oncoming car. Your heart races and you leap out of the way just in time to avoid a collision. When the danger has passed, you are overwhelmed by a feeling of fear and the realization that you could have been killed. The pattern of physiological reactions that took place in order to get you out of harm's way is clearly separate from the feeling of fear that you later experience. Thus, in a general way a feeling is a perception of an internal emotional state. Damasio (1999) suggests that: 'Feelings are the mental representation of the physiological changes that occur during an emotion'. It can also be argued that feelings are the mental representation of the physiological changes that occur during a mood state.

WHAT AND HOW DO WE FEEL?

It is somewhat surprising that the amount of research conducted on feelings lags way behind research on other aspects of emotion (Scherer, 2004). This is partly to do with the historical tendency to use the terms 'emotion' and 'feeling' as synonymous. However, many researchers (e.g., LeDoux, 1996, 2000) now emphasize the importance of distinguishing between emotions and feelings and this distinction may be one of the primary reasons that emotion has now assumed 'center stage in neuroscience' (Winston and Dolan, 2004, p. 204). Another reason why the study of feelings has lagged behind is that the necessity of relying on the use of verbal self-report has led cognitive psychologists and neuroscientists to avoid the topic. However, there seems little doubt that the only way to directly measure the contents of a subjective representation of an emotion or mood is to ask people to report on their own mental state (Feldman Barrett, Mesquita et al., 2007). There is growing evidence that emotions and moods are represented in consciousness primarily as states of pleasure or displeasure (Feldman Barrett, Mesquita et al., 2007; Edelman and Tononi, 2000).

It is important to point out that the subjective perception of emotion depends not just on a perception of how we feel at a subjective level, but also on a self-perception of other components of emotion such as physiological changes. In agreement with this, studies using self-report measures indicate that, in addition to pleasure/displeasure, many mental representations of emotions and moods also include some arousal-based content. Thus, the mental representation of an emotion often indicates whether the degree of pleasantness (or unpleasantness) was weak or strong. Klaus Scherer, in particular, has argued that feeling has a special status as a component of emotion because it plays an important role in integrating and regulating the component process itself (Scherer, 2000b, 2003, 2004). Thus, feeling is a complex combination of information coming from a variety of different systems and seems to represent valence and arousal in consciousness awareness. It is of interest to note that we do not seem to report different emotions when asked to report on our affective feelings, instead we seem to report broad dimensions of pleasure/displeasure and arousal.

Antonio Damasio (1999) has attempted to provide a conceptual analysis of feelings by considering the neural mechanisms necessary to allow for the conscious mental representation of emotions. He agrees with William James in assuming that feelings are essentially an awareness or consciousness of bodily states. He postulates two levels of bodily representation that are arranged in a hierarchical manner.

First-order bodily representations: In order to experience feelings our brain must first have a way in which to represent our body as a distinct unit. Our body, as a unit, is mapped in our brain, in structures that regulate life and signal the status of our internal states continuously. Likewise, the characteristics of an external object that might elicit an emotion (i.e., an emotionally competent stimulus) are also mapped within our brain in the sensory and motor structures that are activated by the interaction of the organism (our body) with the external object (e.g., a snake or someone we love). Both the body and the external object are mapped as neural patterns, and it is these patterns that Damasio considers to be first-order maps. The key is that the changes in these sensory-motor maps which relate to the external object can cause changes in the maps pertaining to the body (organism). These changes can then be re-represented in other maps which represent the relationship of the external object and the organism. These are what Damasio calls 'second-order maps'.

Second-order bodily representations: The neural patterns formed in second-order maps can become mental images in the same way as the neural patterns in first-order maps. Damasio argues that because of the body-related nature of both first- and second-order maps, the mental images that describe the relationship are feelings. This second-order re-representation of the first-order representations (of the body and of the external object) help to provide integrated feedback which in turn can be modified through our ongoing experience, and therefore can be exploited in terms of guiding behaviour.

Damasio (1999) argues that 'consciousness is the critical biological function that allows us to know sorrow or know joy, to know suffering or know pleasure, to sense embarrassment or pride, to grieve for lost love or lost life' (p. 4). In other words, he makes the case that one cannot actually experience (feel) an emotion unless there is consciousness. Thus, while there are coordinated responses that constitute an emotion and subsequent brain representations that constitute a feeling, we can only really know that we feel an emotion when we sense that emotion as occurring within our own bodies. Knowing that we have a feeling can only occur, according to Damasio, *after* we have built the second-order representations necessary for core consciousness. While Damasio's theory of consciousness is outside the scope of this chapter the argument that feelings are dependent on consciousness (which is one of the most difficult and elusive topics within science) goes some way towards explaining the difficulties inherent in investigating the nature of feelings, or how we come to know our emotions.

Measurement of the neural and physiological correlates of feelings

There have been some attempts to uncover the neuronal basis of feeling states (see Winston and Dolan, 2004, for review). A real difficulty in this endeavour relates to the fact that feelings are, by definition, private mental states, although no more so than any other mental state. Another difficult problem is that feelings occur *after* emotions in most models of feelings and emotions, making it very difficult to separate out the functional neuroanatomy of the feeling from that of the emotion (Winston and Dolan, 2004). This means that many experiments tend to confound emotions and feelings.

The most common method to investigate the neural correlates of feeling states is to induce one mood or the other in people by presenting them with stimuli known to produce particular mood states. Note that a further confusion here is the induction of mood states, rather than emotions, in these studies. While there may be much overlap between emotions and moods, as discussed in the previous section, they are almost certainly not identical states. In one of the first studies of this kind, George et al. (1995) presented happy, sad and neutral faces as well as asking people to recall personal real-life events in order to induce feelings of sadness and happiness. While people were experiencing these mood states, the regional blood flow within the brain was measured by means of fMRI. Widespread increases and decreases in *regional cerebral blood flow* (rCBF) were found in frontal, temporal and cingulate regions depending upon the mood elicited. In a similar study, participants were asked to recall happy, sad or disgusting events or to watch films designed to elicit happy, sad or disgusted feelings while PET scans were being taken (Lane et al., 1997). Brain activity during these conditions was compared to activity during neutral conditions and a variety of common and distinct patterns of activity were observed. However, as pointed out by Winston and Dolan (2004), no direct comparisons were made between the happy, sad and disgusted conditions so the authors could not draw any strong conclusions regarding differences between the different feeling states.

Damasio et al. (2000) used PET scanning and also asked people to generate the feelings of fear, happiness, sadness, and anger. Unfortunately, like the study reported by Lane et al. (1997), no direct comparisons of the different feeling states were made, rather each feeling state was compared with a neutral baseline. It is of interest that rCBF increased in brain-stem (pons) and hypothalamic areas *regardless* of which mood was being experienced. This, of course, supports the view that feelings are associated with changes in ANS functions, which are controlled by these brain areas (Damasio, 1999). A number of cortical areas (orbitofrontal, anterior and posterior cingulate, and secondary somatosensory cortices) were also activated in response to feeling states (Damasio et al., 2000). There are two problems with this study. First, the temporal resolution of PET is quite poor, making it difficult to know whether the activity in the various brain areas occurred before or after the conscious experience of the feelings. Second, because the feelings were self-generated it is possible that people deliberately attempted to modulate their own bodily states in order to produce the required mood state. If this happened, the rCBF in the various brain areas would be due to the physiological activation and not to the feeling state *per se*. A number of recent papers by Hugo Critchley and his colleagues have provided more direct support for the notion that changes in bodily states are critical to the generation of feelings and that the insula may play a crucial role in the elaboration of affective feelings. Some key studies from this group are presented in Box 2.2.

BOX 2.2

Neural basis of feeling states

Damasio has hypothesized that the cerebral representation of bodily states is the substrate for emotional feelings. This model proposes a first-order autoregulatory representation of bodily state at the level of the pons, and a second-order experience-dependent re-mapping of changes in bodily state within structures such as the cingulate cortex.

This model was directly tested in a study reported by Critchley et al. (2001a). They used PET scanning and tested people with a rare neurological disorder called *pure autonomic failure (PAF)* as well as control participants. PAF is usually acquired in middle age and only affects the ANS. People with PAF cannot modulate their bodily state via the ANS but they have no other neurological deficits. Because of this, the role of peripheral autonomic feedback in emotional processing can be selectively studied in these patients. Critchley et al. (2001a) presented participants with a variety of mental and physical stress tasks and found that increases in both blood pressure and heart rate occurred for the control participants but not for the PAF participants as expected. The PET scanning demonstrated significantly increased activity in dorsal pons for the PAF participants compared to controls. Moreover, PAF patients also showed increased anterior cingulate activity associated with increased exertion. This suggests that the anterior cingulate modulates ANS function and integrates it with feedback about ongoing autonomic changes. In PAF patients cingulate activity is increased in the absence of ANS changes in an attempt to generate a task-appropriate autonomic tone (Winston and Dolan, 2004). Most crucially, the authors also found subtle deficits in emotional experience when they compared PAF patients with those with Parkinson's disease who were similarly disabled. Patients with PAF reported fewer emotional experiences in general. This study provides empirical support for the notion that there is a hierarchical representation of bodily states.

BOX 2.2 continued

In a subsequent study, a backward masking paradigm was used in which angry faces were presented to PAF and control patients while undergoing fMRI scanning. One of the angry faces was accompanied by a short burst of white noise (CS+) on 30% of the trials, while the other face was never accompanied by the aversive stimulus (CS–). Critchley et al. (2002) found that both the right and left amygdalae responded to masked CS+ faces, whereas only the right amygdala responded to unmasked CS+ faces. Importantly, the right amygdala response to unmasked faces was modulated by ANS arousal, whereas the amygdala response to the masked faces was not modulated by ANS arousal. The most interesting result, however, was that increased activity in the insula in response to CS+ faces statistically interacted with both masking and ANS arousal. These results suggest that the insula plays a crucial role in integrating affective processing with representations of bodily states, which ultimately results in feelings (see Morris, 2002, for discussion). The suggestion is that the amygdala may be involved in the early translation of sensory processing into automatic affective responses, whereas the insula is involved with the transfer of these automatic affective responses into subjective feelings (Critchley et al., 2002; Morris, 2002).

Summary

Research on the neural and physiological correlates of feelings has lagged behind research on emotions and moods. One difficulty is that emotions and moods have not been distinguished in many studies. Subjective measures using verbal report are the only way to directly ascertain how someone is feeling at a given moment. An important theoretical question concerns whether each distinct emotion or mood state has a distinctive feeling, or whether we have broad good and bad feelings, which might also vary in terms of intensity. The evidence from studies using self-report measures suggests that the latter is the case.

CHAPTER SUMMARY

This chapter outlines the distinction between *emotions*, *moods* and *feelings*. Emotions and moods are primarily dissociated on the basis of duration and intensity as well as being focused on a specific event (emotions) rather than being more diffuse and 'objectless' (moods). Feelings refer to the subjective mental representation of both emotions and moods. The content of these mental representations tends to involve elements of *valence* (pleasure versus displeasure) and *arousal* (strong versus weak). A key feature of emotions is that they are coordinated sets of responses (behavioural, autonomic, neural) to a specific set of circumstances. Hence, they tend to have a rapid onset and only last for a brief time. In contrast, moods are less intense and may last for a very long time. Indeed if mood states endure for more than a couple of weeks they are usually considered to have become *mood disorders*. Much of what we know about the neurochemistry of mood comes from the investigation of abnormal mood states such as clinical depression and mania. In general, emotions may have more to do with behavioural and expressive responses, while moods may have more to do with ongoing cognitive evaluations of one's situation in life. Interestingly, frequent negative mood states appear to be more related to negative health outcomes than frequent emotion episodes. A large number of measurement techniques have been developed to assess the different components of emotions and moods and these were also briefly discussed.

RECOMMENDED READING

An excellent discussion and commentaries on the distinctions between emotions and moods is provided in:

Paul Ekman and Richard J. Davidson (1994) *The Nature of Emotion*. New York: Oxford University Press. (Question 2: pp. 49–96).

A number of edited books are available containing relevant chapters by different authors. These are:

Tim Dalgleish and Mick Power (1999) *Handbook of Cognition and Emotion*. Chichester: Wiley.

Richard J. Davidson, Klaus R. Scherer and H. Hill Goldsmith (2003) *Handbook of Affective Sciences*. New York: Oxford University Press.

Michael Lewis and Jeannette M. Haviland-Jones (2000) *Handbook of Emotions*, 2nd edn. New York: Guilford Press.

J.A. Coan and John J.B. Allen (2007) *The Handbook of Emotion Elicitation and Assessment*. New York: Oxford University Press.

The following article provides an excellent overview of the conscious experience of emotion:

Lisa Feldman Barrett, Batja Mesquita, Kevin Ochsner and James Gross (2007) 'The experience of emotion', *Annual Review of Psychology*, 58, 373–403.

3 INDIVIDUAL DIFFERENCES IN EMOTIONAL REACTIVITY AND REGULATION

Temperament, Personality and Affective Style

When we look around ourselves and our friends it is clear that there are *individual differences* in how people respond to affective stimuli. Some people may cry profusely during a sad movie, while others remain unmoved. This individual variation has often been ignored in both cognitive and neuroscience studies where the focus is frequently on how people *in general* perform on a range of tasks. However, as confirmed by our everyday experience, it is evident that there is really no such thing as a 'general' or 'average' response. Instead, emotional reactivity differs markedly between people. In order to understand *emotions*, *moods* and *feelings*, therefore, we also need to understand how people might differ in their capacity to *experience* these affective states, as well as how people might differ in terms of how they *process*, *respond to* and *regulate* affective situations.

TEMPERAMENT

Much research on individual differences in emotionality has been conducted under the rubric of *temperament*. Temperaments can be construed as dispositions to react in certain ways to a variety of situations and it is, of course, likely that these dispositions are associated with particular neural circuits in the brain. Mary Rothbart, for example, has conducted influential research on temperament in young infants. She argues that the ease of arousal when stimulated and the ability to control that arousal are the two fundamental aspects of temperament that emerge very early in infancy (Rothbart, 1989). The ease with which an infant responds to stimulation in terms of motor activity, crying, vocalization, smiling and physiological responses – *reactivity* – can be measured in terms of the speed of response, the intensity or magnitude of the response, and the time to the peak magnitude of the response. The capacity to control that arousal – self-regulation – refers to a range of processes such as attentive mechanisms, approach behaviours, avoidance, attack and so on.

These two components of temperament map rather nicely onto the idea that the brain contains both *excitatory* (approach) and *inhibitory* (withdrawal) circuits (Kagan, 1994). Thus, a reactive infant would be assumed to have an excitable brain, whereas the infant who can regulate her/his reactivity and not become distressed would be assumed to have a strong inhibitory system. Consistent with this view, there is now

BOX 3.1

History of the concept of human temperament

The idea that people have enduring temperaments is not new. For example, in a book entitled *Character*, the Greek philosopher Theophrastus (372–287 BC) described many different types of people such as the flatterer, the dissembler, the tactless, the mean, the avaricious, and the garrulous. He argued that people could use their will power to determine their character.

Even earlier, the Greek physician Hippocrates (c. 460–377 BC), known as the father of modern medicine, also advocated a dispositional approach to explain human character and behaviour. He suggested that the clear variations between people's emotional reactivity, rationality and behaviour could be explained by reference to the balance between the four bodily fluids or 'humours'. These humours were: black bile, yellow bile, blood and phlegm. The idea was that a delicate balance between these bodily fluids created a tension or opposition between two pairs of qualities – 'warm' versus 'cool' and 'dry' versus 'moist' – that resulted in four different temperaments: *melancholic, sanguine, choleric* and *phlegmatic*. Melancholia (sadness) was due to too much black bile, whereas the sanguine (happy) temperament was due to an excess of blood. The phlegmatic (calm) temperament was related to excessive phlegm while the choleric (irritable) temperament was attributed to too much yellow bile.

Some 500 years later the philosopher and physician, Galen (131–201 AD), further developed these ideas and described nine temperamental types, each of which was tied closely to a physical condition. These ideas have had a profound influence on both philosophy and medicine down through the centuries.

These ideas were also instrumental in influencing early scientific psychology (Krohne, 2003). For instance, the father of experimental psychology in Europe, Wilhelm Wundt (1903), developed the temperament typology into a dimensional system. Wundt distinguished between people on the basis of the *speed* and *intensity* of their emotional arousal, allowing him to combine two levels of each dimension (a) speed: fast versus slow, and (b) intensity: strong versus weak. This resulted in a typology of emotional reaction tendencies that was closely related to the four temperaments of Hippocrates and Galen. Phlegmatics, for example, were characterized by *slow* and *weak* emotional arousal.

substantial evidence for the existence of both excitatory and inhibitory systems in the brain. From this perspective, temperament can be defined as 'constitutionally based individual differences in reactivity and self-regulation, in the domain of affect, activity, and attention' (Rothbart and Bates, 2006). Thus, in a general way, temperaments refer to fairly stable emotional reactions to a range of situations, they appear early in life and are assumed to comprise a significant genetic component (e.g., Kagan, 2003).

An historical overview of the study of *temperament* is presented in Box 3.1. The concept of temperament went out of favour in mainstream science until the late 1950s and early 1960s (Kagan, 1994, 2003; Krohne, 2003). In an important development,

TABLE 3.1 The nine dimensions of infant temperament

(a)	General activity level
(b)	Regularity of basic functions
(c)	Reactions to unfamiliarity
(d)	Ease of adapting to new situations
(e)	Responsiveness to stimulus events
(f)	Amount of energy associated with an activity
(g)	Dominant mood
(h)	Distractibility
(i)	Attention span

Source: Thomas and Chess (1977).

which helped to revitalize the concept of temperament, Thomas and Chess (1977) conducted extensive and detailed interviews with 85 well-educated parents of infants aged 3 to 9 months in New York City. Information was gathered on a range of the infants' characteristics, which resulted in the identification of nine different temperamental dispositions (see Table 3.1).

As acknowledged by the authors, these nine dimensions are not independent from each other. For instance, the child who reacts well to unfamiliar situations (category c) is likely to find it much easier to adjust to a new situation (category d). However, by examining the patterns of correlations between the various dimensions, Thomas and Chess identified three higher-level categories: the *easy child*, the *slow-to-warm-up child*, and the *difficult child*. The most common category was the easy child, accounting for about 40% of the infants, while around 15% were categorized as slow-to-warm-up. Around 10% of the sample were categorized as 'difficult', and these children were most likely to develop psychiatric symptoms when they were older. The remaining 35% of the infants were difficult to categorize because they did not fit easily into any of the three 'types'. The finding that difficult children were more likely to develop psychiatric problems in later life illustrates the notion that variations in temperament may lead to different vulnerabilities to develop emotional disorders. Subsequent research has used a variety of techniques and, although not everyone agrees on a single classification of childhood temperament, almost all taxonomies assume that the degree to which emotions are expressed and the regulation of emotions form the basic components of temperament (Rothbart and Bates, 2006; Rothbart and Derryberry, 1981; Rothbart and Sheese, 2007).

PERSONALITY

The related concept of *personality* has been used interchangeably with *temperament*, although there are some historical differences in how the concepts have been addressed. For example, temperament has most frequently been studied in the context of child development with the emphasis on the role of biological, especially genetic, factors in influencing individual differences in temperament. In contrast, personality has usually been investigated in adults, often those who are suffering from some form of mental problems. Many investigators have assumed that a person's *personality* characteristics can have a profound influence on affective experiences, especially as a factor in determining emotional reactivity as well as influencing regulatory processes. It is, therefore, important for students of emotion science to understand the distinction between temperament and personality.

Early theories of personality were based to a large extent on the clinical case notes of psychiatrists and psychologists who studied damaged and mentally disturbed people (Hall and Lindzey, 1970). Questionnaire-based measures are another common methodological approach in the study of personality. Self-report instruments have been used to identify the key personality factors or *traits* that can tell us something about the *uniqueness* of a person as well as illustrating how people *differ* from each other. One of the first psychologists to employ a trait approach to the study of personality was Gordon Allport (1937, 1961). He argued that personality describes what is most typical and characteristic of an individual. A more formal definition is 'the dynamic organization within the individual of those psychophysical systems that determine his [or her] characteristic behavior and thoughts'. The use of the term *psychophysical* reflects Allport's belief that personality is a blend of both mental and biological aspects, and that these are so fused together that it makes little sense to try and separate them. Extensive research indicates that, although thousands of different trait terms are used in everyday language, we employ a relatively small number when we try to describe a person. For example, we might describe someone as being 'friendly', 'ambitious', 'reliable' and so on. According to Allport, traits should not be seen merely as adjectives that label various behaviours, but as neuropsychological structures that actually exist within the person (1961). This view puts a high degree of emphasis on *individuality*. No two individuals behave or think exactly alike and therefore no two people have exactly the same personality. Nevertheless, there are a number of common traits that help us to categorize people in more general terms such as 'cheerful', 'depressive', 'reliable' and so on.

The notion of *traits* is important in contemporary emotion science because it suggests that people have a number of core aspects of their personality that can influence how a particular situation might be perceived or appraised, and this, in turn, can influence behaviour. Thus, two people may perceive and interpret the same situation in ways that are unique to them and, therefore, are likely to react in very different ways.

The trait approach to personality

If you are asked to describe what another person is like you will almost certainly use a number of adjectives that describe that person's typical behaviour. Thus, you may use such terms as relaxed or excitable, careful or reckless, friendly or unfriendly, warm or cold, reliable or irresponsible and so on. Indeed, Allport identified almost 18,000 different terms in the dictionary relating to personality traits! Many of these terms may be synonyms and it is also likely that many groups of traits tend to go together. Raymond B. Cattell was a psychologist who made a significant advance in our understanding of personality. He argued that there are three important sources of data about human personality: the life record, or *L-data*; the self-rating questionnaire, or

Q-data; and the objective test, or *T-data*. L-data might include a range of records, such as school records, and ratings from other people (e.g., teachers, friends, counsellors etc). Q-data, in contrast, provides a person's *self-report* by asking people (either in interviews or by questionnaire) to provide a description of themselves and their behaviour. Finally, T-data provides information on a variety of tests (e.g., perceptual tasks) that can be objectively measured. However, it is Q-data sources, especially the use of questionnaire measures of personality, that are most commonly used in emotion science.

Cattell (1957b) developed a questionnaire in which he asked a large number of college students to describe their friends using a choice of over 200 adjectives. He found that many of these adjectives tended to be used together. If someone was described as 'friendly' for example, it was likely that adjectives such as 'cheerful', 'outgoing' and 'talkative' would also be used. Not surprisingly, the same person would not tend to be described as 'reserved', 'sober' or 'quiet'. Thus, groups of adjectives tended to cluster together into higher-order groups. A statistical technique known as *factor analysis* was used to identify a smaller group of higher-order *factors* describing personality. A person's responses on a number of self-descriptive trait-adjectives were coded and then examined for sets of responses which correlated with each other. On this basis, 16 core personality traits were identified and included in a 16 Personality Factor Questionnaire, or *16-PF scale*. Each of the 16 traits represents a continuum between two extremes, e.g., reserved–outgoing, as shown in Table 3.2.

While Cattell's 16-PF is still widely used a number of significant problems with the scale have been identified. Norman (1963) found that the 16 different personality traits could be broken down into 5 core factors: *extraversion* (talkative, outgoing etc),

TABLE 3.2 The sixteen factors derived by Cattell and measured on the 16-PF Questionnaire

Reserved	Outgoing
Less intelligent	More intelligent
Affected by feelings	More emotionally stable
Humble	Assertive
Sober	Happy-go-lucky
Expedient	Conscientious
Shy	Venturesome
Tough-minded	Tender-minded
Trusting	Suspicious
Practical	Imaginative
Forthright	Shrewd
Placid	Apprehensive
Conservative	Experimenting
Group-dependent	Self-sufficient
Casual	Controlled
Relaxed	Tense

Source: Adapted from Conn and Rieke (1994).

TABLE 3.3 The 'Big Five' factors of personality and the subordinate traits

Factor	*Constituent traits*
Openness to experience	Appreciation for art and adventure Unusual ideas Imaginative High degree of curiosity
Conscientiousness	Tendency to show self-discipline Dutiful and responsible Planned rather than spontaneous behaviour Aim for achievement
Extraversion	Tendency to experience positive emotions easily Tendency to seek company of others Talkative and outgoing Energetic Tendency to seek stimulation
Agreeableness	Tendency to be compassionate Co-operative Trusting of others Accepting of others
Neuroticism	Tendency to experience negative emotions easily Often nervous and anxious

agreeableness (cooperative and good-natured etc), *conscientiousness* (hard-working, reliable etc), *emotional stability* (composed, calm etc), and *cultural awareness* (artistic, creative, imaginative etc). More recent research has converged on this notion that personality can be completely described by five core traits (John, 1990). The most influential and widely accepted *five-factor* model of personality was presented by McCrae and Costa (1985). On the basis of extensive empirical evidence they proposed that there are five core traits underlying human personality – openness to experience, conscientiousness, extraversion, agreeableness, neuroticism – and developed a questionnaire (NEO-Personality Inventory or NEO-PI) to measure these five factors (Costa and McCrae, 1985; McCrae and Costa, 1987). Each of the 'Big Five' contains a range of more specific subordinate constructs as shown in Table 3.3.

Criticisms of the trait approach

The trait approach has proved very useful as a framework in personality research. However, the five-factor model does not include some important aspects of personality, such as religiosity, manipulativeness, honesty, masculinity/femininity, sense of humour and so on, that might affect a person's response to affective situations. Moreover, some research has indicated that the five factors may not be completely independent of each other (Hogan et al., 1997). Another problem relates to the fact that the five-factor model of personality was developed primarily in Western countries. As we saw in Chapter 1, cultural models of emotion propose that emotional reactivity to situations is often determined by the surrounding context and culture; on *external* factors rather than on *internal* factors such as personality traits. A trait approach to personality, of course, assumes that there are enduring features of the person – personality traits – that remain relatively consistent across different situations. This may well be true in Western cultures where the *'independent self'* is primary and the emphasis is very much on the individual, often at the expense of group cohesion. In contrast, many Eastern cultures give priority to the *'interdependent self'* and emphasize the importance of maintaining harmony and balance within a group, often at the expense of individual happiness or achievement (Markus and Kitayama, 1991; Triandis, 1989). In support of this view, there is some evidence that personality traits are good predictors of behaviour in individualist cultures, but are less accurate in collectivist cultures (Church and Katigbak, 2000). Nevertheless, a number of studies have found that the Big Five factors do seem to exist in many collectivist cultures such as China and the Philippines, although other unrelated factors, such as *tradition* in China, are also apparent (Cheung and Leung, 1998; Katigbak et al., 2002). These factors need to be taken into account in a complete scientific account of human emotion.

Some influential theories of personality

Eysenck's model

Hans Eysenck (1953) developed a model of human temperament, based primarily on questionnaire studies and detailed clinical interviews, which indicated that there were two major dimensions of personality: introversion/extraversion and neuroticism/stability. *Introverts* were characterized as being somewhat reclusive, less socially active, quiet and reserved, introspective and generally preferred books to people. In contrast, *extraverts* were characterized as being gregarious, socially active, happy, impulsive, and generally assertive. We can call this personality dimension *extraversion-positive affectivity (E-PA)*. An independent trait of *neuroticism* was also identified. This consists of a range of negative emotional states (anxiety, depression, tension etc) and tends to correlate very highly with standard measures of trait-anxiety. This dimension has subsequently been called *neuroticism-negative affectivity (N-NA)*. All of these dimensions can be measured by means of the Eysenck Personality Questionnaire (EPQ) (Eysenck and Eysenck, 1975b), which is still widely used in personality and emotion research. A third factor of *psychoticism* was later added. It is characterized by egocentric, aggressive and impulsive behaviour. People high on this factor tend to appear impersonal and cold, and lack empathy for others. A revised version of the EPQ (r-EPQ) (Eysenck et al., 1985) was developed to measure all three dimensions. An important point to note is that the three dimensions of extraversion, neuroticism and psychoticism are not correlated with each other. In other words, they are independent (or orthogonal) factors. Two of the traits – extraversion and neuroticism, or E and N – are consistent with two of the five traits identified in the five-factor model of personality.

Eysenck argued that genetic factors were important in determining an individual's degree of introversion/extraversion, neuroticism, and psychoticism. Subsequent research with identical twins reared apart has confirmed that genetic factors do account for a significant proportion (about 40%) of the variance in personality factors (Plomin et al., 1997). To determine how genetics may influence the three personality dimensions identified by the EPQ, great efforts have been made to uncover the underlying psychophysiological mechanisms. A key proposal was that introverts have more active cortical arousal and activity than extraverts and that this is regulated by the *ascending reticular activating system* (ARAS) in the brain (Eysenck, 1967). The empirical evidence generally supports this hypothesis. For example, a comprehensive review of EEG studies concluded that introverts were significantly more cortically aroused than extraverts in 22 out of 33 studies (Gale, 1983). The theory suggested that neuroticism should be associated with increased activity in what was termed the *visceral brain*, which comprises the amygdala, hippocampus, cingulate, septum and hypothalamus. Studies using *indirect* measures such as heart rate and skin conductance responses have generally not found support for this view (Fahrenberg, 1992). However, more recent studies using *direct* measures of brain activity, which are more sensitive to changes than indirect measures, have identified specific patterns of activation related to E-PA and N-NA (see Canli, 2006, for overview).

Kagan's model

Jerome Kagan has developed a two-dimensional model of temperament based on years of research to monitor the development of infants, through childhood into adulthood (Kagan, 1994). His main interest was to determine how young infants and children respond to unfamiliar situations (people or objects). Most of us have witnessed how some children become fearful and distressed when introduced to something novel and try to avoid the situation. In contrast, other children seem less fearful, and are more likely to explore new situations and interact with unfamiliar people. Kagan used the terms '*inhibited*' and '*uninhibited*' to describe these two categories of children. His model of temperament was based on an extensive body of research showing that all species demonstrate genetically-based variations in the propensity to approach or avoid unfamiliar situations or objects (e.g., Schneirla, 1959). As discussed in his book *Galen's Prophecy*, Kagan (1994) found that a large proportion of children (about 40%) could be categorized as 'uninhibited' in that they were slow to become aroused, but when they did become aroused they tended to be excitable and engaged in much babbling and smiling. The majority of these infants went on to become highly sociable and relatively fearless children. In contrast, about 20% of infants could be categorized as 'inhibited': they appeared to be very easily aroused when presented with new situations and tended to become distressed in novel surroundings. The majority of these infants developed into relatively fearful and cautious children. These broad temperamental types become clear when an infant reaches about 1 year of age, and remain reasonably stable throughout childhood

TABLE 3.4 Kagan's main behavioural characteristics of inhibited and uninhibited children

Inhibited children	*Uninhibited children*
Shy with strangers	Highly sociable
Tend to avoid unfamiliar situations, people or objects	Tend to approach unfamiliar situations, people or objects.
Distress in unfamiliar situations	Spontaneous activity in unfamiliar situations
Subdued emotion in new situations or when meeting new people	Expressed positive emotion in new situations or when meeting new people

Source: Adapted from Kagan (1994).

and into the adolescent and adult years. The main features of these temperamental categories are summarized in Table 3.4.

Research suggests that there are clear differences in physiological response between inhibited and uninhibited children (Kagan, 1994, 2003). In a longitudinal study, 450 infants were tested when they were 4 months old, and a proportion of these children were tested again when they were 14 months, 21 months, 4.5 years, and 7.5 years of age. On the basis of these data, it was suggested that some babies are born with a very low threshold of excitability in the amygdala and its projections to the ventral striatum, hypothalamus, cingulate and other brain areas. During a 40-minute session in which they were presented with a number of unfamiliar stimuli these '*high reactive*' infants demonstrated a high degree of muscle tension, intense muscle activity, and frequent crying. One particularly interesting finding was that, when these reactive babies were tested again at around 1 or 2 years of age, they were much more likely to express fear in unfamiliar situations. In contrast, the '*low reactive*' group of children showed much lower levels of motor arousal and minimal distress (e.g., crying) in the same 40-minute test with unfamiliar items. When tested later, this group of children was more likely to show few signs of fear in unfamiliar situations. When they were tested at 7.5 years of age, the children who had been categorized as 'high reactive' at 4 months were most likely to have acquired symptoms of anxiety (e.g., fear of the dark, fear of animals, extreme shyness with strangers etc), making up 45% of the group with anxious symptoms. In contrast, only 15% of the group who showed anxious symptoms at 7.5 years had been categorized as low reactive when they were 4 months old (Kagan et al., 1999). Thus, high reactivity in the first few months of life seems to predispose children to being 'inhibited' and more fearful during childhood. These children are more likely to develop anxiety symptoms when they are around 7 or 8 years of age.

To summarize, this model of temperament is centred upon the concepts of approach and avoidance, which manifests as *inhibited* and *uninhibited* temperamental styles in childhood. There also seems to be a clear biological basis to these different psychological profiles. However, it is important to note that our biology is not necessarily our destiny since the links between a temperamental disposition and emotional expression are strongly modulated by each individual's particular experiences in life, as well as the cultural context in which an individual develops (Kagan, 2003).

Gray's model

Jeffrey Gray (1982) developed a theory of personality based on decades of experimental work, primarily investigating the effects of anti-anxiety drugs in rats. He concluded that there are *three* fundamental emotion systems in the brain: a *Fight or Flight System* (F/FLS), a *Behavioural Activation System* (BAS), and a *Behavioural Inhibition System* (BIS). Early studies examined the effects of common anti-anxiety drugs on animals and found that the effects of these drugs could be best understood by the concept of the BIS. The central idea is that this brain system controls the inhibition of ongoing behaviour, increases vigilance towards the source of potential threat, and also results in an increase in arousal. Imagine a rat happily foraging and feeding when it notices the scent of a cat. As soon as the dangerous odour is detected the BIS becomes activated, which immediately inhibits the foraging behaviour and increases arousal and attention towards the possible location of the cat. A diagrammatic representation of the BIS is shown in Figure 3.1.

The idea is that all of the inputs lead to *conflict* in the sense that the current situation conflicts with ongoing goals. Thus, in our example of the rat smelling the cat, the input is an innate fear stimulus representing danger, which conflicts with the ongoing activity of feeding. This conflict activates the BIS, which leads to various outputs: the rat stops what it is doing; it becomes vigilant, attempting to locate the cat; and physiological arousal increases in order to facilitate flight or fight responses. Thus, the BIS is assumed to operate as a *comparator* that constantly monitors the *current* state of the world in terms of whether it matches the *expected* state of the world. Any conflict that is detected will result in the activation of the BIS. Extensive research by Gray and his colleagues, as well as many others, has shown that almost all anti-anxiety drugs have consistent effects on behavioural outputs in animals (see Gray, 1982; Gray and McNaughton, 2000, for reviews). In cases of pure fear, such as those elicited by the immediate presence of a predator, the typical behaviours are active avoidance (escape), defensive attack (fight) or behavioural freezing, which is common in many

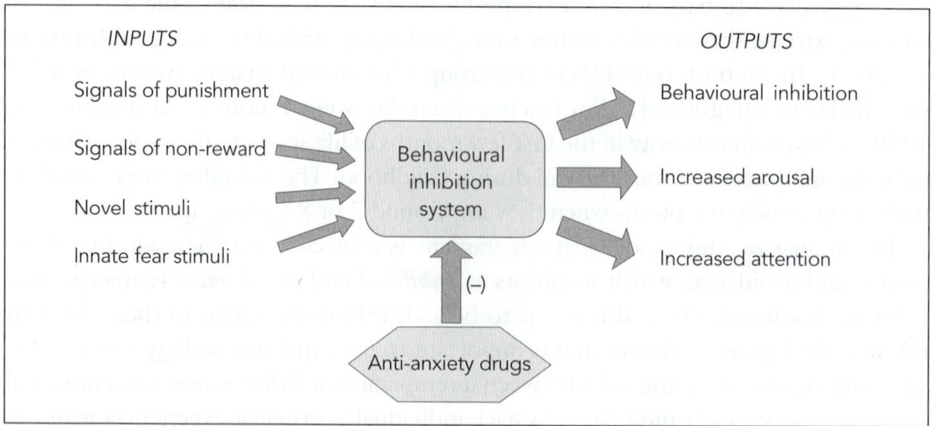

FIGURE 3.1 The key inputs and outputs of the behavioural inhibition system
Source: Gray (1982).

species such as rats and rabbits. It is interesting to note that the most common type of anti-anxiety drugs – benzodiazepines – have no effect on these behaviours. Thus, giving a rat a drug such as Valium does not decrease the amount of fear behaviour expressed in the presence of a predator. However, in situations where there is a clear *approach–avoidance conflict* the anti-anxiety drugs have a strong impact. They tend to shift the balance from avoidance towards approach. When an animal is assessing a potential risk (e.g., is there a predator present?) there is a clear conflict between the benefits of rapid escape and the benefits of further exploration (e.g., finding a mate). The interesting result is that when rats are under the influence of anti-anxiety drugs this balance is shifted so that they spend relatively more time exploring and 'assessing risk'. The evidence indicates that this class of drugs has clear anti-anxiety effects in humans as well as animals. Thus, anxious patients report a significant reduction in anxiety when compared with a placebo condition (dummy pill). Likewise, physician-ratings also indicate that anxiety is reduced when patients are treated with this type of drug.

An important step towards identifying the neural mechanisms underlying 'anxiety' was the finding that damage to the *septo-hippocampal* region of the brain affects the behaviour of rats in conflict situations in a very similar way to anti-anxiety drugs. This suggests that the septo-hippocampal system is crucial for anxiety. In a general way then, the BIS is assumed to be located in the septo-hippocampal region and is considered to control behavioural inhibition in response to aversive stimuli (see Gray and McNaughton, 2000, for a comprehensive review).

In contrast to the BIS, the *fight–flight system* (F/FLS) is involved in cases of pure fear and controls active fight or flight behaviour in response to aversive stimuli. The decision to actively avoid danger or to fight is very much dependent on what has been termed the *defensive distance* between a danger and the animal (Blanchard and Blanchard, 1990b). This reflects the obvious observation that different types of behaviour are appropriate at different distances from threat. If we go back to our example of the rat and the cat, it is clear that fighting is only appropriate when the cat is very close and escape is not possible. However, if the cat is relatively far away then vigilance and assessment of the danger is more important. The role of the F/FLS is to allow the rat to actively avoid the cat or to fight if necessary. There is some evidence that this system is controlled by the amygdala and is probably analogous to panic and simple phobias in humans. This contrasts with the BIS, which appears to be analogous to anxiety in humans because it controls aspects of cognitive appraisal such as risk assessment (Gray, 1982; Gray and McNaughton, 2000). The inputs and outputs of the F/FLS are shown in Figure 3.2(a).

The third system identified by Gray is concerned with responses to appetitive stimuli and has been called the *behavioural approach system* (BAS). The inputs to the BAS are signals of reward and non-punishment, as shown in Figure 3.2(b). When activated, the BAS results in active approach behaviours.

The basis of anxiety reactions is considered to be the activation of the BIS by means of the *simultaneous* activation of the FFS and the BAS. Imagine the situation in which an animal is faced with an approach–avoidance conflict. This is fairly common in

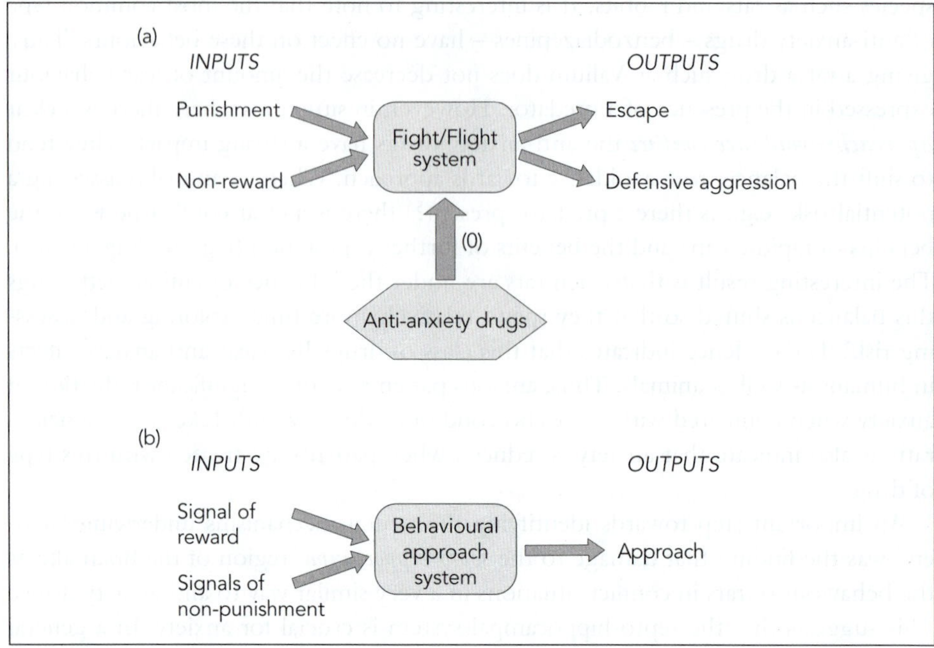

FIGURE 3.2 The inputs and outputs of (a) the fight–flight system, and (b) the behavioural approach system

Source: Gray (1982).

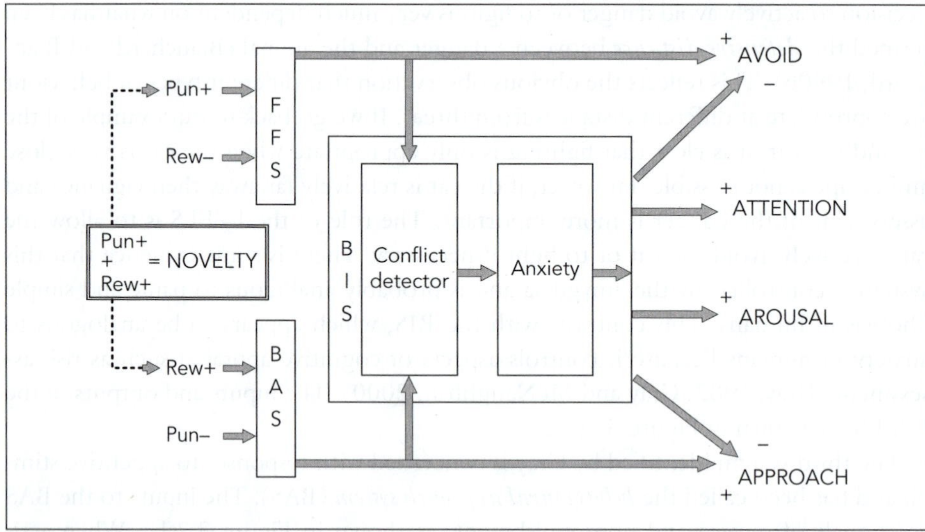

FIGURE 3.3 A simplified overview of the relations between the three emotion systems

Source: Adapted from Gray and McNaughton (2000).

normal behaviour (e.g., simultaneous presence of a potential mate and a predator). In this situation, simple approach and simple avoidance are both inhibited and replaced by active scanning of the environment, an internal scanning of memory, as well as a variety of general risk assessment behaviours. Since all of these processes are designed to increase the salience of potentially dangerous stimuli one consequence of the activation of the BIS is to shift the balance between approach and avoidance behaviours more in the direction of avoidance. The relations between the three fundamental emotional systems are illustrated in Figure 3.3.

As can be seen in Figure 3.3, the F/FLS is activated by the presence of punishment (Pun+, e.g. a predator) or the absence of a reward (Rew–, e.g. absence of food or potential mates) and, once activated, this system directly increases avoidance behaviour. The BAS, in contrast, is activated by the presence of a reward (Rew+, e.g. presence of food) and the absence of punishment (Pun–, e.g. no predator or obvious danger) and, once this system is active, the approach behaviours are increased. However, if both systems are activated at the same time (e.g., presence of a predator and a mate) then conflict occurs and the BIS becomes activated. In this situation, both simple avoidance and simple approach are inhibited and are replaced by increased attention: increased scanning of the environment, risk assessment and internal scanning of memory. All of these operations are, of course, aimed at detecting negative information and lead to an increase in the salience of such information. Thus, a clear consequence of activation of the BIS is a shift of the balance between approach and avoidance tendencies in the direction of increased avoidance.

Gray and his colleagues have conducted extensive research to identify the neural substrates of these three fundamental emotion systems (see Table 3.5).

Two questionnaires have been developed to provide self-report measures of the BIS and BAS in humans (Carver and White, 1994). These scales contain items such as 'Even if something bad is about to happen to me, I rarely experience fear or nervousness' or 'When I want something, I usually go all out to get it' and each item is answered on a 4-point scale ranging from 1 (very true for me) to 4 (very false for me). People who score highly on the BAS tend to be more sensitive to rewards, whereas those who score highly on the BIS are relatively more sensitive to punishment. Moreover, scores on BIS scales are correlated with the degree of neural activation to affectively significant stimuli (Mathews et al., 2004) (see Table 3.5).

TABLE 3.5 Gray's model of emotional systems

System	*Neural structures*
Flight–Fight (F/FLS)	Amygdala, hypothalamus, central grey
Behavioural inhibition (BIS)	Septo-hippocampal circuits
Behavioural approach (BAS)	Basal ganglia, dopaminergic tracts

Source: Gray (1994).

Cloninger's model

Cloninger (1987) also developed a psychobiological model of temperament based on the idea that there are three primary temperamental types. These are functionally organized within the brain as independent systems concerned with the *activation*, *maintenance* and *inhibition* of behaviour in response to specific classes of stimuli. These *temperamental* factors are assumed to involve automatic responses to stimuli that essentially reflect consistent biases in information processing. Cloninger's three dimensions of personality or temperament are presented in Table 3.6.

The temperamental types outlined in Table 3.6 are assumed to be organized in a hierarchy and, as is typical of many complex systems, can be broken down into stable subsystems that evolved in a sequential way. Thus, the idea is that the phylogeny of temperament began with the development of a *behavioural inhibition system* (harm avoidance) in all animals, which was then followed by a *behavioural approach system* (novelty seeking) in more advanced animals, and then various subsystems were added in order to *maintain* a number of behaviours (reward dependence) in reptiles and later phyla (Cloninger and Gilligan, 1987). Extensive research into the mechanisms underlying these three components of temperament or personality suggests that the avoidance of danger or harm is related to the *norepinephrine* (NE: also known as *noradrenaline*) system, novelty seeking is linked with *dopaminergic* (DA) systems, whereas reward dependence is related to the functioning of the *serotonin* system (5-HT).

A self-report questionnaire called the *Tridimensional Personality Questionnaire (TPQ)* was developed in order to measure these three components of temperament. Subsequent analysis revealed that these factors were psychologically independent of each other. In addition, a fourth dimension of '*persistence*' was identified (Nixon and Parsons, 1989). Large-scale twin studies have provided additional evidence that these four dimensions of temperament are independent of each other, and that they are associated with different genetic profiles (Heath et al., 1994; Stallings et al., 1996). The main characteristics of the four temperamental components are outlined in Table 3.7.

TABLE 3.6 Cloninger's three primary temperamental types

Harm avoidance (HA)	HA is viewed as a heritable bias in the inhibition of behaviours such as persistent worry and rumination on the possibility of future problems. The more passive avoidance mechanisms such as fear of uncertainty and shyness of strangers are also part of this temperament.
Novelty seeking (NS)	NS is viewed as a heritable bias in the initiation or activation of behaviours such as frequent exploration of new environments or situations, impulsive decision-making, extravagance in approaching positive stimuli such as rewards. In addition, this temperament is characterized by a quick loss of temper and the active avoidance of frustration.
Reward dependence (RD)	The main aspect of this temperament is a dependence on social rewards. RD is viewed as a heritable bias in the maintenance or continuation of ongoing behaviours and is generally manifested as sentimentality, social attachment, and dependence on the approval of others.

Source: Cloninger (1987).

TABLE 3.7 Cloninger's model of temperamental types

Temperamental dimension	*High score on TPQ*	*Low score on TPQ*
Harm avoidance	Careful and cautious Fearful and apprehensive Tense Doubtful and timid Easily discouraged Insecure Passive Pessimistic	Carefree and relaxed Courageous and daring Composed Optimistic Outgoing and bold Confident Dynamic Vigorous
Novelty seeking	Exploratory Excitable Curious Quick-tempered Enthusiastic Impulsive Easily bored	Indifferent Uninquisitive Unemotional Slow-tempered Unenthusiastic Reserved Orderly
Reward dependence	Loving and warm Tender hearted Sensitive Dependent and sociable Dedicated	Tough minded Practical Cold Content to be alone Socially insensitive
Persistence	Hardworking and industrious Persistent and stable Frustration seen as a challenge Ambitious	Inactive and unreliable Unstable and erratic Gives up easily when frustrated or criticized Not ambitious

TPQ = Tridimensional Personality Questionnaire

Source: Cloninger (1987).

It is important to remember that each of these factors are themselves multifaceted, and consist of a number of lower-order traits. For instance, harm avoidance consists of an amalgam of scores from subtraits including: anticipatory worry versus uninhibited optimism; fear of uncertainty; shyness with strangers; and fatigue versus vigour. The four temperamental components identified by means of subjective self-report scales are hypothesized to be genetically-based, become obvious early in life and involve pre-conceptual biases in learning.

Cloninger et al. (1993) have subsequently extended this model based on a synthesis of information from research in social and cognitive development and descriptions of human personality derived from humanistic psychology traditions. For example, the four temperaments defined on the TPQ do not account for traits such as *compassion* and *social cooperation*. The evidence indicates that as human beings mature many of the commonly-seen response biases are related to concepts of the *self*. Thus, in the teenage years, questions relating to 'who we are' and 'why we are here' are very common. Questions of this type are clearly more *conceptually-driven*, and responses to them can often be modified by changes in the salience and significance of stimuli that are determined by our own sense of identity (Cloninger et al., 1993). The *self-concept* is an important aspect of a person's personality. It deals with an individual's sense of his or her own identity as distinct from others, and with his or her unique combination of characteristics. How these aspects of the *self-concept* might develop can be distinguished in relation to the extent to which a person identifies the self as (1) an autonomous individual, (2) an integral part of humanity or society, and (3) an integral part of the universe or the unity of all things. As we saw in Chapter 1, culturally-based approaches put a particular emphasis on the fact that these facets of personality will differ markedly depending on the type of culture in which an individual develops. If one is growing up in a highly collectivist culture then the self-concept may be much more involved with notions of being an integral part of society. In contrast, those living in a highly individualist society might be more likely to develop a concept of the self containing the notion that the individual is autonomous and independent.

An extended questionnaire called the Temperament and Character Inventory (TCI) has been developed to measure the four temperaments (HA, NS, RD, and P) in addition to three new *character* dimensions (Cloninger, 1994):

1 self-directedness – a measure of individual self-acceptance,
2 cooperativeness – a measure of the degree of acceptance of other people, and
3 self-transcendence – a measure of the degree to which an individual feels a part of the universe and nature as a whole.

This seven-factor model provides a much more comprehensive structure of human personality. It is based on the idea that perceptual memory processes which relate to *temperament* operate independently of more abstract and intentional processes which define conceptual memories. Subsequent research has verified that the seven-factor model can explain a greater degree of the variance in personality than the four-factor model alone (e.g., Gillespie et al., 2003).

How do the various theories of temperament and personality relate to each other?

We have discussed four influential theories of temperament or personality in this section. In spite of the fact that these theorists use data from a variety of disciplines – behavioural neuroscience studies with rats; questionnaire studies with humans, studies of the developing child using parents' reports and so on – there is actually a remarkable degree of overlap among the four theories. If we take Gray's proposal of three primary systems as standard we see that the BIS and the BAS overlap considerably with Kagan's notion of inhibition and lack of inhibition. Gray himself argued that the underlying causal dimensions of Eysenck's personality components of neuroticism and extraversion–introversion were the BIS/Anxiety dimension (see Figure 3.4). Likewise, the BAS or impulsivity system lay between neuroticism and extraversion (Fowles, 2006; Gray, 1970, 1973). This theoretical description indicates that *neuroticism* is a reflection of increased sensitivities to *both* reward *and* punishment (Fowles, 2006). Likewise, extraversion can be considered to reflect a greater sensitivity to reward than punishment, while introversion reflects a greater sensitivity to punishment than to reward.

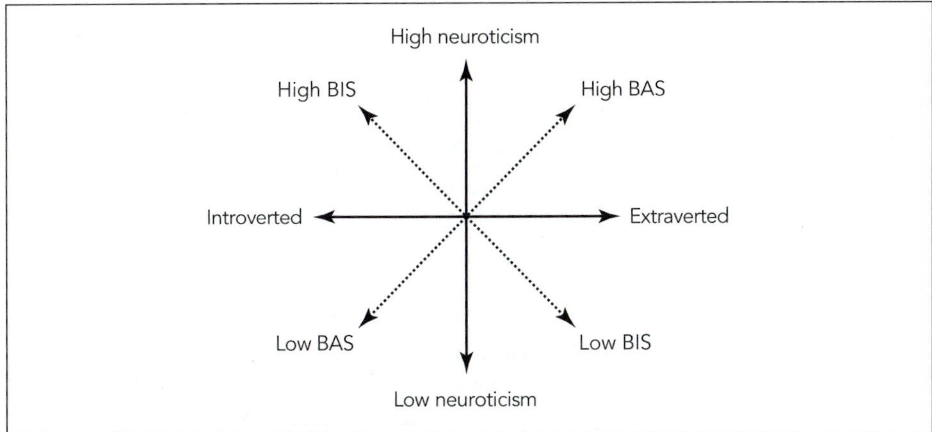

FIGURE 3.4 The structure of personality on the basis of Eysenck's neuroticism and introversion–extraversion dimensions with Gray's notion of the BIS/Anxiety and BAS/Impulsivity systems overlaid

Source: Gray (1970).

It seems then that the theories of Gray, Kagan and Eysenck can be fairly easily reconciled. The dimensions suggested by Cloninger also seem to overlap to a large extent with this structure. Thus, harm avoidance is close to the notion of the BIS, while novelty seeking is similar to the BAS. Reward dependence almost certainly relates to extraversion, which in turn is related to the BAS. The fourth dimension of persistence is less obviously linked to Gray's proposal. Also, the wider traits relating to character in Cloninger's model cannot easily be reconciled with the other dimensions of personality.

Maslow's hierarchy of needs

The theories of personality that we have discussed so far have been influential in emotion science but, with the exception of Cloninger's approach, have tended to focus on *negative* affective experiences such as anxiety, and often stemmed from work with mentally disturbed individuals. In contrast, Maslow argued that in order to understand human personality it was essential to focus on people's *positive* characteristics. He proposed that the ultimate goal or *need* of a human being was to be *self-actualized* and that the need for personal growth motivated much of human behaviour (Maslow, 1954, 1970). The concept of self-actualization refers to the notion that people have a need to strive for their full potential. Thus, a person needs to be what he can be: the artist must paint, the writer must write and so on. If people do not fulfil whatever potential they have then they are not self-actualized. However, in order to reach this ultimate goal there are a range of more basic needs that need to be addressed. At the bottom of the hierarchy, shown in Figure 3.5, are the *physiological* needs relating to food, water, sleep, sex, and elimination. These are all needs directly related to survival and are, therefore, considered to be fundamental. Next up in the hierarchy are the

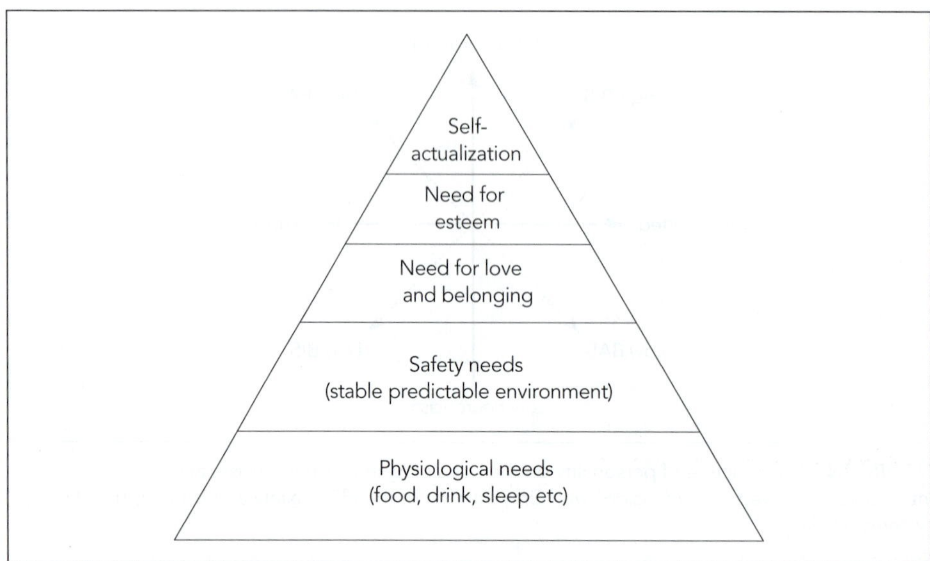

FIGURE 3.5 Maslow's hierarchy of needs
Source: Maslow (1954).

needs for personal safety. Once these needs have been satisfied the higher-level needs of being loved and feeling that we belong to a group can be addressed. Further up the hierarchy are needs for personal recognition and respect that lead to self-esteem and finally, at the top of the hierarchy, is the need to fulfil one's own potential.

Maslow (1970) studied people who he considered to be self-actualized, including many who were well known figures such as Abraham Lincoln, Albert Einstein, Eleanor Roosevelt and so on. On the basis of these studies he concluded that a self-actualized person is characterized by having a need for privacy, a realistic orientation to life, and a general acceptance of themselves and others and of the world as it is. They tend to be spontaneous, independent and deal with situations in a fresh and flexible manner rather than in a stereotypical way. In particular, these people have often had profound mystical or spiritual experiences or so-called *peak experiences* of ecstasy or awe. Most importantly they are secure in who they are and are not overly affected by other's negative opinions about them. They tend to have a few deeply-felt intimate relationships. Clearly the drive to achieve one's potential can influence the affective quality of one's life. This approach focuses on the individual in terms of their personal growth rather than focusing on a small number of traits that might influence reactivity across a variety of situations. Maslow's theory is very much embedded in a Westernized view of what is considered the ultimate human achievement. For him, the individual reaching his full potential is the ultimate. Thus, at least in Western societies, this theory suggests that the need to fulfil one's potential is a strong motivating force underlying human behaviour. This perspective implies that this need is likely to influence responses to affective situations – and indeed determine what constitutes affective situations – in a number of ways.

AFFECTIVE STYLE

The previous sections discussed a number of influential theories and research concerning individual differences in temperament and personality. A related construct is the notion of *affective style*, which relates to the extent to which each and every one of us experiences *positive affect* (PA) and *negative affect* (NA) in our daily lives. While related to previous research on temperament and personality traits, the notion of affective style has been developed to more directly address individual differences in how people *react* to affective situations as well as differences in how people *regulate* their affective responses (e.g., Davidson, 1998a). A large body of research indicates that individual differences in affective style can play an important role in the degree to which we experience positive and negative emotions. Depue and Monroe (1986), for example, reviewed a wide range of literature and concluded that people with different temperaments may actually create different environments and stressors for themselves. They called this the 'person–environment covariance'. It is similar to Bolger and Zuckerman's (1995) 'differential exposure' model of neuroticism, which demonstrates that people scoring high in neuroticism experience negative events far more frequently than those with low scores on neuroticism. Let us consider how this might happen. If we think of someone who is very depressed and sad, he or she is generally not much fun to be with and may receive criticism from other people for lying in bed all day. A happy person on the other hand is outgoing and may travel to other countries where he or she meets other outgoing people who like to travel. In other words, the way in which people react to the world can have a profound impact on the type of social world that they inhabit.

Investigations in realistic situations as well as laboratory-based studies indicate that when people (or animals) are presented with similar incentives and challenges, the resulting emotional reactions differ widely across different individuals. This is an important point and illustrates that the degree to which we experience PA or NA is dependent upon (a) our appraisal of a particular situation, and (b) our emotional reactivity to the situation. It is the range of these differences that Davidson (1992b, 1998a) has referred to as *affective style*.

Components of affective style

Many components of affective style have been studied in diverse research literatures. Table 3.8 summarizes some of the domains of emotion processing that may vary between individuals. At the level of *emotion perception* cognitive processes can be biased towards either positive or negative stimuli. Individual differences can also occur across the *response systems* of the body – subjective, behavioural, physiological and so on – as well as at the level of neural reactivity. Indeed, research in emotion science has led to exciting discoveries about fundamental individual differences in how the brain responds to emotional stimuli (e.g., Canli et al., 2001) and how these individual differences may be linked to very specific changes at a genetic level (e.g., Lesch et al., 1996). The increasing convergence of behavioural and neuroimaging methodologies,

TABLE 3.8 Some domains of emotion processing

Emotion component	*Examples*
Emotion perception	Detection of threatening information Selective allocation of attention towards positive or negative information
Emotion production	Changes in response to emotional situations. These can operate at behavioural, autonomic, neural and subjective levels
Emotion regulation	There are a variety of processes that may amplify or reduce the expression of emotion at behavioural, physiological, neural and subjective levels
Emotion memory	A number of processes may result in the selective remembering of either positive or negative information

in addition to genetic analyses, holds great promise for significant advances in our understanding of emotions and emotional disorders.

In addition to the range of potential differences at perceptual/cognitive levels, as well as at response and neural levels, a number of processes are also involved in *regulating* emotional responses, and these can also differ across individuals. Indeed, it is very difficult to determine precisely when an emotion ends and regulation begins because it is likely that regulatory processes are recruited every time an emotion is generated (Davidson, 1998a). Emotion regulation refers to a range of processes that serve to *amplify*, *reduce* or *maintain* the magnitude of emotional reactions (Thompson, 1994). While we have separated out perceptual, response and regulatory processes for ease of discussion, it is obvious that these processes are tightly interrelated and interact in highly dynamic ways. In order to respond to an emotional stimulus, for example, we need to perceive and appraise the stimulus and the probability of doing this may be influenced by regulatory mechanisms. For example, if we become very frightened (response) when watching a horror movie (perception), we may shut our eyes (regulation), so that we are less likely to see the next terrifying scene and our response then reduces. All of these different processes are, of course, interacting in a fast and dynamic way and the *causal* relationship between the different processes is very difficult to determine.

Individual differences in emotional responding

There are a number of different ways in which we can *respond* to emotional situations. In response to a funny story we may laugh (*behavioural output*) and feel happy (*subjective experience*), and if the story is really funny we may even cry and get a pain in our stomach (*physiological response*). A range of neural and biochemical responses may also be occurring which we cannot directly observe or experience. There may be individual differences in any of these response systems. Davidson (1998a) also argues that an individual difference in a particular response system does not necessarily transfer between different emotions. For example, a person who is highly expressive when given good news may not necessarily be highly expressive when given bad news.

As shown in Table 3.9, there may be individual differences in the *threshold* at which particular components of an emotional response are elicited. For example, one person

TABLE 3.9 Davidson's components of emotional response

Threshold differences	Differences in the threshold of eliciting components of a particular emotion
Peak or Amplitude	Differences in the maximum intensity of a given response
Rise time to peak	Differences in the time between onset of a stimulus and the maximum response
Recovery time	Differences in the time to return to baseline following perturbation in a particular system
Duration of the response	Total length of time from onset of the response to a return to baseline

Source: Davidson (1998a).

might be very sensitive to sour milk so that the smell of milk that is just one day out of date may cause intense revulsion and a disgust reaction. In contrast, another individual may only have this degree of reaction when the milk has been off for a couple of days. Threshold differences have been reported between the level of threat at which people will appraise a stimulus as threatening. In one study, people were grouped according to their score on self-report measures of trait anxiety. All groups were found to be vigilant for extremely threatening pictures, while only the highly anxious group were vigilant for mildly threatening stimuli (Mogg et al., 2000). Thus, there are individual differences in the perceived threat value of a given stimulus, which, in turn, is likely to influence the physiological response. It is also possible that different people may make a similar appraisal of a stimulus but show individual differences in their *response* to that appraisal. Unfortunately, there has been very little systematic research on establishing threshold differences in different emotional response systems.

In addition to threshold differences, there are also differences between the *magnitude* of people's responses, or what is technically called the peak (or amplitude) of the response. While sitting in a dentist's chair, for example, some individuals may experience elevations in their heart rate of 60 beats per minute, whereas another individual may feel equally apprehensive but his or her heart rate may increase by just 20 beats per minute. Once again, Davidson (1998a) cautions that such individual differences may be highly specific to a particular response system and may not be generalized to other response systems, even within the same emotion. In the example above, both people may show the same facial expression of fear (both may look highly anxious), yet they differ in terms of the cardiovascular response to anticipating dental treatment. The *rise time to the peak of the response* is also likely to vary dramatically between different individuals. For example, upon discovering that their mobile phone has been stolen, some individuals might get extremely angry within milliseconds, whereas others may take seconds or even minutes to generate an anger response. Davidson (1998a) speculates that there may be a relationship between the rise time to peak and the peak of the response, such that people with a high amplitude of response may also rise to that peak more quickly. However, this is another area in which there is very little empirical evidence.

The final two components of individual differences in emotional responding are the *recovery time* and the *duration of the response*. Once an emotion has been elicited and a variety of orchestrated responses have taken place, some people are much faster to recover and return to a baseline than others. Anger is a good example. Some people may recover from an angry episode very quickly, while others may simmer for hours afterwards. As we discussed in Chapter 2, temporal duration is an important way in which emotions proper and mood states differ. If the recovery time from an emotion is very slow, this may transfer into an ongoing mood state. The overall duration of an emotion obviously depends on variations in the other components, and may also be on the borderlines between emotions and moods.

Neural correlates of individual differences in affective style

In terms of *individual differences* in affective responding most of the focus has been on asymmetries in prefrontal cortical (PFC) activity (Davidson, 1995). For example, in an early EEG study it was found that 10-month old infants who cried when they were taken away from their mothers were more likely to have greater *right-sided* prefrontal activity and less *left-sided* prefrontal activity compared with infants who did not cry in response to being separated from their mothers (Davidson and Fox, 1989). This pattern of results suggested that the left PFC was involved with the experience of PA, whereas the right PFC was more associated with the experience of NA. This hypothesis has been supported by EEG results with adults. When people viewed emotional videos or pictures the left anterior PFC became activated during the experience of PA, whereas the right anterior PFC became activated during NA (see Davidson, 1992b).

An important discovery was that individual differences in prefrontal activity remained stable across a three-week period, with test–retest reliabilities in the range of 0.65 to 0.75 (Tomarken et al., 1992). This stability indicates that individual differences in prefrontal asymmetry can be adequately treated as a trait-like measure. Indeed, a review of the literature (Coan and Allen, 2004) concludes that frontal EEG asymmetry can serve as both:

1 an individual difference variable which is related to emotional responding and which may be a risk factor for emotional disorders, and
2 a state-dependent concomitant of emotional responding.

Coan and Allen (2004) caution that we should be careful to make a distinction between frontal brain *activity* and frontal brain *activation*. Frontal activity, as measured by EEG, refers to a tonic (or general) level of cortical processing, whereas frontal activation refers to an increase in cortical response to a specific stimulus. Thus, we can find individual differences in frontal asymmetries in baseline brain *activity* as well as individual differences in frontal asymmetry in response to an emotional challenge (or reward). It seems that relatively greater *left* frontal *activity* is associated with a trait propensity to approach or engage with an emotional stimulus, whereas relatively greater *right* frontal activity is associated with trait tendencies to withdraw or disengage from a stimulus (Coan and Allen, 2004; Davidson, 1993). One interesting line of evidence derives from studies of sociability in young children. For example, Nathan Fox et al. (1995) found that children with relatively greater *right* frontal activity at rest were less competent socially and generally more inhibited in social interactions. In contrast, children with relatively greater *left* frontal activity were more outgoing and sociable. In adult studies, a similar pattern has been found. People with greater right frontal asymmetry tended to be shy and withdrawn, whereas those with relatively greater left frontal asymmetry were more sociable and socially competent (Schmidt, 1999).

Research with rhesus monkeys has attempted to establish the neurophysiological mechanisms that might underlie these individual differences in prefrontal activity. Animals with extreme right frontal EEG activity were found to have higher circulating levels of cortisol relative to animals with less right frontal activity (Kalin et al., 1998). Three groups of animals were selected: 12 were classified as extreme left frontals, 11 as extreme right frontals, and 16 were a middle group with no obvious EEG frontal asymmetry. The animals with greater right-sided frontal symmetry had significantly higher levels of plasma cortisol in comparison with the extreme left-sided group. However, interestingly, it was found that the middle group had *lower* levels of cortisol in the extreme left frontal group, rather than increased cortisol in the extreme right frontal group. In other words, the level of cortisol in the middle group did not differ from that in the extreme right-frontal group (Kalin et al., 1998). As pointed out by the authors, this finding is not consistent with the traditional view that increased fearfulness is associated with increased cortisol levels. In contrast, reduced fearfulness appears to be associated with lower cortisol levels. In addition to these between-group differences in circulating cortisol, the extreme right-frontal monkeys were also found to engage in greater amounts of freezing and defensive behaviour in response to a human intruder test. This finding is consistent with studies of human children and adults which have found that extreme right-frontal activity is associated with increased emotional distress (see Davidson, 1995, for review).

Human studies have found that extreme right and left frontal activity is related to the level of PA or NA reported. For example, Tomarken et al. (1992) found that people who were classified as having extreme left frontal asymmetry based on frontal EEG activity reported significantly more PA on the trait version of the PANAS (Positive and Negative Affect Scales, see Table 2.7), while the extreme right asymmetry group reported relatively more NA on the PANAS. Sutton and Davidson (1997) reported an even stronger association between prefrontal asymmetry and scores on the BIS and BAS scales. The concepts of BAS and BIS are essentially identical to the notion of approach and withdrawal systems and it is not too surprising to find that people with relatively greater left-sided frontal activity report higher BAS scores, whereas those with greater right frontal activity report higher BIS scores (Sutton and Davidson, 1997). Subsequent research has confirmed this relationship for the BAS, but evidence for the link between right frontal activity and higher BIS is less well established. For example, two subsequent studies have found a strong association between left frontal asymmetry and higher BAS scores, but no association between right frontal asymmetry and BIS scores (Coan and Allen, 2003; Harmon-Jones and Allen,

1997). One possible explanation is that the withdrawal system is probably somewhat less complex than the BIS. The withdrawal system comprises a number of processes that allow efficient withdrawal from aversive stimulation. The BIS is also thought to facilitate withdrawal, but in addition interrupts and inhibits ongoing behaviour as well as increasing arousal and attention (Gray, 1994). Many of these processes (e.g., increasing vigilance and attention) may have nothing to do with simple withdrawal. In contrast, there seems to be a great deal of overlap between Davidson's approach system and Gray's BAS.

The association between left frontal activity and the approach (or BAS) system has been supported by the case of trait anger. Anger is an interesting emotion to investigate in this context because it is a negatively valenced emotion, but is clearly approach-related rather than withdrawal-related. Harmon-Jones and Allen (1997) found that people with relatively greater left frontal activity reported higher levels of trait-anger than those with greater right frontal activity, in spite of the fact that anger was rated as a negative emotion. This is an important demonstration that greater left frontal activity is not necessarily always related to higher levels of PA, but may be more specifically related to *approach* mechanisms. Thus, it seems that activity in left frontal regions may subserve *approach-related positive affect*, whereas brain activity in right frontal regions may subserve *withdrawal-related negative affect.*

A real difficulty in examining the impact of affective style is in drawing a distinction between *emotion reactivity* and *emotion regulation.* People may react differently to both incentives and threats. However, it is also clear that there are marked differences in how people regulate their emotional reactions to both incentives and threats (Gross, 1998b; 2007). Making a distinction between reactions and regulatory processes is an important area that needs to be developed to fully understand how individual differences in affective style lead to fundamental differences in emotional experience.

AFFECT REGULATION STRATEGIES

There are many different ways in which emotions and moods can be regulated in everyday life. If someone is feeling very sad, for example, he may try to enhance his mood by going shopping or listening to very up-beat music. Anger might be suppressed by counting to ten and taking several deep breaths. A real challenge for emotion science is to find a conceptual framework that can incorporate all of the various aspects of affect regulation. A useful framework has recently been put forward suggesting that *affect regulation* consists of four main overlapping constructs (Gross and Thompson, 2007). They make the point that in some sense all goal-directed behaviour can be seen as an attempt to maximize pleasure (*approach*) and minimize pain (*avoidance*). This means that almost all behaviour is about affect regulation in some way. To allow for more coherent investigations, it is therefore useful to break affect regulation down into the four focused groups of processes that are outlined in Figure 3.6: coping, emotion regulation, mood regulation and defences.

Coping refers to a set of processes that are focused on reducing negative affectivity. Thus, if somebody is very stressed at work, she may take up jogging or some other

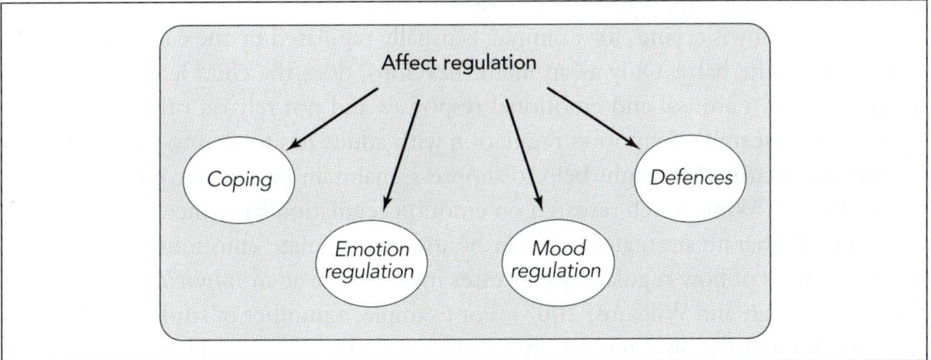

FIGURE 3.6 Four main sets of processes related to affect regulation
Source: Gross and Thompson (2007).

form of exercise to help reduce the negative physiological and psychological aspects of the situation. Another important aspect of coping is that these processes are usually involved with fairly long periods of time (e.g., coping with the death of a loved one). *Emotion regulation*, in contrast, refers to those processes that can be implemented to regulate specific *emotions. Mood regulation* refers to a set of processes for regulating enduring mood states rather than brief emotions. Since moods are often not directed at specific objects or situations, and have less well defined sets of behavioural responses than emotions, these processes are often more concerned with altering emotional *experience* rather than *action tendencies.* Mood repair strategies form an important part of many psychological therapies, for example, in helping people to imagine and think about more positive situations in an attempt to elevate their mood. Finally, the *defences* are processes for regulating sexual or aggressive impulses, and the negative affectivity that is often associated with these impulses. These four categories clearly overlap to a large extent and all (along with many other processes) are important in terms of understanding behaviour. In this chapter, we will concentrate primarily on empirical work on *emotion regulation.* Work on *mood regulation* will be introduced in Chapters 9 and 10 when we are considering the determinants of emotional disorders and well-being.

Emotion regulation

The investigation of how emotions are regulated is a thriving area in emotion science. Emotion regulation involves a range of processes that act to *amplify*, *reduce* or *maintain* the magnitude of emotional reactions (Thompson, 1994). Research on this topic initially focused on trying to understand how children learn to regulate their emotions (e.g., Thompson, 1990) and there have been many studies on how adults regulate emotions (e.g., Gross and Levenson, 1993). It is interesting to note that developmental studies with children have often focused on *external* factors that operate to regulate emotions (e.g., Cole et al., 2004). This makes a lot of sense, of course, as parents and teachers often play a strong role in encouraging young children to regulate (usually suppress) their emotions. The attempt to control arousal and distress when a baby is crying, for example, is usually regulated by the caregiver holding and cuddling the baby. Only as an infant develops, does the child learn to begin to regulate his own arousal and emotional responses and not rely on others to do this. In contrast, research on emotion regulation with adults has tended to focus primarily on *internal* factors that might help to suppress, maintain or enhance emotions (e.g., Gross, 1998a). While much research on emotion regulation has concentrated on *conscious* and deliberate strategies that can be used to regulate emotions there are also many examples of how regulatory processes may operate at an *implicit* or *unconscious* level (e.g., Bargh and Williams, 2007). For example, a number of studies have shown that emotion regulation can occur in a fairly automatic way (e.g., Haas et al., 2007).

Five sets of emotion regulation processes have been identified. Figure 3.7 shows how each impacts at different stages in the generation of emotions (Gross, 1998a; Gross and Thompson, 2007). Four of these emotion regulation families occur before appraisals result in an emotional response, and are called *antecedent-focused* strategies. In contrast, *response-focused* processes are those emotion regulation processes that occur after a response is generated (Gross and Munoz, 1995). It is important to remember that emotion regulation processes can operate at any time from the very earliest point at which a potentially emotive situation is identified, through the deployment of attention to the situation and the generation of a range of appraisals regarding its affective significance, right up to the point where a response takes place.

Situation selection and situation modification are both emotion regulation strategies that can help to shape the characteristics of a situation. For example, a person of a nervous disposition may avoid going to a horror movie with a group of friends because she knows that she will become distressed (situation selection). In other words, these processes involve taking actions to ensure that we are either more or less likely to be in a situation that will probably be emotional in some way. The closely related processes of situation modification involve attempts to change the situation in some way. For example, instead of going alone to a party where you know few people, you

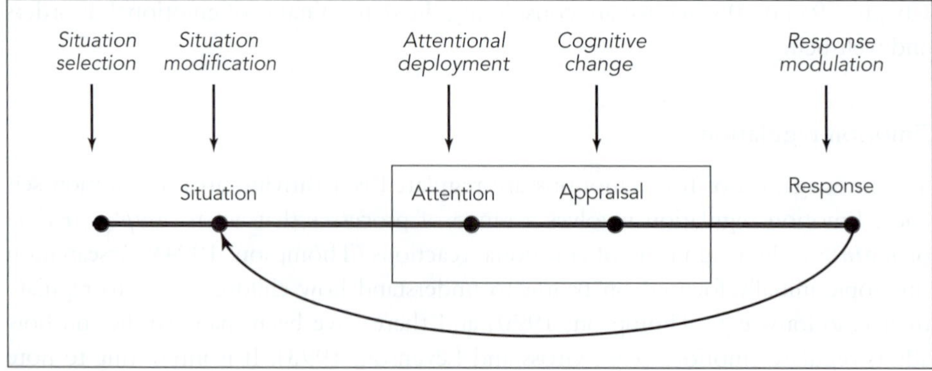

FIGURE 3.7 A process model of emotion regulation showing five families of emotion regulation strategies

Source: Gross and Thompson (2007).

might ask a friend to come along. One emotion regulation strategy that can be used in a given situation is attentional deployment. For example, when lying in the dentist's chair we may invoke thoughts of a forthcoming holiday to deflect attention from the current negative emotional state. There are many forms of attentional deployment, such as completely withdrawing attention by closing the eyes during a scary movie or re-directing attention by means of distraction (e.g., thinking about something else). These are highly effective cognitive ways of regulating emotions.

Cognitive appraisal or reappraisal strategies are also commonly used to change the meaning of a situation so that the emotional impact is altered. For example, in the early work of Richard Lazarus (1966) a number of experiments presented people with stressful video images of young boys being circumcised. However, negative emotional responses were reduced dramatically by telling some participants that the people on the video were all actors and that no real pain was involved. In other words, the external situation was not changed but the way in which the events were interpreted was reappraised, and this was an effective way to regulate emotions. Finally, *response modulation* occurs very late in the process after a response has been initiated. Examples of emotion regulation strategies operating at this stage can include the use of drugs and exercise to modulate the physiological and experiential aspects of emotions. Thus, for example, alcohol may be used to reduce the physiological signs of nervous energy and tension in a social situation. In Figure 3.7, a feedback arrow goes from the emotional response back to the situation. Obviously, an emotional response, such as crying during an argument, can alter the situation but the feedback arrow also emphasizes the dynamic nature of emotion regulatory processes.

Most of the research on emotion regulation has concentrated on conscious and strategic forms of regulation. However, *unconscious* processes have also been shown to play an important role in the regulation of emotions and moods (see Bargh and Williams, 2007, for review). For example, interacting directly with another person creates the tendency to behave in a similar way oneself. If you look at somebody who smiles it is likely that you will also smile although you may well be unaware of this. Cognitive neuroscience research has found that this tendency to mimic others' actions is coordinated by what have been called '*mirror neurons*' in the brain. Giacomo Rizzolati and his colleagues discovered this by accident when they were investigating the actions of particular groups of motor neurons in the brains of monkeys. These experiments involve the surgical implantation of electrodes into the monkey's brain to monitor the activity of individual neurons. Once the anaesthetic has worn off the monkeys are free to roam around normally. The researchers noticed that some motor neurons were very specific in that they responded to particular actions such as reaching out and picking up a peanut. However, they then made the accidental discovery that the same neurons fired when the monkey saw the experimenter reach out and pick up a peanut (di Pellegrino et al., 1992; Rizzolatti et al., 1996). They called these *mirror neurons* and speculated that they might be important in helping us develop *empathy* for other individuals. Subsequent research has confirmed the existence of mirror neurons in both monkeys and humans. The idea is simple but far-reaching. If watching a particular action and performing that action activates the same group of neurons, then it seems likely that watching an action and performing an action will elicit the same *feelings* in people. The important point for present purposes is that mirror neurons might provide a neural basis for a form of non-conscious emotion regulation that is likely to be extremely important in coordinating social interactions. For example, in an intense conflict situation somebody moving in a very calm manner might activate the mirror neuron system and have the effect of calming an individual in an automatic way. There is currently no research on whether there are individual differences in the operation of the mirror neuron system.

Individual differences in emotion regulation

The processes that regulate affective responses seem to develop in a fairly consistent way during childhood. For example, infants rely on caregivers to regulate their emotions, but as they grow older they learn to modulate their own arousal and distress in fairly simple ways. Over the first couple of years of life, children develop a range of *effortful control strategies* that they use to delay gratification according to social expectations. These control strategies gradually become used in a variety of more flexible ways (Kopp, 1982). Effortful control processes are defined as the ability to inhibit a dominant response in order to perform a less dominant response (Rothbart and Rueda, 2005). For instance, a child may delay the desire to eat a sweet so that she can complete a task. There are wide individual differences in the development of these effortful control processes. For example, both parents' and teachers' reports indicate that children differ from each other in terms of their abilities to control their impulses and emotions, and that these differences remain fairly stable across childhood (Eisenberg, Sadovsky et al., 2005). The differences can be categorized as *overcontrolled*, *undercontrolled*, and *optimally controlled*.

Importantly, these different styles of control have been linked with the ability to adjust to a variety of situations, and with social competence in a more general way. For example, high levels of effortful control (as long as they are not overcontrolled) are associated with better adjustment and better social skills. The ability to modulate or re-direct attention is linked with the capacity to maintain optimal levels of arousal in stressful situations. This allows a child (or an adult) to process information in a more even-handed way and to plan and behave in a way that is appropriate for the given situation. In contrast, a difficulty with controlling attention is likely to result in *over* arousal in a stressful situation, with the resulting biases in perception, poor planning and inappropriate behaviour (see Eisenberg, Sadovsky et al., 2005 and Eisenberg, 2007, for further discussion).

As we have seen previously, many theoretical approaches link temperament to underlying biological processes (e.g., Cloninger, 1987; Davidson, 1992b; Eysenck, 1953; Gray, 1982; Kagan, 1994). While theories differ, most assume that the systems that support *defensive* and *harm-avoidance* behaviour or *approach* and *appetitive* behaviour represent the aspects of temperament most related to emotional reactivity (Derryberry and Rothbart, 1997). In situations that present potential rewards as well as potential punishments (e.g., Gray, 1982) both withdrawal and approach systems are activated, and compete with each other to influence perceptual processes in addition to physiological arousal and basic action tendencies. The assumption is that these systems are mutually inhibitory so that one can dominate the other. It is not surprising, however, that the withdrawal system often predominates, since it is generally more important in terms of survival to avoid threat than to achieve a reward. However, the interesting point is that strong individual differences have been observed in the degree to which these systems inhibit each other (Ito and Cacioppo, 2005). Thus, people with a strong withdrawal system – those who score high on the BIS scale – find it more difficult to prevent the activation of this system, while those with high scores on the BAS scale find it more difficult to suppress the approach system. The degree to which effortful control strategies can be implemented is clearly an important determinant of emotional reactivity.

The ability to control emotional reactivity, as long as it is not overcontrolled, is associated with better social relations and higher degrees of *empathy*. The ability to suppress one's own arousal may help a person to focus more on other people (Rothbart et al., 1994). The effective use of effortful control processes is also associated with the use of more verbal methods of managing anger, whereas children with poor control skills often deal with anger by means of overt aggression (Eisenberg et al., 1994). Thus, individual differences in the use of effortful control processes to regulate emotions can lead to very different sets of social skills.

In theoretical terms, individual differences in temperament can operate at each of the five stages of the emotion generation process, as shown in Figure 3.7. However, very little research has been conducted on this. One exception is a body of work showing individual differences in the extent to which people can use *reappraisal* and *suppression* strategies (Gross and John, 2003). Reappraisal can, of course, influence the entire emotion sequence including the experience of more positive and less negative emotions. In contrast, individual differences in suppression operate much later in the process and generally modify the behavioural aspects of emotional responses without necessarily changing the *experience* of emotion. We might also expect that the big five personality traits may influence emotion regulation strategies. While there is some speculation about how the traits of conscientiousness, extraversion, neuroticism, openness, and agreeableness might influence each of the five stages of emotion regulation (John and Gross, 2007), there is no direct research on this question. This is an important area that needs to be developed within emotion science.

Neural correlates of emotion regulation

The *prefrontal cortex* (PFC) and the *anterior cingulate cortex* (ACC) play an important role in the regulation of emotion (see Ochsner and Gross, 2005, for review). In an early study, participants were presented with a series of negative photographs. In order to induce an *attend* condition they were asked to pay attention to the photos but not to modify their feelings in any way. In contrast, a *reappraise* condition required people to reinterpret the photographs in a positive way so that their negative feelings would be reduced (Ochsner et al., 2002, 2004). The results showed that people who were better able to reduce negative affective feelings, as measured by self-report, demonstrated a greater degree of activation of the dorsal part of the ACC, measured by fMRI. Attempts to reduce negative affect were also associated with activation of various areas within the left ventromedial PFC (vmPFC) and a reduced activation in the right amygdala. Thus, it seems that the left vmPFC may be involved in emotion regulation, and that successful regulation suppresses the activation of the amygdala.

This hypothesis was tested in a more recent study. Participants were again presented with negative photographs and asked to enhance, maintain or suppress their emotional responses using reappraisal strategies that they had learned in an earlier session (Urry et al., 2006). The results showed that there were reliable changes in the amygdala (both left and right) as a function of regulation instruction. As expected, the instruction to *enhance* the emotional response correlated with an increase in amygdala activation compared to the control (maintain) condition, whereas the instruction to *suppress* the emotional response was associated with a reduction in amygdala activity. More importantly, these changes in amygdala activity were correlated in a reciprocal way to signal changes in large areas of the vmPFC. Thus, participants who showed greater activation of the vmPFC during suppress relative to the maintain condition also showed greater reductions in amygdala activation contemporaneously. There are some limitations to studies examining the neural correlates of emotion regulation (see Davidson et al., 2007; Ochsner and Gross, 2005, for reviews). For example, in many studies the emotion regulation instructions are given to participants *before* the emotion eliciting stimulus is presented and, therefore, it is difficult to know whether the instructions are suppressing an emotional response or preventing it occurring in the first place. Research that more directly relates neural signal changes to emotion regulation at each of the five stages outlined in Figure 3.7 would be very useful. Moreover, most studies have examined the regulation of negative emotions, and there is a need for more work on the neural correlates of regulating positive emotions. Nevertheless, the research to date does suggest that the vmPFC and the amygdala form a neural circuit that plays an important role in the regulation of negative affect.

CHAPTER SUMMARY

This chapter has looked at the role of individual differences in temperament, personality traits, and affective style in determining emotional reactivity to everyday events. Research on regulatory processes that can modulate emotions was also discussed. A range of enduring personality differences between people have been identified and it seems that the 'big five' traits of conscientiousness, extraversion, neuroticism, openness and agreeableness are the main factors that underlie personality, at least in Western countries. The individual differences in temperament or personality that are apparent at subjective and behavioural levels are related to individual differences in general biological systems (e.g., approach versus avoidance; behavioural activation versus behavioural inhibition). Naturally occurring variations in these systems can have profound effects on a person's experience of positive and negative affect. In other words, how a person responds to affective situations and how they feel in these situations can be determined to a large extent by enduring personality characteristics. Thus, a complete science of emotion needs to take these individual differences into account. There is some evidence that different patterns of activity within the frontal lobes are important correlates of individual differences in the degree to which positive and negative affect is expressed and regulated.

RECOMMENDED READING

A highly readable introduction to the study of temperament, with a particular emphasis on his own work is provided in:

Jerome Kagan (1994) *Galen's Prophecy: Temperament in Human Nature*. London: Free Association Books.

Two excellent books provide detailed discussions of research on the biological and genetic bases of individual differences in personality/temperament, and the processes involved in emotion regulation:

Turhan Canli (ed.) (2006) *Biology of Personality and Individual Differences*. New York: Guilford Press.

James J. Gross (ed.) (2007) *Handbook of Emotion Regulation*. New York: Guilford Press.

4 CATEGORICAL APPROACHES TO THE STRUCTURE OF AFFECT

EMOTIONS AS DISCRETE CATEGORIES

Many emotion scientists view emotions as instances of discrete categories such as anger, fear, sadness, happiness and so on. Frequently associated with such a view is the additional assumption that a small number of emotions might be *basic* or *primary* in some way. These conclusions are drawn from empirical evidence from a variety of research traditions. Their assumption is that different emotions have different neurological structures, and that these are activated fairly directly and automatically by the appropriate stimuli and/or appraisals (Dolan, 2002; LeDoux, 1996; Panksepp, 1998). As would be expected from this perspective, some emotions seem to appear in all cultures, as well as across many animal species. This suggests that at least some emotions may be *primary* or *basic* in that they are given to us by nature and represent biological phenomena that exist independently of our perception of them. As argued by Panksepp 'these systems constitute the core processes for the "natural kind" of emotion' (2000, p. 143).

We should be careful, however, not to take the term *basic emotion* too literally. While theorists often talk of a set of biologically basic emotions such as anger, fear, happiness, sadness, and disgust, they are usually referring to a group of related affective states (e.g., emotion families) rather than to specific emotions (Ekman and Davidson, 1994). The term '*emotion family*' refers to a set of phenomena which are related to each other by a number of common characteristics (Ekman, 1992a). Each emotion family is assumed to consist of a primary *theme* as well as a number of *variations* (Ekman, 1992a; Ekman and Friesen, 1975). The *theme* comprises the characteristics that are unique to that emotion family: commonalities in physiological activity, in expression and action patterns; in the nature of the antecedent events that elicit the emotions; and the appraisal processes. In contrast, *variations* on a central theme can be produced by a range of factors:, individual differences in biology and genetic inheritance; different learning experiences; differences in the contexts in which an emotion might occur and so on.

What do we mean by basic emotions?

The term 'basic' has many different meanings in the context of emotions (e.g., Averill, 1994; Ortony and Turner, 1990). In everyday language, the term 'basic' usually implies that an object is considered fundamental if it fulfils an important function. With regard to emotions, the 'basic' emotions might be those that are critical for the survival of:

(a) the species – *biological criterion*,
(b) the society – *social criterion*, or
(c) the self – *psychological criterion*.

As pointed out by Averill (1994), the biological criterion is the most common interpretation within emotion science (Darwin, 1872/1998; Ekman and Friesen, 1971; Izard, 1977; Tomkins, 1962, 1963). Since human beings, along with other species, are the product of millions of years of evolution many assume that biological mechanisms are more fundamental in some way than social, cultural or psychological mechanisms.

This notion has been challenged, however, on the basis that biological mechanisms only set loose constraints on behaviour. A culturally-based concept assumes that the particular form of emotions is constructed to a large extent by social factors (Averill, 1980; Mesquita, 2003). Thus, some emotions are specific to particular cultures and may even be defining features of that culture. Examples are the emotion of *amae* – contentment arising from complete acceptance by another person – in Japan and the emotion of *liget* –the feeling of exhilaration when taking a head – among the head-hunting Ilongot people of the Philippines. *Liget* is considered to be a basic emotion in this society, but does not exist in any other cultures. Thus, there are many emotions that may be basic in a social sense that may not be basic in a biological sense.

The notion that different emotions represent different *categories*, some of which may be more basic than others, remains the dominant approach within emotion science (Ekman, 1973, 1992a; Izard, 1977, 1993, 2007; LeDoux, 1996; Panksepp, 1998; Plutchik, 1980; Tomkins, 1962, 1963). Izard (2007) has recently argued that basic emotions involve internal bodily activities and expressive capacities that derive from evolved neural structures. They are elicited by emotionally competent stimuli, and have unique regulatory properties that can modulate both cognitive processes and action tendencies. Izard also assumes that each basic emotion has a unique *feeling*. A central assumption behind discrete emotions approaches is that (at least some) emotions are products of our evolution and therefore have a strong biological basis. The crucial element that distinguishes one emotion from another is the fact that 'our appraisal of a current event is influenced by our ancestral past' (Ekman, 1999, p. 46). Many discrete emotions theorists rely primarily on animal data (LeDoux, 1996; Panksepp, 1998). Others focus on research with humans, often emphasizing the *universality* of the physiological and expressive correlates of emotion (Ekman and Friesen, 1975). Many cognitive appraisal models of emotion also suggest that emotions are organized into discrete categories, even though they do not necessarily assume that these emotions are primitive in a biological sense (Frijda, 1986; Lazarus, 1991; Scherer, 1984). A brief historical overview of discrete emotions approaches is presented in Box 4.1.

BOX 4.1

A brief overview of some influential approaches assuming the existence of a set of discrete emotions

The discrete emotions approach is a very old method of trying to understand emotions. Descartes, for example, assumed that there were only 6 primary emotions, or passions, and that all others were composed of mixtures of these six. He suggested that *love, hatred, desire, joy, sadness* and *admiration* were primary emotions, but gave no rationale for his choice.

It was Charles Darwin who set the stage for scientific theories of discrete emotions in his now classic book *The Expression of Emotions in Man and Animals* (Darwin, 1872/1998). Darwin was fascinated with the fact that the same facial expressions seemed to occur in a wide variety of cultures, and even across different species, and he interpreted this as indicating that some emotions must indeed be universal or basic (see Figure 4.1). Darwin was one of the first scientists to propose that there are a small number of innate emotional states which can be communicated to others by means of expressive behaviours (facial, vocal, and so on). The evidence he presented for this view was that:

1 some facial expressions appear in similar form in lower animals, especially primates;
2 some facial expressions are seen in infants and young children in the same form as in adults;
3 some facial expressions are shown in identical ways by people who are born blind and those with normal vision; and
4 some facial expressions appear in similar form in widely distinct races and groups of humans.

These arguments inspired a still vibrant research tradition and lively debate on the relationships between emotions and facial expressions (Ekman, 1992b, 1994d; Russell, 1994, 1995).

Categorical emotions approaches are usually infused with the notion that emotions evolved because they were adaptive in dealing with a number of *fundamental life tasks* that are common to all members of a species (and are often common across species as well). One influential cognitive theory, for example, proposed that each emotion is associated with a specific predicament or what can be termed a '*core relational theme*' (Lazarus, 1991). The experience of loss, for example, is the core relational theme relevant to *sadness*, whereas facing uncertainty and threat is the core relational theme underlying *fear*. Johnson-Laird and Oatley (1992) have also argued that universal human experiences such as losses, achievements, frustrations have led to the evolution of specific emotions. These specific emotions have been adapted over the life of a species to help deal with a number of common predicaments. From this perspective, basic emotions are considered to be *biologically primitive* in the sense that they relate to needs that must be met if an individual or a species is to survive. Happiness, for example, might be related to the need to reproduce, fear to the need for protection, sadness to the need to maintain possession of a pleasurable object (Plutchik, 1962).

BOX 4.1 continued

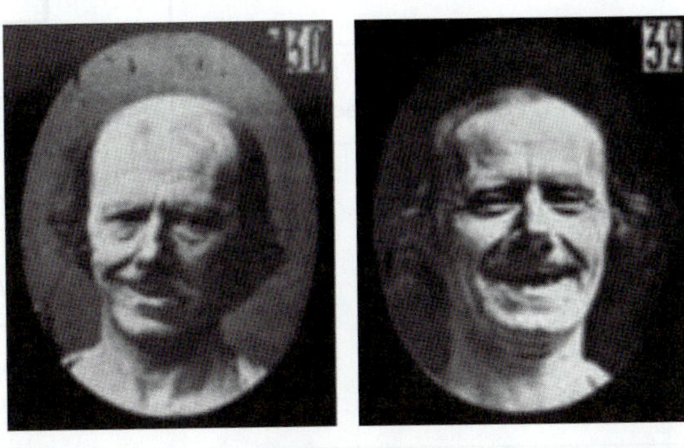

FIGURE 4.1 Some common facial expressions noted by Charles Darwin
These images were initially published by Guillaume Duchenne in his 1862 book *Mechanisme de la Physionomie Humaine* and later republished by Charles Darwin in *Expressions of Emotions in Man and Animals* (1872/1998).

Other discrete emotions theorists have concentrated on trying to uncover the *neural circuits* underlying emotions, and have primarily conducted experiments with rats (Gray, 1990; LeDoux, 1996; Panksepp, 1998). This neurobiological research suggests that a number of separate emotions have been constructed by natural selection rather than by the experiences gained during the lifespan of the individual. Thus, researchers with a neurobiological background who primarily study rodents (Gray, 1990; Panksepp, 1998) and those with a cognitive background who primarily study humans (Izard, 1977; Johnson-Laird and Oatley, 1992; Lazarus, 1991) converge on the same conclusion: the primary *function* of basic emotions is to mobilize the individual to respond to fundamental and universal life tasks. The key point here is that the individual is *prepared* to respond to these life events in ways that have been adaptive in the past history of both the species and the individual's own life.

CRITERIA FOR BASIC EMOTIONS

The central idea underlying a discrete emotions approach is that once an emotion is triggered a set of easily recognizable behavioural and physiological responses is produced. These responses are coordinated in time and correlated in intensity. A schematic model of emotion is shown in Figure 4.2. The model follows Levenson (1994) and assumes that once an emotion has been activated a set of subroutines for the various response systems is then activated, much as we might find in a computer program (Tomkins, 1962, 1963). As shown in Figure 4.2, an emotion can be activated directly from an environmental event or by means of an appraisal of this event. The resulting activation of a specific neural circuit, in turn, activates a set of behavioural and physiological responses to the emotion. The subroutine for 'feeling' has been separated out

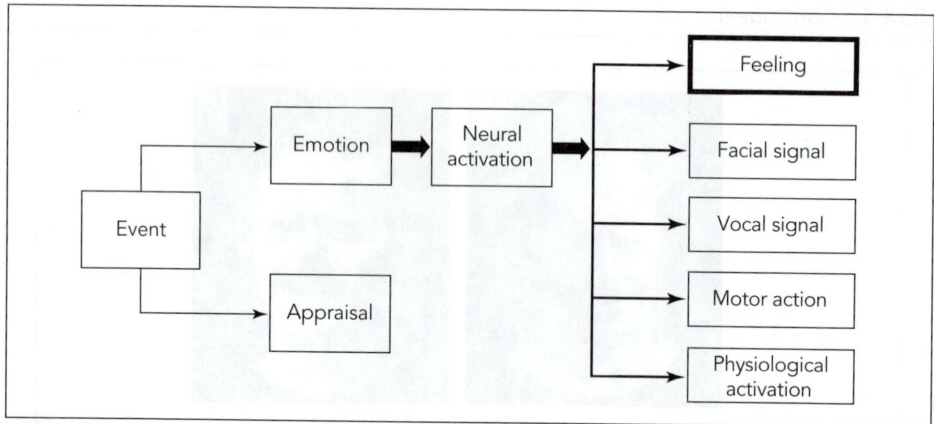

FIGURE 4.2 A schematic model of emotion from a discrete emotions perspective

Source: Adapted from Levenson (1994).

in Figure 4.2 because it is not clear how direct is the association between the activation of emotion neural circuits and the resulting feeling state.

Different emotions such as anger, sadness and happiness are assumed to be associated with different coordinated response patterns. However, no clear set of criteria has been used consistently to identify the basic emotions. Different theorists often use different criteria and therefore include different emotions in their lists of 'basic' emotions. Ortony and Turner (1990) have claimed that this lack of agreement calls into question the entire notion of 'basic emotions'. This seems to be an exaggerated response. While the lack of consensus cannot be denied, there is actually much more agreement than Ortony and Turner acknowledge. For example, in spite of wide differences in the criteria used – distinctive universal signals, distinctive physiology, and

TABLE 4.1 Criteria for distinguishing basic emotions from each other and from other affective phenomena

Criteria	*Distinguish between discrete emotions*	*Distinguish emotions from other affective phenomena*
Distinctive universal signals	✓	
Distinctive physiology	✓	
Universal antecedent events	✓	
Dedicated neural circuits	✓	
Presence in other primates		✓
Coherence among response systems		✓
Quick onset		✓
Brief duration		✓
Automatic appraisal		✓
Unbidden occurrence		✓

Source: Based on Ekman (1992a, 1999).

distinctive appraisal scenarios – many theorists have converged on happiness, fear, anger, disgust and sadness as prototypical examples of basic and discrete emotions.

Nevertheless, it is important to develop a clear set of criteria so that basic emotions can be distinguished from each other and from other affective phenomena, such as moods and feelings. Paul Ekman (1992a and b) outlined nine criteria: three which can be used to distinguish between the different basic emotions, and six which are used to establish whether an emotion is basic. The latter criteria may occur in all of the basic emotions, so they cannot be used to distinguish between emotions. However, they can be used to distinguish basic emotions from moods and feelings. Ekman and others have added additional criteria to distinguish basic emotions (Ellis and Toronchuk, 2005; Panksepp, 1998). Table 4.1 lists the criteria outlined by Ekman in 1992, with the addition of 'dedicated neural circuits', which was added in 1999.

OVERVIEW OF EMPIRICAL EVIDENCE FOR DISCRETE EMOTIONS

Distinctive signals

Expressing emotions by means of various signals is widespread in nature. Animals use loud noises, flapping of wings, the laying down of scent and so on as a way of indicating their affective state to other animals. Many emotions that are opposites are expressed by means of opposing actions or postures (Darwin, 1872/1998). Comprehensive reviews and discussions of how emotions are expressed across species are available (Darwin, 1872/1998; Snowdon, 2003).

Tomkins (1962, 1963) was one of the first to suggest that each discrete emotion in humans was characterized by a very specific response pattern which was produced by an innate neuromotor programme. This hypothesis was subsequently translated into the idea that one of the outcomes of these neuromotor programmes is to elicit discrete and distinctive facial and vocal signals for each of the different emotions (Ekman, 1972; Izard, 1971, 1977). There is a large body of research designed to investigate whether universal signals of emotions do, in fact, occur. Most of this research has been concerned with *facial expressions of emotions* (Ekman, 1992c), while some work has also been conducted on *vocal expressions of emotion* (Scherer et al., 2003).

Recognizing different facial expressions

From the earliest research, an important question has been the possibility that some emotions might have similar facial expressions across cultures, and even across species. Early studies investigated how accurate people were in labelling the emotions expressed in photographs of faces. The typical technique was to photograph an actor expressing a range of different emotions and then to ask people from different cultures to say what emotion was being expressed. The results were not satisfactory. The main problem was that people used a large number of words to describe the different expressions. For example, in one study the posed picture for 'hate' was variously identified as mental pain, disgust, dread and so on. This led researchers to present people

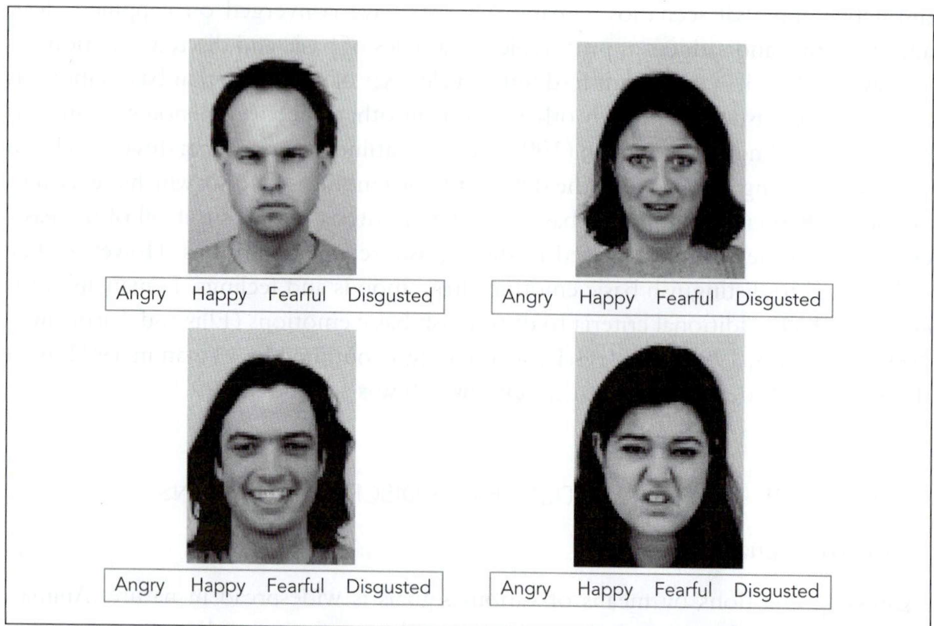

FIGURE 4.3 An example of a typical method used to assess the universality of emotion recognition Images taken from Karolinska Directed Emotional Faces (KDEF) developed by Lundqvist et al. (1998).

with a limited number of words from which to select the most appropriate label for the posed expression. As shown in Figure 4.3, usually up to six words are given (e.g., disgusted, angry, happy, fearful, neutral, surprised).

The accuracy and reliability of people's recognition of different emotional expressions improves considerably when a limited number of labels is available. In one study, 69 photographs of facial expressions were prepared, showing typical examples of either a neutral expression or interest, joy, surprise, distress, fear, shame, disgust, and rage (Tomkins and McCarter, 1964). Participants were given the photographs in a random order and were asked to match each image with the appropriate label. A high degree of agreement was found among participants.

Given that people can identify emotions fairly well from photographs within their own culture, the next question was whether the same result would be found in cross-cultural studies. Ekman and his colleagues showed a large number of photographs of Caucasians to people from different countries (USA, Brazil, Japan, New Guinea and Borneo) and found that the majority of people in each culture agreed on the emotion being expressed by each face (Ekman et al., 1969). This study did not provide conclusive support for the idea that emotional expressions are universal, however, because people in the preliterate societies had lower levels of agreement than those from the Western countries. They may also have been influenced by Western-made movies.

To get around this problem, Ekman and Freisen (1971) conducted a now classic study with members of the Fore linguistic cultural group of New Guinea. Until 1960 these people were an isolated 'stone age' culture who had had little or no contact with Westerners. The people taking part in the study were selected precisely because they had seen no movies, did not understand English or pidgin, had not lived in any government towns, and had never worked for a Caucasian. On the basis of these criteria, 180 adults and 130 children were tested, which is a relatively large sample. Each person was read a simple story and then shown 3 different photographs. He or she was then asked to select the photograph in which the person's face best described the emotion described in the story. All of the stories were straightforward and short such as 'his/her child has died and she is feeling very sad' or 'she/he is looking at something that smells very bad'. Using this technique, high agreement was found for both adults and children for almost all of the emotion expressions. For adults, the median agreements were:

happiness	92%
anger	87%
sadness	81%
disgust	83%
surprise	68%
fear	64%

In a follow-up study, the authors obtained pictures of posed emotional expressions in these same New Guineans and showed them to US college students. The US students also judged the correct emotion in almost all cases. These results are powerful and led Ekman and Freisen (1971) to draw the conclusion that 'particular facial expressions are universally associated with particular emotions.' In a summary of much of this cross-cultural work, Ekman (1992a and b) has argued that there is now substantial evidence that six basic emotions can be identified on the basis of universally recognized facial expressions: happiness, surprise, fear, sadness, anger, and disgust combined with contempt.

While research on facial expressions provides strong evidence for the universality hypothesis, there have been a number of critiques of this body of research. For example, presenting people with a small number of emotion labels and asking them to make a forced choice may lead to an inflated estimate of the level of agreement in the choice of emotion terms (Russell, 1994). Indeed, as we have seen, agreement is not as good when people are asked to use their own terms to describe the emotions being expressed. Ortony and Turner (1990) have also questioned the validity of research on the universality of facial expressions on slightly different grounds. They raise the possibility that it may not be the facial expressions themselves that are universal signals, but rather that some *components* of facial expressions (e.g., furrowed brows) may be the universal signals. As yet there has not been an extensive study to investigate whether particular components of expressions are universally recognized. Until further evidence is available, we must accept that, at least some, facial expressions may be universal and are readily recognized across different cultures.

Recognizing emotional prosody and vocalizations

Another way of signalling emotions is, of course, by means of vocalizations. Some of these also may be universal; for example, the 'yuck' sound we make when we taste something unpleasant (indicating disgust), or the scream which conveys fear or terror. The typical methodology used to determine the recognition of emotional vocalizations is similar to that used in the research on facial expressions. A professional actor is usually asked to read out standard phrases or nonsense syllables in a particular emotional tone – depressed, happy, angry and so on. These recordings are then played in a random order to participants who are asked to indicate the emotions being expressed. As in the facial expression literature, people are usually provided with a set of standard labels for each of the segments. Klaus Scherer (1989) reviewed this literature and concluded that the agreement between observers was around 60%, which is about five times higher than would be expected by chance. Of course, many of the same criticisms that were made of the facial expression recognition literature also apply here. Several studies, for example, used a small number of emotions and provided people with a set of labels, so that agreement may have been somewhat overestimated. Moreover, early studies did not take into account differences in intonation between variants of the same specific emotion. For example, 'hot' anger and 'cold' anger may have quite different vocal characteristics but nevertheless refer to the same specific emotion of anger (Scherer, 1986).

Banse and Scherer (1996) attempted to deal with this problem by asking professional actors to portray a number of specific emotions in which at least two variants of the emotion families were expressed. They found that the accuracy of emotion recognition between emotion families was 55%, whereas chance accuracy would have been 10%. This demonstrates that the recognition of emotion from standardized vocal portrayals is well above what would be expected by chance. Unfortunately, there are very few cross-cultural studies of vocal recognition, but those that do exist indicate that recognition of some emotions by means of vocal portrayals may be universal (Frick, 1985). It should be noted, however, that in a recent study the accurate identification of emotions, while high, did decrease as the similarity in language from the actors' native language (German) got more distant (Scherer et al., 2001). This was the case even though language-free speech samples were used. These results suggest that the portrayal of emotion by the voice is probably influenced by culture. While there is some evidence for cultural specificity in these data, a review has pointed out that there is still a striking similarity in the patterns of errors that occur across the different languages. Thus, there is some evidence that the recognition of discrete emotions by vocalizations may be universal (see Scherer et al., 2003, for review).

Emotional prosody also enhances neural activity in the auditory cortex (Grandjean et al., 2005). Participants in an fMRI study wore headphones and had to selectively attend to either the right or the left ear on different trials and make a gender decision on the voice that they heard. The voices produced word-like but meaningless utterances that were delivered in either an *angry* or a *neutral* prosody. As shown in Figure 4.4, the *angry* speech prosody increased neural activity in the superior temporal sulcus

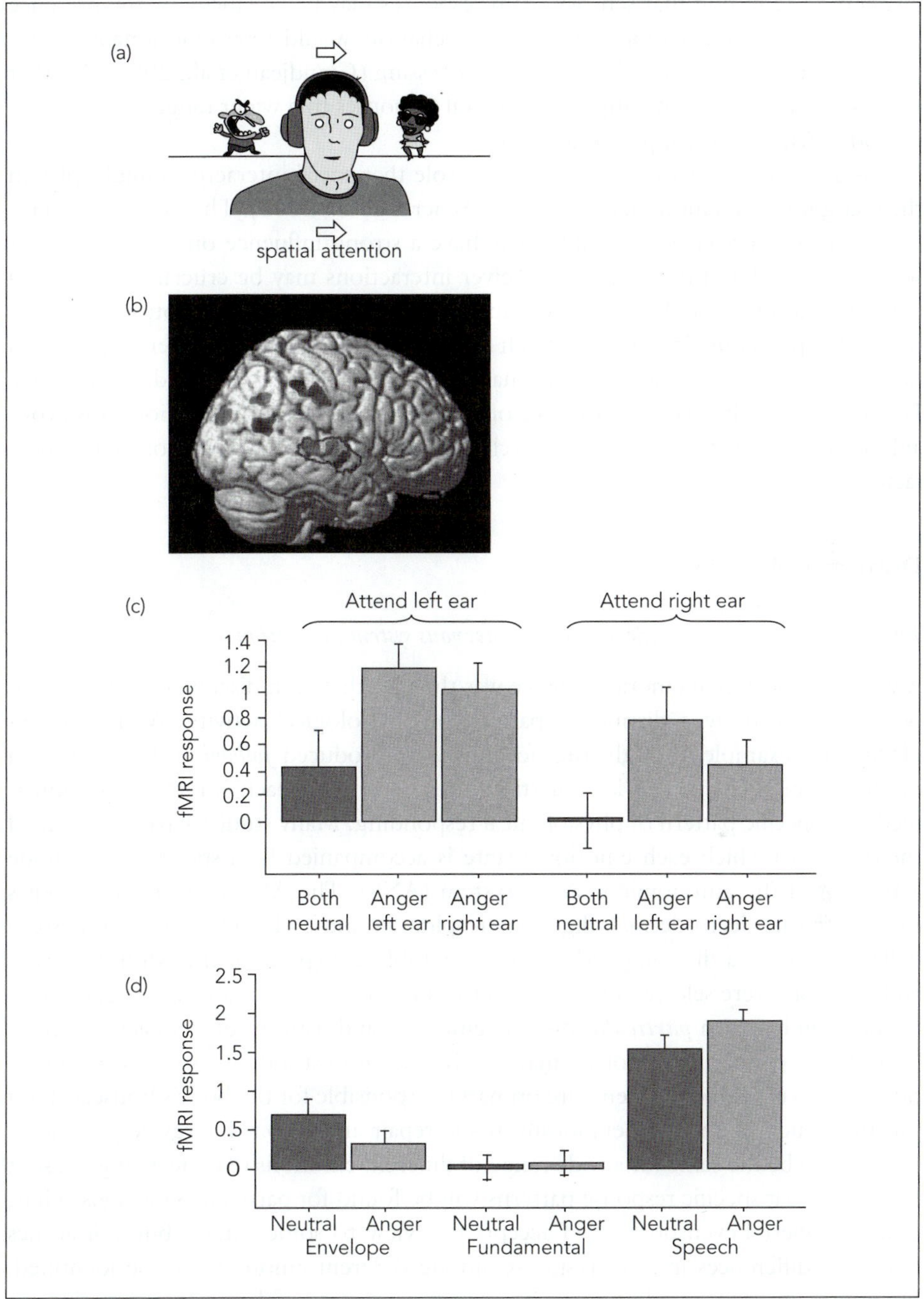

FIGURE 4.4 Cortical activations elicited by spatial attention and emotional prosody

Source: Grandjean et al. (2005).

bilaterally, suggesting that sensory brain responses may be enhanced by the presence of threat-related information. This neural mechanism would allow emotionally significant stimuli to be prioritized for further processing (Grandjean et al., 2005). Further studies are required to investigate the neural responses to a wider range of emotional prosody such as fear, happiness and so on.

It is also important to acknowledge the role that social interactions might play in the recognition of emotional intonation (Scherer et al., 2003). The hearing requirements of the receiver, for example, may have a strong influence on how the sender sends the signal and these sender–receiver interactions may be crucial in emotional communication. A similar caveat was applied to the signalling of emotion by means of facial expressions. It is very difficult to include dynamic social interactions, with rapidly changing expressions and intonations etc, into laboratory-based experiments. However, given the likely importance of these sender–receiver interactions it is probably necessary to develop new research methodologies that can incorporate these factors.

Distinctive physiology

Evidence for emotion-specific autonomic nervous system activation

A very early notion in emotion science was the idea that each discrete emotion might be accompanied by a distinctive pattern of physiological activity. William James (1884), for example, thought that feelings were produced *following* the perception of physiological changes. A key question, then, is whether each emotion is accompanied by a specific pattern of physiological responding. Many studies have investigated the degree to which each emotional state is accompanied by a specific and unique activation of the autonomic nervous system (ANS). The ANS regulates the body's cardiovascular, electrodermal, digestive, respiratory and endocrine organs and essentially operates as a 'life-support' system (see Table 2.2 (p. 27)). If ANS functioning and emotions were selected by evolution for survival, it is reasonable to expect a close relationship between *particular* discrete emotions and patterns of ANS activation.

ANS and endocrine responses may not be the clearest indicators of specific emotions, however, as these systems are primarily responsible for the body's housekeeping functions such as energy metabolism, tissue repair and so on. Energy requirements are likely to be the same for a wide range of different emotions (e.g., fear, anger), so it is unlikely that specific response patterns will be found for particular emotions (Gray, 1987). Robert Levenson (1988) accepts this view to some extent, but still argues that clear differences in ANS response among different emotions can be identified. He points out that, in addition to its main function in regulating homeostasis (i.e., to maintain a consistent and stable internal bodily state), the ANS provides support for behavioural demands. If the *function* of emotions is to organize and coordinate the response to some environmental demand, and if this synchronization requires the mobilization of particular adaptive behaviours, then specific patterns of activation would be necessary to support that behaviour. Levenson has demonstrated that ANS activation is associated with specific behavioural requirements with the assumption that emotion specificity will occur only when particular emotions require particular behaviours (Levenson, 2003).

In early work the emotions of anger and fear were experimentally induced by means of carefully scripted interactions between the study participants and trained confederates (Ax, 1953). For example, the experimenter would act in a highly incompetent manner in order to induce anger in the study participants. Various measures of autonomic function were then obtained and it was found that different patterns of ANS activation occurred between the anger and the fear conditions. More recently, Ekman and his colleagues induced a number of emotions in study participants by asking them to produce facial expressions related to anger, fear, sadness, and disgust (Ekman et al., 1983). As an interesting aside, the Directed Facial Action task used in these studies involves giving participants precise instructions to produce a facial configuration typical of a basic emotion (anger, disgust, fear, happiness, sadness, or surprise). People may be told to 'raise your eye-brows' or 'move your lips slightly upwards' and so on. The fascinating aspect of this technique is that once a person has produced a good prototypical facial expression they then report experiencing the relevant emotion on over 60% of the trials. In other words, producing a typical facial expression of fear or anger is an effective way of inducing subjective experience of that particular emotion. For the present purposes, the interesting part of the Ekman et al. (1983) study was the finding that each emotion could be distinguished by means of specific patterns of ANS activation. These findings have now been replicated in a group of people from a very different culture – the Minangkabau tribe of Western Sumatra in Indonesia, which is a fundamentalist matriarchal Muslim society – suggesting that particular patterns of ANS activity may be universal (Levenson et al., 1992).

Empirical evidence suggests that a small number of discrete emotions are associated with specific patterns of ANS activation. This area of research has always been controversial, however, and some reviews of the literature have concluded that the evidence for ANS specificity is weak when a range of different emotions are taken into account (Cacioppo et al., 1997). One possible reason is that ANS activation is primarily related to motor outputs, rather than to the other aspects of emotion (Ekman, 1992a and b). Thus, certain patterns of ANS activation are likely to have been selected because they were effective for specific motor responses (e.g., freezing, fighting). These responses subsequently also became adaptive for specific emotions such as anger, fear or disgust. If this is the case, we would not necessarily expect to find emotion-specific ANS activity for emotions which did not require specific motor activity for survival. Ekman (1992a and b) argues that sadness and happiness, for example, can be included in this category. The lack of empirical evidence for specific ANS patterns of activation for these emotions, then, does not necessarily damage the universality hypothesis.

Distinctive neural circuits

If a small set of *basic* and *discrete* emotions exist, then we would expect to find patterns of neural activation that are relatively specific to each of these emotions. It has been suggested, for example, that the best criterion to identify basic emotions is the 'specification of brain circuits that generate coherent emotional behaviours along with valenced states in animal models that have homologous counterparts in human brains' (Panksepp, 2004, p. 138). Research on animal models of emotions takes this approach. More recently, there has also been an explosion of research using brain-imaging methodologies to investigate the neural correlates of specific emotions in humans.

Animal research

Some research has focused on identifying neurochemical systems that influence emotional responses (e.g., Panksepp, 1998). Others have concentrated on the role of specific anatomical structures in influencing the learning and expression of specific emotions, especially fear (e.g., LeDoux, 1996).

Panksepp (1998) hypothesizes that affective processes arise from *subcortical* emotional action systems. The assumption is that these subcortical circuits are shared by all mammals, have been shaped during evolution, and lead to unique affective *experiences* or *feeling*. If human feelings arise from the same subcortical structures as all other mammals (and many other species as well), the clearest understanding of feelings is likely to come from detailed neurobiological studies with animals such as rats. This is a controversial position on a number of grounds. First, many investigators doubt whether many species have feelings at all (as opposed to emotions) (Rolls, 2005). Second, many neuroscientists argue that feelings are 'red herrings' in terms of the scientific understanding of emotions (LeDoux, 1996). In their view, feelings are responses produced by the activation of an emotion circuit and are of no more importance to the overall emotion than other components, which might be behavioural or physiological. Other neuroscientists argue that feelings are likely to be implemented by cortical brain areas and are unlikely to arise directly from subcortical structures (Berridge, 2003; Rolls, 2005). Finally, many emotion scientists would argue that it is easier to study feelings in humans where they can be measured more directly.

Panksepp's approach: emotional action systems

Panksepp (1998) argues that the functioning of neurotransmitter systems lies at the heart of emotional action systems which have evolved over many millennia. Since the original discovery of chemical synaptic transmission more than 50 neurotransmitters and neuromodulators have now been identified in the brain. Most of these substances fall into one of three broad chemical categories: amino acids, amines, and peptides. Table 4.2 shows some of the major neurotransmitters, most of which are involved in emotions. A brief overview of the principles of neurotransmission is presented in Box 4.2.

The logic of Panksepp's approach is that we should study animals under fairly naturalistic conditions (playing, fighting etc) so that those neurotransmitters that are important for particular affective systems can be identified. These neurotransmitters can then be manipulated in humans by means of psychoactive drugs to investigate how variations in levels of different neurotransmitters can affect subjective feelings.

TABLE 4.2 Major neurotransmitters

Amino acids	*Amines*	*Peptides*
Gamma-amino butyric acid (GABA) Glutamate (Glu) Glycine (Gly)	Acetylcholine (ACh) Dopamine (DA) Epinephrine Histamine Norepinephrine (NE) Serotonin (5-HT)	Cholecystokinin (CCK) Dynorphin Enkephalins (Enk) Neuropeptide Y (NPY) Somatostatin Substance P Thyrotrophin-releasing hormone Vasoactive intestinal polypeptide (VIP)

BOX 4.2

The principles of neurotransmission

It is important to understand how information is transferred around the brain. There are many different anatomical parts of the brain, as we have already seen, and many of these regions are connected to each other by means of nerve fibres and groups of brain cells (*neurons*). It was once thought that neurons communicated with each other only by means of electrical impulses. Waves of electrical activity moving from neuron to neuron can be observed in the brain, and are measured by EEG. However, it is now known that these electrical impulses can be produced by the action of *chemicals*, often called *neurotransmitters*. When one of these chemicals interacts with receptor cells on a neuron this can result in the firing of that neuron.

In the 1920s, Otto Loewi provided definitive evidence that information is transmitted around the nervous system primarily by means of chemicals rather than electrically. He made this discovery by means of an ingenious experiment. It was known at the time that activating the vagus nerve led to a slowing of the heart. The question was whether this happened because of an *electrical* signal from the nerve to the heart, or by means of a *chemical* signal from the nerve to the heart. Loewi isolated a frog's heart with the vagal nerve left intact. He stimulated the vagal nerve and found that, as expected, the heart rate slowed down. He then took the solution that had bathed this heart and applied it to a second isolated frog's heart. This heart also slowed down, providing definitive evidence that the solution contained a chemical which affected the functioning of the second heart. The chemical that Loewi had isolated was *acetylcholine* (ACh), and it is now well-established that information is almost always passed around the nervous system by means of chemical transmission.

Many different *neurotransmitters* have been discovered. They are generally held in synaptic vesicles within neurons, and are released into a small gap between neurons when a particular neuron is stimulated. These neurotransmitters then drift across the small gap between the pre-synaptic and the post-synaptic neurons

continued overleaf

BOX 4.2 continued

where they react with *receptors* on the neighbouring neuron. If the chemical structure of the neurotransmitter provides a good fit with the receptor – a bit like a lock and key mechanism – this neuron then fires. It releases its own neurotransmitters and so the message moves onwards. A diagrammatic representation of this process is shown in Figure 4.5.

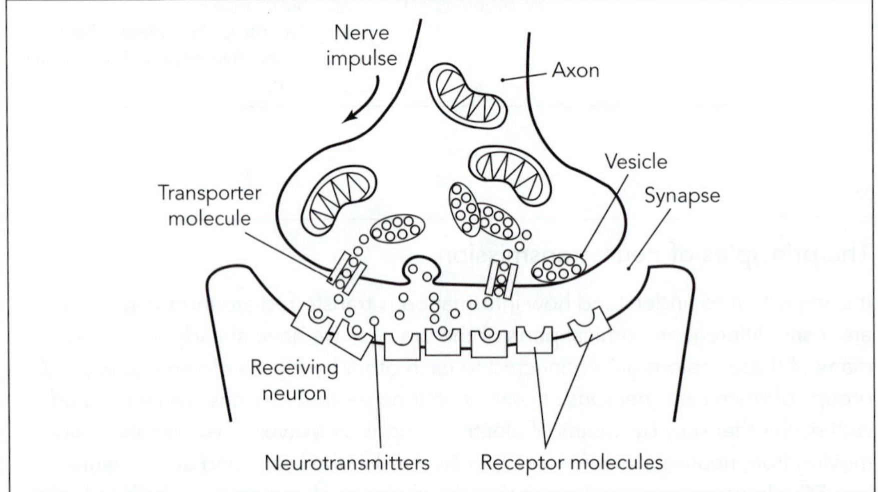

FIGURE 4.5 Neurotransmission

Source: Levitan and Kaczmarek (1997).

Panksepp (1998) proposes that affective processes in the brain can be divided into three general categories, which differ in level of complexity. As shown in Table 4.3, the proposed outline is very similar to Paul MacLean's (1990) notion of a triune brain going from the brain stem (lower functions) to mid-brain limbic systems (emotions) to cortical areas (higher cognitive functions). The 'Blue-ribbon, grade A emotions' are called 'basic emotions' in other taxonomies.

On the basis of many years of animal research, Panksepp (1998) has concluded that there are seven primary 'affective systems' which can be considered 'basic' and are gifted to us by evolution. All of these affective systems seem to be influenced by serotonin (5-HT) and norepinephrine (NE), which have fairly general effects. However, some systems are also affected by specific neurotransmitters depending on where they are within the brain. These seven systems and key neurochemicals are outlined in Table 4.4.

Oxytocin, maternal care and romantic love

To illustrate how emotional systems might be identified on the basis of the underlying neurochemistry we will focus on the care system. The peptide, *oxytocin*, appears to be crucial for the development of maternal behaviour, pair-bonding and perhaps even

TABLE 4.3 Three levels of complexity in affective systems

	Reflexive affects	*Blue-ribbon, grade A emotions*	*Higher sentiments*
Examples	Startle reflex Gustatory disgust Pain Homeostatic distresses (e.g., hunger) Pleasures (good tastes)	Fear Anger, Sadness Joy Affection Interest	Shame Guilt Contempt Envy Humour Empathy Sympathy
Brain structures	Brain stem regions	Mid-brain regions (e.g., periaqueductal grey PAG)	Frontal cortex

Source: Based on Panksepp (1994).

TABLE 4.4 Basic emotional systems of the mammalian brain with some key neuroanatomical and neurochemical components

Basic emotional systems	*Key brain areas*	*Key neurochemicals*
Seeking	Nucleus accumbens-VTA Mesolimbic mesocortical outputs Lateral hypothalamus-PAG	(DA)+, glutamate (+), many neuropeptides, opiates (+), neurotensin (+)
Rage	Medial amygdala to BNST Medial and perifornical hypothalamus and dorsal to PAG	Substance P (+), ACh (+), glutamate (+)
Fear	Central and lateral amygdala to medial hypothalamus and dorsal PAG	Glutamate (+), many neuropeptides, CCK, NPY
Lust	Corticomedial amygdala BNST Preoptic and ventromedial hypothalamus Lateral and ventral PAG	Steroids (+), vasopressin and oxytocin, CCK
Care	Anterior cingulate, BNST, Preoptic area, VTA, PAG	Oxytocin (+), prolactin (+), DA (+), opioids (+/–)
Panic	Anterior cingulate BNST and preoptic area Dorsomedial thalamus Dorsal PAG	Opioids(-),oxytocin(–), prolactin (–), CRF (+), glutamate (+)
Play	Dorsomedial diencephalon Parafascicular area Ventral PAG	Opioids (+/–), glutamate (+), ACh (+)

Notes:
The monoamines 5-HT and NE are not listed because they influence all emotions in non-specific ways. For the same reason, the higher cortical regions of the brain, which are also involved in emotionality (mostly frontal and temporal areas) have also been omitted.
ACh, Acetylcholine; BNST, bed nucleus of stria terminalis; CCK, Cholecystokinin;
CRF, Corticotrophin-releasing factor; DA, Dopamine; NPY, Neuropeptide Y; PAG, Periaqueductal grey; VTA, Ventral tegmental area; –, inhibits prototype; +, activates prototype.

Source: Adapted from Panksepp (2006), using data from Panksepp (1998).

romantic love. Oxytocin is important for female sexuality, and also plays an important role in childbirth and breastfeeding. However, it also has a wider role in the development of nurturance and maternal behaviour. For example, most rat species show wide individual differences in maternal behaviour, such as licking and grooming of pups. These differences seem to be directly related to variations in oxytocin receptor expression. It has been found that oxytocin receptor levels were much higher in the bed nucleus of the stria terminalis (BNST) and medial preoptic areas of rats who engaged in more licking/grooming behaviour compared with those mothers who engaged in low levels of licking and grooming (Francis et al., 2000). A follow-up study found that female rats who received higher levels of licking and grooming as pups had a higher number of oxytocin receptors in the BNST and the central nucleus of the amygdala. These females went on to become far less fearful and more maternal than rats with lower levels of oxytocin receptor binding (Francis et al., 2002). Moreover, when the action of oxytocin was blocked by injecting a receptor antagonist into the VTA region of the rat brain, the onset of maternal behaviours was also blocked (Pedersen et al., 1994). This provides a very strong indication that the release of oxytocin is crucial for the development of normal maternal behaviours. It is interesting to note that oxytocin is also involved in the panic system, which is closely related to separation distress. If a young animal gets separated from its mother or from the group he or she will send out distress signals. The injection of oxytocin into the brain leads to a dramatic reduction in the number of such distress calls (see Panksepp, 1998, for discussion). Thus, an increase in the level of oxytocin results in increases in maternal behaviour and decreases in separation distress calls. Conversely, reductions in oxytocin lead to a reduction in caring and nurturance and to an increase in separation distress.

This is a good demonstration of a *double dissociation* between two systems and the underlying chemistry. It makes absolute sense, of course, that the panic system and the care system should be linked in this way, but it is also an important illustration of how difficult it can be to identify *separate* neural circuits for different emotions. It is almost certain, for example, that each neurochemical is involved in a number of different emotions. We already know that 5-HT and NE seem to be involved in all emotions. As shown in Table 4.4, glutamate also seems to be involved in most of the primary emotional systems. This is not surprising when we consider how evolution works. Natural selection operates on the basis of small and gradual changes in biological systems or processes, so a particular neurochemical is likely to become involved in a range of different behaviours. Oxytocin is an excellent example of this. Its original role was almost certainly to maintain female sexuality and to induce milk production in the breast. However, as we now know, oxytocin seems to play a role in mediating maternal urges and, perhaps also, feelings of romantic love as well as maternal love.

It is, of course, extremely difficult to know whether oxytocin is really affecting maternal *feelings* of love, rather than acting directly on specific maternal behaviours (e.g., grooming). Many of these behaviours can, of course, occur in the absence of feelings. For example, licking and grooming and retrieving young if they fall out of the nest are fairly stereotypical responses that may or may not be associated with specific feelings. Studies with prairie voles, however, have provided an intriguing indication that oxytocin may play an important role in the development of pair-bonding. Prairie voles are of particular interest because they tend to pair for life and are strictly monogamous. In one experiment, oxytocin was injected directly into the brains of these voles. They went on to establish social bonds far more quickly than usual. However, when a receptor antagonist was injected into the voles' brains so that oxytocin could not act in the normal way, they became highly promiscuous (Cho et al., 1999). These findings show that oxytocin is critical for the development of pair-bonding. These experiments can still not tell us, however, whether this pair-bonding is really mediated by feelings.

In human studies using fMRI, groups of mothers were asked to look at pictures of their own baby and photographs of other babies that they had known for a similar amount of time. In addition, people who reported that they were 'deeply in love' observed photographs of their boyfriend/girlfriend and photographs of other friends while the fMRI machine was scanning their brain. It was found that a wide range of subcortical areas rich in oxytocin receptors (e.g., PAG, VTA), as well as areas of the insula and cortex, were activated to a greater extent when photographs of the loved ones were being observed (Bartels and Zeki, 2004). Unfortunately, there was no measure of subjective feelings in this study and no direct measure of oxytocin levels. It is therefore difficult to draw conclusions about the role of oxytocin in generating feeling states. Nevertheless, research with rats, prairie voles, and humans all indicate that oxytocin is clearly important for the development of social attachments and pair-bonding, sexual behaviour, as well as the development of maternal care.

It would be interesting to conduct studies that deliberately increase or decrease oxytocin production in humans and then examine the resulting changes in people's reports of how their feelings change. No such study has yet been conducted. However, a relevant study has reported that oxytocin reactivity is correlated with the behavioural displays of romantic love (Gonzaga et al., 2006). A group of women were asked to recall a vivid love-related experience and a number of behavioural markers and subjective reports were taken. During these recall periods a series of blood samples were also obtained so that the degree of oxytocin reactivity could be measured. Interestingly, oxytocin reactivity did not correlate with subjective feelings, even though it did correlate with behavioural indicators of love. This evidence is preliminary but it does suggest that oxytocin is not directly related to feelings.

LeDoux's approach: fear conditioning

Much of what we know about the neural pathways involved in the fear system has come from studies of *fear conditioning*, and Joseph LeDoux has been a leading exponent of this approach. Fear conditioning is a simple procedure in which an external stimulus (usually an auditory tone) is used as the *conditioned stimulus* (CS), and this is paired with an *unconditioned stimulus* (US) such as a mild electric shock to the foot. This is a very useful and elegant procedure because the US is associated with a clear unconditioned response (UR) such as freezing in rats. Once a tone has been presented with a foot-shock on a couple of occasions, the rat will begin to exhibit a *conditioned response* (CR) to the presentation of the tone alone. The use of this simple procedure with rats has demonstrated that the amygdala is a crucial neural structure in

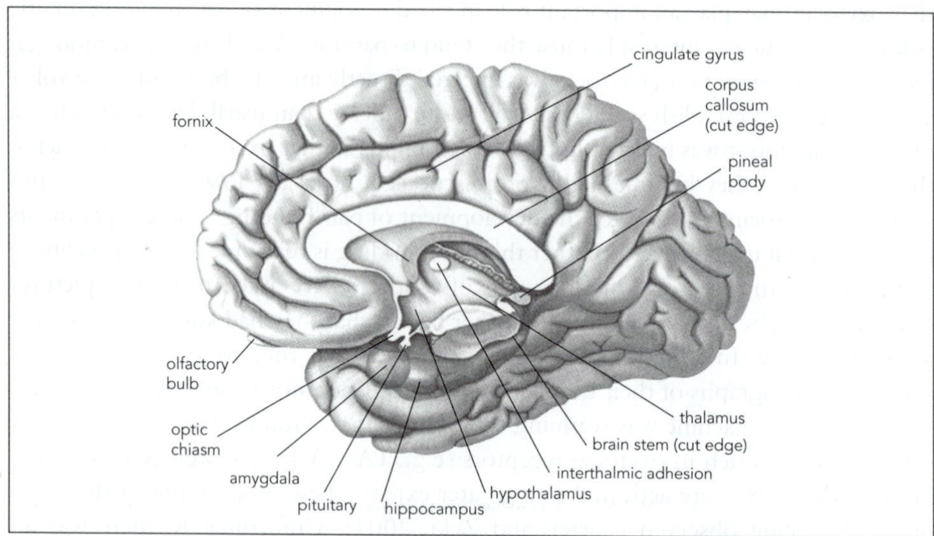

FIGURE 4.6 The position of the amygdala and hippocampus within the human brain
Source: Bear et al. (2001).

the processing of fear. Figure 4.6 shows the position of the amygdala within the brain, along with other nearby structures such as the hippocampus.

Anatomical studies have shown that there are up to 13 different sections of the amygdala, all of which may serve different functions. However, it is common to group these sections into three major parts (see Figure 4.7): the corticomedial nuclei, the basolateral nuclei and the central nucleus. LeDoux has conducted numerous experiments with rats, and has proposed that there are two different routes from an initial (auditory) fear stimulus to the amygdala. When a sound is detected by specialized cells in the ear, a signal is sent to the thalamus, which is the part of the brain that integrates sensory signals. Once in the thalamus, this signal can be sent *directly* to the amygdala, which is a very fast route or the so-called 'quick and dirty route' (LeDoux, 1996). Alternatively, the signal can go from the thalamus to the auditory cortex and from there to the amygdala by bundles of nerve fibres. This route is slower (although still fast) and has sometimes been called the 'high road', in contrast to the faster 'low road', to a fear response (LeDoux, 1996). A schematic diagram of the anatomical connections between the auditory system and the amygdala is shown in Figure 4.7.

Research with rats confirms that the amygdala is critical to the learning of danger signals, which is a crucial survival mechanism. If the basolateral nuclei of the amygdala are surgically removed, or if amino acid receptors in this region are inactivated, then rats do not acquire a conditioned fear response (LeDoux and Phelps, 2004). In other words, while they react normally to the US (electric shock) they do not develop a fear response to the CS (tone). Thus, the basolateral nuclei appear to be crucial for fear learning.

Research has also shown that the *context* in which particular associations are learnt is important for the overall process of learned associations. For instance, in fear

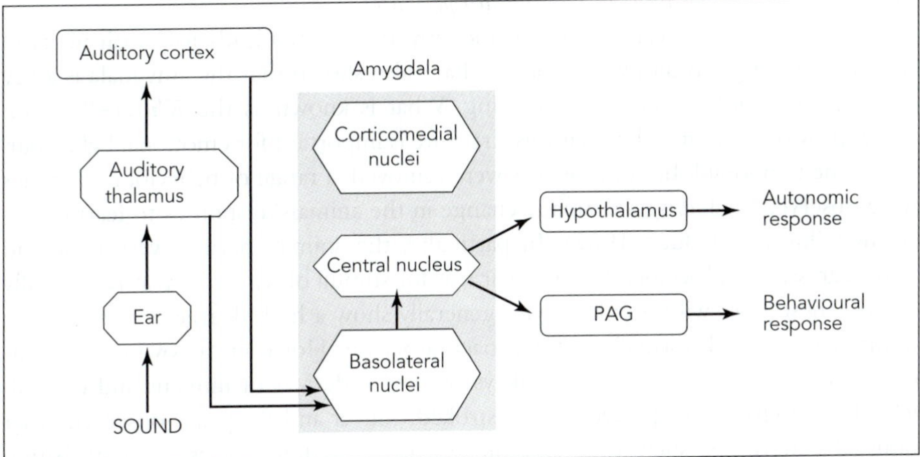

FIGURE 4.7 A neural circuit for learned fear

Sound waves enter the ear where they pass through the auditory system to the thalamus. The signal is then transmitted from all regions of the auditory thalamus to the auditory cortex. The signal can go directly from the thalamus to the amygdala, or it can go via the cortex. In both cases, the signal enters the sensory input region of the amygdala, the basolateral nuclei. Information within the amygdala is constantly integrated and updated with information coming from other areas of the brain (not shown in diagram) and then transmitted to the central nucleus of the amygdala. The central nucleus is the main output region of the amygdala and from here signals can be sent to numerous brain areas including the hypothalamus and the periaqueductal grey (PAG), which control a range of individual responses such as hormone release, changes in blood pressure, and freezing behaviour.

conditioning experiments rats often develop fear reactions to the particular chamber in which the fear conditioning takes place, even in the absence of the CS (Phillips and LeDoux, 1992). It turns out that the development of these *contextual fear associations* depends upon the functioning of the hippocampus, which is also known to be heavily involved in episodic memory. If the hippocampus is damaged prior to conditioning, normal conditioning to the CS can occur, but the rat does not acquire a CR to the *context* (Phillips and LeDoux, 1992).

In addition to the development of specific associations between a fear response and a particular stimulus or context, the *maintenance* of fear is also important. Once a fear response has been learned it tends to be fairly persistent unless the CS is presented many times in the absence of the US. Thus, for example, a rat may have been conditioned to associate foot-shock (US) with a tone (CS), but if that tone is presented many times *without* the accompanying shock to the foot the fear response will gradually diminish and disappear. This is an active process, which is technically called *extinction*. It seems that a number of areas within the PFC are important for this process. If the medial PFC is damaged in rats, the extinction process is impaired and the fear response persists over long periods of time (Morgan and LeDoux, 1995). This suggests that the medial PFC, in conjunction with other cortical areas, is important in terms of regulating how the amygdala and hippocampus respond to situations and stimuli based on their current affective significance (Phelps et al., 2004).

Effects of amygdala damage in non-human primates

As we have seen, surgical removal of the amygdala in rats leads to impairments in fear conditioning. Studies with monkeys have also shown that the amygdala is a key structure for normal emotion processing. What is known as the *Kluver–Bucy syndrome* provided an early clue that this structure is important for emotional behaviour. When the temporal lobes of monkeys were removed, a range of behavioural changes were observed, including a dramatic change in the animals' responses to fearful situations (Kluver and Bucy, 1937). In particular, the animals became very tame and non-aggressive, and seemed to lose their fear for stimuli of which they were normally afraid. These were wild monkeys who generally show a high degree of fear towards humans and would normally not approach a person. However, following the bilateral temporal lobectomy, these monkeys showed little fear of humans and even allowed themselves to be picked up and stroked. Kluver and Bucy also observed other unusual behaviours, such as hypersexuality (increased frequencies of masturbation and homosexual and heterosexual acts) and a tendency to eat a variety of non-food items such as faeces and rocks. In interpreting these results, we need to be aware that the entire temporal lobes were removed and not just the amygdala. Thus, some of the behavioural changes may have been due to the removal of regions other than the amygdala. However, later research has shown that the amygdala does seem to be the key structure for determining the affective significance of particular sensory stimuli (Weiskrantz, 1956). For instance, it has been demonstrated that monkeys show a reduced fear response to snakes following ablation of just the amygdala. This seems to be a genuine reduction in the experience of fear as it is associated with a reduction in the facial expressions and vocalizations that are associated with an acute fear response (Kalin et al., 2001).

Experimental work with monkeys, in which parts of the frontal lobes were damaged, has also shown that this region is important in modulating emotional responses. Bilateral damage to the PFC, for example, results in profound deficits in emotional displays (facial expressions etc) in monkeys, and also leads to severe disruption in a number of social behaviours (Franzen and Myers, 1973). More recently, Raleigh and Brammer (1993) have found very high concentrations of particular types of serotonin (5-HT) receptors in the amygdala and in the vmPFC of monkeys who were very competent in social behaviours (e.g., grooming, cooperation etc). In contrast, the levels of 5-HT receptors in these brain regions were very low in monkeys which did not have good social skills. These findings illustrate the importance of the connection between subcortical and cortical regions (the amygdala and vmPFC) and emotional responses, and emphasize how the adequate functioning of both of these systems is critical to the development of social behaviour.

While the amygdala is an important structure in the development and maintenance of fear responses, other adjacent areas also play important roles in fear. For example, a number of structures extending from the temporal lobe and amygdala, through the anterior and medial hypothalamus, through the periaqueductal grey area (PAG) and then down to the brain stem, and the lower brain stem and spinal cord, control many of the physiological symptoms of fear (e.g., HR and BP response, startle response).

In addition, all of these areas are richly connected to other brain regions, including cortical areas. When these brain systems are stimulated electrically, rats demonstrate a range of fear-like behaviours. At low levels of intensity a freezing response is likely to occur, whereas with higher levels of intensity a flight response is more likely. Panksepp (1998) points out that these are precisely the type of fear behaviours that rats show when a danger such as a predator is either far away (freezing) or close (flight).

Human research

Lesion studies

Much of what we know about how emotions are implemented in the human brain comes from studies of people who have received damage to the brain, often by means of a stroke, a tumour or an accident. One of the most famous case histories in neurology is the story of Phineas Gage. Phineas Gage worked as a foreman on the Vermont railroad and at the age of 25 suffered a bizarre accident, which he was lucky to survive. While tamping gunpowder into a hole to prepare for construction work his tamping iron hit a rock and the powder exploded sending a metre-long rod straight through his head. The tamping iron entered his brain just below the left eye, passed through his left frontal lobe and exited from the top of his head, damaging both frontal cortices. Remarkably, Phineas Gage survived the accident and recovered with language and memory functions intact. However, following the accident it became clear that all was not well. While Gage had made a good physical recovery, his physician, Dr John Harlow, noted that Gage's personality had changed in a profound way. Before his accident he had been a reliable and hard worker and was liked and respected by all who knew him. However, following the accident he became 'fitful, irreverent, indulging at times in the grossest profanity (which was not previously his custom), manifesting but little deference for his fellows, impatient of restraint or advice when it conflicts with his desires' (Harlow, 1868, p. 339). In general, his personality had changed from an organized hard-working man to someone who was frequently socially inappropriate and unreliable. In the words of Harlow, Gage was 'no longer Gage'. In 1994, Hanna Damasio and her colleagues examined Gage's skull which is still preserved in a museum at the Harvard Medical School. By reconstructing the passage of the iron rod through his skull, they were able to determine that the most damaged area of Gage's brain was the vmPFC, especially on the left side (Damasio et al., 1994). The personality changes that Phineas Gage experienced following his injuries suggested that the prefrontal cortex plays an important role in regulating emotions in humans as well as in other primates. Figure 4.8 shows the nature of the damage that Phineas Gage sustained, based on a model developed by Hanna Damasio. Both the model and the actual skull are on display at Harvard University in Boston.

Many studies of people with damage to the prefrontal cortices have shown that these cortical areas are involved in a number of different aspects of emotional functioning. However, on the basis of research with animals, many subcortical structures are also likely to be important for specific discrete emotions (LeDoux, 1996; Panksepp, 1998). A number of studies have examined people with damage to subcortical

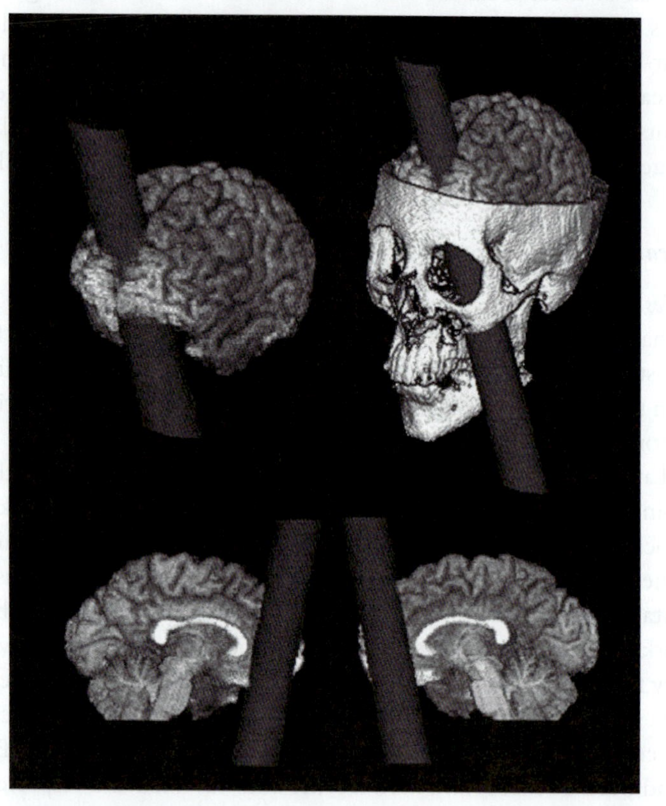

FIGURE 4.8 Model of damage sustained by Phineas Gage
Source: Damasio et al. (1994).

structures, with most research focusing on damage to the human amygdala. The most common consequence of amygdala damage in humans is a change in emotional behaviour, although it is interesting to note that the effects are not as dramatic as those seen in monkeys with lesions to the amygdala (Aggleton, 1992). In terms of evidence for discrete emotions, one of the most interesting consequences of amygdala damage in humans is a very specific deficit in the recognition of fear displays, with recognition of other emotions being left intact. Andy Calder and his colleagues tested two patients with amygdala damage with some standardized facial expression recognition tests. One patient, called DR, had had both the left and right amygdala removed surgically for the treatment of intractable epilepsy. The other patient, SE, had suffered damage to both amygdalae (and some other regions of the right temporal lobe) due to encephalitis. Both patients were shown a series of faces from the Ekman and Freisen (1976b) set and asked to indicate which expression was being presented. Both DR and SE could recognize most emotional expressions easily, but had severe difficulties in recognizing fear expressions, and to a lesser extent anger expressions (Calder et al., 1996). Other studies have confirmed that amygdala damage seems to be related to very specific deficits in the recognition of fearful expressions (Adolphs et al., 1994). It should be noted, however, that, while a reduced ability to recognize fearful facial expressions and/or vocalizations is a key aspect of amygdala damage in humans, amygdala-damaged patients may have a range of deficits and there are some individuals who do not have any problems at all with recognizing or expressing fear (see Calder et al., 2001). These findings indicate that the role of the amygdala is far more complex than being simply a fear detector. Nevertheless, it is clear that the recognition of fearful facial expressions does seem to be dependent on a functioning amygdala (Adolphs et al., 1995; Calder et al., 1996).

In contrast, damage to the insula and basal ganglia regions of the brain seems to be associated with a particular difficulty in recognizing facial expressions of disgust. In a detailed study of a single patient, known as NK, who had lesions in insula and basal ganglia regions (primarily in the left hemisphere) very specific problems in recognizing facial as well as vocal signals of disgust were found. However, NK's recognition of other emotion categories appeared to be normal (Calder et al., 2000). Moreover, NK filled out a number of questionnaires which showed that his *experience* of both fear and anger was normal, while severe abnormalities were reported in his subjective experience of disgust. This finding indicates that the insula and basal ganglia regions are involved in both the *recognition* and the *experience* of disgust. The association of the insula and feelings of disgust are consistent with a report that electrical stimulation of the insula in conscious patients undergoing surgery for epilepsy resulted in highly unpleasant sensations in the stomach as well as unpleasant tastes and feelings of nausea (Penfield and Faulk, 1955).

Further evidence supporting a distinction between fear and disgust comes from studies of people with Huntington's disease. This is a neurogenetic disorder that, in the early stages of the disease, affects a region of the basal ganglia called the striatum. Sprengelmeyer and colleagues (Sprengelmeyer et al., 1996, 1997) presented the facial expression recognition test to people with Huntington's. The participants had problems with recognizing a number of emotions, but they had particular problems in recognizing the facial signals of disgust. As we saw earlier, evidence on recognition of disgust also comes from a study of a single patient who had focal lesions within the insula and the basal ganglia of the left hemisphere (Calder et al., 2000). These studies, among others, indicate that there may well be different neural circuits underlying fear and disgust, even though there is likely to be some overlap of neural areas. More recently, it has also been reported that lesions to the ventral basal ganglia are associated with selective deficits in the ability to recognize anger (Calder et al., 2004).

While problems in recognizing emotion in others is well established in patients with various types of brain damage, it is important to ask whether the damage to these structures also influences the person's subjective experience of emotion. Can people with this type of damage still *feel* fear or disgust in the appropriate situations? There is not very much evidence available to answer this question, but it has been found that when the amygdala is electrically stimulated during surgery for epilepsy a feeling of fear is often induced (Halgren, 1992). This finding is difficult to assess, however, as many other reactions are also common with this type of stimulation. Nevertheless, studies of electrical stimulation to the wider fear system – amygdala, PAG, hypothalamus, brain stem – show that people tend to report strong feelings of foreboding when these areas are stimulated. For example, one patient reported that 'Somebody is now chasing me, I am trying to escape from him' (Panksepp, 1985). Anecdotal reports also suggest that the experience of fear is abnormal in people with amygdala damage. For example, the husband of one woman with amygdala damage reported that when they were surrounded by a group of youths who tried to mug him, his wife was relaxed and said that they were just 'larking around'. However, on another occasion she became terrified when two actors in a television programme were mildly aggressive towards each other (see Calder et al., 2001, for review). There is also some evidence from patient NK that damage to the insula and basal ganglia interferes with the subjective experience of disgust (Calder et al., 2000).

To summarize, studies of patients with brain lesions have shown that amygdala damage may lead to specific deficits in the recognition and experience of fear (Calder et al., 1996), damage to the insula and basal ganglia results in deficits in recognizing and experiencing disgust (Calder et al., 2000; Sprengelmeyer et al., 1996, 1997), and damage to the ventral striatum can impair the recognition of anger (Calder et al., 2004). This body of research suggests that discrete emotions are associated with specific brain areas both in terms of recognition of different emotion categories as well as the subjective experience of these emotions.

Fear conditioning with brain injured patients

In addition to tests of emotion recognition, the fear-conditioning paradigm has also been used successfully in human research. Photographs of faces, coloured squares or tones are most commonly used as the CS, while mild electric shock or an aversive burst of noise is the most common US. The typical response measured in human studies is the skin conductance response (SCR), which provides a good index of ANS function. Several studies have shown that the amygdala is indeed crucial for the development of conditioned fear in humans. It has also been found that the hippocampus is essential for the explicit learning of a fear response in humans. A clear dissociation has been reported between patients with amygdala damage and patients with hippocampal damage on a fear-conditioning paradigm (Bechara et al., 1995). In this study, a patient with selective bilateral damage to the amygdala was easily able to learn which visual and auditory stimuli (CS) were linked with the US. However, this individual did not develop a conditioned response to the CS as measured by SCR, which is very unusual. In other words, even though the patient could remember which tone would lead to an electric shock, no anticipatory fear occurred when this tone was presented. In contrast, a patient with selective bilateral damage to the hippocampus was unable to learn the association between the CS and the US, but nevertheless did develop a normal conditioned fear response as measured by SCR. This patient showed anticipatory fear when the crucial tone was presented even though the individual could not remember that this particular tone was associated with the shock. Thus, one patient was able to learn an explicit association between a CS and a US but did not develop a normal fear response to the CS, while another patient could not learn the explicit association but did develop a normal fear response to the CS. This demonstrates a classic double dissociation, which is an important technique in neuropsychology. Finally, as an important control, Bechara and colleagues found that a patient with bilateral damage to both the amygdala and the hippocampus was not able to learn either the explicit association or the fear response. In an elegant way, this study demonstrates that the amygdala and the hippocampus can operate independently of each other, allowing us to acquire different types of representations of the aversive consequences of particular events. These different kinds of representations, explicit/hippocampal and implicit/amygdala are likely to be useful in a range of different situations. For example, it is sometimes important to respond to threat instantly even if we do not explicitly *know* what the threat is (e.g., a snake hidden in the grass). At other times, it is important to know that danger may occur in a particular situation even if we have never experienced that situation directly. Thus, if I tell you that there is an aggressive dog living beside a path in your local park you will probably experience a fear reaction if you happen to walk down that path, even though you have never experienced any threatening event in that location. Research indicates that the amygdala and the hippocampus may play different roles in modulating these different aspects of fear (Phelps, 2004).

Evidence of how important explicit knowledge can be in the development of a fear response was reported by Elizabeth Phelps and her colleagues in another elegant study (Funayama et al., 2001). Participants were told that there was a possibility that they would receive an electric shock when they saw a particular coloured square (e.g., a blue square) but that no shock would occur when other coloured squares were presented. Even though no shock was ever administered throughout the experiment, normal participants (i.e., non-brain-damaged) understood that a blue square might indicate a forthcoming shock and, as we would expect, they developed a normal fear response (as measured by SCR) any time the blue square was presented. In marked contrast, patients with amygdala damage did not develop this SCR to the blue square even though they could easily report the explicit link between the blue square and the possibility of getting a shock. This study is important in demonstrating two things. First, the study shows that the amygdala modulates the fear response but that it, in turn, is modulated by the hippocampus. Because no shock was ever administered, the fear response can only have developed in response to the *explicit knowledge* of the CS–US (blue square–electric shock) link. This explicit memory is, of course, controlled by the hippocampus, which must have sent a signal to the amygdala so that the amygdala itself responded as soon as the blue square was presented. Second, for the people with amygdala damage, the amygdala could not respond and therefore a fear response did not develop. This demonstrates the crucial role that the amygdala plays in the development of a normal fear reaction.

Is the amygdala specific to fear?

While the amygdala has been implicated in both the recognition and the experience of fear, it is also clear that this structure is involved in a number of other emotions. For example, when electrodes were implanted into the dorsolateral amygdala of monkeys, it was found that specific neurons within this region were activated by stimuli that indicated reward to the same extent as stimuli that indicated punishment (Sanghera et al., 1979). It has also been found that the amygdala responds to a range of positive stimuli (e.g., happy faces) but that this response is strongly modulated by a person's personality traits (Canli et al., 2002). Thus, it is clearly not the case that the amygdala is involved only in fear. Instead, this neural structure may play a wider role in a range of different emotions. This makes it difficult to establish whether the amygdala is part of a neural circuit that is specific to fear, or whether it may be part of a neural circuit underlying any significant affective stimuli.

Brain imaging of emotions

Lesion studies can be problematic to interpret since damage frequently affects a number of different brain areas. This makes it difficult to attribute particular functions to specific brain regions. However, advances in brain imaging technology have opened up new ways of investigating the hypothesis that individual emotions such as fear, anger, sadness, disgust, happiness are associated with specific neural circuits. In particular, PET and fMRI allow us to observe which brain areas are involved in emotion in conscious healthy individuals. A problem with many brain imaging studies of emotion, however, is that the researchers do not make a clear distinction between emotions, moods and feelings (the subjective experience of emotions). In addition, they often do not make a distinction between the *perception* of emotion and the *expression* of emotion in either behavioural outputs or feelings. These different aspects of emotions (or moods) may have different neural substrates and this is important to bear in mind when evaluating neuroimaging studies of emotion (Murphy et al., 2003).

Many neuroimaging studies have examined emotion perception by presenting people with emotional stimuli (usually visually) and then examining which brain areas are differentially activated to different emotions. While a wide range of stimuli can be used (e.g., positive and negative pictures; positive and negative words; aggressive and calm prosody etc), most studies have used photographs of different facial expressions. These are useful stimuli because:

(a) they are highly significant social stimuli that are familiar to everyone,
(b) the same individual's face can be used so that there is a good control between different emotional expressions. In other words, the same person can be presented expressing anger, happiness, fear, disgust and so on. This degree of matching would be much more difficult to achieve using pictures of different scenes, and
(c) different facial expressions may relate to different basic emotions, as suggested by the work of Paul Ekman. Thus, examining the neural correlates of processing different facial expressions might tell us something about the neural circuits underlying different basic, or discrete, emotions.

In an early study, photographs of faces with fearful and happy expressions were presented one by one to participants while their brain activity was monitored by means of PET (Morris et al., 1996). There was a clear differential activation of the left amygdala to fearful relative to happy faces. Two recent studies, have examined a wider range of emotional expressions (fear, disgust, happiness and sadness) but these studies report a conflicting pattern of results. Surguladze, Russell et al. (2003) found that the amygdala was activated by high intensity fearful expressions, while the hippocampus, anterior insula, and putamen were activated to increasing intensities by fearful, disgusted and happy expressions, respectively. Moreover, linear decreases in hippocampus and putamen responses occurred to increasing intensities of sadness. In contrast, a similar study, also using fMRI, did not find any differential activation among these different emotions. Instead, it found that a number of brain regions tended to respond to increasing intensities of emotion, rather than individual emotions (Winston et al., 2003).

Given the relative newness of neuroimaging studies of emotion and the low participant numbers in each study (usually around 12 participants), it is difficult to draw conclusions from any single study. For this reason, the use of meta-analysis is a useful technique. Meta-analysis is a statistical technique that reviews a large number of studies using similar methodologies so that a greater degree of statistical power can be used to draw conclusions across several studies. The effect sizes found in each individual experiment can be entered into a statistical analysis so that overall patterns that may not be obvious in any individual study can be investigated. Two comprehensive meta-analyses on the functional neuroanatomy of emotions have been reported (Murphy et al., 2003; Phan et al., 2002).

We will focus on the Murphy et al. (2003) meta-analysis because it includes a larger number of studies ($n = 106$) than the earlier analysis conducted by Phan et al. (2002). Murphy and colleagues directly tested the hypothesis that the pattern of neural activity would differ for the basic emotions of fear, anger, disgust, happiness, and sadness. They examined all of the relevant studies (106 were identified) and then determined the most consistently activated brain region for each emotion. Some support for the basic emotions approach was found, with some brain regions being more consistently activated for particular discrete emotions:

1 *fear* – amygdala;
2 *disgust* – insula/operculum and globus pallidus;
3 *anger* – lateral orbitofrontal cortex (OFC);
4 *happiness* – rostral supracallosal ACC/dorsomedial prefrontal cortex (dmPFC);
5 *sadness* – rostral supracallosal ACC/dmPFC.

This analysis included studies examining emotion perception as well as those examining the subjective experience of emotion. Further statistical analysis showed that three of the discrete emotions (fear, disgust and anger) could be distinguished from all others, while the pattern of neural activation did not differ between sadness and happiness. A similar pattern of findings was found in a more focused analysis of studies that investigated only the recognition of facial expressions of emotion (i.e., emotion perception). The results of this analysis are shown in Table 4.5.

As can be seen in Table 4.5, the number of studies for each emotion is relatively small. Nevertheless, there seems to be evidence for separate spatial distributions of

TABLE 4.5 The regions most consistently activated when processing facial expressions of the basic emotions

	Fear *(8)*	*Disgust* *(5)*	*Anger* *(4)*	*Happiness* *(4)*	*Sadness* *(3)*
Amygdala	63	19	0	0	25
Insula/operculum	0	100	22	0	0
Globus pallidus	23	80	22	0	0
Lateral OFC	61	19	100	23	0
rs ACC	38	19	23	50	0
dmPFC	38	19	23	50	0

The number of studies included in the meta-analysis is shown in brackets.
Source: Adapted from Murphy et al. (2003).

neural activity for the emotions of fear, disgust, and anger. In contrast, no significant difference between the spatial distribution of neural activity for happiness and sadness could be detected. It is important to note that regions of the anterior cingulate and mPFC (rsACC and dmPFC) were activated in most of the discrete emotions studied, suggesting a more general role for these brain areas (see Murphy et al., 2003, for further discussion). It is possible that some brain areas may play a general role in both the perception and experience of emotions, while other regions play a more specific role for individual discrete emotions. On the basis of their meta-analysis, in conjunction with evidence from brain damaged individuals, Murphy et al. (2003) conclude that there are partially separate neural systems underlying fear, disgust, and anger. This conclusion is broadly consistent with the discrete emotions approach that at least some basic emotions can be separated at both psychological and neural levels of representation.

Distinctive antecedent events

Another criterion assumed to be important in determining whether an emotion is 'basic' is that the emotion should be elicited by a distinctive antecedent event (see Table 4.1). If basic emotions evolved to help us deal with fundamental life tasks, then it is clear that there should be some common elements in the contexts in which particular emotions occur. Boucher (1983) argued, for example, that the loss of a significant other was an antecedent to sadness in most cultures. While there may be cultural variations in what person is a 'significant other', the death of that individual will generally result in sadness.

There are two general types of events that elicit specific emotions: biologically primed stimuli and stimuli that elicit responses through learning experiences. For example, we have seen how rats can quickly and easily learn to fear a tone that is associated with an electric shock. However, research also shows that rats will demonstrate a classic fear response to the smell of a cat, even if they have had no prior experience with cats (Panksepp, 1998). In most situations, it is likely that emotional responses to particular situations are the result of the joint contributions of evolution and social learning. An elegant study by Susan Mineka and her colleagues demonstrates this very nicely. They studied young rhesus monkeys that had been born and raised in the laboratory and had had no prior experience of snakes. Snakes, of course, represent a real danger to monkeys in the wild. In the experiment, the young monkeys were presented with realistic toy snakes, as well as a bunch of flowers as a control. The monkeys showed no particular fear of either the toy snakes or the flowers, showing that the sight of a snake is not hard-wired for monkeys in the way that the smell of a cat seems to be for rats. The researchers had obtained a video of an adult monkey demonstrating a classic fear response to a real snake in the wild. A copy of the video was then edited: the snake was replaced with a bunch of flowers so that it looked like the adult monkey was displaying fear to the bunch of flowers. Both versions of the video were then presented to two groups of naive monkeys who had never seen either snakes or bunches of flowers before. Remember that the video of the adult monkey's fear reaction was identical in both cases, so that if social learning was the *only* factor in eliciting the emotion of fear then the naive monkeys should develop a fear response to *both* the flowers and the snakes. Following the video, the naive monkeys were presented with a toy snake and a bunch of flowers. The naive monkeys developed a strong fear response only to the toy snake, while no fear reaction developed to the bunch of flowers. Moreover, the fear response to the snake was very persistent and difficult to extinguish (Mineka et al., 1984). This experiment nicely demonstrates that just one exposure to an adult exhibiting fear towards a snake is enough to induce a strong fear of snakes in young monkeys. This is clearly a *selective* learning process because the identical fear display to a bunch of flowers did not elicit a fear reaction. Thus, biological evolution seems to have provided us with a variety of stimuli which represented great dangers and/or advantages to our ancestors, and which are still important antecedents to emotional responses today (Mineka and Öhman, 2002; Öhman, 1986). It is no surprise, for example, that the most common phobias are the fear of spiders and the fear of open spaces – neither of which represent a particularly common danger in the modern world.

Appraisal models of emotions

The work of Mineka and others show that there are particular stimuli which are more easily associated with the induction of specific emotions. However, it is also clear that no one set of antecedent events is likely always to elicit the same emotions in everybody (Stein and Trabasso, 1992). Instead, many psychologists have argued that it is the *appraisal* of the situation which gives it a particular meaning, and this, in turn, will elicit a specific basic emotion. For example, Nancy Stein and her colleagues have argued that the *basic emotions* can really be reduced to *basic appraisal scenarios* (Stein and Trabasso, 1992). They argue for the existence of a small set of high-level goals associated with a core set of appraisal and action processes, which relate in a fairly direct way to the attainment of particular goals. These core goals are shared across cultures and, therefore, the appraisals linked to these goals are fundamental cognitive processes that result in basic emotions. Thus, the evaluation or appraisal of an event (e.g., interpreting somebody's comment as an insult) is seen as the key mechanism that leads to an emotion (e.g., anger).

It was Magda Arnold (1960) who first argued that *appraisal* was the crucial immediate evaluation of a situation that could account for the qualitative differences among emotions. In other words, discrete emotions are produced because of variations in fundamental appraisals of situations. She suggested that people evaluated particular situations on three key dimensions: Is the situation beneficial or harmful? Is an important object present or absent? Is the object difficult to approach or avoid? The idea that emotions are elicited by appraisals is reasonable given that we do not tend to become emotional about situations or people that we do not care about or that have no special significance for us. Therefore, the evaluation or appraisal of the way in which something is significant is an important determinant of the type of discrete emotion that is experienced. Arnold (1960) argued that all organisms constantly evaluate the environment for changes that might have relevance for their own well-being. These appraisals then result in specific action tendencies which are experienced as emotions. The component process model in Figure 4.9 outlines four major appraisal objectives that occur in a particular sequence (Scherer, 2001, 2004). Each type of appraisal – relevance, implication, coping potential, and normative significance – unfolds sequentially over time and receives input from a variety of motivational and cognitive processes such as attention, memory, reasoning and the concept of the self. Thus, various evaluation criteria as well as stored information are considered crucial for the appraisal process (see Scherer, 2001).

The central assumption of an appraisal perspective is that organisms constantly evaluate their environment for personal significance. This means that different emotions are produced by a cumulative sequence of appraisals or stimulus evaluation checks (Ellsworth and Scherer, 2003; Scherer, 1984). Appraisal theories differ from many categorical theories of emotion (Izard, 1977) in that they do not assume that distinct basic emotions are produced by innate hard-wired neural circuits. In contrast, appraisal models assume that there are as many different emotions as there are reliably differentiated appraisals. Nevertheless, many appraisal-based models do argue that a

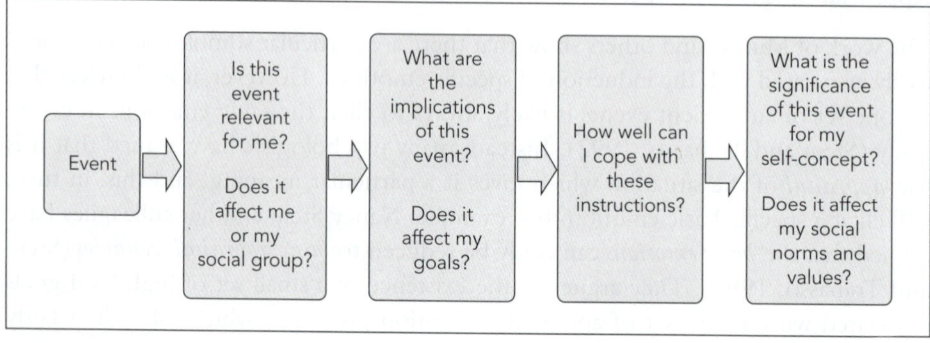

FIGURE 4.9 The component process model

Source: Scherer (2001).

smaller number of emotions are important in helping the organism to adapt to important events that have consequences for survival and well-being. This is the primary reason why Klaus Scherer (1994) has suggested that these should be *modal* emotions, rather than *basic* emotions. This is a useful concept since these are the emotions most commonly experienced across cultures. In addition, most cultures have distinctive verbal labels in their languages to refer to these 'modal' emotions which are elicited by a fundamental appraisal. There are many appraisal-based models of emotion and we do not have the space to provide a comprehensive overview here (for an excellent review see Ellsworth and Scherer, 2003). Instead, we will consider in some detail two influential models of emotion which both hold that cognitive appraisal is at the heart of the emotion process.

Richard Lazarus (1966, 1991)

Richard Lazarus proposed a *cognitive–motivational–relational* theory (1991) in which each discrete emotion is associated with what is called a 'core relational theme'. The core relational themes and the emotions they elicit are outlined in Table 4.6. Each discrete emotion is elicited by an appraisal of one of the core relational themes, all of which are common situations in which we might find ourselves. Few people would object to this list but, as pointed out by Power and Dalgleish (1997), the 'core relational themes' are more or less equivalent to a list of dictionary definitions of different emotions. It also seems to be rather circular in the sense that we might define anger as the emotion that occurs when we appraise a situation as being demeaning to us. This is, of course, exactly the core relational theme that Lazarus identifies as leading to anger. Moreover, we might also imagine that anger and aggression are likely to occur in situations where we are in danger (core relational theme associated with fear) and where there is no escape. Indeed, animal research shows that there is a close

TABLE 4.6 Examples of some core relational themes and the discrete emotions with which they are associated

Core relational theme		*Resulting emotion*
A demeaning offence against you or your family	⇒	Anger
Faced with an uncertain threat	⇒	Anxiety
Faced with an immediate overwhelming danger	⇒	Fright
Faced with a transgression of a moral value	⇒	Guilt
A failure to live up to an ideal	⇒	Shame
Wanting to have what somebody else has	⇒	Envy
Resenting someone for loss of another's affection	⇒	Jealousy
Being faced with an indigestible object (or idea)	⇒	Disgust
Progressing towards a wanted goal	⇒	Happiness
Being moved by another's suffering	⇒	Compassion

Source: Based on Lazarus (1991).

relationship between fear and defensive aggression. Thus, this list does not seem to have a high degree of explanatory power because we can simply keep adding themes or situations that we think might be linked to a specific emotion.

Oatley and Johnson-Laird (1987)

Oatley and Johnson-Laird proposed a cognitive theory of emotions, in which they argued that a primary *function* of discrete emotions is to provide a means by which important life goals can be pursued. An important aspect of Oatley and Johnson-Laird's theory is that they acknowledge the *functional* nature of emotions while also accepting that cognitive evaluation is critical for the elicitation and differentiation of different emotions. The basic idea is that an event is appraised in relation to various goals. These appraisals are considered to occur automatically and without conscious awareness, and are driven by a small set of basic emotions. They argue that relatively complex organisms such as mammals are faced with two major problem areas: personal goals and the unpredictability of their surroundings.

First, every organism has multiple goals: not being injured or killed; finding food; finding a mate; finding shelter and so on. At any given moment each of us has many different goals, all competing for priority. For example, you may have a higher-level goal of passing your exams at the end of the year, but you may also have a lower-level goal of having lunch in a hour or so, and then another goal of going out at the weekend. The problem is that these goals have to be prioritized in some way. You cannot actively pursue all of them at the same time, and it is often the case that different goals may be incompatible with each other. For example, you may hope to gain a place on a college sports team, and this involves training at least three times a week. Thus, going out training is compatible with your goal of getting on the team. However, let us imagine that you have a slight injury that seems to be getting worse the more you train. The goal of staying injury-free would indicate that you should cut back on your training, but this is probably incompatible with the goal of getting a place on the team. Life is full of conflicting goals like this, and, according to Oatley and Johnson-Laird, emotions play a key role in prioritizing and organizing these goals.

A second problem facing every mammal is the fact that the world is an unpredictable place. If everything that happened from moment to moment could be accurately predicted then life would be very simple. However, life is not like this and therefore our cognitive systems need to be highly flexible in order to cope with a changing world. According to Oatley and Johnson-Laird (1987), this is precisely why emotions have evolved: to help us to coordinate competing goals in a flexible way. The emotion signal is very old in evolutionary terms. It sets the entire cognitive system into a specific mode but, when some environmental event indicates that a change in this mode is necessary, then the critical emotion signal forces a change from one mode to another.

On the basis of the work of Ekman (1973) and others, Oatley and Johnson-Laird (1987) propose that at least five basic emotions have evolved to enable complex cognitive systems to assign priorities to specific goals in a flexible way. Emotions are

TABLE 4.7 Junctures and the five basic emotions associated with them

Juncture of goal or plan		*Basic emotion*
Sub-goals or goals being achieved	⇒	Happiness
Failure or loss of plan or goal	⇒	Sadness
Self-preservation goal threatened	⇒	Anxiety
Plan or goal frustrated or blocked	⇒	Anger
Gustatory goal violated	⇒	Disgust

Source: Oatley and Johnson-Laird (1987).

important when a key juncture occurs between plans or goals because they allow the system to switch rapidly from one mode to another. The key junctures in goals and plans that are associated with specific basic emotions are outlined in Table 4.7. The important point is that these key junctures are identified by cognitive appraisals or evaluations.

CHAPTER SUMMARY

This chapter has reviewed evidence from a wide variety of sources indicating that, at least some, emotions are 'gifts of nature'. *Discrete emotions approaches* hypothesize that some emotions are crucial for adapting to common and important life events and have evolved to help us deal swiftly with these universal situations. For this reason, these *basic emotions* would be expected to have key expressive signals which are likely to elicit them. These signals may well be universal, fairly unique physiological responses and neural circuits, and common antecedent events. A number of important criteria for basic emotions were outlined and evidence ranging from neurobiology to psychological models of appraisal provide some evidence for the hypothesis.

Many emotion scientists are confident that fear can be categorized as a basic emotion. This chapter has focused on research into fear in both animals and humans because it is the basic emotion that has been studied most intensively. The assumption is that similar evidence will be found for the other basic emotions once the appropriate research has been done.

RECOMMENDED READING

Excellent discussion and commentaries on the question of whether there are basic emotions is provided in:

Lisa Feldman Barrett (2006) 'Are emotions natural kinds?', *Perspectives on Psychological Science*, 1, 28–58.

Lisa Feldman Barrett et al. (2007) 'Of mice and men: Natural kinds of emotions in the mammalian brain? A response to Panksepp and Izard', *Perspectives on Psychological Science*, 2, 297–312.

Paul Ekman and Richard J. Davidson (1994) *The Nature of Emotion*. New York: Oxford University Press. (Question 1: pp, 7–47).

Carol E. Izard (2007) 'Basic emotions, natural kinds, emotion schemas, and a new paradigm', *Perspectives on Psychological Science*, 2, 260–80.

Jaak Panksepp (2007) 'Neurologizing the psychology of affects', *Perspectives on Psychological Science*, 2, 281–96.

An older series of articles published in the journal *Psychological Review* also provide an overview of different opinions on the question of whether basic emotions exist.

Paul Ekman (1992) 'Are there basic emotions?', *Psychological Review*, 99, 550–3.

Carol Izard (1992) 'Basic emotions, relations among emotions, and emotion–cognition relations', *Psychological Review*, 99, 561–5.

Andrew Ortony and Terence Turner (1990) 'What's basic about basic emotions?', *Psychological Review*, 97, 315–31.

Jaak Panksepp (1992) 'A critical role for "affective neuroscience" in resolving what is basic about basic emotions', *Psychological Review*, 99, 554–60.

Terence Turner and Andrew Ortony (1992) 'Basic emotions: Can conflicting criteria converge?', *Psychological Review*, 99, 566–71.

5 DIMENSIONAL APPROACHES TO THE STRUCTURE OF AFFECT

A DIMENSIONAL VIEW OF AFFECT

Many emotion scientists view emotions and moods as reflections of general dimensions of experience rather than as discrete categories. The focus of this approach is often on how the world is *experienced* and much of the research in this tradition uses self-report as the primary data. An underlying assumption is that emotions are defined to a large extent by the verbal labels we use to describe them. One of the functions of a language is to provide labels for particular states and events which can be readily understood by speakers of that language. Thus, we know what people mean when they say they are 'madly in love', or that they are 'angry'. A genuine problem for science, however, is that these everyday labels often describe very broad and 'fuzzy' semantic categories that may not necessarily represent facts of nature (Russell and Feldman Barrett, 1999). In other words, while we know roughly what is meant when people say that they are sad, it is not clear if our concept of sadness actually refers to a natural biological or psychological category. Research that traces the development of emotion concepts in children, for example, has found that even very young children can discriminate between different emotions. However, it seems that the basis of this discrimination is along the dimensions of pleasure and arousal rather than the more adult categories labelled fear, anger and so on. This has led some investigators to argue that children need to *learn* these more refined categories by exposure to numerous social situations (e.g., Russell and Lemay, 2000).

In an extensive review, Russell (1991) concluded that emotion categories in the English language are similar to emotion concepts in other languages but, importantly, they are not identical. Moreover, the number of labels referring to emotion categories also varies widely from language to language. This raises the possibility that emotions may also vary widely from culture to culture. In other words, if our understanding of emotions is generated by the linguistic terms available in our culture, then our *experience* of emotions may also be determined by our language and culture. An extreme form of this view is that emotions are learned or socially constructed, rather than given to us by nature (Averill, 1980; Feldman Barrett, 2006a). This is an assumption underlying many theories that take a *dimensional* approach to the understanding of emotion.

WHAT DO WE MEAN BY DIMENSIONS?

Many emotion scientists argue that the *human experience of emotion*, or the *feelings* associated with emotions, is the main phenomenon to be explained. This emphasis on people's feelings has led to the hypothesis that the world is experienced along broad dimensions, rather than as discrete categories of different emotions. Research on a number of different emotion components (subjective report; physiological response; neural activity) has converged on the notion that affect can be described along two broad dimensions. These have been variously called *arousal* and *valence* (Russell, 1983), *approach* and *avoidance* (Davidson, 1994b), or *positive affect (PA)* and *negative affect (NA)* (Watson and Tellegen, 1985).

A number of different terms have been used to refer to the *arousal* dimension in different theoretical accounts: *activation*, *tension*, *energy*, *activity* and so on. However, these terms are almost certainly referring to the same underlying construct. In terms of subjective experience, *arousal* or *activation* is often interpreted as the amount of energy we feel we have available. This can range from deep sleep and drowsiness, through feeling relaxed, alert, active, hyperactive, to frenetic excitement at the top end of the scale. It is often argued that these subjective feelings of activation or arousal represent a summary of our true physiological state at any given time (e.g., Russell and Feldman Barrett, 1999). Arousal rises and falls throughout the day and is dependent on a range of environmental factors such as the time of day, the weather, physical activity, intake of drugs and so on, in addition to general personality differences (Thayer, 1989, 1996). These variations are *felt* or experienced as changes in what has been called *core affect* and form an important dimension of our subjective experience of affective states (Feldman Barrett, 2006a; Russell, 1980; Russell and Feldman Barrett, 1999). This conceptualization of arousal and how it is experienced is close to the definition of mood states that we outlined in Chapter 2.

A sense of *valence* (positive versus negative) or *pleasure* has also been identified as an important dimension of affective experience. This term has been variously referred to as *hedonic tone*, *positive* and *negative affect*, *pleasant* and *unpleasant* feelings, *approach* and *avoidance*, and so on.

Extensive research has shown that the dimensions of valence and arousal appear to be universal human experiences occurring in all cultures (Osgood et al., 1975; Wierzbicka, 1995). In particular, a number of bipolar dimensions such as tense–calm, happy–sad, excited–depressed have been found in all the languages that were examined (Osgood et al., 1975). This indicates that people commonly describe their subjective experiences along a number of bipolar dimensions, and that we experience the world around us in terms of these bipolar concepts – 'I was very happy/very sad'; 'The situation was very relaxed/very tense' and so on. Subsequent theories have focused primarily on the two broad dimensions of valence (positive–negative) and arousal (relaxed–excited). These seem to be the most salient dimensions, and it has been difficult to draw a distinction between arousal and a possible third dimension of *tension*, *dominance* or *potency* (Russell, 1983). Taken together, this line of research suggests that these two dimensions do indeed represent the fundamental building blocks of our emotional experience.

A dimensional approach has also emerged from behavioural research with animals. In particular, Konorski (1967) proposed a model based on two broad types of reflexes: *preservative* and *protective*. Preservative reflexes relate to the preservation of health and well-being and include nurturing the young, ingestion of food, and sexual activities. Protective reflexes relate to survival: avoiding and withdrawing from dangers and the rejection of noxious substances (poisons etc). These are all ***unconditioned responses*** – we do not have to learn how to do them. An important point to remember is that Konorski emphasized that arousal or activation modulates *both* of these types of reaction.

This view was extended by Dickinson and Dearing (1979), who developed the dichotomy between preservative and protective reactions into two opposing motivational systems: *attractive* and *aversive*. The idea is that these systems can be activated by a wide range of unconditioned stimuli, and tend to oppose each other – when one is active the other is inhibited. These two motivational systems are seen as fundamental to the learning of new responses to unconditioned stimuli. Many other lines of research have supported the hypothesis that two motivational systems – attractive–aversive and approach–avoidance – exist in the brain (e.g., Davidson, 1994b; Depue and Collins, 1999; Rolls, 2005).

It is very likely that the two neurobiological systems overlap considerably with the valence dimension discovered in human research. In other words, the attractive or approach system may be involved in generating feelings of positive affect (PA), while the aversive or withdrawal system may generate feelings of negative affect (NA). It is often assumed that these two motivational systems (approach–avoidance) can account for the salience of the valence dimension in our subjective experience, and that arousal accounts for variations in the activation of both systems (Lang, 1995). The important point here is that arousal is not seen as a separate substrate in the brain, but, rather, is considered to reflect variations in the valence dimension. A brief overview of dimensional approaches to understanding emotion is presented in Box 5.1.

CRITERIA FOR IDENTIFYING GENERAL DIMENSIONS OF AFFECT

Since emotional experience is at centre stage in most dimensional accounts it is not surprising that subjective report of feelings is a primary criterion for the dimensions approach. The notion that we experience blends of broad dimensions such as pleasant or unpleasant rather than discrete emotions seems somewhat counterintuitive because our perception of emotions as discrete categories is very powerful. Imagine a situation in which you were very angry and contrast that with one in which you were very afraid. At first it might seem that these two states felt very different. However, the evidence suggests that if you really try to describe how the two states *feel* it is difficult to get beyond descriptions of arousal and valence. The argument is that what distinguishes the two states is the *perception* and *interpretation* of the surrounding context

BOX 5.1

A brief overview of dimensional approaches to understanding affect

One of the earliest attempts to provide a description of the fundamental dimensions of how we experience the world was put forward by Wilhelm Wundt (1874/1905). Wundt was a German scientist – a contemporary of William James – who is widely considered to be the founder of experimental psychology in Europe. He established the world's first laboratory of psychological science at the University of Leipzig in 1879.

Wundt asked people to describe their inner experiences (a method known as *introspection*), and concluded that emotional experience (feelings) could be understood by looking at three different dimensions: *valence* (positive–negative), *arousal* (calm–excited), and *tension* (tense–relaxed). Moreover, he argued that these dimensions were likely to be related to measurable physiological states of the body. Subsequent evidence confirms that valence is indeed a salient aspect of our experience of the world. For example, people find it very easy to report on how good or bad they feel, and liking or disliking something is likely to result in either approach or withdrawal, which are two important behavioural dimensions observed in even the simplest organisms (Schneirla, 1959). Likewise, it seems to be an easy task for most people to report on how arousing or intense an experience is, showing that arousal is also an important dimension of subjective experience. William James (1884, 1890/1950) also assumed that arousal represented an important dimension of the subjective experience of emotions.

Subsequent research in emotion science using self-report data has confirmed that arousal and valence are both important components of how affect is experienced (e.g., Russell, 1980; Russell and Feldman Barrett, 1999). Measures of physiological responding have also highlighted the importance of these two dimensions. A particularly useful development has been the construction of a large database of photographs by Peter Lang and his colleagues. These photographs have been rated by hundreds of people along the dimensions of valence and arousal (Bradley and Lang, 1994; Lang, 1980) and are available to emotion researchers as the *International Affective Picture System (IAPS)* (Lang et al., 2005). This standardized set of stimuli is extremely useful because the same material can be used by different laboratories, making it much easier to draw comparisons across different studies. In order to achieve normative ratings, each individual is presented with a large number of photographs one at a time and asked to rate each photograph according to (a) how pleasant or unpleasant it is, and (b) how arousing it is. People generally have no problem in separating these dimensions and subsequent research has shown that each dimension is associated with different patterns of psychophysiological response (Lang et al., 1993). Figure 5.1 shows how some images are typically organized in the two-dimensional space defined by valence and arousal. As can be seen, a photograph of a cute baby is generally rated as being highly pleasant and medium in terms of arousal, whereas an erotic image might be judged as being equally pleasant but more arousing. Likewise, a picture of a snake is generally judged as fairly arousing but also fairly unpleasant.

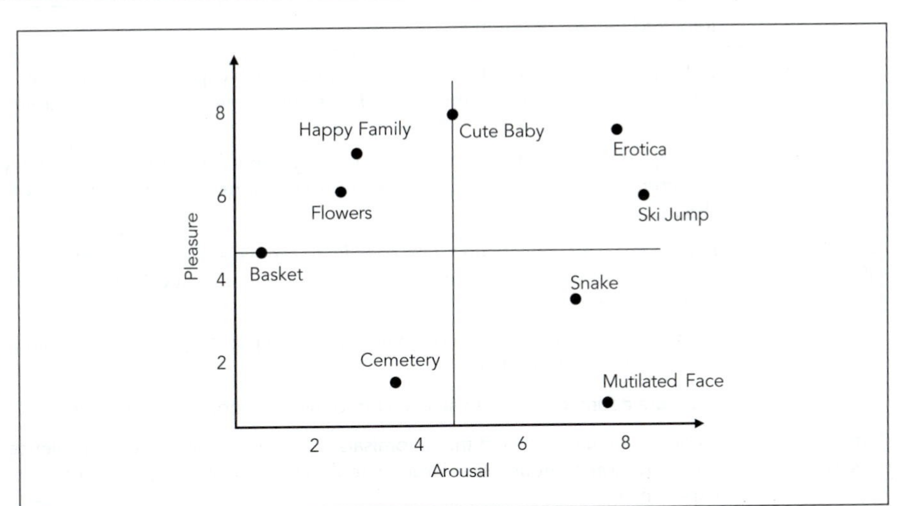

FIGURE 5.1 Typical distribution of images from the IAPS set

Source: Adapted from Lang (1995).

Standardized sets of affective sounds (Bradley and Lang, 1999b) and words (Bradley and Lang, 1999a) have also been developed. These have also been successfully rated along the dimensions of valence and arousal. Thus, it seems that people find it easy to judge images, sounds and words in terms of how arousing they are (most calm to most exciting) as well as how pleasant or unpleasant they are (valence).

(Feldman Barrett, 2006a; Schachter and Singer, 1962). Therefore, self-report data is an important method for identifying dimensions.

A broader criterion for the authenticity of the approach as a whole comes from evidence showing that the cognitive interpretation of general feelings is a major determinant of how emotions are categorized. Other important criteria in the identification of affective dimensions comes from research examining the physiological and neural circuits that might underlie emotional responses (Davidson, 1984; Lang, 1995; Rolls, 1999). Some key criteria to identify affective dimensions are outlined in Table 5.1.

OVERVIEW OF EMPIRICAL EVIDENCE FOR DIMENSIONS

Subjective report

Description experience sampling measures of affective experience

A key criterion to establish that subjective experience is based on two broad dimensions is to demonstrate that this is how people actually report their emotional experience. One method is the *Descriptive Experience Sampling* procedure (DES) (Hurlbert, 1997). This involves testing large numbers of people across different situations and asking them to report how they feel in each situation.

TABLE 5.1 Criteria for the dimensional approach to understanding emotion

Criteria	*Required pattern of results*
Subjective report	Self-report studies should demonstrate that people's experience of emotion is described primarily in terms of two dimensions rather than several discrete emotions.
	Self-report measures between the various negative emotions should be highly intercorrelated. Likewise, correlations between reports of positive emotions should be high.
Physiological specificity	Physiological responses should be specific to the dimensions of valence and arousal, and responses to these dimensions should be relatively independent of each other.
	Physiological indicators among the negative (and positive) emotions should be correlated with each other.
Neural circuits	Separate neural circuits for valence and for arousal should be identified
Cognitive appraisals	Evidence should be found that appraisals occur for the dimensions of valence and activation or arousal to a larger extent than for other dimensions of experience.
	Additionally, it is important for this approach to establish that cognitive appraisal or conceptualization is necessary to explain reports of discrete emotion categories.

Generally, people can report their experiences easily, although individual differences have been found. For example, some people tend to report their experiences in very broad, global terms whereas others characterize their experiences more along the lines of discrete emotion terms (Feldman Barrett, 2004). One student's response to the terrorist attacks of 9/11 in New York City was 'Maybe anger, confusion, fear. I just felt bad on September 11th, Really bad' (Feldman Barrett, 2006c, p. 38). Another student used more precise discrete emotion labels by saying 'My first reaction was terrible sadness ... But the second reaction was that of anger, because you can't do anything with the sadness'. At first sight, this evidence seems to go against the hypothesis that emotions are experienced along two broad dimensions. However, subsequent analysis supports the dimensional perspective in that *all* participants in eight different studies described their momentary emotional state in terms of pleasure or displeasure, while people differed widely in the use of discrete emotion terms (Feldman Barrett, 2006c). In other words, while *everyone* can easily describe the difference between a pleasant and an unpleasant feeling, there are large individual differences in the understanding and use of discrete emotions labels. This suggests that valence (pleasure and displeasure) may be a more fundamental property of affect than discrete emotion terms. It is interesting to note at this point that it is often not clear from this research whether people are reporting their subjective experience of emotions or moods, or both.

Other studies using the DES methodology have found that people report feeling some degree of affect almost all of the time (Diener et al., 1991) and that emotional experiences are almost always reported in terms of being either pleasant or unpleasant. It is, perhaps, encouraging to note that most people report that they experience positive affect (pleasant feelings) most of the time (Diener and Diener, 1996). In support of a dimensional approach, however, it is not clear that everyone experiences anger, sadness, fear and so on as qualitatively different states (e.g., Feldman Barrett, 2006b; Larsen and Cutler, 1996). For example, when people's reports of their daily emotional experiences over several weeks are analyzed, it becomes obvious that many individuals describe their experience in very broad, global terms, whereas others characterize their experiences in more discrete emotion terms (Feldman Barrett, 1998). Feldman Barrett (2004) points out that people who report their experiences in global terms often use discrete emotion labels to refer to broad affective states (pleasant versus unpleasant). She describes these people as being low on *emotional granularity*. Those who are high in emotional granularity, however, tend to use discrete emotion labels in a more precise way to capture the distinctiveness of a word's meaning. These data seem to indicate that people differ in terms of how good they are at accessing and/or describing their own internal states. A difficulty in describing differences among distinct internal states does not, of course, necessarily mean that these states do not exist.

Nevertheless, when people are asked to describe their experiences of emotion the evidence from DES techniques suggests that anger, sadness, fear etc are often not experienced as distinct and separate states. In order to get round potential problems in verbalizing experiences, a more common method of acquiring self-report data is to present people with standardized questionnaires relating to affective experience. When these data are analyzed by sophisticated statistical techniques it seems that the various discrete emotion terms can be broken down into more fundamental or primitive components relating to valence and arousal (e.g., Russell, 1980).

Questionnaire measures of affective experience

A typical research methodology is to obtain self-report data about how affective states (moods and emotions) are consciously experienced. For example, people may be asked to describe their experience of emotion by selecting representative adjectives (cheerful, happy, sad, irritable etc). If emotions are experienced as discrete categories (anger, sadness, fear etc) then these data should cluster around a small number of categories with different factors for each basic emotion. However, a large body of data indicates that this is not the case. When self-reports of emotional experience are projected into geometric space by means of sophisticated statistical techniques the data almost invariably take on a *circumplex structure* as shown in Figure 5.2.

Figure 5.2 is based on Russell's model, with arousal or activation on the vertical axis and valence on the horizontal axis. Feelings are characterized in terms of pleasantness and intensity, and basic emotion categories only fall in certain regions of the circumplex (Feldman Barrett, 2006b; Russell, 1980; Russell and Feldman Barrett, 1999). These data suggest that affect is best conceptualized as variations along a number of dimensions – intensity, degree of pleasure, degree of activation – rather than in terms of discrete categories. In the case of fear, for example, being attacked by a large dog would usually be more intense and less pleasurable than the fear experienced on a

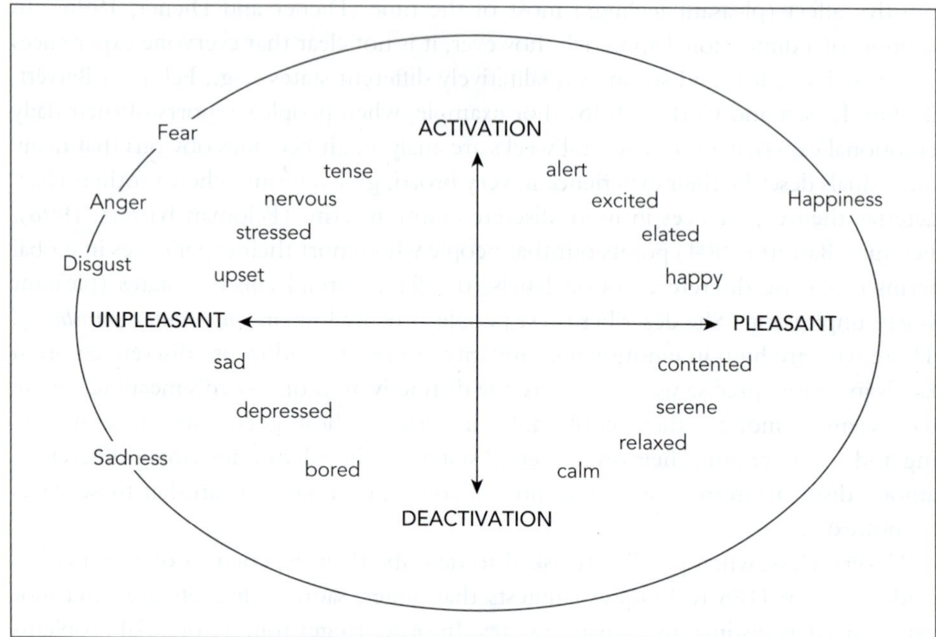

FIGURE 5.2 A graphical representation of Russell's two-dimensional model of emotion
Source: Adapted from Russell (1980).

roller coaster ride. Both are instances of fear, but the two experiences can be rated along these dimensions in quite different ways. Thus, rather than there being a set of separate discrete emotions with clear boundaries between them, the idea is that each emotion can be situated as a specific point along the two dimensions of *pleasantness* and *activation* (Russell and Feldman Barrett, 1999).

Russell's (1980) circumplex model proposes two bipolar dimensions of experience with one ranging from positive to negative affect (i.e., PA to NA), and the second reflecting variations in arousal. This perspective implies that obtaining ratings along two scales – pleasant–unpleasant and active–passive – is sufficient to capture the differences between emotions. The key proposal is that every emotion can be understood as a combination or blend of these two dimensions.

An alternative view suggests that PA and NA represent separate and unrelated (*orthogonal*) dimensions of experience (Watson and Tellegen, 1985). This *independent* model views both PA and NA as distinct constructs (least to most positive, and least to most negative). At first sight, it might seem that PA and NA have to be linked in a bipolar way because it is hard to imagine someone in a state of high NA and high PA at the same time. However, empirical research has found that the bipolar relationship seems to apply only for very intense levels of emotional experience. Thus, people reporting very high levels of NA do indeed tend to report relatively low levels of PA, just as high levels of PA are associated with reports of low levels of NA (Diener and Iran-Nejad, 1986; Watson, 1988).

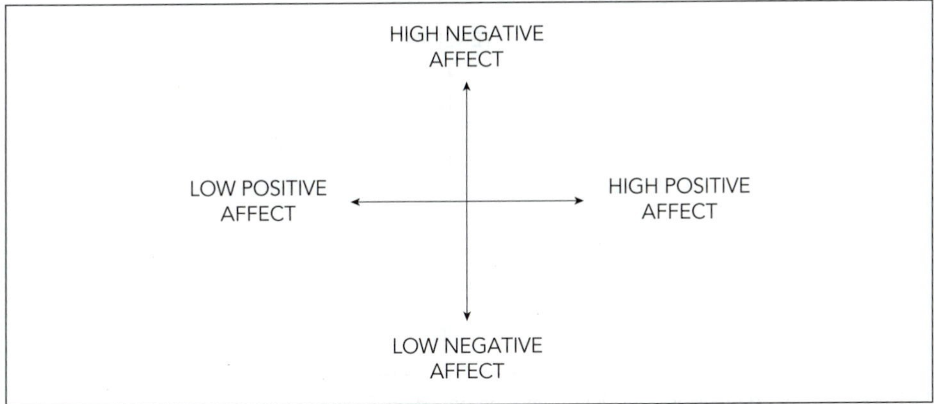

FIGURE 5.3 Two-dimensional model of emotion based on Watson and Tellegen (1985)

However, under the more typical everyday circumstances when emotional experiences are less intense, PA and NA actually seem to be strikingly independent of each other (Diener and Emmons, 1985; Watson, 1988). Thus, somebody who is experiencing a low level of NA (e.g., fairly relaxed) is not necessarily feeling happy. In fact, scores on PA can occur anywhere along the continuum. Early work found, for example, that people's self-reports of sadness and happiness are not correlated (Nowlis, 1965). Moreover, as noted by Watson and Clark (1994), PA and NA can sometimes become dissociated even under more intense conditions. For example, when we actively try to experience NA (e.g., watching a horror movie, parachute jumping, or riding on a roller coaster) this can also lead to high levels of excitement and pleasure. Further evidence for the independence of PA and NA is the fact that negative mood states are highly correlated with each other, and positive mood states are highly correlated with each other (Watson et al., 1988). Thus, people who are in an apprehensive mood are also likely to report feelings of depression, tension etc.

In contrast to Russell's model (see Figure 5.2), in which activation and valence are seen as two separate dimensions, the structural model proposed by Watson and Tellegen (1985) has two *independent* dimensions of *valence* (PA and NA). As shown in Figure 5.3, this structure suggests that affective space can best be conceptualized in terms of two separate dimensions of positive and negative affect. Thus, happiness might be represented as relatively high on PA and relatively low on NA, while excitement might be rated higher on PA but at the same level of NA.

Yet another description of affective space considers that the two critical aspects are independent dimensions of *activation*: tension vs energy (Thayer, 1989, 1996). A schematic diagram of this model is presented in Figure 5.4.

In summary then, the structures of affective space that emerge from questionnaire studies have been interpreted as:

representing two dimensions of *valence* (Watson and Tellegen, 1985);
representing two dimensions of *activation* or *energy* (Thayer, 1989); or
comprising both *valence* and *activation* (Russell, 1980).

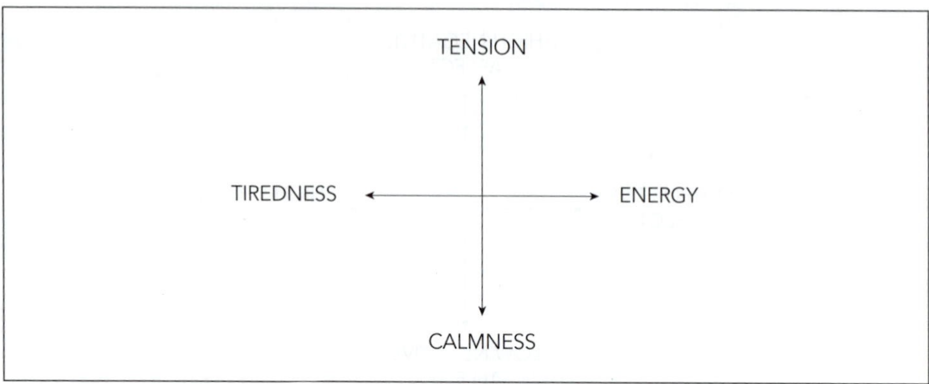

FIGURE 5.4 Two-dimensional model of emotion based on Thayer (1989)

Do these results indicate fundamentally different structures underlying the conscious experience of affect? In spite of apparent differences, it has been argued that all of these models are actually describing the same affective space (Russell and Feldman Barrett, 1999). For example, Watson and Tellegen's (1985) notion of PA and NA implicitly involves the notion of *activation* in that both PA and NA are considered to vary in *intensity*. This seems to effectively incorporate the notion of activation or arousal into the structure. Likewise, Thayer's (1989) two activation dimensions also implicitly incorporate *valence*.

Empirical evidence using complex structural equation modelling of self-report data supports the hypothesis that all of these structures are indeed describing the same thing (Feldman Barrett and Russell, 1998; Yik et al., 1999). They reported that the pleasant–unpleasant and activated–deactivated dimensions accounted for 92% of the variance in PA and 97% of the variance in NA. Similarly, when Thayer's dimensions were examined, it was found that the pleasant–unpleasant and activated–deactivated dimensions accounted for 80% of the energy–tired dimension, and 73% of the tense–calm dimension. Thus, it seems that in spite of using different labelling these structures are actually measuring the same underlying components of subjective experience and that valence and activation are both critical dimensions of our experience (Russell and Feldman Barrett, 1999). In terms of the two criteria for self-report data outlined in Table 5.1, it is clear that the data do support both assumptions:

(a) people report their emotional experience in terms of valence and arousal, and
(b) there are high inter-correlations between self-reports of negative emotions and positive emotions.

Physiological specificity

If dimensional models are correct, then we would expect to find fairly consistent patterns of physiological activation in relation to the dimensions of valence and arousal. In psychophysiological research it has often been argued that emotions are best understood as being organized around an underlying motivational base (Bradley and

Lang, 2000b; Lang, 1995). The idea is that the appetitive (or approach) and the aversive (or withdrawal) systems can account for the valence dimension in the expression of emotions. Most models assume that approach and withdrawal systems are mutually inhibitory so that when one is activated the other is inhibited (Dickinson and Dearing, 1979; Konorski, 1967). These models do not generally see arousal as a third system that is modulated independently of the approach and withdrawal systems. In contrast, arousal is seen as the metabolic and neural activation of either approach or withdrawal systems, or the co-activation of both together (Cacioppo and Berntson, 1994). The brain's approach and withdrawal systems are therefore considered to represent the neuroanatomical foundation of both valence and arousal effects in animals and humans. If emotions are indeed organized by the brain's motivational systems of approach and withdrawal, we might expect that the physiological responses to affective stimuli should reflect this organization. In other words, as indicated in Table 5.1, the response of physiological systems should co-vary with subjective judgments of valence and arousal. Thus, we should be able to find physiological responses that are activated by increasing levels of arousal, but not affected by valence. Likewise, increasing levels of valence should activate certain physiological responses independently of variations in arousal.

A typical methodology to assess the relationship of physiological responses to subjective reports of valence and arousal is to first require participants to evaluate a large number of stimuli such as IAPS pictures on the basis of valence and arousal. The pictorial stimuli can then be ranked from high to low for each individual on the basis of their own judgments. The next step is to examine the degree of activity in each physiological measure for each rank (collapsed across participants) in terms of valence and arousal. This strategy optimizes the possibility of detecting changes in physiology which correlate with changes in affective judgements (Bradley and Lang, 2000a; Lang et al., 1993). Research using this methodology has focused on the action of facial muscles, skin conductance and heart-rate responses, as well as electrocortical activity and the startle reflex.

Facial muscle action

Several major groups of muscles in the face are important for the expression of different emotions (Ekman and Friesen, 1986; Fridlund and Izard, 1983). For example, the *corrugator muscles* are important for lowering and contracting the brows and this expression is a reliable indicator of distress. The *zygomatic muscle*, in contrast, is important for the smile response and activity in this muscle indicates expressions of happiness. A clear prediction then is that if a stimulus (e.g., a picture, a word or a sound) is judged to be unpleasant then we should detect activity within the corrugator muscle, whereas if a stimulus is judged to be pleasant then activity in the zygomatic muscle is more likely. Contractions of these facial muscles can be measured by means of the electromyographic activity (EMG) detected by small electrodes placed on these muscles. As shown in Figure 5.5, significant activation of the corrugator muscle does indeed occur when a picture is rated as unpleasant. Figure 5.5(a) shows the degree

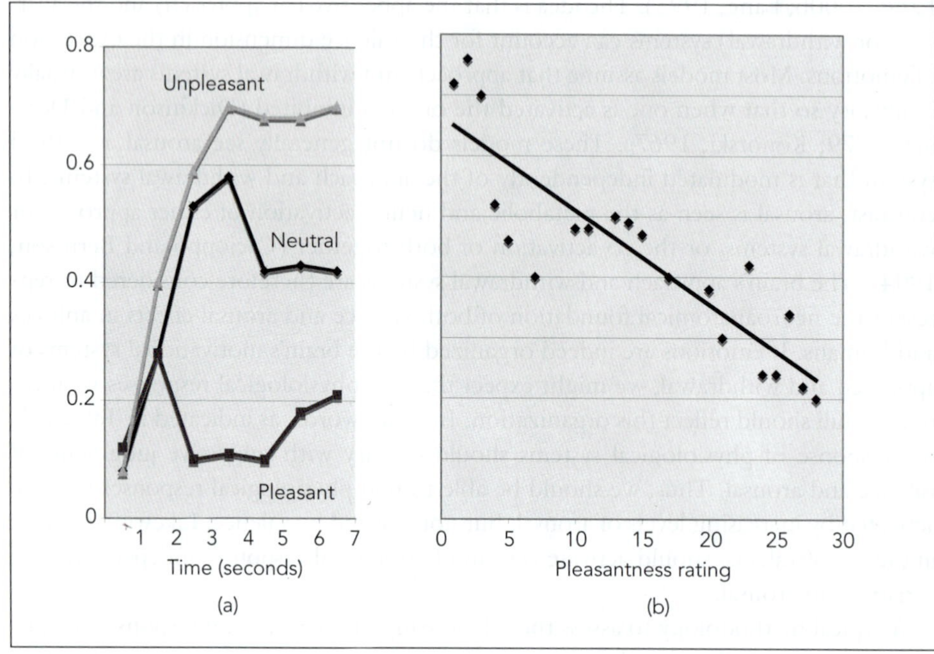

FIGURE 5.5 Patterns of facial corrugator EMG activity
(a) As a function of prior valence ratings of IAPS pictures (left panel)
(b) The correlation between an individual's ratings of pleasure with the corrugator EMG response to viewing IAPS pictures.

Source: Adapted from Lang et al. (1993).

of activation of the corrugator muscle when viewing pleasant, neutral and unpleasant IAPS pictures. The corrugator muscle is activated by all types of picture, but at some point there is a clear divergence based on the rated valence of the picture. For the neutral items, EMG activity is intermediary between the pleasant and unpleasant pictures. The degree of activation is increased for unpleasant pictures, whereas the degree of activation is decreased for the pleasant pictures relative to neutral pictures. Moreover, as shown in Figure 5.5(b), the negative correlation between self-reports of valence and corrugator EMG activity is very high ($r = -0.90$) (Lang et al., 1993). The degree of change in corrugator activity systematically decreases as the pleasantness ratings of the pictures increase. This supports the notion that activity of the corrugator muscle does indeed provide a good index of the *valence* of a stimulus.

As expected, the opposite pattern occurs for activity of the zygomatic muscle (smile response). As shown in Figure 5.6, there is a strong positive correlation between activity in the zygomatic muscle and self-reported ratings of valence. As the ratings of pleasantness increase the degree of activity in the zygomatic EMG also increases ($r = 0.56$) (Lang et al., 1993). It is interesting to note that there are significant gender differences in this paradigm. About 75% of women show the expected pattern compared with only 25% of men showing this pattern. A very similar data pattern has been reported (including the gender difference) when participants were asked to imagine

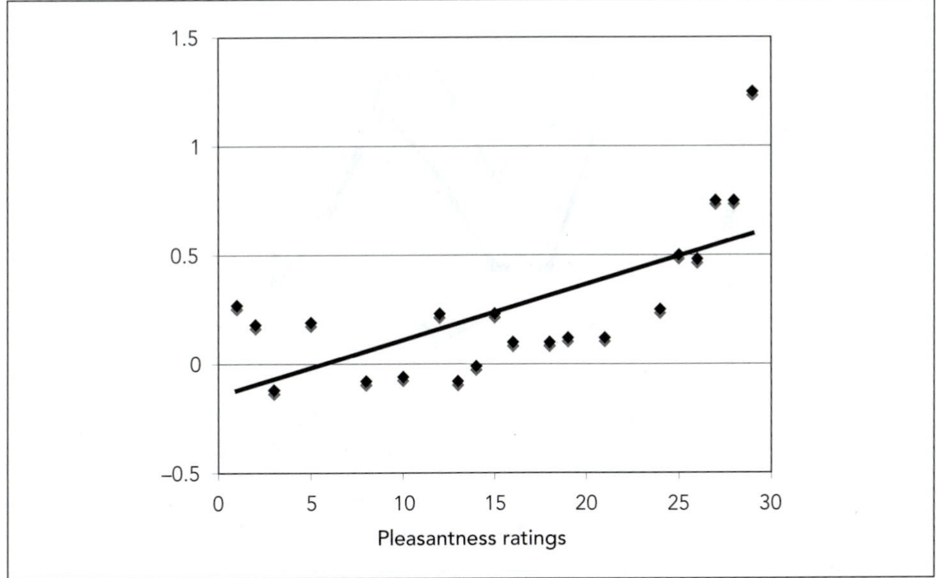

FIGURE 5.6 The correlation between individual's affective judgments of pleasure with their zygomatic EMG response when viewing IAPS pictures

Source: Adapted from Lang et al. (1993).

different positive and negative scenes rather than actually viewing the pictures. Once again, facial EMG responses in the zygomatic muscle increased with increasing pleasantness (Schwartz et al., 1980). It is difficult to interpret the gender difference here, but it suggests that women might be more facially expressive than men when experiencing positive and negative affect. The data shown in Figure 5.6 are collapsed across male and female participants, which explains the relatively modest correlation ($r = 0.56$).

Heart rate and skin conductance

The first point to note is that there are a number of difficulties in using heart rate as an index of emotional state. Several physical factors, such as posture, height and weight, an individual's fitness level and so on, all have a significant impact on the underlying heart rate, as well as the degree of variability in heart rate. In addition to physical factors, it has also been found that heart rate varies according to different mental processes. For example, when orienting to external stimuli heart rate tends to decelerate, whereas when attempting to recall some item from memory the typical heart-rate response is one of acceleration (Lang et al., 1990). Thus, a range of both physical and psychological factors can influence the heart-rate response, making it difficult to use as an index of response to affective stimuli.

Nevertheless, when careful controls are put in place a classic heart-rate response can be observed when viewing affective pictures. When a picture is first presented the heart rate tends to slow, probably reflecting attentional orienting. The second stage

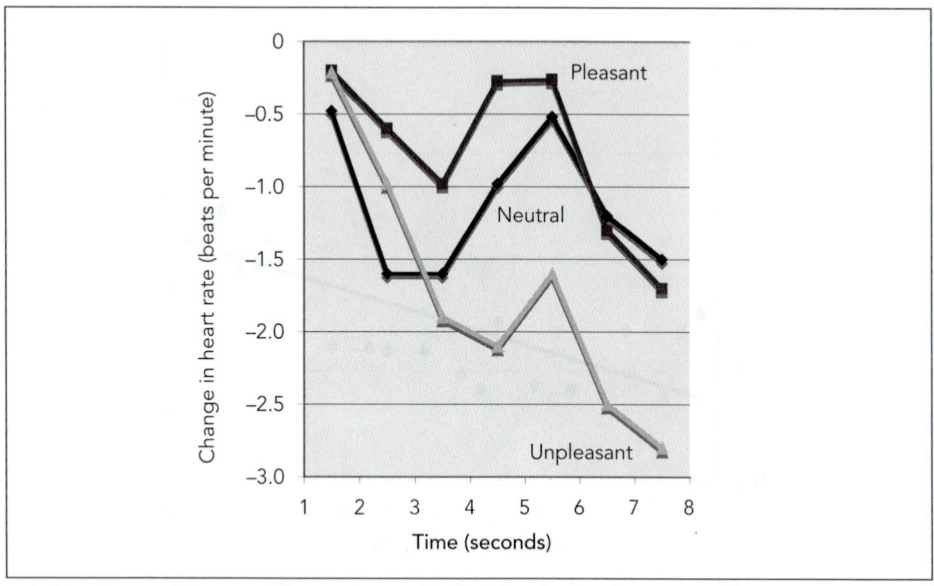

FIGURE 5.7 Pattern of heart-rate response as a function of the prior valence ratings of IAPS pictures

Source: Adapted from Lang et al. (1993).

involves an acceleration of heart rate, followed a few seconds later by a secondary deceleration. As shown in Figure 5.7, the valence of the stimuli influences this standard pattern. Unpleasant stimuli produce the greatest degree of initial deceleration and acceleration, while pleasant stimuli produce greater peak acceleration (Lang et al., 1993). Correlational analysis has also shown a high positive correlation between the peak heart-rate acceleration and the individual's affective judgements of pleasure ($r = 0.76$) (Lang et al., 1993).

A more reliable measure of arousal is the *skin conductance response* (SCR). As shown in Figure 5.8(a) the degree of SCR activity tends to increase linearly as ratings of arousal increase, regardless of the degree of emotional valence. While activity does not change much over 7 seconds for neutral pictures, strong increases are observed for both pleasant and unpleasant pictures as arousal increases. In addition, as shown in Figure 5.8(b), there is a strong positive correlation ($r = 0.81$) between self-report ratings of arousal and changes in skin conductance (Lang et al., 1993).

In summary, the data measuring facial muscles, heart-rate response and skin conductance response are consistent with the hypothesis that there are specific physiological responses to the self-reported dimensions of valence and arousal. Activity in corrugator and zygomatic muscles as well as heart-rate response are all indicative of variations in the valence of stimuli. In contrast, skin conductance activity is a good index of variations in the self-reported arousal of stimuli In addition, changes in cortical activity, as measured by evoked potentials, and overall viewing time are also indicative of arousal as opposed to valence. Thus, we tend to look longer at arousing pictures, regardless of whether they are positive or negative.

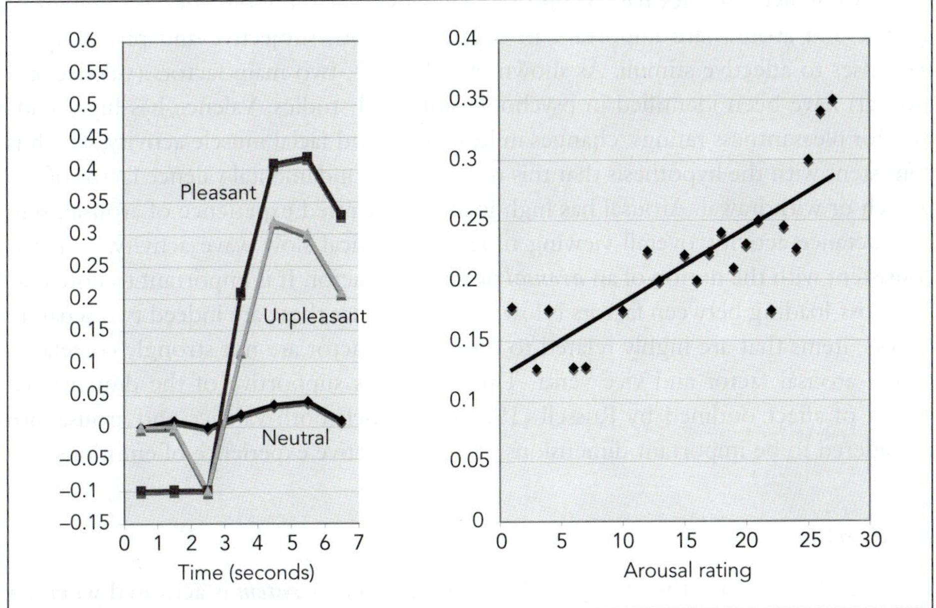

FIGURE 5.8 Patterns of skin conductance activity
(a) As a function of prior valence and arousal ratings of IAPS pictures
(b) The correlation between individual's ratings of arousal with the changes in skin conductance response to viewing IAPS pictures

Source: Adapted from Lang et al. (1993).

TABLE 5.2 Loadings of dependent measures from two factor analyses of measures of emotional picture processing

Measure	*Valence*	*Arousal*
From Lang et al. (1993)		
Valence ratings	0.86	–0.00
Corrugator muscle	–0.85	0.19
Heart rate	0.79	–0.14
Zygomatic muscle	0.58	0.29
Arousal ratings	0.15	0.83
Interest ratings	0.45	0.77
Viewing time	–0.27	0.76
Skin conductance	–0.37	0.74
From Cuthbert et al. (1998)		
Valence ratings	0.89	0.07
Corrugator muscle	–0.83	–0.10
Heart rate	0.73	–0.02
Arousal ratings	–0.11	0.89
Cortical slow wave	–0.06	–0.79
Skin conductance	0.19	0.77

Source: Bradley and Lang (2000b).

Factor analytic studies have supported the view that the motivational variables of valence and arousal are important in organizing both subjective and physiological responses to affective stimuli. As shown in Table 5.2, two main factors (valence and arousal) have been identified in psychophysiological studies. Valence has high loadings for pleasantness ratings, changes in heart rate, and facial muscle activity, which is consistent with the hypothesis that this represents a fundamental valence factor of approach or withdrawal. Arousal has high loadings for rated experience of arousal, skin conductance activity, overall viewing time, and cortical slow wave activity, which is consistent with the notion of an *arousal* or intensity factor. It is important to note that the cross-loading between factors is low, indicating that these are indeed two separate factors: items that are highly related to the valence factor are not strongly correlated to the arousal factor and vice versa. This analysis is supportive of the dimensional model of affect outlined by Russell (1980), in which both valence and arousal are considered to be important dimensions of our subjective experience of emotions.

Startle response

Lang (2000) has hypothesized that the brain's *avoidance system* is activated when an organism reacts to an aversive stimulus, while activation of this system will be reduced when an appetitive stimulus is being processed. The assumption is that both of these priming effects – potentiation and reduction of response – are likely to be influenced by the overall level of activation. Measurement of the *startle response* has proved to be an easy-to-measure defensive reflex which is useful for testing this hypotheses. The startle response is a primitive defensive reflex that plays a protective role such as protection of the eye in the eye-blink reflex. It interrupts ongoing behaviour so that the potential threat can be attended to and processed (Graham, 1979). According to the *motivational priming hypothesis* (Lang, 1995), this defensive startle reflex should be faster and of greater strength when the aversive motivational system is already activated. Imagine that you are alone in a dark house late at night and are feeling nervous. A loud noise outside is likely to result in a stronger startle response than if you were relaxing with friends in the daylight.

This hypothesis was first studied in a fear conditioning experiment with rats (Brown et al., 1951). During the extinction period, when the unconditioned stimulus is no longer presented with the conditioned stimulus and the fear response to the conditioned stimulus gradually declines, the rats were startled by shots from a toy pistol. The degree of startle was measured by a stabilimeter in the floor of the cage. The animals reacted more strongly when the startle stimuli were presented during the fear-conditioned signals than during presentations of neutral stimuli. An extensive series of studies by Davis and his colleagues has shown that fear-conditioned startle is modulated by a neural circuit of which the amygdala is an important part. This circuitry is shown in Figure 5.9 (Davis, 1986; 1989; Davis et al., 1987).

In animal studies, the whole body startle response is generally measured, whereas in human studies the typical methodology is to measure just the eye-blink reflex. An eye-blink typically occurs 30 to 40 milliseconds after the onset of a stimulus and

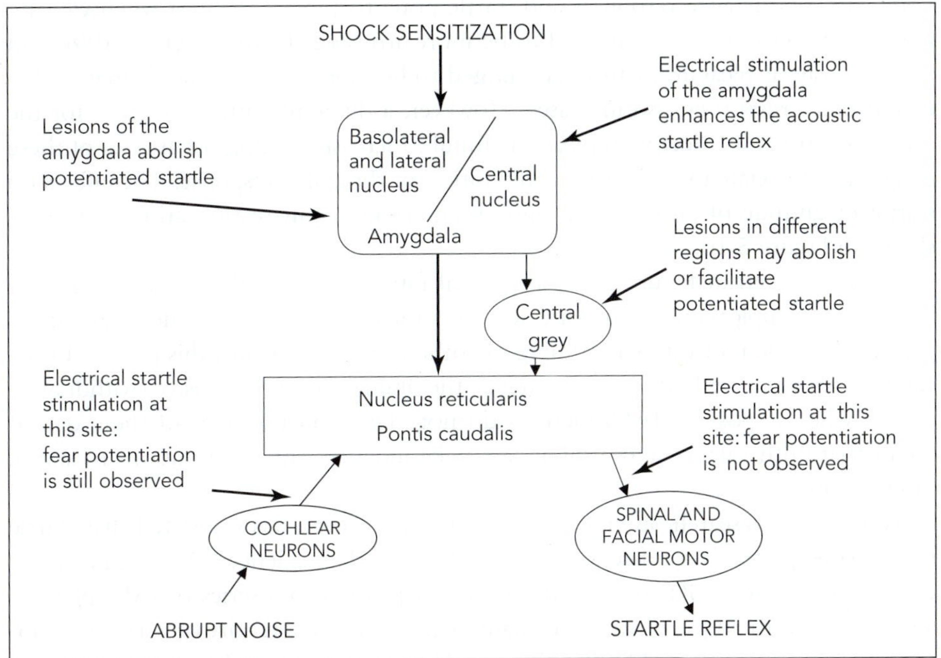

FIGURE 5.9 The neural pathway between a startle probe input and its effector output
Source: Adapted from Lang (1995).

this provides a reliable index of the startle reflex. The latency and magnitude of this response can be measured by placing small electrodes just below the lower eye-lid to detect small changes in the facial muscle that surrounds the eye. The stimulus used to evoke an eye-blink response in humans is usually a 50-millisecond burst of white noise at around 95 decibels (db). This stimulus is fairly innocuous and does not interfere with ongoing tasks, but is still sufficient to induce an eye-blink reflex. Many studies have confirmed that the eye-blink response to a startle probe is enhanced during exposure to shock-conditioned stimuli relative to an unconditioned stimulus. This is a similar result to the findings of startle studies with rats (Hamm et al., 1991). This suggests that the same neural structures might be responsible for controlling startle potentiation in both rats and humans (Lang, 1995).

Lang's *motivational priming hypothesis* proposes that when an organism is processing an unpleasant scene the brain's aversive defensive system is activated and any defensive reflexes will be enhanced. However, since the aversive and appetitive systems are considered to be mutually inhibitory, it follows that when pleasant stimuli are being processed the aversive system should be suppressed, and therefore the magnitude of defensive reflexes should be diminished (Lang, 1995; Lang et al., 1990). This hypothesis has been tested directly on people viewing IAPS pictures. As expected, when viewing unpleasant pictures (e.g., snakes, pointing guns, etc) the startle response is at its strongest, whereas when viewing pleasant pictures (e.g., happy babies, attractive nudes, etc) the startle response is at its minimum (Bradley et al., 1990). Moreover, both skin conductance responses and startle potentiation are greatest when viewing unpleasant pictures that are judged to be more arousing (Cuthbert et al., 1996). In a similar way, as pleasant pictures are judged to be more arousing the degree of skin conductance responses also increases. However, a different pattern emerges for the startle potentiation effect with pleasant stimuli. Increasing ratings of arousal of these images are associated with a greater inhibition of the reflex response. The effects on startle magnitude of pleasant and unpleasant stimuli of increasing arousal rating is shown in Figure 5.10.

As can be seen in Figure 5.10, as arousal rating increases the startle magnitude increases for unpleasant stimuli but decreases for pleasant stimuli. This is exactly as predicted by the motivational priming hypothesis, which explains this pattern by assuming that negative IAPS pictures engage the brain's aversive defensive (withdrawal) system whereas positive IAPS pictures do not. Thus, on the basis of these data it seems that both valence and arousal can make independent contributions to startle modulation.

More recent research on emotion regulation, however, has suggested that startle seems to be primarily a reflection of arousal rather than valence (Dillon and LaBar, 2005). Dillon and LaBar presented their participants with a series of IAPS pictures and instructed them to enhance, maintain or suppress the intensity of whatever emotional response was elicited by the pictures. The prediction was that if arousal is critical then enhance instructions should lead to a greater magnitude of eye-blink startle relative to either maintain or suppress instructions, and this should happen for both

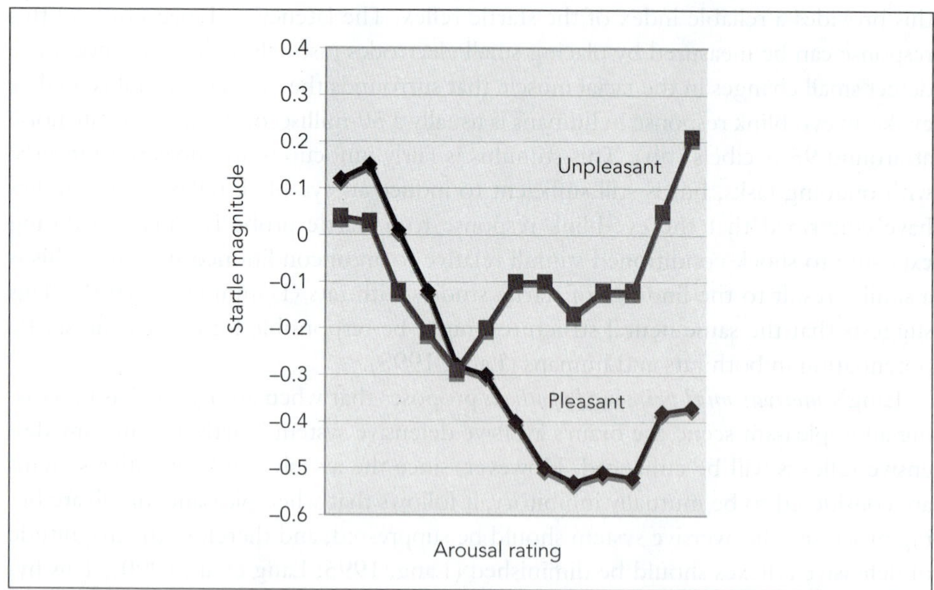

FIGURE 5.10 The magnitude of startle potentiation for both pleasant and unpleasant IAPS pictures as a function of increases in self-reported ratings of arousal

Source: Bradley and Lang (2000b).

positive and negative pictures. However, if valence is more important then a different pattern should emerge, based on Lang's motivational priming hypothesis. In this case, because the aversive system is activated when viewing negative pictures, enhance instructions should lead to increased startle when compared to maintain or suppress instructions. Conversely, because the aversive system is assumed to be inhibited when processing positive pictures, then enhance instructions should attenuate startle relative to maintain or suppress instructions. This is because positive affect is assumed to be highest when the emotional responses from viewing positively valenced pictures are enhanced. Dillon and LaBar's results are presented in Figure 5.11.

As can be seen in Figure 5.11, the emotion regulation instructions led to an increased startle response for enhance relative to maintain and suppress instructions. However, while the suppress instructions produced a reduced startle response compared to maintain instructions, this did not reach statistical significance. The most important finding, however, is that the general pattern of enhance > maintain > suppress was the same for both negative and positive IAPS pictures. Thus, conscious attempts to increase and decrease the emotional response to pictures had similar effects on the startle response regardless of valence. These results are inconsistent with the motivational priming hypothesis. They fit Dillon and LaBar's hypothesis that arousal may be more important than valence in modulating startle.

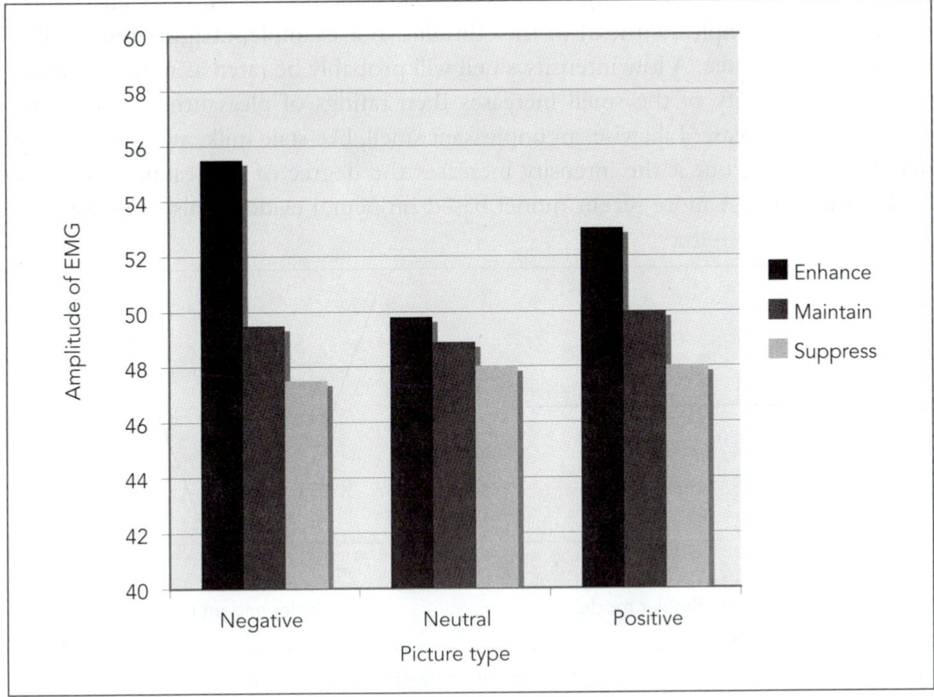

FIGURE 5.11 Eye-blink startle responses as a function of emotion regulation cues

Source: Adapted from Dillon and LaBar (2005).

To summarize, there is evidence that physiological measures reflect two underlying dimensions that can be termed valence and arousal. Activity in facial muscles and variations in heart rate show specific patterns of responses for the *valence* dimension, while measures of skin conductance and the startle reflex provide an index of *arousal.* Thus, based on the criteria outlined in Table 5.1, there is reasonably strong physiological evidence for a dimensional approach.

Neural circuits

Investigation of the dimensions approach by measuring neural activity is somewhat problematic because there are essentially three different models. The overall level of neural activity could be assessed. If arousal is coded by the brain as a separate dimension from valence, as predicted by some models (Russell, 1980), then we would expect to observe some brain areas that activate in response to arousal and not to valence. The neural assessment of valence is even more complicated because it is not clear whether valence is a single bipolar dimension going from most unpleasant to most pleasant that is independent of arousal (Russell, 1980), or whether PA and NA are independent dimensions with varying levels of arousal for each (Watson and Tellegen, 1985). A diagrammatic representation of these models is outlined in Figure 5.12.

As shown in Figure 5.12(b), Watson and Tellegen's (1985) model combines valence and arousal by allowing both PA and NA to vary in intensity. This makes intuitive sense because increasing the intensity of something often does change the pleasantness (or unpleasantness) of the stimulus. For example, imagine the smell of freshly ground coffee. A low intensity smell will probably be rated as mildly pleasant, and as the intensity of the smell increases then ratings of pleasantness will almost certainly also increase. Likewise, an unpleasant smell, like stale milk, at a low intensity may be tolerable, but if the intensity increases the degree of unpleasantness is also likely to increase. A more recent model based on neural evidence also suggests that

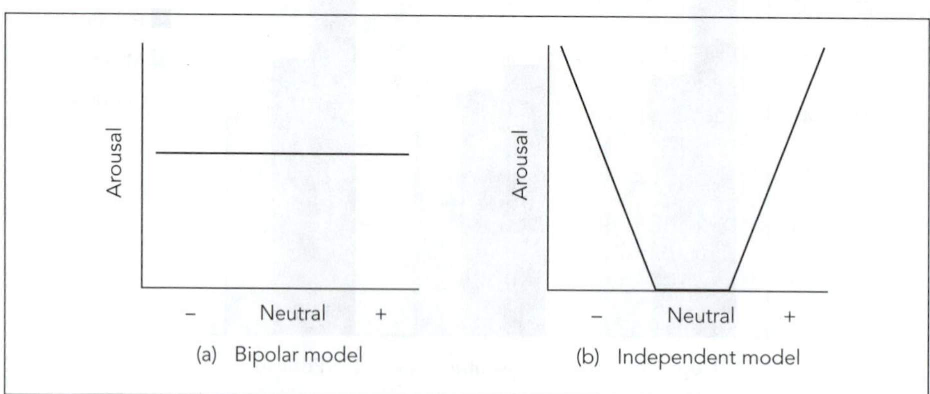

FIGURE 5.12 Diagrammatic representation of two different models of valence

(a) The bipolar model assumes that activation increases from most negative to most positive (e.g., Russell, 1980)

(b) The independent model assumes that activation increases independently for both positive and negative valences (e.g., Watson and Tellegen, 1985).

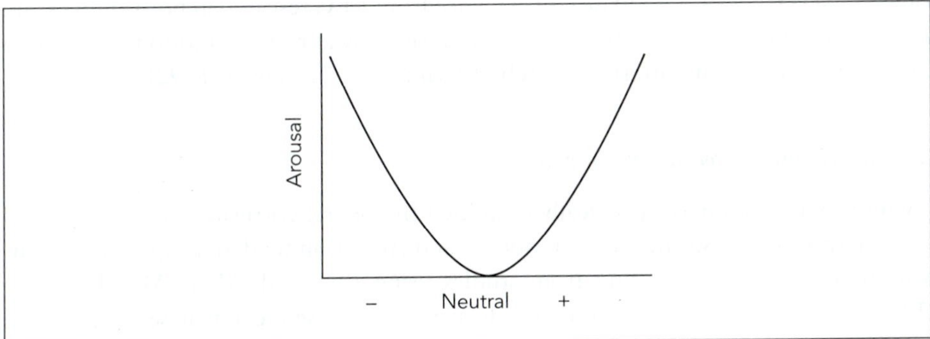

FIGURE 5.13 Winston et al.'s (2005) model relating intensity and valence
Source: Lewis et al. (2007).

intensity and valence may be integrated in the representation of a stimulus (Winston et al., 2005). This model suggests that valence increases from most neutral to most intense regardless of being positive or negative, which gives the U-shaped relationship shown in Figure 5.13.

EEG studies of the neural correlates of valence

Richard Davidson and his colleagues have used EEG to measure cortical activity in the left and right hemispheres in order to index valence (see Davidson, 1984, 1992b, 1998a, for reviews). The *valence asymmetry* model suggests that the right and the left prefrontal cortices of the brain play different roles in how we perceive and experience positive and negative emotions. Electrophysiological data show that approach-related positive emotions (e.g., happiness) are associated with greater activation of the left-sided PFC, while withdrawal-related negative emotions (e.g., fear) are associated with greater right-sided PFC activity (Davidson, 1992b). EEG studies with monkeys have shown a very similar pattern of asymmetrical cortical activation (Kalin et al., 1998). This research indicates that PA and NA are associated with activation of the left and right cortices, respectively (Davidson, 1992b, 1998a; Davidson et al., 1990).

While positive and negative emotions are often equated with approach and withdrawal mechanisms, it is important to note that these are not identical constructs. Many positive emotions are approach-related (e.g., happiness, curiosity), but some, such as contentment, are not. Likewise, while many negative emotions are related to withdrawal (e.g., fear and disgust), others, such as anger, are related to approach mechanisms. Even the emotion of fear, which is often considered to be a prototypical aversive or withdrawal-based emotion, can also be associated with the tendency to approach a place of safety. Thus, it is overly simplistic to equate positive emotions with approach and negative emotions with withdrawal. Davidson (1998a) has suggested that it is therefore useful to emphasize the action tendencies related with different emotions. It is difficult to determine how much this differential activation of the two cerebral hemispheres is due to individual differences in response to affective stimuli (affective style) rather than to a momentary response to particular situations or objects. Nevertheless, a good deal of evidence from EEG research in both animals and humans has shown that approach-related and withdrawal-related emotions do seem to be related to different patterns of cerebral asymmetry (Davidson, 1992b, 1998a).

The functional neuroanatomy of valence

Two meta-analyses have specifically examined the neural correlates of (a) emotional valence (positive versus negative emotions) and (b) action tendency (approach versus withdrawal emotions) coming from studies using PET and fMRI (Murphy et al., 2003; Wager et al., 2003). Unfortunately, neither of these meta-analyses assessed the neural correlates of arousal. The majority of work at that time had concentrated on investigating valence with relatively little research being conducted on the correlates of arousal. Moreover, many of the studies investigating valence have actually confounded valence and arousal. Thus, we will begin by reviewing studies assessing the neural correlates of emotional valence and then we will consider some more recent studies specifically examining both valence and arousal.

Murphy et al. (2003) assessed 81 studies that examined negative emotions and 30 studies that examined positive emotions. They hypothesized, on the basis of the valence asymmetry model, that greater left-sided activation of the prefrontal cortex should occur for positive emotions, whereas greater right-sided activation should occur for negative emotions. Against expectation, no statistically significant differences were found in the degree of lateralization observed between positive and negative emotions. However, some support was found for the hypothesis that different neural systems are involved in approach and withdrawal action tendencies. Approach-related emotions were associated with greater activation within the left PFC. However, no laterality differences were reported for withdrawal-related emotions. Thus, this meta-analysis provides only partial support for the valence asymmetry model.

The meta-analysis conducted by Wager et al. (2003) included a larger range of studies and did find differences in neural activation for valence. Positive emotions were associated with greater activation of the left lateral PFC as well as the basal ganglia, whereas negative emotions were associated with increased activation of the insula. In agreement with Murphy et al.'s analysis, greater activation of the left lateral PFC was related to approach emotions, as was activation of the medial PFC. A range of brain areas was correlated with withdrawal-related emotions: amygdala, left medial PFC as well as the anterior cingulate, in addition to the basal ganglia, left insula and left fusiform and superior occipital cortices.

Thus, we can see that these two meta-analyses give a rather inconsistent picture. This is perhaps not too surprising as studies included in the analyses differed widely in terms of the type of tasks that people were undertaking when their brain was being scanned (e.g., rating IAPS pictures, passively viewing emotional facial expressions, recalling positive and negative situations and so on). In addition, given that prefrontal cortical areas are also involved in a range of cognitive processes it is often very difficult to separate out the effects of cognitive and emotional processes in these types of studies.

A number of studies conducted since these meta-analyses have shown that valence does appear to be associated with increased activation of the vmPFC as well as the dlPFC and vlPFC (Anders et al., 2004; Anderson et al., 2003; Dolcos et al., 2004a; Small et al., 2003). A potential confounding factor, however, is that these same regions are also involved in cognitive processes such as attention and evaluative judgement. In other words, if the simple act of judging a photograph can activate the vmPFC, then it is very difficult to isolate any additional activation that might be due specifically to the valence of the photograph. This problem was tackled directly in an fMRI study that explicitly controlled for preceding attention as well as cognitive processes like judgment (Grimm et al., 2006). The researchers compared the pattern of brain activity when people were simply passively viewing emotional pictures with when they were judging emotional pictures. The pattern of brain activity due to the process of judgment could then be distinguished from the brain activity associated with the valence of the pictures. A large number of IAPS pictures were used and participants either had to judge whether each picture was positive or negative during a 4-second presentation or to passively view each picture for 4 seconds. Following scanning, each participant rated all of the images for both arousal and valence on a 1 to 9 scale. These ratings revealed that the positive and negative pictures did not differ in terms of arousal. The fMRI analysis demonstrated that activation within the vmPFC did indeed correlate positively with valence. More positive ratings were associated with a greater degree of activation in the vmPFC for both positive and negative pictures. In other words regardless of whether a picture was negative (e.g., a growling dog) or positive (e.g., a smiling baby) increasing ratings of positivity were associated with increased activation of the vmPFC. This neural activity seemed to be specifically related to emotional valence since vmPFC activity and valence did not correlate when people were judging the photographs.

This study is important because it shows that emotional pictures can activate the vmPFC in the absence of any cognitive task. In addition, this relation is independent of valence. Grimm et al. (2006) conclude that activity in the vmPFC may reflect affective value or significance in a general sense regardless of whether it is positive or negative. This study also found that valence was correlated with activity in both left and right dlPFC, but only during an unexpected judgment condition. This is consistent with another report that activity in the dlPFC seems to be involved in emotional judgment (Dolcos et al., 2004b). These results are important and suggest that a number of distinct prefrontal cortical regions might contribute to different aspects of emotional stimulus processing. In particular, the vmPFC may relate to the affective significance of an emotional stimulus whereas the dlPFC may relate to the evaluative aspect of valence.

The functional neuroanatomy of arousal and valence

The previous section discussed the regions within the prefrontal cortex that are associated with the valence of a stimulus. However, so far we have not looked at studies examining both valence and arousal. As we have seen, EEG studies have shown that increased cortical activity is associated with increasing arousal (Lang et al., 1997). In addition, the fact that the startle response is enhanced as arousal increases provides indirect evidence that the amygdala might be involved in arousal, because the amygdala has been shown to control startle in animal work (Lang, 1995; LeDoux, 1996). More recent studies using fMRI have provided direct evidence that the activation of the amygdala is correlated specifically with emotional arousal (Anders et al., 2004; Anderson et al., 2003; Dolcos et al., 2004a; Williams et al., 2001). Anderson et al. (2003) presented people with a number of odours that were rated for both valence and intensity. A clear double dissociation was found. The activity of the amygdala varied with the intensity of the odour, but it did not react to its valence. In contrast, valence was associated with increased activity in the orbitofrontal cortex (OFC) but this region did not react to differences in intensity. A very similar dissociation has been reported for different tastes, with the amygdala responding to increases in intensity and the OFC responding to variations in valence (Small et al., 2003).

Another study reported a double dissociation between the neural mechanisms underlying intensity and those underlying valence using word stimuli (Lewis et al., 2007). A variety of words were selected from the ANEW set (Affective Norms for English Words), which are rated on a 1–9 scale for both valence (1 = very unpleasant, 9 = very pleasant) and arousal (1 = not arousing, 9 = very arousing) (Bradley and Lang, 1999a). Each word was presented for 1 second and people had to decide (by pressing a button) whether the word could be used to describe themselves (yes/no). The results supported previous work by showing that parts of the OFC responded strongly to the valence of the word whereas responses in insula, basal ganglia and amygdala varied in line with the arousal ratings of the words (Lewis et al., 2007). This functional dissociation between brain regions that are modulated by valence (orbitofrontal cortex) and brain regions that are modulated by arousal (amygdala and associated area) suggests that these two dimensions may well be processed in a distinct manner, supporting some dimensional models of emotion (e.g., Russell, 1980).

Lewis et al. (2007) found a more complex relationship, however, in that different sub-regions of the OFC responded to negative and positive valence. Increasing positive valence was related to enhanced activity in the right lateral OFC as well as in the anterior insula. In contrast, increasing negative valence was related primarily to increased activity in the posterior insula and the ACC, as well as the right OFC and right medial OFC. This pattern of brain activity is more supportive of the dimensional models proposing separate coding of PA and NA (Watson and Tellegen, 1985).

However, Lewis et al. also found that large areas of the brain were activated by the conjunction of valence and arousal, which suggests that valence and arousal may be integrated into a single representation (Watson and Tellegen, 1985; Winston et al., 2003). For example, a number of areas within the left medial OFC and striatum were activated in response to the interaction between valence and arousal, although this occurred only for negative words (Lewis et al., 2007). This valence-specific brain response to arousal supports the idea that emotional content influences the way in which we respond to arousal.

The neuroscience of reward and punishment

Edmund Rolls (1999, 2005) has developed a valence-based model of emotions from research examining responses to *reinforcement* and *punishment.* Following on from the behavioural tradition in psychology (Watson, 1919), the model proposes that emotions are essentially coordinated responses to *reinforcing* stimuli. In behavioural terminology, *instrumental reinforcers* are stimuli that can alter the probability that an action will be produced. For example, if positive reinforcement is delivered (e.g., food) then an animal or human will work to achieve that reward. However, if the reward is not delivered then there is less probability of action. Rolls' scheme classifies emotions in terms of reinforcing effects as shown in Figure 5.14. In Figure 5.14, the vertical axis describes emotions associated with the delivery of a reward (up) or punisher (down). The horizontal axis describes emotions associated with the non-delivery of an expected reward (left) or the non-delivery of an expected punisher (right).

It should be made clear that Rolls explicitly states that his classification system is not intended to represent a dimensional scheme, since the parameters plotted on the vertical and horizontal axes do not represent *independent* dimensions. This means that the four directions shown in Figure 5.14 can be at least partly independent of each other. In other words, an individual's sensitivity to a reward (S+) might be completely separate from his or her sensitivity to punishment (S–). With this caveat, Rolls' model

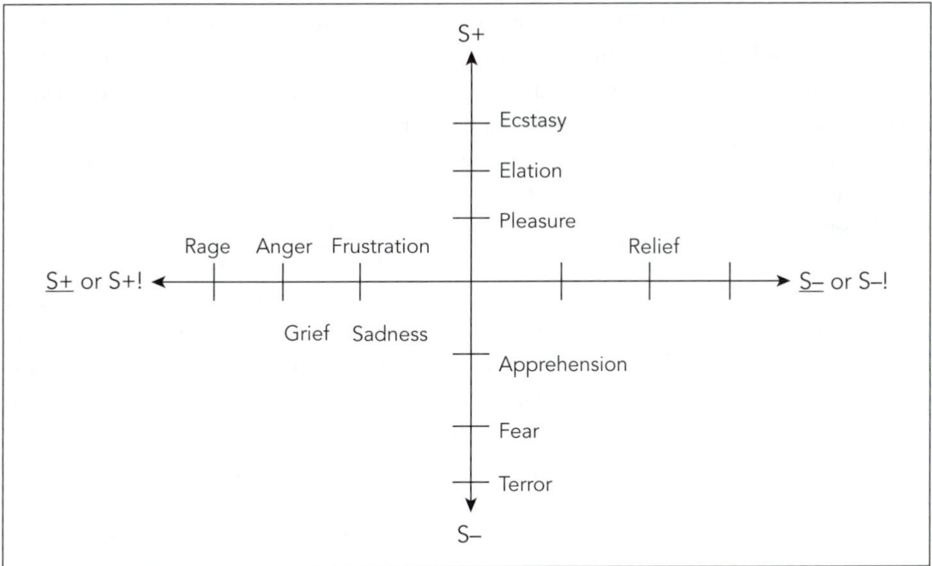

FIGURE 5.14 Rolls' classification of emotions according to different reinforcement contingencies
S+ = delivery of a reward
S– = delivery of a punisher
S+ = omission of a reward (extinction)
S+! = termination of a reward (timeout)
S– = omission of a punisher (avoidance)
S–! = termination of a punisher (escape).

Source: Rolls (2005).

can be considered a dimensional approach in so far as emotions are explained in terms of responses to valence (pleasure and displeasure) as well as arousal or intensity.

Much research suggests that the OFC plays a crucial role in coding stimuli that relate to reward and punishment (Rolls, 2005). For example, in studies of monkeys with electrodes implanted deep within the OFC, it has been found that neurons in this region fire vigorously when a monkey tastes a favourite food or even if the monkey sees an item that is related to the food (see Rolls, 2005 for review). There is evidence that these neurons do indeed code what might be called the 'hedonic value' (i.e., pleasantness) of the food. If the monkey is allowed to eat the food until it is satiated, the firing of the OFC neurons declines in line with the decrease in the food's pleasantness. Functional imaging studies with humans have shown that the OFC becomes similarly activated in response to pleasant foods. In one study, for example, people were asked to rate the pleasantness of the taste of chocolate milk and of tomato juice. They were allowed to drink these drinks until they were satiated and, not surprisingly, the ratings of how pleasant the drinks were declined significantly when the items had been consumed. The interesting finding was that the activation of the OFC decreased as the pleasantness rating decreased (Kringelbach et al., 2003). Importantly, however, the OFC still remained activated to the flavour of food that had not been consumed because the person was satiated, showing that the OFC does indeed seem to code the valence or the pleasantness of the food, rather than other sensory aspects of it.

Rolls and his colleagues have also found that different regions within the OFC respond to pleasant and unpleasant flavours, providing further support for the notion that positive and negative stimuli are coded separately in the brain. For example, activation of the medial OFC correlated with an individual's rating of the pleasantness of a flavour, whereas the unpleasantness of a flavour was correlated with activation in the lateral OFC. A meta-analysis of the literature has confirmed that rewarding (pleasant) stimuli modulate medial parts of the OFC whereas stimuli associated with non-reward (unpleasant stimuli) activate more lateral parts of the OFC in humans (Kringelbach and Rolls, 2004). One study showed a double dissociation between these regions using fMRI in which activation of the medial OFC was associated with a monetary reward, whereas a monetary loss resulted in activation of the lateral OFC (O'Doherty et al., 2001). This pattern of results is consistent with the notion that the medial OFC plays a role in decoding the reward value of a stimulus and that the lateral OFC is involved in evaluating punishers (Rolls, 2005).

The OFC is also anatomically connected to the nucleus accumbens (NAcc), which is situated at the front of the subcortical part of the forebrain. This area has been implicated in the neural representation of both reward and punishment. The NAcc is heavily innervated by both dopamine (DA) and opioid neurotransmitter systems and is often considered to be the 'pleasure' centre of the brain, or the site of positive affect. In many studies with rats, the release of DA in the NAcc region has been shown to be associated with the sight and taste of pleasant food, anticipation of intrinsically rewarding drugs such as heroin or amphetamines, and with the chance of engaging in sexual activities (for review see Berridge, 2003). DA release also appears to be related to reward in humans. One study using PET showed that DA systems in the NAcc were activated when people won money during a computer game (Koepp et al., 1998). To summarize, research using surgical techniques with animals (rats and monkeys) as well as neuroimaging techniques with humans demonstrates that the OFC and the NAcc are important regions for coding aspects of reward and punishment.

As we have seen, the reward system seems to be controlled by the action of DA in the brain. However, it turns out that 'reward' or 'pleasure' is actually much more complex than we might have thought. The psychological models of valence we have discussed generally talk of pleasant versus unpleasant stimuli, and the assumption is that pleasant stimuli are rewarding, while unpleasant stimuli are related to non-reward or to punishment. However, it seems that reward is not, in fact, a unitary concept, but consists of many different psychological components (Berridge and Robinson, 1998). Berridge and Robinson (2003) argue that three processes are necessary for a stimulus to acquire rewarding properties. First, the individual has to be *motivated* to act and learn. Second, he or she must *learn* about the relationships among stimuli and the consequences of actions relating to these stimuli. Finally, the consumption of a reward can produce hedonic *consequences* in terms of pleasantness. Figure 5.15 shows these different components of reward (Berridge, 2003; Berridge and Robinson, 1998). The categories of motivation, learning and emotion or affect each consist of different psychological components, as shown in Figure 5.15. It is important to note that there are both explicit and implicit components in each category. Thus, explicit processes (e.g., explicit desire, expectation, or pleasure) are consciously experienced, whereas implicit processes (incentive salience, habits, and liking responses) may not be accessible to conscious awareness.

Berridge and Robinson (2003) review evidence indicating that different brain systems can influence the components independently of each other. Thus, some brain manipulations can alter the motivational process without influencing how well an

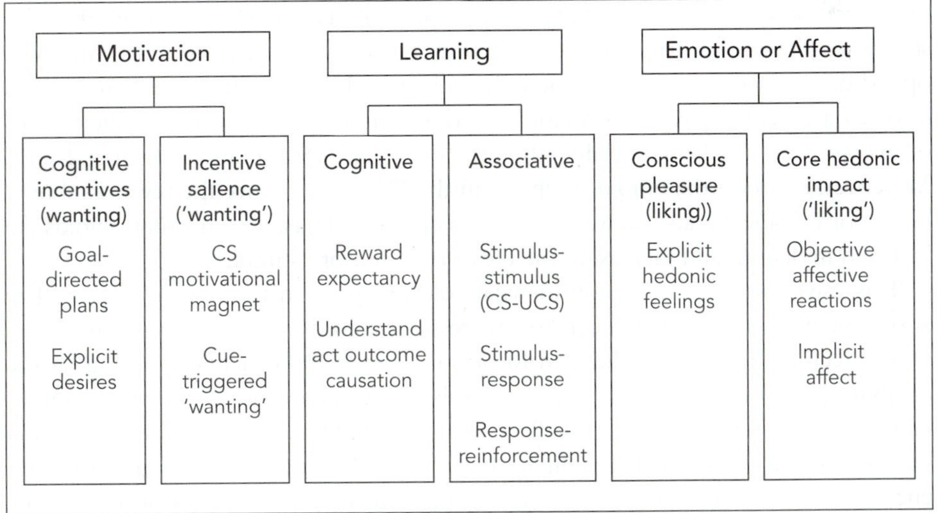

FIGURE 5.15 Berridge and Robinson's components of reward

Source: Based on Berridge and Robinson (2003).

organism can learn the associations between stimuli and actions. An important point made by Berridge and Robinson is that both motivational and emotional components can occur without any conscious awareness of them. Imagine a situation in which you may react to a rewarding stimulus (e.g., a cigarette or a chocolate) without necessarily being aware of your hedonic reaction. This is common in smokers, who often smoke out of habit and may not be aware that they are smoking. Experimental evidence for such implicit emotion comes from a study in which happy facial expressions were presented subliminally so that people were not aware of them. Subjective ratings of mood and feelings did not change when happy expressions were presented, confirming that the stimuli were indeed outside awareness. However, the subliminal presentation caused thirsty people to drink a greater quantity of a fruit drink a few moments later and also led to them rating the drink higher in terms of 'pleasantness' (Berridge and Winkielman, 2003).

An abundance of evidence indicates that DA systems, especially in the NAcc, are important in controlling the brain's reaction to rewarding stimuli. However, several studies have found that administering drugs that lead to a reduction in brain DA does not necessarily impair a rat's hedonic reaction to a sweet taste. Many species, including rats, produce a distinctive 'liking' facial response (e.g., tongue protrusions) in response to sweet drinks, whereas bitter tastes elicit gaping 'disliking' facial responses (Berridge, 2000). When brain dopamine was reduced the rats' facial responses did not indicate that their enjoyment of the drink was affected. Indeed, even massive lesions that eliminated almost all of the DA in the NAcc and striatum failed to disrupt taste 'liking' (Berridge and Robinson, 1998). Conversely, injections of amphetamine into the shell of the NAcc, which leads to an increase in DA, failed to lead to an increase in 'liking' responses to a sweet taste.

Research with humans has also shown that drugs that block the action of DA do not seem to affect the subjective pleasure of either amphetamines (Brauer et al., 2001) or cigarettes (Wachtel et al., 2002). This work suggests that DA does not affect the subjective pleasure of drugs or tastes in either rats or humans. In contrast, however, opioid drugs do seem to hit the 'hedonic hotspots'. Injections into the NAcc of rats leads to a reliable increase in 'liking' responses, and rats will work for the reward of injections of amphetamine directly into their NAcc (Smith and Berridge, 2005). Moreover, blocking the opioid receptors in the NAcc can reduce the reward value of heroin or cocaine to rats (Stewart and Vezina, 1988). Thus, it seems that opioids are involved in 'liking' and increasing the pleasure of sensory stimuli.

This leaves open the question of what role DA plays in the reward system. The answer seems to be that DA affects the processes involved in 'wanting' without necessarily affecting 'liking'. Berridge and Robinson (1998, 2003) define 'wanting' as the attribution of *incentive salience*. They base this definition on findings that the manipulation of DA systems has powerful effects on motivated behaviour (e.g., consumption of rewards) but does not change liking behaviours. The attribution of incentive salience to a sensory input transforms that stimulus into a wanted target of motivation. Incentive salience or 'wanting' is strongly influenced by DA, but also depends on other brain structures such as connections between the NAcc and the amygdala and

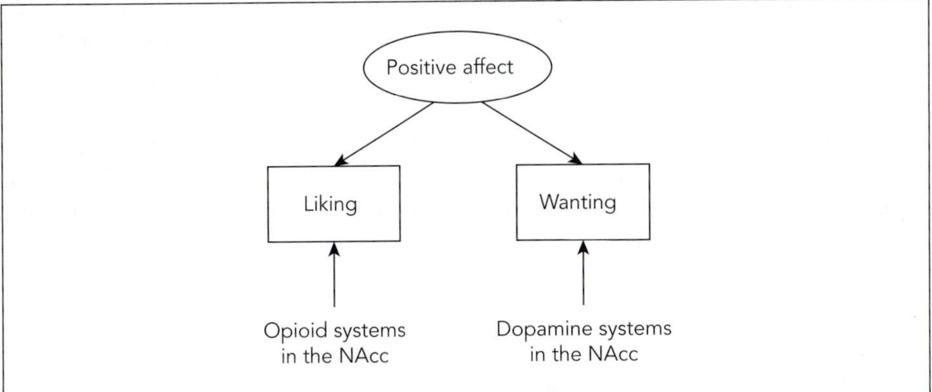

FIGURE 5.16 Berridge et al.'s components of positive affect

parts of the cortex. Stimuli that have been attributed with incentive salience become what Berridge calls '*motivational magnets*' because they elicit appetitive approach and even consumatory behaviour. The relations between wanting and liking and neurotransmitter systems in the brain are clearly complex. However, the important point for our current purposes is the demonstration that even something as apparently straightforward as positive affect can be broken down into different component parts and that these components are modulated by different neurochemical systems. This structure is shown in Figure 5.16.

Cognitive appraisals

If emotions are structured primarily in terms of valence and arousal as dimensional models suggest, then cognitive appraisals should occur *primarily* for the dimensions of arousal and valence. Since people do report a number of distinct emotions it is also important for dimensional theories to demonstrate that cognitive appraisal can lead to the impression of discrete emotions (see Table 5.1).

Are valence and arousal the dominant dimensions of appraisal?

Almost all forms of appraisal theory assume that a simple appraisal of valence is the very first step in the process. For example, the work of Robert Zajonc demonstrates that stimuli of which we are not aware (but have been presented subliminally) tend to be *preferred* over stimuli to which we have not been exposed. Somewhat ironically, he argued on the basis of this *mere exposure effect* that emotions do not require any cognitive processes, but rather, can be elicited directly from the stimulus. However, as pointed out by Ellsworth (1994b), the preferences demonstrated by Zajonc correspond very closely to the simple appraisal of valence: is something *good* or *bad*. As we saw in Chapter 4, many appraisal theories assume that specific appraisals lead to specific discrete emotions (Lazarus, 1991; Stein and Trabasso, 1992). Phoebe Ellsworth has argued, however, that these approaches fail to capture the *similarities* among emotions because they focus almost exclusively on the *differences.* As we have seen previously, there are strong similarities among emotions at a subjective level. While anger and fear can be readily distinguished from each other on the basis of facial expression etc, the evidence suggests that they seem to be *experienced* as fairly similar (i.e., unpleasant and arousing). Ellsworth (1991) has argued that a dimensional approach to cognitive appraisals is required in order to capture these similarities among emotions as well as their differences. She argues that in our emotional experience we often move rapidly from one state to another (e.g., anger to fear to guilt) and that discrete emotions models of appraisal cannot easily account for this. These are important theoretical issues and are consistent with the evidence from questionnaire-based studies that there are high positive correlations among negative emotions and positive emotions: if you score high on fear on a questionnaire, you are also likely to score highly on sadness.

Craig Smith and Phoebe Ellsworth have developed a theory of cognitive appraisal that attempts to provide a better account of the similarities among emotions, as well as the differences (Smith and Ellsworth, 1985, 1987). In an extensive analysis of the semantic content of a wide range of emotions, they derived eight different dimensions of meaning that are important appraisal processes in producing a range of emotions. People were asked to recall past experiences that were associated with each of 15 emotions. Once people had recalled key episodes they were asked to describe these episodes in as much detail as possible. They were then asked about their experiences using questions that were designed to tap into the eight different appraisal dimensions listed in Table 5.3. These dimensions had been derived from previous theories and studies. Analysis of the ratings showed that people reliably used six broad dimensions to differentiate among the 15 different emotions. These six dimensions were pleasantness, human agency, certainty, attention, effort and situational control. Importantly, for most of the 15 emotions a *unique* pattern of cognitive appraisals could be identified.

As shown in Table 5.3, appraisals of valence (pleasantness) and arousal (anticipated effort) were included in the list. However, a number of other appraisals were also identified. The important finding from this study is a strong relation between the cognitive interpretation of an event and the emotional reaction to it. However, it is important to note that we cannot draw any *causal* conclusions from this study. People were asked to recall an emotional experience from the past and then report the appraisals that were involved in that situation, so the results rely on a retrospective report. This leaves open the question of whether appraisals like these remembered ones actually occur in an ongoing situation. Parkinson et al. (2005) have criticized these studies on the basis that they examine people's theories about what causes their emotions rather than the actual causes of the emotions themselves. Nevertheless, the appraisal dimensions uncovered by Smith and Ellsworth do illuminate the ways in which people construct their own emotional experience and it seems that arousal and valence are just two of the dimensions used.

Theories of cognitive appraisal differ in terms of which appraisals are considered to be most important. However, appraisals such as novelty, intrinsic pleasantness,

TABLE 5.3 The eight dimensions of appraisal identified by Smith and Ellsworth

Dimension	*Description*
Attention	Degree to which you focus on and think about the situation
Certainty	Degree to which you are certain about what is going to happen
Control–coping	Extent to which you have control over the situation
Pleasantness	The degree to which the event is positive or negative
Perceived obstacle	Extent to which the pursuit of your goals is prevented
Responsibility	Extent to which you are responsible for events
Legitimacy	Extent to which the event is perceived as fair or unfair
Anticipated effort	Extent to which you must expend energy to respond to the event

certainty or predictability, goal significance, agency, coping potential, and compatibility with social or personal standards are common across a range of theories (see Ellsworth and Scherer, 2003, for review). This body of work therefore does not generally support two-dimensional models since people seem to consider many dimensions in the construction of their emotional experience. Thus, in terms of the criteria outlined in Table 5.1, it would seem that research on cognitive appraisals does not support the notion that valence and arousal are the primary ways in which people construe their emotional experience.

Does cognitive interpretation of affective states result in the impression of distinct emotions?

From a cognitive appraisal viewpoint, the second criterion outlined in Table 5.1 is the notion that people's reports of discrete emotion categories must come from a particular cognitive conceptualization of affective experiences. As we have seen, there is evidence that we are able to subjectively experience variations in our physiological state. Indeed, this notion was the basis of one of the earliest theories of emotional experience (James, 1884). William James proposed that the conscious experience of emotion results from one's perception of autonomic arousal. This theory placed an emphasis on the *physiological* determinants of emotional experience and proposed that people can distinguish among different emotions on the basis of the physical reactions they experience. Thus, when we perceive an object of fear (a bear in the woods for example), our body responds to this and the *feeling* of these bodily changes is the emotion. However, this theory has some difficulty with the fact that physiological arousal can occur without the experience of emotion (Cannon, 1927). For example, when we engage in vigorous exercise we might become very aroused in a physiological sense but will probably not experience any particular emotion. Cannon also argued that physiological changes are simply too slow to precede the conscious experience of emotion. A further problem is that people experiencing very different emotions, such as fear and anger, often show almost identical patterns of autonomic arousal. Finally, Cannon reported several experiments in which the spinal cord of animals was surgically cut so that no physiological sensations could be experienced below the

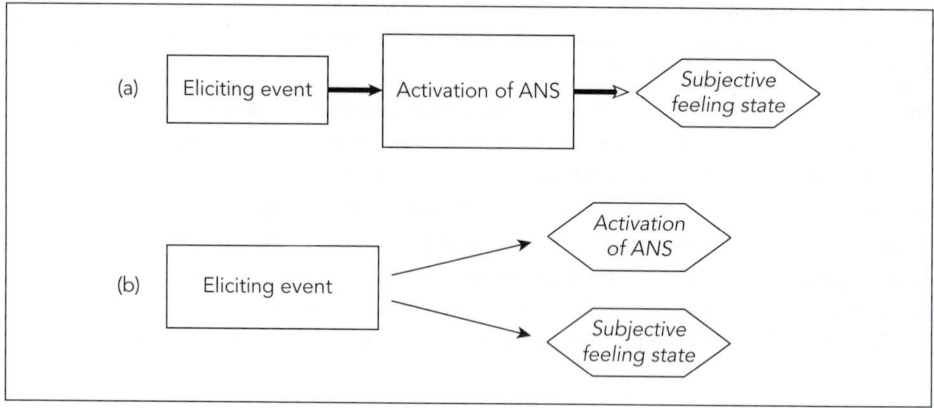

FIGURE 5.17 Theories of emotional experience
(a) James–Lange
(b) Cannon–Bard

level of the cut. In spite of this absence of bodily sensations, however, it seemed that these animals still expressed emotions. On the basis of this evidence, Cannon (1927) argued that *emotion occurs when the thalamus sends signals simultaneously to the cortex (creating the conscious experience of emotion) and to the autonomic system.* His main argument was that physiological changes were very similar across different emotions and therefore could not be used to distinguish among different feeling states as suggested by James. Figure 5.17 illustrates the key differences between the James–Lange and the Cannon–Bard theories.

Subsequent evidence has suggested that there may be some differences in ANS activity between different emotions, and some of the critiques raised by Cannon have been overturned by subsequent evidence (Damasio, 1999). Nevertheless, the fact that many emotions seemed to have relatively similar patterns of physiological arousal presented a problem for the James–Lange hypothesis and formed part of the inspiration for a now-classic experiment conducted by Stanley Schachter and Jerome Singer in 1962.

Schachter and Singer – two factor model

Schachter and Singer (1962) proposed that the experience of emotion depends on two factors: autonomic arousal and cognitive interpretation of that arousal. They hypothesized that when you experience physiological arousal you search your environment for an explanation. Thus, there is some agreement with James' theory in accepting that emotion is inferred from arousal. However, there is also agreement with Cannon's position that different emotions were thought to yield indistinguishable patterns of arousal. These views were reconciled by the suggestion that people look to *external* rather than to *internal* cues to differentiate and label their specific emotions. Thus, an emotional experience is considered to have two parts: a physiological element, much as described by William James, and a cognitive appraisal element, much as described by Magda Arnold (1960). This is illustrated in Figure 5.18.

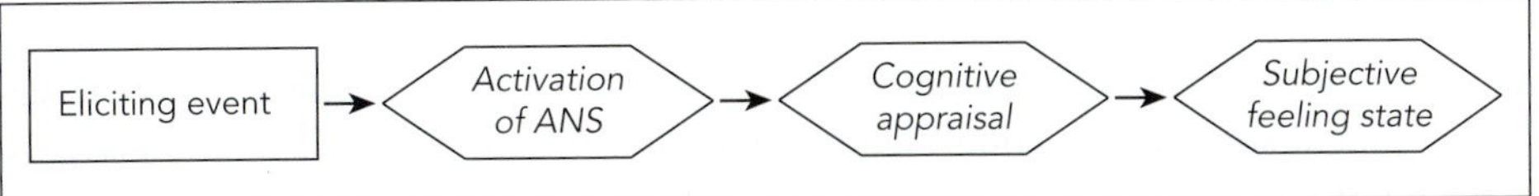

FIGURE 5.18 Schachter and Singer's two-factor model

This hypothesis was tested in an intriguing experiment (Schachter and Singer, 1962). Male college students were led to believe that they were participating in an experiment about the effects of a vitamin injection on vision. Some participants were then injected with adrenaline, which is known to produce autonomic arousal, while others received a saline injection, which has no effect on arousal. Some of the participants in the group receiving adrenaline (*informed* group) were told that the 'vitamin' produced certain side-effects such as a pounding heart, tremors, and a flushed feeling – the typical effects of an injection of adrenaline. However, other participants were told that the drug would have no side effects (misinformed). Individuals who had received the placebo were also told accurately not to expect any side effects (informed) or to expect arousal effects (misinformed). After receiving the injection, the participants were asked to wait in a room with one other participant, who was actually a confederate of the experimenter. The confederate behaved in one of two ways: in the *euphoric condition* he was very active and playful, running around the room and making paper aeroplanes and so on; in the *angry condition*, however, he was disagreeable and constantly complained about having to fill out questionnaires.

The affective responses of the participants were assessed by the experimenters through a one-way mirror as well as by subjective questionnaire. The first finding was that the informed subjects showed very few signs of experiencing emotion. Of more interest, however, was the finding that the misinformed individuals generally described and labelled their mood in accordance with the situational manipulations. In other words, those who had received adrenaline and experienced physiological arousal without any adequate explanation tended to feel either euphoric or angry depending on the confederate's behaviour. However, those who had received adrenaline and experienced physiological arousal but had an adequate explanation for their symptoms did not experience any emotion. Thus, the emotional experience was not determined by physiological arousal alone, but rather by physiological arousal in combination with an appraisal of the situation. If I feel aroused and my companion is very angry then I will tend to interpret my own arousal as anger. However, if I feel aroused but know that this is because I have taken adrenaline then I will be less likely to be influenced by another's emotional behaviour.

This experiment has been highly influential in psychology, even though a number of problems have been noted. For example, in spite of several attempts, no study has been able to fully replicate the effects (Marshall and Zimbardo, 1979; Reisenzein, 1983). Thus, although this theory has had a very strong influence on subsequent research, it does not appear to be valid. Nevertheless, it was important in focusing the attention of researchers on the role of *cognitive factors* (i.e., a person's interpretations) in determining emotional states.

Misattribution of arousal

While the full Schachter and Singer (1962) experiment has not been replicated, several subsequent studies have confirmed that the misattribution of physiological arousal is an important phenomenon and can indeed influence our emotional experience. In one experiment participants engaged in intense physical activity, which resulted in physiological arousal, and then rested until they thought that their arousal had subsided. It was found that participants rated erotic images as more arousing and cartoons as being much funnier than people who had not recently engaged in physical activity (Zillmann, 1979).

A similar misattribution of arousal has been reported in an imaginative real-life experiment. Dutton and Aron (1974) interviewed men who had crossed over the Capilano River in Vancouver, Canada by one of two bridges. One bridge was a wide sturdy wooden bridge, which was about 10 feet above the water. However, the other was a suspension bridge, which was almost 200 feet above the water and consisted of boards and steel cables with very low hand-rails. The entire bridge swayed alarmingly and people generally felt fairly nervous when crossing. In the experiment, men who had just crossed the river were approached by a female researcher who asked them to fill out a survey on local scenic attractions. A key part of the experiment, however, was that the interviewer gave each participant her telephone number and suggested that he get in touch if he would like to talk further. More phone calls were made by men who had crossed over the suspension bridge than by men who had crossed over the low bridge. Dutton and Aron (1974) concluded that the arousal produced by the bridge was misattributed to attraction to the woman interviewer. This line of research demonstrates that bodily arousal is indeed used to colour our subjective experience of the world. However, this arousal is interpreted in terms of current context and may not necessarily provide an accurate reflection of what caused the arousal in the first place.

Recent neuroscience studies have provided potentially relevant data showing that the amygdala only seems to respond to arousing stimuli in a particular emotional context. This suggests that the amygdala and nearby structures, such as the ventral striatum which includes the NAcc, may respond to the general affective significance of a stimulus rather than to arousal or valence specifically. For example, some studies have shown that activity within the NAcc increases in response to generally salient stimuli regardless of whether they are positively or negatively valenced (Breiter et al., 1996; Liberzon et al., 2003; Phan et al., 2004). The NAcc is anatomically connected to a number of regions within the PFC as well as to a range of subcortical regions such as the amygdala. Therefore, it is possible that the NAcc may play an important role in determining the *affective significance* or *salience* of a stimulus (Berridge and Robinson, 1998).

The conceptual act model

Lisa Feldman Barrett has developed the *conceptual act model*, which proposes that discrete emotions are an illusion created by a cognitive process of categorizing what she calls *core affect* (Feldman Barrett, 2006b; Russell and Feldman Barrett, 1999).

This is essentially an updated version of the Schachter and Singer (1962) model. The hypothesis is that what we *perceive* and *experience* as individual emotions (anger, fear, sadness etc) actually emerge from more basic or fundamental psychological processes. Thus, rather than an emotion like anger being truly discrete in the sense of having a distinct neural circuitry etc which can be contrasted with sadness, which will have another distinct neural circuitry, the emotion we term anger is actually constructed by how we perceive and categorize changes in a more fundamental and general *core affective system*. It is this general affective system that is hypothesized to be the fundamental or basic building block of emotional life (e.g., Feldman Barrett, 2006a and b; Russell, 1980, 1991; Russell and Feldman Barrett, 1999).

Russell and Feldman Barrett (1999) do, however, distinguish what they call *prototypical emotional episodes*, which correspond to *emotions* (i.e., a synchronized set of events concerned with a specific object) as defined in this book. They point out that these *prototypical emotional episodes* are very rare, and contrast them with *core affect*:

> We use the term core affect to refer to the most elementary consciously accessible affective feelings (and their neurophysiological counterparts) that need not be directed at anything. Examples include a sense of pleasure or displeasure, tension or relaxation, and depression or elation. Core affect ebbs and flows over the course of time. (Russell and Feldman Barrett, 1999, p. 806)

The notion of core affect is the same as the concept of mood as defined in this book. Therefore, the hypothesis is that our background mood states are experienced along the general dimensions of valence and arousal, and that these states are categorized into discrete emotion categories based on a cognitive appraisal of the current context. Feldman Barrett (2006b) reviews extensive evidence that conceptual knowledge can and does influence the subjective experience of emotions and moods (see also Dutton and Aron, 1974; Schachter and Singer, 1962). Thus, the second criterion for dimension models as outlined in Table 5.1 does appear to have been fulfilled.

COMPARING DISCRETE AND DIMENSIONAL APPROACHES

Lisa Feldman Barrett (2006a, 2006b; Feldman Barrett, Mesquita et al., 2007) has recently argued that progress in emotion science has been limited by the assumption that a core set of basic emotions is given to us by nature. She suggests that the hypothesis of discrete emotions is not supported by the evidence and a dimensional perspective, in combination with the notion of conceptual categorization of core affect, provides a better explanation of the data. However, as illustrated in Table 5.4, emotion scientists taking discrete emotions or broad dimensions as the fundamental building blocks of affect frequently are studying quite different aspects of affect. Discrete emotions theorists often focus on the neural or physiological underpinnings of *emotions* or *moods* (often in rodents). Some even argue that the subjective experience of the emotion is irrelevant to the understanding of the emotion itself. In contrast,

TABLE 5.4 The contrast in emphasis between discrete emotions approaches and dimensional approaches in investigating the fundamental nature of emotion.

Type of approach	*Typical core data*	*Assumed underlying mechanisms*
Discrete emotions	RTs to prototypical stimuli (e.g., angry, happy, fearful expressions etc) Recognition of prototypical facial expressions ANS specificity to particular emotions Activation of specific neural circuits	Cortical-subcortical neural circuits with the emphasis on the subcortical structures Cognitive appraisal
Dimensions	Subjective report of feelings ANS response to general dimensions (e.g., positive versus negative affect) Neural activation to general dimensions	Cortical-subcortical neural circuits with the emphasis on the cortical structures Cognitive appraisal

those adopting a dimensional approach are more likely to focus on subjective report of feelings as the main dependent variables. While there are exceptions, researchers in the two traditions tend to:

(a) focus on different aspects of affect (e.g., feelings versus neural or cognitive structures);
(b) use different paradigms to study what they consider to be emotion (e.g., questionnaires versus fMRI); and
(c) study different species to address these (different) questions (e.g., rodents versus humans).

The problem arises when a theory developed from one of these traditions is then generalized in an attempt to explain 'emotion' as a whole.

It is difficult at this point to determine whether discrete emotions perspectives or dimensional perspectives provide a more accurate view of emotions and moods and how they are structured. A key challenge is to examine these different research traditions and determine whether the empirical evidence from both approaches can be integrated in a sensible way to provide a comprehensive understanding of affect. In Chapter 11, the conclusion is drawn that research from both traditions is important and essentially provides information from different *levels of analysis* (e.g., subjective report versus neural activation). If emotion scientists are careful to define the different elements of affect (emotions, moods, feelings, emotion schemas) then data from both of these approaches can be integrated to provide a more comprehensive overview of affect.

A further complication is that individual differences in how people respond to different situations are usually not considered in research on the structure of affect. These consistent differences in people's *responses* to emotional situations, as well as differences in how they *perceive* and *interpret* emotional situations, however, are likely to be influential in terms of how affective life is structured.

CHAPTER SUMMARY

Chapter 5 discussed evidence that our affective experience is structured around a small number of underlying dimensions. Evidence from self-report data suggests that valence and arousal emerge as important elements of our subjective experience. However, on examination of the pattern of cognitive appraisals that people make, it seems that a wide range of dimensions are used. This does not support the view that a small number of dimensions are primary. Nevertheless, physiological responses do seem to be related to the broad dimensions of valence and arousal, and brain-imaging studies have also found that valence and arousal are coded within the brain. Importantly, however, neurobiological research has found that valence may not be as fundamental as some researchers have assumed. In particular, *positive affect* can be broken down further into sub-components such as 'wanting' and 'liking'. There is some evidence for both the discrete emotions view and the dimensional view, although it must be remembered that these theories and the experiments designed to test them are often aimed at different levels of analysis (e.g., subjective experience or feelings versus coordinated physiological responses).

RECOMMENDED READING

An excellent overview of the structure of emotion in terms of self-report data is provided in:

James A. Russell and Lisa Feldman Barrett (1999) 'Core affect, prototypical emotional episodes, and other things called emotion: Dissecting the elephant', *Journal of Personality and Social Psychology*, 76, 805–19.

A recent series of excellent articles by Lisa Feldman Barrett also provides a detailed discussion of dimensional approaches to emotion and questions whether discrete emotion categories can be considered as 'natural kinds'.

Lisa Feldman Barrett (2006) 'Are emotions natural kinds?', *Perspectives on Psychological Science*, 1, 28–58.

Lisa Feldman Barrett (2006) 'Solving the emotion paradox: Categorization and the experience of emotion', *Personality and Social Psychology Review*, 10, 20–46.

Lisa Feldman Barrett and Tor D. Wager (2006) 'The structure of emotion: Evidence from neuroimaging studies', *Current Directions in Psychological Science*, 15, 79–83.

Critiques of this approach are provided by:

Carol E. Izard (2007) 'Basic emotions, natural kinds, emotion schemas, and a new paradigm', *Perspectives on Psychological Science*, 2, 260–80.

Jaak Panksepp (2007) 'Neurologizing the psychology of affects', *Perspectives on Psychological Science*, 2, 281–96.

Excellent discussions of the brain mechanisms involved in the reward system is provided in the following sources:

Kent Berridge and Terry Robinson (2003) 'Parsing reward', *Trends in Neurosciences*, 26, 507–13.

Edmund T. Rolls (2005) *Emotions Explained*. Oxford: Oxford University Press.

6 AFFECT–COGNITION RELATIONS: PERCEPTION, ATTENTION AND JUDGMENT

THE RETURN OF AFFECT IN PSYCHOLOGY AND NEUROSCIENCE

There was speculation about the relations between affect and cognition in philosophical circles long before the foundation of scientific psychology. Plato discussed the uncontrollable and pervasive aspects of emotion, which led to a general sense that emotions or 'passions' as they were often called, disrupted and interfered with cognition or 'reason'. It was in the Enlightenment period of the 1800s that philosophers drew a distinction between *cognition* (or understanding), *affect* (or feeling) and *conation* (will). Philosophers such as Immanuel Kant argued that human mental faculties could be divided into these three elements: 'pure reason' that corresponds to intellect or cognition; practical reason, which Kant equated with will and action; and judgment, which was related to feeling pleasure and pain (see Hilgard, 1980, for overview). This tripartite division of mental faculties was readily accepted by the founders of experimental psychology (e.g., Wundt and Titchener), although they were careful to emphasize that, while the three components could be assessed separately by means of introspection, they combined together to form a *unitary* psychological experience.

Unfortunately, subsequent research did not adhere to this unitary view, so cognition, affect, and conation were studied in isolation from each other until fairly recently. One exception to this was the 'New Look' in perception research, which came to the fore in the 1940s and 1950s. This approach very much emphasized the potential influence of affective states and motivations on the fundamental mechanisms of perception and attention (e.g., Bruner, 1957). The New Look movement is described in Box 6.1.

While some studies on affect–cognition relations did take place during the early part of the 20th century (e.g., Bruner, 1957; Razran, 1940; Izard, 1964), intensive investigation of affect–cognition really only came back into the mainstream of scientific investigation in the 1980s. This revival was driven by a number of factors, including demonstrations by empirical programmes in social psychology that affective reactions could influence a variety of social judgments and decisions (e.g., Zajonc, 1980). Around that time, experimental cognitive psychologists also became interested in how affective states could influence cognitive processes such as memory and learning (e.g., Bower, 1981; Bower et al., 1981). Cognitive approaches were also being applied to the study of emotional disorders (Dalgleish, 2003; Williams et al., 1988, 1997; Yiend, 2004, for reviews). These developments in psychology were complemented by subsequent developments in neurobiology which began to show that the neural structures underlying affect were essential components in coordinating

BOX 6.1

The New Look in perception

The New Look in perception was a programme of research conducted in the 1940s and the 1950s. The basic argument was that the emotional meaning of a stimulus could be responded to before the stimulus was consciously perceived, and that the reaction could determine the content or form of the resulting conscious percept. This is similar to the argument Zajonc (1980) presented almost 30 years later. At the time it was radical and controversial to suggest that fundamental mechanisms of perception could be influenced by affect. As Bruner (1992) points out, the New Look idea was that perception was not a neutral registration of what was 'out there'. It was, rather, an activity affected by other concurrent processes of thought, memory and so on.

Empirically, the New Look approach was concerned primarily with the notion of *perceptual accentuation* – what makes some features of the world more salient than others? Early experiments found that positive stimuli were often perceived as being bigger (e.g., valuable coins), brighter or louder than they actually were. Conversely, people often took longer to respond to negative stimuli. In some early experiments a series of words was presented very rapidly and participants were required to name the words as quickly as possible. The results showed that subjects took longer to name taboo words such as 'fuck' than neutral words like 'bird'. Bruner and Postman (1947) interpreted these results as being a measure of 'perceptual defence'. The negative valence of the taboo word was processed very early after sensory registration, and activated a defence mechanism which led to slower perception of the word. The important point is that the affective significance of the word was determined *prior* to the perceptual identification of the word. An obvious flaw with these experiments, however, was that the results may have been due to a *response bias* rather than to a perceptual mechanism. In other words, student participants may have been reluctant to shout out taboo words in front of their professors. Thus, the taboo and neutral words may have been perceived just as quickly as each other but an inhibition of response might have resulted in the slower naming times for the taboo words. This is a plausible objection to these experiments. Nevertheless, at the time, these experiments were important and radical demonstrations that the valence of stimuli was an important potential determinant of perception and/or the response to a stimulus.

Unfortunately, following this interesting start, the New Look movement never really got going. This was due to a variety of historical reasons. First, the notion of unconscious perceptual processes attracted the attention of psychoanalytically-oriented theorists and gave the New Look a bad name in mainstream cognitive psychology. Moreover, just around this time the information-processing model became the dominant approach in cognitive psychology. As we have seen, there was little place for the involvement of emotional reactions in perception, and virtually no place for the idea of non-conscious or pre-attentive processing prior to the resolution of a conscious percept, in the early days of cognitive psychology.

continued overleaf

BOX 6.1 continued

The return of the New Look

Times have changed, and the traditional focus of the original New Look – the role of motivation and affect in basic perceptual processes – is now at the centre stage of both psychological and neuroscientific inquiry. Much of the development of cognition and affect as a dynamic subject area, for example, is due to the re-emergence of these issues in contemporary cognitive psychology.

Niedenthal and Kitayama (1994) argue that one of the reasons for this change is the realization that, even though the processes of the mind can be described in terms of rational, computer-like operations, they have nonetheless been shaped by their effectiveness in adapting to the biological, social and cultural environments. Thus, a focus on functionalism has returned, and much of cognitive psychology is now concerned with addressing the *adaptive* functions of mental operations. From this perspective, theoretical and empirical enquiries into affect are essential to make sense of the workings of cognitive mechanisms themselves. Many of the questions currently under investigation were first raised in the 1940s and 1950s when such hypotheses as relations between affect and cognition were simply not acceptable to the scientific community. See Bruner, 1992, 1994; Erdelyi, 1974; Greenwald, 1992; Niedenthal and Kitayama, 1994, for discussions about the New Look.

adaptive cognitive responses (e.g., Adolphs et al., 1998; Damasio, 1996). Moreover, there was a growing realization that affect and cognition were closely integrated and that an understanding of one would almost certainly require an understanding of the other (e.g., Oatley and Johnson-Laird, 1987). Thus, there was a burgeoning of theoretical and empirical work focusing specifically on the nature of affect–cognition relations. The results of this body of work in cognitive and social psychology meant that Bruner was able to assert with confidence in 1994 that:

> Everybody agrees, I think, that there is both evidence for as well as adaptive advantages to fast, direct affective arousal that can preadapt and then steer subsequent cognitive processing. (1994, p. 273)

THE INTERACTION OF AFFECT AND COGNITION

In the history of affect–cognition relations, there has been a tendency for investigators interested primarily in emotions to focus on the cognitive antecedents and appraisal strategies that people use to generate emotional responses (Forgas, 2001). In contrast, those who are primarily interested in more pervasive mood effects have typically studied the consequences of mood states on cognitive processes such as attention, memory and social judgments. These different research fields often had minimal relations with each other leading to the impression that cognition and affect were two separate domains. However, on examination of the neural circuits and mechanisms underlying the processes that are involved in affect and cognition, it becomes clear that the processes are intimately connected at multiple levels (Lane and Nadel, 2000;

Phelps, 2006). In the following sections, we will review the classic debate between Robert Zajonc and Richard Lazarus before considering more recent empirical work in some detail.

The Zajonc-Lazarus debate

In a series of articles in the 1980s, Robert Zajonc reviewed a wide range of evidence that he interpreted as supporting the proposition that affect can be independent of cognition (Zajonc, 1980, 1984). He was careful to point out that affect was not always independent of cognition, but that affective and cognitive processes were co-ordinated by separate systems and, therefore, could potentially operate entirely independently of each other. His hypothesis was that the affective tone of a stimulus is generally identified within the first few milliseconds following sensory registration and is assessed rapidly prior to 'cognitive' processing (Zajonc, 1980). The evidence came from a variety of sources, all demonstrating that our affective and evaluative reactions to particular objects or situations are usually very rapid and are often remembered for much longer than other details of the situation.

Subsequent evidence supports the view that affective reactions are fast (LeDoux, 1996) and play an important role in determining social reactions (Zajonc, 2000). One piece of empirical evidence for the primacy of affect was the mere exposure effect; that repeated exposure to an object leads to increased positive affective reactions towards it, even if people have no explicit recollection of having seen it (Zajonc, 1968; Kunst-Wilson and Zajonc, 1980). In a typical experiment, a large number of meaningless shapes were presented one by one for less than 5 milliseconds each. The short exposure time ensured that people were not aware of what was being presented and, sure enough, when asked to pick out the shapes that had been presented from similar shapes that had not been presented, the success rate was just 50%, indicating chance responding. Thus, people did not recognize the shapes that had been presented previously. However, more interesting results were found when the instructions were changed slightly for a different group of participants. They were asked to pick out the shapes that they preferred. This group of people now chose around 60% of the shapes that had been presented previously. Even though this does not seem like a large increase, 60% is significantly above what would be expected by chance, leading Zajonc (1980) to conclude that 'preferences need no inferences'. In other words, affective reactions (preferences) do not require cognition (recognition).

This view did not go unchallenged, however, and Richard Lazarus (1982, 1984), in a series of articles written in response to Zajonc, argued for the opposite extreme. He believed that an emotion could not be produced without a prior cognitive appraisal. In other words, cognition was considered to be necessary for emotion. Indeed, it has been pointed out that the preference demonstrated in the mere exposure effect is actually very close to the concept of a simple appraisal of valence. The first step in stimulus analysis is the appraisal of whether the object is 'good' or 'bad' (Ellsworth, 1994a). Lazarus addressed many of the points made by Zajonc in addition to presenting other evidence for the *primacy of cognition* in affect–cognition relations. As one example, he argued that the mere exposure effect does not represent evidence for the primacy of affect because a preference does not constitute good evidence for an affective reaction. If someone expresses a preference for Coca-Cola over Pepsi, for example, this is a clear preference but almost certainly does not indicate a strong affective reaction towards either Pepsi or Coke. In addition to challenging the interpretation of much of Zajonc's evidence, Lazarus also presented evidence that cognitive appraisals are crucial for determining the type and intensity of affective response. In a series of now-classic studies, the way in which people appraised a video clip of an aboriginal circumcision ceremony was manipulated by means of different sound tracks (Lazarus, 1966). Participants who were told that the events on the screen showed real boys who were in much pain experienced more intense negative affective reactions, as measured by both self-report and by physiological response, than those who were told that the boys were all actors and that no real pain was involved. Thus, the way in which the video was appraised determined the emotional response to the video.

The debate between Zajonc and Lazarus in the 1980s was useful in terms of putting affect–cognition relations back onto the scientific agenda. However, the debate fizzled out, primarily because of confusion over semantic issues. This was especially true in relation to the definition of 'cognition'. Modern-day cognitive psychologists have no problem with the idea that many cognitive processes can operate outside conscious awareness. Thus, the evidence that preferences do not need conscious awareness would not necessarily be interpreted as evidence that affect is being processed independently of cognition. Many cognitive processes (e.g., implicit memory, subliminal perception etc) have been shown to be independent of conscious cognition. In addition, many appraisal theorists have argued that appraisals can be automatic and unconscious (e.g., Leventhal and Scherer, 1987). Contemporary research, therefore, tends to view the Zajonc–Lazarus debate as creating a rather false dichotomy between affect and cognition.

An alternative way to conceptualize the relations between affect and cognition is to view affect as being an integral part of cognition (Adolphs and Damasio, 2001). This view is supported by a growing body of empirical evidence that affective processes can modulate information processing in a number of domains, including attention, memory, reasoning and decision-making. Moreover, cognitive appraisal theorists also acknowledge that, while emotional responses are usually dependent on prior appraisals, the emotional reactions of a person in a given situation can also influence how that situation will be interpreted (Ellsworth and Scherer, 2003). Affect–cognition relations have been studied extensively in social (Forgas, 2001), cognitive (Bower, 1981), and clinical psychology (Williams et al., 1988) as well as in cognitive neuroscience (Armony and LeDoux, 2000). A selective review of evidence across these disciplines will be undertaken in this chapter and in Chapter 7.

Cognitive models of affect

Appraisal-based models propose that the experience of emotion is determined to a large extent by the way in which a situation is interpreted or appraised by the individual. However, many appraisal models do not provide a particularly good account of the evidence that differentiated emotions can be elicited very rapidly and with little conscious awareness of the nature of the stimulus that elicited the emotion in the first place. While some theories view appraisals as being dynamic components of emotion rather than necessarily being the antecedents of emotion (Ellsworth and Scherer, 2003), there have been relatively few attempts to provide empirical evidence for the mechanisms of automatic appraisal (Smith and Kirby, 2001). However, some *process-based* models have now been developed. Rather than visualizing a single 'appraisal' of a situation, these models propose that appraisals can occur in parallel at multiple levels ranging from very low-level action tendencies right up to high-level conscious decisions (Leventhal and Scherer, 1987; Smith and Kirby, 2000). This is a welcome development, but many of the empirical studies to investigate how cognitive appraisals might elicit emotional responses still tend to rely on subjective self-reports. While subjective evaluations are important and of interest in their own right, it is difficult to see how they can inform us on how automatic appraisal processes might be operating.

The techniques of cognitive neuroscience can be profitably used to investigate the neural correlates of appraisal processes. David Sander and his colleagues, for example, have argued that the amygdala may operate as a *relevance detector*, thus providing a neural structure for a fundamental component of appraisal models: *fast automatic detection of relevance* (Sander et al., 2003, 2005). Brain imaging methodologies provide the opportunity to investigate appraisal processes as they happen rather than relying on later subjective evaluations. To illustrate, one fMRI study has shown that the appraisal of context modulated the magnitude of the amygdala response to a specific event (Kim et al., 2003). In this study, the interpretation of a surprised facial expression was modified by presenting a simultaneous negative 'she has just lost $500' or positive 'she has just won $500' sentence. A negative interpretation of the face was associated with greater signal changes in the right ventral amygdala, while a positive interpretation was associated with greater signal changes in the vmPFC. Thus, the researchers were able to establish a systematic inverse relationship between amygdala and vmPFC activity that was directly related to differences in appraisal (Kim et al., 2003).

Information-processing approaches in cognitive psychology have largely developed quite independently of appraisal-based models. They tend to focus on behavioural methods designed to determine how people orient towards and remember different events and objects in their environment. These models emerged from the so-called 'cognitive revolution' in psychology (Miller, 2003), which defined cognitive psychology as the scientific exploration of the way in which information is collected, modified, interpreted and stored. This approach focused on the direct measurement and analysis of actual cognitive processes rather than focusing on people's subjective interpretation of their own cognitive processes. In general, however, information-processing models of cognition tended to exclude the role of affective states, partly because the overriding metaphor was the computer analogy, and this did not generally incorporate a consideration of emotions and moods (Neisser, 1967). A number of investigators,

BOX 6.2

Information-processing models in cognitive psychology

Cognitive psychology is the scientific discipline that studies mental activities, and cognitive psychologists try to understand the nature of the information processing that underlies our mental activity. Smith and Kosslyn (2006) point out that two concepts are particularly important: mental representations and the processes that operate upon them. A *representation* is a physical state that conveys some meaning or information about the state of the world. For example, words on a page are representations, as are patterns of connections between neurons within the brain. A representation has two key elements. First, the representation has a specific *form*. Thus, we can have a written description of a table and we can have a photograph of a table. The same object is being represented by two different forms. In addition to the form of a representation, we also have the *content* or the *meaning* of the representation. A mental representation does not represent anything unless it occurs within a particular processing system. In other words, mental representations have to be processed in some way in order to convey meaning. A sentence written in Spanish conveys meaning if you understand the language (i.e., you know how to *interpret* the representations). Without the knowledge of how to interpret the words, they remain meaningless lines on a page. Thus, a process is something that transforms information from one form into another. Imagine the example of voice

however, realized that the information-processing approach had a number of advantages for the investigation of affect–cognition relations (e.g., Williams et al., 1988; Eysenck, 1992a). Interestingly, while appraisal theorists use 'appraisal' as the explanation for emotions, information-processing models attempt to understand why appraisal itself is often biased. In other words, the 'explanation' in one theory is the subject matter for another theory. The information-processing models simply took as given the fact that an affective outcome was related to cognitive appraisals and interpretation; the question was why and how these biases in appraisal had come about (e.g., Williams et al., 1988).

The application of information-processing models to emotion and emotional disorders has a number of advantages. First, in utilizing a range of behavioural paradigms this approach can examine whether biases are occurring at an implicit or non-conscious level. For example, a sad person might orient naturally towards the negative rather than the positive aspects of a given situation, but this bias might not be available to conscious awareness. In other words, fairly automatic processes and appraisals may result in the allocation of attentional resources towards threatening or negative stimuli that then produce the conscious impression that the world is a dangerous place. An important point to remember, of course, is that the bias itself may not be conscious. This means that a study focusing on subjective report (e.g., by means of interview or questionnaire) may completely miss the role that processing biases may play in eliciting particular mood states and emotions (Eysenck, 1992a; Williams et al., 1988, 1997).

recognition software that can transform the sounds of spoken words into written words. The *input* (voice) is detected and decoded and then transformed into an *output* (written words) following some well-established rules and principles.

Of course, most complex activities cannot be carried out by means of a single process. Instead, multiple processes work together in a processing system in order to achieve some desired outcome. A key assumption of the information-processing approach in cognitive psychology is the conceptualization of the mind as a multipurpose processing system. It is, thus, easy to see why models derived from computer programming were common in the early days of cognitive psychology (Smith and Kosslyn, 2006).

Information-processing models have been developed across all areas of cognitive psychology including studies of low-level visual and auditory perception, attention, memory, written and spoken language, decision-making, reasoning and problem-solving. See Eysenck and Keane, 1995 and Smith and Kosslyn, 2006, for comprehensive introductions to cognitive psychology. While not everyone agrees that information-processing approaches are the best way to study cognition – see Still and Costall, 1991 – these models have been very influential in the development of both theory and research.

Behavioural techniques derived from experimental cognitive psychology can, however, directly access both implicit (non-conscious) and explicit (conscious) biases, giving them a significant advantage over self-report methods. A further advantage of information-processing approaches is that, by focusing directly on how people process information, they can provide an important link between research at a 'lower' neurobiological level and 'higher-level' social-cognitive approaches in psychology (Dalgleish, 2004). Behavioural techniques designed to assess information processing are very easily combined with brain-imaging techniques to determine the neural mechanisms involved at different stages in information processing. To illustrate, components of the *event-related potential* (ERP), can provide a useful index of when attentional resources are allocated to particular types of information (e.g., positive versus negative valence). Information-processing approaches have been very influential in mainstream cognitive psychology (see Eysenck and Keane, 1995; Smith and Kosslyn, 2006, for overviews) and in the 1980s these models began to be applied to the understanding of emotion and emotional disorders (see Dalgleish, 2004; Williams et al., 1988, 1997; Yiend, 2004, for reviews). Box 6.2 outlines some of the key elements of information processing models.

Current cognitive research investigates how comprehensive mental representations of affect unfold in time (Scherer, 1984) and the neuroanatomical correlates of these processes are also being intensively studied (Adolphs and Damasio, 2001; Sander et al., 2005). On this view, affective processing is seen as being an evolutionary antecedent to more complex forms of cognitive processing. However, these complex forms of cognitive processing are presumed to be dependent upon the guidance provided by affective processing. Affect essentially provides the cognitive system with a representation of the *value* or *significance* of a stimulus, and allows for the production of rapid actions and responses to environmental demands. As pointed out by Adolphs and Damasio (2001), a 'key insight is that cognition must include not only representations of external sensory stimuli, but also representations of the organism that is perceiving those stimuli, including a representation of the biological value of those stimuli to the organism' (p. 45). This is a thoroughly cognitive approach, which essentially re-invents the New Look approach of the 1950s, and emphasizes the notion that affective and cognitive processes are intertwined from very low-level perceptual processes up to complex social judgments.

PROCESSING OF AFFECTIVE INFORMATION: EMPIRICAL DATA

In the investigation of how cognitive and affective processes interact, the direction of influence is not always clear. Thus, as shown in Figure 6.1, a particular emotion or mood state is likely to induce a cognitive bias so that mood-relevant material is then prioritized by the processing system. In turn, of course, such a bias is also likely to influence the ongoing mood state and increase the propensity of experiencing related emotions. This dynamic cycle is also likely to be continually influenced by ongoing individual differences in personality as well as external environmental factors.

Each of us has beliefs and understanding of the world that are derived to a large extent by fundamental cognitive processes:

- perception – how we perceive stimuli and events;
- attention – how we allocate processing resources among competing objects and events;
- interpretation – how we interpret ambiguous situations;
- judgment and decision making – how we decide and judge a variety of events, e.g., chances of winning the lottery, or chances of developing a serious illness;
- memory – the nature of the stimuli or events that we are most likely to remember.

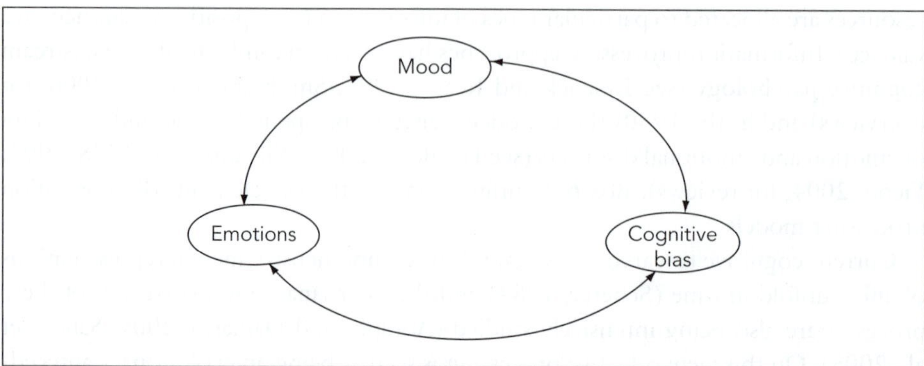

FIGURE 6.1 The relationship between emotions, moods and cognitive bias

Obviously, each of these cognitive processes comprises a range of more detailed subprocesses, and it is clear that a bias in any of these processes is likely to have a strong impact on one's general outlook on life. The following section discusses empirical evidence investigating whether affect modulates early processes of perception and attention. We then go on to discuss studies demonstrating affect–cognition interactions at later stages of information processing (e.g., judgment, decision-making and memory).

Perception and attention

An important problem confronting the sensory systems of any living creature is the need to detect important information among all the irrelevant objects and data that bombard us from moment to moment. Sensory and perceptual processes in the brain are designed for rapid identification and classification of objects across all modalities. Information-processing approaches assume that there are clear limitations and constraints on how much information can be processed at any given time, and this fundamental limitation in capacity leads to a high degree of *selectivity* in attention. Thus, there is a close relationship between perceptual and attentional processes. In other words, our brain is equipped with mechanisms for separating important information from the stream of currently irrelevant information.

One model proposes that once an item has been attended then perceptual mechanisms can more easily identify and classify that object. However, things may not be so simple. There is evidence that extensive perceptual processing may take place *before* attention is allocated to an object. Whether information is identified before or after the allocation of spatial attention is known historically as the early versus late selection debate (see Lavie and Tsal, 1994, for review). The idea that affect might have direct effects on perception is predicated on the notion that the affective significance of an object can be identified prior to attentional processing. Indeed, it is a real puzzle how perceptual processes manage to provide an accurate representation of the external world while at the same time selecting the adaptively relevant features of that world (Bruner, 1994). In addition to being selective, attentional mechanisms need to be highly flexible since what is irrelevant one moment may become relevant the next. Thus, attention needs to be able to move efficiently and speedily from object to object or from location to location (Pashler, 1997; Styles, 1997). It seems reasonable to assume that some processing of affective significance or relevance must take place before perceptual processes have been completed, as was proposed by the New Look psychologists. The determination of what is relevant or salient or what has value is of course crucial to this process and it comes as no surprise to find that many aspects of selective attention do seem to be influenced by the affective significance of sensory events (Vuilleumier, 2005a).

What makes an object or situation affectively significant? Some objects may be affectively significant because they are innate and hard-wired to be always prioritized by the attentional system (e.g., snakes, spiders). Thus, rats do not have to learn to fear cat odour and the scent of a cat tends to command the attention of a rat in a fairly automatic way (Panksepp, 1988). Many stimuli acquire significance because of our learning history and because of the elicitation of selective associations between specific objects and specific emotional responses (LeDoux, 1996). Many factors can determine whether an object becomes infused with affective significance. These include the novelty of a stimulus, its intrinsic pleasantness, its certainty or predictability, the object's general relevance to an individual's goals, the situation's compatibility with personal and social standards and so on. All of these will influence whether a particular object or situation is appraised as significant (see Ellsworth and Scherer, 2003, for review).

A primitive appraisal of valence can ensure that behavioural responses to important stimuli can be prepared rapidly and efficiently (e.g., LeDoux, 1996; Zajonc, 1980, 1998). Thus, the faster the 'good' can be distinguished from the 'bad' the faster an appropriate response can be implemented, leading to greater success in adapting to the environment. This theoretical perspective assumes that a distinction between 'good' (positive stimuli) and 'bad' (negative stimuli) should occur very early in information processing and leads to the hypothesis that an *attentional bias* for negative, especially threat-related, stimuli should be readily apparent. Williams et al. (1988) defined attentional bias as occurring when 'there is a discrete change in the direction in which a person's attention is focused so that he/she becomes aware of a particular part or aspect of his/her stimulus environment' (p. 54). It is important to remember, however, that attentional biases may occur at implicit levels so that people may not always be aware that they have a persistent tendency to selectively notice particular types of information. It is also likely that attentional biases can occur in every sensory modality, although vision has been the most widely studied. Thus, it is likely that biases towards positive (or negative) sounds and smells as well as sights can be identified. Moreover, the evidence indicates that while attentional bias can come under voluntary control in some situations, these biases usually occur automatically.

A bias toward negative or positive material may occur at any stage from very early in sensory processing right up to the explicit evaluation of stimuli. The advantage to the organism in sensing negative material would be likely to induce a bias in the initial allocation of attention. While it is often not easy to determine exactly the point at which a bias might occur, there is a growing body of evidence that negative information is prioritized very early in information processing. To address this issue, we need to make a distinction between direct and indirect influences of affect on perceptual processes. As shown in Figure 6.2, the affective significance of a stimulus could affect perceptual processes indirectly via the enhancement of attentional mechanisms. For example, it is well established that selective attention itself results in improved perceptual processing. Parts of the visual cortex that are involved in the initial registration of stimuli can be activated or enhanced by the allocation of attention to a particular spatial location, and the perception of any object appearing in that location will be enhanced (Brefczynski and DeYoe, 1999). Thus, if the affective significance of a stimulus can lead to increased attentional allocation to itself, then it is likely that perception of that object will also improve. Thus, affect might modulate perception indirectly by influencing attentional processes. It is also possible, of course, that the affective

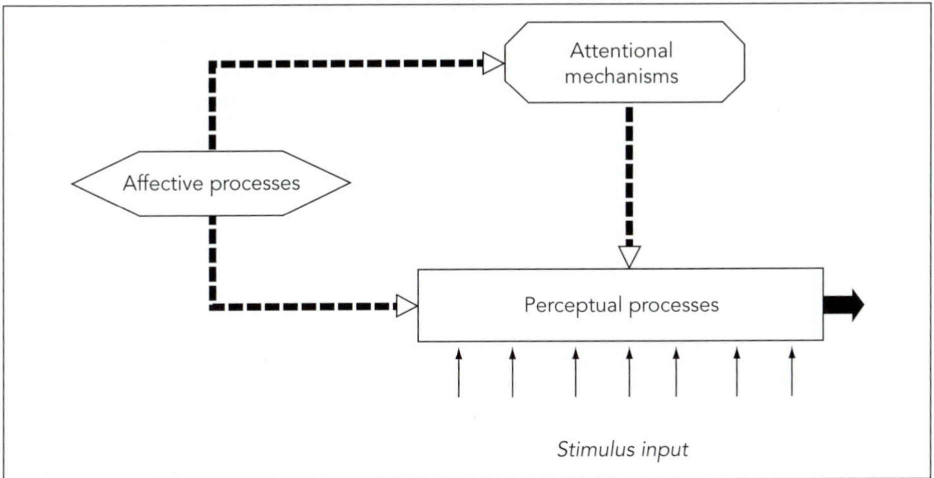

FIGURE 6.2 Direct and indirect effects of affective processes on perceptual processes

significance of a stimulus might have a direct impact on perceptual processes. If affect influences very early processes such as perception and attention then there is of course a large potential for these differences to continue on to later aspects of cognitive processing such as memory, decision-making and social judgment (Phelps, 2006).

Behavioural studies

Within cognitive psychology, several behavioural tasks have been developed to assess the degree to which people may be biased towards a particular type of stimulus (e.g., positive or negative valence – see Table 2.8). Visual search tasks can determine how quick people are to detect a particular class of stimulus. In typical search paradigms, arrays of letters are presented briefly on a computer screen and participants are required to detect a target that might have a particular colour or a particular conjunction of features (e.g., colour and shape). Targets can be presented against backgrounds of varying sizes (e.g., number of background distractors). Typically the time to detect single features such as colour is not affected by display size, whereas the time to detect a conjunction of features is strongly affected by display size (Treisman, 1988). Thus, the speed to detect a red letter among 5 or 30 green letters will be about the same, whereas the time to detect a red A among red and green As and Ts will get progressively slower as the size of the display increases. Anne Treisman and others have argued that these results show that single features 'pop-out' of a crowded display while *conjunctions* of features can only be detected by a slow serial search. Thus, attention must be allocated to each location in the display so that the two features (e.g., red and A) can be bound together (see Styles, 1997, for overview). Visual search tasks have been modified to investigate how quickly negative and positive stimuli can be detected. In other words, do negative items 'pop out of the crowd?' In a typical task, an array of objects is presented on a computer screen (usually for less than 1 second) and

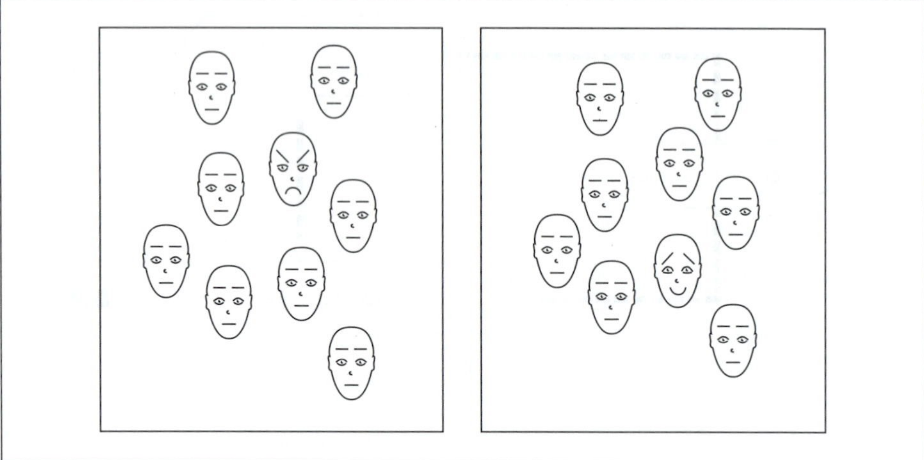

FIGURE 6.3 Example of discrepant displays in a visual search task
The left panel shows a threatening expression among neutral expressions, while the right-hand panel shows a friendly face among neutral expressions. These schematic threatening and friendly faces were developed by Daniel Lundqvist and Arne Öhman at the Karolinska Institute in Sweden and are reproduced here with permission.

the person has to indicate whether a particular object (e.g., angry facial expression) is present or absent by pressing one of two buttons. In studies that vary the affective significance of stimuli it is more common to require people to indicate whether the display contains all the same items by pressing one button or whether there is a discrepant item in the display by pressing another. Examples from discrepant trials with schematic facial expressions are shown in Figure 6.3.

In an early study, visual search was used to assess how quickly people could detect photographs of real faces with angry and happy expressions (Hansen and Hansen, 1988). It was found that people were faster to pick out angry faces relative to happy faces, indicating an allocation of attention towards the angry facial expressions. These findings were referred to as a 'threat-superiority effect' since it seemed that the threatening expression was easier to detect than the friendly expression. Moreover, the results also indicated that the speed of detection of angry expressions was relatively unaffected by increasing display size. On the other hand, the detection of a discrepant happy expression was substantially slower in large (9 items) displays relative to small (4 items) ones. This pattern of results led Hansen and Hansen (1988) to conclude that the angry expression popped out of the crowd.

Following publication of this study, however, a number of potential methodological problems were identified. These problems related to the use of photographs of real expressions in this type of research. It is very difficult to ensure that the faces with different expressions do not differ on some other non-emotional features that may also affect search times. Even when photographs of the same individual are used to represent different expressions there may still be some low-level visual differences between the different expressions. In fact, this was discovered to be the case in the studies reported by Hansen and Hansen (1988). In subsequent research the same authors discovered that the initial results were almost certainly due to dimples and other non-emotional features of the angry expressions (Hampton et al., 1989), leading some researchers to conclude that only 'confounded faces' pop out of a crowd (Purcell et al., 1996).

Given these problems, the schematic stimuli developed by Arne Öhman and his colleagues, and shown in Figure 6.3, are very important. They have been carefully constructed to ensure that there are exactly the same number of visual feature differences between the angry face and the neutral face as there are between the happy face and the neutral face. Thus, any difference in reaction times between these displays must be attributed to differences in the ease with which the emotional expressions are detected or processed. Using displays similar to those shown in Figure 6.3, it has been confirmed that people are indeed faster to respond when the discrepant item is an angry expression compared to trials with a friendly expression as the discrepant item (Eastwood, 2001; Fox et al., 2000; Öhman, Lundqvist et al., 2001). However, these studies show that while angry expressions are detected more efficiently than happy expressions they do not pop out of the crowd. For example, in one study the addition of distracting faces systematically slowed the overall reaction time, although the degree of slowing was less for angry faces than happy ones (Fox et al., 2000).

The results shown in Figure 6.4 indicate that the search for angry expressions is serial in that attention must move from item to item. However, the speed of attention shifts is faster towards angry rather than happy expressions. Thus, the search slope (i.e., the average delay per item added to the display) was 16 ms for angry targets, compared to 29 ms for happy targets, suggesting that angry expressions were detected more efficiently. These results were subsequently replicated (Eastwood et al., 2001; Öhman, Lundqvist et al., 2001) and support the view that negative stimuli (angry expressions) induce an attentional bias to a greater extent than positive affective stimuli

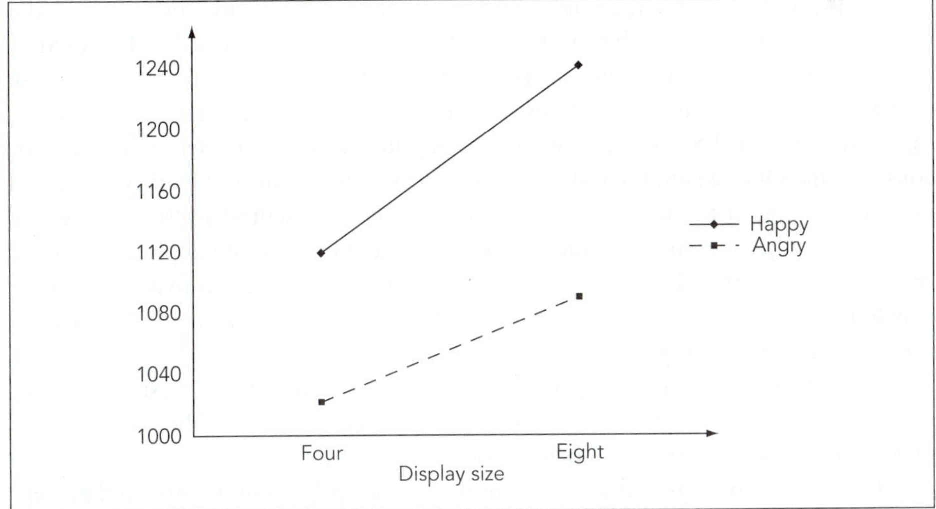

FIGURE 6.4 Speed of detecting angry or happy expressions in a neutral crowd

Source: Adapted from Fox et al. (2000).

(happy expressions). This conclusion was refined by Öhman, Lundqvist et al. (2001) who observed that sad faces did not lead to enhanced detection times. It was only angry expressions that resulted in faster detection. This result suggests that it is the threat value of the angry expressions rather than their negative valence that is driving the results. Although sad and angry expressions are both negatively valenced, only angry expressions are detected more quickly than happy expressions. This result supports the interpretation of Öhman et al.'s findings as threat-superiority effects.

Threat-superiority effects have also been reported with a range of other types of stimuli such as snakes, spiders, guns and syringes (Blanchette, 2006; Brosch and Sharma, 2006; Fox et al., 2007; Öhman, Flykt et al., 2001). Taken together, these results suggest that there may be a default mechanism which rapidly allocates attention toward threat-relevant stimuli. Some of these stimuli may be prioritized because they are innate in that they are of evolutionary significance (e.g., angry facial expressions, snakes, spiders etc), whereas other stimuli may have acquired fear-relevance throughout the life-course (e.g., syringes, guns etc). It is clear, of course, that threat-relevant stimuli are likely to be consistently appraised as highly relevant since they represent potential danger to the organism and therefore these results are also broadly compatible with appraisal-based accounts (Sander et al., 2003, 2005).

In the visual search task, the presence of threat-related material facilitates performance so that responses are speeded when the item is fear-relevant. However, there are a number of paradigms in which the presence of fear-relevant stimuli results in a reduction in performance. These tasks are often called 'interference tasks' as they demonstrate how a particular class of stimulus might interfere with or disrupt an unrelated ongoing task. The prototypical example is the *Stroop task*, which is one of the most widely used attentional tasks in experimental psychology (Stroop, 1935). The original Stroop task presented a series of colour words (red, green, blue etc) printed in different coloured ink and the requirement was to name the colour of the ink as quickly as possible. Not surprisingly, it takes much longer to name the colour of the ink when it conflicts with the meaning of the word (e.g., the word red printed in blue) showing that the meaning of the word interferes with the colour-naming task (see MacLeod, 1991, for review). In the modified version of the Stroop task, often called the emotional Stroop task, words varying in valence are presented in different coloured ink. Once again, the task is simply to name the colour of the ink while ignoring the meaning of the word. Pratto and John (1991) presented a series of negative and positive adjectives in an emotional Stroop task and found that people took significantly longer to name the colours of the negative relative to the positive words. They concluded that there is a general vigilance for negative social information relative to positive social information.

An early bias toward negative material makes a lot of sense, of course, since the consequences of missing a threat such as a predator are far worse then the consequences of missing a positive stimulus such as food. However, the question remains as to whether the affective significance of a stimulus can actually result in improved perception. In other words, in the presence of a negative stimulus are we actually more likely to see or hear better? Research conducted by Liz Phelps and her colleagues indicates

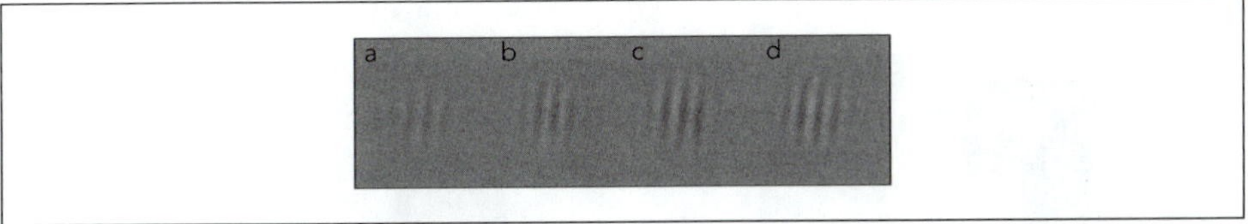

FIGURE 6.5 An example of 'Gabor' stimuli
Source: Phelps et al. (2006).

that the answer to this question is 'yes'. They based their assessment of perceptual acuity on the orientation of Gabor stimuli (see Figure 6.5). The contrast of these images can be varied, thus providing a good measure of perceptual sensitivity.

In their first experiment, a fearful or a neutral face was presented at the centre of the computer screen for 75 ms. Following a blank screen for 50 ms, four Gabor stimuli (1 tilted, 3 upright) were then presented for 40 ms. The 165 ms interval between the onset of the face and the disappearance of the Gabor stimuli was deliberately chosen to ensure that no eye-movements would take place, ensuring that the task was completed under conditions of covert attention. The results demonstrated that the level of contrast needed to perform the orientation discrimination task was lower when a stimulus followed a fearful face relative to a neutral face. These results indicate that the emotional expression of the face can alter a very early visual process: an affective stimulus actually influenced the quality of visual perception (Phelps et al., 2006).

In a second experiment, these authors addressed the question of whether affect would potentiate the effect of covert attention on perception. As shown in Figure 6.6, faces were now used as attentional cues. Participants were instructed to keep focused on the central fixation and either one or four faces were displayed. In a single, or focused cue condition a single face was presented in one of four locations to elicit focused transient attention to that location. In the multiple, or distributed cue condition four faces were presented in each of the four locations so that attention was spread more evenly across the display. The single cues resulted in higher contrast sensitivity than the multiple cues, indicating that focused attention enhanced contrast sensitivity. Observers were also found to be more sensitive to contrast when the faces had a fearful expression than a neutral expression. As in the first experiment, perception was improved by the presence of a fearful expression. However, the more interesting result was the finding that the effects of emotion and attention interacted. Emotion had a greater effect for the single-cue condition than for the multiple-cue condition, and the highest sensitivity occurred when the cue was a single fearful face.

This pattern of results demonstrates that manipulating emotion in conjunction with attention increased contrast sensitivity well beyond the benefits of either emotion or attention alone. In other words, emotion seemed to potentiate or magnify the benefits brought about by the transient allocation of attention. People were better able to see in the presence of emotional stimuli (Phelps et al., 2006). These results provide a strong indication that negative stimuli can have both direct and indirect effects on perception; the indirect effect being the ability to influence perception by

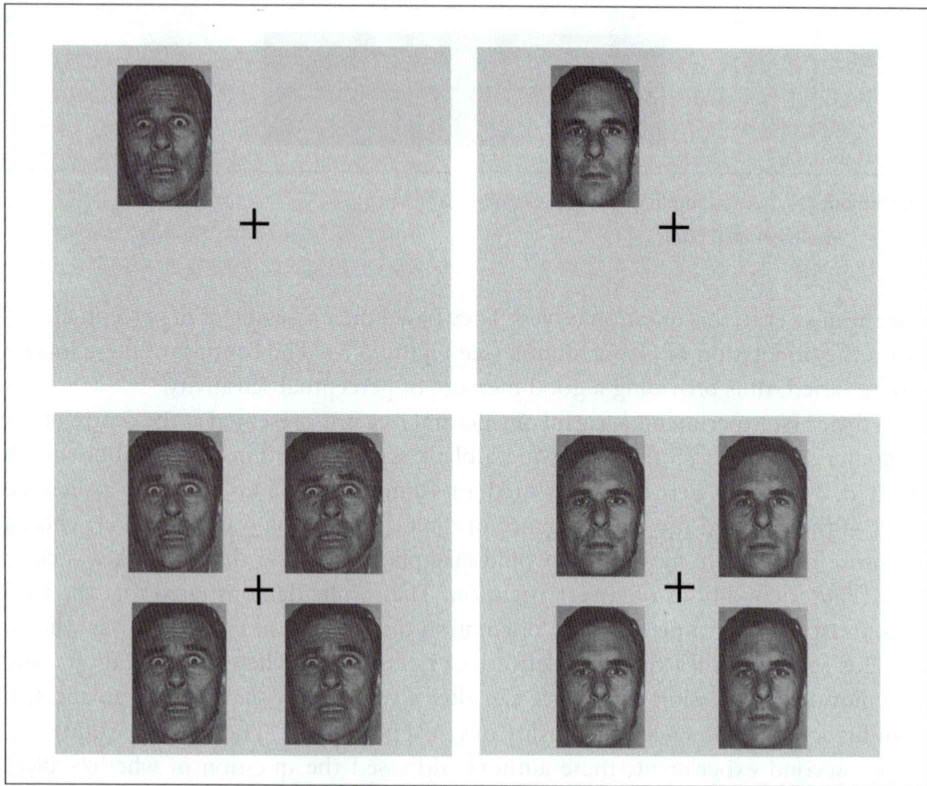

FIGURE 6.6 Cueing conditions
Source: Phelps et al. (2006).

magnifying the impact of attention. The inclusion of positively valenced stimuli to determine whether the negative material has a greater impact on perception than positive material would be an interesting extension to this work. Phelps et al. (2006) only used negative and neutral stimuli, so we cannot tell whether it was the affective nature of the material or the negative valence of the material that influenced perception. Nevertheless, this work provides a clear demonstration that the mere presence of a negative stimulus can have an effect on very basic perceptual processes (Phelps et al., 2006).

Brain imaging studies

The behavioural evidence reviewed above indicates that perceptual acuity can be enhanced by the presence of negative stimuli (Phelps et al., 2006), and that attentional mechanisms are tuned to prioritize negative stimuli relative to positive stimuli (Eastwood et al., 2001; Fox et al., 2000; Öhman, Lundqvist et al., 2001). This prioritization of negative material would also explain why these stimuli are difficult to ignore, and therefore interfere with competing tasks when they are presented as to-be-ignored distractors (Pratto and John, 2001). It makes perfect sense that negative stimuli, especially those representing potential danger, would be prioritized for cognitive processing. In line with this view, there is now substantial evidence that the neural representation of negative stimuli is indeed boosted relative to neutral stimuli (see Vuilleumier, 2005a, for review).

Several neuroimaging studies have shown that amygdala activity correlates with enhanced activity of neurons in the extrastriate cortex in the presence of emotional stimuli. Since the extrastriate cortex is involved with sensory processing, these findings are consistent with the hypothesis that emotional stimuli can boost sensory processing. For example, in early studies photographs of faces were presented to participants and an enhancement of activity in visual cortical areas was observed with both PET (Morris, Friston et al., 1998) and fMRI (Surguladze, Brammer et al., 2003) when the facial expressions related to danger (e.g., fear, disgust). A similar boost of activity in occipital and temporal cortical areas has also been reported for pictures of complex scenes (e.g., IAPS pictures) when they relate to aversive events relative to neutral or pleasant events (e.g., Lane et al., 1998; Lang et al., 1998). All of these studies are consistent with the idea that the affective significance of a stimulus can boost the sensory representation of that stimulus, especially when it relates to threat or potential danger. An important question to ask, however, is whether affective stimuli lead to a general enhancement in cortical activity or whether the sensory processing is enhanced specifically for stimuli associated with the nature of the eliciting stimulus. In other words, if a fearful face increases visual cortical activity (e.g., Morris, Friston et al., 1998) does this occur in regions specific to face processing or is it more general? This question was directly addressed in an important study examining emotion–attention interactions by means of fMRI (Vuilleumier et al., 2001).

Vuilleumier et al. (2001) capitalized on the fact that specific regions of the visual cortex respond to faces (fusiform cortex – sometimes called the *fusiform face area*, FFA) whereas other areas respond to pictures of houses and places (parahippocampal gyrus). As shown in Figure 6.7, pairs of faces and pairs of houses were presented in a vertical and horizontal alignment. Participants were instructed to keep focused on the central fixation and then they had to match either the horizontal or the vertical images. This design allowed for a separate assessment of the effects of spatial attention and the effects of the emotional expression of the faces. Thus, people's attention (i.e., houses or faces) could be assessed, and in addition the impact of the presence of a fearful expression on brain reactivity could be assessed independently of spatial attention. The results showed that, as expected, greater activity occurred in the fusiform gyrus when faces were attended rather than houses, with no increase in activity in the parahippocampal gyrus. Conversely, there was greater activity in the parahippocampal gyrus when attention was paid to houses rather than faces. This modulation of activity occurred equally for both fearful and neutral expressions. However, fusiform activity was also enhanced by fearful expressions, regardless of whether the faces were attended. Thus, the mere presence of a fearful expression resulted in increased activity in the fusiform gyrus even when the faces were not being attended (see Figure 6.8).

A similar pattern of activation was observed for the amygdala. As expected, amygdala activity increased when fearful expressions were attended (e.g., Morris et al.,

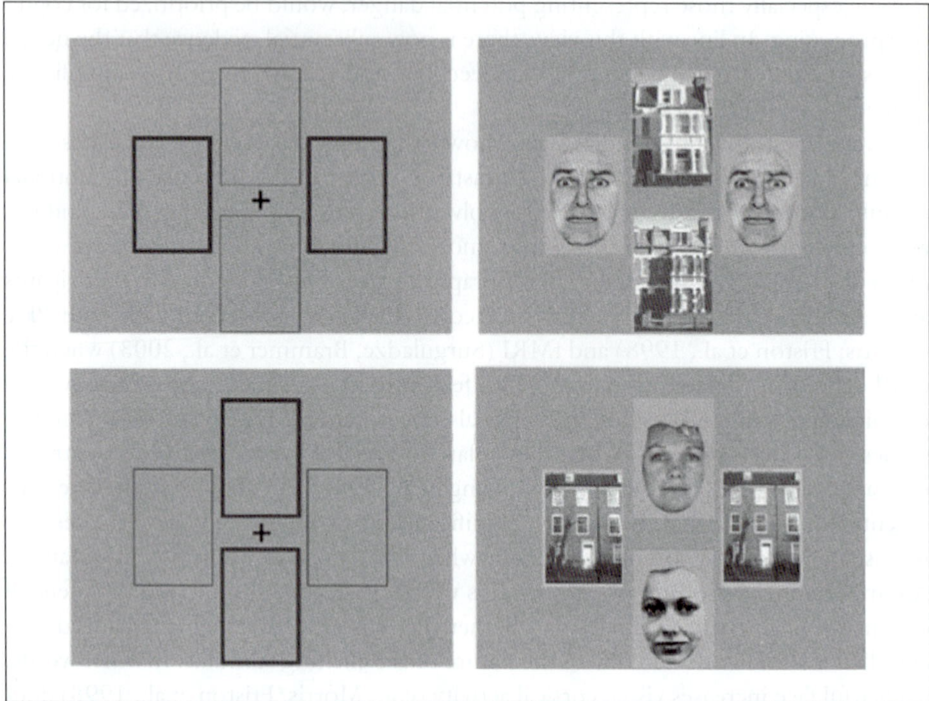

FIGURE 6.7 Interaction between emotions and attention
Source: Vuilleumier et al. (2001).

1998), but Vuilleumier and his colleagues found that the degree of activation was not modulated by spatial attention. As shown in Figure 6.9, the degree of amygdala activity in response to fearful faces did not decrease when the faces were unattended. These results are important in suggesting a potential neural mechanism that would allow the visual system to prioritize the processing of stimuli with threat value (Vuilleumier et al., 2001). The enhancement of responses in the sensory cortex (fusiform gyrus) to fearful relative to neutral faces would allow these stimuli to be noticed before other, less salient, stimuli.

This neural mechanism is unlikely to be specific to the visual modality since a similar pattern of results has recently been reported for the auditory modality. The mere presence of an angry voice enhanced activity in the superior temporal sulcus (STS)

Notes to Figure 6.8

(a) fMRI shows increased activity in the fusiform gyri in both hemispheres when participants attended to faces versus houses, regardless of emotion expression.
(b) Activity in the right fusiform gyrus demonstrating greatly attenuated responses when faces appeared at task-irrelevant locations as compared to relevant locations but still a significant response when task-irrelevant faces had a fearful expression.
(c) Estimates of activity for the right fusiform gyrus in each condition, confirming that its response not only increased when faces were attended, regardless of expression, but also increased when faces were fearful rather than neutral, regardless of the attentional manipulation.

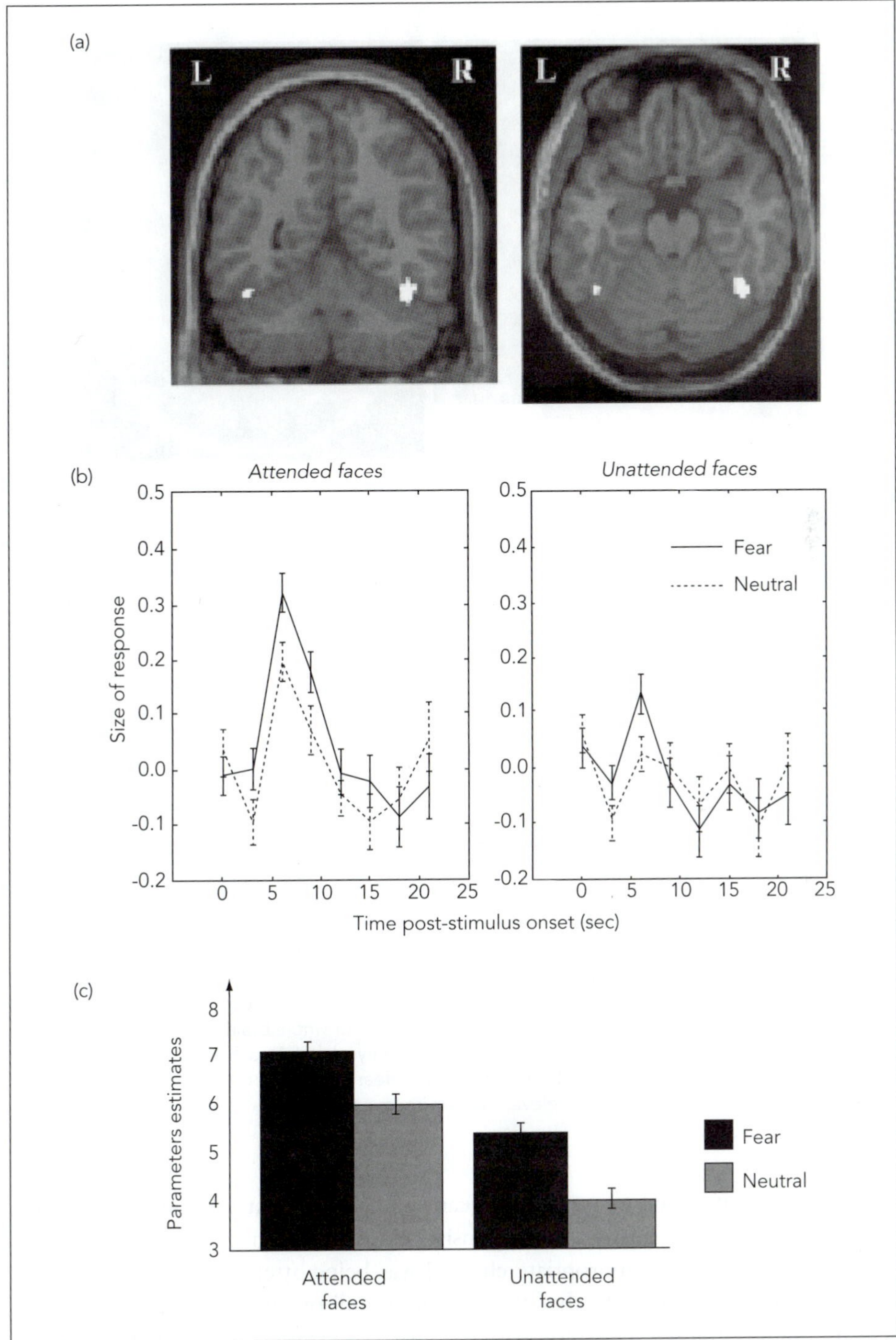

FIGURE 6.8 Activity in the fusiform gyrus caused by emotion–attention interactions

Source: Vuilleumier et al. (2001).

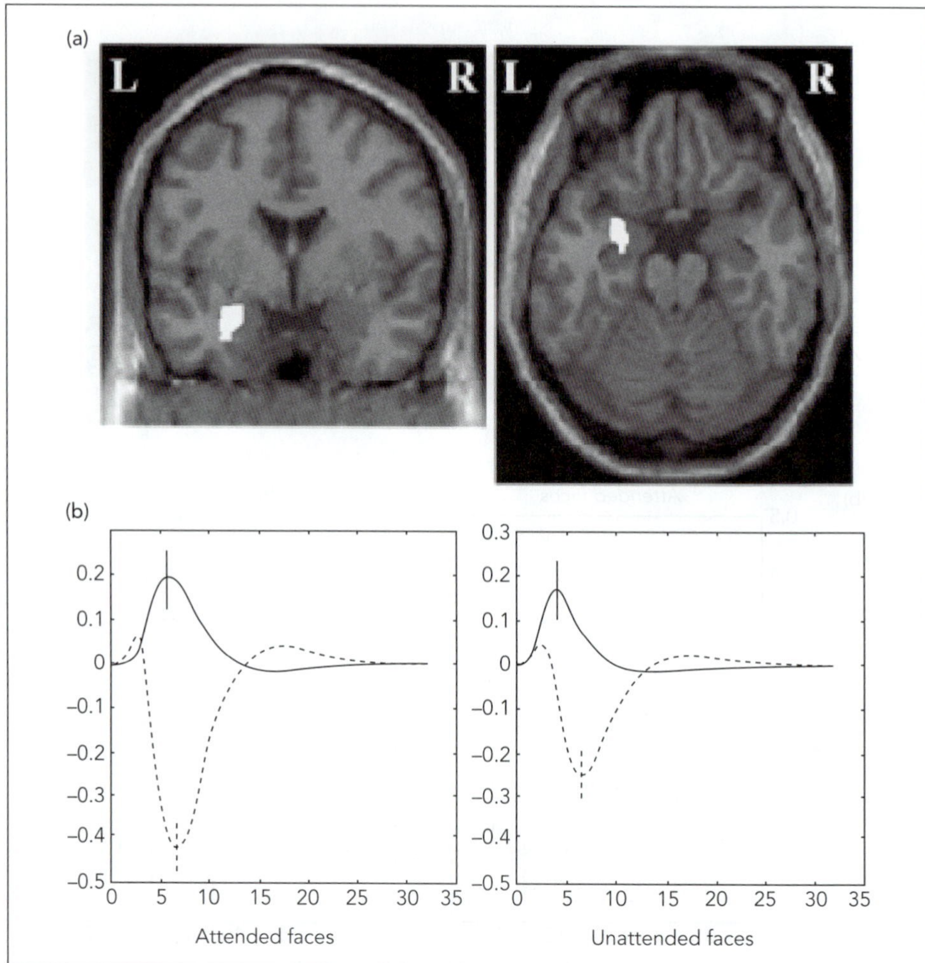

FIGURE 6.9 Activity in the amygdalae caused by emotion–attention interactions

(a) Activation of the left amygdala produced by fearful expression of faces, regardless of the spatial attention manipulation. Group results are superimposed on a single-subject T1-weighted MRI (activated voxels at $p = 0.05$, corrected for whole brain).

(b) Illustration of the hemodynamic response in the left amygdala for each experimental condition, showing that the magnitude of activation elicited by fearful face expression did not significantly differ when faces appeared at the relevant versus irrelevant locations.

Source: Vuilleumier et al. (2001).

whether it was attended or not (Grandjean et al., 2005). At the same time, selective attention also modulated the responsiveness of this region in that activity was always greater when the appropriate channel was being attended (see Figure 6.10). These results clearly indicate that threat-related auditory information can enhance sensory brain responses. Thus, for both the visual modality and the auditory modality, it seems that the mere presence of threat-related information can boost sensory processing. This would provide a neural mechanism allowing for affectively significant stimuli to be prioritized for further processing.

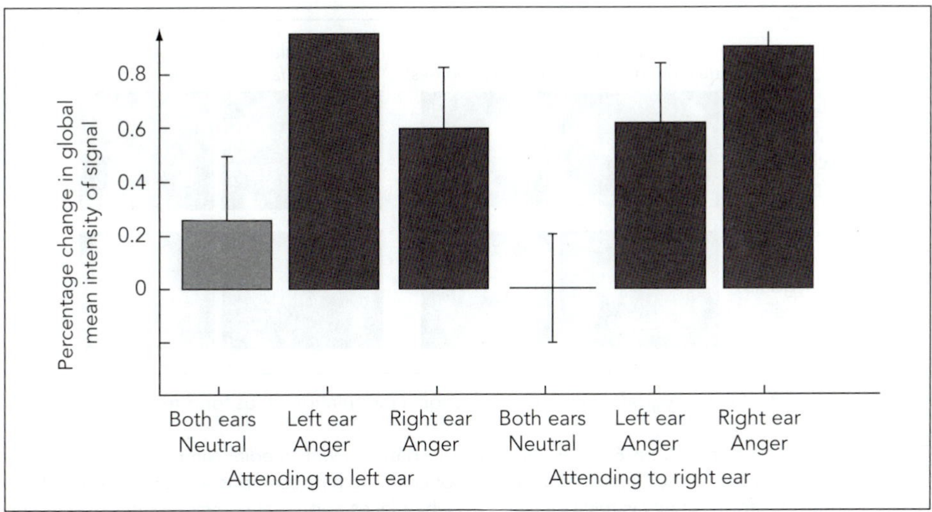

FIGURE 6.10 Estimates of activity in the right STS
Blood oxygenation level-dependent responses were higher for angry versus neutral speech, irrespective of the side of angry speech and the side of selective listening. In addition, responses were also increased during attention to the left compared to the right ear, irrespective of prosody.

Source: Grandjean et al. (2005).

How might the boosting of the neural representation of negative stimuli occur? One clue comes from the findings that activity in cortical sensory areas correlates with amygdala activity in the presence of threat-related visual stimuli (e.g., Morris et al., 1998). This pattern has led to the hypothesis that the amygdala may play a crucial role in modulating the enhanced sensory response to stimuli with a high threat-value. Correlations are very useful in terms of generating hypotheses but they cannot be used to sort out the direction of influence. Thus, it is impossible to determine from many previous studies whether the amygdala is projecting information to the visual cortex, thus enhancing sensory processing, or whether increased activation of the sensory cortex modulates the amygdala response. A recent study by Patrik Vuilleumier and his colleagues directly addressed this question by investigating patients with different types of brain lesions. Twenty-six patients with lesions in the medial temporal lobe were tested in the selective attention task in which attention could be directed towards either houses or faces. All of the patients had lesions within the hippocampus, and half also had damage to the amygdala. The results showed that all patients showed enhanced activity in the fusiform gyrus when they directed attention to the faces, showing that these extrastriate visual areas were intact and normally activated by faces. However, the results for fearful and neutral expressions showed that the enhanced fusiform activity was replicated only for the patients with intact amygdalae. Patients with damage to the amygdala did not show any fear-related increase in fusiform activation (see Figure 6.11). These results strongly suggest that the amygdala can have a direct modulatory role on the visual cortex. In other words, the presence of negative stimuli activates cells in the amygdala, which then results in an increased activation of cells in the sensory cortex.

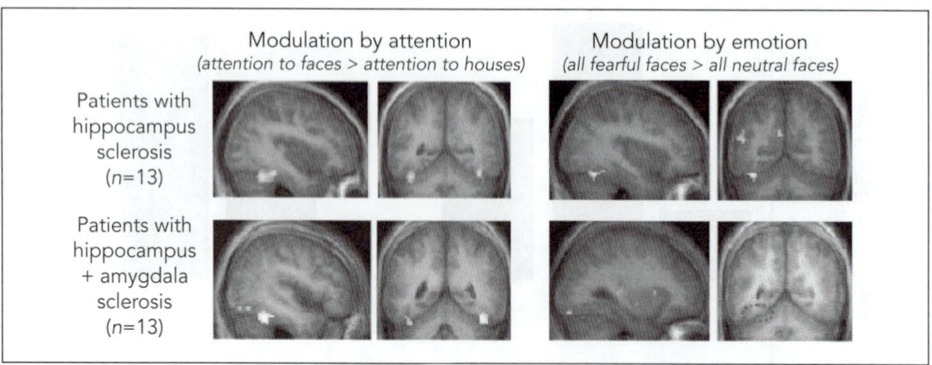

FIGURE 6.11 Effects of amygdala damage on emotional modulation of fusiform responses to fearful faces

The fMRI paradigm from Figure 6.8 was employed in patients with medial temporal lobe sclerosis whose damage involved either hippocampus alone or both the hippocampus and amygdala. In both patient groups, fusiform activity is reliably increased when faces appear at relevant relative to ignored locations (left-side panels), indicating that these face-sensitive visual areas are structurally and functionally intact. By contrast, additive enhancement of fusiform activity by fearful expressions is still observed in patients with hippocampal sclerosis (and intact amygdala), but lost in patients with amygdala sclerosis, revealing distant functional consequences of amygdala damage on intact visual regions.

Source: Vuilleumier and Pourtois (2007).

The foregoing results indicate that affective stimuli can be prioritized by at least two neural mechanisms. First, threat-related stimuli may directly activate the amygdala, which then rapidly modulates the sensory cortex by means of feedback loops to allow more extensive and in-depth processing of the salient stimuli. Second, the affective stimuli might directly activate parietal and frontal regions of the brain that are involved with attentional control, and these areas then project to sensory processing areas. This second mechanism is suggested by the results of the impact of spatial attention on cortical activity. The two mechanisms are, of course, consistent with behavioural evidence for an enhancement of perceptual acuity (Phelps et al., 2006) and an increased allocation of attention (e.g., Fox et al., 2000; Hansen and Hansen, 1988) towards threat-related stimuli.

Further evidence for a direct influence of amygdala on visual cortex comes from studies examining people with damage to the right parietal region who experience left spatial neglect. These patients tend to neglect the left-hand side of space and when two objects are presented to the left and right visual fields at the same time, the object on the left tends to be 'extinguished' or missed. Thus, the mechanisms of spatial attention have gone awry, so that attention is not allocated to the left visual field when there are objects in both visual fields. However, these patients are less likely to extinguish emotional faces relative to neutral faces (Fox, 2002; Vuilleumier and Schwartz, 2001). Put the other way, these patients are more likely to notice faces with emotional expressions. In one study a man with left spatial neglect missed 73% of faces with a neutral expression that were presented to his neglected field. However, he missed only 43% of fearful expressions and 53% of happy expressions (Fox, 2002). A very similar

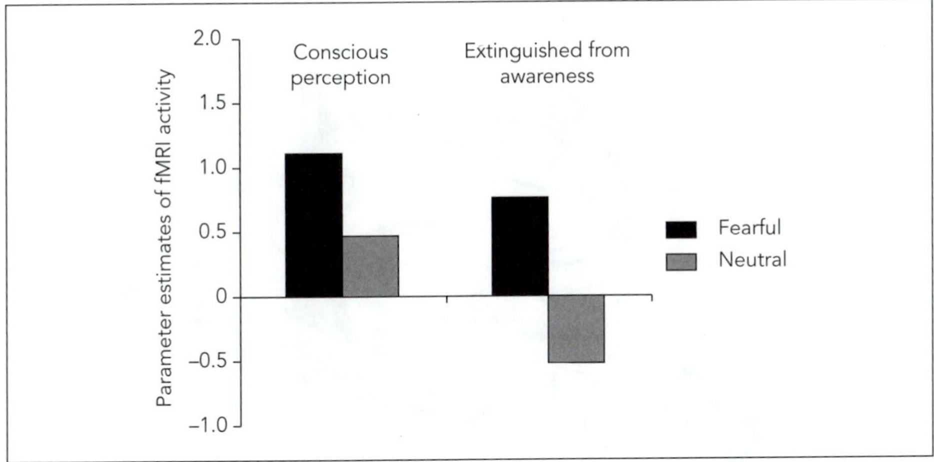

FIGURE 6.12 Activity in right fusiform in a patient with right parietal cortex damage and left spatial neglect

Source: Adapted from Vuilleumier et al. (2002).

pattern of results was reported by Vuilleumier and Schwartz (2001). These results support the hypothesis that affective stimuli can enhance sensory processing even in the absence of spatial attention. It is interesting to note that in both of these studies no difference was found between negative and positive facial expressions.

More direct evidence for the hypothesis that affective stimuli can influence sensory processing without spatial attention was reported in an fMRI study by Vuilleumier and colleagues (2004). A patient with left neglect was scanned while faces were presented to his 'blind' visual field. In spite of damage to the right parietal region, this patient showed a normal enhancement of the right fusiform cortex when presented with fearful relative to neutral expressions in the left visual field. The enhancement was strongest for those faces that were noticed, but, importantly, was still observed when the faces were not consciously seen. The pattern of results found with this individual patient are shown in Figure 6.12. Once again, they show additive effects of spatial attention and emotional expression on activity in the sensory cortex.

There is now substantial evidence from neuroimaging experiments that the amygdala is a crucial structure in the enhancement of affectively significant stimuli. The amygdala is ideally positioned for this role because (1) it receives multiple sensory inputs from every modality, and (2) it sends projections to many subcortical and cortical regions. Thus, the amygdala is capable of influencing (and being influenced by) multiple perceptual and cognitive processes. Figure 6.13 shows direct projections from neurons within the amygdaloid complex to all cortical stages along the ventral visual system. As we have seen, neuroimaging evidence indicates that threat-related visual (Vuilleumier et al., 2001) and auditory (Grandjean et al., 2005) stimuli enhance the activation of the appropriate regions of the sensory cortex, which would explain why perceptual acuity is enhanced in the locations occupied by threat-related stimuli (Phelps et al., 2006).

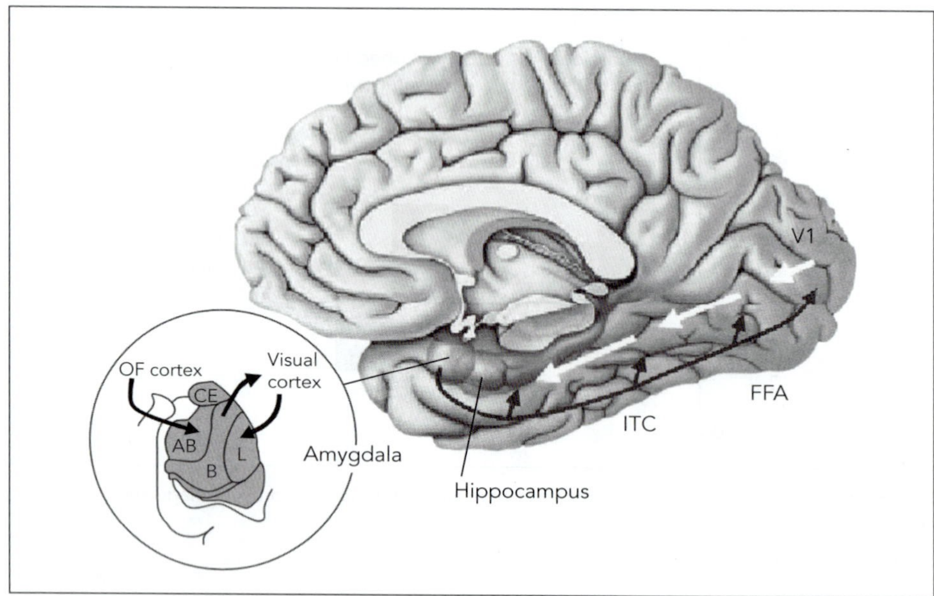

FIGURE 6.13 Feedback connections between amygdala and visual cortex
Source: Vuilleumier (2005b).

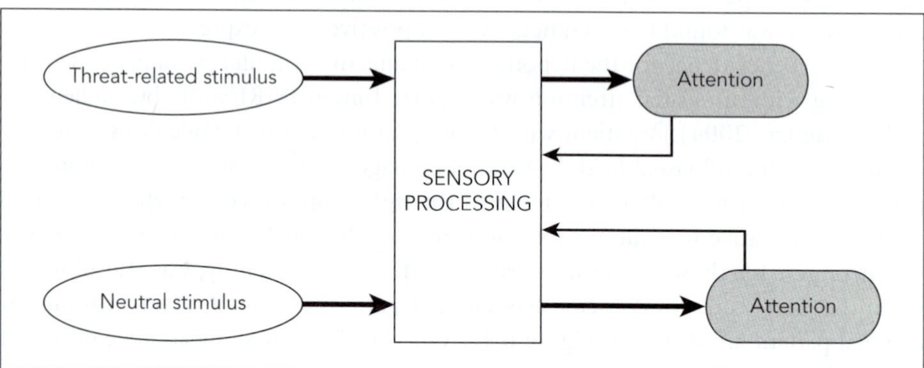

FIGURE 6.14 A simplified model of how threat-related stimuli may be prioritized by neural mechanisms

To summarize, neuroimaging evidence now suggests that the degree of cortical activity occuring in the presence of affective stimuli can be modulated by the activation of the amygdala as well as being influenced by spatial attention. A highly simplified schematic model of how threat-related stimuli might be prioritized for further processing is outlined in Figure 6.14. Sensory processing in cortical areas is enhanced for threat-related stimuli so that these items are more likely to win the competition for attentional mechanisms. This boosting of sensory processing is possibly due to the activation of the amygdala which then modulates sensory cortical areas.

The time course of affective processing

The foregoing evidence from neuroimaging studies suggests that stimuli representing danger are prioritized by an amplification of responses in sensory cortices that is modulated by the amygdala. This prioritization should lead to much faster processing of negative stimuli than positive. A problem with fMRI and PET data is the difficulty in determining the time course of the various stages of information processing, because the temporal resolution of these techniques is poor. The behavioural data do, however, indicate that threat-related stimuli are processed more quickly than positive or neutral stimuli.

However, the temporal resolution of behavioural data is also suboptimal. We know that both affect and attention are typified by very fast subprocesses that occur well within the first 500 millisecs of stimulus onset (e.g., Mangun and Hillyard, 1995). Behavioural indices that rely on reaction times, such as in the visual search and Stroop tasks, almost certainly reflect response selection and preparation processes as well as perceptual processing differences. In other words, in the visual search task attention might be allocated equally quickly toward positive and negative material but responses are then selected more quickly for the negative stimuli. This enhancement of response selection for negative material would, of course, explain facilitation when the negative material has to be detected combined with interference when the same material has to be ignored. The idea that responses might be selected faster for negative stimuli seems a reasonable assumption given that the presence of threat (e.g., a predator) might require more rapid and efficient motor responses than neutral or positive material. Thus, the behavioural data cannot determine whether faster reaction times to negative stimuli are due to faster perceptual or attentional processes, or whether they are due to faster preparation of motor responses.

Direct measures of brain activity that have good temporal resolution can help to address this question. In particular, event-related brain potentials (ERPs) derived from electroencephalographic (EEG) recordings can provide precise moment-to-moment information regarding the temporal allocation of attention. ERPs can be broken down into different components, each of which is assumed to reflect different stages of information processing. To illustrate, the P100 is a positive component of the ERP that is maximal over the occipital lobe and reaches a peak between 100 and 150 msec after the onset of a stimulus. The P100 is produced by neural activity in the striate cortex and is known to reflect changes in the allocation of attention. If participants are instructed to attend to a stimulus in one location and to ignore those in another location, the P100 increases for the occurrence of targets in the attended area (Clark and Hillyard, 1996).

Several studies have examined the P100 component for the early differentiation of positive and negative material that has been suggested by behavioural studies (e.g., Fox et al., 2000; Hansen and Hansen, 1988; Pratto and John, 1991). Participants were required to evaluate a series of both positive and negative IAPS pictures while ERPs were being recorded (Smith et al., 2003). The results showed that P100 amplitudes were indeed larger for negative pictures than for positive pictures. Given that the P100 component measures early attention allocation in the extrastriate cortex, these results support the behavioural evidence for the enhanced detection of negative stimuli being due to the early allocation of attention (Hansen and Hansen, 1988; Pratto and John, 1991). While differences at the stage of response selection may have played some role in the behavioural results, the ERP data indicate that the behavioural results cannot be entirely due to differences in the speed of response selection

A more recent study provides further evidence that negative affective stimuli can modulate very early ERP components (Pourtois et al., 2004). Pairs of faces with fearful and neutral expressions were presented briefly side-by-side on a computer screen, followed by a white rectangular bar on one side or the other. On 'go' trials participants had to categorize the bar as being either horizontal or vertical. Participants were better at detecting the orientation of the bar when it replaced a fearful face than when it replaced a happy face. ERPs were measured on 'no-go' trials to avoid any complications due to motor preparation effects. On these trials the pair of faces was presented exactly as before but participants did not have to respond to the bar. The results showed that the amplitude of the P100 component was significantly larger when the target appeared in the location of the fearful expression relative to the happy face. Thus, it seems that the fearful facial expressions elicited a rapid orienting of spatial attention towards their own location. These results can be explained by two different mechanisms. First, they may be due to an indirect orienting or attentional effect that is driven by fronto-parietal regions of the brain. Second, the results may be due to a direct sensory facilitation for threat-related stimuli (Vuilleumier and Pourtois, 2007).

Other research suggests that emotional stimuli may have direct effects on sensory processing. This is indicated by findings that negative information can lead to enhancement of an even earlier component of the ERP (Pourtois et al., 2004; Stolarova et al., 2006). Research on ERPs has demonstrated that an early negative deflection occurs about 60–90 msec after the onset of a stimulus. This deflection – called the C1 component – is thought to be the earliest response of the primary visual cortex to a stimulus (Di Russo et al., 2003). In the study by Pourtois et al. (2004) discussed above, a C1 component was detected at about 90 msec, which was enhanced for fearful relative to happy faces. A subsequent study discovered that the C1 component was indeed enhanced for negative stimuli that had been learned, and that the enhancement increased as the affective meaning of the stimulus became clearer (Stolarova et al., 2006). This study is important because the C1 component was measured for stimuli that were initially affectively neutral, which then became associated with either aversive or neutral pictures in a conditioning paradigm. To achieve this, a series of IAPS pictures that were either aversive (e.g., mutilated bodies, attack scenes) or neutral (e.g., landscapes, people) were presented as unconditioned stimuli (UCS) in a learning experiment. Some of the checkerboard gratings were always preceded by aversive IAPS pictures (CS+) while others were always preceded by neutral IAPS pictures (CS–). This procedure led to successful conditioning, as confirmed by an enhanced startle response to the CS+ stimuli relative to the CS– stimuli during the conditioning blocks, while no differences in startle occurred at baseline or during an extinction phase. Moreover, over 83% of the participants rated the stimulus used as

CS+ as being less pleasant than the one used as CS–. Thus, even though affectively negative IAPS pictures are a relatively mild threat relative to electric shock or loud noise, they were successful in inducing a conditioned response. These conditioned CS+ stimuli elicited a more negative C1 deflection than the CS– at parietal electrode sites throughout the conditioning blocks, and this C1 component was found to originate in the striate cortex. The enhanced C1 component occurred in response to previously neutral stimuli that had been aversively conditioned. These results thus rule out the possibility that the differentiation of affectively negative stimuli soon after stimulus onset might be due to low-level visual differences between the aversive and neutral stimuli. Importantly, the fact that aversive stimuli can enhance the C1 component 65–90 msec after the onset of a stimulus strongly suggests a direct effect on neurons in the sensory cortex. Because of the short latency of the C1 component, it is unlikely to be directly influenced by either cortical or subcortical feedback (Stolarova et al., 2006). Instead, it seems more likely that sensory processes are being directly enhanced for aversive stimuli, supporting the notion that threat appraisals occur very rapidly (e.g., LeDoux, 1996; Zajonc, 1980). To date, no studies have examined appetitive stimuli, so it is impossible to determine whether this very early enhancement of brain responses to affective stimuli is specific to aversive stimuli or whether it would also occur for approach-related appetitive stimuli. This is an important question for future research.

Judgment and decision-making

Given the substantial evidence that affect can exert strong attention-bias effects on neural mechanisms, it is likely that the same affective features of the environment might also have a profound effect on how we judge and evaluate our surroundings. Making decisions about important life events (e.g., what to study at university, who to marry, whether or not a job offer should be accepted) are crucial and nearly always associated with affective significance. A growing body of empirical research suggests that affect does influence how we make decisions and how we evaluate a variety of social situations. Some evidence has come from the investigation of people who have suffered brain damage, and the loss of certain affective signals has led to a disruption of their ability to make basic decisions. Other work in social psychology has shown that ongoing mood states can have a profound influence on how people evaluate a variety of social situations, as well as how they judge their own general satisfaction with life. Related to this there are a number of empirical studies suggesting that mood states can influence a range of judgments relating to subjective risk.

Is affective processing necessary for effective decision-making?

When we are faced with a risky choice, it is known that a SCR is elicited. Antonio Damasio and his colleagues have argued that this SCR signal can act as a *somatic marker* to provide an important aid to decision-making (Bechara et al., 1994, 1996, 1997; Damasio, 1999). A large body of research has outlined a clear neurobiological mechanism that is hypothesized to underlie everyday decision-making based on 'gut reactions' or 'hunches' (e.g., Bechara et al., 1996, 1997; Damasio, 1994, 1999). The central idea is that somatic states can be generated by both *primary inducers* (i.e., innate or learned stimuli that cause positive or negative emotional states) and *secondary inducers* (i.e., a memory of a real or hypothetical primary inducer, which when brought into working memory can itself induce a somatic state).

Primary inducers (e.g., a venomous snake) are thought to activate the amygdala directly, which in turn triggers a somatic state by causing the release of several neurotransmitters in the brain stem area. The cell bodies of all of the major neurotransmitter systems (e.g., dopamine (DA), serotonin (5-HT), noradrenaline (NA) and acetlycholine (Ach)) are located in the brain stem. The axon terminals of these neurotransmitter systems interact with cells throughout the cerebral cortex as well as in the basal ganglia and thalamus. This neurochemical mechanism therefore provides a plausible means by which somatic states could exert a strong biasing effect on a range of behaviours, feelings and cognitive processes.

While the induction of somatic states from primary inducers is dependent upon the amygdala, the induction of somatic states generated by secondary inducers (e.g., a memory of being bitten by a snake) appears to be dependent upon cortical circuitry of which the vmPFC plays a central role. In particular, it seems that the vmPFC can couple together knowledge of secondary inducers to somatic state patterns that are related to how it 'feels' to be in a given situation. For example, recalling an occasion when you learned that you had passed an important examination could lead to a coupling of that memory with an appropriate somatic state.

Anatomical studies have revealed that there are multiple connections in the brain between the amygdala and the vmPFC, and the cell bodies of the major neurotransmitter systems within the brain stem (Blessing, 1997). One implication of this is that changes in the activity of different neurotransmitter systems can be detected as somatic states which cannot be detected by physiological changes in the body itself. This is what Damasio and his colleagues call the 'as if body loop'. They propose that the activation of representations of somatic states in the brain stem (by means of a secondary inducer) can result in changes in neurotransmitter release without actually engaging the body. In other words, somatic states can be simulated within the brain in the 'as if body loop'. Thus, the amygdala may be involved in emotional situations that require a rapid response, whereas the vmPFC may be engaged in emotional situations driven by thoughts and reflection. Figure 6.15 presents a schematic overview of this framework.

It is important to remember that multiple connections exist between amygdala and vmPFC so that each region can modify the activity of the other, in addition to being able to modulate the output of neurotransmitter systems in the brain stem. As we saw in Chapter 3, there is evidence that the vmPFC can play a role in reducing the activation of the amygdala by emotion-regulation strategies (Urry et al., 2006).

This neurobiological mechanism allows for a very rapid autonomic response when we are faced with uncertain situations. The interesting point is that most of us are able to generate these anticipatory autonomic responses when we are faced with a

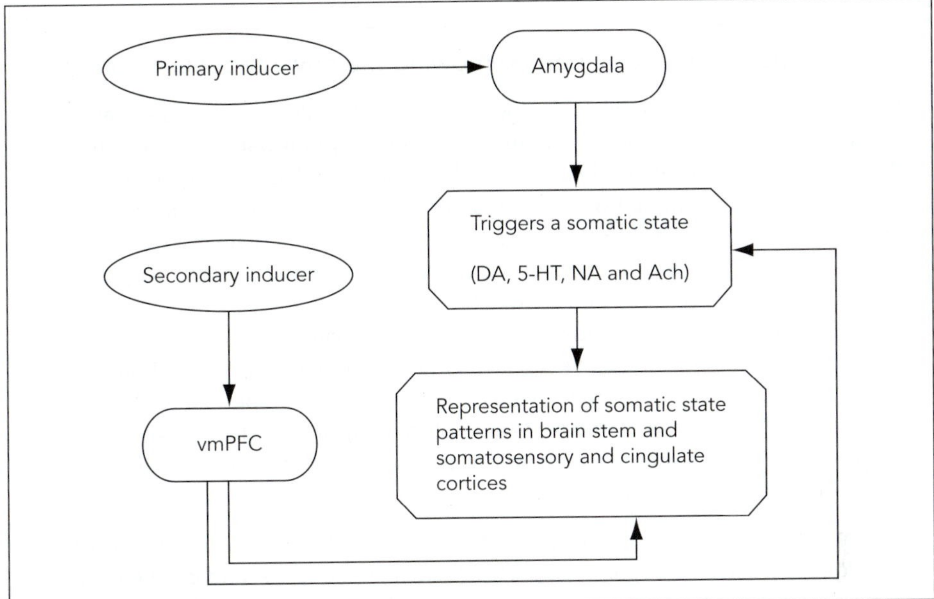

FIGURE 6.15 Schematic overview of how primary and secondary inducers can implement representations of somatic states in the brain (following Damasio, 1999)

risky choice even before we know that it is a risky choice (Bechara et al., 1997). It has long been known that patients with bilateral damage to the vmPFC experience severe problems in personal decision-making. People with injury to this region of the brain often make disastrous choices that can lead to a loss of friends and family, as well as substantial financial losses in their everyday life. A particular problem appears to be that people with this type of damage find it difficult to learn from their previous mistakes. In other words, they tend to repeatedly make decisions that result in negative outcomes. The important point is that these patients show normal reasoning capacity on standard neuropsychological tests. Thus, in spite of a completely normal ability to reason, they tend to make very poor decisions in everyday situations.

Damasio and colleagues have developed the *somatic marker hypothesis* (SMH) to explain this pattern of findings. The SMH suggests that the problems with decision-making in real life are due to a deficit in the emotional mechanism that rapidly signals the probable consequences of an action. This somatic marker is thought to be crucial to the selection of an appropriate and advantageous option. This mechanism is probably best explained by the now-classic experiment reported by Bechara et al. (1997) in which they introduced the Iowa Gambling Task (IGT). This study is described in Box 6.3.

To summarize, The SMH proposes that the induction of somatic states biases cortical processes towards beneficial responses and away from risky decisions. This mechanism seems to be implemented by regions of the vmPFC and is crucial for everyday decision-making. Research, primarily with brain-damaged people, highlights the important role that feelings and hunches can play in assisting good decision-making.

BOX 6.3

Deciding advantageously before knowing the advantageous strategy

Bechara et al. (1997) developed the Iowa Gambling Task (IGT) to simulate real-life decision-making in the way it presented the uncertainty of rewards and penalties. Participants were each given $2000 facsimile US notes and asked to gamble so that they maximized the amount of money that they won. Each player had four decks of cards (A, B, C, and D). Turning over a card carried an immediate reward of $100 in decks A and B and $50 in decks C and D. However, turning over some cards resulted in an unpredictable penalty which were large in decks A and B, and small in decks C and D. The advantageous way to play this game is to select from decks C and D which will lead to an overall gain. On the other hand, selecting from decks A and B will inevitably result in an overall loss. The game is stopped after 100 card selections, but, of course, participants are not told any of this. Thus, players have no way of predicting when a penalty will arise and no way of calculating the net losses or gains from each deck.

The interesting finding was that by about card 50 all of the normal (i.e., non-brain-damaged) participants began to express a 'hunch' that decks A and B were risky and began to avoid choosing from these decks. These participants all generated anticipatory SCRs when they were considering choosing from decks A or B. Moreover, by about card 80, 7 out of 10 people had figured out why decks A and B were riskier. Interestingly, the 3 who did not reach what Bechara et al. called the 'conceptual stage' still made advantageous choices (i.e., they avoided decks A and B).

However, a very different pattern was found for six patients with bilateral damage to the vmPFC. The main finding was that none of these patients generated anticipatory SCRs at any point during the task. Three of these patients did figure out that decks A and B were risky, but remarkably they still continued to select from those decks. Thus, the patients with vmPFC damage did not generate anticipatory SCRs. They tended to make poor decisions and always ended up making a loss (just as they do in real life). Moreover, these bad choices were still apparent even when the patients had explicit knowledge of the risks.

Just as the affective significance of a situation can draw attentional resources in a fairly automatic way, it seems that affective significance can also influence the quality and type of decisions that are made. Damage to the mechanism underlying the detection of affective significance results in a deficit in how well decisions are made (Damasio, 1999).

There are a number of criticisms of the somatic marker hypothesis, based primarily on methodological issues. For instance, the somatic marker hypothesis presumes that people learn to avoid certain 'risky' decks in the IGT in an implicit manner and that these implicit hunches feed into the decision-making process. However, it turns out that information about the riskiness of different decks may be more available to conscious awareness than had previously been thought (see Dunn, 2006, for review).

This raises the possibility that the somatic markers may be a result of making a risky decision, rather than a signal that is used in making the decision. Other theoretical and empirical questions need to be addressed, and these are discussed in a number of papers (Bechara et al., 2005; Dunn et al., 2006; Maia and McClelland, 2005). In spite of these potential problems with the details of the SMH, however, it is clear that this framework provides a useful indication of how affective processing can benefit everyday decision-making. In addition, the neural mechanism underlying the relations between affect and decision-making is especially well specified in the SMH compared to other models.

Does mood influence personal and social judgments?

Complementary results to those discussed above have been reported in social psychological studies with non-brain-damaged people. For example, in one study attraction to another person depended to a large extent on how the person doing the judging reacted physiologically to the attributes of the person being judged (Clore and Byrne, 1974). Thus, if I feel happy and positive when in someone's company I am more likely to find that person attractive than if I am in a situation where that person makes me feel sad and depressed. Many other studies have confirmed that current mood state can have a strong effect on our judgments of objects and people. In one study either a positive or a negative mood state was induced by asking participants to watch either an elating or a depressing movie. Participants were then given a 20-item questionnaire, which they were told had been filled out by another person. The requirement was to read the questionnaire and then to evaluate the person who had completed it on a range of personality traits. The results showed that people who had watched the elating movie were in a more positive mood and also rated the target person more positively than those who had watched the depressing film (Gouaux, 1971). In an early study, participants were asked to evaluate political slogans either following a free lunch or in a room with a foul-smelling odour. Perhaps not surprisingly, the participants who received the free lunch gave much more positive ratings of the slogans than those in the unpleasant room (Razran, 1940). These results can be explained by assuming that people make evaluations that are congruent with their current mood state. For example, network models of mood and memory assume that moods are encoded as specific nodes within semantic networks so that when a particular mood state (e.g., happiness) is activated then all events associated with that mood state also become activated in our memory structures (Bower, 1981).

Mood congruency effects on social judgment have been found in real-life settings. In one study, people were approached as they left a cinema having just watched a happy, a sad, or an aggressive movie. They were asked to answer a series of questions about their level of satisfaction with their own lives as well as recent political events, and were also asked to assess the likelihood that a range of different events would occur. People who had watched a happy movie made much more positive judgments and their estimation of positive events occurring in the future was enhanced when compared with those who had watched the aggressive or the sad movie (Forgas and

Moylan, 1987). Thus, current mood state seems to influence judgment and evaluation in a way that is congruent with the mood. Those in a happy mood tend to make more positive judgments, while those in a negative mood make more negative evaluations.

Other experiments have induced positive mood states by giving passers-by an unexpected free gift. Such a gift has an immediate impact in inducing a positive mood even when the gift is relatively minor. In one study, it was found that people who had received an unexpected gift were more likely to judge that they were highly satisfied with some of their current possessions (e.g., a TV set) compared with those who had not received a free gift (Isen et al., 1978). Estimates of future positive or negative events are also influenced by current mood state. For example, the induction of a negative mood state (sadness) resulted in people estimating that a range of negative life events (e.g., contracting a serious disease; being caught in a fire or being electrocuted; being the victim of violence) were more likely compared to control participants in a neutral mood state (Johnson and Tversky, 1983). The interesting thing about this study is that reading a detailed newspaper report about the death of one person resulted in increases of estimated risk across many causes of death and was not restricted to the particular instance of death related to the newspaper article. This global effect is consistent with network models of mood and memory which would predict that the global increase is a consequence of activation spreading across all events related to a particular emotion node (Kavanagh and Bower, 1985).

As we have seen, current affective state can have a profound influence on our judgment and evaluation of other people. What about judging and evaluating our own competence and abilities? Do affective states also influence these more personal judgments? There is now abundant evidence that a current mood state can indeed play an important role in determining the type of judgments that people make about themselves and their future. For example, people who are currently happy rate themselves as having much higher self-esteem than those who are in more negative or neutral mood states (Wright and Mischel, 1982). Consistent with this, experimental studies have found that when a happy mood state is induced people select more positive trait adjectives to describe themselves, whereas when in a sad mood state more negative self-descriptors are more common (Sedikides, 1995). These effects, however, are significantly modified by whether the self-beliefs relate to peripheral and unusual traits that require people to think about them more deeply. When the traits relate to more familiar central beliefs, current mood state does not have as great an effect (Forgas, 1995).

The affect-as-information approach

Schwarz and Clore (1988) have developed an 'affect-as-information' approach, which proposes that people frequently make judgments by asking themselves 'How do I feel about it?'. The central tenet of this approach is that people use their current affective state as information that can be employed when making a judgment or evaluating something. Thus, if I feel really anxious and afraid then the situation I am in must be dangerous. In this example, the feelings of anxiety are used as important sources of information to evaluate how dangerous a situation might be.

The affect-as-information approach proposes that feelings provide affective feedback that can then guide judgment, decision-making and information processing (e.g., Clore et al., 2001; Clore and Gasper, 2000; Schwarz and Clore, 1988). In contrast to many information-processing models where feelings are pictured as the output arrows, this approach emphasizes the role of feelings as input in information processing. In other words, feelings are assumed to represent the affective significance of a situation that can then be used to guide cognition and behaviour. Just as behaviours such as facial expressions convey emotional appraisals publicly, it is assumed that feelings convey such information internally (Clore et al., 2001). There is a large body of supporting evidence for this hypothesis in social psychology showing that feelings can and do affect social judgments (e.g., Schwarz and Clore, 1983). In addition, the work of Antonio Damasio and colleagues in neuroscience provides some evidence for a neural network that might facilitate this relationship.

However, there are a number of situations in which feelings and moods do not always influence judgments. If the feelings are not attributed to the object being judged, for example, then the relationship disappears. Mood states induced by the weather do influence people's judgment of their future happiness. However, if the current weather is brought to their attention the mood state no longer influences judgments (Schwarz and Clore, 1983). When people can easily attribute their current mood state to the weather it does not influence their general sense of well-being. However, when they do not attribute their mood to the weather then the current mood state has a strong impact on their judgment of general satisfaction with life. This is an important demonstration that the effects of mood on judgment cannot be explained by a simple mood congruency hypothesis which would predict that when one is in a particular mood all information relevant to that mood becomes activated and therefore is likely to influence judgment. However, the fact that this relationship disappears, or at least is reduced, when the source of the mood state is pointed out to people suggests a more complex process. The affect-as-information account proposes that people can use their current affective state as an important piece of evidence that helps in the decision-making process. How you feel about something determines how you evaluate it. This is only the case, however, when the mood state is seen as relevant. Mood congruency accounts cannot easily explain why mood state does not influence social judgments when the individual sees it as having nothing to do with the object being judged. However, such a situation is easily explained by an affect-as-information account.

CHAPTER SUMMARY

This chapter discusses the complex literature on the nature of the relations between affect and cognition. Historically, these two concepts were seen as separate domains and this was illustrated by the debate in the 1980s between Richard Lazarus and Robert Zajonc. Zajonc argued that affect was primary to cognition, while Lazarus argued that a cognitive appraisal was necessary to elicit an affective response. Subsequent research and theoretical development indicates that affect and cognition are actually integral and inseparable parts of each other. The influence of affect (especially moods) on basic perception, attention and judgment is a dynamic field of contemporary research and both behavioural and neuroimaging methods are being employed to address the fundamental questions.

RECOMMENDED READING

There are several edited books containing excellent chapters on the nature of the relations and interactions between affect and cognition:

Tim Dalgleish and Mick Power (1999) *Handbook of Cognition and Emotion.* Chichester: Wiley.

Richard J. Davidson, Klaus R. Scherer and H. Hill Goldsmith (2003) *Handbook of Affective Sciences.* New York: Oxford University Press.

Joseph P. Forgas (2001) *Affect and Social Cognition.* Mahwah, NJ: Lawrence Erlbaum.

7 AFFECT–COGNITION RELATIONS: MEMORY

ARE AFFECTIVE EVENTS BETTER REMEMBERED THAN NEUTRAL EVENTS?

There is a widespread belief that affective events are better remembered than non-emotional events. In fact, it is often precisely the affective quality of the event that is remembered over and above other details of the event. Many experiments show that people tend to remember their affective reactions to particular stimuli even under conditions when they have no conscious recollection of ever having even seen the stimulus before (Zajonc, 1980, 2000). A dramatic demonstration of the dissociation between memory for affect and memory for other details was reported in a study with a group of patients with profound amnesia (Johnson et al., 1985). Photographs of male faces were presented to patients with Korsakoff's syndrome alongside descriptions indicating that the individual in the photograph was either a 'good' guy (e.g., engaged in pro-social behaviours) or a 'bad' guy (engaged in anti-social behaviours). A week or so later when the patients were shown these photographs once again, the patients had no recollection of any of the faces or even of having seen them before. Nevertheless, when asked to judge whether the person seemed like a nice or not-so-nice individual, the evaluations of the patients were consistent with the positive or negative descriptions that they had heard before. In other words, the original positive or negative appraisals of the photographs had had an impact on current judgment. Thus, there was a dissociation of affective and cognitive information in this classic test of implicit memory.

Implicit memory is the impact on current behaviour and judgment of a previous encounter that has now been explicitly forgotten (i.e., people have no conscious recollection of it) (Schacter, 1987). Indeed the first known description of implicit memory is an anecdotal story of a French psychiatrist in the early 1900s. Dr Claparede had a patient with deep amnesia and on one occasion when they shook hands, Dr Claparede pricked the palm of the patient with a drawing pin. On their next meeting the patient had no recollection of ever having met Dr Claparede, but he nevertheless refused to shake hands with him! These results indicate that the affective qualities of a situation may well endure in implicit memory. However, they do not directly assess whether these qualities can lead to an improvement in our conscious recollection (i.e., explicit memory) of events.

Studies of autobiographical memories

There is evidence that the affective qualities of a situation can result in an enhancement of memory for everyday events (Hamann, 2001; Reisberg and Heuer, 1992, 2004). To illustrate, the various emotional events that occur in our lives are often remembered with exceptional vividness and detail. A striking example of this enhancement of memory occurs with what have been called 'flashbulb memories' (Brown and Kulik, 1977). These events, such as the Challenger space shuttle explosion in 1986, the death of Princess Diana in 1997, the O.J. Simpson trial in 1995, or the destruction of the World Trade Center in New York in 2001, are often recalled with a remarkable degree of vividness and clarity. For instance, an early study found a high correlation (0.71) between participants' ratings of the vividness of their memories and their ratings of how emotional the original event had been (Reisberg et al., 1988). Moreover, this relationship remained fairly consistent regardless of whether the event had been positive or negative. Thus, the correlations between vividness and emotionality ratings were 0.89 for sad events, 0.68 for angry events, 0.90 for fearful events, and 0.71 for happy events. Other studies have confirmed this pattern, finding very high ratings of memory vividness for very traumatic events as well as very positive events (e.g., Rubin and Kozin, 1984).

It is interesting to note, however, that, while people's recollections of these flashbulb effects tend to be accompanied by a high degree of confidence that the memory is correct, evidence suggests that these memories are often inaccurate. In one study people were interviewed just days after the explosion of the Challenger space shuttle and asked questions about where they were when they heard about the disaster, who gave them the news, did they witness it on TV and so on. These same people were then interviewed about 3 years later and asked the same questions. Even though people still had very vivid memories and reported these with a high degree of confidence, many of these memories were wrong and in some cases completely misrepresented the original event (Neisser and Harsch, 1992). A more recent study investigating memory of the events of 11 September 2001 in the USA among a group of students also found that people's memories for these highly emotional events differed from memories of neutral events (Talarico and Rubin, 2003). The discrepancies were mostly in terms of vividness and belief in accuracy, rather than in actual accuracy. Thus, it seems that while memory for affective events might be very clear and vivid, the accuracy of these memories may not actually be any better than for more neutral events.

Studies of flashbulb memories are of great interest, but, like all studies of autobiographical memory, they have a real disadvantage when we want to assess whether memory differs for different classes of events (e.g., affective versus neutral). The problem is that we do not know about all of the emotional events that have taken place in a person's life. Thus, if we find that someone recalls far more affective events than neutral events, can we reliably conclude that this individual's memory is really better for the emotional events? It may be the case that more affective events were actually experienced and therefore the results simply represent fact rather than being a bias towards remembering affective events. The need for greater control explains why memory accuracy is often studied within the laboratory setting. Even though the laboratory may seem somewhat impoverished compared with the events of people's everyday life, it does enable scientists to present equivalent numbers of emotional and non-emotional events so that differences in recollection of these events can more easily be investigated. A variety of stimuli have been used in these studies, including IAPS pictures, word lists of positive and negative adjectives as well as events (see Hamann, 2001, for review).

Laboratory-based studies

In one laboratory study, the distinction between 'remember' and 'know' judgments was utilized to investigate the impact of affect on the subjective sense of remembering and accuracy, respectively (Ochsner, 2000). The remember/know paradigm provides measures of two independent processes that are thought to underlie recollection: *remember*, which includes the retrieval of an event along with various contextual details, and *know*, which is a sense that an item is familiar without any precise memory of the contextual details. See Yonelinas, 2002, for review. Participants in these experiments are shown a list of items (e.g., words or pictures) and some time later are presented with the same items, which are now randomly mixed with similar items that have never been presented. For each item, the participant has to first decide whether the item is 'new' (i.e., never presented before) or 'old' (i.e., presented before). For an 'old' judgment, they then have to indicate whether the item is 'remembered' (i.e., recollected with details of the original context in which the item was encoded) or 'known' (i.e., seems familiar but with no recollection of details of the encoding context). In the study reported by Ochsner (2000), people were asked to make these remember/know judgments of pictures from the IAPS set depicting affectively negative and positive images, as well as neutral scenes. The affectively negative stimuli were consistently remembered more accurately relative to either positive or neutral stimuli. In addition to an effect of valence, highly arousing pictures (both negative and positive) were better remembered than neutral pictures. Importantly, the correct recognition of negative stimuli was more likely to be accompanied by a conscious recollection (i.e., remember judgments) whereas feelings of familiarity (i.e., know judgments) did not increase for negative stimuli. These results provide laboratory evidence for the observation that negative events are often remembered with a rich amount of detail and context. This pattern of results is consistent with the previously discussed findings of studies demonstrating the vividness of autobiographical memories for negative events even when accuracy is not any better (e.g., Talarico and Rubin, 2003).

A recent study has confirmed that the affective quality of a stimulus can enhance the *feeling of remembering* and suggests that this occurs because of enhanced activity in the amygdala (Sharot et al., 2004). Participants were presented with 75 negatively arousing and 75 neutral pictures from the IAPS set and then were asked to make remember/know judgments about an hour later when they were in the fMRI scanner. The behavioural results showed that accuracy for the negative pictures (82%) did not differ from accuracy for neutral pictures (84%). However, the negative pictures were characterized by primarily 'remember' judgments (62%) rather than 'know' (29%) judgments. In contrast, remember and know judgments did not differ for the neutral pictures (43% versus 47%). This study provides further evidence that the subjective sense of remembering can be enhanced for affectively negative stimuli even though the accuracy of memory for these stimuli is not enhanced. The fMRI results indicate that this enhanced feeling of remembering can be attributed to an increase in activity in the amygdala during 'remember' judgments for affective pictures. In contrast, enhanced activity within the parahippocampal cortex was associated with 'remember' judgments for neutral pictures. Thus, it seems that the subjective sense of remembering is associated with different neural circuits depending upon whether an affective or a neutral event is being remembered (Sharot et al., 2004).

Memory for the gist of things

A different line of research indicates that affect may enhance the *accuracy* of our memories primarily for what has been called the 'central' aspects or the 'gist' of a scene. See Reisberg and Heuer, 2004, for review. Evidence comes from studies of eye-witness testimonies in which it is common for people to report very detailed memories of a weapon but little about other aspects of the crime, including what the perpetrator looked like. Elizabeth Loftus has called this the 'weapons-focus' effect (Loftus, 1975). She has shown that participants spend a greater amount of time looking at a weapon in a scene and that the amount of time spent looking at a weapon is inversely related to their ability to identify the criminal (Loftus et al., 1987). Similar findings have been reported in the more naturalistic setting of a rubella vaccination clinic (Peters, 1988). Memory for the syringe was very good but people could not remember the nurse who gave them the injection. Moreover, memory for the peripheral details was inversely correlated with the degree of arousal. The more aroused people were by the sight of the needle the less likely they were to identify the nurse who gave them the injection.

These results are consistent with a hypothesis proposed many years ago by Easterbrook (1959) who hypothesized that emotional arousal causes a *narrowing of attention* so that the central part of a scene is processed in detail while the periphery receives little or no processing. The well-established weapon-focus effects would seem to support this hypothesis, with good memory for items that are central to the crime, such as the weapon, accompanied by poorer memory for less central details. Further support for this notion was found in a study that presented participants with a sequence of photographs in which a woman was observed either gathering flowers in a park (neutral version) or lying on the ground having been stabbed in the throat (threat version). Participants were later asked to select which photographs they had seen previously from a range of pictures which had zoomed in on the central scene to different degrees. The aversive pictures were consistently remembered as being more 'zoomed in' than the neutral pictures, indicating that details of the peripheral aspects of the scene were not particularly well remembered (Safer et al., 1998).

Taken together, this body of work suggests that affect can improve the accuracy of memory for the central aspects of a scene but can impair memory for the peripheral aspects. Thus, in terms of answering the question of whether affect can improve the accuracy of memory, the answer very much depends on what aspect of the scene we are considering. The subjective sense of remembering and the vividness of memory, however, are clearly enhanced by the affective significance of a scene or situation.

What factors are involved in the enhancement of memory for affectively significant stimuli? Highly emotional events are generally very unusual and distinctive, and they are also likely to be related to important goals and themes in our life. For this reason, these events may often be thought about much more than neutral events and, therefore, are likely to be rehearsed more frequently. It may well be this extra rehearsal that leads to the improvement in memory for emotional events. Moreover, as we have seen previously, emotional events and stimuli (especially when they are negative) typically attract attention to a far greater degree than neutral events. This enhanced *encoding* of negative stimuli may also result in better memory for these events. Thus, affective events may not enhance memory directly. Instead, these events may be better remembered because of the indirect effects of affect on initial encoding and rehearsal, or the simple fact that they tend to be distinctive and unusual.

This possibility was directly addressed in a study by Christianson and Loftus (1991). They presented participants with a story conveyed by a series of photographs, as shown in Figure 7.1. The neutral stimulus told a story of a woman riding her bicycle; the unusual stimulus told a story of a woman carrying her bicycle; while the negative stimulus told a story of a woman being injured while riding her bicycle. Memory for peripheral details (a car in the background) did not differ between the negative and the unusual story. However, memory for the central details, such as the length of the woman's skirt, was much better for the emotional sequence than the unusual sequence. Thus, this experiment indicates that the effects of negative affect cannot be attributed only to distinctiveness (Christianson and Loftus, 1991).

DOES AFFECT INFLUENCE MEMORY BY MEANS OF AROUSAL OR VALENCE?

Most of the studies of explicit memory for emotional events and experiences have compared memory for neutral events that are not particularly arousing with stimuli that are both highly arousing and at an extreme on the valence dimension (either highly positive or highly negative). Thus, the relative contribution of the arousal dimension and the valence dimension to the memory enhancement effect is often impossible to determine. However, we know that arousal and valence have dissociable effects on the neural processes that are engaged when attending to stimuli (e.g., Anderson et al., 2003). A similar dissociation might be found with regard to the effects of arousal and valence on explicit memory.

Effects of arousal on memory for affective material

It has been proposed that the amygdala is a key structure underlying the enhancement in memory for arousing stimuli. For example, in animal research it has been

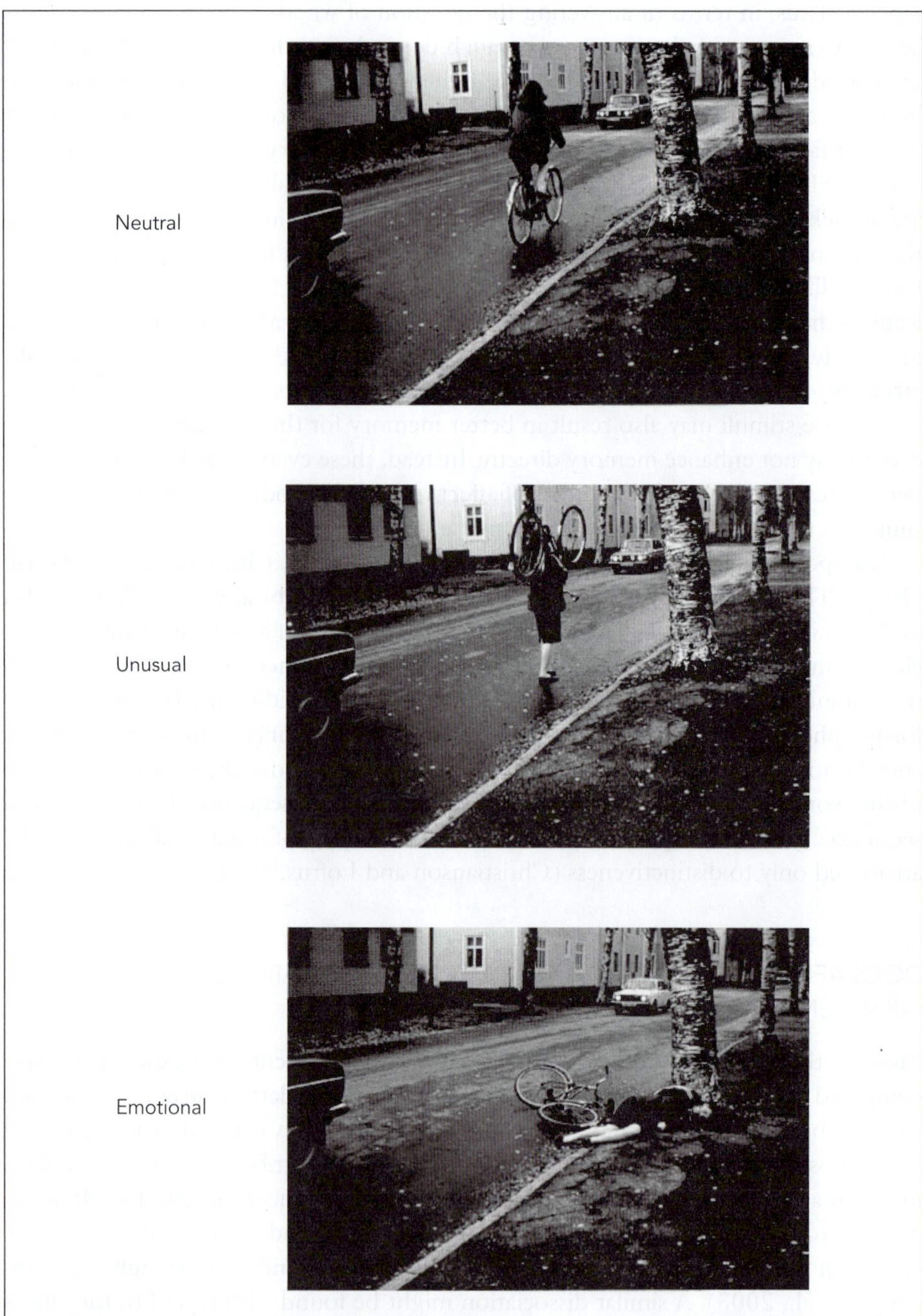

FIGURE 7.1 Examples of the pictures used to go with the stories presented by Christianson et al.
Source: Christianson and Loftus (1991).

shown that physiological arousal leads to an activation of *beta-adrenergic* receptors in the amygdala. This activation, in turn, modulates the activity of the hippocampus in a way that ensures an enhanced *consolidation* of memories for events that elicited an arousal response (see McGaugh, 2000, 2004, for review). Evidence for the role of the amygdala in remembering arousing events was also reported in a patient with selective damage to the amygdala (Cahill et al., 1995). This patient showed relatively normal long-term memory for non-emotional material, but did not show the enhancement of recall that is normally associated with emotional arousal. More direct evidence comes from findings that arousal can enhance the recollection of episodic memories. Pharmacological manipulations of arousal have also been shown to alter memory of events depending on whether arousal was increased (improved memory) or decreased (impaired memory).

In addition, Ralph Adolphs and his colleagues have found that amygdala damage specifically impairs memory for the central aspects of a scene with no impairment of memory for more peripheral aspects (Adolphs, Denburg et al., 2001; Adolphs et al., 2005). This is an unusual pattern since people usually remember the central aspects of arousing scenes more clearly than the peripheral aspects. The trade off between the 'gist' and the periphery is eliminated by amygdala damage, as shown in Figure 7.2. Non-brain-damaged people demonstrated better memory for the gist of aversive events relative to neutral events, but remembered the peripheral details of aversive events less well than those of neutral events. In contrast, a patient with bilateral amygdala damage (SM046) showed poorer memory for the gist of aversive relative to neutral events but had no difference in memory for the details of aversive and neutral events.

The pattern shown in Figure 7.2 suggests some disruption of an attentional focusing mechanism in the patient with amygdala damage. Neuroimaging studies also provide evidence for the role of the amygdala in modulating the effects of arousal on memory. In the first study to investigate the role of the amygdala in explicit memory for affective events, PET scanning was used during the encoding of affective events (Cahill et al., 1996). Eight participants viewed a series of 12 film clips that were emotional and 12 film clips that were neutral while cerebral glucose metabolism was measured by PET. The emotional video clips all related to violence or scenes of mutilation and were rated as eliciting the emotions of fear and disgust. Thus, all of the emotional films were highly arousing but always related to aversive events. Three weeks later, participants returned to the laboratory and were asked to recall as many of the film clips as they could. As expected, participants recalled more of the emotional film clips relative to the neutral clips. The more interesting finding was that the degree of metabolic activity in the right amygdala (during encoding) was highly correlated with the number of emotional films recalled three weeks later ($r = 0.93$, $0 < 0.01$) while there was no relationship between amygdala activity and recall of the neutral film clips ($r = 0.33$, ns). The pattern of results reported by Cahill et al. (1996) is shown in Figure 7.3.

Figure 7.3 indicates that activity in the amygdala during the encoding of an aversive emotional event is strongly correlated with the subsequent recall of that event. In

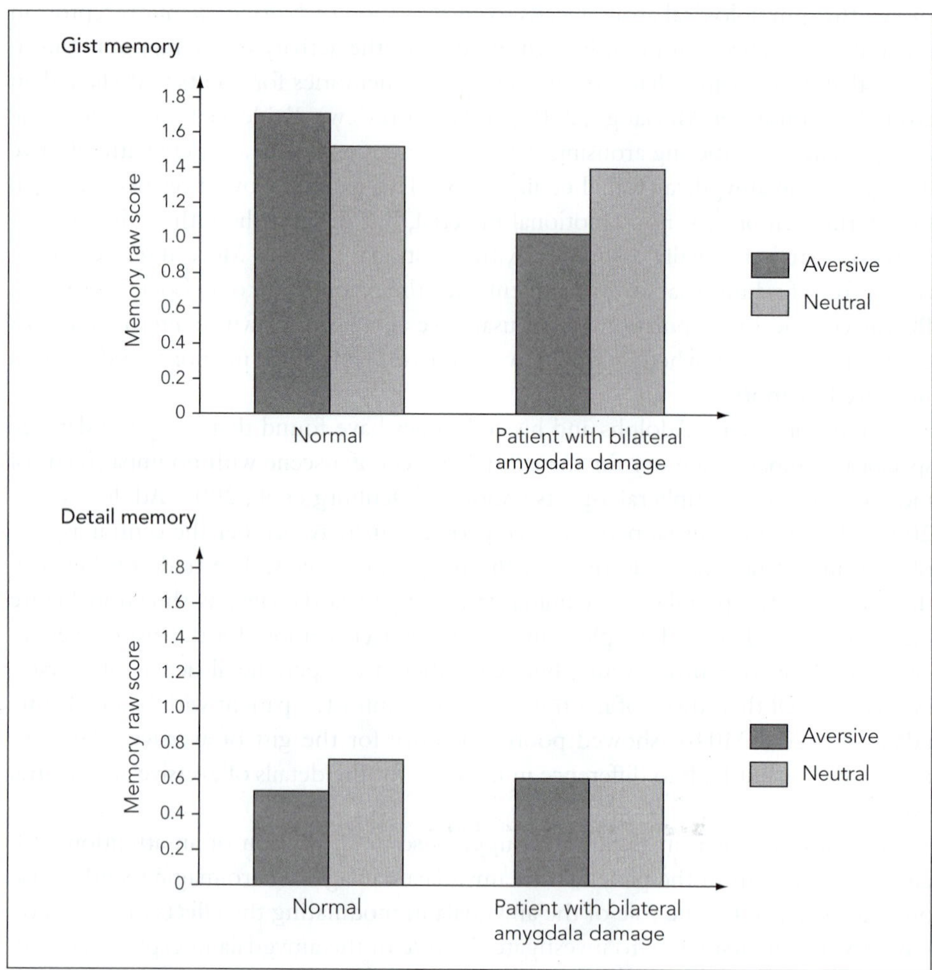

FIGURE 7.2 Memory for the 'gist' and the 'details' of aversive and neutral events
Data show the results for a group of participants without brain damage and a patient with bilateral amygdala damage.

Source: Adolphs, Denburg et al. (2001).

contrast, the activity in the amygdala during the encoding of non-emotional events did not correlate with subsequent recall.

The absence of a correlation between amygdala activity and recall of non-emotional events was replicated in a subsequent study using word stimuli (Alkire et al., 1998). However, in this study, a striking correlation was found between activity in the left hippocampus during encoding of words and subsequent free recall of these words, as shown in Figure 7.4. Eight participants listened to a sequence of unrelated words while in the PET scanner. A day later they returned to the laboratory where they were asked to free recall as many of the words as they could. The degree of activity in the left hippocampal region was strongly correlated with the subsequent recall of words (Figure 7.4). However, the degree of activity in either the left or the right amygdala

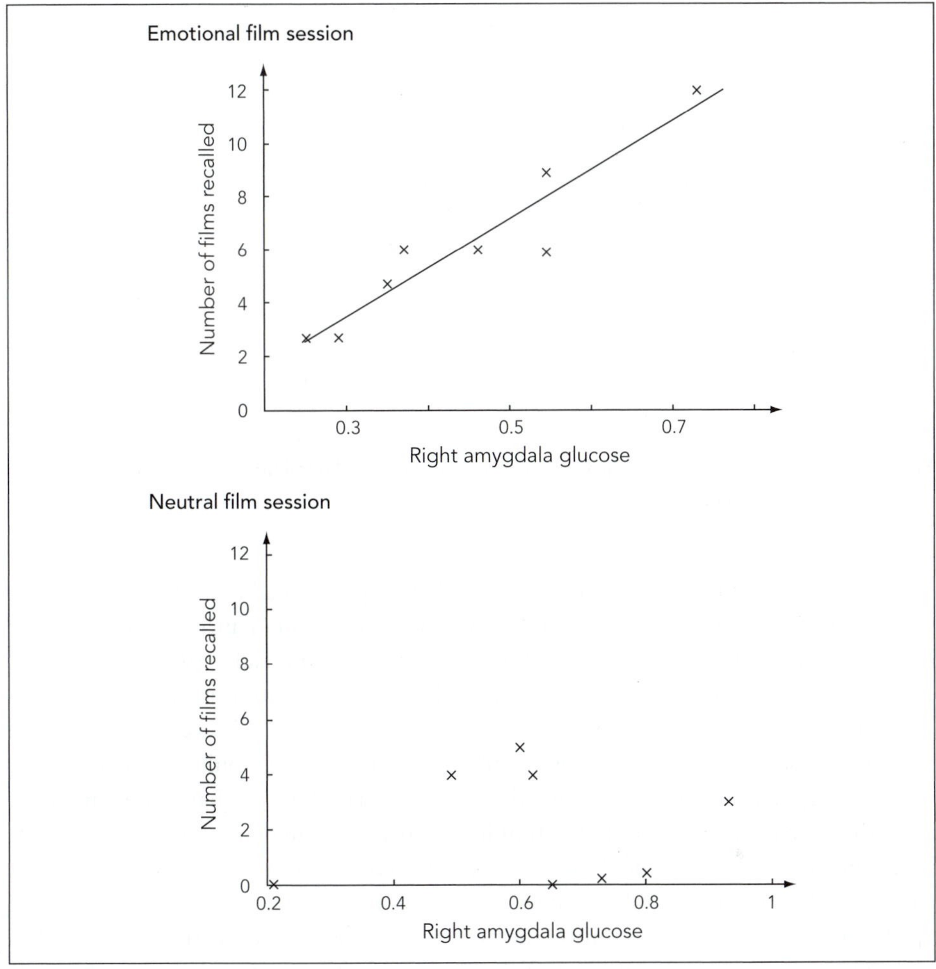

FIGURE 7.3 Right amygdala activity during encoding and subsequent recall of film clips for both emotional and neutral films

Source: Cahill et al. (1996).

did not correlate with subsequent recall of these neutral words. Thus, it seems that amygdala activation during encoding is associated with improved memory for emotional stimuli (Cahill et al., 1996), while activity within the hippocampal region is associated with recall of neutral stimuli (Alkire et al., 1996).

A problem with the results of Cahill and his colleagues for present purposes is that, while the emotional films were rated as being highly arousing, they all depicted aversive scenes. Thus, it may be the case that the amygdala was responding to either the valence or the arousing qualities of the clips. Subsequent research has more directly assessed the activity of the amygdala in relation to arousing stimuli that are both negatively and positively valenced (Canli et al., 1999; Hamann et al., 1999). For example, in one study ten participants viewed aversive, pleasant, interesting and neutral pictures when in the PET scanner. They were subjected to a surprise recall test about

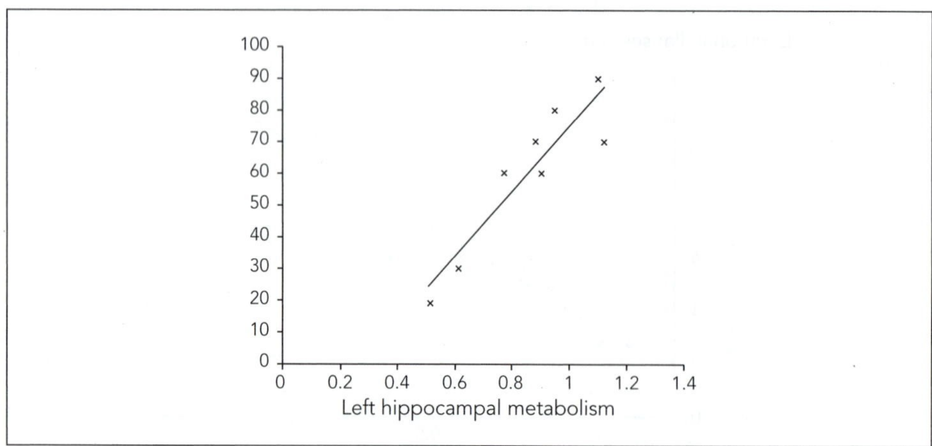

FIGURE 7.4 Activity in the left hippocampal region and recall of unrelated neutral words
Source: Alkire et al. (1998).

10 minutes after scanning had finished. Another surprise recall test and a recognition memory test were presented four weeks later. Memory was enhanced for the aversive (mean correct recall = 47%) and the pleasant (mean correct recall = 39%) pictures relative to the interesting (mean correct recall = 18%) or the neutral (mean correct recall = 19%) pictures at immediate recall. This enhancement for both aversive (21%) and pleasant (17%) relative to interesting (10%) or neutral (6%) stimuli remained at four weeks. Amygdala activity during encoding was correlated with enhanced memory for both the aversive and the pleasant stimuli, which were matched on arousal. Interestingly, this correlation only held for the recognition memory at four weeks and was not significant for either delayed or immediate recall. The correlation between amygdala activity at encoding and recognition memory 4 weeks later suggests that the amygdala plays a role in ensuring that memory for arousing events remains relatively stable over a four-week period. Moreover, amygdala activity was correlated with the arousing qualities of the stimuli regardless of valence (Hamann et al., 1999).

Another study using fMRI also found that the amygdala was engaged during the processing of both positive and negative stimuli, and that the degree of activity was related to subsequent recognition memory for both affective words and pictures regardless of valence (Kensinger and Schacter, 2006). The surprise recognition memory test was presented about 30 minutes after scanning. Thus, in this study there was a correlation between amygdala activity at encoding and subsequent memory for emotional items following a fairly short delay.

Thus, several studies indicate that amygdala activity during encoding is related to improved memory for emotionally arousing material regardless of valence. One mechanism by which the amygdala may achieve this enhancement of memory might be via modulation of the hippocampus. The evidence comes from a number of studies showing that the degree of amygdala activity correlates with the degree of hippocampal activity during encoding of affective stimuli (Hamann et al., 1999; Kensinger

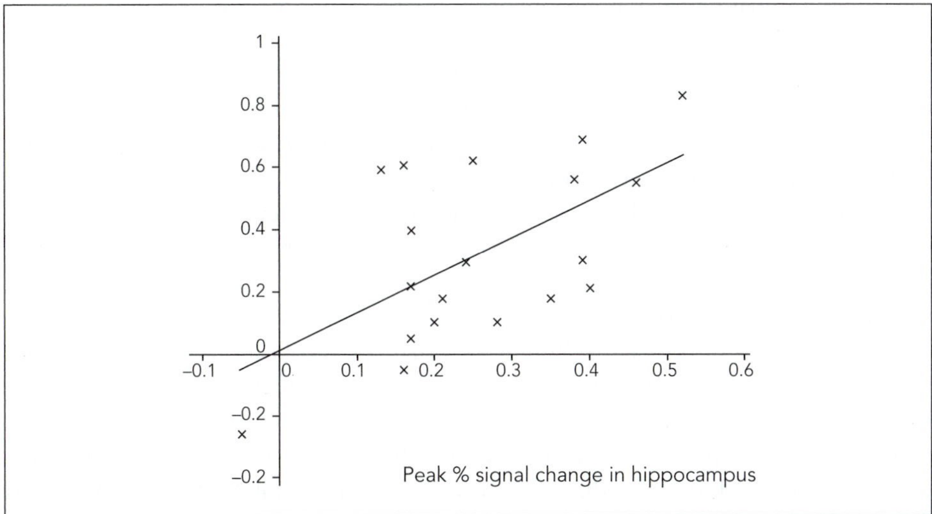

FIGURE 7.5 Activity in the amygdala and hippocampus during encoding of arousing words that were later remembered

Source: Kensinger and Corkin (2004).

and Corkin, 2004). Kensinger and Corkin found that activation of the amygdala and the hippocampus correlated during the encoding of arousing words that were later remembered ($r = 0.60$, $p < 0.01$) as shown in Figure 7.5. This pattern suggests that an amygdala–hippocampal network might underlie the enhanced explicit memory for emotionally arousing stimuli (Kensinger and Corkin, 2004).

Effects of valence on memory for affective material

There are very few neuroimaging studies that specifically examine whether valence influences explicit memory independently of arousal. One such study presented participants with words that were either aversive or neutral (Kensinger and Corkin, 2004). However, the aversive words were subdivided into arousing (e.g., rape, slaughter) and non-arousing (e.g., sorrow, mourning) so that valence could be assessed independently of arousal. Participants remembered more of the negative words regardless of whether they were arousing (87%) or non-arousing (85%) relative to neutral (77%). However, while there was no difference between the two categories of negative words on the behavioural task, it did seem that enhanced memory for these items was associated with different neural networks. Activity in the amygdala and good correlation between amygdala and hippocampal activity (see Figure 7.5) were related to subsequent memory for arousing words. In contrast, activity in the PFC and good correlation between PFC and hippocampal activation were associated with subsequent memory for negative, but non-arousing, words (Kensinger and Corkin, 2004). It is interesting to note, however, that in terms of behavioural outcomes there was no difference in the accuracy or the quality of memory for the arousing and non-arousing negative words in this study. Further research of this nature is required to assess whether the

PFC–hippocampal network is also involved in enhancing memory for non-arousing positive words.

Some of the studies we have discussed indicate that, under laboratory conditions, there is no difference in the accuracy of memory for positive and negative stimuli when they are equally arousing (e.g., Hamann et al., 1999; Kensinger and Schacter, 2006). This pattern of results is consistent with research on flashbulb autobiographical memories in which highly arousing positive and negative events seem to be equally memorable (e.g., Reisberg et al., 1988). However, other studies have found that memory for negative events is sometimes more accurate than for positive stimuli (Ochsner, 2000). Moreover, a number of studies of autobiographical memory suggest that there might be a *positivity bias* such that our recollections of past events are biased towards positive rather than negative events (Walker et al., 2003, for review). We can question whether this is a memory bias at all, however, since it seems that people generally experience far more pleasant than unpleasant events. In one study students were asked to keep a diary for an academic term, while some kept the record for over 2 years. Each day they were asked to indicate a single unique event that had happened and then rate that event as being pleasant, unpleasant or neutral (Thompson et al., 1996). About 50% of the events were rated as pleasant, while roughly 25% were rated as unpleasant. In subsequent research (Walker et al., 1997), participants were asked to keep a diary of events rated for pleasantness at the time that the event occurred. Then at a later time (3.5 months, 1 year, and 2 years later) they were asked to recall how the event had made them feel. It was found that the affective intensity of events faded with time, and that intensity faded more for negative events than positive events. In other words, affective memory for pleasant and unpleasant events seems to fade at different rates. Walker et al. (1997) argue that this differential fading gives our autobiographical memories a rich sense of positivity. This *fading affect bias* means that when people reminisce they usually perceive their lives to be positive rather than negative. In other words, we really do seem to look back with rose-coloured glasses, which is also consistent with the findings of many surveys (Diener and Diener, 1996).

It is difficult to evaluate this research as it is unclear whether there really is a bias toward *remembering* positive rather than negative information. Most studies ask people to rate how they felt when they experienced particular events, which is somewhat different from asking people to recall those events. When surprise recall tasks are given under laboratory conditions it seems that memory for negative and positive events are equivalent (e.g., Hamann et al., 1999; Kensinger and Corkin, 2006).

However, it may be that events which are relevant to us show a bias towards positive information. There is some evidence for this suggestion in studies that investigate memory for behaviours that are either self-relevant or other-relevant. After all, it is safe to assume that the affective events we experience in our everyday lives are likely to be more important for our sense of self, and more clearly related to our life goals, than the simple pictures and words presented in laboratory experiments. In one study a series of 32 behaviours that related to negative (e.g., would pay back money that was borrowed) or positive (e.g., would look after a friend who was ill) descriptions were presented. Half of the participants were told that the statements applied to themselves, while the other half were told that the statements related to another person called Chris (Sedikides and Green, 2000). In a recall test, it was found that more negative core behaviours (e.g., untrustworthy or unkind acts etc) were remembered in the Chris-reference condition than the self-reference condition. Sedikides and Gregg (2003) have suggested that the concept of self is a very rich, positive and motivation-laden structure, and that negative information that is pertinent to the self tends to be processed in a fairly shallow way. In contrast, information that is flattering to the self tends to be processed in a deeper and more elaborative way. This mechanism would, of course, explain better memory for self-relevant positive relative to negative information (Sedikides and Green, 2000), and also provides a potential explanation for the finding that autobiographical memory is often biased in favour of pleasant and positive information (Walker et al., 2003).

DOES AFFECT INFLUENCE MEMORY AT ENCODING, CONSOLIDATION OR RETRIEVAL?

The enhancement of emotional memories might be achieved in a number of ways. First, arousal (or valence) might have a direct influence at the time of *encoding* so that emotionally salient events are processed in more detail and are, therefore, better remembered. Second, the main impact of affect on memory may occur during the *consolidation* of memories, when they are being laid down into long-term memory. Finally, it is also possible that the role of affect may play a part when we are attempting to *retrieve* specific memories. Figure 7.6 shows the time courses and stages involved in experiencing and remembering an affectively arousing event. A variety of encoding processes are likely to be engaged when an event is actually happening (e.g., attentional orienting and engagement; sensory processes etc) to create an initial representation of the event. When the event is complete many of these encoding processes may still be engaged, but other post-encoding processes also come into play (Hamann, 2001). The most well known of these post-encoding processes is consolidation, which is a storage process thought to be involved in making memories more stable over time. A feature of consolidation is that it continues for some time (minutes to hours and more) after the initial event. This means that memory for affectively arousing events is likely to improve relative to neutral events as time goes on. Evidence for consolidation initially came from animal research in which it was shown that the administration of stimulant drugs after a task had been learnt led to a further improvement in memory. Likewise, drugs thought to block the consolidation processes were shown to impair memory even when they were presented after the event had been encoded (McGaugh, 2000, 2004, for reviews). These results support the view that post-encoding processes that continue for some time after a representation of an event has been established can have a powerful effect on memory. As shown in Figure 7.6, *retrieval* can be attempted at any time within this process. One problem is that we do not know how long consolidation processes actually last. Nevertheless, the general hypothesis would be that information retrieval immediately after the event should result in little difference in memory for affective and neutral events. On the

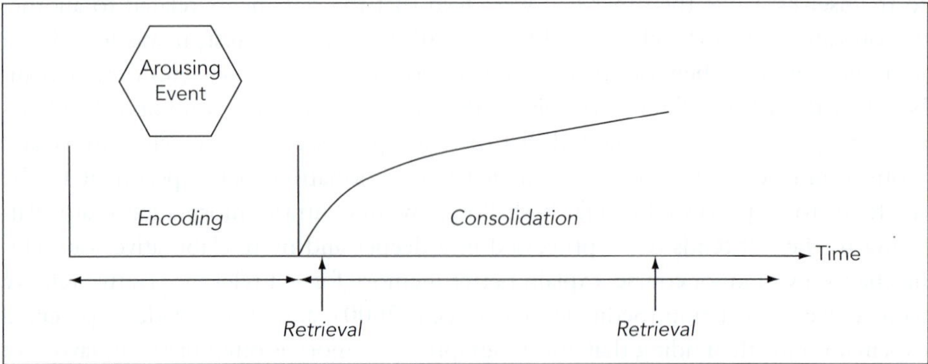

FIGURE 7.6 Stages in laying down affective memories
Source: Adapted from Hamann (2001).

other hand, retrieval some time after the event should result in better memory for affective events. Our memory for arousing events should improve with time relative to our memory for neutral events.

It is important to remember, however, that these various memory stages probably overlap rather than being sequential, and are almost certainly organized by different neural circuits. Moreover, a number of factors such as rehearsals and so on may vary for different events. Highly arousing events, whether they are positive or negative (e.g., getting married, passing final exams, death of a loved one etc), are likely to be ruminated on and thought about far more than less salient events. Therefore, it is very difficult to make precise predictions unless we very carefully control for all of these factors. This, of course, is very difficult even under laboratory conditions, and virtually impossible in real life. Nevertheless, with the relatively innocuous stimuli, such as affective pictures, words or video clips, presented in laboratory studies, differences in degree of rumination and rehearsal should be minimized. It turns out that affect does seem to have an effect on memory during both encoding and consolidation phases, and possibly also has an impact during retrieval. Evidence for each of these hypotheses is reviewed next.

Encoding effects

Behavioural data provides extensive evidence that arousing stimuli (e.g., angry facial expressions) enhance attention to themselves (e.g., Fox et al., 2000; Hansen and Hansen, 1988; Öhman, Lundqvist et al., 2001), and it seems likely that this attentional enhancement will result in a more elaborated mental representation. In one study an emotional Stroop task was presented in which participants were asked to name the colours of a series of threat-related and neutral words (Russo et al., 2006). Following the Stroop task, a surprise free recall test was presented. Participants who showed the greatest degree of attentional bias towards the threat words also showed an enhanced memory for these words. Thus, processes occurring during encoding are likely to play a role in boosting memory for affectively arousing stimuli.

Apparent support comes from the studies we have already discussed showing that the degree of amygdala activity during the encoding of emotionally arousing stimuli is correlated with the subsequent memory for these events (Cahill et al., 1996; Hamann et al., 1999). However, it should be noted that some of these studies assessed recall several weeks after encoding. Indeed, in the study reported by Hamann et al. (1999), when recall was tested just 10 minutes after encoding no correlation was found between amygdala activity at encoding and recall. However, amygdala activity at encoding did correlate with enhanced memory for arousing stimuli 4 weeks later. This pattern suggests that the amygdala activity at encoding may have affected subsequent consolidation processes in some way which would take a little time to develop. Nevertheless, in this study, even though amygdala activity did not correlate with recall after 10 minutes there was a behavioural boost in memory at 10 minutes, which is presumably before consolidation can take place. Similarly, a more recent study found enhanced memory for arousing stimuli around 30 minutes following encoding and this memory boost did correlate with enhanced amygdala activity during encoding (Kensinger and Schacter, 2006). Therefore, it seems that at least some of the effects that have been reported must be due to encoding processes that are acting independently of consolidation.

Consolidation effects

Much of the evidence for the role of consolidation in boosting memory for emotional events comes from animal research. For example, pharmacological manipulations have demonstrated that if stimulant drugs that boost memory are given after training (encoding) they still lead to a further enhancement of memory (McGaugh and Petrinovich, 1965). Importantly, it was found that drugs that are infused directly into the amygdala after training have little effect on performance a couple of hours later, but can influence memory tested 24 hours later (Schafe and LeDoux, 2000). This pattern suggests that the drugs are selectively affecting the consolidation of long-term memory, rather than influencing acquisition or retrieval. Evidence suggests that the adrenal stress hormones (e.g., adrenaline and cortisol) appear to play a particularly important role in the consolidation of memory. For example, drugs that activate ß-adrenergic receptors in the amygdala and other areas have been shown to enhance memory for many types of experience (McGaugh, 2000). The amygdala seems to be critical for mediating the influence of adrenaline and glucocorticoids since lesions of the amygdala can block the effects these hormones have on consolidation. To illustrate, infusions of ß-adrenergic receptor antagonists into the amygdala after training enhance memory, while lesions of the amygdala or infusion of ß-adrenergic receptor antagonists after training block this enhancement of memory (Quirarte et al., 1997).

Supporting evidence has also been reported in human studies. For instance, amphetamine, which is a powerful stimulant with arousing properties, given before and after learning of lists of words results in an improvement in memory for those words (Soetens et al., 1995). Even more direct evidence comes from studies in which people received either a placebo or a ß-adrenergic antagonist just before viewing pictures accompanied by an emotionally arousing story. Those people who had received placebo showed the typical enhancement by remembering best the pictures that occurred during the most emotional part of the story. However, this enhancement for pictures encoded under emotionally-arousing conditions was eliminated by administration of a ß-adrenergic receptor antagonist (Cahill et al., 1994). Moreover, adrenaline given after participants viewed affectively-arousing slides produced an enhancement in the participants' long-term memory of the slides (Cahill and Alkire, 2003).

Thus, extensive evidence from pharmacological manipulations indicates that emotionally-arousing events and stimuli are more likely to be consolidated into long-term memory representations. The mechanisms underlying this consolidation process are probably linked to the actions of a variety of hormones that are modulated by the amygdala. In turn, the amygdala sends projections to a number of other brain regions (e.g., the hippocampus) which are also likely to be important in consolidating memories. As we have seen, some neuroimaging studies with human participants show that an enhanced connectivity between amygdala and hippocampal activity during encoding of arousing stimuli is associated with improved long-term memory of these events (usually tested 3–4 weeks later). These studies are generally considered to support the hypothesis that the amygdala–hippocampal network is directly influencing consolidation (e.g., Kensinger and Corkin, 2004). However, a problem with these studies is that memory is generally only tested once after consolidation is presumed to be well under way and therefore it is difficult to assess whether arousal is primarily influencing consolidation rather than encoding processes.

Retrieval effects

Relatively few studies have examined the impact of affect during the process of retrieval. However, there is some evidence that activation of the amygdala and regions of the anterior temporal pole are involved specifically in the retrieval of affective information (Dolan et al., 2000). Participants were shown a set of positive, negative and neutral IAPS pictures five minutes prior to PET scanning. During scanning, participants were presented with a series of pictures (some old, some new) and asked to either make a recognition judgment or an indoor/outdoor judgment task. It was found that qualitatively different neural networks were involved in the retrieval of neutral information and the retrieval of affective information. For both positively and negatively valenced pictures there was significant activation in the right anterior temporal pole and in the left amygdala. These regions were not activated during retrieval of neutral pictures. The activation of the left amygdala during retrieval of affective items was independent of the valence of the pictures, as has also been found for effects at encoding (e.g., Hamann et al., 1999). A problem with this study is the possibility that the amygdala was activated post-retrieval by the emotional arousal produced by the retrieved memory. In other words, the amygdala may not have played a specific role in retrieving affective stimuli, but rather, it may have been rapidly activated by the retrieved memories.

This problem was overcome to some extent by a study that assessed retrieval of previously neutral items that had been encoded in differing affective contexts (Smith et al., 2004). Participants viewed various neutral pictures superimposed on a background of IAPS pictures that were negative, positive or neutral. During retrieval of these neutral items, there was significant activation of the amygdala, OFC and the ACC for those that had been encoded in affective backgrounds. These structures are known to be associated with affective processing. The fact that they were activated to inherently neutral stimuli that had been learned in affective backgrounds supports the hypothesis that affect can also influence memory by modulating retrieval processes.

However, there is an alternative explanation of these results. It is clear that stimuli that become associated with affective contexts may themselves become affectively toned. Therefore, it may have been the current processing of the now affectively significant item that led to activation rather than the retrieval itself. This problem illustrates the difficulty of isolating the effects of affect on a specific aspect of memory, especially retrieval.

To summarize, there is evidence that affect may well influence memory at all stages. Thus, an affective context may influence the *encoding* of a stimulus as well as the *consolidation* of memories into long-term memory. Finally, it is also possible that the affective context can specifically influence *retrieval* processes, although the evidence is less clear here. These processes are very difficult to separate. Other issues relate to the current emotions and the ongoing mood states being experienced by participants in experiments. In autobiographical studies of emotional memory, for example, it is likely that people are in highly aroused affective states (e.g., excitement or fear) and it may well be these emotions or mood states (rather than features of the events themselves) that impact on memory. Even in laboratory studies that present stimuli which are inherently less arousing (e.g., pictures of mutilated bodies etc) it is nevertheless possible that viewing numerous negative items may induce negative mood states. Indeed, some studies have effectively induced both positive and negative mood states simply by requiring people to process affectively toned pictorial stimuli such as sad and happy facial expressions (Schneider et al., 1994). Therefore, it may be the induction of a particular mood state that influences subsequent memory rather than features of the stimulus or event. In the next section, the large literature on mood and memory is reviewed.

DO MOOD STATES INFLUENCE MEMORY?

The study of how mood might influence memory has a long history (Blaney, 1986; Eich, 1995; Ellis and Moore, 1999; Levine and Pizarro, 2004, for reviews). The general idea is that when we are in a bad or depressed mood, we tend to notice things that are congruent with that mood and also seem to remember the more negative events that have happened to us in the past. In contrast, when we are in a good mood, the world can seem a brighter place and we seem to remember lots of positive and happy memories from our past. By and large, scientific research has provided support for these general impressions. The investigation of mood and memory is a large and complex literature and here we will focus on two phenomena that have been intensively studied: *mood congruent memory* and *mood dependent memory*.

Mood congruency effects occur when we recall primarily negative events from our past when we are in a depressed mood, or when we recall primarily positive events from our past when we are in a happy mood. In other words, what we remember is *congruent* with our current mood state. Thus, recall is facilitated for information that is affectively congruent with our current mood state. In contrast, mood dependent memory occurs when material that was learned while in a particular mood is more likely to be recalled when you are again in that mood. In other words, if we hear a story while we are in a sad mood, then we should be more likely to remember details of that story some time later when we are once again in a sad mood as opposed to being in a happy mood. Thus, the hypothesis here is that memory will be facilitated when there is a match between mood at encoding and mood at retrieval. We will examine evidence for both of these hypotheses in the following sections.

Mood congruent memory

Mood congruent memory can occur at both encoding and retrieval. Investigations of mood congruent memory have generally induced a particular mood state (usually happy or sad moods) in the laboratory and then presented people with some material to learn. Following some delay, a recall or recognition test has then been given. A wide range of methods have been used to induce mood states and some of the more common techniques, along with a representative example of a study using this technique, are outlined in Table 7.1. Mood is usually measured subjectively both before and after the induction procedure by means of a standardized scale such as the profile of mood states (POMS) or simple visual analogue scales (VAS) that require people to mark on a line where they are in terms of a particular mood (e.g., extremely sad at one end to extremely happy at the other). This allows the researchers to confirm that the appropriate mood state has been successfully induced.

The effects of mood at encoding have usually been investigated by inducing either a sad or a happy mood and then requiring people to learn a list of words with either

TABLE 7.1 Common procedures used to induce different mood states in studies investigating the influence of mood on memory

Type of procedure	*Description*	*Example of study using this technique*
Velten mood induction	Series of statements relating to negative or positive mood states are read	Direnfield and Roberts (2006)
Mood induction by music	Snippets of music relating to negative or positive mood are listened to	Gilboa-Schechtmann et al. (2000)
Mood induction by film	Series of positive (e.g., comedy) or negative film clips are watched	Park and Banaji (2000)
Hypnosis	Participants are hypnotized into either a positive or a negative mood	Bower et al. (1981)

a negative or a positive valence. Later, when participants are in a neutral mood state they are asked to recall as many of the words as they can. Increased recall is found for items that were congruent with mood at encoding (e.g., Bower et al., 1981; Rinck et al., 1992). The typical explanation for this effect is that people encode mood congruent information at a deeper level and engage in more elaborative associations for material that is congruent with their current mood state. The *associative network model* (Bower, 1981), for example, predicts that information that is congruent with a person's current mood should be more salient and processed at a deeper level than material that is incongruent with current mood. There is plenty of evidence for this: people in whom a happy mood state is induced tend to spend more time looking at positive versus negative pictures, watch more happy relative to sad television shows, seek out pleasant social experiences rather than relatively sombre activities and spend more time listening to up-beat versus sad music (Eich, 1995, for review). Forgas (1995) has also reported that people in sad or happy moods spend more time studying material that is congruent with their mood state and less time studying material that is incongruent with their mood state, supporting the view that people engage in more elaborative processing of mood congruent material. This provides a good explanation of the influence of mood at encoding since it is well established that an increase in elaborative processing of material is associated with better memory for that material.

While the effects of mood congruency at encoding seem fairly consistent the influence of mood at *retrieval* is less clear. The typical experiment requires people to learn lists of words that vary in valence (positive and negative) while in a neutral mood. A mood state (sad or happy) is then induced at retrieval and participants are required to recall as many words as they can. Under these conditions, some studies have reported no effects of mood on memory (Bower et al., 1981; Gotlib and McCann, 1984) while some report mood congruency effects (Teasdale and Russell, 1983). Studies of autobiographical material, however, have tended to show more consistent results. In this type of study, a mood state is induced and people are asked to recall events from their own life. Generally, the valence of the events recalled is congruent with the mood state induced at retrieval (Blaney, 1986), although some studies have reported better memory for events that are incongruent with the current mood (Parrott and Sabini, 1990). A real problem with studies of autobiographical event memory, however, is that the valence of the material recalled is almost always congruent with the mood state at the time of the event. For example, if a person is induced into a happy mood state she might recall a positively valenced event such as a party that took place the previous year following the news that she had passed her exams. This of course might be evidence that mood congruency at retrieval influenced memory, but it is also highly likely that the person in question was in a very happy and positive mood at the time that the party took place. Therefore, the results of this type of study might just as easily be explained by mood congruency effects occurring at encoding rather than mood congruency effects at retrieval (Blaney, 1986).

Another complication in interpreting the effects of mood on memory, especially for autobiographical events is that the mood at retrieval as well as current appraisals of events may distort memory of past affective experiences. There is evidence, for example, that memories for past affectively-toned events can be reconstructed to some extent based on the current appraisals of the event. In one experiment, students were asked to rate how anxious and nervous they felt before a midterm exam. They were then randomly assigned to one of two groups. Group 1 were told their exam grades before being asked to recall their pre-exam emotions, while Group 2 were asked to recall their pre-exam emotions before being given their grades. In contrast to those who had not yet learned their grades, students who had done well tended to underestimate how anxious they had felt before the exam, whereas those that had done poorly tended to overestimate how anxious they had felt (Safer et al., 2002). Thus, information given after the outcome of an event is known can produce distortions in how well people remember their past affective experiences.

Animal research has found supporting evidence by showing, for example, that over time the memory for the intensity of a fear response can become increasingly malleable. Hendersen (1985) conditioned rats to expect an electric shock when they heard a specific tone. An index of how intensely the rats experienced the shock was obtained by a simple behavioural measure. First, the rats were deprived of water so that they were thirsty. Then when they were given access to water, the degree to which their drinking behaviour was disrupted by the tone provided a measure of the felt intensity of the shock. This simple memory test took place on two occasions, one day after the initial conditioning and again 60 days later. On the day of the memory test, rats were once again exposed to unexpected electric shocks that were either less intense or more intense than the original shock. The interesting finding was that, when the rats were then exposed to the critical tone that was associated with the original shock, those that had just received a more intense shock showed more disruption to drinking than those who had received a milder shock. Importantly, this difference was larger at the longer delay. This experiment provides further evidence that a more recent experience can override memory and result in a bias towards more recent events (Hendersen, 1985). An electric shock will be remembered as less intense if a more intense shock has been recently experienced, whereas it will be remembered as more intense if a milder shock has been recently experienced.

Therefore, just as with memory for non-emotional events, memory for affectively significant events is also subject to distortion and can be influenced by post-event appraisals and experiences. This should not surprise us too much since the function of memory may be to guide future behaviour rather than to keep an accurate record of the past. Thus, the recollection of past negative or positive affective experiences allows organisms to know whether to avoid or to seek out similar situations in the future (e.g., Damasio, 1994; Hendersen, 1985). Since emotional memories are influenced by appraisals of the current affective situation, they may act as a better guide for future behaviour than if they were a more faithful record of the past (Levine and Safer, 2002). This assumption is supported by that fact that, while emotional memories clearly do fade over time and are subject to distortions from post-event reinterpretations, they do still tend to be longer-lasting and more vivid than non-emotional memories (e.g., Reisberg and Heuer, 2004).

In general, mood congruency effects on memory are well established and probably occur both at encoding and retrieval. A number of factors are important in determining whether mood congruency effects will occur. These include: whether or not the material that is encoded is self-referential rather than other-referential and whether or not people are aware that what they are learning is consistent with their current mood (Ellis and Moore, 1999). Another important factor concerns the intensity of the experienced mood state and the intensity of the material. For example, Rinck et al. (1992) found the typical mood congruency effects at encoding when the words to be learned were highly affectively toned. However, when the affective tone of the words was mild they actually found mood *incongruency* effects. The authors argue that when both materials and mood are sufficiently intense they are likely to be noticed and then more elaborative associations are likely to be formed. This explanation accounts for mood congruency effects in intense situations, but does not explain mood incongruency effects with milder material.

There have been a number of demonstrations of mood incongruency effects and it is interesting to question what mechanisms might underlie these effects. Why might people recall more positive information when they are in a negative mood or more negative information when they are in a positive mood? One possibility is that the effects of mood on memory may be modulated by cognitive control strategies such as the attempt to regulate moods. For example, in a study of autobiographical event memory Parrott and Sabini (1990) interviewed people on either bright sunny days (when mood was positive) or dark overcast days (when mood was depressed). On the dark overcast days when people rated themselves as being relatively sad, the first memory retrieved was very often a positive memory. Parrot and Sabini explained this result as the attempt by people to overcome their depressed mood by a mood repair strategy. We all learn to overcome our mood states in order to be more socially desirable (e.g., not to giggle or laugh during a religious service, to feign interest when we are bored etc). Thus, it is plausible that people will engage in a variety of cognitive tricks to overcome mood states and these cognitive strategies may explain mood incongruency effects in memory research. This seems a reasonable explanation for mood incongruency effects in autobiographical memory especially when the current mood is negative and positive retrievals help to restore a more positive mood. However, findings that very mildly affective stimuli can be better recalled when they are mood incongruent (Rinck et al., 1992) are more difficult to explain by this mechanism.

Until recently, studies of mood dependent memory have been restricted to the behavioural domain with little knowledge about the neural mechanisms that might underlie the effect. However, a study reported by Erk et al. (2003) indicates that the strength of activity in emotion-specific brain regions (e.g., amygdala) that was associated with the emotional context at encoding correlated with the probability of correct recall. In this study, all of the stimuli encoded were neutral words, but they were learned within an affective context. This background context was achieved by presenting participants with blocks of either negative or positive IAPS pictures followed by lists of 42 neutral words to be remembered. It is important to note that the authors themselves did not claim to be inducing mood at encoding, although it is likely that their procedure did just this (Lewis and Critchley, 2003). If so, the pattern of results suggests a possible neural basis for the influence of mood at encoding on subsequent recall. In other words, activity in emotion-specific regions of the brain associated with mood state at encoding might influence the probability of recall of words which have become affectively toned by means of the background context.

Mood dependent memory

As we have seen, mood dependent memory is the demonstration that material learned while in a particular mood is more likely to be recalled when the individual is again in the same mood. The important thing to remember here is that it is the *consistency* between mood at encoding and mood at retrieval that is important. This is different from mood congruency effects where it is the consistency between the mood and the material to be remembered that is important. One of the first experiments to investigate mood dependent memory effects used an experimental design that has become a prototype for subsequent studies (Bower et al., 1978). In the first part of the study, half of the participants were induced into a happy mood state while half were induced into a sad mood state by means of hypnosis. Once the appropriate mood state had been induced, participants were given a list of 16 unrelated neutral (List A) words to learn. A second opposite mood was then induced and people were required to learn another list of unrelated neutral words (List B). In the final session some time later, participants were once again induced into either a happy or a sad mood and asked to recall as many items as they could from List A. The crucial aspect of this experimental design was that some people were recalling words that they had learned when in the same mood as their current mood at retrieval, while other participants were now in a different mood than they had been when learning the words. The results from this study are shown in Figure 7.7.

As can be seen in Figure 7.7, recall of neutral words was significantly better when the mood at retrieval matched the mood at encoding. Moreover, the size of this effect was comparable for both sad and happy moods. Unfortunately, however, following several early demonstrations of these mood dependent memory effects, a number of studies failed to replicate the results. For example, Gordon Bower and his colleagues conducted several similar experiments but could find little or no evidence for mood dependent memory (Bower, 1987; Bower and Mayer, 1989). Nevertheless, in spite of these inconsistencies extensive reviews of the literature have concluded that there are certain conditions under which mood dependent effects almost always occur (Eich, 1995; Ucros, 1989).

In a detailed meta-analysis of the literature, for example, it was found that mood dependent memory effects were far more likely to occur with real-life events than with laboratory tasks. It should not surprise us that affect would influence memory to a greater extent when we are dealing with complex social situations and relationships rather than fairly arid stimuli such as meaningless lists of words. In complex social situations, the affective nature of the situation is an inherent part of the event that tends to be highly salient and well remembered. For example, many studies in social

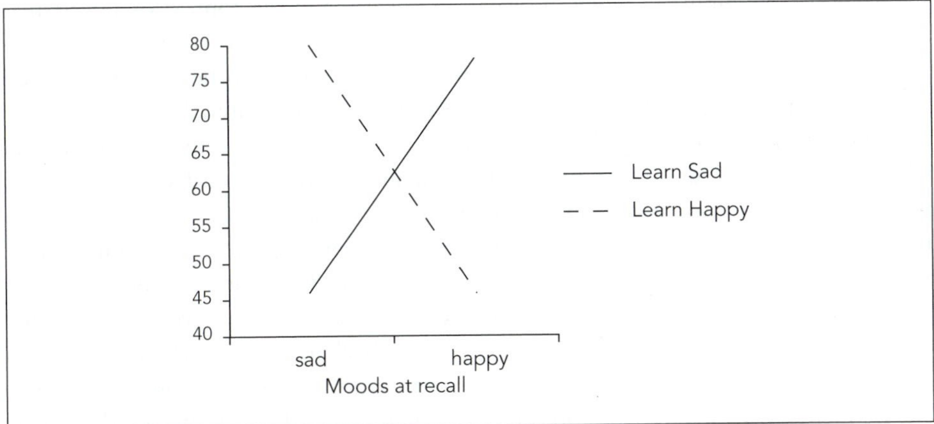

FIGURE 7.7 Recall of neutral words learned when participants were happy or sad, and then recalled when they were feeling happy or sad

Source: Bower et al. (1978).

psychology have shown that a person's mental representation of a social event tends to be dominated by the affective tone of the situation rather than other details of the event. Thus, for example, people may recall a specific event as being 'warm, interesting, dull, tense, calm, rejecting' (Pervin, 1976). Different events may be categorized together on the basis of their affective similarities over and above any other similarities. For this type of material, it is likely that the encounter and the mood experienced during that encounter are perceived as 'belonging together' and it is this grouping of affect and the situation that ensures strong mood dependent memory effects (Bower, 1981; Bower and Forgas, 2001; Eich et al., 1994). Moreover, as we mentioned previously, affective situations encountered in everyday life are also likely to relate to a person's important life goals and are likely to be appraised and interpreted as being especially significant.

For all of these reasons, mood states occurring in real-life situations are generally associated with stronger and more intense mood states than would normally occur under laboratory conditions. It is likely that a stronger mood state at encoding will result in a stronger association with the material to be remembered. Thus, when mood at retrieval *matches* the mood at encoding, the mood itself provides a stronger retrieval cue (Bower, 1981, 1992). This would explain why mood dependent memory is most evident when mood states are intense (Eich, 1995). The point here is that mood can act as a distinctive context that can then have powerful effects on memory. If the context or state is changed it will become harder to remember things that were learned in the past. However, if the original state or context is reinstated then the material once again becomes accessible to memory.

This perspective assumes that mood can act as a retrieval cue in much the same way as other factors can influence memory. For instance, when divers learn a list of words while under water they are more likely to retrieve those words when they are again under water relative to when they try to recall the words on the beach (Godden and

Baddeley, 1975). Similarly, when information is learned in the context of a particular background aroma that information is more likely to be retrieved when the same aroma is presented. State dependent memory effects have also been demonstrated by means of pharmacological manipulations. If people learn material while under the influence of a particular drug they are subsequently more likely to recall that material when in the same drug-induced state. Thus, many environmental factors can act as retrieval cues and mood is just one of them. Evidence that mood is acting as a cue to retrieval comes from findings that mood dependent effects are not generally found when recognition (as opposed to recall) tests are used (Bower and Cohen, 1982, for review). The idea is that the recognition cue itself is a very strong retrieval cue that simply overrides other more subtle cues, such as background mood, aroma etc. In contrast, when retrieval cues are minimal then mood may play a strong role in influencing memory. If this explanation is correct, then it is perfectly understandable why stronger mood states would be associated with stronger mood dependent memory effects.

An alternative explanation as to why mood dependent memory effects are more reliable with real-life events might be because these events are likely to have *internally* generated as opposed to *externally* generated retrieval cues. This hypothesis was tested directly by requiring people to either 'read' or 'generate' words that were later recalled (Eich and Metcalfe, 1989). For the read items, participants had to read a list of word pairs from the same semantic category in which the second word was the target item (e.g., silver-GOLD). For the generated items, the same category pairs were used but this time the participant had to generate the second word (e.g., precious metal: silver-G___). The words that were generated by participants under these conditions were better remembered than words that were read when the mood at encoding (read or generate) matched the mood at retrieval. This pattern of results supports the hypothesis that internally generated events are more easily associated with the current mood state and therefore mood dependent memory effects are more likely. Eich (1995) concluded from his extensive review of the literature that mood dependent memory effects were, in fact, reliable and consistent as long as the moods experienced were strong and stable, especially when people were involved in actively generating the target events that were later remembered. In everyday social situations, of course, this is almost always the case, whereas it is less likely under laboratory conditions. Thus, when mood acts as a highly distinctive state or context then there is ample evidence that mood can exert a powerful effect on memory.

DOES THE TYPE OF MOOD MAKE A DIFFERENCE TO MEMORY?

In the literature we have discussed so far, neither mood congruency effects nor mood dependent effects seem to differ between different mood states. For example, in the early mood congruency studies (Bower, 1981) the magnitude of the effect was equivalent for sad and happy mood states. Likewise, in mood dependent memory studies little difference is observed between sad and happy mood states (Bower et al., 1978). Indeed, as we have seen the intensity of the mood may be more important than the mood itself (Rinck et al., 1992). However, this reliance on the concept of arousal or intensity in mood and memory research has been criticized by Levine and Pizarro (2004). They argue that a more complete understanding of how moods and emotions influence memory will only develop if researchers take seriously the differences between different emotions. The hypothesis is that emotions direct attention towards the aspects of a situation that are functional for that particular set of circumstances. For example, fear is elicited by an appraisal of future harm or threat, and resources will then be attuned to information relevant to potential danger and to the means of avoiding danger. In contrast, anger is elicited by the appraisal of a current obstacle to well-being. Thus, resources will be allocated toward stimuli relevant to the obstacle and its removal. From this perspective, it is impossible to distinguish emotions only on the basis of levels of arousal and type of valence (Ellsworth and Scherer, 2003). In contrast, this view makes the prediction that emotions should enhance memory for those details that are most relevant to the motivations associated with discrete emotions. There is some confusion between emotions and moods here, but the argument does seem plausible if we assume that different mood states are also related to different adaptive functions.

ARE POSITIVE AND NEGATIVE MOODS ASSOCIATED WITH DIFFERENT INFORMATION-PROCESSING STRATEGIES?

What is the evidence that different mood states should enhance memory for events that are relevant to the motivations associated with different moods? One line of research concerns the finding that different information-processing strategies seem to be associated with different moods. For instance, when people are happy they tend to rely on more general knowledge and stereotypes consistent with the notion that happiness occurs when a goal has been attained and there is no immediate problem to solve. In contrast, negative moods are associated with a more detailed evaluation of information with a reduced emphasis on general knowledge. This is consistent with the view that negative moods are experienced when important goals have been threatened or have failed. Klaus Fiedler (1990, 2000, 2001), for example, has presented evidence that different affective states are indeed associated with different information-processing strategies. He proposes that the type of information-processing strategy used in different situations relates directly to the different adaptive functions of different mood states. Thus, the proposal is that positive affective states support the processing of information by means of *assimilation*, which involves the active cognitive elaboration of stimuli using internal schemata and knowledge structures. This information-processing style is particularly useful in appetitive situations where exploration and creativity are important. In contrast, negative affective states induce the processing of information by means of *accommodation*, which is an adaptive process whereby the organism focuses on the demands of the external world. Thus, accommodation involves the careful, exhaustive and detailed perception and analysis of external stimuli. This information-processing style is more relevant in aversive situations in which it is important that the organism does not make mistakes.

There is abundant evidence that these different styles of information processing are indeed associated with positive and negative affective states. Thus, people in happy moods tend to be more creative and are more likely to use top-down processing styles (e.g., Isen, 1984). People in negative moods tend to engage in a more systematic evaluation of information and are less likely to commit memory errors (see Fiedler, 1990, 2000, for review).

There is also evidence that these different information-processing strategies can influence memory. For example, in one study a happy or a sad mood was induced in participants and they were then presented with information about everyday activities such as eating in a restaurant (Bless et al., 1996). The crucial part of the experiment was that some of the information presented was typical of the situation (e.g., 'the hostess placed the menus on the table') while other information was not typical of a particular script (e.g., 'he put away his tennis racket'). In a later recognition test, people who had been in a happy mood were more likely to 'recognize' script-typical material even when it had not been presented. In contrast, participants who had been in a sad mood were more accurate in identifying items that had or had not been presented. Likewise, other studies have shown that people in happy mood states are more likely to endorse ethnic names as being members of stereotypical categories, while those in negative mood states are more accurate in recognition judgments and are less likely to be lured by stereotypical information (Park and Banaji, 2000). Taken together, these studies indicate that positive mood states can result in a greater reliance on general knowledge and stereotypes with a resulting increased number of intrusion errors in memory. This pattern is as predicted by the notion that positive and negative moods promote information-processing styles based on assimilation and accommodation, respectively (Fiedler, 1990).

These findings are difficult to explain purely in terms of general arousal. Instead, it seems likely that people experiencing different emotions and their associated mood states might process information in fundamentally different ways. In turn, these different information-processing styles are likely to have consequences for how well specific types of information are remembered. In particular, positive and negative emotions (and presumably moods) have different motivations and therefore different types of information are likely to be relevant to these emotions. Levine and Pizarro (2004) have outlined the types of information that are expected to be central to different emotions on the basis of appraisal theory. See Table 7.2.

While this is a plausible hypothesis, there is precious little evidence to support the suggestion that different emotional and mood states are associated with enhanced memory for different types of information. Levine and Pizarro (2004) cite a range of evidence from different psychopathological states (e.g., anxiety, depression etc) showing that these states are associated with attentional and judgmental biases towards mood relevant material. Thus, people with spider phobia show enhanced recognition memory for pictures of spiders while depressed people recall more negative autobiographical events than non-depressed people (Williams et al., 1988, for review). This literature will be discussed in more detail in Chapter 9 and is broadly consistent with the notion that different mood states result in cognitive biases for motivationally

TABLE 7.2 Different information-processing strategies associated with positive and negative emotions and the type of information expected to be central for different emotions

Emotional valence	*Motivational state*	*Information-processing strategy*
Positive	Goal attained; no immediate problem to be solved	Flexible processing; increased reliance on general knowledge and heuristics
Negative	Actual or threatened goal failure; change beliefs, plans or behaviours	Analytic, data-driven processing
Discrete emotions	Motivational state	Central information
Happiness	Maintain current state; attain new goals	Broad range of information from general knowledge and the environment
Fear	Avoid or escape threat of goal failure	Sources of threat; means of avoiding threat
Anger	Remove obstacle to goal attainment	Goal; agents obstructing goal attainment
Sadness	Adjust to irrevocable goal failure	Outcomes and consequences of goal failure

Source: Based on Table 1 in Levine and Pizarro (2004).

relevant material. However, for now it is important to point out that these studies generally only investigate a single mood state (e.g., depression or anxiety) and compare this with a matched control group.

What is required to properly test the motivational hypothesis are studies that induce different mood states in the same experiment and then investigate memory for different types of information. There are very few studies of this nature. However, one study did examine recall following the induction of happiness, sadness or anger (Levine and Burgess, 1997). These different mood states were elicited by randomly assigning students a grade 'A' or 'D' on a surprise quiz. Immediately after the quiz, the students took part in what they believed to be a separate study in which they were required to listen to a narrative story about a person's first term at university and then recall as many details as they could from the story. At the end of the study, they were asked to indicate how angry, happy or sad they had felt when they had received their quiz grades. The results on the memory test revealed that those who said they had been happy showed an enhanced memory for narrative as a whole. In contrast, students who said that they had been primarily sad or angry were more likely to recall specific types of information. Those who were sad recalled significantly more information relating to negative outcomes than did angry participants (e.g., 'They received a bad grade on the speech'). In addition, angry students showed a tendency to recall more information about goal states than did sad students (e.g., 'Mary wanted her speech to be really good'), although this difference did not reach statistical significance. Thus, these results provide some evidence that people in different negative mood states (anger versus sadness) tend to recall different types of information that relate to the varying motivations underlying these different affective states. However, more specific studies are required to fully address this hypothesis.

THEORETICAL ACCOUNTS OF MOOD AND MEMORY INTERACTIONS

Associative network models

Various different theories have been developed to explain the pattern of results discussed in the previous sections. One of the most influential is that developed by Gordon Bower based on associative network theories, which have long been popular in cognitive psychology. The basic idea behind associative network theories is that all of the concepts and facts we hold in our long-term memories are stored as *nodes* within a complex network (Anderson and Bower, 1973). Our concept of a dog, for example, is stored as a node alongside many other nodes such as animal, barks, bites, Fido etc. These nodes are connected together by means of semantic relationships so that closely related concepts (e.g., dog-bark) will be closely associated in the network, whereas other concepts (e.g., dog-ship) will be more distantly related. The assumption is that when a particular node is activated (by reading the word 'dog' for example, or thinking about a dog) an activation spreads out around the network like a wave, activating closely related concepts more than more distantly related concepts.

Associative network models provide a good account of *semantic priming effects*, which is the demonstration that our perception of a word or concept can be speeded and improved if a semantically related concept has just been processed. To illustrate, in a typical experiment people may make lexical decisions (i.e., word or non-word decisions) on a series of letter strings presented on a computer screen. The *target* letter strings are usually presented just after another word called the *prime*. The typical finding is that RTs are faster when the prime is semantically related to the target on word trials. Thus, people would be faster to decide that 'nurse' was a word when it followed the word 'doctor' than when it followed the word 'sailor'. This semantic priming effect is often explained by appealing to associative network models. Processing the word 'doctor' results in activation of that concept along with all associated concepts in the network. Thus, closely related concepts (e.g., nurse, hospital, illness, patient etc) will be activated above a baseline level so that, if they are now presented for identification, they will be easier to identify because they are already activated (e.g., Anderson and Bower, 1973).

The insight of Bower (1981) was to propose that mood states could also be stored as nodes within a semantic network, along with other 'cognitive' concepts. Thus, for each particular fact a range of affective states (e.g., emotions and moods experienced in association with that object) may also be linked to the core concept. This means that if a concept is activated in memory then there may well be some activation of the associated mood via the same mechanisms as operate in semantic priming. Similarly, if a particular mood state is activated then concepts and facts associated with that mood will also be activated. It is clear that this model predicts both mood congruency and mood dependent memory effects. If we are in a happy mood, for example, then concepts and facts associated with that mood state also become activated so that mood congruent material is rendered more salient. Likewise, if we attempt to recall information that is linked with a particular mood state (e.g., sadness) and we are currently in the same mood state facts associated with sadness should become more salient, increasing the likelihood of recalling those facts. Mood dependent memory effects are therefore also predicted by an associative network model.

Bower assumed that around six basic emotions are fairly hard-wired into the brain (1981). Each of these would have specific triggers and each trigger would become elaborated and differentiated as an individual's life progressed. Consistent with models of appraisal, he proposed that the process of eliciting an emotion could be understood as a series of production rules that recognized or appraised particular situations that called for the production of a particular emotion. Importantly, the proposal was that, once an emotion node was activated, this activation would spread to a variety of indicators connected with this emotion. These include a variety of autonomic responses, facial expressions and action tendencies, as well as associated concepts such as memories and situations that were connected with that emotion in the past. In other words, a particular memory record is assumed to be stored in association with the emotion evoked and experienced during that event. This means that when people are in a similar mood state to when they learned a particular fact then it should be much easier to recall memories associated with that mood. This, of course, has been found in mood dependent memory studies. A fragment of an associative memory network incorporating two basic emotions is outlined in Figure 7.8. It is interesting to note that the activation of one emotion node (e.g., sadness) is assumed to inhibit other emotion nodes as well as increasing activation of concepts related to the activated emotion. This push-pull mechanism would serve to increase mood congruency effects since related concepts are activated at the same time as concepts related to other mood states are inhibited.

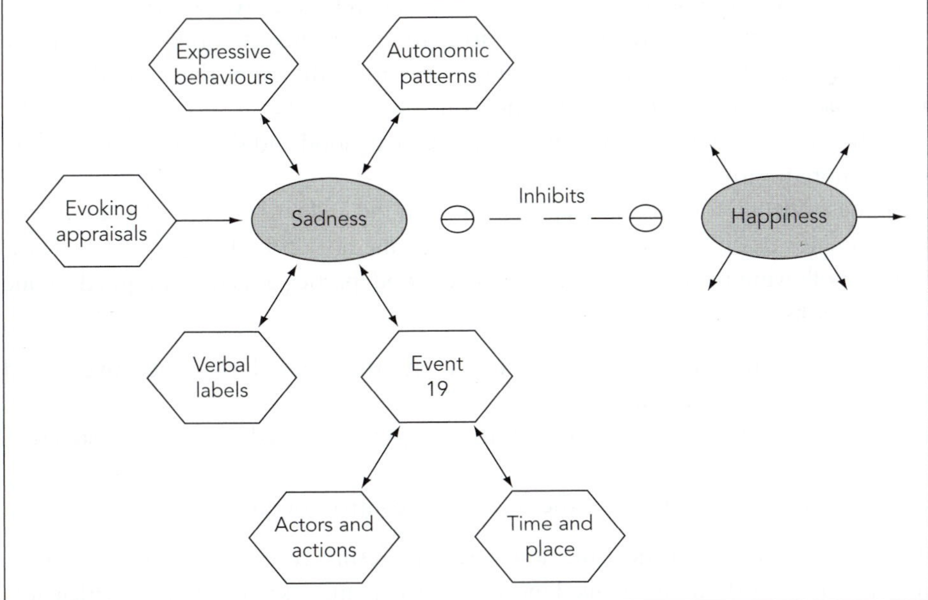

FIGURE 7.8 A fragment of the associative network surrounding an emotion node in memory
Source: Bower (1981).

The associative network model of mood and memory has been highly influential and explains many of the reported mood congruency and mood dependency memory effects. However, there are some problems with associative network theory. One issue is that network models make fairly general predictions of mood congruency effects regardless of the particular mood elicited. However, as we will see in Chapter 8, different mood states seem to be associated with different types of cognitive bias. Thus, depressed mood is associated with mood congruent biases in recall whereas anxious mood states do not seem to elicit mood congruent memory biases. In contrast, anxiety states are associated with mood congruent biases in attention (see Williams et al., 1988, for review). The differentiation of mood congruency effects based on which aspect of cognition is being assessed is difficult to reconcile with a simple network model.

Another criticism of network models is that they do not account for the effects of *motivation* on mood congruent memory effects (Singer and Salovey, 1988). A large literature now suggests that motivation is an important variable in determining mood congruency effects on both memory and judgment. For example, there is a good deal of evidence that people do not passively experience negative affective states. Instead, they use a variety of strategies to regulate affective states either to prolong positive mood states or to reduce or eliminate negative states (e.g., Frijda, 1988; Thayer et al., 1994). One such strategy is *distraction*, which usually involves an active attempt to focus attention on something unrelated to the event that caused the initial negative reaction. The work of Susan Nolen-Hoeksema and her colleagues has shown that distraction is most effective when attention is directed to something mildly pleasant and/or absorbing (Nolen-Hoeksema and Morrow, 1993; Nolen-Hoeksema et al., 1993; Rusting and Nolen-Hoeksema, 1998). Theoretically, the use of strategies like distraction should influence the way information is activated within an associative network. Since distraction draws attention away from the event that caused the initial negative mood and focuses attention on something else, it should interrupt the spreading of activation associated with the negative mood and should instead activate other, more positive, associations in memory.

Some evidence for this was reported in a mood induction study that examined the influence of different strategies on a simple memory test (Rusting and DeHart, 2000). Following the induction of a negative mood, participants were assigned to one of three tasks:

(a) think about their feelings and the event that caused their negative mood (rumination condition);
(b) think about a series of distracting thoughts provided to them (distraction condition); or
(c) list their thoughts freely as they occurred (control condition).

They were then given a short memory test. The results revealed that those who ruminated on their thoughts recalled more negative memories compared to participants in the control condition. However, people in the distraction condition recalled more positive memories than participants in the control condition. These results show that different mood repair strategies can result in either mood congruent (rumination), mood incongruent (distraction) or no mood congruency (control condition) effects. This pattern of results for different cognitive strategies is problematic for simple forms of associative network models.

Affect infusion model (AIM)

When motivations to regulate emotions and moods are present, mood incongruity effects often occur. Numerous studies have shown that mood congruity effects on both memory and judgment are by no means universal and may be influenced by a range of factors such as the context, the nature of the task, the type of mood experienced, and many other features of the situation (Blaney, 1986; Fiedler, 1991; Forgas et al., 1984). In an attempt to bring some coherence to this range of empirical results, Joseph Forgas has developed the affect infusion model (AIM) (Forgas, 1995). His main aim was to provide a more explicit specification of the circumstances in which mood congruity effects are likely or unlikely to occur. The model is based on the assumption that the mood-congruent predictions of associative network models should occur only under conditions that allow an open and unbiased search and processing strategy to operate (Bower and Forgas, 2001).

The AIM identifies four processing strategies in which differing degrees of affect infusion may occur. As shown in Figure 7.9, affect infusion depends on which strategy is adopted in a given situation. The choice of strategy can be influenced by features of the task required, the person and the situation as a whole. Two of these strategies – direct access and motivated – involve closed and directed processing which limits the opportunity for affect infusion. In contrast, the two other strategies – heuristic and substantive – require more open and constructive processing styles, allowing more opportunity for affect infusion. Thus, the AIM proposes that different information processing strategies play a central role in determining the nature of affect–cognition relations.

The AIM defines affect infusion as the process by which affectively salient information becomes incorporated into cognitive and behavioural processes and exerts a congruent influence. As shown in Figure, 7.9, affect infusion is most likely to occur when one of the high infusion strategies is adopted, that is, when the overall situation promotes an open, elaborate and constructive information-processing style (Fiedler, 1991; Forgas, 1995). The AIM leads to the counterintuitive prediction that affect infusion will occur primarily when more substantive processing is required. This prediction has been supported by findings demonstrating that people show larger mood congruity effects when they are required to make judgments on atypical people, dating couples that were not well-matched or serious and complex conflicts. In contrast, when the judgments were on typical people, well-suited couples and straightforward conflicts then mood congruity effects were minimized (Bower and Forgas, 2001; Forgas, 1995, for review).

Affect infusion is defined as the mechanisms by which affectively toned information becomes incorporated into and exerts a congruent influence on cognitive processes

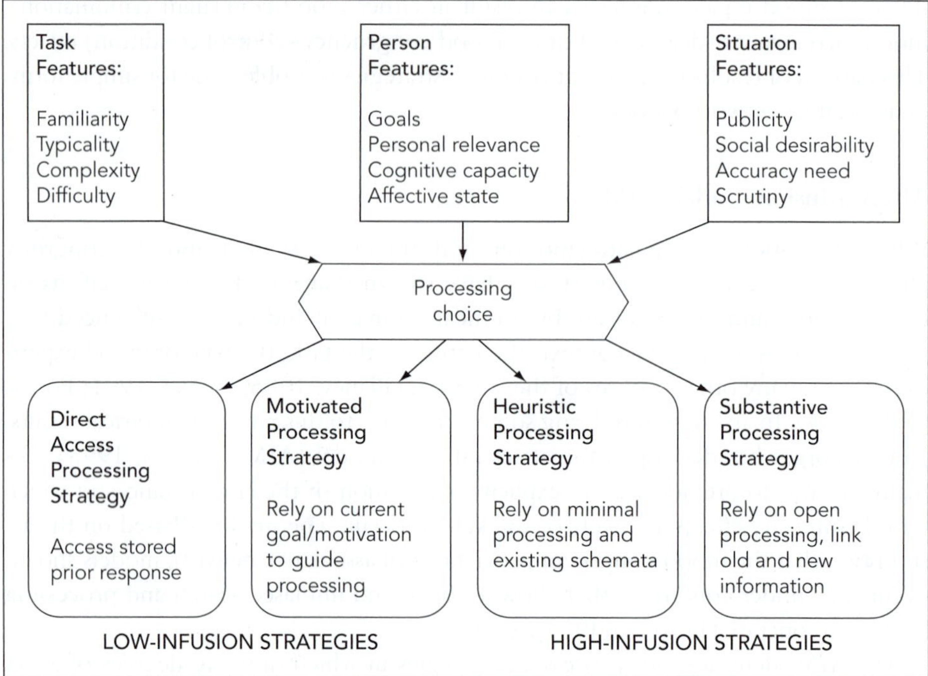

FIGURE 7.9 Outline of the multi-process AIM
Source: Forgas (1995).

(Forgas, 1995, 2001). The AIM proposes that the incorporation of affectively loaded information into cognitive processes will occur only when constructive and highly elaborate information processing strategies are used. This is because these strategies facilitate the inadvertent use of affective information. In contrast, if the situation calls for a simple pre-existing response or when a particular motivational objective is dominant, then affective information has little impact on cognitive processing. The AIM assumes that:

(a) the extent of affect infusion and hence mood congruity effects depends on the type of information processing style that is adopted; and
(b) all other things being equal, people should adopt the simplest processing strategy that requires the least effort.

As shown in Figure 7.9, the AIM identifies four different processing strategies. The *direct access strategy* involves the direct retrieval of a pre-existing response, and is likely to be used when the task is familiar and no strong motivational or other cues call for more elaborate processing. The *motivated strategy* is directed by a specific motivational objective, and involves a very targeted and selective information search relevant to that objective. As we have seen earlier, negative mood states may trigger motivated processing in the interests of mood repair. Both the direct access and the motivated processing styles tend to limit the amount of incidental affect infusion that can occur.

However, when there are no simple responses available or when there is no direct motivation to guide a response, then people may rely on heuristics or cognitive short-cuts to achieve a constructive response with minimal effort. Thus, in situations where there are no motivational pressures for more detailed processing and where the task is simple, familiar or of little personal relevance, then a *heuristic strategy* is likely to be adopted. Affect infusion can occur with this processing style as long as people rely on affect (e.g., mood state) as the heuristic cue. When the three simpler strategies are not adequate to deal with the situation then people are likely to adopt a *substantive processing strategy*. This strategy is most likely to be adopted when the task is difficult or complex or when it is novel and there is no motivational goal to guide processing. Affect infusion effects are very likely to occur with this strategy because of the reliance on constructive and generative processes that may selectively prime access to affectively congruent thoughts, memories and interpretations.

In addition to specifying different information processing strategies the AIM also outlines a range of contextual variables that influence processing choices. These include variables related to the person doing the processing, the situation and the task required. Moreover, as we have seen earlier in this chapter, there is evidence that different mood states may induce different types of processing strategy. Thus, positive affective states generally induce a more top-down and heuristic processing style, whereas more negative mood states tend to elicit more bottom-up, detailed and vigilant processing strategies (e.g., Bless, 2000; Fiedler, 2000). The AIM accommodates this evidence that affect itself can influence processing choices. In summary then, a key prediction of the AIM is the *presence* of mood congruity effects when heuristic and substantive processing strategies are adopted, and the *absence* of affect infusion when direct access or motivated processing is used. Thus, the AIM extends associative network models by specifying more explicitly the conditions under which affect infusion and hence mood congruent and mood dependent memory effects are most likely to occur (Bower and Forgas, 2001; Forgas, 1995, 2001).

CHAPTER SUMMARY

This chapter has reviewed some of the large literature indicating that affective events are better remembered than neutral events. Evidence for this hypothesis has been found for autobiographical memory (e.g., flashbulb memories), as well as within laboratory studies. However, while these emotional memories are highly salient they are not necessarily more accurate than any other type of memory. The question of whether affective material is remembered because of the effects of intensity or arousal or because of the valence of the material was addressed. Substantial evidence was also presented suggesting that affect can influence memory at both *encoding* and during the *consolidation* of material. There is also some evidence that affect can play a role at *retrieval* but there is less research on this component.

A brief overview of the literature addressing the effects of ongoing mood states on memory was also discussed, demonstrating evidence for both mood congruent memory effects as well as mood dependent memory effects. Bower's *associative network model*, which can account for many of the findings on the nature of the relations between affect and memory, was presented. Network-based theories do have some problems. However, at least some of these can be overcome by the *affect infusion model* developed by Forgas, which was also described.

RECOMMENDED READING

Although rather dated the following articles provide an excellent commentary and review of mood and memory research:

Blaney, P.H. (1986) 'Affect and memory: A review', *Psychological Bulletin*, 99, 229–56.
Bower, G.H. (1981) 'Mood and memory', *American Psychologist*, 36, 129–48.

A more recent review can be found in:

Parrott, W.G. and Spackman, M.P. (2000) 'Emotion and Memory', in M. Lewis and J. Haviland-Jones (eds), *Handbook of Emotions.* New York: Guilford Press, 2nd edition.

A number of edited books are also available containing many excellent chapters by different authors. These are:

Richard J. Davidson, Klaus R. Scherer and H. Hill Goldsmith (2003) *Handbook of Affective Sciences.* New York: Oxford University Press.
Paula Hertel (2004) *Emotion and Memory.* Oxford: Oxford University Press.

8 INDIVIDUAL DIFFERENCES IN EMOTION PROCESSING

DO COGNITIVE BIASES INFLUENCE EMOTIONAL REACTIVITY?

Chapter 3 presented evidence that different temperaments and personality traits are associated with different degrees of emotional reactivity. This chapter considers whether these differences may relate to personality congruent biases in cognitive processing. The hypothesis is that variation in *temperament* may shape how we see and interpret the world around us. In other words, do particular temperamental dimensions *bias* cognitive processes so that people attend to, interpret, and remember information that is congruent with their personality? What has been termed the 'trait congruency hypothesis' and assumes that all personality traits should predispose people to preferentially process information that is congruent with that trait (e.g., Bargh et al., 1988). Thus, constructs related to one's personality should be more easily accessible to cognitive processes and therefore will influence information processing over time.

AN OVERVIEW OF EMPIRICAL EVIDENCE

It is easy to imagine that a highly extraverted person might enjoy and actively seek out social opportunities since these are *perceived* and *interpreted* as being fun and rewarding. In contrast, a neurotic (or anxious) individual might interpret exactly the same situation as being very threatening and unpleasant. Thus, the impact of everyday events and situations can vary in consistent ways due to fundamental differences or *biases* in how people process the same information. There is a burgeoning literature showing how individual differences in affective style or temperament can bias a variety of cognitive processes (see Bargh et al., 1988; Mathews and MacLeod, 2005; Rusting and Larsen, 1998; Williams et al., 1988, 1997; Yiend, 2004, for reviews). One difficulty in trying to determine how individual differences in personality traits influence cognitive processing is that almost all of the research has focused on negative personality traits, emotions and mood states. This is understandable, of course, since a major research interest has been to determine whether cognitive biases are significant risk factors for the development of emotional disorders. This gap is beginning to be filled, however. There is a growing body of empirical work focusing on the impact of positive cognitive biases on general well-being and happiness. This work is especially interesting because it allows us to begin to identify the range of factors that might influence *resilience* to the stresses and strains encountered in everyday life.

This chapter discusses research investigating the association between natural variations in personality traits or temperament (e.g., extraversion, neuroticism etc)

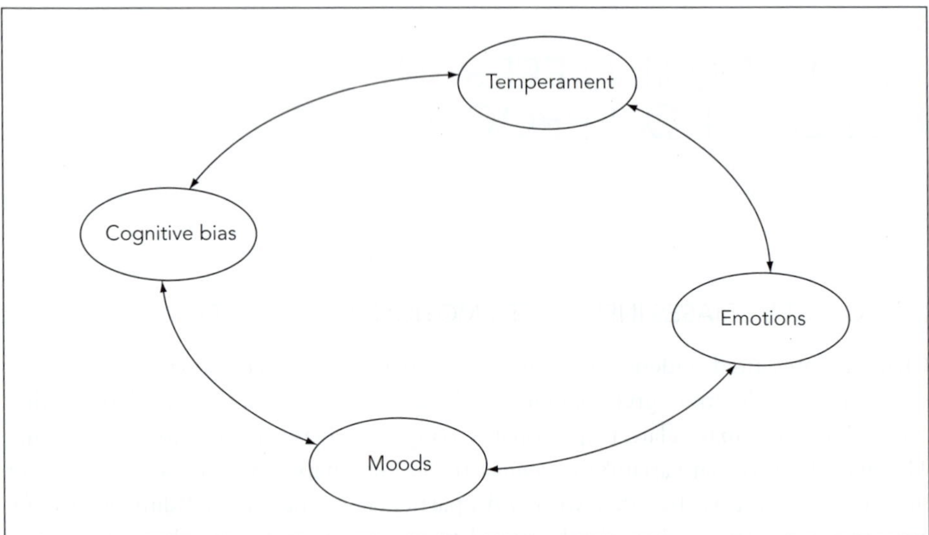

FIGURE 8.1 The reciprocal nature of the relationship between temperament, emotions, moods and cognitive biases

and fundamental biases in how information is processed. It is important to keep in mind, however, that the relationship between temperament and cognitive bias is bi-directional, as illustrated in Figure 8.1. A personality trait such as extraversion might induce a cognitive bias such that positively valenced information is prioritized by the cognitive system. Conversely, a pre-existing cognitive bias such as the tendency to selectively process either positive or negative information may result in the development of particular personality traits such as extraversion or neuroticism, respectively.

INTERACTIONS BETWEEN PERSONALITY TRAITS, EMOTIONS AND MOOD STATES

A difficult issue is how to separate the effects of *temperament* on cognitive processing of emotional information from the effects of *current mood state*. Enduring personality traits are, of course, strongly correlated with the propensity to experience particular emotions and mood states. This means that many of the apparent effects of temperament on cognitive processing may actually be due to mood states and emotions. In other words, if we find that extraversion is associated with enhanced processing of positive events, it is difficult to determine whether this is due to the mood state (happiness) or to the more enduring personality trait (extraversion), or to a combination of both (e.g., processing is enhanced for positive material in extraverts only when they are in a positive mood state).

In most everyday situations it is likely that personality traits and mood states will interact to modulate the strength of affect–cognition relations. Thus, we might expect that a temperamental dimension such as E-PA might be associated with the selective processing of positively valenced information, but that this will be particularly obvious when people are in a positive mood state. Likewise, a negative temperamental dimension such as N-NA should be associated with selective processing of negative information and this should be particularly noticeable when people are in a negative mood state. In other words, the type of mood congruency effects that we discussed in Chapters 6 and 7 are likely to be amplified when there is a match between the affective tone of enduring personality traits and more transient mood states. This is an important point and means that studies of mood congruency that do not take personality traits or temperament into account may well be missing a large part of the picture (Rusting, 2001).

First, cognitive processing may be modulated directly by variations of a range of personality traits or temperaments. Second, personality traits may modulate transient emotions and mood states that, in turn, influence cognitive processing. In other words, personality traits may bias cognition *indirectly* by influencing the intensity and frequency of mood states experienced. Third, it is also likely that personality traits and mood states will interact with each other to intensify the nature of cognitive biases. The three possible ways in which personality traits may influence cognitive biases are illustrated in Figure 8.2. To make matters even more complicated, we also need to keep in mind that the relations among all of these factors are likely to be bi-directional.

In the next section, we will selectively review the empirical evidence investigating the role of personality traits in modulating affect–cognition relations. Many information-processing studies have investigated whether trait (personality-based) and state-like (mood-based) individual differences in affective style are associated with particular

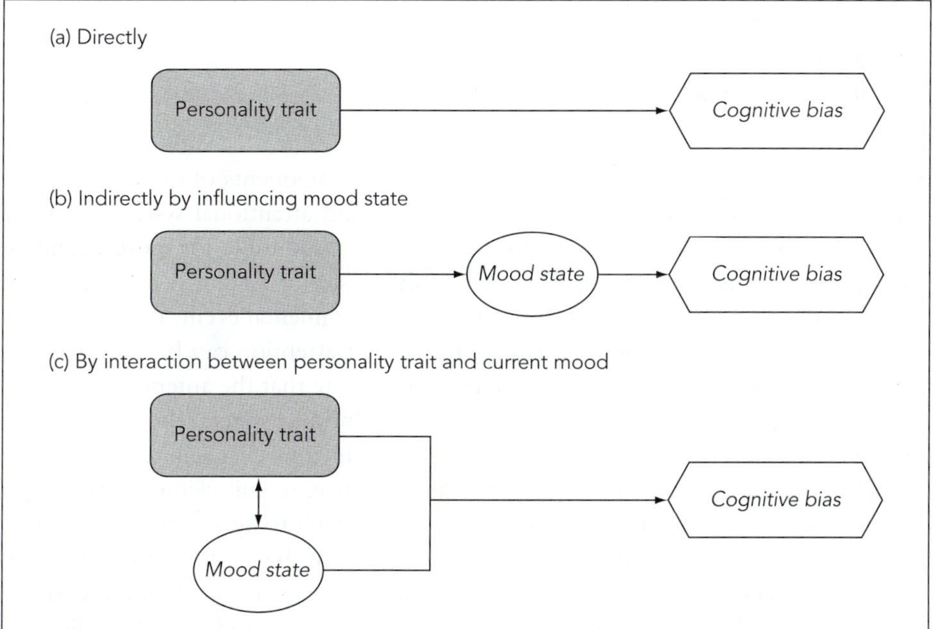

FIGURE 8.2 Three ways in which personality traits might influence cognitive bias

cognitive biases. Most empirical work has focused on negative traits (neuroticism, negative affectivity, trait-anxiety etc) and, therefore, most of the examples relate to negative emotions. Nevertheless, the assumption we make is that the same relations should hold for positive personality traits and biases towards positive information. We discuss a representative selection of studies that examine individual differences in cognitive processing in the domains of perception and attention, memory, and interpretation and judgment. In the final section, we discuss research investigating individual variations in *neural reactivity* to affective stimuli.

PERCEPTION AND ATTENTION

Various forms of *arousal* can serve to alert the organism to particular information. However, *attention* operates in a much more specific manner in terms of highlighting or amplifying the more important sources of information in a given situation. As we saw in Chapter 6, material with a negative valence tends to attract attention to a greater extent than positively valenced material. Thus, the bad often outweighs the good in terms of getting noticed. However, personality traits can modulate the degree to which each class of stimuli (positive versus negative valence) draws attention. Before examining some experiments in more detail, let us first discuss an important distinction between two attentional systems that has been made by Michael Posner and his colleagues (Posner and Petersen, 1990; Posner and Raichle, 1994). The *posterior attention system* is a reactive system that is involved with the orientation of attention from one spatial location to another. Thus, when a new object appears (or disappears) this system becomes activated. There are three subsystems within this overarching system that are responsible for three component operations:

(a) attention must *disengage* from the current focus;
(b) attention then *moves* to the new location;
(c) attention then *engages* with the new location.

Separate neural systems seem to underlie the three components of disengage, move and engage (Posner and Petersen, 1990). The second attentional system is known as the *anterior attentional system*, and this system is responsible for more voluntary and flexible attentional control. Thus, while the posterior system is often reflexive and responds in a fairly automatic way to some environmental event, the anterior attentional system plays a more regulatory role so that attention can be allocated in a voluntary and deliberate manner. It is important to note that the anterior attentional system can modulate the activity of the posterior attentional system, thereby ensuring that an organism is not always at the mercy of environmental events in terms of where attention gets allocated. Many cognitive tasks, of course, recruit elements from both of these systems and therefore it is sometimes very difficult to figure out which system is primarily involved in a particular experiment. Most of the studies examining individual differences have focused on tasks that primarily engage the posterior attentional system. We will discuss some of these studies first and then consider some studies that have investigated individual differences in attentional control mechanisms.

Personality congruent biases

If E-PA and N-NA are indeed associated with cognitive biases to process different classes of information then we should find fundamental personality-related differences in the operation of the posterior attentional system when stimuli relate to reward and punishment. Specifically, E-PA should be associated with a tendency for the system to be more activated in response to positively valenced information. On the other hand, N-NA should be associated with a tendency of the system to be more activated in the presence of negatively valenced stimuli. Thus each of the three components of this system – disengage, move, engage – should be biased in a way that is congruent with a particular personality trait.

There are surprisingly few studies examining biases in attention for negative and positive information in which measures of both E-PA and N-NA are available. In one study, participants' personality traits of E (extraversion) and N (neuroticism) were assessed on the Eysenck Personality Questionnaire (EPQ) (Eysenck and Eysenck, 1975a) and they were then presented with a series of faces and words to which affective judgements had to be made (Rusting and Larsen, 1998). The participant had to indicate by pressing a button whether the face was 'positive', 'negative' or 'neutral'. Faster reaction times (RTs) reflect faster encoding of a stimulus and are often considered to also reflect a speedier orienting of attention to it. Overall, people were slower to categorize negative relative to positive or neutral stimuli, regardless of whether they were words or pictures. This indicates that positive material is generally encoded more quickly than negative material. In order to examine the role of personality traits in determining performance on this task, correlations were then computed between E-PA and N-NA and RTs for positive, negative, and neutral items. The pattern of correlations is shown in Table 8.1. Extraversion was negatively correlated with RT to positive stimuli but not with RT to negative or neutral items. Thus, as expected, higher scores on extraversion were associated with faster RTs to positive words or faces indicating faster encoding of positive material. However, against expectation, no correlations were found between RTs to negative stimuli and degree of neuroticism.

TABLE 8.1 Standardized correlations (beta scores) predicting performance on an affective decision task from the personality factors of extraversion and neuroticism

	Extraversion	*Neuroticism*
Word stimuli		
Positive	–0.23*	–0.12
Negative	–0.01	–0.17
Neutral	0.04	0.03
Face stimuli		
Positive	–0.19*	0.05
Negative	0.15	–0.18
Neutral	0.09	0.00

Source: Data are taken from Rusting and Larsen (1998).

This study also obtained a self-report measure of current mood state on the Positive and Negative Affect Schedule (PANAS) (Watson et al., 1988). However, the results showed that mood state had no impact on the nature of processing in the attentional task. This may seem surprising given the research we discussed in Chapters 6 and 7. We should remember, however, that mood state was not induced in this study. Instead, the person's current mood was measured by means of the PANAS and we might expect that these natural mood states were not as intense as those experienced following a very specific mood induction. The important point from this study is that there was a correlation between extraversion and a positive attentional bias, even when current mood was taken into account.

Gomez et al. (2002) also investigated both neuroticism and extraversion in the same study. An index of these personality traits was measured by means of the EPI and three different measures of information processing were presented to participants. The researchers found that extraversion was associated with enhanced attentional processing of pleasant information, while neuroticism was associated with preferential processing of unpleasant information. In another study a variation of the Posner cueing task (Posner, 1980) was used, in which signals of either reward (gaining points) or punishment (losing points) were presented at different locations on a computer screen (Derryberry and Reed, 1994). Extraverts were slower to disengage their attention from the location where a positive incentive had been presented, while introverts were slower to move their attention away from a location where a negative incentive had been presented. Importantly, these biases were strongest in those participants with high scores on N. This study demonstrates that there seems to be no simple relationship between extraversion and signals of reward, and neuroticism with signals of punishment, as would be predicted by a straightforward two-factor model of how personality traits might influence cognitive processing. Instead, it seems that scores along the extraversion–introversion dimension are associated with sensitivity to both types of cue and that these biases are intensified by neuroticism. Thus, neurotic introverts were slow to disengage from negative locations, while neurotic extraverts were slower to disengage from positive locations (Derryberry and Reed, 1994).

Further support for an interaction between E and N was found in a study in which participants had to rapidly categorize word-pairs that 'best went together'. The word-pairs were organized so that they could be categorized as 'pleasant', 'unpleasant' or 'neutral' (Rogers and Revelle, 1998). The results showed that E was positively correlated with the number of pleasant items chosen, while N was correlated with the number of unpleasant items chosen. However, as shown in Figure 8.3, the relationship between N and choice of unpleasant pairs was strongly influenced by scores on E, while the relationship between E and the choice of pleasant word-pairs was modified by scores on N. Once again, this is not the pattern that would be expected from a simple two-factor model with two independent dimensions of N and E. Rather, it seems that both extraversion and neuroticism influence the responses towards affective stimuli in a highly interactive way.

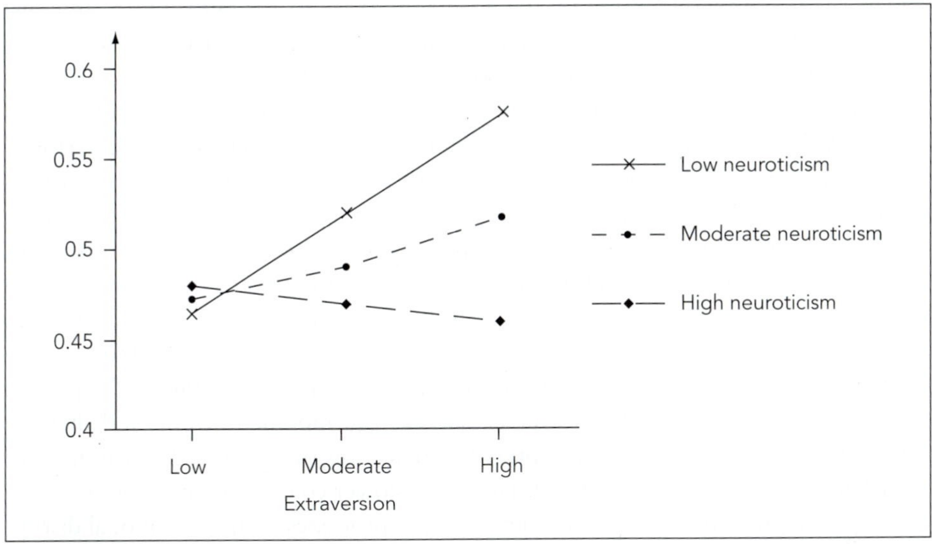

FIGURE 8.3 Proportion of pleasant over unpleasant word-pairs as a function of extraversion and neuroticism

Source: Rogers and Revelle (1998).

Neuroticism and selective processing of negative information

While there are very few studies that measure both E-PA and N-NA in attentional studies, there is a large literature examining attentional biases in relation to N-NA. To determine whether high levels of trait-anxiety or N-NA is characterized by an attentional bias towards negatively valenced information, many researchers have used interference tasks that require people to perform some central task while attempting to ignore distracting information. The classic Stroop colour-naming task (Stroop, 1935) has been modified so that emotionally valenced words can be presented in different colours. Higher levels of negative affectivity are consistently found to be associated with longer RTs to name the colours of negative words, relative to positive or neutral words (see Williams et al., 1996, for review). In an early study people who scored high or low on the Beck Depression Inventory (BDI) (Beck et al., 1961) were required to name the colours of depressive, positive or neutral words (Gotlib and McCann, 1984). The valence of the words made little difference to the response times of those scoring low on the BDI. However, those with higher scores (who were mildly depressed) took significantly longer to name the colours of negative words relative to either positive or neutral words. Other studies have shown that increased Stroop interference occurs for words related to a person's ongoing worries (e.g., social threat and physical threat) relative to neutral words (Mathews and MacLeod, 1985).

Watts and colleagues (1986) presented participants with both a general emotional Stroop task with words such as death, grief etc and a modified Stroop task containing words relating to spiders (e.g., crawl, hairy etc). People who reported a high fear of spiders showed little disruption on the general negative words but showed large disruption on the words related to spiders. Similar findings were reported in a study conducted with people who had recently taken a drug overdose. Greater disruption was found for words that related to drug use and suicide than more general threat-related words (Williams and Broadbent, 1986). Thus, the evidence suggests that performance on the emotional Stroop task is particularly disrupted when the negative words relate to a person's particular concerns or personality traits. Interference effects have also been found using a *dichotic listening* paradigm in which people have to shadow (repeat aloud) words presented in one ear, while ignoring words being presented in the unattended ear. People with higher levels of trait-anxiety (N) experience more disruption to the shadowing task when threat-related words are presented to the non-shadowed ear (Foa and McNally, 1986; Mathews and MacLeod, 1985). The pattern of results reported in interference tasks, such as the modified Stroop and dichotic listening tasks, has often been interpreted as reflecting the enhanced distribution of spatial attention to negative material. However, slower colour-naming times to negative words might actually reflect a variety of other processes such as emotional disruption effects, or a delay in disengaging attention from the negative content, rather than indicating an increased tendency to orient towards negative material.

Because of the problems in establishing the mechanisms underlying increased Stroop effects to negative words, researchers have turned toward *attentional probe* paradigms to assess individual differences in the distribution of spatial attention. Most attentional probe (sometimes called *dot-probe*) paradigms involve presenting negative-neutral pairs of stimuli on a computer screen for about 500 ms. Figure 8.4 shows a typical sequence of events in a single trial using the attentional probe paradigm. This display is immediately followed by a probe target (: or ..) that must be categorized by pressing one of two buttons. The probe may appear in the previous location of either the negative or the neutral stimulus. Reaction times for the two trials can then be compared. If spatial attention is preferentially oriented towards negative material, the detection of the probe should be much faster when the probe appears behind the location of the negative stimulus than when it appears behind the location of the neutral stimulus. This would be the expected result for people with high levels of trait-anxiety.

In one of the first studies to use this paradigm, pairs of negative and neutral words were presented and participants were simply required to detect the presence of a target probe that could appear in either location. Only those reporting high levels of anxiety were faster to detect probes following negative words than those following neutral words. Those with lower levels of anxiety showed no difference in probe detection between the two conditions (MacLeod et al., 1986). Subsequent research has confirmed these initial findings with word stimuli as well as with emotional pictures and photographs of different emotional facial expressions (e.g., Bradley et al., 1998; Bradley et al., 2000; Broadbent and Broadbent, 1988; Fox, 1993, 2002; MacLeod and Mathews, 1988). These results support the hypothesis that elevated levels of N-NA are associated with the increased allocation of attention toward negatively valenced stimuli.

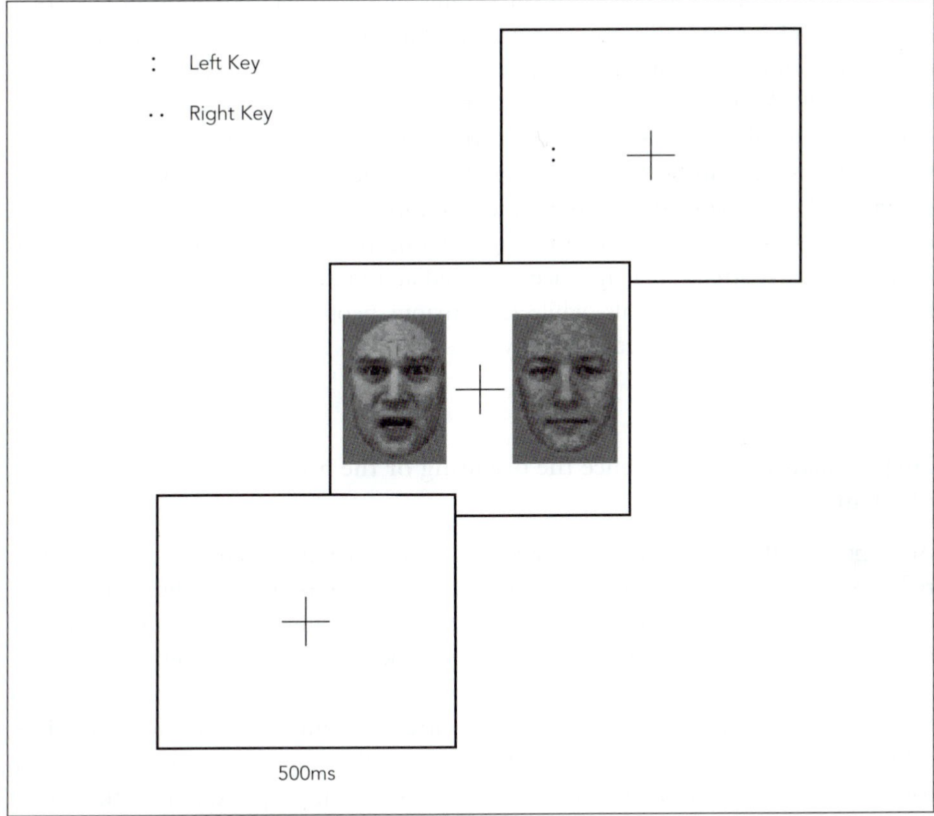

FIGURE 8.4 An example of a typical trial in an attentional probe experiment

There is also evidence that these personality congruent processing effects are intensified when people are in an anxious mood state. MacLeod and Mathews (1988) assessed each participant's level of trait-anxiety and tested this group of students early in the academic year when self-reported state-anxiety was low. They tested them again a few weeks prior to an important examination when self-reported state-anxiety was significantly increased. The results showed that those who reported high trait-anxiety (i.e., high N-NA) demonstrated the strongest tendency to selectively attend towards negative material when state-anxiety was elevated. In other words, there was an interaction between temperament and current mood state in determining the selective processing of threat-relevant information.

In general then, there is substantial evidence that personality traits can influence the allocation of attention towards negative material, especially if people are also in an anxious mood state. It is also clear, however, that everyone should allocate attention to really dangerous events. If a situation is truly dangerous and threatening then we would expect personality traits to have relatively little impact as there should be a general bias for everyone to orient towards the source of threat. Personality traits are likely to influence the *threshold* at which attention switches into a more vigilant mode.

Thus, at high levels of intensity threat stimuli should attract attention in everyone. At lower levels of intensity people reporting higher levels of trait-anxiety would be expected to allocate attention towards threat to a greater extent (Mathews and Mackintosh, 1998; Mogg and Bradley, 1998). Evidence for this proposal has been found in the attentional probe task with threat stimuli that have been modified so that they vary in threat intensity from low to high. This can be achieved, for example, by morphing facial expressions so that the same face can be transformed into low intensity, medium intensity and high intensity anger. Using this intensity manipulation, it has been found that attentional vigilance occurred at a moderate level of threat intensity for highly anxious individuals, while less anxious people only showed vigilance for threat at high levels of threat intensity (Mogg et al., 2000; Wilson and MacLeod, 2003).

Do personality traits influence the orienting or the holding of attention?

An important theoretical issue is whether the findings with the attentional probe task reflect attention being drawn towards the locus of threat, or whether the results reflect a difficulty in disengaging from the threatening material. Given that stimuli are usually presented for around 500 ms in attentional probe experiments it might be the case that people switch attention several times between the two locations and once threat has been noticed, there is then a difficulty in disengaging from this location (Fox, 2004). Evidence for anxiety-related differences in disengaging from threat has been found in experiments using modifications of Posner's cueing paradigm. In this task, a single cue is presented on either the left- or the right-hand side of a computer screen and is followed by a target probe in one of the two locations. In the original version, the cue was a brief flickering of one of the boxes and the perception of targets was enhanced if the target appeared in a cued location (Posner, 1980). In a modification of this paradigm, faces with either angry, happy, or neutral expressions were presented as cues, and individual differences in terms of how quickly people oriented towards valid cues or disengaged from invalid cues were examined (Fox et al., 2001; Fox et al. 2002). The sequence of events in an invalid trial with an angry face as the cue is shown in Figure 8.5, and the typical pattern of results found is shown in Figure 8.6.

As can be seen in Figure 8.6(a), there were no differences across the three facial expressions for the valid cue trials. In other words, neither the low nor the high anxious group were faster to detect targets that were cued by an angry expression relative to a neutral or a happy expression. The results for the invalid trials were quite different (Figure 8.6(b)). There was now a clear difference between the two anxiety groups. The low anxious group showed no difference across the three cue types, while the high anxious group were significantly slower to detect a target that appeared in an invalidly cued location when the cue was an angry facial expression. It is interesting to note that in this study the delay in disengaging from threat was more strongly related to the level of current mood state as measured by state-anxiety, although the same pattern was apparent for variations on trait-anxiety. In subsequent experiments

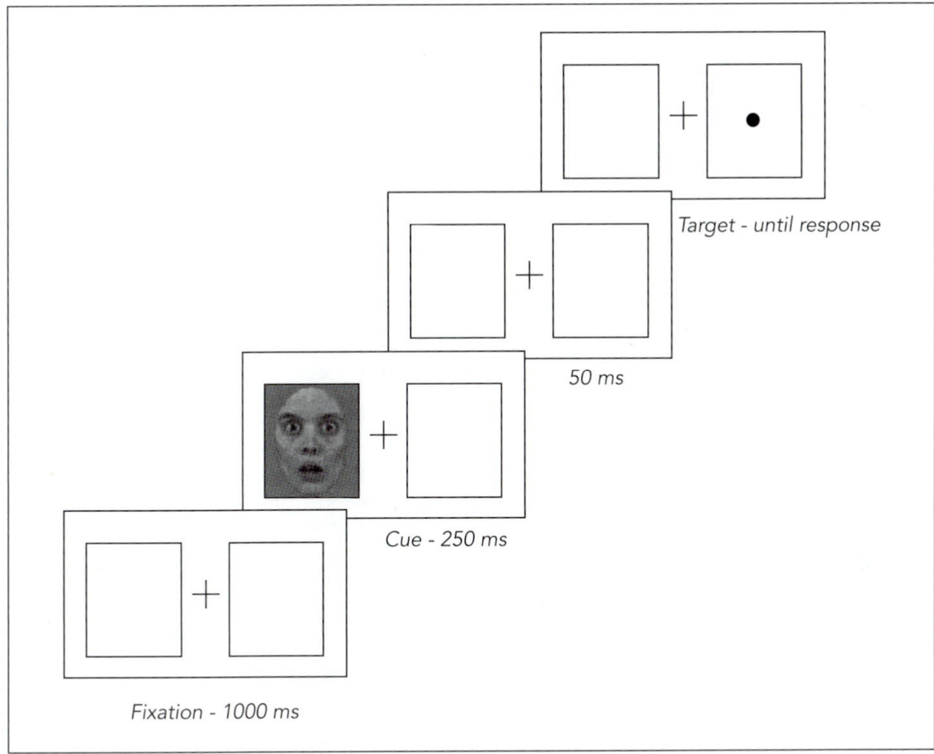

FIGURE 8.5 Example of the sequence of events in an invalid trial with a threat-related cue
Source: Fox et al. (2001).

using a very similar task, the delay in moving attention away from threat was found to be related to the participants' N-NA personality trait as measured by means of trait-anxiety (Fox et al., 2002).

A similar delay in disengaging attention from personality congruent material has been found when positive and negative IAPS pictures were used as the cue (Yiend and Mathews, 2001). These results suggest that trait-anxiety is associated with a tendency to delay disengaging attention from the location of a threat-related cue. They are consistent with findings that variation in E-PA and N-NA are related to a tendency to disengage more slowly from locations associated with positive and negative incentives, respectively (Derryberry and Reed, 1994).

It is important to point out, however, that these results cannot be taken to demonstrate that there is no enhanced movement of attention towards personality congruent material. This is because a sudden onset cue appearing on its own in a visual field tends to capture attention automatically regardless of its semantic content. Just as a loud noise automatically captures your attention, so does a sudden flash of light. This means that single cues are noticed very rapidly and accurately (e.g., just over 300 ms in the results shown in Figure 8.6). Since spatial attention is rapidly allocated to the sudden onset cue, this provides an excellent measure of the subsequent disengagement of attention when the cue appears in the invalid location. However, it is unreasonable to

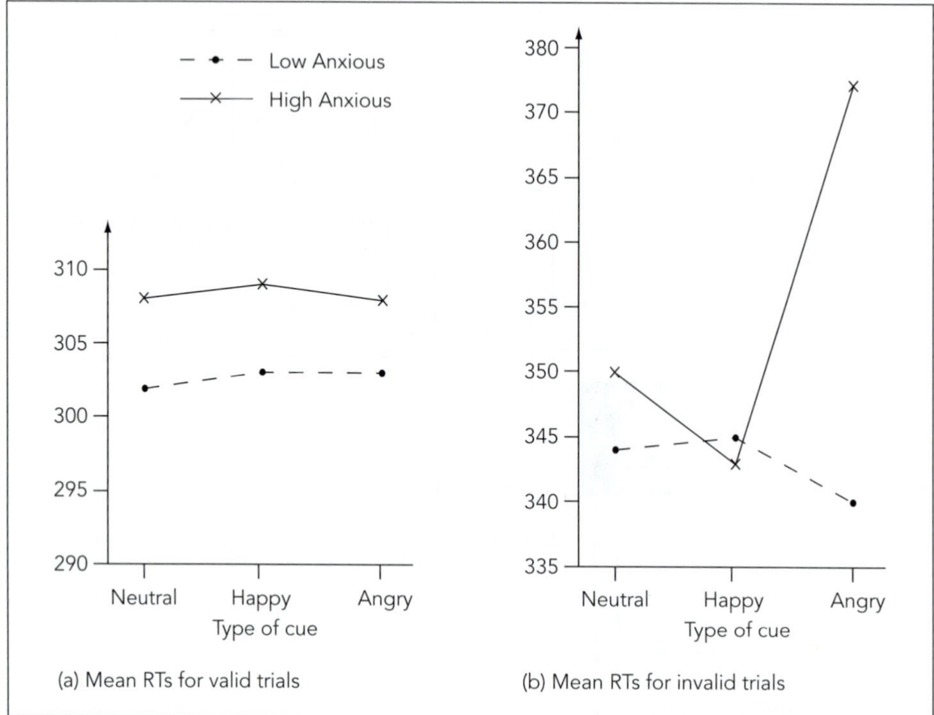

FIGURE 8.6 The typical pattern of results found in the modified emotional version of the Posner cueing task

Source: Adapted from Fox et al. (2001).

expect that attention can be moved more quickly towards threat-related material since the speed of response is probably already as fast as it can go.

In the traditional version of the attentional probe task it is impossible to distinguish between the movement of attention towards threat and the disengagement (or engagement) of attention with threatening stimuli. When two objects are presented simultaneously spatial attention is allocated to both locations instantly. This means that we do not know where attention is focused, so it is impossible to determine whether differential probe detection times are due to the faster allocation of attention towards threat, or due to the slower disengagement of attention from threat, or both. The Posner task with a single cue, however, allows us to examine the disengagement of attention since we know when attention starts. Another task is required, however, to determine whether there are also differences in the speed of moving attention towards threat depending on a person's personality.

An obvious task to examine is the visual search task. We might expect personality traits to influence the speed of detecting material that is congruent with a particular trait. Thus, extraverted people might be quicker to notice stimuli relevant to their own concerns, for example, friendly facial expressions rather than threatening or negative facial expressions. In contrast, people with a tendency towards neuroticism might be faster to notice negative facial expressions. There is some empirical evidence for this hypothesis from research conducted with people diagnosed with social anxiety. When presented with arrays of facial expressions, socially phobic individuals showed an enhanced ability to detect faces with angry expressions whereas this tendency was not apparent for a matched control group who did not have social phobia (Gilboa-Schechtman et al., 1999). Likewise, people with a phobic fear of snakes (or spiders) show an enhanced ability to detect photographs of snakes (or spiders) relative to photographs of mushrooms and flowers when compared with matched control participants (Öhman, Flykt et al., 2001). Thus, it seems that a general propensity to detect threat rapidly and efficiently can be enhanced by individual differences in personality. Results are somewhat mixed, however. Other studies have found no relationship between levels of self-reported trait anxiety and the speed to detect angry facial expressions (Fox et al., 2000). It may be the case that such individual differences are stronger with specific phobic fears (e.g., spider phobia) than more general variations in levels of trait-anxiety (see Fox, 2004, for further discussion).

Other paradigms that may provide a better measure of the ability of particular classes of stimuli to capture attention include the *attentional blink* task and the *eye-gaze cueing* task. The *attentional blink* paradigm is a behavioural task that requires people to identify two successive targets (T1 and T2) in a stream of items, usually letters or words, that are presented very quickly one after the other. The effect is revealed by a difficulty in detecting the second target (T2) when a response is required to the first target (T1) compared to when no response is required to T1. However, this only occurs when T2 is presented within about 500 ms of T1, hence the assumption that attention really does seem to *blink*. The attentional blink effect probably reflects attentional capacity limitations when two targets are presented in rapid succession (Raymond et al., 1992; Shapiro et al., 1997). Attentional blink effects are common for words and other people's names. However, if your own name is presented as T2 then a blink often does not occur. In other words, one's own name gets noticed even during the period that attention is supposed to have blinked (Shapiro et al., 1997). This result suggests that affectively salient stimuli, such as your own name, can automatically attract attention and therefore may be immune to attentional blink effects. In support of this, T2 words with a very strong negative valence were found to produce no attentional blink and were identified more frequently than neutral words in healthy individuals. In contrast, a patient with amygdala damage showed equivalent blink effects for negative and neutral words suggesting that the amygdala-mediated mechanism to boost affective stimuli is necessary to detect salient stimuli under these difficult conditions (Anderson and Phelps, 2001).

The attentional blink task was adapted to determine whether affectively salient facial expressions are more detectable than neutral faces and whether these effects are related to individual differences in the degree of self-reported N-NA (Fox et al., 2005). *Rapid serial visual presentation* (RSVP) streams of distractors were presented and participants had to categorize T1, which was a picture of either mushrooms or flowers. T2 was either a fearful or a happy facial expression embedded in a stream of faces with neutral expressions. Participants simply had to press a button if an 'emotional' face appeared in the stream. As shown in Figure 8.7, a trial consisted of a rapid

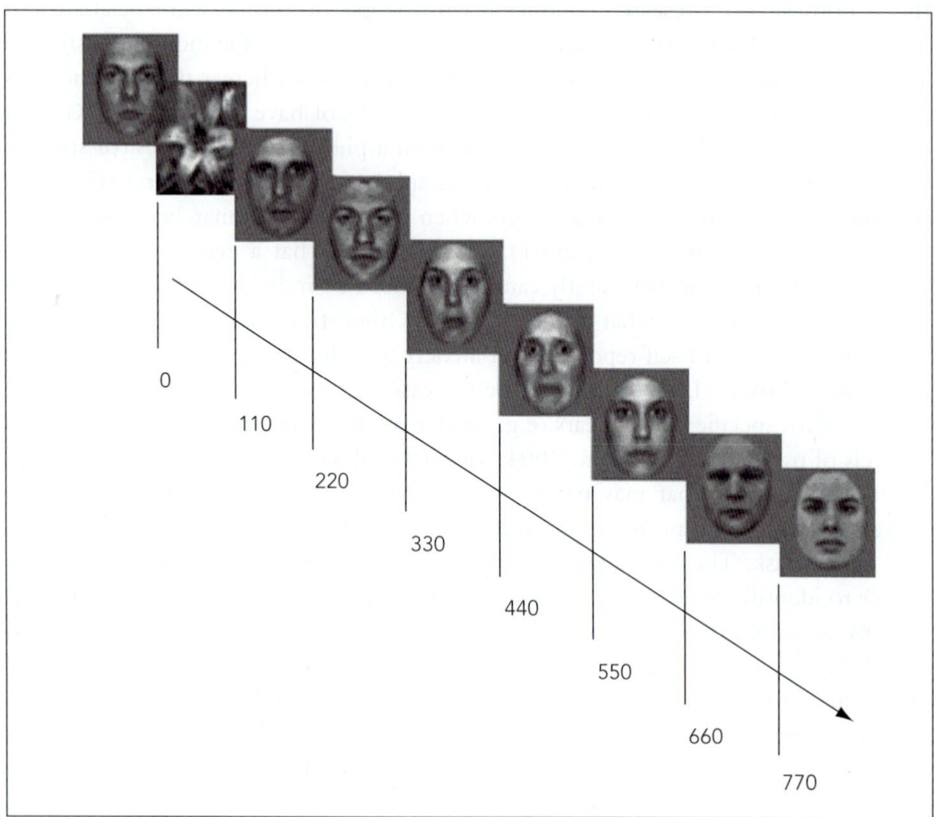

FIGURE 8.7 An example of a typical trial to investigate the attentional blink effect
Source: Fox et al. (2005).

serial presentation of fifteen photographs presented for 110 ms each. On the critical *dual task* trials, the requirement was to detect whether a fearful or a happy facial expression had been presented (T2) and then to categorize non-facial stimuli as either mushrooms or flowers (T1). On the control *single task* trials, the pictures of mushrooms or flowers (T1) were simply to be ignored and a response was required only for T2 (did an emotional expression appear in the stream?).

If high levels of N-NA do modulate the orienting of attention towards negatively valenced stimuli then the detection of fearful facial expressions should be subject to a weaker blink effect for high-anxious individuals than for low-anxious individuals. This is exactly what was found (see Figure 8.8). While a significant attentional blink did occur for both happy and fearful expressions, it was significantly reduced for fearful expressions in people reporting high levels of trait- and state-anxiety compared to those reporting low levels of anxiety. This pattern suggests that the attentional system is more rapidly allocated to negatively valenced stimuli when levels of trait-anxiety or neuroticism increase.

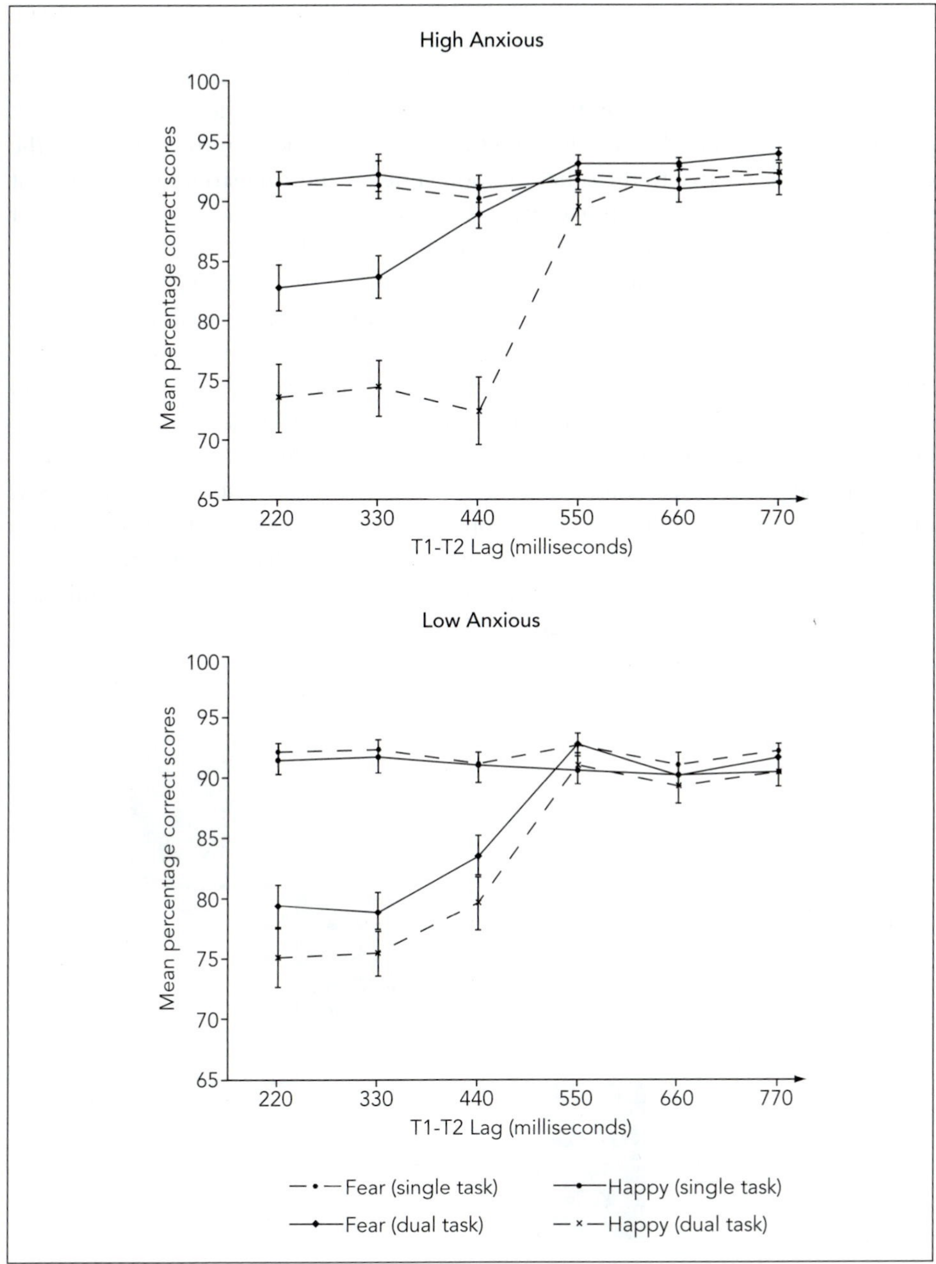

FIGURE 8.8 How self-reported anxiety can modulate the degree of attentional blink
Performance was high when no T1 task was required. When T1 had to be attended a substantial blink occurred for emotional expressions (happy and fearful) for both high and low anxious groups. However, for the high anxious group the degree of blink was significantly reduced for the fearful facial expressions.

Source: Data from Fox et al. (2005).

The gaze cueing task has also been used to assess whether personality traits can modulate the differential engagement of attention with personality congruent material. In this task, a face is presented at the centre of a computer screen and then the eyes shift to either the left or the right of the screen. If a response to the target is required, performance is enhanced when the target appears in the location towards which the eyes are looking relative to the other location (Friesen and Kingstone, 1998). Recent studies have varied the emotional expression on the central face, and shown that higher levels of trait-anxiety are associated with greater allocation of attention to the location cued by the fearful face (Fox, Mathews et al., 2007; Mathews et al., 2003; Putman et al., 2006; Tipples, 2006). Figure 8.9 shows a typical trial in this type of task. Figure 8.10 shows that the enhanced cueing effect is specific to fearful expressions for those reporting high levels of trait-anxiety. The pattern of results found in the gaze cueing task suggests that people reporting higher levels of N-NA are more likely to orient their attention towards a locus of implied threat.

In summary, there is considerable evidence that personality traits (especially N-NA) can have an important influence on the operation of the *posterior* attentional system in processing of affective material. In particular, it seems that personality traits can influence emotional processing after attention has moved and engaged a significant stimulus (Derryberry and Reed, 2003). Thus, people who are highly neurotic or

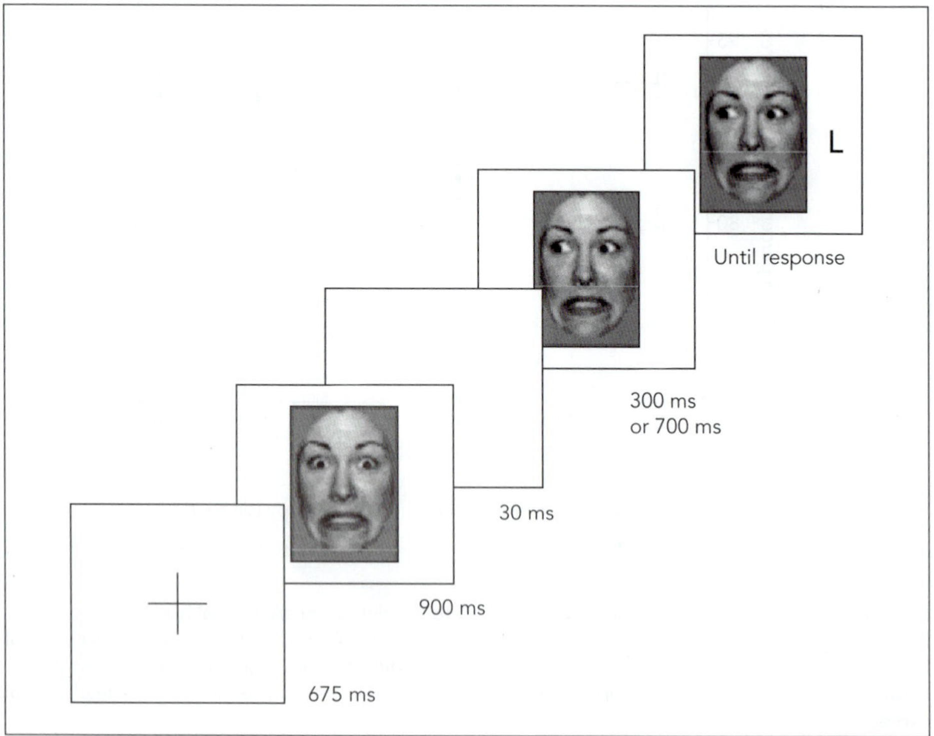

FIGURE 8.9 Typical sequence of events in a gaze cueing experiment
This example shows an incongruent averted gaze condition with a fearful expression.
Source: Fox, Mathews et al. (2007).

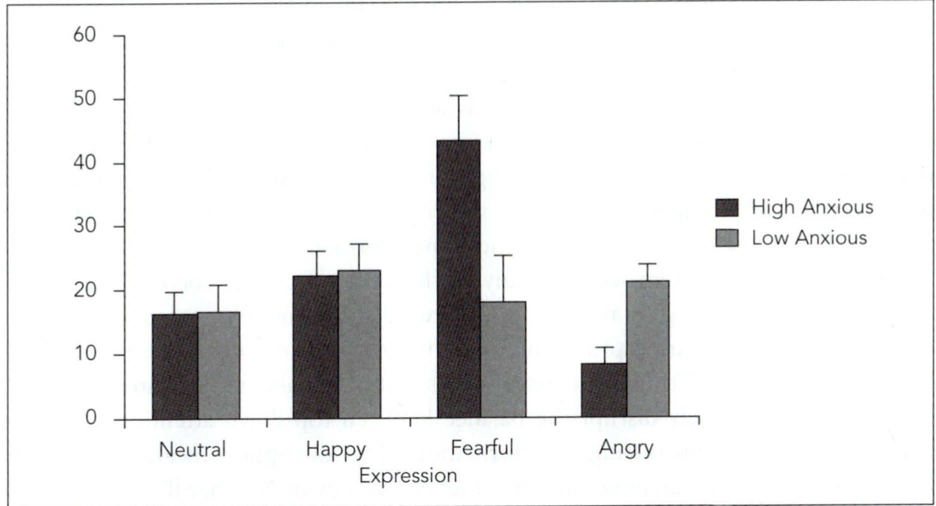

FIGURE 8.10 Mean congruency effect as a function of trait-anxiety and facial expressions
Source: Fox, Mathews et al. (2007).

anxious (especially if they score low on extraversion) are slow to disengage from locations associated with threat (Derryberry and Reed, 1994, 2002; Fox et al., 2001, 2002; Yiend and Mathews, 2001). Extraverts (especially if they score high on neuroticism) are slower to move their attention away from rewarding locations (Derryberry and Reed, 1994). It seems that, once a stimulus has been engaged, the engagement deepens, resulting in delays in disengaging and moving away, and these processes are modulated by personality traits. There is also some evidence that personality might boost the early allocation of attention towards threat locations. This hypothesis is supported by findings that those scoring high on measures of trait-anxiety are faster to move attention towards a location of implied threat (Fox, Mathews et al., 2007; Mathews et al., 2003; Putnam et al., 2006; Tipples, 2006) and are less likely to miss threat-related stimuli under difficult processing conditions (Fox et al., 2005).

Personality traits and attentional control

Some research has also examined the role of personality traits in modulating the *anterior* attentional system. As we have seen, the anterior attention system allows for more voluntary and flexible control or 'effortful control' (Derryberry and Reed, 2003; Rothbart et al., 1994). Derryberry and his colleagues have investigated attentional control in adults by means of a self-report measure. Using a modification of the Posner cueing task, they required participants to engage in a 'game' in which some locations were 'threatening' (where points would be lost) whereas other locations were 'safe' (points were generally won). They found that anxious individuals with poor attentional control showed a delay in disengaging their attention from the threatening locations. However, highly anxious participants with good attentional control were better able to shift their attention away from the threatening locations and towards the safe locations (Derryberry and Reed, 2002). This interesting research indicates that attentional control may also vary in systematic ways between people, and that this is independent of the degree of anxiety or neuroticism reported.

To conclude, attentional biases towards affectively salient information is heavily influenced by individual differences in temperament or personality. Many of these effects occur at fairly automatic levels (e.g., orienting towards and disengaging away from threat) and are likely to be under the control of the posterior attentional system. Individual differences in temperament may also modulate the operation of the anterior attentional system so that many of the early effects may be either boosted or suppressed depending on the degree of flexible and voluntary control that can be exerted. These effects are captured nicely by the *attentional control theory* proposed by Eysenck et al. (2007). This theory proposes that personality traits related to N-NA (trait-anxiety) effectively disrupt the balance between top-down attentional control and stimulus-driven processing of information. This disruption means that, when confronted with a threatening stimulus, higher degrees of N-NA will be associated with an enhanced allocation of attentional resources toward threat relative to other types of information.

MEMORY

Evidence from both autobiographical and laboratory research indicates that temperament can influence the type of material that is best remembered. A real problem in this research, of course, is that it is very difficult to separate out the effects of personality traits and mood. We know that mood states can affect memory, and we also know that personality traits can influence the frequency and intensity with which particular mood states are experienced. Thus, if we find that extraverts recall more positive material and neurotics recall more negative material it is difficult to determine whether this due to the underlying personality traits or to the more frequently experienced mood states.

The study reported by Rusting and Larsen (1998: Study 2) is important in this regard because it examined the effects of E-PA and N-NA on simple recall while controlling for current mood state. Levels of E-PA and N-NA were measured on the EPQ (Eysenck and Eysenck, 1975a) and current mood state was measured by means of the Positive and Negative Affect Scales (Watson et al., 1988). As discussed in the previous section on personality congruent biases, participants were presented with a reaction-time task in which they had to categorize a list of words and pictures as being 'positive', 'negative' or 'neutral'. Following this task, they were given a surprise recall test in which they were given four minutes to write down as many words as they could from the reaction-time test. Overall it was found that extraverts selectively recalled more positive than negative or neutral words, while neurotics selectively remembered more negative words. Importantly, as shown in Table 8.2, the correlations between extraversion and neuroticism and selective recall of differently valenced material were still significant when current mood state was controlled statistically. This means that, regardless of current mood, extraverts tended to remember positive material while

TABLE 8.2 Standardized correlations (beta scores) predicting performance on free recall from personality factors and current mood

	Extraversion	*Positive mood*	*Neuroticism*	*Negative mood*
Positive words	0.19*	0.10	–0.06	–0.15
Negative words	–0.06	–0.10	0.19*	0.12
Neutral words	–0.05	0.05	0.07	–0.05

Source: Data are taken from Rusting and Larsen (1998).

neurotics selectively remembered the negatively valenced material. Even though they were given the same event, the experienced memory of that event had quite a different affective tone. Interestingly, current mood state did not predict selective memory in this study when personality traits were taken into account, although personality did predict the selective recall of personality congruent material. In other words, there were personality congruent memory effects but no mood congruent memory effects.

In a subsequent experiment, mood states were induced (Rusting, 1999). Once again, strong effects of personality (E and N) were found in influencing the recall of positive and negative material, respectively. However, when positive and negative mood states were actively induced current mood became a stronger predictor of selective recall than personality traits. Thus, a strong mood state can lead to mood congruency effects in recall. In addition, more enduring personality traits such as extraversion and neuroticism can also determine the nature of selective recall to a significant extent.

Separate effects of depression and anxiety on recall

There is evidence that temperament can influence autobiographical memory although once again most of the research focuses on N-NA and selective memory for negative material. To illustrate, it has been found that depressed individuals have a tendency to report negative autobiographical memories (Clark and Teasdale, 1982).

To better investigate whether there are personality congruent effects in memory it is necessary to present the same events under more controlled conditions and then see whether there are differences in what people recall. In other words, given a mixed list of positive and negative material, are there personality-related differences in what people remember? There is substantial evidence for this hypothesis when depression is assessed. For example, when people are required to encode a word in terms of how it relates to themselves, those who score highly on standardized measures of depression demonstrate a strong retrieval advantage for negative relative to positive or neutral material (Denny and Hunt, 1992; Watkins et al., 1992; Williams et al., 1997, for review).

Intriguingly, however, it has proved more difficult to demonstrate selective memory for negative material in those scoring high on scales of trait-anxiety (e.g., Mogg et al., 1989). This is interesting because measures of depression and anxiety are usually highly correlated with each other, and both are important aspects of N-NA. It seems that when only shallow or incidental encoding is required there exists a selective bias in free recall that is modulated by the level of self-reported trait-anxiety (Russo et al., 2001; 2006). When participants had to either count the number of syllables in a word or simply name the colour of a word at encoding those with high trait-anxiety scores selectively recalled negative, relative to positive or neutral, words. This difference disappeared, however, when participants had to rate each word at encoding for pleasantness (Russo et al., 2001). The pleasantness rating was assumed to promote a deeper semantic analysis and when this occurred no selective memory advantage was found. However, selective memory for negative material is found under exactly these conditions when people differ in terms of depression. These findings suggest that depression and anxiety may have different impacts on explicit memory.

Empirical work examining rumination is also consistent with this view. For example, it is known that individual differences in depression are related to the tendency to ruminate about negative emotions, and that these tendencies tend to maintain depressive mood states (Nolen-Hoeksema, 1991; Nolen-Hoeksema and Morrow, 1993). Indirect evidence that personality differences in the propensity to ruminate can lead to selective recall of negative material has been reported (Rusting and deHart, 2000). This study found that participants who were required to focus on a negative mood state that had been experimentally induced and ruminate about it recalled more negative memories than participants in a control condition. This effect was particularly strong for those people who said that they were poor at controlling their mood states. Thus, since we know that depression is associated with difficulties in controlling negative mood states as well as excessive rumination on negative events, this study provides indirect evidence that individual differences in depression are related to the selective recall of negative material.

The influence of mood repair strategies on selective recall

This brings us to the role of mood repair strategies in modulating selective memory biases. As we saw in Chapter 7, motivational variables are critical in determining whether mood *congruent* or mood *incongruent* memory biases are found (Forgas, 1995; Isen, 1985; Parrott and Sabini, 1990; Singer and Salovey, 1988). Motivational theories propose that an individual's motives are of paramount importance to the type of memories that are recalled. In contrast to associative network models of memory, which often view memories as static nodes within a network, motivational theories view memories as dynamic aspects of the developing individual. From this perspective, memories are actively retrieved to help in maintaining or altering a current mood state, especially in relation to one's overall goals and plans (Singer and Salovey, 1996). Thus, the self-regulation of mood states is one important motive that has been investigated.

First, there is evidence that recalling particular types of memory can indeed regulate mood (Parrott and Hertel, 1999). Second, there is also evidence for individual differences in the ability to repair moods. In one study, for example, a sad mood was induced by playing participants a segment of a sad movie. Immediately after watching the melancholy movie each participant was asked to recall two strongly emotional memories (Josephson et al., 1996). As predicted, all participants tended to recall a sad memory at first. Thus, a general mood congruency effect was found in the first memory recalled. However, the valence of the second memory recalled was influenced by the individual's scores on a measure of depression. Those who were mildly depressed tended to recall a second sad event, whereas those with low scores on depression tended to recall a positive event. Almost all participants said that they deliberately tried to recall a positive memory in order to improve their current mood state, although only those with low depression scores actually recalled one (Josephson et al., 1996). It is clear that these individual differences in the use of mood repair strategies can play an important role in determining the nature of mood congruency effects in memory. Some people find negative mood states to be particularly aversive, and may try to regulate them by substituting negative thoughts and memories with positive ones. These differences in regulatory strategies can also influence the nature of memory recall to a significant extent.

INTERPRETATION AND JUDGMENT

In everyday life we are often faced with complex and ambiguous situations that require interpretations of emotional content. For example, are they laughing at me or with me? Is that facial expression a smile or a smirk? Given what we have learned about temperamental differences so far, we would expect to find strong effects of personality traits on the interpretation of such ambiguous situations. It is extremely difficult to conduct research in real-life settings. Experimental psychologists have, therefore, developed a range of tasks that can be conducted under controlled laboratory conditions that are supposed to simulate what occurs in dynamic social situations. One straightforward way to investigate the *interpretation* of ambiguity is to present people with a list of homophones and then ask them to write down what they heard. Homophones are words that sound the same but have two different meanings, for example, 'taught' and 'taut'. There is available a selection of homophones that have both a neutral and a threatening meaning (e.g., pain–pane, die–dye). In an early study, it was found that people who scored relatively highly on self-report measures of trait-anxiety were more likely to provide a negative interpretation than a neutral one. This bias did not occur for low-anxious individuals (Eysenck et al., 1987). In a subsequent study, high- and low-anxious groups were required to read sentences that had either a threatening or a non-threatening interpretation (e.g., 'The doctor examined little Emily's growth'). It was found that people with higher levels of trait-anxiety were more likely to interpret these sentences in a negative way – relating growth to a tumour rather than height – whereas low-anxious groups made more benign interpretations (Mathews et al., 1989). A problem with experiments using homophones, however, is that the results might be due to a response bias rather than to an interpretation bias. In other words, it is possible that both meanings might come to mind automatically but that anxious people may then be more likely to select and report the more negative interpretation.

To get around this potential response bias problem, Richards and French (1992) used a lexical priming task to access the semantic activation of each meaning of an ambiguous word when it is presented. Participants undertook a series of trials in which homographs were presented as prime words. Homographs are words that have the same spelling but have two different meanings with different emotional valences (e.g., arms, shot, beat, stroke). When the gap between the prime word and the target lexical decision task was relatively long (i.e., more than 750 ms) it was found that highly trait-anxious participants showed a larger priming effect for the negative meaning of the homographs. No such effect was found, however, when the time from prime to target was reduced to 500 ms, suggesting that the effects may not have been automatic. Nevertheless, these results do suggest that people who are temperamentally more anxious have a tendency to interpret ambiguous words in a more negative way (see also Calvo and Castillo, 2001).

In a more general study, ambiguous homophones were used to assess biases in interpretation for people with varying measures of both *extraversion* and *neuroticism*. Rusting (1999) developed a number of homophones that have either positive or neutral meanings (e.g., bridal–bridle; peace–piece; won–one) as well as homophones that have either negative or neutral meanings (e.g., bored–board; fined–find; poor–pour). Scores on extraversion were highly correlated with the tendency to provide positive rather than neutral interpretations of homophones, while higher scores on neuroticism were correlated with the tendency to interpret homophones in a more negative way. Thus, for both negative affectivity (as measured by trait-anxiety or N) and positive affectivity (as measured by E) there is empirical evidence for selective interpretation biases. People who are more neurotic tend to interpret ambiguous material in a more negative way, whereas people who are highly extraverted are likely to interpret ambiguous material in a more positive way.

Estimates of risk

Apart from the interpretation of ambiguous situations, it might also be expected that estimates of risk for future events are influenced by personality traits to some extent. Kahneman and Tversky (1973) proposed that, when people make judgments about the likelihood of an event occurring in the future, they generally use the ease with which they can construct mental models of the event to influence their judgement. In other words, if the scenario of obtaining top-class marks in your next examination comes to mind much more easily than the scenario of not obtaining top marks, then it is likely that you will overestimate the chances of success and underestimate the chances of failure. Kahneman and Tversky (1973) originally called this the *availability heuristic* and later renamed it the *simulation heuristic* (Kahneman and Tversky, 1982).

The cognitive networks of people high in E-PA should be especially tuned to the signals of reward and, therefore, should contain a good deal of elaboration of positive affect. In contrast, the cognitive networks of high N-NA people should be tuned towards the signals of punishment or non-reward and, therefore, a greater elaboration of negative affect should occur. The empirical evidence generally supports this hypothesis. For example, in an early study Butler and Mathews (1987) required students to rate the subjective risk of a range of examination-related and other negative events happening to either themselves or another person. For those who scored high on a measure of trait-anxiety (i.e., high N-NA) all positive events were judged to be less likely to happen to themselves relative to others. In contrast, all negative events were judged to be more likely to happen to themselves. This supports the notion that individual variation in N-NA is related to different estimates of positive and negative events occurring.

In a related study, the simulation heuristic was applied to the pessimism that is associated with chronic worriers. Participants were required to rate the subjective likelihood of a range of positive and negative events occurring, and were also asked to think of reasons why some events would come about and others would not (MacLeod et al., 1991). The results showed that the speed at which people could think of a reason was strongly correlated with their judgement of how likely the event was. In other words, those who were chronic worriers (i.e., high on N-NA) were quicker to think of a reason why a negative event might occur, and also judged this event to be fairly likely. In contrast, the same people took longer to think of a reason why a positive event would occur, and judged this event to be less likely. These results provide support for the notion that the simulation heuristic differs between different personality traits, resulting in consistent individual differences in the estimates of subjective risk. A follow-up study confirmed that anxious and depressed individuals judged future negative events to be more likely and gave more supporting reasons for their occurrence relative to control participants. The opposite pattern was observed for positive events: lower subjective probability estimates were given and fewer supporting relative to contradictory reasons were given for their occurrence (MacLeod et al., 1997). This line of work provides evidence that various aspects of N-NA (e.g., trait-anxiety or chronic worry) are associated with a high degree of pessimism about the future. These people expect negative events to happen and tend to underestimate the probability of positive events occurring.

As is often the case in this area of research the emphasis has been on negative affectivity and neuroticism rather than on positive affectivity and extraversion. However, very similar results have been reported for both extraverts and neurotics in line with theoretical expectations (Zelenski and Larsen, 2002). In this study, self-report measures of E-PA and N-NA as well as current mood state were obtained and participants were asked to estimate the likelihood that positive and negative future events would occur. The results showed that E-PA was associated with the expectation that positive events would occur, whereas N-NA was associated with the subjective judgement that negative events were relatively more likely. Importantly, this study found that the influence of personality traits on subjective judgement was not modulated by current mood states. Taken together, these results indicate that stable personality traits such as extraversion and neuroticism include stable cognitive networks that can bias affective judgements in affect congruent directions. Thus, personality traits can bias the current interpretation of ambiguous events as well as shifting the perceived likelihood of future good and bad events occurring.

NEURAL REACTIVITY

A number of theorists suggest that fundamental differences in the reactivity of the approach and avoidance systems are a core part of what constitutes personality. If so, a strong correlation between E-PA and psychophysiological reactivity to positive events (signals of reward) and between N-NA and psychophysiological reactivity to negative events (signals of punishment) would be expected. It is also possible, of course, that both E-PA and N-NA relate to constructs that are much wider than psychophysiological reactivity, but are still related to activity in these different neurobiological systems in an intimate way. Either way, strong correlations would be expected between self-report measures of E and N and direct measures of physiological and neural reactivity to valenced stimuli. A study by Catherine Norris and colleagues reported evidence for this hypothesis in showing a strong correlation between self-reported neuroticism and the magnitude of SCRs to unpleasant relative to pleasant or neutral IAPS pictures (Norris et al., 2007). While a measure of extraversion was obtained in this study, the relationship of scores on E and autonomic response to pleasant pictures was not reported. Nevertheless, the pattern of psychophysiological response to negative images and neuroticism supports the hypothesis that neuroticism involves a hyper-activation of the limbic system with a consequent low tolerance for aversive stimuli (Eysenck, 1967).

Neuroimaging studies

Several studies have made use of neuroimaging technologies to investigate brain activation in response to stimuli that are either positive or negative in relation to the personality traits of E-PA and N-NA. Canli et al. (2001), for example, have investigated whether the reactivity of the brain to emotional stimuli is influenced by personality. Fourteen women were given the NEO-FFI, which provides separate measures for the 'big five' personality dimensions (neuroticism, extraversion, openness to experience, agreeableness and conscientiousness). Each participant watched alternate blocks of positive and negative pictures selected from the IAPS set (Lang et al., 2005) while brain reactivity was monitored by means of fMRI. The results showed that brain reactivity to positive pictures (relative to negative pictures) correlated significantly with participants' E scores in both cortical (frontal and temporal) and subcortical (amygdala, caudate, putamen) regions. Brain activation to negative pictures correlated significantly with participants' N scores in left frontal and temporal cortical regions. These fMRI results provide evidence that individual differences in brain activation when faced with emotional stimuli are associated with specific personality traits, and suggest a possible neural mechanism for the association between personality traits and emotions in everyday life (e.g., Bolger and Zuckerman, 1995; Costa and McCrae, 1980).

This type of research holds great promise for shedding light on the neural basis of human individuality. For example, the different patterns of brain activation arising from identical pictures for different individuals are almost certain to result in quite different subjective interpretations of the same objective experience. As argued by Canli et al. (2001), a positive emotional interpretation may be biased by fairly automatic brain responses to the positive elements of experience, whereas a negative emotional interpretation may be biased by brain responses to the negative aspects of experience. It is also possible, of course, that brain processes may themselves be biased by differences in cognitive interpretations. Thus, the direction of causality is not always clear in studies examining cognitive biases and neural correlates.

An interesting feature of Canli et al.'s study, however, was that correlations between brain activation and E scores were exhibited in both cortical and subcortical regions, suggesting that the neural systems associated with personality are represented *at all levels of neural processing*. In other words, it is not just subcortical areas (e.g., the limbic system) that differ between people. Rather, differences in activation occur at multiple levels throughout the brain.

In another study, fMRI was again used to test the hypothesis that the amygdala would be activated in response to happy facial expressions primarily for those people expressing a high degree of E (Canli et al., 2002). This hypothesis was derived from earlier findings that the amygdala fired consistently in response to fearful facial expressions, but its response to happy faces seemed to be very inconsistent (e.g., Morris et al., 1996; Whalen et al., 1998). Canli et al. (2002) speculated that this inconsistency of amygdala activation to happy faces might be due to individual differences in extraversion. This was a reasonable hypothesis given that their earlier study had shown that amygdala activation to positive IAPS pictures varied as a function of E (Canli et al., 2001). They presented blocks of angry, fearful, happy, sad and neutral faces to fifteen participants who had completed the NEO-FFI. The results are shown in Figure 8.11.

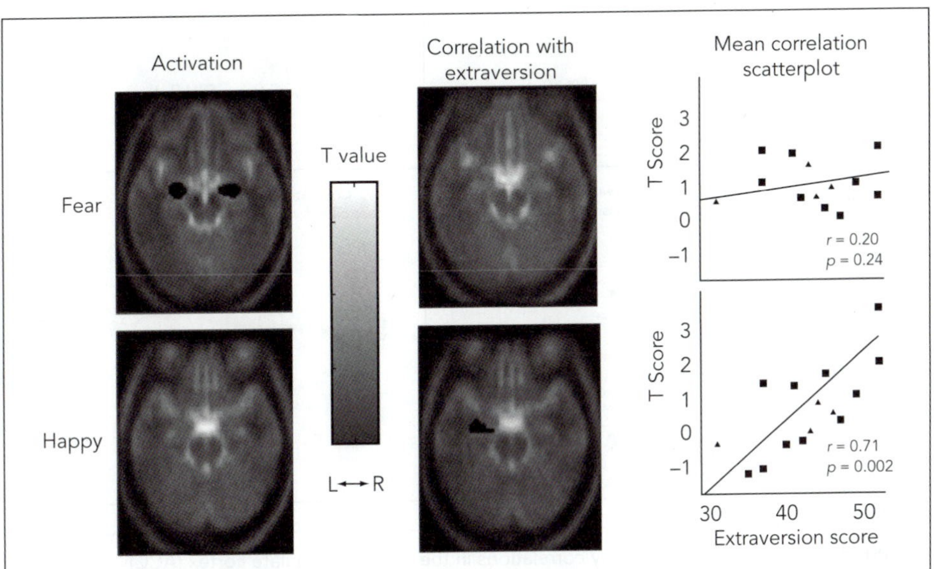

FIGURE 8.11 Response of the amygdala to emotional faces
(a) Significant amygdala activation to fearful, but not happy, faces (dark black blobs)
(b) Correlation of extraversion with left amygdala activation to happy, but not fearful, faces (dark black blob)
(c) Mean activations (in T scores) as a function of extraversion

Source: Canli et al. (2002).

There was a bilateral activation of the amygdala to fearful facial expressions which did not correlate with scores on E (or indeed with any of the other personality traits). In contrast, there was activation of the left amygdala in response to happy facial expressions which correlated very strongly ($r = 0.71$) with scores on E.

On the basis of these results, Canli and his colleagues (2002) suggest that two processes are involved in the amygdaloid region:

1 Detection of potential danger signals (such as fearful faces) which is engaged consistently across people;
2 An approach-related activation of the amygdala in response to positive stimuli (such as happy faces) which is engaged variably across people as a function of extraversion.

The fact that the amygdala activation to happy expressions was left lateralized is, of course, consistent with the work of Richard Davidson and others discussed in

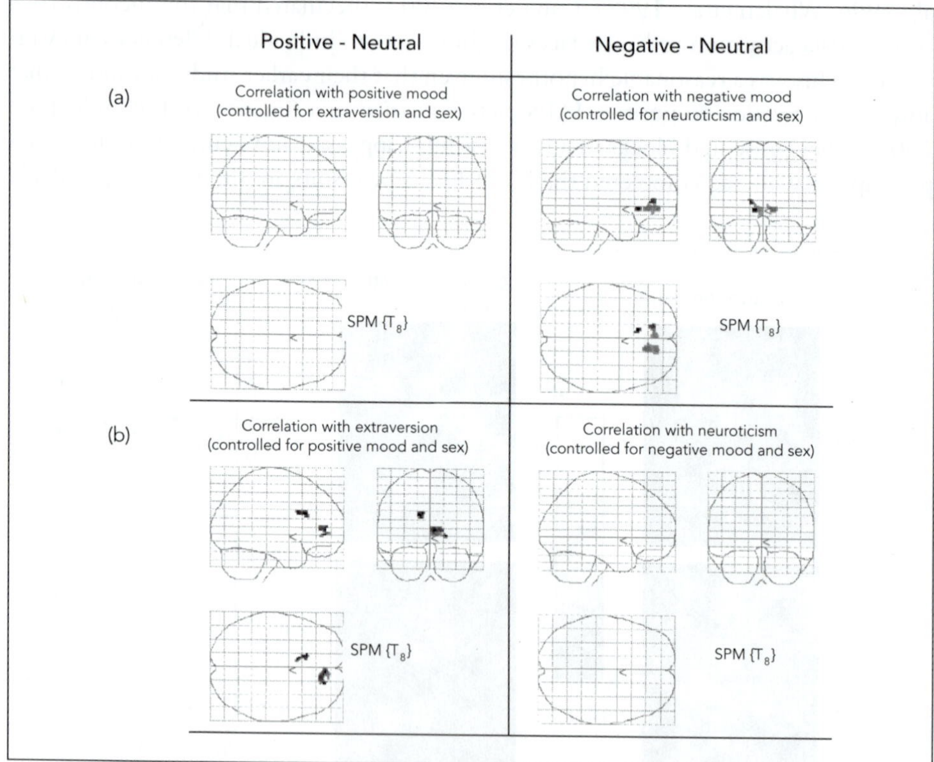

FIGURE 8.12 Mood and personality correlations in the anterior cingulate cortex (ACC)
(a) Sagittal, coronal and axial view of significant correlation clusters within the ACC: regions where increased activation in AC to positive or negative words was significantly correlated with mood state (controlling for personality traits and for sex)
(b) Sagittal, coronal and axial view of significant correlation clusters within the ACC: regions where increased activation in ACC to positive or negative words was significantly correlated with personality (controlling for mood state and for sex).
SPM=Statistical Parametric Mapping

Chapter 3, and indicates that this neural mechanism may contribute to the outgoing sociable style of extraverts. In other words, these individuals are more likely to engage the approach-related neural systems that are associated with positive emotions in response to reward-related stimuli.

Canli et al.'s (2002) results are a good illustration of how personality traits can influence some neural responses to emotionally-relevant perceptions but not others. It is of particular interest that N did not correlate with amygdala activation to fearful or angry facial expression, as might have been expected. An earlier study (Canli et al., 2001) also failed to find any correlation between N and amygdala activation to negative IAPS pictures (although there were significant correlations with N in cortical regions). However, one study has reported a significant correlation between activation of the amygdala to negative images (pictures of snakes) and a self-report measure of dispositional pessimism using PET as a measure of brain activation (Fischer et al., 2001). Thirteen female participants who were not snake phobic viewed video clips of

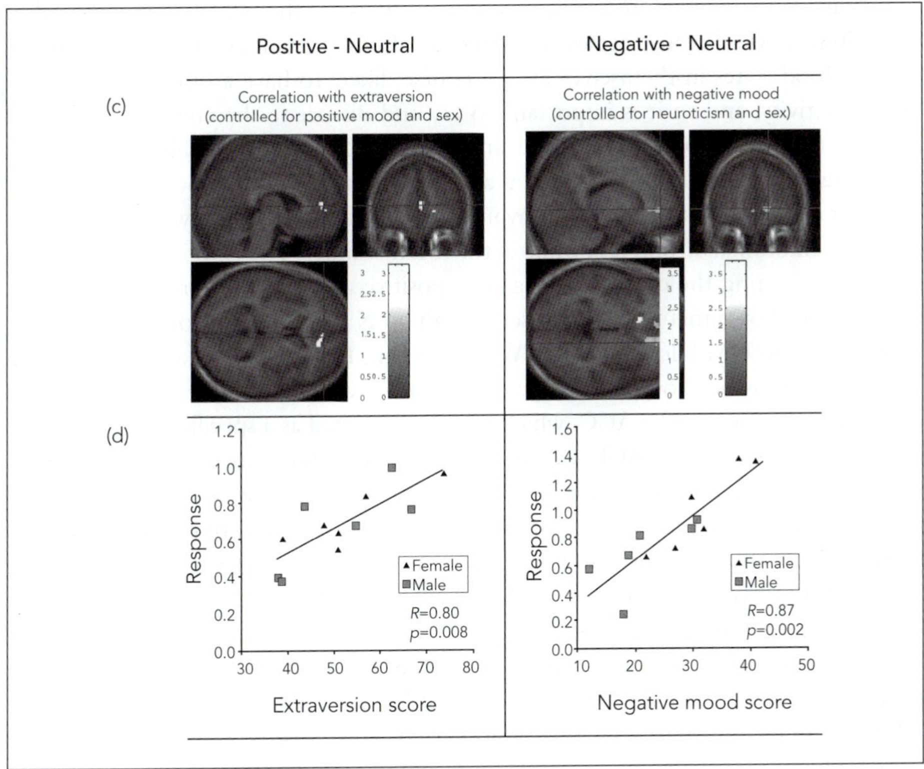

(c) Projection of correlation clusters onto averaged structural image of all participants. Crosshairs are placed on the most prominent activation clusters within the ACC that were associated with extraversion ($p < 0.01$) or with negative mood ($p < 0.025$)

(d) Scatter plots show response values (predicted, fitted response plus error) as a function of extraversion and negative mood scores.

Source: Canli et al. (2004).

moving snakes while undergoing PET scanning. Each participant also completed the Seligman Attributional Style Questionnaire (SASQ) (Peterson et al., 1982), in which low scores indicate relatively more pessimism. People who score high on pessimism on this scale (i.e., low scores) also tend to score highly on a number of measures of N-NA. Thus, dispositional pessimism is highly correlated with negative affectivity, trait-anxiety and neuroticism. As predicted by Fischer et al. (2001), there was bilateral activation of the amygdala in response to the snake videos and the degree of activation as measured by rCBF was correlated with pessimism scores for both the left ($r(13) = -0.53$, $p < 0.032$) and the right ($r(11) = -0.60$, $p < 0.0141$) amygdala. Remember that negative correlations in this case indicate that higher pessimism was related to greater activation of the amygdala. These results indicate that neuroticism (as indexed by pessimism) can modulate the strength of amygdala activation to negative stimuli. Thus, while amygdala activity may occur fairly automatically and consistently to negative (especially threat-related) stimuli, this study provides evidence that even this response may vary in relation to individual differences in personality traits.

Just as with cognitive processes, it is difficult to assess the influence of personality on brain reactivity because personality traits are also important determinants of mood states. Mood states in themselves are, of course, likely to have a direct influence on brain reactivity, and so it is important to try and dissociate the effects of personality traits from those of mood states. Canli et al. (2004) addressed this issue directly. They presented the NEO-FFI as well as a self-report measure of mood states (POMS) (McNair et al., 1992) to twelve healthy individuals. Each participant was then subjected to the emotional Stroop task while in the fMRI scanner. The emotional Stroop task involves indicating the colours of negative, positive and neutral words and previous research has shown that people who score high on N are generally slower on negative words than those with low N scores (Williams et al., 1996). Canli et al. (2004) found an intriguing dissociation between personality traits and mood states in terms of the degree of activation of the ACC, which they had selected as a specific region of interest (ROI). The degree of ACC activation to positive stimuli varied as a function of E (while controlling statistically for mood state) but did not vary as a function of positive mood state (while controlling for E). In contrast, the ACC response to negative words varied significantly as a function of negative mood state (when controlling for N) but did not vary as a function of N (when controlling for negative mood state). These results are shown in Figure 8.12.

In addition, negative mood states (but not N) were found to increase the functional connectivity between the ACC and the left middle frontal gyrus and the left inferior parietal lobe during the presentation of negative words. These findings are intriguing because they demonstrate that enduring personality traits and more transient mood states may have different effects (Hamann and Harenski, 2004). ACC activation seems to be associated with mood state for negative affective states, while activation of the ACC in response to positive stimuli seems more related to a trait personality factor (E). Canli et al. (2004) speculate that negative mood states may modulate the activation of the ACC, which in turn can enhance sensory selection and stimulus anticipation. This fits well with findings of enhanced cognitive processing of negative stimuli during dysphoric (negative) mood states (e.g., Bradley et al., 1993; Gotlib et al., 1988). In contrast to the rather dynamic effects of mood state on processing, the finding that ACC activation to positive words is a function of E (and not positive mood state) suggests a neural mechanism for more enduring and consistent differences between people (Canli et al., 2004). As we have seen, the literature suggests a much more consistent relationship between the activation of brain areas (e.g., amygdala) in response to positive stimuli as a function of extraversion, but brain activation to negative stimuli does not appear to be reliably related to individual differences in neuroticism. The work of Canli et al. (2004) suggests the hypothesis that enhanced brain activation to negative stimuli may be determined to a greater extent by mood states rather than personality traits.

GENETIC DETERMINANTS OF INDIVIDUAL DIFFERENCES IN EMOTIONALITY

It has long been known that genetics makes an important contribution to individual differences in personality, even though the contribution of individual genes to personality is likely to be relatively modest. This issue can be investigated by examining measures of E and N in pairs of identical twins who have been raised in different families and environments. These studies have generally established that genetic factors contribute about 40–60% of the variance in N and E, as well as other personality traits (e.g., Heath and Martin, 1994; Plomin et al., 1994; Reif and Lesch, 2003). However, in some of the first studies to examine the role of a single gene in terms of individual differences in emotionality, the contribution of the *serotonin transporter gene* (5-HTT) to personality traits was estimated at just about 8% (Lesch et al., 1996), while variation in the *D4 dopamine receptor gene* (D4DR) was estimated at 3–4% (Benjamin et al., 1996). Even though this contribution might seem relatively small, the search for variations within single genes is important. It has been pointed out, for example, that personality is a complex trait that is likely to be underpinned by many genes (Bouchard, 1994; Savitz and Ramesar, 2004a and b).

In the unravelling of the human genome around 45,000 genes have been identified and over 30,000 of these are expressed in the brain (Paterson et al., 1999). This means that the sheer number of different possible determinants of personality (both genetic and environmental) is so large that the pursuit of what are known as *dimensional* approaches to behavioural genetics has become increasingly common (Plomin et al., 1994). The idea is that, while there may not be specific genes for complex emotional disorders (such as depression or anxiety), there may be genes that underlie particular behavioural dimensions (such as neuroticism, extraversion, introversion and so on). An appropriate strategy for investigation would be to examine how variations within single genes might influence specific behavioural dimensions or personality traits. A huge amount of research effort in emotion science is now being directed towards the search for potential candidate genes that may underpin different emotion-related personality traits.

An important first step in this research process is the development of coherent methods to identify potential candidate genes. Several key criteria have been established in order to facilitate this process. First, the gene must be *polymorphic*, which means that there is a variant (or what is technically known as an *allele*) of the gene that can be linked to a personality trait. Second, the polymorphism should have some relevance to the personality trait in question. For example, if high levels of neuroticism are thought to be linked with low levels of serotonin (5-HT) then polymorphisms resulting in reduced levels of 5-HT in the brain would be obvious candidates (see Deary et al., 1999). The first studies to report links between genetic polymorphisms and personality traits were published in 1996. In one study, a polymorphism of the 5-HTT gene was shown to be linked to neuroticism (Lesch et al., 1996), while two studies reported an association between a polymorphism of the D4RD gene and novelty-seeking behaviour (Benjamin et al., 1996; Ebstein et al., 1996). Following these pioneering studies, there has been a flood of reports of genetic polymorphisms linked to specific personality traits (see Savitz and Ramesar, 2004b, for review). While many studies have failed to establish any links and many positive results have not been replicated, Savitz and Ramesar (2004b) nevertheless conclude that there is more than enough evidence to suggest a genuine link between genetic variation and personality traits. Since most work has been conducted on polymorphisms of genes involving the 5-HT and the DA systems, we will selectively review these studies along with related studies that provide converging evidence for the role of polymorphisms in the development of personality traits.

Serotonin and variation in emotional reactivity

The study reported by Lesch et al. (1996) on the serotonin transporter (5-HTT) gene provides an excellent example of the search for a *candidate* gene. There are two variants (alleles) of this gene. One variant is physically longer (l) due to the inclusion or deletion of a number of base pairs in the promotor region of the gene. The shorter (s) variant has a range of functions but tends to produce less of the transporter molecule that is responsible for removing 5-HT (serotonin) from the synaptic cleft. While it might be expected that this would result in more 5-HT in the brain, the evidence suggests that the s-allele is actually associated with reduced 5-HT function (Greenberg et al., 1999; Williams et al., 2003). It should be noted, however, that this may only be true of Caucasian men and further research is required with women and different ethnic groups (Williams et al., 2003).

Anatomically, it has been established that several 5-HT receptor subtypes are located within the amygdala, and animal research has shown that 5-HT levels in the amygdala increase during fear conditioning (Inoue et al., 1993), while 5-HT enhancing drugs reduce the acquisition of fear conditioning (Inoue et al., 2004). Thus, the evidence seems to suggest a complex relationship between emotional reactivity and brain 5-HT levels. Nevertheless, on the basis of a wide range of evidence Stutzmann and LeDoux (1999) have suggested that a reduction of 5-HT functioning is related to an increase in the processing of aversive stimuli. This is caused by a reduced ability to inhibit sensory processing which is normally modulated by 5-HT. Each of us carries two copies (alleles) of each gene, one from each of our parents. Thus, a given individual can be homozygous for s (s/s), homozygous for l (l/l), or heterozygous (s/l). Lesch et al. (1996) found that people who carry at least one copy of the s-allele (i.e., s/s or s/l) reported significantly higher levels of neuroticism on standardized questionnaires. This study has inspired a number of studies linking molecular genetics with individual differences in emotionality. It should be noted, however, that there have been some concerns about the strength of the evidence for the role of allelic variation in the 5-HTT gene and neuroticism because a number of studies have failed to replicate the original results (see Reif and Lesch, 2003; Savitz and Ramesar, 2004b, for reviews). Questions have been raised about these replication attempts, however, as many studied much smaller samples that the original ($N > 500$), and many also used unusual populations such as violent offenders, alcoholics, and drug addicts (Reif and Lesch, 2003).

Further evidence for the role of 5-HTT polymorphisms in neuroticism has come from a pioneering study combining functional imaging and genotyping in a single study. Hariri et al. (2002) hypothesized that if the 5-HTT polymorphism is associated with N, then it should also be associated with individual differences in how the brain responds to fear-related stimuli. They tested this hypothesis by presenting people with a series of angry and fearful facial expressions while the activation of the amygdala was observed using fMRI. People who carried the s-allele of the 5-HTT gene demonstrated significantly greater amygdala activation in response to angry and fearful faces compared with those who were homozygous for the l-allele. This result was found in two separate samples of 28 people (Hariri et al., 2002), and has been replicated with a larger sample (Hariri and Weinberger, 2003). Thus, individual differences in amygdala activation to fear-related stimuli is determined to a significant extent by variation in the 5-HTT gene.

A more recent study extends these results by demonstrating that, in addition to stronger activation of the amygdala in carriers of the s-allele, these individuals also show a greater degree of coupling between the amygdala and the ventromedial prefrontal cortex (vmPFC) (Heinz et al., 2005). Twenty-nine participants were genotyped: 9 were homozygous for the l-allele of the 5-HTT gene (l/l), 9 were homozygous for the s-allele (s/s), and 11 carried both the s-allele and the l-allele (s/l). Participants were exposed to blocks of unpleasant, pleasant and neutral pictures from the IAPS set while their brain activity was measured by means of fMRI. Bilateral amygdala activation to the negative pictures was found and this correlated significantly with genotype. The number of s-alleles positively correlated with the magnitude of amygdala activation to negative (relative to neutral) pictures, replicating the findings of Hariri et al. (2002). Of more interest, coupling between the amygdala and the vmPFC was found to be stronger in participants carrying an s-allele (s/s, s/l) compared to those with an l/l genotype. In other words, activity in both the amygdala and the vmPFC was increased in s-allele carriers when processing negative information. This study provides further support for the hypothesis that the 5-HTT gene may play a key role in the development of neural circuits that are implicated in the high levels of negative affectivity (Heinz et al., 2005).

A study by Canli et al. has indicated that the 5-HTT gene may have a much broader role in emotional and cognitive processing than previously thought (Canli, Omura et al., 2005). These authors point out that most work in this area demonstrates that carriers of the s-allele show enhanced amygdala activation to negative images in comparison with neutral images (e.g., Hariri et al., 2002; Heinz et al., 2005). On logical grounds, this means that the results could be due to either (a) enhanced activation of the amygdala in response to negative stimuli, or (b) reduced activation of the amygdala to neutral stimuli. Because no previous study included a passive baseline condition, the second possibility (b) could not be tested. Canli, Omura et al. (2005) presented 41 participants with a modified Stroop task in which blocks of negative, neutral and positive words were presented and participants had to indicate the colour of the words by pressing the appropriate button. In addition, a passive control condition was included in which participants simply looked at a fixation cross and did not have to respond. Twenty-eight of the participants carried the s-allele (s/l or s/s) while thirteen were homozygous for the l-allele (l/l). As predicted and found in previous studies, there was significantly greater activation of the right amygdala in response to the negative relative to the neutral words for participants carrying the s-allele. However, when the fixation control was used as the comparison condition it was found that participants carrying the s-allele showed significantly less activation than those carrying the l-allele when responding to neutral Stroop words. Critically, when the negative word blocks were compared to the fixation control condition, there was now no difference in amygdala activation between the s-allele and the l-allele groups. These results suggest that greater amygdala activation to negative stimuli in s-allele carriers is due to decreased activation to neutral stimuli, rather than increased activation to negative stimuli.

As Canli, Omura et al. (2005) point out, it is important for future research to determine whether this finding generalizes to other tasks beyond the Stroop effect. If this is the case, then clearly the 5-HT genotype is playing a much wider role in cognitive and emotional processing than the simple notion that it renders the amygdala more sensitive to negative stimuli. Canli, Omura et al. (2005) suggest that the 5-HTT s-allele could be associated with either (a) a tonic increase in amygdala activation during an inactive rest condition, or (b) with a phasic decrease in amygdala activation in active conditions, and this is illustrated in Figure 8.13. This is an important focus for future research. It should be noted, however, that, even if a reduction in amygdala activation to neutral stimulation turns out to be the key mechanism underlying the role of the 5-HTT s-allele in emotional reactivity, it is still the case that, over time, carriers of the s-allele do experience a relatively greater degree of amygdala activation to negative stimuli compared to those who are homozygous for the l-allele.

Differences in emotional reactivity between people who carry the s-allele and the l-allele of the 5-HTT gene are assumed to be due to a reduction in 5-HT function in the brain. A study by Cools et al. tested this hypothesis more directly by pharmacologically reducing the amount of 5-HT in the brain and assessing whether this made any difference to the amygdala response to threat-related faces (2005). They also

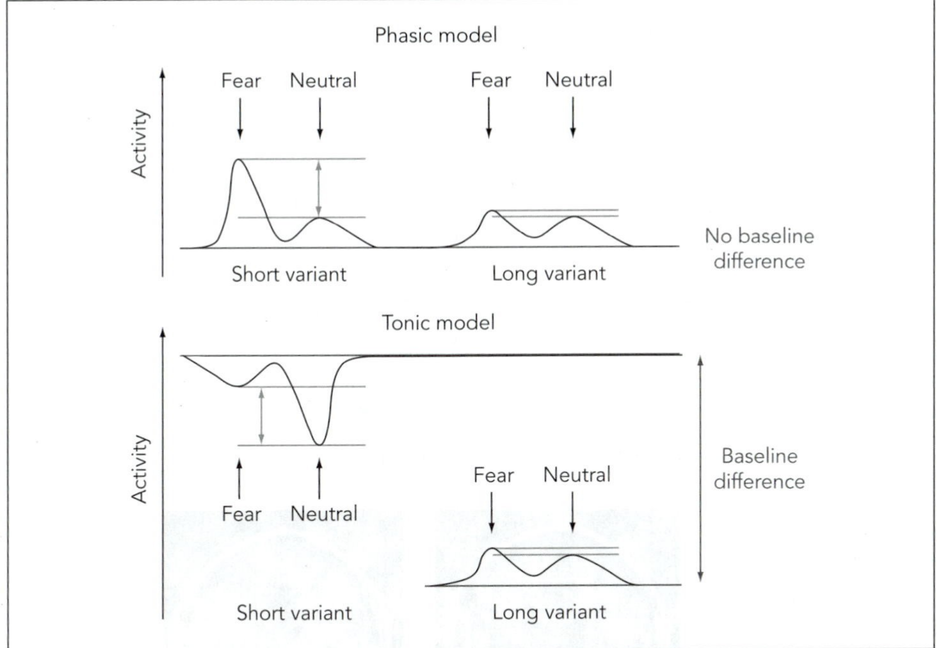

FIGURE 8.13 The standard 'phasic' versus the 'tonic' model of 5-HTT dependent modulation of brain activity

Source: Canli and Lesch (2007).

examined the role of self-reported threat-sensitivity, as measured on the BIS scale (Carver and White, 1994), on modulating the effects of the 5-HT depletion. The acute depletion of brain 5-HT was induced in 12 male participants by means of the acute tryptophan depletion (ATD) procedure, which has been well established as a means of lowering brain levels of serotonin. Participants were tested on two occasions and were given a tryptophan depleting drink or a balancing amino acid drink under double-blind conditions (i.e., neither the experimenters nor the participants were aware of which drink they had been given). About five hours after the drink (to ensure low tryptophan levels in the experimental group), participants were asked to categorize a series of faces as male or female while undergoing an fMRI scan. Fearful, happy and neutral facial expressions taken from the Ekman and Friesen (1976a) set were presented in alternating blocks. The results showed that the ATD procedure had no significant effect on amygdala activation to fearful faces when all participants were considered as a single group. However, when individual differences in threat-sensitivity were taken into account enhanced right amygdala activation to fearful faces (relative to happy faces) was found in those participants with higher scores on the BIS. The results are shown in Figure 8.14.

Thus, this study shows that 5-HT depletion resulted in an increase in the responsiveness of the right amygdala to fearful faces as a function of individual differences in threat sensitivity (Cools et al., 2005). It is an intriguing example of how different

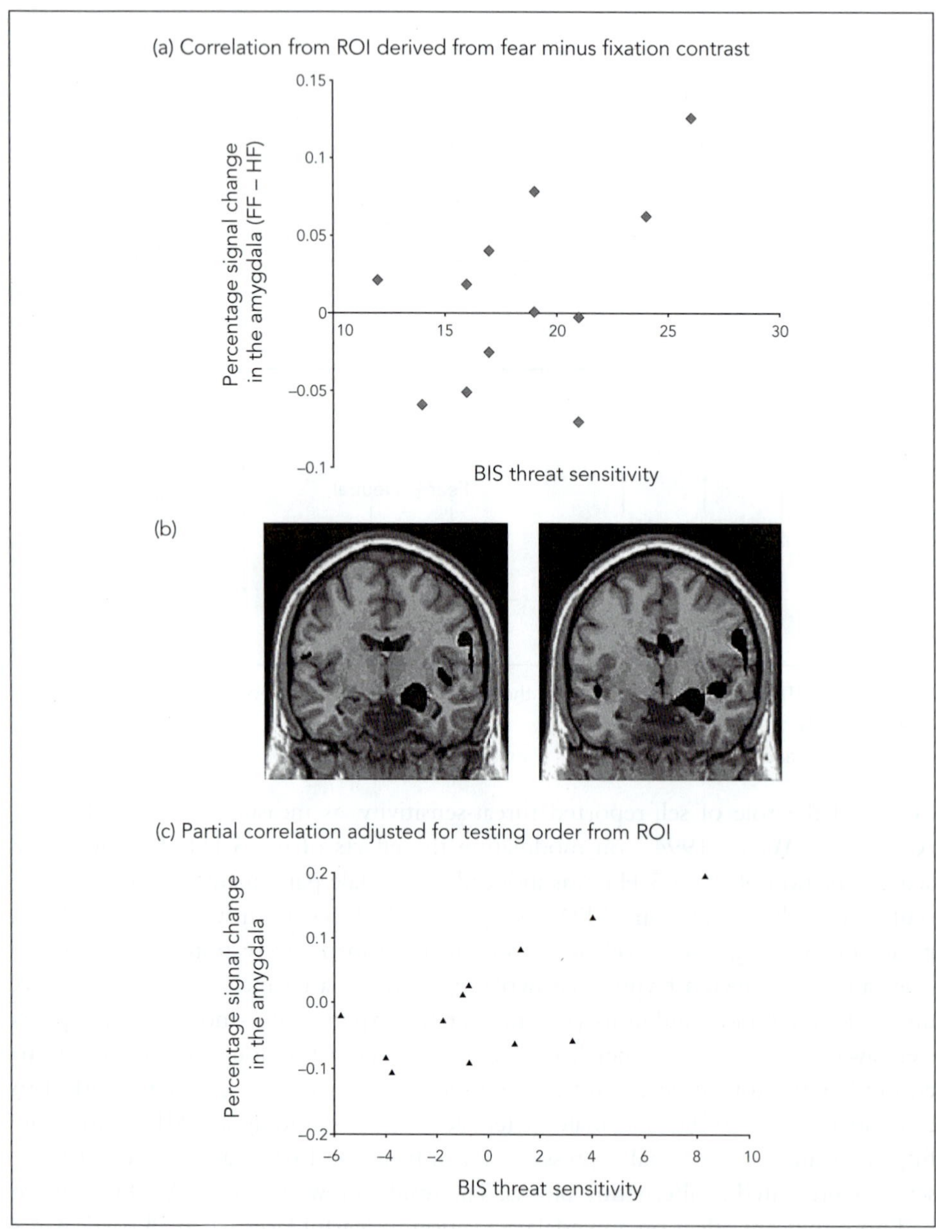

FIGURE 8.14 Results of Cools et al.'s (2005) study to assess the impact of ATD on amygdala response to threat-related stimuli

(a) Individual scores on the BIS threat sensitivity scale against percentage signal changes in right amygdala activation: fearful faces (FF) compared with happy faces (HF)
(b) The anatomical locations of the association between threat sensitivity and ATD effects superimposed on two coronal slices from a single brain image
(c) Threat sensitivity scores against percentage signal changes in right amygdala activation after correction (partial correlation) for testing order

Source: Cools et al. (2005).

individuals can respond quite differently to drug interventions that affect brain neurotransmitter levels. Reduction of brain levels of serotonin did not affect everyone in the same way, but those with high levels of N-NA (as indexed by high BIS scores) were especially reactive to a reduction in levels of brain serotonin and became highly reactive to aversive stimuli under these conditions.

Other work has examined polymorphisms in the *human tryptophan hydroxylase-2* (hTPH2) gene in terms of amygdala activation to aversive stimuli (Canli, Congdon et al., 2005; Brown et al., 2005). Tryptophan hydroxylase (TPH) is an enzyme that can influence the amount of 5-HT that is produced in the brain. There is a single nucleotide polymorphism (G(-844)T) on this gene such that people can be homozygous for G (G/G), homozygous for T (T/T) or heterozygous (G/T). Brown et al. (2005) presented a series of fearful and angry faces, as well as geometric shapes as control stimuli, while participants were in the fMRI scanner. Participants were genotyped based on the hTPH2 gene into two groups: G/G homozygotes ($n = 11$) and T-allele carriers (G/T, $n = 9$; T/T, $n = 2$). Importantly, it was confirmed that the two groups did not differ in their 5-HTT genotype status. Greater bilateral amygdala activation occurred in response to the fearful expressions in people who were hTPH2 T-allele carriers in comparison with G-allele homozygotes. This work was extended by Canli, Congdon et al. (2005), who found greater amygdala activation to fearful and sad, relative to neutral, facial expressions in T-allele carriers. In addition, however, it was also found that the T-allele was associated with a greater activation of the amygdala to happy faces. On the basis of these results, Canli, Congdon et al. speculated that allelic variation of the hTPH2 gene might modulate amygdala responsiveness as a more general function of emotional *arousal* rather than *negative valence*.

The confusing aspect of these two studies, however, is that the T-allele of the hTPH2 gene seems to be associated with an increase in brain 5-HT synthesis (Brown et al., 2005), and yet people who carry this version of the gene exhibit enhanced amygdala activation in response to aversive stimuli. Thus, a genotype associated with higher brain levels of serotonin is linked with enhanced neural reactivity to negatively valenced stimuli. In marked contrast, the s-allele of the 5-HTT gene seems to be associated with reduced 5-HT synthesis in the brain but is also associated with enhanced amygdala activity to aversive stimuli (Hariri et al., 2002; Heinz et al., 2005). In line with later studies, the acute depletion of TPH (and the resulting depletion of brain 5-HT) has also been shown to be associated with enhanced amygdala activity to aversive stimuli, at least in those who report high degrees of threat sensitivity (Cools et al., 2005). It is not clear how this paradox can be explained and it is an important focus of future research.

One difficulty with this area of research is that often very small samples have been tested and, therefore, we do not yet have enough data to firmly establish the nature of the links between specific allelic variation and variations in brain neurochemistry. This is clearly an exciting and important area of research that should shed light on the complex links between genotypes, brain biochemistry, and personality characteristics.

Dopamine and variation in emotional reactivity

Turning now to the dopamine (DA) system, a number of genes and receptors which appear to be potential candidate genes that might underlie specific personality traits have been identified (Savitz and Ramesar, 2004b). Indeed, two of the very first studies to examine a link between genetic polymorphisms and personality traits examined polymorphisms of the dopamine D4 receptor gene (D4DR) (Benjamin et al., 1996; Ebstein et al., 1996). To illustrate, Ebstein et al. genotyped 124 people in Israel and found that 34 carried a long (l) allele of polymorphic exon III repeat sequence of the D4DR gene (i.e., l/l or l/s), while 90 were homozygous for the short (s) allele (s/s). All participants completed Cloninger's Tridimensional Personality Questionnaire which, as we have seen in Chapter 3, gives measures of four different dimensions of temperament: novelty seeking (NS), harm avoidance (HA), reward dependence (RD) and persistence (P). The key finding was that those carrying the long allele of the D4DR gene scored significantly higher on NS compared to those who did not carry the l-allele. The other three personality dimensions did not differ between the genotype groups. Another study using the NEO-PPI found that those carrying the l-allele of the D4DR gene scored significantly higher on extraversion and significantly lower on conscientiousness than those not carrying the l-allele (Benjamin et al., 1996). Benjamin et al. also estimated scores on novelty seeking from the combination of scores on the NEO-PPI and replicated the results of Epstein et al. (1996) that possession of the l-allele resulted in higher novelty seeking estimates. These two studies provide evidence for a link between polymorphisms of the D4 dopamine receptor gene and novelty seeking.

A more recent experimental study has provided laboratory-based evidence for the role of individual differences in extraversion, as well as genetic variation, in determining the degree of response to positive rewards (Cohen et al., 2005). As we have seen, one of the key characteristics of people who score high on measures of E is that they are hypothesized to be highly sensitive to rewards (e.g., Depue and Collins, 1999). Dopamine (DA) is known to be heavily involved in the brain's reward system (Baxter and Murray, 2002). In particular, the dopamine D2 receptor gene (D2DR) has been implicated in processes of reward (e.g., Blum et al., 1996; Berridge and Robinson, 2003). The A1 allele in particular has been associated with reduced levels of D2 receptors in the brain (Jonsson et al., 1999) and with clinical disorders of reward insensitivity and alcoholism. Cohen et al. (2005) used fMRI to investigate whether individual differences in extraversion would predict the degree to which the brain's dopaminergic reward system would be activated, and whether these differences are related to the A1 allele on the D2DR gene. Sixteen participants took part in the study and were divided into two groups: those with one or two copies of the A1 allele ($n = 9$) and those without the A1 allele ($n = 7$). All participants completed the NEO-PPI questionnaire and were then asked to take part in a gambling task while brain activation was assessed by means of fMRI. On each trial, participants had to choose either a high-risk (i.e., 40% chance of winning \$2.50 and 60% chance of winning \$0.00) or a low-risk gamble (i.e., 80% chance of winning \$1.25 and 20% chance of \$0.00), and then there was a

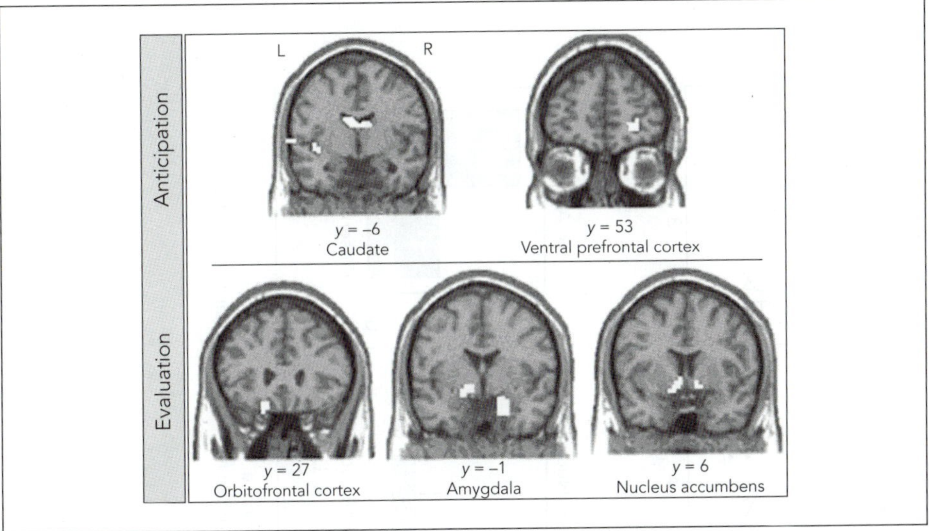

FIGURE 8.15 Activation (white blobs) related to reward anticipation and reward evaluation
(a) Regions in the striatum, insula, and prefrontal cortex were active during an anticipation period prior to receiving a reward
(b) Regions in the orbitofrontal cortex, amygdala, and nucleus accumbens showed greater activity when receiving rewards than when not receiving rewards (evaluation period)

Source: Cohen et al. (2005).

7.5 second delay before they were informed of what they had won or lost. During this anticipation period, there were significant activations in dorsal caudate nucleus, right vmPFC, insula, bilateral PFC and right parietal cortex. E scores did not correlate with activation of any of these regions (Cohen et al., 2005: Study 2). However, when the reward was actually given significantly greater activation was observed in bilateral medial OFC, right amygdala, bilateral nucleus accumbens and left hippocampus (see Figure 8.15). Of more interest, however, the reward response was significantly greater in 5 out of 6 of these regions of interest (ROI) for those scoring high on E relative to those with lower scores on E. Next, the two genotyped groups were compared and, as shown in Figure 8.16, the brain's reward response was significantly reduced in those participants who carried a copy of the A1 allele.

The results reported by Cohen et al. (2005) are consistent with those fMRI studies which show that E is associated with greater amygdala and PFC activation when viewing positive images (Canli et al., 2001, 2002). Cohen et al.'s results, however, provide more direct evidence that these brain areas are activated to a greater extent in extraverts when they have actually received a reward. Moreover, this study demonstrated that the brain's reward system was less activated by a reward for those individuals carrying the A1 allele of the D2DR gene, supporting the notion that a reduced concentration of D2DR in the reward system leads to a reduction in sensitivity to rewards. It is interesting to note, however, that the presence of the D2DR A1 allele was not related to E scores in this study. Cohen et al. (2005) conclude that the link between this allele and extraversion might be subtle and is likely to be influenced to a

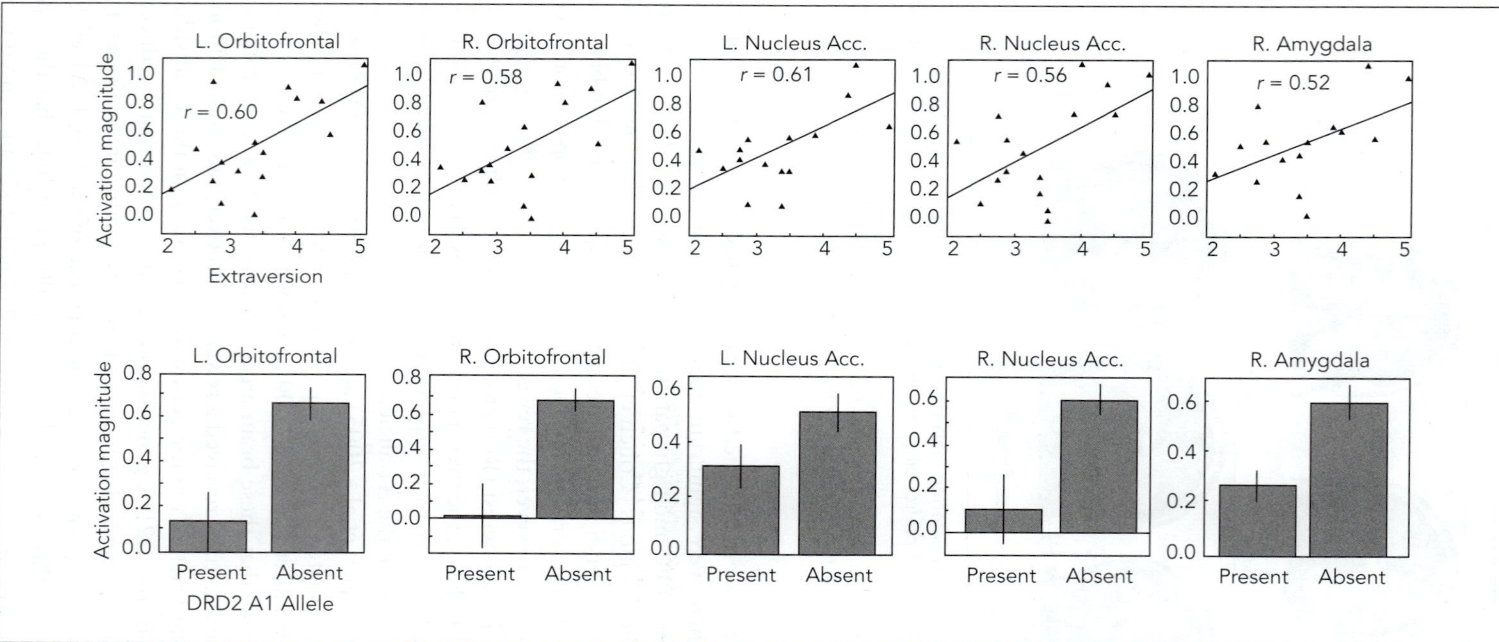

FIGURE 8.16 Extraversion and DRD2 variability predict neural reward responses during an evaluation phase
(a) Relationship between extraversion scores and reward responses in regions showing greater activity in the reward > no reward contrast during the evaluation phase
(b) Reward responses in subjects with and without the DRD2 gene polymorphism

Source: Cohen et al. (2005).

large extent by both environmental (e.g., amount of stressful life events in childhood) and other genetic events. It is also the case that the sample size was relatively small and larger samples may be required to establish associations between particular genotypes and scores on personality questionnaires.

In this section we have discussed selected highlights of research looking at whether specific genetic polymorphisms are related to particular personality traits. In a wider context, the findings that subtle variations in 5-HTT, D4DR or D2DR genotypes can result in differences in the degree to which neural circuits become activated in response to emotional stimuli are important. This work is especially exciting because it suggests hypotheses at the molecular level about the development of the neurobiological circuits underlying processing biases in how people perceive and respond to affective stimuli. It seems clear that research using a combination of behavioural and functional neuroimaging methodologies is likely to lead to significant advances in our understanding of emotions and emotional disorders, particularly when combined with genotyping.

CHAPTER SUMMARY

This chapter considered evidence that personality traits can influence the fundamental mechanisms of information processing. Most research focuses on two of the *big five* personality traits. *Neuroticism* is one trait that has been associated with the enhanced processing of negative, especially aversive, stimuli and is often measured by self-report indices of trait-anxiety, trait anger and depression, as well as more general measures of neuroticism and negative affectivity. In contrast, individual variation on self-report measures of *extraversion* has been linked with the enhanced processing of positive stimuli, especially those that are related to reward. A key difficulty is the separation of the effects of personality traits from their related mood states when examining biases in cognitive processing. Empirical evidence looking at biases in attention, memory, judgement and interpretation, and how they relate to different personality traits was examined. Finally, individual variation in neural reactivity to affective stimuli was discussed in relation to individual differences in personality traits as well as variations at the level of genotypes.

RECOMMENDED READING

Some excellent general overviews of the role of personality-related differences in information processing are available in the following sources:

Andrew Mathews and Colin MacLeod (1994) 'Cognitive approaches to emotion and emotional disorders', *Annual Review of Psychology*, 45, 25–50.

Jenny Yiend (2004) (ed.) *Cognition, Emotion, and Psychopathology.* Cambridge: Cambridge University Press.

Joseph P. Forgas. (2001) (ed.) *Affect and Social Cognition.* Mahwah, NJ: Lawrence Erlbaum.

For overviews of the work on neuroimaging and genotyping the following edited book provides many relevant chapters:

Turhan Canli (2006) (ed.) *Biology of Personality and Individual Differences.* New York: Guilford Press.

Finally, the following article provides a readable overview of the association between the serotonin transporter gene and personality traits:

Turhan Canli and Klaus-Peter Lesch (2007) 'Long story short: The serotonin transporter in emotion regulation and social cognition', *Nature Neuroscience*, 10, 1103–9.

9 DETERMINANTS OF EMOTIONAL DISORDERS

All of us go through periods of distress and sadness in our lives. However, for some people the levels of distress and sadness reach a point where they can no longer cope with everyday tasks. What factors are involved in leading some people to develop an emotional *disorder*? There are, of course, wide cultural variations in what is considered 'normal' or 'abnormal' in terms of emotional behaviour. For example, the wild pig syndrome that we discussed in Chapter 1 is considered quite normal for men of a certain age in Gururumban society, but would be considered quite odd in most other places! Moreover, even within a particular culture there may be wide variation in what is considered acceptable or 'normal' within different subcultures. People in Western cultures, for example, are given tremendous leeway in their behaviour when they are considered to be 'in love'.

In spite of these differences there have been attempts to provide classification systems for mental disorders. The best-known example is the *Diagnostic and Statistical Manual of Mental Disorders* published by the American Psychiatric Association. This was first published in 1952 and the most recent version is the fourth edition published in 1994 (*DSM-IV*). This manual provides five different scales or axes showing a range of symptoms and characteristics of more than 200 mental disorders, and is widely used by psychiatrists as an aid in diagnosis. The first three axes are *always* used in assessment, while the last two are optional and can be used depending on the judgement of the psychiatrist. A brief summary of the five axes is presented in Table 9.1.

TABLE 9.1 The five axes of the *Diagnostic and Statistical Manual of Mental Disorders*

Axis 1	Clinical disorders	Allows a particular disorder to be diagnosed based on a range of specific symptoms (e.g., worry etc).
Axis 2	Personality disorders and mental retardation	Identifies particular patterns of long-term dysfunction that are known to be related to personality disorders or mental retardation.
Axis 3	General medical conditions	Identifies any physical conditions or illnesses that are likely to affect emotional state and the ability to function effectively.
Axis 4	Psychosocial and environmental problems	Identifies any major stressful or important event that occurred with 12 months of the onset of the mental disorder.
Axis 5	Global assessment of functioning	Provides a 100-point scale that can be used to assess the individual's overall level of functioning at work and at home.

One benefit of DSM-IV is that disorders are defined by observable symptoms rather than features believed to cause each disorder. In addition, each diagnostic category differentiates between those characteristics which are considered essential and those that are not. For example, in order to make a diagnosis of Generalized Anxiety Disorder (GAD), the presence of excessive worry and anxiety is essential, while just three of the following symptoms need to be present: restlessness, being easily fatigued, difficulty concentrating, irritability, muscle tension or sleep disturbance. While DSM-IV is useful, it also has a number of problems. In particular, it does not take much account of differences across different cultures and therefore is most relevant for Western societies. It also provides a strictly *categorical* classification scheme in which people are assumed to either have or not have a specific disorder. The reality is, however, that many symptoms (e.g., rumination) are common across a variety of different disorders and therefore it has been suggested that a *dimensional* approach might be more appropriate. This is similar in some ways to the discussion regarding categorical and dimensional approaches to emotion. Rather than assuming that there are distinct and separate categories of mental disorder with specific causes and specific treatments it may be more accurate to assume that people experience a variety of symptoms to varying extents. Nevertheless, the diagnostic categories identified in DSM-IV are widely used in both the assessment and the treatment of mental disorders around the world. In this chapter we will focus on just two broad diagnostic categories that have variously been called *emotional*, *affective*, *mood* or *distress* disorders. These disorders along with their characteristics are outlined in Table 9.2.

Emotional disorders are relatively common, occurring in around 20% of the population. Thus, approximately 1 in 5 people will suffer from an anxiety or depression-related disorder during their life, meaning that millions of people around the world experience problems relating to the affective system. The National Comorbidity Survey (NCS) (Kessler et al., 1994) conducted in the United States found that the *prevalence* (i.e., the proportion of the population experiencing a particular illness) of mood disorders is generally much higher among women than men, while other disorders are more common in men (see Table 9.3). A more recent assessment of the NCS found that the lifetime risk of MDD is 7–12% for men and 20–25% for women (Kessler et al., 2005). The risk of experiencing at least one anxiety disorder is around 28% (Greenberg et al., 1999). In the UK, the Psychiatric Morbidity Survey estimates that 19.4% of the adult population suffers from mood disorders and the World Health Organization (WHO) estimates that in both the US and Western Europe almost 40% of all disability (mental and physical) is due to mental illness (London School of Economics, 2006). Another salient fact is the high degree of *co-morbidity* that occurs between depression (MDD) and the anxiety disorders. One study, for example, reported that almost 90% of people with anxiety disorders experience at least one episode of clinical depression during their life (Gorman, 1996). Emotional disorders impose a huge cost for the individuals concerned as well as for their families and society at large. It is no surprise, then, that a substantive research effort has been dedicated to the task of trying to understand what causes emotional disorders and how they can be best treated.

TABLE 9.2 The main *DSM-IV* diagnostic categories relating to affective and anxiety disorders

Diagnostic category	*Typical features*
Depression-related disorders	
Major depressive disorder (MDD)	Five of the following symptoms must occur almost every day for at least a 2-week period: sad, depressed mood; loss of pleasure and interest in usual activities; difficulties in sleeping; changes in activity level; weight loss or gain; loss of energy and tiredness; negative self-concept, self-blame and self-reproach; difficulties in concentrating; recurring thoughts of suicide or death.
Bipolar disorder	A condition in which individuals alternate between experiences of both severe depression and mania (i.e., a mood state involving elation, intense activity, talkativeness and unjustified high self-esteem).
Anxiety-related disorders	
Panic disorder	A panic attack involves intense fear and discomfort with at least four bodily symptoms suddenly appearing, for example, accelerated heart rate, feeling of choking, nausea, sweating, chest pains, shortness of breath, palpitations, feeling dizzy and fear of dying. The diagnosis is given if people experience a number of unexpected panic attacks and have ongoing worries about: (a) having another panic attack, (b) changes in behaviour because of the panic attack, and (c) the implications of the attack.
Post-traumatic stress disorder (PTSD)	PTSD is triggered by a specific event such as a natural disaster or a war. The three main types of symptoms relate to: (a) re-experiencing the traumatic event (e.g., intrusive thoughts that cause intense emotional distress), (b) avoidance of situations and thoughts related to the triggering event, (c) increased arousal (e.g., increased startle response, difficulties with sleep, difficulty with concentration). Experiences of intense anger, anxiety, depression and guilt as well as explosive violence are also common in PTSD.
Generalized anxiety disorder (GAD)	GAD is defined by persistent and uncontrollable worry and anxiety that has been present for at least six months.
Social phobia	Social phobia is diagnosed if a person shows the following: (a) an intense and persistent fear of one or more situations in which there is exposure to unfamiliar people or to scrutiny, (b) the feared social situation almost always induces intense anxiety, (c) it is recognized that the fear and anxiety is excessive and out of proportion to the situation, (d) the feared social situations are either avoided or responded to with intense anxiety, (e) the phobic reactions interfere with working and/or social life.
Specific phobia	The main symptoms of a specific phobia involve (a) an intense and persistent fear of a specific object or situation, (b) a recognition by the individual that the degree of fear is excessive, (c) the feared object is either avoided or responded to with intense anxiety, (d) the phobic reactions interfere with working and/or social life and cause distress. Phobias can occur to a variety of objects but the most common relate to heights, open or enclosed spaces, spiders, snakes, dogs.
Obsessive compulsive disorder (OCD)	OCD is characterized by persistent obsessions (i.e., intrusive anxious thoughts) as well as compulsions (e.g., repeated actions and rituals). These can occur to a variety of situations. However, obsessions about being contaminated by germs are common and this is usually related to compulsive hand washing and cleaning. Performing the action results in a temporary reduction in anxiety but this does not typically last for very long and the action has to be repeated again and again.

TABLE 9.3 The lifetime prevalence of depression and anxiety-related disorders in males and females in the USA, percentages

Disorder	*Male*	*Female*	*Total*
Depression-related disorders			
Major depressive disorder	12.7	21.3	17.1
Manic episode	1.6	1.7	1.6
Anxiety-related disorders			
Panic disorder	2.0	5.0	3.5
Generalized anxiety disorder	3.6	6.6	5.1
Social phobia	11.1	15.5	13.3
Specific phobia	6.7	15.7	11.3
Other disorders			
Alcohol or drug addiction	35.4	17.9	26.6
Antisocial personality disorder	5.8	1.2	3.5
Schizophrenia	0.6	0.8	0.7

Source: Kessler et al. (1994).

RISK FACTORS FOR ANXIETY AND DEPRESSION

The first risk factor that may leave people more vulnerable to developing emotional disorders is *stressful environmental or life events.* Second, some of the *temperamental or personality traits* that we discussed in Chapter 8 have been associated with mood disorders. Third, the development of emotional disorders has been linked with different patterns of neural activity. A reduction in the level of certain brain chemicals has also been identified as a *neurobiological* factor associated with the development of emotional disorders. Fourth, a number of *cognitive processes and biases* have been identified as possible risk factors for both anxiety and depression. Fifth, there is evidence that some people may be predisposed to developing an emotional disorder because of their *genetic make-up.*

These factors are not independent of each other, of course, and it is likely that they will interact to enhance an individual's vulnerability to becoming anxious or depressed. For example, a particular set of life events (e.g., domestic violence) may modify the temperament of a child leaving that individual more likely to react negatively to violence in later life. Similarly, a particular genotype or a severe life event (e.g., death of a loved one) may result in a reduction in levels of certain neurotransmitters leaving people more vulnerable to the development of emotional disorder. The interactive quality of these factors is captured in what is known as the *diathesis-stress* model of psychopathology. This model assumes that a psychological disorder occurs because of two things:

(a) a *diathesis* – a predisposition or vulnerability to a particular disease or disorder. This may be a genetic vulnerability, or it may relate to a social vulnerability, and
(b) *stress* – the occurrence of some severe environmental or life event.

The crucial point is that both the stressful environmental event and the predisposition are necessary for a disorder to develop.

In this chapter a brief overview of the evidence for each of the important vulnerability factors for emotional disorders is presented. The five factors are: environmental or stressful life events, temperamental dimensions, cognitive processes, neurobiological processes, and genetic make-up. The importance of *environment–gene–personality interactions* in determining emotional disorders is also considered.

ENVIRONMENTAL EVENTS

Very traumatic life events may play an important role in setting up people's vulnerabilities to emotional disorders. This potential determinant of emotional disorders is often overlooked in cognitive and neuroscience models. The causal link between environmental effects and emotional disorder is perhaps most obvious in *post-traumatic stress disorder (PTSD)*. As we saw in Table 9.2, the trigger for PTSD is usually a specific event such as being in a war zone or experiencing a major accident. Almost everybody experiences a number of symptoms typical of PTSD *immediately* after a serious trauma. Thus, following a road traffic accident or a violent assault, most people will experience anxious arousal along with various symptoms of fear and avoidance as well as possibly experiencing 'flash-backs' and images that result in a mental re-experiencing of the trauma. Following rape, for instance, the vast majority of victims suffer the symptoms of PTSD immediately afterwards, but these decline substantially a month later, and occur in less than 40 per cent of victims 3 months later (Rothbaum et al., 1992). Indeed, the lifetime prevalence of PTSD following rape or violent assault is between 35% and 39% (Kilpatrick and Resnick, 1993). These figures tell us that, while the traumatic event itself is important in setting up a specific vulnerability for PTSD, other factors must also be involved in the development of the disorder (see Craske, 2003, for review).

There is substantial evidence that stressful encounters are associated with subsequent emotional disorders. First, there is evidence that stress has a direct effect on the brain, especially in causing a substantial loss of neurons (*neuronal atrophy*) in a number of brain regions including the hippocampus (McEwen, 2000). Second, human studies have shown that children who experience stress in early life are at an increased risk of developing emotional disorders. For example, one study found that women who were abused as children were much more likely to develop anxiety and depression disorders when they were adults than women from similar backgrounds who had not experienced childhood abuse (McCauley et al., 1997). Large-scale epidemiological studies have also reported that depression in adulthood is significantly associated with the amount of stress and trauma experienced in childhood (Heim et al., 2004). A more recent longitudinal study found that severe physical or sexual abuse in childhood is an important risk factor for later anxiety and depression disorders (Collishaw et al., 2007). It is interesting to note that the experience of stress, trauma and hardship in childhood is linked to a wide variety of emotional disorders – many anxiety disorders as well as depression – in addition to other mental conditions such as schizophrenia (see Craske, 2003; Fumagalli et al., 2007, for reviews). This suggests that stress may affect broad neurophysiological systems rather than being specific to particular emotions. The adverse effect that stress in childhood has on subsequent mental health further suggests that many emotional disorders may have a developmental origin. In other words, it is possible that exposure to stressful life events in childhood may set up vulnerabilities that leave people more susceptible to the development of both depression and anxiety in later life.

The number of stressful life events experienced in adulthood is also associated with a variety of illnesses including depression and anxiety (e.g., Brown and Harris, 1978). Many studies have used the *Social Readjustment Rating Scale*, which was developed in 1967 and asks people to say which out of 43 life events has happened to them over the past year (Holmes and Rahe, 1967). All of these life events – death of a spouse; child leaving home; going on vacation; birth of a baby; divorce and so on –) are rated according to the degree of adjustment that they require, taking account of the fact that both positive (e.g., birth of a baby) as well as negative (e.g., divorce) changes can be stressful.

Stress in these studies is usually defined as the degree of adjustment that is required to cope with the event. Scores on this scale are highly correlated with the degree of anxiety and depression experienced. There are, however, a number of obvious problems with this approach. For example, a correlation cannot determine the *causal* relationship between two factors. Thus, while a high number of stressful life events may indeed cause the onset of depression or anxiety, it is equally possible that the presence of depression or anxiety may cause a number of stressful life events (e.g., divorce, sexual difficulties etc). In addition, the actual impact or stress value of different life events is likely to vary dramatically from person to person. While most people would consider divorce to be a very stressful experience, someone who has been deeply unhappy for many years might feel mainly relief upon getting divorced and may not rate this event as being particularly negative or stressful. To get around this problem, researchers have now developed more detailed semi-structured interview techniques to help to get a clearer idea of the impact that particular events might have on people's lives. Using these more time-consuming but accurate methods, research has confirmed that there does seem to be a strong relationship between the onset of emotional disorders and the number and severity of stressful life events that have been experienced (Brown and Harris, 1978).

It is interesting to consider the potential mechanism that would allow stressful life events to generate a vulnerability to emotional disorders. One possibility is that the experience of major stress, especially at a young age, may modify the neurobiological mechanisms that help the body cope with adverse events. It has been found, for example, that people who are diagnosed with either an anxiety disorder or with a major depressive disorders often have an overactive *hypothalamic-pituitary-adrenal* (HPA) system. This hyperactivity is almost certainly due to a reduction in the level of *glucocorticoid receptors* expressed in the brain (Plotsky et al., 1995). Depression itself might lead to a reduction in the level of these receptors, or it might be the case that a lower level of these receptors results in depression and anxiety. Experimental research, often with animals, has played an important role in trying to determine the direction of causality.

One experimental strategy is to examine how stress occurring very early in life affects the functioning of the HPA axis. For example, one group of young rats may be assigned to an experimental group where they are deprived of maternal care for a couple of hours each day. The functioning of the HPA axis in these animals can then be compared with a control group that has been assigned to normal maternal care. A consistent finding in these studies is that both prenatal stress and stress during infancy lead to an alteration in the activity of the HPA. For example, baby rats that have been stressed develop fewer glucocorticoid receptors in the brain and show an enhanced responsiveness to subsequent stress (see Fumagalli et al., 2007, for review).

Experimental research such as this has led to theoretical models suggesting that the experience of stressful life events, especially at a young age, can lower a person's threshold for stress activation by affecting the neurobiological mechanisms involved with the response to stress. One model proposes, for instance, that intense and chronic stress can result in fundamental changes in processes involving the amygdala that lead to an 'easy to trigger' or hyper-reactive state (Rosen and Schulkin, 1998). Heim and Nemeroff (1999) also propose that exposure to stressful events in early life results in a permanent change in the functioning of the HPA. This leaves people more vulnerable and reactive to stressful events that might occur later in life.

As pointed out by Michelle Craske (2003), the experience of adversity and stress in early life can also have a profound effect on the development of temperament. People with more negative experiences in childhood are more likely to develop a more neurotic personality. As we will see in the next section, the temperamental dimension of N-NA is itself associated with an increased vulnerability to emotional disorders. The fact that the effects of stress on subsequent vulnerability to emotional disorders might be mediated through the effects of stress on temperament might explain why the effects are fairly non-specific. In other words, broad changes in temperamental characteristics related to N-NA would be expected to have effects on a wide range of negative emotions. The type of mediation effect envisaged is shown in Figure 9.1.

The nature of the relationship between stressful life events and the development of emotional disorders is considerably more complicated than that illustrated in

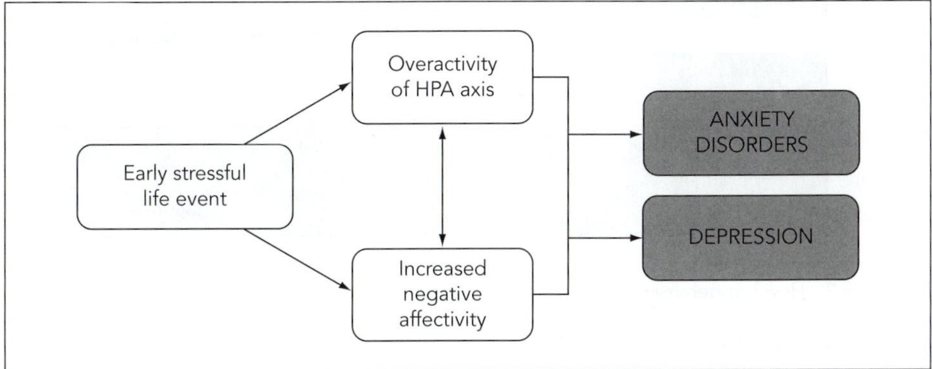

FIGURE 9.1 Possible mechanisms underlying the relationship between stressful life events experienced in childhood and the development of subsequent emotional disorders

Figure 9.1. For example, research with both animals and humans has shown that, while adverse early experience is clearly a strong predictor of subsequent emotional disorders, there are clear individual differences in who goes on to develop severe depression and anxiety reactions. As we will discuss later, an individual's specific *genotype* (e.g., Caspi and Moffit, 2006) as well as more general *temperament* (e.g., Clark, 2005) are both important determinants of how a person will react to an adverse situation. For the time being, however, we can conclude that adverse life events are an important factor in the development of emotional disorder and that these effects may be exerted both directly and indirectly.

TEMPERAMENT AND PERSONALITY

As shown in Figure 9.2, there are four ways in which temperament might affect the development of clinical disorders such as anxiety and depression. First, the *vulnerability* or predisposition model proposes that temperamental dimensions (e.g., N-NA) play a direct casual role in the development of psychopathology. In other words, the temperament acts as a predisposition so that, given the appropriate environmental event, a disorder may develop. To illustrate, the experience of being lost in the supermarket as a child may trigger the onset of agoraphobia (fear of open spaces), but only for those with a temperamental predisposition to disorder.

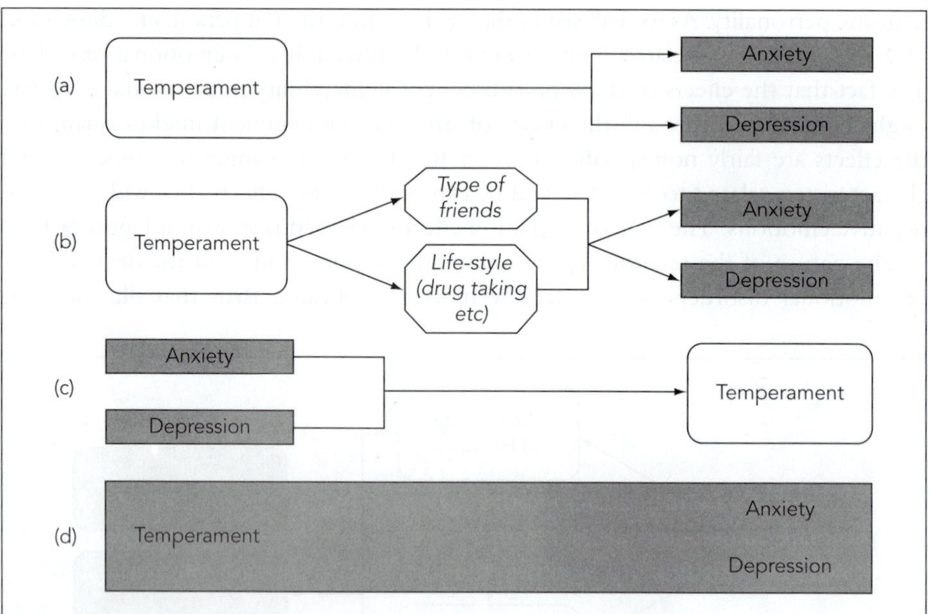

FIGURE 9.2 How temperament might be associated with the development of emotional disorders
(a) vulnerability model
(b) pathoplasty model
(c) scar or complication model
(d) continuity or spectrum model

Second, the *pathoplasty* model proposes that a temperamental dimension may modify the course of a disorder without necessarily playing a direct causal role. Instead, the temperament plays an indirect role in emotional disorders. This might be due to an influence on the social environment, for example, which in turn may influence the onset of psychopathology. To illustrate, a nervous and inhibited child may deliberately seek out quiet environments which do not involve a lot of social interaction, and this may ultimately play a role in the development of social phobia. Thus, whilst the temperament is clearly important in the development of disorder it has not played a direct role.

Third, the *scar* or *complication* model proposes that the relationship might run in the other direction so that temperament may be altered by the experience of an emotional disorder. Thus, the experience of severe anxiety or depression might lead to fundamental changes in personality such as increased insecurity or increased dependency on others.

Finally, the *continuity* or what is sometimes called the *spectrum* model proposes that both temperament and emotional disorder reflect the same underlying processes. Thus, temperament lies at the normal end of a spectrum of traits that are essentially sub-clinical manifestations of a clinical disorder. Put the other way around, the idea is that emotional disorders are extreme manifestations of normal personality traits.

The models outlined in Figure 9.2 are not mutually exclusive, and indeed evidence exists to support all four models (Clark, 2005; Clark et al., 1994; Mineka et al., 1998; Tackett, 2006). For example, the experience of severe life events, especially if they occur in childhood, can enhance the degree of N-NA, thus changing the fundamental temperament of the individual. However, it is also the case that a high degree of N-NA can increase the likelihood of experiencing adverse life events, and also amplify the general impact of these events on the person. Thus, a cycle is established whereby temperament can influence the type of events an individual might experience, which in turn can either increase or decrease the level of N-NA expressed.

Are temperamental dimensions risk factors for emotional disorders?

While there is evidence for all four models of how temperament and emotional disorder might be related (Figure 9.2), many influential theories support some version of the vulnerability or pathoplasty models (e.g., Clark, 2005). There are a number of significant methodological issues which make it very difficult to firmly establish the direction of causality. For instance, investigations of anxious and depressed populations cannot test the vulnerability, pathoplasty or scar models because an emotional disorder is already present and, therefore, we do not know the nature of the temperamental dimensions and/or personality traits before the onset of the disorder. To confirm that temperament plays a causal role in the development of emotional disorders it is necessary to conduct large-scale longitudinal studies in non-clinical populations in which temperament is measured at a very young age before the onset of any clinical disorder. This cohort can then be followed over many years to determine which individuals go on to develop emotional disorders and whether temperament and/or personality traits are a strong predictor of subsequent disorder. A particular advantage of such large-scale longitudinal studies is that they help to identify higher-order temperamental dimensions that transcend the features of specific disorders. The identification of higher-order temperaments is particularly useful in helping to account for the significant degree of overlap or co-morbidity that has been observed among anxiety and depressive disorders (Brown, 2007). The two affective dimensions of *neuroticism-negative affectivity* (N-NA) and *extraversion-positive affectivity* (E-PA) have emerged most consistently from longitudinal studies as playing an influential role in the development of emotional disorders.

Neuroticism-negative affectivity (N-NA)

N-NA is considered to be a high-order dimension of personality that has effects on mood, cognition, neurobiological processes and behaviour, and also has a significant genetic component (Clark and Watson, 1991; Watson and Clark, 1984b, 1994). As illustrated in Figure 9.3(a), it can be assumed that N-NA represents a broad dimension that incorporates the *behavioural inhibition* system (BIS) (Gray, 1982), which in turn incorporates the more narrowly focused construct of *behaviourally inhibited* temperament (Kagan, 1994). There is good evidence that these constructs are closely related to a neurobiological circuitry relating to aversion or avoidance of harm (e.g., Cloninger et al., 1993; Gray, 1982; Kagan, 1994). In particular, there is strong evidence for a relationship between N-NA and the structure and function of subcortical structures such as the amygdala and hippocampus, as well as regions of the prefrontal cortex including the DLPFC and the ACC (see Whittle et al., 2006, for comprehensive review). A wide range of scales relating to negative mood states that measure aspects of both anxiety and depression are almost certainly measuring this more general dimension of N-NA. Therefore, it is not surprising that there is a strong correlation between measures of anxiety and depression or that there is a high degree of co-morbidity between disorders of anxiety and depression.

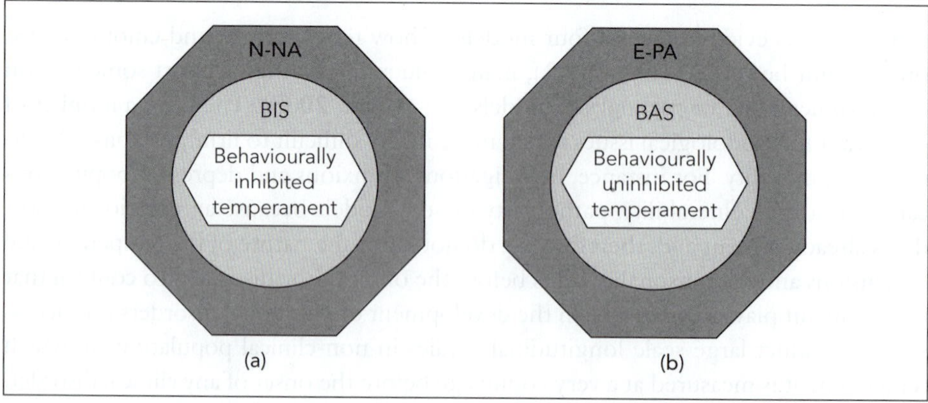

FIGURE 9.3 Relationship between identified temperament in infants, the BIS and BAS systems, and the higher-order dimensions of N-NA or E-PA

A central hypothesis to explain the high degree of co-morbidity between anxiety and depression is the assumption that N-NA plays an overarching role in both sets of disorder. Longitudinal studies have generally found that N-NA is a good predictor of subsequent anxiety and depression disorders (Craske, 2003; Tackett, 2006, for reviews). For example, in a review of five separate studies it was found that N-NA was the only factor that was consistently related to depression (Gunderson et al., 1999). Another comprehensive review concluded that N-NA is a risk factor for both depression and a range of anxiety disorders including panic disorder, specific phobias, social phobia and PTSD (Clark et al., 1994). Subsequent studies have mainly confirmed these findings. Thus, in one four-year prospective study the level of N-NA was a strong predictor of major depression as well as panic attacks in a cohort of adolescents (Hayward et al., 2000). The large-scale 'Dunedin' epidemiological study under way in Australia has also found that children classified as 'inhibited' at age three are more likely to experience depression in their twenties (Caspi, 2000).

As illustrated in Figure 9.3, the behaviourally inhibited temperament studied in young children (e.g., Kagan, 1994) is likely to be a behavioural manifestation of the broader dimension of N-NA (Craske, 2003; Turner et al., 1996). Behaviourally inhibited temperament is itself a good predictor of subsequent emotional disorders. For example, one longitudinal study found that up to 30% of behaviourally inhibited children went on to develop a range of anxiety disorders (Biederman et al., 1990). Other studies have found that, while around 15% of children with healthy parents are categorized as having a behaviourally inhibited temperament, up to 85% of children of parents with panic disorder fall into this category, as do around 50% of the children with parents with major depression (Rosenbaum et al., 1988). Similarly, a study following a group of adolescents who had been characterized as being either inhibited or uninhibited when they were two years of age found significant associations between behavioural inhibition and subsequent social phobia twelve years later (Schwartz et al., 1999).

In further research with this group it was shown that those who had been categorized as inhibited when they were two years old demonstrated a stronger amygdala response to novel (compared to familiar) faces when they were young adults. Moreover, three of the 15 adults categorized as inhibited when they were infants were subsequently diagnosed with social phobia, while none of those categorized as uninhibited were diagnosed with any anxiety disorder (Schwartz et al., 2003). These results would seem to support a vulnerability model because the differences in observed brain reactivity (e.g., increased amygdala activation to novelty) might represent a predisposing factor related to high N-NA, rather than something that develops after the onset of the disorder (e.g., scar model).

Several reviews have concluded that behavioural inhibition is a significant risk factor for both anxiety and depression (Craske, 2003; Tackett, 2006). It is important to remember, however, that the majority of behaviourally inhibited children do not develop emotional disorders. Behavioural inhibition probably leads to a *tendency* to respond more intensively to stressful events (*vulnerability* model), possibly due to changes in the physiological and regulatory systems (Craske, 2003). Then, depending upon the type and number of stressful life events that are experienced, an emotional disorder may or may not develop. For example, there is evidence that behavioural inhibition is associated with a lowered threshold of response in the amygdala and hippocampal regions of the brain (Kagan et al., 1987; Schwartz et al., 2003), which would explain a heightened reactivity to stress.

Research with children and adolescents, therefore, largely supports a predisposition model suggesting that high levels of N-NA set up a vulnerability for the development of anxiety and depression. However, it is very difficult to separate the vulnerability model from the continuity or spectrum model. As pointed out by Tackett (2006), longitudinal research interpreted as evidence that personality traits may be a risk factor for emotional disorders could equally be interpreted from a spectrum model perspective. Thus, the evidence that N-NA predicts later emotional disorders could be evidence that anxiety and depression lie on a similar continuum, or dimension, with N-NA. The finding of similar neural circuits in healthy individuals with high levels of N-NA and in those with anxiety and depression disorders also supports a continuity model. The implication is that the development of an emotional disorder out of a temperamental dimension could indicate that a person's point on the underlying continuum can change over time, rather than indicating that these are two mutually exclusive constructs with one causing the other. One method of separating the vulnerability from the continuity model might be to identify a common influence such as genetic factors. The spectrum model would predict that common genetic factors should be associated with both the temperament and the emotional disorder, while the vulnerability model would not necessarily predict this relationship.

Moving back to adult research, a more recent study examined the stability of both temperament (N-NA, E-PA) and specific disorders (depression, GAD, social phobia) in 606 outpatients with anxiety and depression disorders over a two-year period (Brown, 2007). The interesting finding was that the temperamental dimension of N-NA changed significantly across the period, and also accounted for the largest changes in treatment effects. In other words, those patients with very high levels of N-NA prior to treatment showed the poorest response to treatment. This is consistent with previous findings that depressed patients who relapse following treatment tend to have higher levels of N-NA (Frank et al., 1987). Taken together, these results suggest that N-NA poses a significant risk factor for emotional disorders.

One implication of the finding that scores on scales measuring N-NA change in response to treatment (e.g., Brown, 2007) is that N-NA scores might also reflect the current influence of *state* mood in addition to a more stable personality dimension. It has been pointed out that measures of both negative and positive affectivity tend to include both trait and state variance, which are of course highly correlated with each other. However, it has also been found that, when these are separated, the trait measure provides a better predictor of future emotional disorder (Clark, 2005, for review). It is important to include and evaluate the influence of state mood in longitudinal and treatment outcome studies. Nevertheless, the evidence to date suggests that the broad temperamental dimension of N-NA does affect the likelihood of developing an emotional disorder, predicts how long the disorder is likely to last, and predicts the likely response to treatment (Brown, 2007; Clark, 2005; Clark et al., 1994; Craske, 2003; Tackett, 2006). Importantly, N-NA seems to play a role across a wide variety of anxiety disorders as well as depression.

Extraversion-positive affectivity (E-PA)

As illustrated in Figure 9.3(b), it can be proposed that E-PA subsumes the *behavioural approach system* (BAS) as portrayed by Gray (1982), which in turn incorporates the *uninhibited temperament* observed in children by Kagan (1994) and others. There is evidence that E-PA is related to neurobiological circuitry that is rich in dopaminergic projections. These include some subcortical structures such as the amygdala and nucleus accumbens (NAcc), as well as cortical structures including the ACC and the DLPFC (see Whittle et al., 2006, for review).

Unlike N-NA, the empirical evidence suggests that E-PA is not associated with a range of emotional disorders, but, instead, appears to be specific to depression (and perhaps social phobia). An obvious characteristic of a person with severe depression is the apparent inability to enjoy life or to experience pleasure. This has led to the hypothesis that depression is associated with a deficit in the E-PA system (e.g., Davidson, 1994a). Several lines of evidence support this hypothesis. First, there is substantial evidence that low levels of E-PA are associated with depression (Clark and Watson, 1991). Second, the variations in positive mood states that occur in clinical depression appear to be greatly exaggerated versions of the normal daily variations in positive mood that occur in healthy individuals (Clark et al., 1989). Third, experimental studies have shown that depressed individuals are less responsive to positive stimuli such as pleasant scenes (Dunn et al., 2004) or amusing film clips (Rottenberg et al., 2002). Fourth, some evidence suggests that depressed individuals are specifically hyporeactive (i.e., under-reactive) to reward incentives. For example, in one study a memory task was presented to people under reward (gain money), punishment (lose money), and neutral incentive (neither gain nor lose money) conditions (Henriques et al., 1994). Using signal detection analysis non-depressed control participants were found to have quite a liberal response bias in both reward and punishment conditions; they were more likely to consider a stimulus as a signal if they were rewarded for correct hits or punished for misses. The interesting thing was that the depressed participants showed a similar response pattern in the punishment condition but behaved in a very different way in the reward condition. Specifically, the depressed participants did not change their response bias when they were rewarded. These results indicate that the depressed individuals were less responsive to rewards relative to the control participants. A more recent study has reported converging support for this notion by demonstrating differences between people with early onset depression and controls in frontal brain asymmetry when anticipating a reward (Shankman et al., 2007). When expecting a reward on a gambling type task, control participants demonstrated the expected increase in left frontal activity, measured by EEG (Davidson, 1994a). This was not observed in participants with early onset depression, suggesting that this group had a deficit in the approach-based appetitive system that underlies E-PA (Shankman et al., 2007). These results provide some support for Davidson's (1994a, 1998b) hypothesis that depression is associated with a low approach affective style due to a dysfunction in an incentive motivation system.

Finally, longitudinal studies also provide support for the notion that depression is specifically associated with a deficit in the system underlying E-PA. A number of studies have found that depressed patients who remained depressed following treatment had lower initial E-PA scores than patients who recovered, while other studies have found that low E-PA scores predicted depression four years later (see Clark et al., 1994, for review). Interestingly, however, there is some indication in these studies that high levels of E-PA might actually act as protection against depression (i.e., an invulnerability factor) rather than low E-PA acting as a vulnerability factor.

Thus, there is a good deal of evidence that low levels of E-PA are associated specifically with depression but do not seem to be linked to anxiety disorders. There is, however, an exception in that some studies have found that low E-PA might be a characteristic of social phobia (e.g., Amies et al., 1983; Brown et al., 1998). One study that followed a large sample of anxious and depressed patients over a 2-year period found that low E-PA was related to both depression and social phobia but not GAD (Brown, 2007). In contrast, high N-NA was associated with all three disorders (depression, social phobia and GAD). In general then, an inability to experience pleasure and positive mood states would seem to represent a significant risk factor for clinical depression, and possibly also social phobia, but not other anxiety disorders.

Tripartite model of personality-psychopathology relations

One of the more influential models of the relations between temperament/personality and emotional disorder is the *tripartite model* (Clark and Watson, 1991; Mineka et al., 1998). This model was developed to explain the high degree of co-morbidity that occurs between anxiety and depression disorders, and to account for the clear distinctions that occur among the different types of emotional disorder. The proposal is that a broad distress factor (captured by the notion of N-NA) is common to both depression and anxiety. However, low levels of E-PA are proposed to be specific to depression, while a hyperarousal (i.e. over-reactive arousal system) of the autonomic nervous system is considered to be specific to the anxiety disorders.

As we have seen, there is considerable evidence that N-NA is an important factor in both depression and anxiety disorders, and that low E-PA is a risk factor more specifically for depression and also social phobia. There is also evidence for the third factor in the tripartite model: anxiety disorders are characterized by a heightened degree of autonomic arousal, which is manifested by a range of symptoms such as rapid heartbeat, shortness of breath, dizziness, trembling and so on. It is generally thought that hyperarousal is not really a temperamental dimension in the same way as N-NA or E-PA. In this context, it is interesting that the construct of *anxiety sensitivity* has been proposed as a potential personality analogue of anxious arousal (Clark et al., 1994). Anxiety sensitivity is a high degree of fear of the symptoms of anxiety itself (e.g., rapid heart-beat, shortness of breath etc) and is thought to be a significant risk factor for the development of anxiety disorders (McNally, 1990; Reiss, 1991). Anxiety sensitivity is not the same thing as N-NA. People reporting high anxiety sensitivity generally do not respond with fear and anxiety to a broad range of stressors as is typical of those reporting high N-NA. Instead, they respond with fear specifically to the symptoms of their anxiety (McNally, 1989, 1990; Reiss, 1991). Thus N-NA relates to a higher order dimension of responding to a wide range of negative stimuli, while anxiety sensitivity is a more specific type of reactivity that only correlates moderately with N-NA (Clark et al., 1994). In general, the tripartite model seems to provide a good explanation of how temperament might be involved in the development of emotional disorders.

NEUROBIOLOGICAL FACTORS

Emotional disorders, such as depression and anxiety, are characterized by significant disruptions to neural circuits underlying emotion (Ressler and Mayberg, 2007). As with temperament, it is very difficult to determine the causal direction of this relationship. Many studies show that anxiety disorders are associated with increased activity within the amygdala (e.g., Drevets, 1999). However, it is not clear whether this is a result of experiencing an anxiety disorder, or whether an over-reactive amygdala might be a causal factor in the development of anxiety disorders. Much of the necessary research to answer this question – such as longitudinal studies measuring premorbid amygdala activity in a large cohort – is not yet available.

Frontal brain asymmetries and emotional disorders

Neuropsychological case studies have shown that damage to the left hemisphere of the brain often results in depressed mood states, whereas damage to the right hemisphere is associated with euphoric mood states (Borod, 1992; Gainotti, 1972). A similar pattern has been noted in non-brain-damaged individuals who have been subjected to the Wada test, which induces a temporary inactivity of one hemisphere by injecting sodium amytal into the brain. Using this method, it has been reported that deactivation of the left hemisphere results in a depressed mood, while a euphoric mood is more common following deactivation of the right hemisphere (Lee et al., 1987). In addition, studies of brain-damaged individuals have shown that damage to the left PFC is more likely to induce depression than damage to any other brain area. The degree of depression experienced is more severe in those sustaining damage nearer to the front pole of the frontal cortex (see Robinson and Downhill, 1995, for review). These observations formed the basis for the hypothesis that particular types of frontal asymmetries might constitute a risk factor for emotional disorders (Davidson, 1992b; Davidson and Irwin, 1999; Heller et al., 1998).

A large body of research does suggest that resting prefrontal asymmetry may indeed serve as a risk factor for the development of depression. For example, studies using EEG measures have found that depression is associated with decreased activity in the left PFC (e.g., Henriques and Davidson, 1991). Using other neuroimaging techniques such as PET, some studies have reported a pattern of decreased blood flow or metabolism in left prefrontal activity at rest in people diagnosed with clinical depression (see George et al., 1994, for review). Consistent with these findings, it has been reported that relatively greater right frontal resting activity is associated with higher scores on the Beck Depression Inventory (a measure of N-NA) in a group of undergraduate students (Schaffer et al., 1983). Thus a pattern of asymmetry with decreased left PFC activity and increased right PFC activity seems to be a marker of depression. However, it should be noted that some large-scale studies have failed to replicate this association (Reid et al., 1998). One possible explanation is that prefrontal asymmetry may tap into only one of several different risk factors for depression.

While most of the research on prefrontal asymmetry and psychopathology has focused on depression, some studies have also examined anxiety disorders. For example, monkeys with extreme right frontal asymmetries have higher levels of circulating cortisol relative to those with extreme left asymmetries (Kalin et al., 1998). In humans, greater right prefrontal asymmetries are associated with the experience of more negative affect, while those with greater left asymmetries tend to report more positive affect (Tomarken et al., 1992; Sutton and Davidson, 1997). Work with children also indicates that the right PFC seems to be more involved with the experience of negative affect, especially as related to anxiety (e.g., Davidson and Fox, 1989). The role of the right PFC might be primarily involved with the coordination of vigilant attention that is, of course, a common feature of anxious mood states. Consistent with this, increased activation of the right frontal and parietal cortex was observed in a group of people diagnosed with social phobia during a period when they were anticipating a major stressor (i.e., giving a public speech) (Davidson, Marshall et al., 2000).

In contrast to many of the foregoing studies, however, anxiety is sometimes also associated with relatively greater left frontal activity (Heller et al., 1998). On the basis of these apparently inconsistent results, a revised '*valence*' model of frontal asymmetries and anxiety has been proposed (Heller and Nitschke, 1998). The central hypothesis of this model is that anxiety consists of two distinct, though related, processes: *anxious apprehension* and *anxious arousal.* It is proposed that these separate processes are reflected in frontal EEG asymmetries as relatively greater left frontal activity in anxious apprehension, with relatively greater right parietal activity occurring in anxious arousal (Nitschke et al., 1999). This model is consistent with the finding reported by Davidson et al. (2000) that people with social phobia exhibit greater right frontal activation when anticipating a social threat, as the participants in Davidson's study were also aroused as measured by autonomic functions. The evidence suggests that individual differences in prefrontal asymmetry may render people more vulnerable to both depression and anxiety. There is a need for ongoing research using neuroimaging, behavioural and genetic techniques to attempt to elucidate the potential mechanisms underlying these associations.

Cortical-subcortical circuits in emotional disorders

Work on prefrontal asymmetries has relied on data from EEG. It is difficult to determine the source of the neural activity with EEG methods because electrical activity is measured from the surface of the scalp. However, neuroimaging methods such as PET and fMRI can provide information regarding the activation of subcortical structures and can also help to identify particular neural circuits that might be involved in different negative affective states and clinical disorders. In particular, the development of *circuits* or patterns of connections between cortical and subcortical structures is now thought to be crucial in the development of emotional disorders. This comes from the fact that it is becoming increasingly clear that individual brain regions do not operate in isolation from each other. Instead, there are strong anatomical connections among different brain regions so that changes in one region are likely to affect activity levels in many other regions (Friston, 2000).

In a comprehensive review of the human literature, three subcortical structures (amygdala, hippocampus and nucleus accumbens) and three cortical structures (orbitofrontal cortex, anterior cingulate cortex and the dorsolateral prefrontal cortex) have been identified as being particularly important for the psychopathologies related to N-NA and E-PA (Depue and Collins, 1999; Mayberg et al., 1999; Whittle et al., 2006). These hypothesized circuits are shown in Figure 9.4. The circuit underlying N-NA is assumed to be primarily right lateralized, while the E-PA circuit is assumed to be primarily left lateralized.

The data reviewed by Whittle et al. (2006) suggests that negative affective states (i.e., high N-NA) such as anxiety and depression are associated with enhanced activity and activation in the amygdala and hippocampal regions as well as with a reduction in prefrontal activity, especially areas of the right DLPFC. This fits with the general hypothesis that increased activation of the prefrontal cortex is involved with

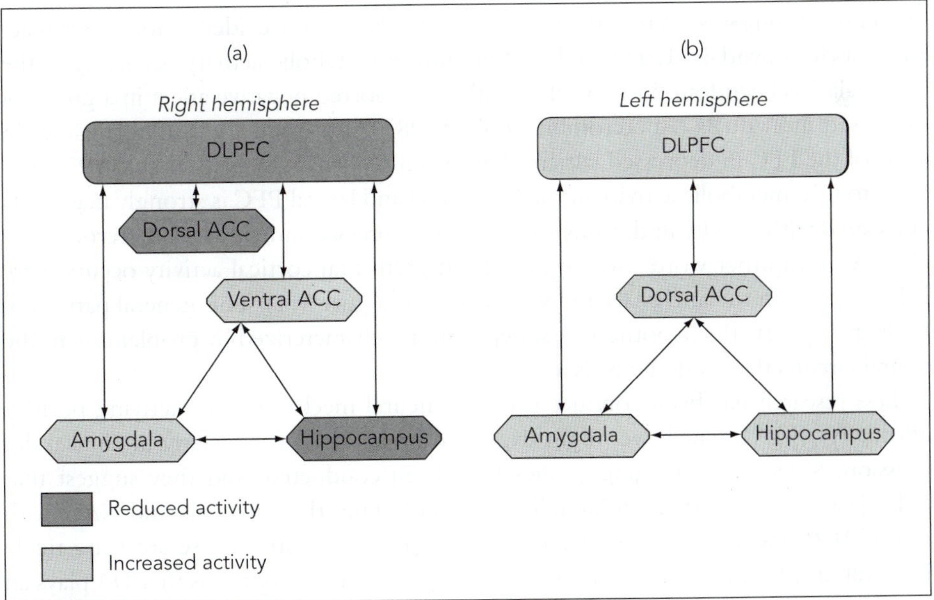

FIGURE 9.4 The neural circuits proposed to underlie the temperamental dimensions of (a) N-NA and (b) E-PA

the attempt to inhibit negative mood states (e.g., Lévesque et al., 2003). This leads to the hypothesis that anxiety and depression are associated with increases in activity within the amygdala and hippocampus that then tends to go unchecked because of a failure to recruit inhibitory regions within the prefrontal cortex. Emotional regulation studies have provided additional support in demonstrating that successful attempts at decreasing negative affective states is associated with decreases in amygdala activity and increases in activity in prefrontal cortical regions (Ochsner et al., 2004; Phan et al., 2005).

As an example, Scott Rauch and his colleagues have proposed that PTSD is underlain by a hyper-reactive amygdala in combination with an under-recruitment of areas of the medial PFC (especially the affective division of the ACC) (Rauch et al., 1998). Thus, PTSD may develop because there is an absence or weakness of top-down control over the strong fear conditioning that is mediated by the amygdala. Consistent with this proposal, it has been shown that when PTSD symptoms are provoked there is a correlated increase in amygdala activity and a decrease in activity in the medial PFC (Shin et al., 2006).

Thus, while neuroimaging studies have identified a number of brain areas (e.g., amygdala, hippocampus, medial and dorsolateral PFC, OFC, ACC) that are implicated across a wide range of different anxiety disorders (Rauch, 2003), it is becoming clear is that it may not be the functioning of these areas in themselves that is important for the development of emotional disorders. Instead, it may be problems with functional circuits among a subset of these areas. A key neurobiological marker of anxiety disorders may be a deactivation of prefrontal regions when faced with a stressful encounter alongside an increased activation of the amygdala and related regions. This is clearly an area that requires further research.

Neuroimaging research with depression has also found evidence for hyper-reactivity of the amygdala. Using PET the amount of metabolic activity occurring in the amygdala has been found to correlate with self-reported negative affect in a group of depressed individuals (Abercrombie et al., 1998). Also using PET, abnormalities in parts of the PFC in depressed patients have been reported (Drevets et al., 1997). Related to this, metabolic activity in the left medial and lateral PFC is strongly negatively correlated with activity in the amygdala in non-depressed individuals (Abercrombie et al., 1998). In other words, when greater left prefrontal cortical activity occurs there is less activity in the amygdala and vice versa (see Figure 9.4). This general pattern of findings supports the hypothesis that depression is characterized by problems with the neural circuits that underlie N-NA.

Less research has been conducted on the neural mechanisms underlying positive affectivity (E-PA), which we might expect to be involved particularly in clinical depression. Some neuroimaging studies have been conducted, and they suggest that E-PA is associated with a left-lateralized circuit linking the amygdala and NAcc with dorsal ACC and DLPFC activity, as shown in Figure 9.4(b). These areas are richly innervated with dopamine (DA) neurons, supporting the hypothesis that DA plays an important role in positive affective states.

Some studies have reported decreased activity in the left DLPFC in patients with major depressive disorder. Moreover, the degree of activity decreases even further as negative symptoms become more severe (e.g., Galynker et al., 1998). This finding supports the hypothesis that depression is associated with a deficit in a left-lateralized positive affectivity circuit. Further support is provided by research using EEG in which people with early onset depression failed to show increased activation of the left PFC when they were anticipating a reward in contrast to normal controls (Shankman et al., 2007). These findings provide some support for the hypothesis that depression might be at least partly associated with a deficit in an approach-based appetitive system that underlies E-PA (e.g., Davidson, 2000).

In conclusion, this is a complex area in need of much more research. However, the evidence to date does seem to indicate that a hyperactivity of the amygdala may be a characteristic of both anxiety and depressive disorders. The differences between these conditions may be more to do with functioning of prefrontal cortical areas and the development of specific neural circuits that characterize the different disorders. See Rauch, 2003; Whittle et al., 2006, for further discussion.

Regulation of neurotransmitter systems in emotional disorders

It has been suggested that the HPA is the main system allowing for interactions between genetic and environmental factors that play a *causal* role in emotional disorders (Nemeroff, 1998). In particular it is also widely believed that problems with several neurotransmitter systems may lie at the heart of many emotional disorders. Much of the work has focused on *noradrenaline*, which is also called *norepinephrine* (NE), *serotonin* (5-HT) *dopamine* (DA) and *gamma-aminobutyric acid* (GABA). The manipulation of these neurotransmitter systems by drugs is also the main pharmacological approach to treating depression and anxiety disorders. The neurochemistry of emotional disorders is a complex area and only a brief overview is presented here (see Garlow and Nemeroff, 2003, for review).

Much of the empirical work has focused on depression, and has found that both NE and 5-HT seem to play an important role in MDD. DA is also implicated, although probably to a lesser extent. Put very simply, it has been suggested that a reduction in the levels of these neurotransmitters is a major cause of depression, while an increase leads to euphoria (Schildkraut and Kety, 1967). A number of converging lines of evidence support this hypothesis. First, the finding that *reserpine*, which depletes brain NE, produces depression in many patients led to the suggestion that low levels of NE were critical to depression. This hypothesis was supported by the discovery that the *tricyclic anti-depressants* (e.g., imipramine), which lead to an increase in brain levels of NE, are also effective in alleviating many of the symptoms of depression. Much attention has also focused on the role of 5-HT in depression. Experimental studies have found that lowering the level of l-TRP (and by implication the brain level of 5-HT) by dietary manipulations leads to a short-term depressed mood (e.g., Delgado et al., 1994). It is also interesting to note that the response to tryptophan depletion is much more dramatic in people who have recovered from depression. These individuals show a strong return of depressive symptoms when l-TRP is depleted. Moreover, even the first-degree relatives of people with depressive disorders show an enhanced response to tryptophan depletion, suggesting that the response to l-TRP may be a trait vulnerability factor for depression (Garlow and Nemeroff, 2003).

Further support for the suggestion that a reduction in 5-HT might play a causal role in the development of depression is the finding that drugs that increase the levels of 5-HT in the brain provide an effective treatment for depression (e.g., the *selective serotonin reuptake inhibitors (SSRIs)*). A paradox, however, concerns the fact that the pharmacological effects of the SSRIs (e.g., Prozac) occur within hours, while the improvement in depression does not occur for about six weeks. It is not clear how to explain this paradox, but one possibility is that the SSRIs have an effect on a range of 5-HT receptors in the brain, often blocking the immediate action of 5-HT. It is thought that this blocking of the effect may habituate after several weeks, explaining the delay in the antidepressant effects. Major depression has also been found to be associated with variations in the DA system, although this has not received the same degree of attention as NE and 5-HT in the etiology of depression. Nevertheless, as reviewed by Garlow and Nemeroff (2003), there is evidence that increases in brain DA (e.g., in patients with Parkinson's disease) is associated with an elevation in mood while reduced levels of DA can result in depressed mood states.

Most research on the neurochemistry of anxiety has focused on the actions of *gamma-aminobutyric acid* (GABA), which is the most widespread inhibitory neurotransmitter in the brain. For example, the *benzodiazepine* drugs (e.g., temazepam, diazepam), which are used to treat anxiety disorders, act by increasing the affinity of the GABA receptor, and thereby increasing the actions of GABA in the brain. The fact that GABA works throughout almost all areas of the brain makes it very difficult to determine where the anti-anxiety actions may be occurring. To confuse matters further, there are drugs that increase GABA but do not appear to have any anti-anxiety effects. Thus, it is difficult to determine exactly how the actions of drugs such as the benzodiazepines have their effects on anxiety. However, as we have seen earlier GABA receptors within the amygdala and hippocampal regions are likely candidates (e.g., Gray and McNaughton, 2000).

However, some drugs can have anti-anxiety effects without influencing the GABA system. To illustrate, *buspirone* is as effective as the benzodiazepines in the treatment of anxiety but does not increase the effects of GABA. Instead, buspirone seems to act primarily on 5-HT receptors, as well as influencing levels of brain NE and DA. Thus, buspirone has both anti-anxiety and anti-depressant effects, further supporting the suggestion that there is a high degree of overlap among these disorders. In line with this suggestion, it has been found that the tricyclic anti-depressants are at least as effective as the benzodiazepines in the treatment of GAD.

One of the most obvious features of studies examining the neurochemistry of emotional disorders is that many different neurotransmitter systems seem to be involved. This complexity contrasts with the broadly similar symptoms of depression and anxiety that are expressed in most people. A potential problem with research on the neurochemistry of emotional disorders is that it is conducted to a very large extent with animals, especially rodents (see Gray and McNaughton, 2000). There are good animal models of both depression and anxiety and new drugs are usually tested on them to see whether they are effective in alleviating the symptoms of these conditions. While there is clearly a high degree of continuity from animal to human anxiety and depression, there are also likely to be some differences. In particular, it has been pointed out that animal models of anxiety cannot take into account the specific cognitive biases that have been found in humans to be potential risk factors for emotional disorders (Eysenck, 1992b).

Another problem with research on the neurochemistry of emotional disorders is that often the focus is on discovering new drugs that are then compared to an existing treatment. There has been a relative absence of research focusing on how neurotransmitter systems might operate within the specific brain areas known to be involved with emotion and emotional disorders. There is clearly much to be learned about the neurochemistry of depression and anxiety and it is hoped that future research will attempt to relate the effects of various drugs to changes in specific brain regions in more detail.

COGNITIVE FACTORS

A central feature of emotional disorders is the presence of distorted and irrational beliefs and thoughts. In one study 80% of patients with an anxiety disorder endorsed the statement 'It is essential that one be loved or approved of by virtually everyone in his community' compared with only 25% of people who did not suffer from an emotional disorder (Newmark et al., 1973). In the various studies of emotional disorders from a clinical perspective four broad classes of 'thought' have emerged as being particularly important. These are *worry*, *negative automatic thoughts*, *intrusive thoughts* (or *obsessions*), and *over-general memories.*

Worry

Tom Borkovec is one of the leading researchers on the nature and functions of worry and he has defined worry as:

> a chain of thoughts and images, negatively affect-laden and relatively uncontrollable. The worry process represents an attempt to engage in mental problem-solving on an issue whose outcome is uncertain but contains the possibility of one or more negative outcomes. Consequently, worry relates closely to fear processes.
>
> (Borkovec et al., 1983; p. 9)

As we can see in Table 9.4, worry is associated particularly with GAD but also occurs across a range of other anxiety and depressive disorders (Sanderson and Barlow, 1990).

People commonly worry about two major areas: *social evaluation* (e.g., relationships, lack of confidence, aimless future etc), and the possibility of *physical harm* or

TABLE 9.4 Responses to the question 'Do you worry excessively about minor things?' by patients with various anxiety disorders

Anxiety disorder	*Percentage responding 'yes'*
Generalized anxiety disorder	91
Obsessive-compulsive disorder	59
Panic disorder	41
Specific and social phobias	32

Source: Sanderson and Barlow (1990).

illness (see Eysenck, 1992, for review). It is important to remember that all of us worry at some point or another. What distinguishes the worry experienced by people with emotional disorders, however, is that it tends to be continuous and repetitious. In contrast, the type of worry experienced by the normal population tends to be limited to more short-term thoughts and images.

Borkovec and his colleagues have argued that worry reflects a way in which people with GAD learn to cope with the world by the predominant use of *conceptual* activity. The problem with this strategy in terms of mental health, however, is that the worry can be used as a form of cognitive avoidance so that people do not deal directly with their problems. This is supported by findings that people with emotional disorders often do not consider worry to be a problem even when it is intrusive. Instead, they often consider that worry is a very useful way of solving their problems *if only they could find the solution* (Nolen-Hoeksema, 1991). This is a potentially toxic belief, however, because it means that people never really adapt to potentially distressing thought contents and this means that the material's emotional significance tends to be maintained. For example, if we worry about something for only a short period – for example, will I pass my exams? – then during the periods where we are not thinking about it the emotional significance of potentially not passing tends to decrease and the negative material gradually becomes less salient. However, for the person with clinical depression the constant worry and rumination about what might happen if they do not pass keeps the negative thoughts in mind and ensures that they remain salient. Thus, it seems that one of the consequences of worry is to maintain the vigilance towards threat-related cues that is typical of GAD as well as other anxiety disorders (Mathews, 1990).

Negative automatic thoughts

One of the most common symptoms of emotional disorders is what Aaron Beck (1967) has called *negative automatic thoughts*. These thoughts (or images) come into mind in a seemingly involuntary way and they are often instantly elicited by a particular situation. For example, in a social situation a person with social phobia might instantly think 'I am unattractive' or 'I am not interesting to talk to'. These automatic thoughts are very difficult to control and they are intrusive, repetitive and intuitively plausible (Beck et al., 1985). These thoughts occur so rapidly that the person is often unaware of their occurrence, although they are amenable to conscious introspection. Clinical observation suggests that negative automatic thoughts are typical of the stream of consciousness that occurs in anxious and depressed patients.

Automatic thoughts differ in a number of important ways from worry. In particular, negative automatic thoughts seem to be more compressed and less consciously mediated than worry. For example, it has been argued that worry represents an attempt to examine new answers and formulate coping responses to particular problems, while automatic thoughts are more habitual and routinely negative answers to 'What-if' questions (Wells and Matthews, 1994). While negative automatic thoughts are characteristic of emotional disorders, it is interesting to note that there is no evidence that the general use of automatic thinking itself is any more frequent in emotional disorders (Hollon and Garber, 1990). Cognitive psychology has established that automatic processes are common and that all of us engage in automatic processes to a greater extent than more conscious and deliberate thinking processing (Smith and Kosslyn, 2006). What does differ in psychopathology, however, is that the *content* of the thoughts is almost always negative rather than being positive or benign. For example, in depression negative automatic thoughts often relate to themes of loss and failure, while anxiety is characterized by thoughts of future danger and threat (Beck and Clark, 1988).

Obsessions

Another class of thoughts frequently observed in emotional disorders are intrusive thoughts or obsessions. Clinical obsessions are defined as 'repetitive thoughts, images, or impulses that are unacceptable and/or unwanted. They are generally accompanied by subjective discomfort' (Rachman, 1981, p. 89). Rachman offers three criteria to identify obsessions:

(a) the patient reports that the thought constantly interrupts ongoing activity;
(b) the thought or image is usually attributed to an internal origin;
(c) the thought is difficult to control.

As we have seen, there are many cognitive phenomena that might fit these criteria. However, an important feature of obsessions that differentiates them from worry and automatic thoughts is that they are often experienced as senseless and unacceptable (see Wells and Matthews, 1994 for further discussion).

Over-general memory

Another way in which thought processes seem to differ in emotional disorders is in terms of the *specificity* of autobiographical memory. To illustrate, Williams and Broadbent (1986) asked a group of people who had recently attempted suicide to provide examples of situations in which they were 'happy', 'safe', 'interested', 'hurt', 'angry' and so on. They found that this group of depressed individuals tended to give very general memories rather than specific instances in response to these cues. For example, in response to 'happy' the depressed people gave a response such as 'I used to walk the dog every day' whereas a non-depressed person would be more likely to give a specific example (e.g., my son's first birthday party). In fact, it was found that over 40% of the memories offered by the depressed individuals could be described as over-general, compared to around only 16% of a control group (Williams and Broadbent, 1986). Subsequent research has shown that the tendency to retrieve over-general autobiographical memories is indeed a characteristic of depression (see Williams, 2004, for review). It is of interest, however, that over-general memory does not seem to occur in anxiety disorders, suggesting that it may be a feature of depression rather than being typical of emotional disorders more generally (Wessel et al., 2001).

We might ask why a tendency to produce a greater proportion of over-general memories is a problem and why should it relate to depression? At least part of the answer seems to relate to the fact that specific memories are often used as a means to reinterpret past events. For example, let's imagine that a shop-assistant is very rude to me in a store. If I later think about this incident in a specific way it might become clear that she seemed to be tired, it was a busy day, she seemed hassled etc and therefore I might reinterpret the event as relating to the fact that she was hassled rather than that she disliked me in any way. However, if the retrieved memory is very general – shop-keepers are rude to me – then it is much easier to maintain the interpretation that I am not liked or respected.

Cognitive biases

In addition to a range of thoughts and processes that are characteristic symptoms of emotional disorders, a range of cognitive *biases* is also considered to play a causal role in the development of emotional disorders. These biases frequently operate at an implicit level so that people may not be aware that they have a persistent bias to interpret information in a particular way. Several excellent reviews of this literature are available (Bar-Haim et al., 2007; Mathews and MacLeod, 2005; Mineka et al., 2003) and just a selective overview will be presented here.

Many theories assume that mood congruent cognitive biases are a central feature of emotional disorders, playing an important role in both the development and the maintenance of the disorder (e.g., Beck, 1976; Eysenck, 1992; Williams et al., 1988, 1997). Cognitive biases may indeed play a causal role in emotional disorders (e.g., vulnerability model). Alternatively, cognitive biases may themselves be caused by emotional disorders (scar model). It is also possible, of course, that cognitive biases may be produced by an independent factor that is also related to the etiology of the disorder (e.g., pathoplasty model). Therefore, an important focus of research is to try and determine the nature of the causal relationship between emotional disorders and cognitive biases.

Biases in attention

Beck (1967, 1976) proposed that the bias towards processing negative information is a feature of current state depression, and is also a vulnerability factor for the development of depression and anxiety. Thus, the depressed or anxious patient might constantly notice negative stories in the newspaper and on TV, and have a tendency not to notice more positive items of news. Using tasks such as the emotional Stroop and the dot-probe, there is strong evidence that attentional biases do occur across all of the major anxiety disorders such as PTSD, social phobia, specific phobias, panic disorder, OCD and GAD (see Bar-Haim et al., 2007; Mathews and MacLeod, 2005; Mineka et al., 2003, for extensive reviews). Studies of people with GAD have shown that these threat-related attentional biases also occur when the material is presented subliminally (e.g., Bradley et al., 1995; Mogg et al., 1993; Mogg et al., 1995). In other words, even when people are not consciously aware of what is being presented there is still a tendency for attention to be captured by threatening information. These findings indicate that these biases are operating at an automatic level of information processing and may therefore be difficult to control.

A number of studies have found that successful psychological therapy for anxiety disorders can eliminate the characteristic attentional bias for threat. For example, an attentional bias that was present before treatment was not present after treatment in both GAD (Mathews et al., 1995) and social phobia (Mattia et al., 1993). In addition, it has been reported that the magnitude of the reduction of the attentional bias measure in patients who had recovered from GAD was strongly correlated with a reduction in the number of anxious thoughts experienced (Bradley et al., 1995). In other words, the greater the reduction in attentional bias, the greater the reduction in worry. These results raise the possibility that attentional bias for threat may be a marker of the state-anxiety elevations that occur in clinical anxiety disorders, rather than being a trait-like characteristic of people who are vulnerable to anxiety disorders. They also suggest that attentional bias is unlikely to be caused by the experience of an anxiety disorder (scar model).

In an important meta-analysis, Bar-Haim et al. analyzed all studies using the Stroop, dot-probe or modified Posner task that were published between 1986 and 2005 (Bar-Haim et al., 2007). An interesting finding was that attentional bias for threat was characteristic of anxiety states, but that the magnitude of this effect was not any greater for clinically anxious groups when compared with non-clinically high trait-anxious groups. This supports a spectrum-like view that anxiety is associated with biased attention, but that this varies in a continuous way across clinical and non-clinical levels of anxiety. Another striking finding in this meta-analysis was that the magnitude of the bias did not differ across a range of different clinical conditions (e.g., GAD, social phobia, panic disorder, OCD, and simple phobia) in spite of the fact that these conditions differ from each other in a number of salient ways. Thus, it seems that a tendency to selectively attend toward negative information is a characteristic of high levels of N-NA and is a consistent feature of individuals with clinical anxiety disorders.

One important issue in the study of attentional bias in anxiety is the *time-course* of the bias. As we have seen, there is evidence that anxious individuals orient towards threat-related material very early in information processing, even when stimuli are presented subliminally. In fact, a number of studies have suggested that anxiety is characterized by an initial vigilance for threat followed by a rapid avoidance of threat (see Craske, 2003; Mogg and Bradley, 1998, for reviews). For example, one study found that spider phobic individuals initially moved their eyes towards pictures of spiders relative to non-threatening pictures but that this was quickly followed by an avoidance of the spider pictures (Hermans et al., 1999). Mogg and Bradley (1998) have argued that this *vigilant-avoidant* pattern may be instrumental in maintaining anxiety. To illustrate, the initial rapid orientation towards threat may result in the repeated detection of threat without allowing for habituation to occur. In a more recent study (Mogg and Bradley, 2006) evidence for the rapid allocation of attention towards pictures of spiders in spider-fearful individuals was found. As shown in Figure 9.5, a strong attentional bias for pictures of spiders, relative to pictures of cats, was found for the high spider fear group only when the stimuli were presented for 200 ms. This early vigilance was not long-lasting because no significant vigilance was found with either 500 ms or 2000 ms exposure times. While the tendency for avoidance of the spider pictures was not significant at 2000 ms in this study, other studies have found the reported vigilance-avoidance pattern (e.g., Rinck et al., 2005). To summarize, it is clear that attentional biases toward threat-relevant stimuli is a central feature of all anxiety disorders (Bar-Haim et al., 2007). Moreover, the time scale of this bias seems to be an early vigilance for threat followed by an avoidance of threat with longer exposures. This pattern may help to maintain anxiety states, as it provides no opportunity for habituation to threat to occur (Mogg and Bradley, 1998).

In contrast to the fairly widespread evidence for attentional bias in anxiety disorders, the evidence in depression is much more mixed. In spite of some evidence that attentional bias does occur, even with subliminal presentation (Mathews et al., 1996), there have been several failures to find evidence for attentional bias in depression (e.g., MacLeod et al., 1986; Mogg et al., 1993). However, there is growing evidence that depressed individuals do selectively attend to negative information when that information is presented for a relatively long time. For example, most dot-probe experiments expose the critical stimuli for around 500 ms or less. However, when the presentation time is doubled to at least 1 second, there is evidence for a depression-

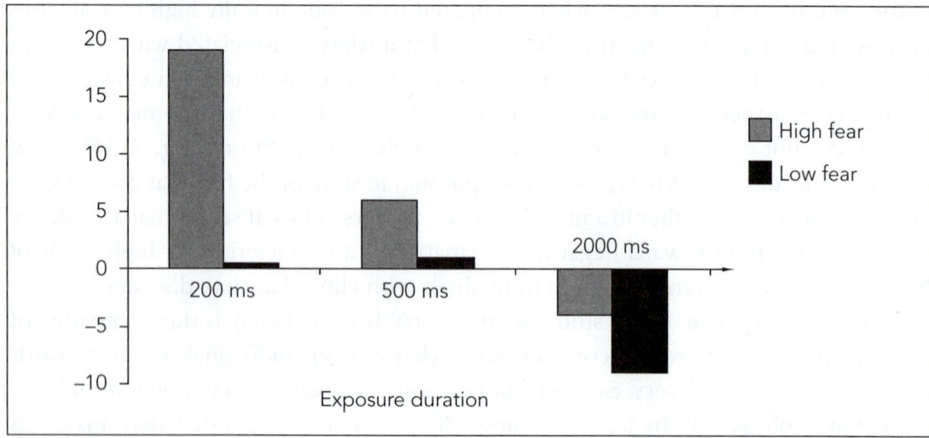

FIGURE 9.5 Attentional bias for spider pictures (relative to cats) in high and low spider-fear groups
Source: Data estimated from Mogg and Bradley (2006).

related attentional bias towards threat in clinically depressed people (e.g., Gotlib et al., 2004; Joormann and Gotlib, 2007). In an interesting study, attentional bias towards sad versus happy facial expressions (relative to neutral) was investigated in a group of people with a current major depressive disorder (MDD). These results were compared with a group who had recovered from a MDD as well as a matched control group who had never experienced any previous anxiety or depressive disorders. The experience of a MDD is itself a significant risk factor for future depressive episodes and therefore this design allows for an examination of attentional bias in a group known to be vulnerable, but not currently depressed. Joormann and Gotlib (2007) found evidence for a small but significant attentional bias towards sad faces (presented for 1 second) in both the currently depressed and the recovered group. In contrast, the normal controls tended to avoid sad faces but oriented towards happy expressions under the same conditions. This pattern of results is presented in Figure 9.6.

The pattern of results shown in Figure 9.6 is important because it shows that both currently depressed and formerly depressed individuals orient their attention toward sad faces when these are presented for a relatively long time. This indicates that attentional bias may not be a marker of state or current depression, but might represent a more enduring trait-like characteristic of depression. The authors are cautious in drawing this conclusion, however, because the attentional bias might be a *consequence* of experiencing a major depressive episode, as predicted by a scar model (Joormann and Gotlib, 2007). A longitudinal design in which attentional biases are measured before the onset of a first depressive episode is necessary in order to confirm that attentional bias is a vulnerability factor for depression. Another interesting finding shown in Figure 9.6 is the fact that the control individuals seemed to selectively avoid the sad faces but showed vigilance for happy expressions. This pattern of avoiding negative stimuli but orienting towards positive material may be a marker of healthy functioning.

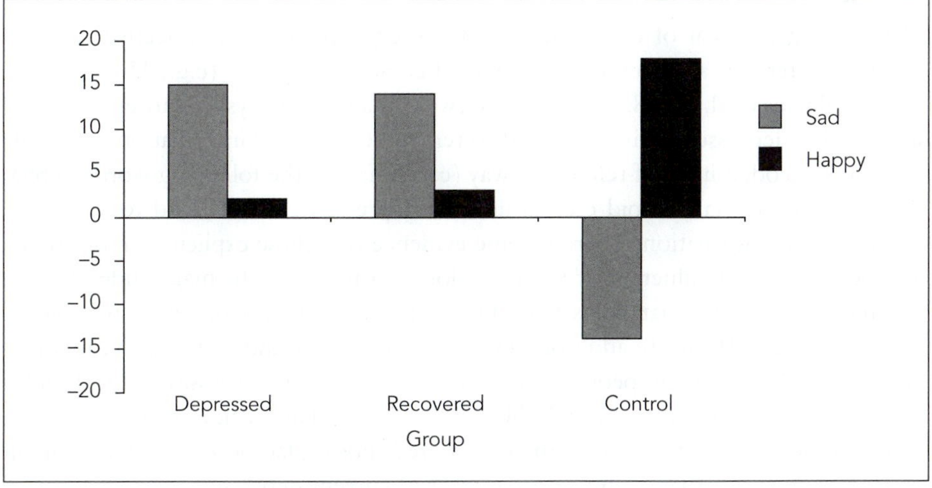

FIGURE 9.6 Attentional biases for sad and happy faces presented for 1 second for currently depressed, recovered and never depressed groups

Source: Data estimated from Joormann and Gotlib (2007).

Biases in judgment and interpretation

In contrast to the controversy surrounding the question of whether attentional biases differ between anxiety and depression, there is fairly general agreement that biased judgments and interpretation are common across all emotional disorders. For example, both anxious and depressed individuals have been found to judge more negative events as being more likely to happen in the future relative to controls (MacLeod, 1999). However, the reduced anticipation of positive future events appears to be more specific to depression (MacLeod and Byrne, 1996), which is consistent with the suggestion that low levels of E-PA is a central feature of depression but not anxiety.

Other studies have shown that both anxious and depressed individuals have a tendency to interpret ambiguous situations in a more negative fashion (e.g., Butler and Mathews, 1983). Several experiments have been conducted to assess the on-line interpretation of ambiguity, but these studies have tended to focus on anxious populations rather than on depression (Mineka et al., 2003). The general finding is that when ambiguous homophones (e.g., pain–pane) or sentences (e.g., 'the doctor examined little Emily's growth') are presented, anxious individuals are more likely to make the negative interpretation relative to non-anxious controls (Mathews and MacLeod, 2005; Williams et al., 1997, for review). It is likely that similar biases in interpretation will be found in clinical depression but further research is required before this question can be answered. The central hypothesis is that the tendency to interpret ambiguous situations in a negative way (e.g., interpreting a facial expression as a smirk rather than a smile), as well as the tendency to judge that negative future events are most probable, is likely to contribute to the maintenance of both anxiety and depression. The tendency to judge the likelihood of positive events as being less likely may, however, be specific to depression.

Biases in memory

There is a great deal of empirical evidence suggesting that the selective recall of negative material is a central characteristic of clinical depression (e.g., Mineka et al., 2003; Williams et al., 1988, 1997, for reviews). In a meta-analysis, Matt et al. (1992) showed that depressed individuals tend to remember negative information, especially when it is encoded in a self-referential way (e.g., imagine the following words in relation to yourself – fail, stupid etc), while non-depressed controls tend to selectively recall positive information. There is some evidence that these explicit memory biases may be a marker of vulnerability to depression. For instance, the magnitude of a bias to remember negative material is a good predictor of a subsequent depressive episode (Bellew and Hill, 1990). In addition, several studies have found that negative memory biases are still observed in people who have recovered from depression (e.g., Bradley and Mathews, 1988; Gilboa and Gotlib, 1997; Hedlund and Rude, 1995). This suggests that negative memory biases may be a predisposing factor for the development of depression rather than being a state marker of current depression.

There is also evidence for *over-general* memory effects in depression (Williams, 2004). Thus, in response to being asked to recall times when they had 'fun' a depressed person may report something like 'whenever I play soccer' rather than 'when I played soccer last Saturday' (Williams et al., 1997). Interestingly, this tendency to report over-general memories does not seem to be specific to negative memories, but also occurs for positive memories, as in the example just given. A number of studies have also found selective memory biases for negative material when *implicit* tasks are used (Mineka et al., 2003). In one study depressed individuals demonstrated an enhanced implicit memory for depression relevant words, whereas non-depressed controls had an implicit memory bias for positively valenced words (Watkins et al., 1996). In summary, there is extensive evidence that clinical depression is associated with explicit and implicit memory biases for negative information. In addition to this selective bias to remember material of a more negative tone, there is also evidence that retrieval tends to be rather general in depressed individuals relative to controls regardless of whether the material being recalled is negative or positive in valence.

In contrast to the body of evidence for selective memory biases in depression the evidence for biased memory in anxiety disorders is more mixed. This is surprising given the fact that anxious individuals selectively attend toward threat-related material. It might be expected that, if a particular type of information is attended to, it might also be better remembered. However, several studies have failed to find any evidence for explicit memory biases in clinically anxious groups, with the possible exception of panic disorder (see Becker et al., 1999; Mineka et al., 2003; Williams et al., 1997, for reviews). To illustrate, one study compared groups of anxious patients (GAD), depressed patients, and a control group who had not experienced any emotional disorder (Bradley et al., 1996). Significant memory biases for negative material on both explicit and implicit tasks were found for the depressed group. However, no memory bias was apparent on either task for the GAD or the control group. This study is especially important because it shows that the tasks used were sensitive enough to detect biases since the depressed group did show a selective bias. Occasional reports of explicit memory biases in anxiety have been reported, but they are rare and may have been due to concurrent high levels of depression (Mineka et al., 2003). In general, it appears that while anxious groups showed a heightened attentional vigilance for threat they do not show a heightened tendency to remember threat-related material. It is possible that this is because anxiety may be associated with a tendency to avoid extensive elaborative processing of threatening material (Williams et al., 1997). In summary, it seems that depression, but not anxiety, is associated with the tendency to selectively remember negative material.

Causal status of cognitive biases

A critical question concerns whether biases in cognitive processing represent a significant risk factor for the development of anxiety and/or depression. Both anxiety and depression are strongly associated with mood-congruent biases in information processing, although the specific type of bias (attention versus memory) may differ across conditions (Becker et al., 1999; Mathews and MacLeod, 2005; Mineka et al., 2003; Williams et al., 1988, 1997, for reviews). It is not clear, however, whether such biases in cognitive processing are a cause or a consequence of emotional disorder. This is a classic chicken-and-egg situation. A bias to selectively process negative information may be one of the *outcomes* of experiencing a particular emotional disorder. In contrast, a persistent bias to process negative information may be a pre-disposing risk factor for the development of emotional disorders. Determining the direction of influence is difficult and longitudinal studies in which cognitive biases are assessed in a large cohort before any emotional disorder is apparent are required.

These studies are, of course, time-consuming and expensive to conduct. However, the development of various methods to *modify* cognitive biases provides a potential alternative method for addressing the causality question. These *cognitive bias modification* (CBM) procedures are simple computerized or paper-and-pencil techniques designed to induce biases that mimic those observed in anxious people. The logic behind CBM is that if a cognitive bias is a predisposing factor for an emotional disorder then inducing such a bias should increase emotional vulnerability. In contrast, decreasing or eliminating such a bias should reduce the vulnerability to emotional disorders.

Several studies have indicated that both attentional and interpretative biases may play a causal role in the development of anxiety. For example, Andrew Mathews and his colleagues (Grey and Mathews, 2000; Mathews and Mackintosh, 2000; Yiend and Mathews, 2002) developed a CBM paradigm to induce a negative interpretative bias in a group of people with anxiety scores in the mid-range. In a typical experiment, 100 ambiguous descriptions of realistic situations were presented to participants (Mathews and Mackintosh, 2000). The last word of each scenario was a word-fragment that had to be completed by the participant. This fragment always resolved the emotional meaning of the text in either a positive or a negative direction depending on the training condition. For example, the following scenario might be presented: 'Your partner asks you to go to an anniversary dinner that their company is holding. You have not met any of their work colleagues before. Getting ready to go, you think that the new people you will meet with find you...' In the condition designed to induce a negative bias the word fragment to be completed would be 'bo_ _ ng' (boring) while in the condition designed to induce a positive bias the word fragment would be 'fri_ _ d_y' (friendly). In this way, participants repeatedly made either negative or positive/neutral interpretations (usually around 100 scenarios) according to the assigned condition. The critical test was a subsequent recognition test, in which a set of new ambiguous social descriptions was presented. The critical difference now was that the scenarios remained ambiguous – there were no disambiguating word-fragments. Participants were then shown a series of sentences that they had to rate according to how similar they were to the ambiguous scenarios. Sentences were endorsed more strongly when they corresponded to the emotional interpretations that matched the CBM condition (positive or negative), showing that an interpretative bias had been successfully induced. Moreover, measures of state-anxiety given before and after CBM demonstrated significant changes in anxious mood that were congruent with the direction of the CBM training (positive or negative). Subsequent studies have reported that these effects can last for at least 24 hours (Mackintosh et al., 2006).

To address the question of whether these induced biases change an individual's emotional vulnerability it is necessary to demonstrate that the induced bias can affect reactions to a subsequent stressful event. Empirical support for this hypothesis has been reported (Wilson et al., 2006). Individuals were trained on a CBM procedure that successfully induced both positive and negative interpretative biases. Those induced to interpret ambiguous material in a negative way became more anxious when they later viewed a series of short video clips depicting real-life accidents and injuries, relative to those in whom a positive bias had been induced (Wilson et al., 2006). These results indicate that CBM can have causal effects both on mood and subsequent emotional responses to new events. The reported pattern of results suggests that interpretative biases represent a significant pre-disposing risk factor for the development of anxiety disorders, at least in that they show that an induced bias can modify anxious reactivity to a stressful encounter.

Selective attentional biases have also been induced using a CBM technique developed by Colin MacLeod and his colleagues (MacLeod et al., 2002). This was achieved by manipulating the traditional dot-probe paradigm. Once again, participants reporting mid-level anxiety scores and no evidence for attentional bias were selected. Those assigned to the *attend-threat* (AT) group received almost 600 trials on which the probe always appeared in the location occupied by a threat-related word. Those assigned to the *attend-neutral* (AN) group received exactly the same trials except that the contingency was reversed. Now, the probe always appeared in the location previously occupied by the neutral word. The results demonstrated that:

(a) The appropriate attentional bias was induced by this procedure: a vigilance for threat-related words was induced in the AT groups on the normal dot-probe task following the CBM procedure. In contrast, those in the AN group showed an attentional bias for neutral words following the CBM procedure.
(b) The induced attentional bias influenced how participants responded to a subsequent stressful task. All participants were required to resolve very difficult anagrams following CBM, and it was found that those in the AT condition were significantly more stressed by this task than those who received the AN condition.

Importantly, these results occurred even though the CBM procedure had no effect on modifying participants' mood. These findings suggest that attentional biases do indeed play a causal role in mediating anxiety reactions.

The efficacy of CBM in reducing attentional biases towards threat-related words in patients with social phobia has also been examined (see MacLeod et al., 2004). All patients received 384 'training' trials every day over a two-week period. The experimental group were presented with the AN condition, which is designed to induce an avoidance of threat-related words, while the control participants received a condition in which the probe appeared equally often in the threatening and neutral locations. Over the two-week period the degree of bias towards threat was reduced in the experimental CBM group. Importantly, this group showed a significant reduction in their anxiety symptoms over the two-week period while no differences were observed in the control participants. Once again the indication is that attentional bias plays a causal role in anxiety disorders. The results also raise the exciting prospect that CBM procedures might be a useful treatment strategy for the reduction of anxiety symptoms.

Taken together, the studies using CBM procedures support the hypothesis that cognitive biases may play a causal role in the development of anxiety. There is much to be learned about these procedures and there are still gaps in our knowledge. For example, there is a need to develop studies with a wider range of outcome measures (e.g., physiological, neural) as well as assessing the impact of induced biases on vulnerability to depression as well as anxiety (see Mathews and MacLeod, 2002; Koster et al., 2008, for review).

Cognitive theories of emotional disorders

Cognitive models assume that explicit deficits in thought processes are important characteristics of psychopathology. For example, Ellis (1962) has argued that *irrational beliefs*, especially when they relate to the self-concept, are key features found in emotional disorders. He proposed that irrational beliefs (e.g., 'nobody will ever like me') are important factors in determining a person's emotional well-being. Since these beliefs can be expressed in a verbal, propositional form this allows them to be addressed in an explicit way in therapy. This notion led to the development of 'talking therapies' such as *cognitive behavioural therapy* (CBT), which is one of the most effective therapies for anxiety and depression (e.g., Beck and Clark, 1988). Information-processing models of psychopathology propose that emotional disorders are also associated with implicit biases to selectively process upsetting or negative material (e.g., Williams et al., 1988). Since these biases are not available to conscious awareness they are much harder to address in therapy. However, there is now some hope that it might be possible to modify these implicit cognitive biases by CBM techniques (Koster et al., 2008).

Beck's notion of dysfunctional schemas

An influential account of emotional disorders from a cognitive perspective has been presented by Aaron Beck. Beck's model was developed from clinical observation rather than from experimental research, and is centred on the notion of a *schema*. This term is used in cognitive psychology to describe how we organize our beliefs and memory structures. Beck and Clark (1988), for example define schemas as 'functional structures of relatively enduring representations of prior knowledge and experience' (p. 24). The idea is that schemas can operate as cognitive shortcuts so that we do not always have to process every detail of a situation from scratch. Within a schema for 'supermarket', for example, we might have representations relating to 'products on shelves', 'background music', 'busy on a Saturday', 'cashier near the door' etc. The proposal is that if part of a schema is activated then the entire schema becomes activated in a fairly automatic way. Thus, information that is not present in the initial input tends to be filled in automatically by the personal schema. This mechanism is very useful, allowing us to operate efficiently without having to process every detail of every situation every time we encounter it. Instead, we rely on our prior experience of similar situations.

In terms of affect, the proposal is that schemas relating to important social relationships and personal goals can also become activated in a similar way, which leaves a lot of room for personal biases to be automatically elicited. The key hypothesis is that emotional disorders can develop if some critical life event takes place that results in the activation of a *dysfunctional* schema. Once a dysfunctional schema has been set in motion it then tends to dominate and override more functional schemas leading to a cycle of automatic thoughts and other symptoms that help to maintain the emotional disorder (see Figure 9.7). In depression, for example, dysfunctional schemas relate specifically to the *cognitive triad* (Beck, 1976). Thus, depressed people are characterized by negative automatic thoughts relating to the *self* (e.g., 'I am worthless'), the *world* (e.g., 'The world is full of obstacles to knock you down') and the *future* ('There is no chance of the future being any better than the past'). In contrast, people with anxiety disorders are characterized by negative thoughts relating to the possibility

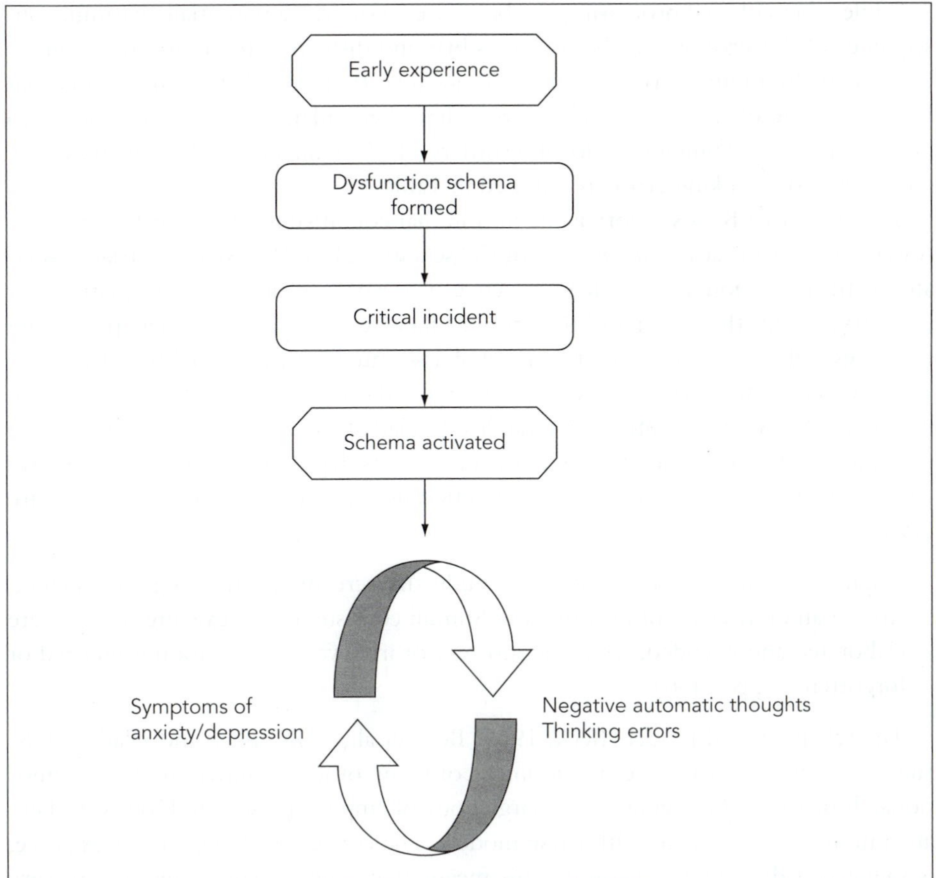

FIGURE 9.7 Schematic outline of Beck's model of emotional disorders

TABLE 9.5 Some common thinking errors observed in clinical emotional disorders

Arbitrary inference	The tendency to draw a conclusion in the absence of sufficient evidence
Selective abstraction	The tendency to focus on a single aspect of a situation while ignoring more important features
Magnification and minimization	The tendency to either enlarge or reduce the importance of events
Over-generalization	The tendency to apply a conclusion to a wide range of events when it is based on an isolated incident
Personalization	The tendency to relate external events to the self when there is no basis to do so
Dichotomous thinking	The tendency to evaluate experiences in all-or-nothing terms

Source: Beck et al. (1979).

of future harm and their own inability to cope with these eventualities. This model assumes that the nature of cognitive processing is similar between anxiety and depression, what differs is the *content* of the thoughts.

While schema-based processing can be very economical, a potentially harmful consequence of this economy is that it allows bias and distortion to enter into cognitive processing. In addition to the automatic negative thoughts that we have discussed before, a range of specific 'thinking errors' have been identified that are thought to play a role in maintaining emotional disorders (Beck et al., 1979). A summary of the more common thinking errors is outlined in Table 9.5.

The essence of Beck's theory is the notion that cognitive resources will be directed towards material that is *congruent* with the schema. Thus, the cognitive triad associated with depression will result in selective processing of negative information relevant to the self, the world and the future. Likewise, in anxiety disorders processing resources will be allocated towards material associated with potential threat and the inability to cope with danger. Psychopathology is therefore thought to result from an interaction between cognitive vulnerability (maladaptive schemas) and exposure to relevant life stressors. Once activated, the proposal is that dysfunctional schemas have an impact on every level of cognitive functioning. As expressed by Beck and Clark (1988):

> Cognitive structures (i.e., schemas) guide the screening, encoding, organizing, storing and retrieving of information. Stimuli consistent with existing schemas are elaborated and encoded, while inconsistent or irrelevant information is ignored or forgotten. (pp. 24–6)

The schema-based model (Beck, 1967; Beck et al., 1979; Beck and Clark, 1988) laid the groundwork for the development of many other cognitive models of emotional disorders and has generated a large body of empirical research. However, there are a number of problems with these models. The concept of 'schema', for example, is vague and difficult to measure. This means that schema-based theories are very difficult to disprove. The evidence for schema-based processing in both anxious and depressed groups is also not as extensive as would be predicted by the theory (e.g., Eysenck, 1992). Thus, anxious patients often do not show schema-congruent retrieval biases, while depressed patients often do not show strong schema-congruent attentional or perceptual biases. In other words, the differences between anxious and depressed individuals in terms of cognitive biases is far greater than would be expected by the content specificity hypothesis. This is one of the reasons why Williams et al. (1988) incorporated fundamental differences in processing style into their model of depression and anxiety.

Williams et al.'s (1988, 1997) cognitive model of anxiety and depression

Mark Williams and his colleagues argued that the *information-processing* methodologies developed within experimental cognitive psychology provide an opportunity to assess both explicit and implicit biases in emotional disorders (Williams et al., 1988). In developing a model of how emotional disorders might develop, they drew on a distinction between *integration* and *elaboration* made by Graf and Mandler (1984). Integration refers to cognitive processes that result in the *strengthening* of a particular representation. For example, the appearance of a spider may recruit perceptual and attentional mechanisms in a fairly automatic way. In a person with spider phobia, these automatic tendencies (e.g., rapid orienting towards the spider) or integrative processes may be intensified. Elaboration, in contrast, refers to processes that come into play later in information processing. These are more resource-demanding and controlled processes that help to connect a particular representation with many other representations. The key hypothesis was that 'anxiety preferentially affects the passive, automatic aspect of encoding and retrieval, whereas depression preferentially affects the more active, effortful aspects of encoding and retrieval' (Williams et al., 1988, pp. 173–4). As we have seen, there is some evidence that anxiety is associated with attentional biases towards anxiety-congruent material, with less evidence for the selective recall of these items. In contrast, clinical depression is characterized by selective recall of negative material relative to positive or neutral material, but often attentional biases towards the same material are not observed unless the presentation time is long (Mathews and MacLeod, 2005; Williams et al., 1988, 1997, for review).

A diagrammatic outline of the Williams et al. (1988) theory is presented in Figure 9.8. An *affective decision mechanism* (ADM) assesses the *valence* (e.g., threat value) of an item at a very early stage in information processing and this is considered to be automatic. The outcome of this decision then establishes priorities for subsequent processing, so that resources are oriented either towards or away from the source of the stimulus at a very early stage of processing. Transient changes in state mood (state-anxiety) can influence the activity of the ADM. However, enduring personality traits (e.g., trait-anxiety) are assumed to have a more permanent influence in directing attention in a more persistent and personality-congruent way. Williams et al. (1988, 1997) did not speculate on the possible neural mechanisms underlying the ADM. However, it is clear that the amygdala, as a key structure involved in the detection of threat, is likely to be a part of the proposed ADM. An important assumption of the

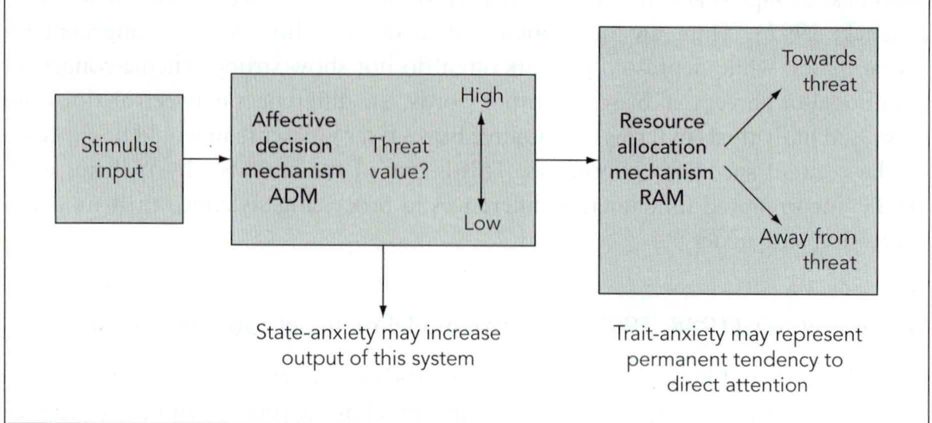

FIGURE 9.8 Resource allocation at the pre-attentive stage of information processing according to the model outlined by Williams et al.

Source: Williams et al. (1988).

model is that attentional biases for threat-relevant information are dependent on the *interaction* between levels of trait- and state-anxiety, and evidence for this has been reported (MacLeod and Mathews, 1988).

Figure 9.9 illustrates the model's assumptions with regard to the later stage of resource allocation. This takes place during the more resource-demanding *elaboration* stage of information processing. The output from the pre-attentive process outlined in Figure 9.8 is input to a later stage of processing that relies primarily on elaboration. Rather confusingly the authors also call the initial process at this stage an *affective decision mechanism* (ADM) that is followed by a *resource allocation mechanism* (RAM). The important point to note is that the ADM and the RAM at this later elaborative

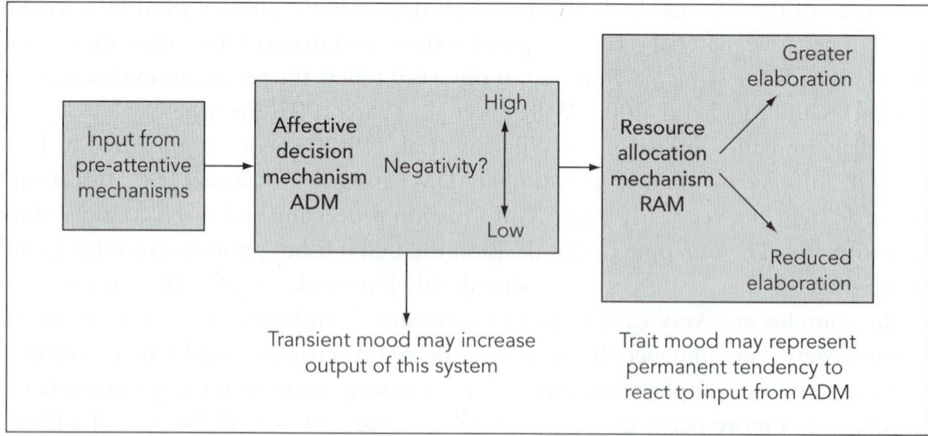

FIGURE 9.9 Resource allocation at the elaboration stage of information processing according to the model outlined by Williams et al.

Source: Williams et al. (1988).

stage are primarily influenced by depressive mood states and personality traits related to depression rather than anxiety.

Subsequent theoretical developments (e.g., Mathews and Mackintosh, 1998; Mogg and Bradley, 1998) have indicated that this model exaggerates the role of personality traits in determining the allocation of attention towards threat. An extremely threatening stimulus will command attention regardless of personality traits. Individual differences in anxiety play a role in determining the *threshold* at which people switch into a more vigilant mode (Mogg et al., 2000; Wilson and MacLeod, 2003). In the second edition of *Cognitive Psychology and Emotional Disorders* Williams et al. (1997) suggested that the notion of an ADM as an 'on' or 'off' decision mechanism was probably incorrect. A more plausible idea is that the ADM can be modelled as a connectionist or parallel distributed-processing network. Thus, the activation of units that represent a threatening stimulus can be enhanced by an 'emotional tag'. This 'tag' may be due to biological preparedness (e.g., evolutionarily-relevant stimuli such as snakes always carry a tag), or prior experience can also result in a threat tag being associated with a particular stimulus. Such 'threat-tagged' units would have a distinct advantage over other competing stimulus units within the same network, and this would automatically increase the chance that they would trigger the secondary RAM. The nature of what a 'tag' is and how it leads to greater activation of units representing threatening stimuli is not entirely clear, as pointed out by Mathews and Mackintosh (1998). Research on how such a tag could be implemented at a neural level is an important question for future research.

GENETIC FACTORS

The role of genes and gene–environment interactions in the development of depression and anxiety is an exciting area of research and there has been a recent call to integrate these research areas with neuroscientific approaches (Caspi and Moffitt, 2006). Figure 9.10 shows the four main methodological approaches to understanding how variation at the genetic level is associated with the expression of emotional disorders (Caspi and Moffitt, 2006).

The first approach, shown in Figure 9.10(a), assumes that there is a fairly direct and linear relationship between a specific genotype and a particular disorder. The typical type of methodology used within this approach is to correlate emotional disorders, such as anxiety and depression, with different genotypes. Progress has been slow in this area because the direct impact of genes on a complex disorder such as depression or anxiety is likely to be relatively minor and therefore difficult to identify.

The second approach (Figure 9.10(b)) links genes with intermediate endophenotypes (e.g., temperament, neurophysiological systems etc) on the basis that these endophenotypes have more straightforward links with genes than the disorder itself. This approach has had some success and still assumes a causal relationship from genes to disorder.

In contrast, the third approach (Figure 9.10(c)) assumes that environmental factors (e.g., sexual or physical abuse) are the main cause of emotional disorders, but

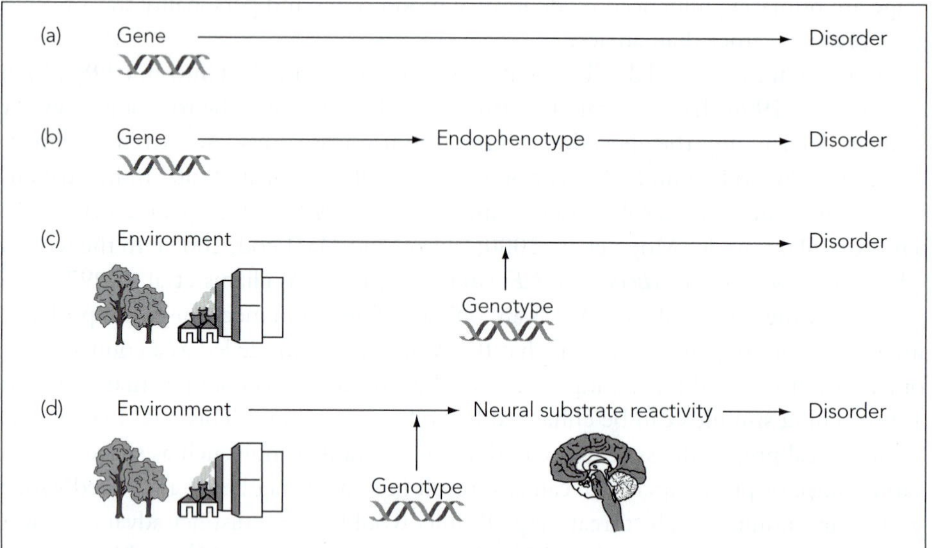

FIGURE 9.10 Four approaches to investigating the links between genes and emotional disorder

(a) Gene–disorder – there are direct relations between specific genes and the disorder.

(b) Endophenotype – there are direct relations between genes and intermediate phenotypes that are themselves linked to the disorder.

(c) Gene–environment interaction – the environment is related to the disorder, but the impact of environmental factors is moderated by genes.

(d) Gene–environment–neural system interaction – the environment affects disorder but is mediated by genes which have a moderating effect on neural circuits that in turn can influence the expression of an emotional disorder.

Source: Caspi and Moffitt (2006).

that genes influence the susceptibility of the person to the negative consequences of the environmental situation. Thus, this approach assumes that there is a dynamic interaction between genes and the environment (G X E interaction) and does not expect a direct link from genes to disorder in the absence of an environmental factor. It takes on board the fact that various stressful life events can play a causative role in the development of emotional disorder and that an individual's genetic make-up can also predispose him or her to develop anxiety or depression. The important point is that each factor is not sufficient on its own, it is the *interaction* between the two that forms a critical risk factor.

Finally, the fourth approach, outlined in Figure 9.10(d), proposes the integration of the endophenotypic approach with the gene–environment interaction approach. In particular, the proposal is that by examining the effects of gene–environment interactions on specific neural circuits (endophenotype) it should be possible to develop a better understanding of the biological mechanisms involved in the development of disorder (Caspi and Moffitt, 2006).

A central feature of the *gene–environment–neural systems* interaction approach is that the biological impact of a particular gene variant becomes progressively weaker as we move from molecular mechanisms to neural structures to behaviour and disorder

(Hariri et al., 2006; Hariri and Weinberger, 2003). Thus, functional genetic polymorphisms such as the short and long allele carriers of the serotonin transporter (5-HTT) gene are expected to be weakly related to complex behaviours, and even more weakly related to the symptoms of emotional disorders. However, these polymorphisms are expected to be more strongly related to reactivity within specific neural systems, and even more strongly related to changes within individual cells. In other words, the action of a gene may be closer to the level at which a neural circuit works than a more remote phenotype such as self-report (Canli and Lesch, 2007). The increasingly divergent pathway from a genetic polymorphism to an emotional disorder is illustrated in Figure 9.11.

The starting point for this 'imaging genetics' approach is the identification of a meaningful polymorphism in a candidate gene that is expected to have relevant effects on specific neural structures (Deary et al., 1999). For example, the variation in the gene for the serotonin transporter (5-HTT), that is known to affect the level of 5-HT present in the brain, would be expected to have an influence on the amygdala because the amygdala contains numerous 5-HT receptors. Abnormalities within this neural structure and related circuits, and how these relate to complex behaviours and emotional disorders, can then be understood in terms of biological mechanisms (see Canli and Lesch, 2007; Caspi and Moffitt, 2006; Hariri et al., 2006; Savitz and Ramesar, 2004, for reviews).

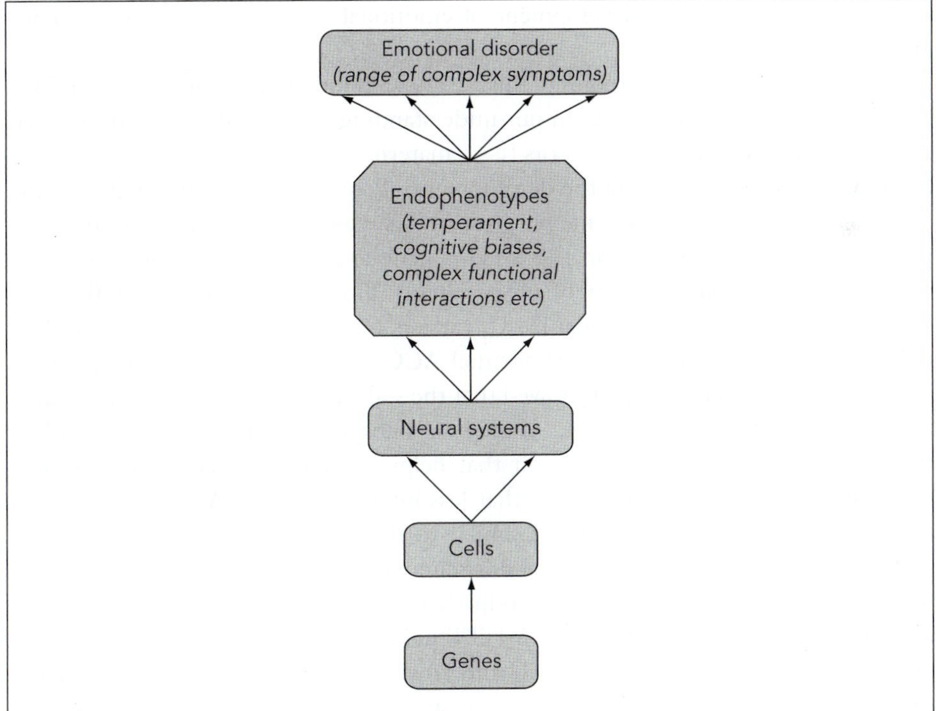

FIGURE 9.11 The path from genes to behaviour and emotional disorder

Source: Adapted from Hariri and Weinberger (2003).

A clear prediction from the imaging genetics approach is that functional polymorphisms in genes that influence neurotransmitters and neural circuits known to be involved in affect should confer greater vulnerability (and of course resilience) to the development of emotional disorders. There is growing evidence from epidemiological studies that this is the case. In a now-classic study it was found that the functional polymorphism on the 5-HT transporter gene had a strong moderating effect on stressful life events in the development of depression (Caspi et al., 2003). In this longitudinal study, a large sample ($N = 1037$) was genotyped and followed over a 23-year period. A number of stressful life events were recorded, which included bereavements, romantic break-ups and divorce, job loss, serious illness and childhood maltreatment. Interestingly, over the 23 years people with the s-allele did not experience a greater number of stressful life events than those who were homozygous for the l-allele. However, it was found that a higher proportion of those who carried the s-allele responded to these stressful life events with depressive symptoms, and they were more likely to be diagnosed with clinical depression. To illustrate, 17% of the respondents who were homozygous for the l-allele became depressed if they experienced more than four stressful life events. However, for carriers of the s-allele, 33% became depressed if they experienced more than four stressful life events. These results provided some of the first evidence for an environment–gene interaction between life stress and the s-allele of the 5-HTT gene as predictors of depressive symptoms. Subsequent research has confirmed that various genetic polymorphisms can significantly moderate the influence of life events on the development of emotional disorders (Caspi and Moffitt, 2006).

Combining longitudinal studies of this nature with functional neuroimaging is likely to lead to significant advances in our understanding of the complex pathways that exist between environmental stressors (e.g., maternal separation), genetic predispositions (e.g., s-allele carrier) and the development of complex disorders like depression and anxiety. There is already some progress in this regard. For example, in one study participants were genotyped on the 5-HTT gene and carefully screened to ensure that no participant had a history of any psychiatric illness (Pezawas et al., 2005). Using both structural and functional fMRI, carriers of the s-allele were found to have reduced grey matter in both the subgenual ACC and the amygdala. Perhaps more importantly, functional imaging showed that the s-allele carriers demonstrated a functional disconnection or uncoupling of the links between the ACC and the amygdala. In other words, the functional circuit that helps to inhibit the amygdala response to negative stimuli was disrupted, so that less inhibition by the ACC led to greater activity within the amygdala. This is similar to the work we discussed earlier (e.g., Rauch, 2003) showing that emotional disorders may be associated with interruptions to the functional neural circuits that modulate the response to affective stimuli. Thus, it seems that polymorphisms of the 5-HTT gene can influence the connectivity of important circuits (e.g., between ACC and amygdala). In particular, s-allele carriers show a functional uncoupling of the amygdala and parts of the ACC so that overactivity of the amygdala in response to affective stimuli may be due to reduced control from prefrontal cortical areas.

Turhan Canli and his colleagues (Canli et al., 2006) conducted an important study to investigate gene–environment interactions at the level of specific brain systems. They found that the absolute level of activity within the amygdala was higher in s-allele carriers compared to those who were homozygous for the l-allele. This is consistent with the notion that the short variant of the 5-HTT gene is associated with a heightened and persistent vigilance. Of particular importance, this study also found significant gene–environmental interactions for both the amygdala and the hippocampus. Life stress affected neural reactivity in both s-allele and l-allele carriers but *in opposite directions*. To illustrate, the activation of the amygdala to neutral stimuli in response to life stress was negative for s-allele carriers but positive for l-allele carriers. Thus, as the number of stressful life events increased for the s-allele carriers the activation of the amygdala in response to neutral faces (relative to a fixation) decreased. Thus, the over-activity of the amygdala to negative stimuli (e.g., fearful faces) was not due to increased activation to the negative relative to neutral stimuli. Rather, it was due to a relative decrease in activation to the neutral faces (Canli et al., 2006). This finding suggests that the frequently observed finding that the short variant of the 5-HTT gene is associated with elevated amygdala activation to negative stimuli may be due to decreased activation to neutral stimuli rather than increased activation to negative stimuli. In contrast, the positive correlation between the number of stressful events and activation of the amygdala in those homozygous for the long variant of the 5-HTT gene suggests that these individuals start out with a lower activity in the amygdala region that only increases in response to stressful events. These results are consistent with a *tonic activation model*, which proposes that the s-allele does not enhance amygdala activation to negative stimuli but rather enhances amygdala activity at rest (Canli et al., 2005; 2006). This model proposes that such a tonic activation of the amygdala could have widespread effects, including a baseline change in state of arousal, increased vigilance to threat, enhanced memory for affective material, reduced extinction of fear-related memories and so on. All of these could contribute to the development of emotional disorders, especially given the appropriate environmental conditions (Canli and Lesch, 2007).

CHAPTER SUMMARY

This chapter has discussed research on five classes of variables that appear to be important risk factors for the development of emotional disorders: *stressful life events*, *temperament*, *cognitive processes*, *neurobiological processes* and *genetic make-up*. These factors are not independent of each other and the potential development of an emotional disorder is usually due to several of these factors interacting with each other. Thus, while stressful environmental events (e.g., child abuse) are associated with the development of emotional disorders, these events primarily induce disorder only in those with a particular genotype (e.g., s-allele carrier on the serotonin transporter). Both genetic and environmental factors can also modify an individual's temperament while temperament itself (e.g., N-NA, E-PA) can influence the type of environment experienced and therefore the type of genes more likely to be expressed. All of these factors can modify specific neural circuits (e.g., prefrontal cortex–amygdala connections), which in turn can determine the nature of the body's response to stressful life events (e.g., functioning of the HPA-axis). Similarly the possession of a specific cognitive bias or pattern of neural reactivity to negative events can also render people more or less vulnerable to emotional disorder. Persistently attending towards negative material, as well as selectively remembering negative relative to neutral or positive information, is especially important because a person's environment becomes more negative if they are biased to process the negative material. While objectively this may not be true (e.g., a depressed person may not actually experience any more negative events than a more positive person), it is the *subjective cognitive biases* that really do change the nature of the environment that is experienced. In other words, the depressed individuals experience life in a more negative way *because* of their cognitive bias.

It is extremely difficult to determine the causal nature of how the five classes of risk factors interact with each other (as well as with many other factors such as social support, financial stability etc) to influence the development of emotional disorders. However, the current trend to study gene–environmental interactions in association with the investigation of specific endophenotypes (e.g., cognitive biases, neural circuits) holds great promise for unravelling the complex interplay of events that lead some people to develop severe problems in regulating their emotional reactions to life.

RECOMMENDED READING

Several chapters in the following edited books are useful for the material in this chapter:

Richard J. Davidson (2000) (ed.) *Anxiety, Depression and Emotion*. New York: Oxford University Press.

Richard J. Davidson, Klaus R. Scherer and H. Hill Goldsmith. (2003) (eds) *Handbook of Affective Sciences*. New York: Oxford University Press.

The following provides an excellent introduction to the information processing perspective on emotional disorders.

Mark Williams, Fraser Watts, Colin MacLeod and Andrew Mathews (1997) *Cognitive Psychology and Emotional Disorders*, 2nd edition. Chichester: Wiley.

The following articles provide more detailed reviews of particular sections of this chapter:

Avshalom Caspi and Terrie E. Moffitt (2006) 'Gene-environment interactions in psychiatry: Joining forces with neuroscience', *Nature Reviews Neuroscience*, 7, 583–90.

Lee Anna Clark (2005) 'Temperament as a unifying basis for personality and psychopathology', *Journal of Abnormal Psychology*, 114, 505–21.

Andrew Mathews and Colin MacLeod (2005) 'Cognitive vulnerability to emotional disorders', *Annual Review of Clinical Psychology*, 1, 167–95.

Kerry J. Ressler and Helen S. Mayberg (2007) 'Targeting abnormal neural circuits in mood and anxiety disorders: From the laboratory to the clinic', *Nature Neuroscience*, 10, 1116–24.

Sarah Whittle, Nicholas Allen, Dan Lubman and Murat Yucel (2006) 'The neurobiological basis of temperament: Towards a better understanding of psychopathology', *Neuroscience and Biobehavioral Reviews*, 30, 511–12.

0 DETERMINANTS OF RESILIENCE AND WELL-BEING

Historically, there has been a strong bias in emotion science to study negative rather than positive emotions. This almost exclusive focus on pathology rather than well-being has meant that relatively little is known about what makes life worth living and even less about the factors involved in how normal people flourish (e.g., Seligman and Csikszentmihalyi, 2000). There are many understandable reasons for this. Positive emotions are usually experienced when goals have been achieved and things are going well. Therefore, we do not tend to pay too much attention to positive emotions and mood states. In contrast, negative emotions are usually elicited in response to some problem such as a threat (e.g., fear), or an obstruction to our plans (e.g., anger) that needs to be dealt with immediately. Moreover, negative emotions *feel* unpleasant and people are generally motivated to change them. When negative emotions and feelings develop into emotional disorders there are enormous costs to the individual concerned as well as to friends, family and the wider society. Thus, with some exceptions (e.g., Eysenck, 1990; Myers, 1992), scientific interest has tended to focus almost exclusively on the negative side of our emotions and moods. This was confirmed in a survey of scientific papers on emotion published in peer-reviewed journals up to 1995, which found that the ratio of negative to positive emotions was about 17:1 (Myers and Diener, 1995).

Five years later, in a call for a new science of *positive psychology*, Seligman and Csikszentmihalyi noted that little research within psychological science had been conducted on the positive features of life such as hope, creativity, wisdom, courage, spirituality and many other aspects of existence that seem important for the 'good life' (2000). The relative lack of scientific research on happiness and well-being is in marked contrast to popular culture where happiness is given a high priority. On almost every street corner we see advertisements encouraging us to buy products that will make us happy. At least in Western cultures, most people claim that being happy is one of the main aims of life and the 'pursuit of happiness' is even one of the core rights enshrined in the American constitution. The one-sided emphasis on negative affectivity and negative emotions is now beginning to change, however, with an increasing focus on positive psychology and a search for the determinants of well-being (e.g., Cloninger, 2004; Diener et al., 2003; Diener et al., 1999; Kahneman et al., 1999; Myers, 2002; Seligman and Csikszentmihalyi, 2000; Seligman et al., 2005). The remit of the new discipline of positive psychology, was outlined by Martin Seligman and Mihaly Csikszentmihalyi in 2000 as follows (p. 5):

> The field of positive psychology at the subjective level is about valued subjective experiences: well-being, contentment, and satisfaction (in the past); hope and optimism (for the future); and flow and happiness (in the present). At the individual level, it is about positive individual traits: the capacity for love and vocation, courage, interpersonal skill, aesthetic sensibility, perseverance, forgiveness, originality, future mindedness, spirituality, high talent, and wisdom. At the group level, it is about the civic virtues and the institutions that move individuals toward better citizenship: responsibility, nurturance, altruism, civility, moderation, tolerance, and work ethic.

Much of the empirical work within positive psychology has centred around the notion of *subjective well-being* (SWB). This is the systematic study of how people evaluate their lives. Often SWB is evaluated for relatively long periods (e.g., one year) but it has also been investigated in the moment (Diener, 1984; Diener et al., 2003). To all intents and purposes SWB is equivalent to the concept of *happiness*, which we can broadly characterize as the experience of contentment and joy, especially when combined with a sense that life is meaningful and worthwhile. As the name implies, SWB is always measured by self-report and there really is no other way to assess whether or not a person is happy. As Daniel Gilbert (2006) has pointed out in his popular book *Stumbling On Happiness*, it does not matter how many types of indices of happiness we have (e.g., physiological measures etc), unless people tell us that they are happy (or sad) we have no way of correlating the physiological measures with the emotion or mood state. Interestingly, SWB is often measured on a very simple Satisfaction with Life Scale that was developed by Edward Diener and his colleagues (Diener et al., 1985). See Table 10.1. In spite of the simplicity of this scale, it correlates highly with other measures of happiness rated by the same person as well as ratings from their friends and family.

In spite of the rapid increase in research on the determinants of SWB (e.g., Seligman et al., 2005), we still know relatively little about what makes us happy in comparison with our knowledge of the development of pathology. Therefore, there are many fundamental questions to which we simply do not know the answer as yet. Second, it is not clear whether it is best to discuss SWB in terms of a general dimension of positive affectivity (e.g., E-PA) or whether it is best to discuss the experience of discrete positive emotions (e.g., joy, enthusiasm, contentment, gratitude, compassion). Third, it is important to draw a distinction between *resilience* and *well-being*. Resilience is the capacity of people to overcome adversity. This means that some trauma or negative event needs to occur in order for resilience to be revealed. The ability to overcome adverse situations and stresses is clearly important in terms of an individual's overall mental health. However, SWB or happiness can be distinguished from resilience because it is important to understand what makes people happy and contented in the absence of trauma. As pointed out by Seligman and Csikszentmihalyi (2000), we know very little about what makes people flourish under benign conditions. The first part of this chapter will discuss research on resilience and the second part of the chapter will discuss the determinants of happiness or SWB.

TABLE 10.1 The Satisfaction with Life Scale developed by Edward Diener

For each question the level of agreement is rated on a 1–7 scale with 1 being 'strongly disagree' and 7 being 'strongly agree' while 4 is 'neither agree nor disagree'. A score of 20 is the neutral point on the scale so that any score above that is 'happy' whereas a score below 20 would indicate an absence of happiness.

Statement	*Rating*
In most ways my life is close to my ideal	1 – 2 – 3 – 4 – 5 – 6 – 7
The conditions of my life are excellent	1 – 2 – 3 – 4 – 5 – 6 – 7
I am satisfied with my life	1 – 2 – 3 – 4 – 5 – 6 – 7
So far I have gotten the important things I want in life	1 – 2 – 3 – 4 – 5 – 6 – 7
If I could live my life over, I would change almost nothing	1 – 2 – 3 – 4 – 5 – 6 – 7

Source: Diener et al. (1985).

RESILIENCE TO STRESS

A range of adverse and stressful events happen to people during their lives, and it is remarkable that the vast majority of people do not develop emotional disorders. We are often far more resilient than we might think, and an important fact that has emerged is that there are significant *individual differences* in how people respond to stress. Many struggle with ongoing anxiety and/or depressive reactions. Some suffer for a shorter period of time, while some seem to cope remarkably well, often being able to move on from the event very quickly. In fact, there are even a reasonable number of people who claim that they have benefited from adverse events, a phenomenon known as *post-traumatic growth* (Linley and Joseph, 2004).

It seems that resilience is the norm rather than the exception. For example, of the American adults who are exposed to a severe trauma during their lifetime, about 8–20% develop PTSD (Kessler et al., 1995). In other words, the majority do not suffer ongoing serious reactions. Even in instances of very severe trauma in childhood (e.g., physical and sexual abuse), around 30% of victims do not go on to develop severe problems such as PTSD and other emotional problems. An important research endeavour therefore concerns the attempt to identify the factors that determine resilience (Hoge et al., 2007; Rutter, 2006).

The concept of resilience is usually considered at the positive end of individual differences in overcoming significant stress or adversity. Resilience is therefore different from the concept of positive mental health or happiness, even though high levels of positive affect might of course be an important component of resilience. Some have argued that there may be a resilient personality trait that can be measured, such as Kobasa's (1979) concept of *hardiness*, while others argue that resilience can only be measured in terms of responses to stressful events and cannot be conceptualized as a personality trait (Rutter, 2007). Michael Rutter essentially makes the case that what people *do* in a stressful encounter may be far more important than who they are. The development of coping skills in the face of a crisis may be particularly important in determining an individual's resilience to adversity (see Skinner and Zimmer-Gembeck, 2007, for review). In the following sections, we will briefly review some work on the concept of resilience with a particular emphasis on prospective longitudinal studies. Following this, the evidence for gene–environment interactions in determining resilience will be discussed. Finally, we will look at some evidence for the notion that there may be a resilient personality type.

Resilience to psychopathology: Longitudinal studies

Much of the research on resilience has been in the context of children and adults who develop PTSD or other types of psychopathology. Within these studies, there is usually a group of people who do not develop PTSD in spite of experiencing very similar trauma to those who do. As shown in Figure 10.1, three sets of factors appear to influence resilience in children (Garmezy, 1993):

(a) temperamental dimensions;
(b) family cohesion;
(c) availability of support systems outside the family.

In terms of temperamental or dispositional factors, as we might expect, a high degree of positive affectivity (i.e., E-PA) seems to be important. In addition, an *internal locus of control* has been shown to be important. This is the belief that the outcomes and prospects for a person's life are very much within their own control. In some ways, an internal locus of control is opposite to the notion of *learned helplessness*, in which people who believe themselves to be powerless often become passive and fail to cope with even minor hassles (Abramson et al., 1978). To illustrate, one study investigated adolescents living in an inner-city suburb who were exposed to varying degrees of life stress and found that a belief in an internal locus of control acted as a buffer against the negative effects of stress (Luthar, 1991).

Many studies of resilience have been criticized for their reliance on *retrospective* reports of both the degree of stress experienced as well as the availability of support

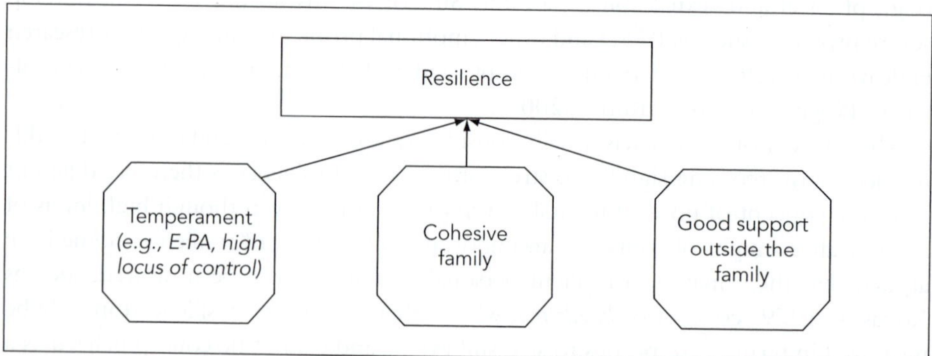

FIGURE 10.1 Factors known to lead to increased resilience in children following a traumatic event

networks (see Hoge et al., 2007, for review). People's memory of stressful events is likely to be vulnerable in these situations and therefore it is important to conduct prospective studies, in which people can be assessed before, during, and after the experience of trauma. Unfortunately, however, these studies are rare and emotion scientists often have to rely on less than perfect data. However, the publication of two longitudinal studies with large sample sizes has added important information to the development of an understanding of resilience (Collishaw et al., 2007; Jaffee et al., 2007).

A major epidemiological study in child psychiatry was begun in the Isle of Wight in 1964. All children born from 1953 to 1955 on the island, which is off the south coast of England, were first assessed when they were 9–10 years of age ($N = 2307$) (Rutter et al., 1970). This cohort was interviewed by the research team on two subsequent occasions; when they were adolescents (14–15 years) and again when they were in middle adulthood (44–45 years). Collishaw et al. (2007) reported data from this cohort that explicitly examined resilience to the experience of childhood sexual and physical abuse. In total, 20 men and 24 women reported retrospectively that they had been the victims of severe maltreatment during childhood. The results showed that the prevalence of depression and anxiety, as well as other aspects of psychopathology, was significantly higher in those who had experienced abuse when compared with those who had not. However, a significant proportion of those who had been abused (44.5%, $N = 14$) reported no psychopathology over the 30 years of adult life prior to the interview and this group were classified as 'resilient'. Factors that most clearly distinguished the resilient group from those who developed psychiatric problems were good parental care, good interpersonal relationships with friends as adolescents, and the quality of adult relationships. In other words, strong and supportive relationships with other people was an important determinant of resilience. The resilient group were also characterized by low scores on a measure of neuroticism. The conclusions that can be drawn from this study are constrained, however, by a number of factors. First, the sample size was relatively small. Second, the reports of childhood abuse were retrospective. Third, no measures of actual coping abilities were measured and these are likely to be important in resilience (Skinner and Zimmer-Gembeck, 2007). Nevertheless, this study is important in demonstrating that the impact of severe sexual and/or physical abuse is associated with an increased risk of psychopathology throughout adolescence and adulthood. More important for the current discussion was the finding that having good interpersonal skills and a supportive social network provided an effective buffer against the negative consequences of this severe life stress.

Studies of the impact of trauma on adults have also identified perceived social support and family cohesion as strong predictors of resilience (Hoge et al., 2007). For example, in a group of 1632 Vietnam veterans, higher levels of social support were associated with lower levels of PTSD (King et al., 1998). Similarly, in a group of Kosovan Albanian refugees who were now living in the UK, significantly lower levels of PTSD were found in those reporting that they had a highly cohesive family (Turner et al., 2003). Thus, it seems that a strong and cohesive family, especially in addition to social support from friends and other organizations, can play an important role in promoting resilience to stressful life events.

Does experience of stress confer protection?

Interestingly, some studies have indicated that exposure to stress might under some circumstances have a protective effect for people later exposed to a new trauma. For instance, in one study it was reported that repeated exposure to traumatic events could actually increase a firefighter's internal locus of control (Regehr et al., 2000). What seems to be important here is the ability to engage in a constructive way with the traumatic event. For instance, there is a lot of evidence that an *avoidant coping style* is associated with an increased risk of PTSD while a more *action-oriented coping strategy* (e.g., 'I made a plan') is associated with resilience (see Hoge et al., 2007, for review). As Rutter (1987a) has pointed out, the impact of a trauma can very much depend on whether the individual avoids or engages with the stressful event.

A recent study with animals has highlighted a potential neural mechanism for the development of resilience (Amat et al., 2006). It has long been known that rats exposed to a series of *inescapable* electrical shocks to the tail later fail to learn to escape from a shock to the feet and show exaggerated fear conditioning – the classic 'learned helplessness' response. However, rats exposed to a similar number of shocks that they can escape from do not show these changes. Those rats who had some behavioural control over a stressor (electric shock) seemed to develop a resilience or a 'behavioural immunization' when faced with a new stressor. These behavioural changes have been linked to changes in the brain stem region especially in the dorsal raphe nucleus (DRN), which is modulated by 5-HT. Inescapable shock leads to a greater degree of activation of the DRN compared to the same amount of escapable shock (Maier and Watkins, 2005).

However, Amat et al. (2006) pointed out that the DRN is a lower brain region that is unlikely to play a role in the detection of whether or not a stressor is controllable. They hypothesized that a higher brain region such as the vmPFC must be involved in regulating lower regions such as the DRN. To demonstrate this they replicated the classic behavioural immunization response to controllable stress. However, when the vmPFC of the rats was inactivated chemically during exposure to the controllable shock their behavioural immunization (or resilience) was completely eliminated. Further experiments demonstrated that the experience of control blocked the intense activation of 5-HT cells in the DRN that are normally associated with exposure to an uncontrollable stress. Moreover, activation of the vmPFC was essential for this effect to occur. Thus, this study provides direct evidence from animal research that the enhancement of inhibitory control over subcortical regions by areas within the prefrontal cortex may be an important neural mechanism in the development of resilience to stress (Amat et al., 2006).

This research is consistent with human research discussed earlier showing that cortical-subcortical circuits are disrupted in people with PTSD (e.g., Rauch, 2003). The implementation of top-down control by the PFC during a stressful encounter is assumed to help prevent the negative consequences of stress. In other words, a strengthening of the cortical-subcortical neural circuits involved in processing negatively affective information may be a critical neural mechanism in the development of resilience.

Gene–environment interactions in resilience

It is somewhat surprising that very little research on resilience has investigated the potential role of gene–environment and indeed gene–environment–personality interactions. As we saw in terms of the development of emotional disorders, there is now growing evidence that gene–environmental interactions are important (Caspi and Moffitt, 2006). Indeed one of the first gene–environment interaction studies investigated the degree to which the maltreatment of children (e.g., physical and sexual abuse) would result in the development of a cycle of violence (Caspi et al., 2002). Caspi et al. examined a functional polymorphism in the monoamine-oxidase A (MAOA) gene. This gene promotes an enzyme that deactivates a set of amine-based neurotransmitters in the brain, thereby leading to lower levels of these neurotransmitters in the brain. The results showed that children who were maltreated and were carriers of the low expression form of the MAOA gene were more likely to be diagnosed with conduct disorder and engage in antisocial behaviour and violent crime. This study once again shows that both maltreatment *and* the possession of a particular genotype are important in the development of emotional problems. The study also found that maltreated children who were carriers of the high expression form of the MAOA gene were less likely to become involved in antisocial behaviour and violent crime. Thus, possession of the high activity MAOA gene may confer some protection against the adverse effects of childhood abuse.

Interestingly, the MAOA gene is a sex-linked gene positioned on the X chromosome. Females have two X chromosomes (one inherited from each parent), whereas males have a single X chromosome (inherited from their mother) and a Y chromosome (inherited from their father). If a female has a low activity MAOA gene on one of her X chromosomes but a high activity MAOA gene on the other , then the negative effects of the low MAOA gene can be moderated. In contrast, if a male has a low activity MAOA gene on his X chromosome then the effects of the gene will not be moderated. This genetic difference may be one of the reasons why violence and aggression, especially in those who are maltreated, is far more common in males than in females. Caspi et al. (2002) found that the effects of the low activity MAOA gene were reduced in girls relative to boys, even though the effects operated in a similar way. Thus, the impact of an environmental stressor such as physical abuse on subsequent antisocial behaviour was magnified by the presence of the low activity MAOA gene, unless its effect was moderated by the presence of the high activity MAOA gene on the other X chromosome. As pointed out by Oatley et al. (2006) this study begins to make sense of the large sex difference in violent and aggressive behaviour.

Is there a resilient personality type?

Rutter (2007) has argued that resilience cannot be considered as a trait-like characteristic since the key influences may lie outside the person (e.g., social support networks etc). Nevertheless, it is possible that particular temperaments or personality traits may influence factors that have a subsequent impact on resilience. For example, people with high E-PA are likely to have a wider network of friends and therefore may indirectly have access to good social support, which is an important buffer against stress.

An emerging research literature addresses the question of why some people do seem to be more resilient to the effects of stress than others and directly searches for evidence of a trait-like characteristic that may confer some protection from the adverse effects of stress. This research defines resilience in terms of the ability to adapt successfully to adverse situations. For example, it has been suggested that the ability to maintain a clear boundary between negative and positive emotions may be one way in which successful adaptation to ongoing stress, such as bereavement, may occur (Zautra et al., 2001). The ability to recover rapidly from the effects of stress may also be an important component of adaptability (Davidson, 2000), and this ability is also likely to differ in consistent ways between people. In support of this hypothesis, resilient individuals have been found to show a much faster physiological recovery from a stressful encounter. Moreover, these individuals also experience fewer depressive symptoms following exposure to situations such as the aftermath of the terrorist attacks of 9/11 (Fredrickson et al., 2003; Tugade and Fredrickson, 2004).

The early work of Jack and Jeanne Block (1980) defined 'ego resiliency' as the ability to adapt flexibly to changing circumstances, and they considered that this was likely to be a stable personality trait. *Trait resilience* from this perspective is effectively the ability to overcome adversity and to bounce back quickly following a major trauma or setback. This concept seems to be related to the notion of *effortful control* that we discussed in Chapter 3 (see Eisenberg et al., 2007). Individuals who have a good degree of effortful control (as long as they are not over-controlled) are generally found to have better social skills and usually adapt better to difficult situations. In other words, effortful control or trait resilience allows people to respond adaptively and therefore plan and behave in a way that is appropriate for a given situation.

Positive emotions are an important component of trait resilience

Recent conceptualizations have argued that the experience of positive emotions forms a crucial part of trait resilience (Fredrickson et al., 2003; Tugade and Fredrickson, 2004; Tugade et al., 2004). The idea here is that resilient people use positive emotions as a way of coping with stressful and difficult situations. People who cannot use positive emotions in adverse circumstances may be less capable of adapting to stress. The work of Anthony Ong and his colleagues has provided empirical evidence that the experience of positive emotions does indeed play a role in the recovery from stress, and that resilient people are especially likely to experience more emotions, both positive and negative, in the face of adversity (Ong et al., 2004, 2006). For example, one study found that both positive and negative emotions occur frequently during a period when people are dealing with the death of a spouse (Ong et al., 2004). Several other studies have shown that adverse events like bereavement are associated with a higher degree of positive emotions than people generally expect (see Bonanno, 2004, for discussion). Further research with a group of elderly individuals confirmed that the experience of positive emotions during periods of increased stress was an important coping strategy that helped to regulate negative emotions Moreover, three different studies found that resilient individuals experienced much higher degrees of positive affectivity than did low resilient people (Ong et al., 2006). Thus, there is evidence that people differ in terms of the degree to which they can regulate negative emotions during periods of stress. Furthermore, the ability to experience positive emotions under these circumstances plays an important role in helping people to adapt to adverse situations.

Positive emotions seem to provide significant physical health benefits in addition to help in coping with chronic stress (e.g., Folkman, 1997; Ong et al., 2004, 2006). For example, those experiencing more positive emotions are less likely to suffer from a stroke in older age (Ostir et al., 2001). Elderly nuns who expressed the most positive emotions when they were young adults lived an average of 10 years longer than nuns who expressed the least positive emotions in early adulthood (Danner et al., 2001). What is the mechanism through which positive emotions can have such widespread benefits? One explanation was proposed by Barbara Fredrickson in her 'broaden-and-build' theory of positive emotions. Positive emotions *broaden* an individual's momentary thought-action repertoires, which allows them to *build* a variety of personal resources that facilitate long-term adaptation to adverse circumstances (Fredrickson, 1998, 2001). Empirical evidence for the broaden-and-build hypothesis comes from demonstrations that positive emotions have specific effects on cognitive processing, making people more open to new ideas and more flexible and creative in their thinking (e.g., Isen, 2000). Another study demonstrated that a video clip producing positive emotions resulted in a more global (relative to local) perceptual bias than a neutral video clip, suggesting that positive emotions do indeed broaden attentional focus (Fredrickson and Branigan, 2005).

Does a repressive coping style promote resilience?

A personality trait often called the 'repressive coping style' has been associated with an enhanced ability to cope with certain adverse situations. To illustrate, there does seem to be a clear individual difference in terms of how people respond to threat as well as the corresponding negative feelings. Bruner and Postman in 1947 referred to 'defensive' individuals who were thought to avoid threat and negative emotions, while 'sensitizers' were assumed to attend to threat and their negative feelings. For a variety of historical reasons, the notion of defensiveness or what is more usually called a *repressive coping style* became associated with the notion that avoiding threat is a bad thing (see Derakshan and Eysenck, 1997, for an excellent review). However, as we have seen in the section on attentional biases, there is solid evidence that vigilance for threat is a characteristic of people with high levels of anxiety and distress. Therefore, the tide has turned somewhat and investigators are now addressing the notion that a repressive coping style may actually be of benefit in adapting to stressful situations (e.g., Bonanno, 2004). A key characteristic of a repressive coping style is dissociation between self-report (indicative of low anxiety) and physiological response (indicative of high anxiety). *Repressors* are often distinguished from genuinely low-anxious individuals on the basis of scoring low on anxiety scales but high on a measure of defensiveness. In contrast, low-anxious people score low on both anxiety and defensiveness, while high-anxious people score high on anxiety and low on defensiveness.

Using the above criteria, there is evidence that repressors are characterized by attentional biases to avoid threat-related stimuli (e.g., Bonanno et al., 1991; Fox, 1993), as well as a tendency to selectively recall positive relative to negative information in memory tasks (e.g., Cutler et al., 1996; Myers and Derakshan, 2004). For example, in the dot-probe task Fox (1993) found that high-anxious people showed the usual vigilance for threat-related words (see Chapter 8), low-anxious individuals showed no bias either towards or away from negative words, but repressors showed a strong bias to avoid threat-related words. This automatic attentional avoidance of threat may be a protective mechanism serving to keep levels of state-anxiety low in stressful situations.

Several studies have shown that these avoidant biases are most obvious when there is a threat to self-evaluation (Derakshan and Eysenck, 1997). These findings have led to the suggestion that a repressive coping style may operate primarily as a means of preserving a positive self-image that is dependent on maintaining low levels of distress and negative affectivity (Derakshan and Eysenck, 1999). If all of this is correct then it may be the case that a repressive coping style can promote resilience to aversive events by means of the automatic avoidance of the more negative and distressing aspects of stress.

This hypothesis was directly addressed in a series of studies reported by George Bonanno and his colleagues. Repressive coping was defined by the presence of low levels of negative affect coupled with high levels of autonomic responding when people were discussing a threatening topic. In a longitudinal design, repressive coping was found to be associated with reduced psychological symptoms (depression, anxiety, PTSD) and better overall adjustment in a group of bereaved adults (Bonanno et al., 1995). The association between repressive coping and good adjustment to stress was still present even when the initial degree of psychological distress was matched statistically. This result strongly suggests that repressive coping may promote resilience in response to the stress of bereavement. In more recent research these effects were replicated and extended (Coifman et al., 2007). Once again it was found that bereaved participants who exhibited a repressive coping style had fewer symptoms of psychopathology and better general health, as well as being rated as being better adjusted by their friends than those who did not exhibit repressive coping. Thus, taken together these results strongly suggest that repressive coping in times of stress may serve a protective function.

These results are interesting but appear to conflict with the findings that an avoidant coping style is associated with a number of maladaptive consequences, such as an increase in PTSD symptoms following a trauma (Hoge et al., 2007). Likewise, experimental studies have shown that the deliberate avoidance of negative affect can actually increase negative affectivity (e.g., Gross and John, 2003). However, the work of Nazanin Derakshan and her colleagues has helped to clarify this issue. To illustrate, a series of studies has shown that repressive coping behaviours are different from the deliberate act of avoiding negative affect (Derakshan et al., 2004; Myers et al., 2004). The main difference seems to be that the avoidance of negative affect in repressive coping is automatic and occurs without any conscious control. This automatic tendency to avoid threat, as observed in both selective attentional and memory biases, might provide a protective function in contrast to deliberate efforts to avoid threat (see Derakshan et al., 2007, for extensive review).

HAPPINESS AND WELL-BEING

Large international surveys have consistently found that people's rating of how happy they are tends to be on the positive side of neutral, suggesting that most people are happy (Diener and Diener, 1996). There is some variation, however, between individualist and collectivist cultures as we might expect. Thus, countries such as the USA and many in Western Europe tend to put a high value on subjective well-being and happiness, while more collectivist societies like Japan tend to value the well-being of others more highly.

The measurement of happiness

An important question to address concerns how SWB or happiness can be measured. The majority of research has used a range of general self-report instruments such as the Satisfaction with Life Scale shown in Table 10.1. These instruments essentially measure happiness as an enduring mood state rather than as a momentary emotion. However, decades of research have shown that SWB remains reasonably stable across time and different situations (see Diener and Lucas, 2000, for review). While emotions and moods clearly fluctuate across time they do tend to move around a mean level that varies among people. In other words, while specific life events may shift mood in a positive or negative direction, when these moods are averaged across longer time periods they average out to reveal a person's mean level of positive affect. This mean level has often been considered to be equivalent to a hedonic 'set-point' to which people inevitably return (e.g., Brickman and Campbell, 1971). It is this mean level or set-point that is thought to be captured by global measures of SWB, and evidence suggests that it is the mean level that remains stable across time and situations (Diener and Larsen, 1984).

Daniel Kahneman (1999) has argued that happiness research should emphasize people's momentary affective experiences rather than relying on more global reflections of satisfaction and well-being. To some extent this is because of potential methodological problems in asking people to report retrospectively on how happy they have been over a given period of time. A body of evidence shows that people take certain types of information into account to a greater extent than other types of evidence when they are asked to make a global judgment of SWB (Kahneman, 1999). For instance, the peak and the end experience of a situation tend to be given most importance when making overall judgments. This was illustrated in a study with people undergoing a colonoscopy, an unpleasant medical procedure in which a scope is inserted

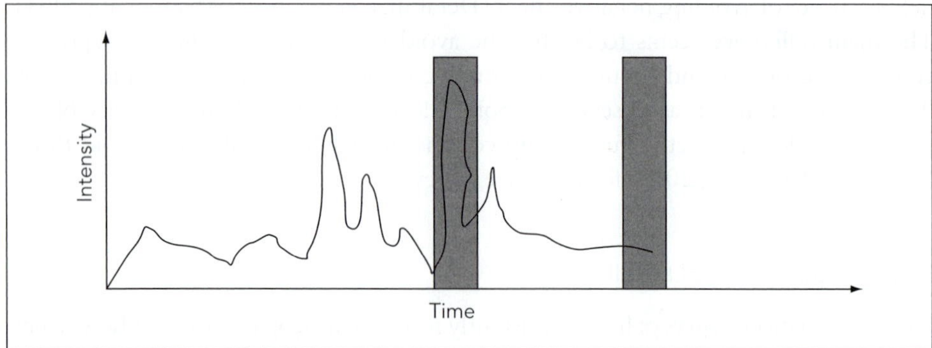

FIGURE 10.2 Influence of peak and end experiences in global judgments of the pleasantness of a situation

into the colon. Redelmeir and Kahneman (1996) found that when the colonoscopy examination was extended, by simply holding the scope still for a short period before removing it at the end of the examination, people rated the overall procedure as being less painful than when the scope was removed at an earlier and more painful part of the test. Thus, even though the latter condition was a longer experience, the last event tended to dictate the overall rating. Similar findings were reported in a laboratory-based study (Fredrickson and Kahneman, 2003). Each participant watched a series of pleasant video clips (e.g., a puppy playing) and they rated their degree of pleasure continuously by means of a pointer and a dial. When the video was completed, each participant was asked to provide a rating of their overall pleasure when watching the movie. As with the medical examination, it was found that the peak and the end experiences were the best predictors of the overall rating. An illustration of the influence of peak and end experiences is shown in Figure 10.2. The moral of this story is that if you want people to have a favourable overall impression of you (e.g., in a job interview or on a date), it is important to ensure a relatively high peak experience and make sure the ending is positive!

The work of Schwarz and Clore (1983) that we discussed in Chapter 6 raises some potential problems with self-report measures of SWB. They found that transient positive mood states had large effects on ratings of global life satisfaction, at least when people did not attribute the mood to some other factor. Thus, we can assume that if people are in a good mood when they are providing a global rating of their SWB their evaluations are likely to be inflated. Researchers need to pay particular attention to current mood states when asking people to make global evaluations of their well-being. To date, the field of SWB has been heavily dependent on self-report measures rather than more objective measures. In one sense this is necessary if we want to understand *subjective* well-being. However, we also need to be mindful of the various self-report and judgmental biases that may confound subjective measures. The development of other measures, such as neurobiological markers of happiness that may not be affected to the same extent as these confounding variables, is therefore important for the future development of happiness research.

In spite of the findings that peak experiences influence the overall judgment of SWB (e.g., Fredrickson and Kahneman, 2003), it has been argued that the *intensity* of positive affective experiences does not seem to play a strong role in the overall assessment of SWB (Diener and Lucas, 2000). Instead, it seems that it is the *frequency* of positive emotions and moods that influences a person's overall judgment of how happy they are (Diener et al., 1991). This may be because intense emotions are relatively rare and therefore may not be considered so relevant to global assessments of well-being. It is also the case, however, that people who experience very intense positive emotions also experience very intense negative emotions, and thus the benefits of positive affect may be counterbalanced by the costs (Diener and Lucas, 2000). This is an area that needs more work to find out just how important intense or peak experiences are in influencing global judgments of SWB. In evaluating the pleasantness or otherwise of relatively short procedures, peak or intense experiences do seem to be important (e.g., Fredrickson and Kahneman, 2003; Redelmeir and Kahneman, 1996). However, when evaluating longer periods of time the frequency of the experience seems to be relatively more important than the intensity of positive experiences (e.g., Diener et al., 1991).

Thus, some happiness researchers argue that the emphasis in measurement should be on the momentary experiences that people have rather than on more global measurements (e.g., Kahneman, 1999). However, Martin Seligman (2002) has argued that what makes people happy in small doses does not necessarily add up to overall happiness. He argues that the emphasis on moment-to-moment experiences is likely to miss the deeper aspects of happiness by focusing only on positive affective experiences. As illustrated in Figure 10.3, Seligman (2002) proposes that happiness is made up of three components each of which should be measured in any study of SWB. The first component is the degree of *positive affectivity* experienced, that is often emphasized in happiness research. The second component relates to the degree to which people are *engaged* in their lives. The work of Mihaly Csikszentmihalyi (1990) has conceptualized this degree of engagement with life as a state of *flow* or optimal experience. This state is well known among sports people who often talk about being 'in the zone'. Csikszentmihalyi points out that often we do not have too much choice about the kind of life we lead. Many people, for example, have to endure boring and tedious

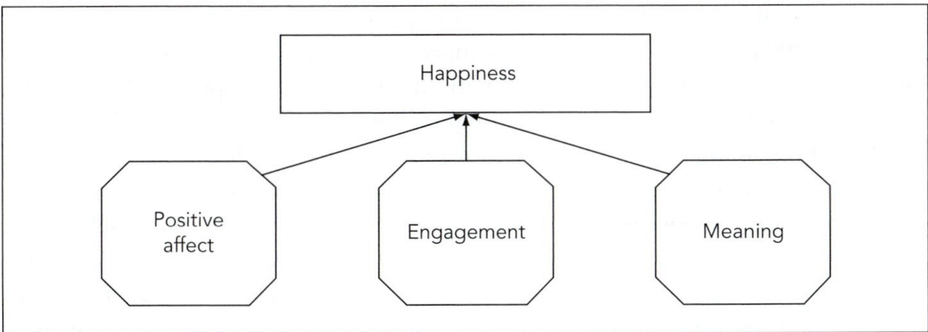

FIGURE 10.3 The three components of happiness as outlined by Seligman (2002)

jobs. However, he has discovered that people can gain a high degree of meaning in their life by really engaging with and taking pride in even very simple tasks. The state of flow is characterized by a sense of being fully engaged in a task, and a degree of creativity and purpose allows the sense of self and the activity to become merged. As stated eloquently by the Irish poet William Butler Yeats in his poem 'Among School Children' when watching a skilled dancer:

> 'Oh body swayed to music, oh brightening glance,
> How can we tell the dancer from the dance?'

The third component refers to a person's sense of how *meaningful* their life is on a broader scale than the day-to-day things. In other words, happiness is not just about seeking pleasure. It is also about taking some control over our lives and being creative in seeking to obtain a degree of engagement and meaning from a range of activities. A series of studies has shown that people differ in reliable ways along all of these dimensions, and that the happiest people are those who orient their life around the pursuit of all three: positive affect, engagement and meaning. Importantly, this research indicates that the greatest impact on overall happiness comes from engagement and meaning, rather than from pleasure (Peterson et al., 2005). Thus, the endless pursuit of pleasure may not be the most direct way to achieve happiness. The pursuit of meaning and engagement and optimal experience may be more important. It is interesting to note that what Seligman called 'peak experiences' were a hallmark of the fully self-actualized people studied by Maslow (1954).

As we have noted, there has been almost total reliance on self-report in happiness research. Many argue that self-report is essential in order to get an impression of *subjective* well-being (e.g., Diener and Lucas, 2000; Gilbert, 2006). It is clear that subjective report really is the only way that we can ensure that a person is experiencing positive rather than negative emotions. However, it is also clear that there are problems with relying solely on subjective report. Throughout emotion science there have been consistent attempts to measure as many of the components of affect as possible (e.g., behaviour or actions; physiological response; neural response; cognitive processes etc). To date, however, there have been relatively few attempts to move beyond subjective report in happiness research. There are some exceptions, of course, such as the demonstration that a left-sided asymmetry in prefrontal cortical activity is a marker of positive affect (Sutton and Davidson, 1997).

Diener (1994) has suggested that it is imperative for researchers to develop a wider range of measures that could include methods such as peer report and non-verbal indicators in order to provide a more complete understanding of SWB. Many of the neural and physiological markers of positive valence that we discussed in Chapter 5 could also be usefully applied more generally in happiness research. While it is often difficult to obtain physiological and behavioural measures in addition to self-report, this is just as important an endeavour in the study of positive emotions as it is in the study of negative emotions. Once a variety of measures is available the patterns or lack of correlations between them can provide important insights into the complexity of our affective lives. However, such measures are likely to tap into positive affectivity primarily, thereby reflecting only one of the Seligman's components of SWB. Therefore, it is also important to develop valid and reliable measures of the degree of engagement and sense of meaning that people have in their lives.

The determinants of happiness

The ability to experience a greater number of positive relative to negative emotions in a good predictor of SWB. For instance, keeping a ratio of about 3:1 (i.e., 3 positive emotions to every 1 negative emotion) seems to be essential for maintaining a state of well-being or flourishing (Fredrickson and Losada, 2005). This is consistent with research reported by Gottman and Levenson (2000) on happiness within marriages. In a series of studies, they have analyzed the patterns of speech interactions between husbands and wives when discussing a conflict (e.g., difficulties with finances). They have found that there are four toxic behaviours – criticism, defensiveness, stonewalling and contempt – that turn out to be very good predictors of which couples will stay together and which will divorce. However, in the present context the more interesting finding is that couples whose marriages have lasted a long time tend to maintain ratios of at least five positive affective interactions to one negative with their partners (Gottman and Levenson, 1992, 2000). Thus, keeping a balance so that positive emotional experiences outweigh negative emotional experiences is an important determinant of happiness. It is important to remember, however, that external factors (life events) and temperamental or personality differences are not independent of each other. Instead, temperament can moderate the influence of external events by means of a range of processes such as cognitive biases and patterns of neural reactivity.

External factors and life events

It is widely believed that factors such as good health, wealth, and a supportive and loving marriage are all predictors of a high degree of subjective well-being (e.g., Argyle, 1999; Eysenck, 1990). However, somewhat surprisingly, the research generally shows that these objective determinants of happiness explain a remarkably small percentage of the variance (e.g., Argyle, 1999; Diener et al., 1999; Eysenck, 1990; Myers, 2000). Take money as an example. In the Western world at least, most of us try to maximize the amount of money we have and generally believe that we would be happier if we had more. However, the general finding is that, while wealth and income does significantly improve SWB, this is only true at very low levels of income (e.g., Diener and Seligman, 2004; Layard, 2005; Myers, 2000). In other words, if people are living in poverty then an increase in income will have a significant impact on their well-being. Beyond that basic level, however, extra money and wealth actually seem to have a very small effect on happiness.

The failure of objective variables to predict SWB was made clear in a now-classic study reported by Brickman and colleagues (1978). They interviewed three groups of people and asked them to rate their level of happiness in the past, at present, and how happy they expect to be in the future. One group had recently won large sums of money in the Illinois Lottery, another group had been permanently paralyzed in accidents, and a control group had experienced no major life events. The startling finding was that the lottery winners did not end up being any happier than the control participants. While the paralyzed individuals did have a somewhat reduced level of SWB, even they tended to bounce back to close to their baseline level.

Brickman et al. (1978) explained these results in terms of a *hedonic adaptation theory*. People react to good and bad events immediately after they happen but that adaptation occurs rather quickly and they soon return to a neutral set-point. Just as we rapidly adapt to sensory stimuli (e.g., smell or taste), the hypothesis is that the affective system reacts to life changes but that all reactions adapt after a period of time. Thus, even winning the lottery does not lead to permanent changes in happiness. As pointed out by David Myers in *The Pursuit of Happiness* (1992), all enjoyable experiences (e.g., passionate love, the exhilaration of success) are transitory and we adapt to them rapidly.

Substantial research following the report of Brickman et al. (1978) has tended to broadly confirm this hedonic adaptation theory. For example, while people report primarily negative emotions following a serious spinal injury, within about two months the dominant emotions reported tend to be positive (Silver, 1982). Likewise, it has been found that both good and bad life events only had a major impact on happiness if they had occurred within the previous two months (Suh et al., 1996). However, a number of facts have emerged that have led to the original adaptation theory being revised. For example, Diener et al. (2006) have pointed out that the notion of a *neutral* set point is wrong. Instead, it seems that the set-point is generally above neutral in that people report that they are happy (and experience more positive relative to negative emotions) most of the time (Diener and Diener, 1996). Another finding is that there are strong individual differences in set-points, and these are probably related to genetically-based temperamental differences. For example, the degree of similarity in self-reported happiness was much higher in identical twins reared apart than in non-identical twins reared apart, suggesting an important genetic component (Tellegen et al., 1988).

Perhaps the most important finding in subsequent research is that happiness can change to a much greater extent than might be expected by the hedonic adaptation theory. As discussed by Diener et al. (2006), while people do adapt to many life changes there is evidence that some life events can lead to more enduring changes in the set-point. The death of a spouse and unemployment, for example, have been found to result in significant reductions in SWB. Even though some adaptation does occur this can take up to 8 years and even then SWB may not get back to the original baseline. This pattern of partial adaptation is shown in Figure 10.4. What Figure 10.4 does not show, of course, is the role of individual differences in adaptation to both good and bad events. Updated versions of hedonic adaptation theory are now incorporating more individual difference variables in order to provide a more complete explanation of the data (e.g., Diener et al., 2006; Wilson and Gilbert, 2005). Moreover,

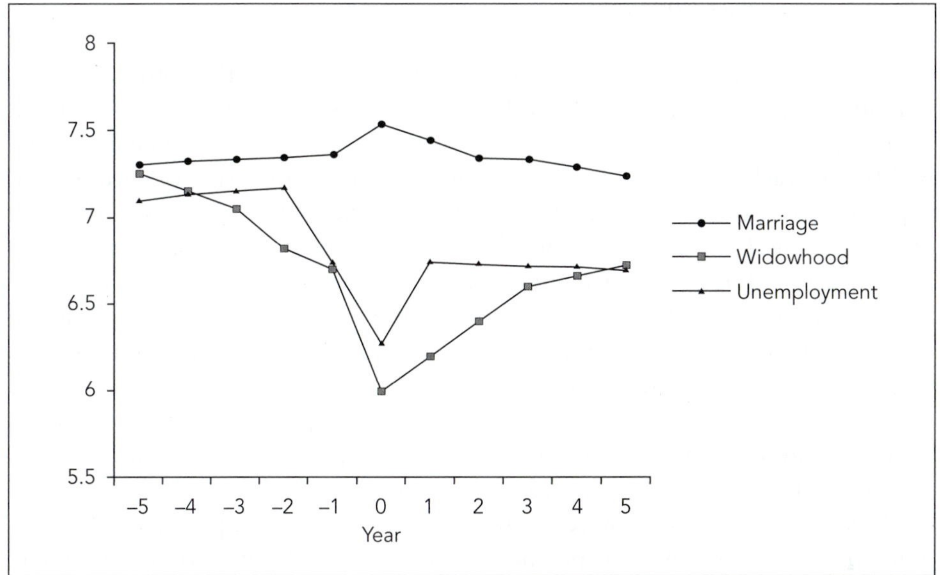

FIGURE 10.4 How people adapt to good and bad events over a 5-year period
Source: Data modified from Diener et al. (2006).

some more recent large-scale panel studies have found long-term changes in SWB in people who have developed long-term disabilities (e.g., Lucas, 2007a). While some adaptation does occur, events such as death of a spouse, divorce or unemployment are associated with lasting changes in SWB. Lucas (2007b) emphasizes that there are considerable individual differences in the extent to which people adapt to major life changes. So, once again the role of temperament and other differences needs to be taken into account when assessing the impact of life events on long-term happiness.

We have discussed a range of external factors that seem to have relatively little impact on SWB, and it also seems that people can adapt to most events even if they are very positive (e.g., winning the lottery). Nevertheless, some factors have consistently emerged as being strong predictors of well-being and happiness. In particular, spending time with other people is a major source of SWB (see Myers, 2000, for review). For example, in one study the characteristics of students who scored in the top 10% on a happiness questionnaire were examined (Diener and Seligman, 2002). A key feature of these happy individuals was their strong commitment to spending time with family and friends, and they did spend more time with friends than those with lower happiness scores. It is interesting that having a cohesive family unit and a supportive social network has also been identified as one of the major factors for resilience in the face of adversity. Clearly, the quality of our social interactions is important in helping us to cope with adversity as well as generally enhancing our subjective well-being. Religious belief and practice has also been found to increase happiness, although it is not clear whether this is due to faith in a higher being or the enhanced levels of social interactions and support networks often involved in organized religions (Myers, 2000).

The importance of perceived control

Some environments give people a far greater degree of control than others, and this is another important factor for SWB. Indeed some researchers have concluded that the feeling of control is one of the primary well-springs of positive mental health and well-being (Taylor and Brown, 1988). There is strong empirical evidence for this hypothesis from a variety of research areas. Many studies of mental health in the work place have found that perceived control is an important predictor of an employee's SWB (Spector, 2002). In one study a group of nurses was investigated over a five-year period (Ganster et al., 2001). Those nurses who were found to have a high degree of perceived control over their various job tasks were reported to have better mental health and used fewer medical services over the 5 years.

In a more direct experimental investigation, having a degree of control over one's life was found to be an important determinant of happiness and health in a group of elderly people (Langer and Rodin, 1976; Rodin and Langer, 1977). To illustrate, the residents of a nursing home were given a house-plant and each participant was randomly assigned to one of two experimental conditions. In the high control condition, people were told that they were responsible for the plant and could water and feed it whenever they liked. In contrast, the low control group were told that a member of the nursing home staff would look after the plant. Over a 6-month period the degree of SWB was higher in the high control than the low control group. More dramatic was the finding that, while 30% of the low control group had died after 6 months, only 15% of the high control group had died after this period.

Further evidence that control can play an important role in enhancing happiness was reported by Schulz and Hanusa (1978). Once again, the elderly residents of a nursing home were studied and each participant was told that a student volunteer would visit on a regular basis. Those in the high control group were allowed to determine the date and time of the student's visit, while those in the low control group were simply given a date and a time for the visit by the research team. Although the number of visits and degree of contact was similar for the two groups, those in the high control group had substantially higher measures of SWB two months later. Once again, having some degree of control over one's life seems to be important for well-being and mental health.

The interesting finding is that the benefits of control for SWB are still strong even when the perception of control is illusory. In other words, even when people just think they are in control they tend to be happier (Taylor and Brown, 1988). Thus control – whether real or illusory – is crucial for happiness. When people lose the ability to control things in their lives they often become depressed and helpless (Seligman, 1975). This was demonstrated inadvertently by a tragic outcome to the study we discussed above by Schulz and Hanusa (1978). Several months after the study had ended the researchers discovered that an unusually large number of people who had been in the high control group had died. It seemed that losing the control, which had been of such benefit to these participants, had had drastic consequences for their well-being and ultimately their physical health. As discussed by the participants, these findings raise a number of important ethical issues that need to be thought about carefully by researchers conducting these types of experiments. When an intervention has an important benefit on SWB, we need to make sure that taking this benefit away when the study is complete does not have disastrous consequences.

As pointed out by Gilbert (2006), the desire to be in control is very powerful and rewarding for most people and almost certainly plays a role in maintaining well-being. This 'illusion of control' is so strong, that people often behave as if they could control the uncontrollable. For example, people are more likely to think that they have a better chance of winning the lottery if they can choose the number on their ticket rather than allow a computer to randomly generate a number (see Langer, 1975, for review). These findings are consistent with experimental evidence that an absence of happiness, as found in depression, is associated with an absence of the illusion of control. This was illustrated in a classic study reported by Alloy and Abramson (1979). People were asked to press or not press a button following which a green light would appear. The contingency between the button press and the onset of the light was controlled by the experimenter who then asked each study participant to estimate the degree of control they thought they had over the onset of the light. The results showed that people who were mildly happy tended to overestimate the degree of control they had when the outcome was positive. In contrast, this group tended to underestimate the degree of control they thought they had when the outcome was negative. In other words, these mildly happy people were inaccurate in estimating the amount of control they had, but thought that they had much more control than they actually had when the outcome was positive. This result is consistent with the widespread illusion of control that most relatively happy people report in their everyday lives (Langer, 1975). The interesting finding came from a second group of people who were mildly depressed. This group turned out to be surprisingly accurate in determining how much control they had in the contingency task (Alloy and Abramson, 1979). The results were interpreted as a *depressive realism* effect. suggesting that depressed people were 'sadder but wiser'. Mildly happy people, on the other hand, were deluded into thinking that they could control positive outcomes. Is this true? Is it the case that depressed people are more accurate in estimating control in their everyday life? This assertion seems to contradict the widespread reports that depression is associated with a range of selective negative biases and distortions (see Chapters 8 and 9).

Subsequent research has resolved this apparent contradiction by demonstrating that depressive realism only occurs when depressed people are judging their own behaviour. When depressed people are asked to estimate the degree of control that other people have in a similar task they tend to overestimate the degree of control (Martin et al., 1984). Thus, the notion that depressed people are 'sadder but wiser' is inaccurate. It does seem to be the case that depressed people do not show the normal 'illusion of control' effect when they are judging their own actions. Instead, depression is associated with a bias to think that other people have more control than they actually have while judging (accurately) that they personally have little control. In contrast, happy people have a bias to think that they have far more control than they actually have, especially when the outcome is good. In terms of the enhancement of SWB and happiness, then, it seems that having some degree of control – even if this is illusory – is vital.

Errors in affective forecasting

Daniel Gilbert and his colleagues have approached the question of what makes us happy by means of what they call *affective forecasting* (e.g., Gilbert and Wilson, 2007; Wilson and Gilbert, 2003). The main finding is that people are very inaccurate at determining what is likely to make them happy or sad. The *impact bias* is the tendency for people to overestimate the duration as well as the intensity of their emotional reactions to future events. In other words, we tend to overestimate how bad we will feel if something bad happens (e.g., if a relationship breaks up), and we also tend to overestimate how good we will feel if something good happens (e.g., winning a large amount of money). Behind this is almost certainly the fact that we do not appreciate how much we can adjust to even very major life events. It is clear that both adverse and highly positive events do affect us, but the reality is that we adapt to these changes within a relatively short period of time (e.g., Brickman et al., 1978; Diener et al., 2006; Taylor, 1983).

In one study people were asked to say how unhappy they would feel two months after a romantic relationship ended (Gilbert et al., 1998). Another group of people who had actually experienced the break-up of a romantic relationship were asked to say how unhappy they felt two months after the end of their relationship. The results clearly showed that those who had not experienced a break-up significantly overestimated how bad they thought that they would feel. Those who had experienced this negative event actually reported that they were happier than the other group thought they would be. This is a classic example of an error of affective forecasting and implies that we do not really know the extent to which external events are going to make us happy or unhappy.

The impact bias is important because, in order to keep engaged with a particular task, people need to be able to predict the valence (positivity or negativity) of future events as well as how strong their emotional reactions are likely to be (Wilson and Gilbert, 2005). Since engagement is important for current happiness, these future predictions are crucial for current well-being. The irony, however, is that we are not generally very good at knowing what is likely to make us happy or unhappy in the future. As another example, it was found that college students overestimated how happy they would be if they were assigned to a desirable dormitory and how unhappy they would be if they were assigned to an undesirable dormitory (Dunn et al., 2003). As can be seen in Figure 10.5, the self-reported happiness of these students a year later was unaffected by the dormitory they were actually assigned to. Wilson and Gilbert (2005) have argued that there are a number of reasons why people make these errors in affective forecasting. For example, we often fail to realize how quickly we will make sense of things that happen to us and this, of course, aids recovery. We also tend to

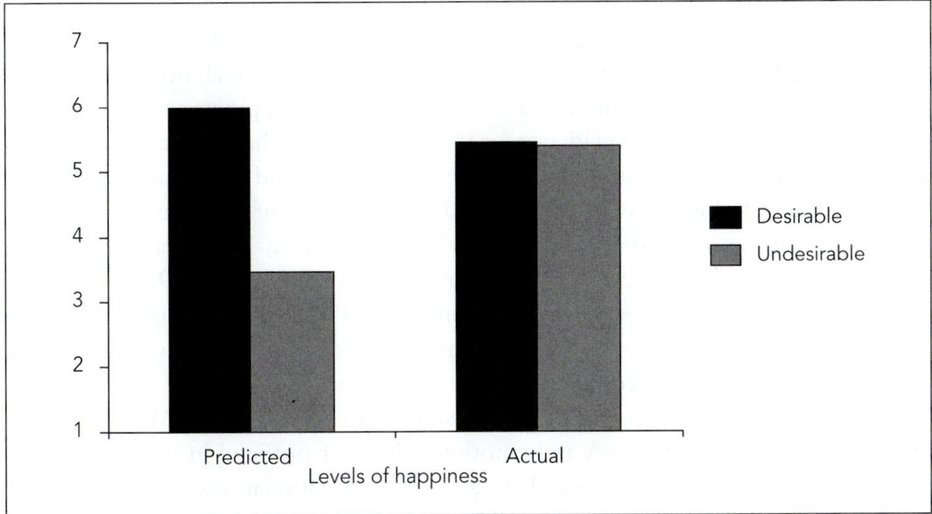

FIGURE 10.5 Predicted and actual levels of happiness for college students after they had been assigned to either desirable or undesirable dormitories

Source: Adapted from Dunn et al. (2003).

underestimate the degree to which events other than the main event will modulate our reactions to the main event. Thus, when assessing the impact of external events on our lives, we need to take a range of factors into account, including the fact that these events are often not as good or bad as we think they will be.

In summary then, it is clear that some external factors, such as having friends and supportive social networks, do have an important impact on happiness. The more internal factor – illusion of control over environmental events – is also an important component of feeling happy. However, many external factors that seem like they should increase our SWB actually have a relatively small effect. One reason for this, of course, is that individual differences in temperament and personality are likely to modulate the effect of a range of factors on SWB. In addition, the general tendency to overestimate the degree to which events will affect us (*impact bias*) is important. Moreover, the degree of engagement and meaning that one has in life is also likely to override many external factors. As pointed out by Diener and Lucas (2000), if a person living in a high crime area or in a very poor neighbourhood becomes actively involved in community politics to improve their area, they may be very happy because their life has a deep meaning even though the objective external factors of their life may be fairly grim. Thus, when investigating SWB and happiness it is important to keep in mind that the *context* and the *individual* are crucial parts of the equation that may override more objective external factors.

TEMPERAMENTAL AND PERSONALITY FACTORS

We have reviewed extensive evidence throughout this book that E-PA is a higher-order temperamental dimension that is associated with the experience of a greater number of positive moods and emotions (e.g., Clark, 2005; Watson and Clark, 1995). People with a high E-PA are more reactive to positive stimuli at neural and cognitive levels, and a very low degree of E-PA is associated with an inability to experience pleasure. Thus, high E-PA should be a strong predictor of happiness and the ability to experience pleasure. There is evidence for this hypothesis in that a variety of measures relating to E-PA – extraversion, neuroticism, self-esteem, and optimism – are highly positively correlated with SWB (Diener and Lucas, 1999). For example, in one longitudinal study it was found that people with a high degree of E-PA (extraverts) actually did experience more positive events than introverts (Magnus et al., 1993). Magnus et al. suggested that the link between temperament (E-PA) and SWB might have been indirect: extraverts are more likely to gain more rewards from their environment and social interactions, and hence experience greater degrees of happiness.

Figure 10.6 shows four types of relationship between E-PA and SWB that parallel the relations between N-NA and emotional disorder outlined in Figure 9.2. The models shown in Figure 10.6(a) and (b) propose a causal relationship between temperament and SWB that can either be *direct* (enhancement model) or *indirect* (facilitation model). They are functionally equivalent to the vulnerability and pathoplasty models of how temperament and emotional disorder might be related. The *consequence* model (Figure 10.6(c)), which is equivalent to the scar model, indicates that SWB itself may play a role in causing a high degree of E-PA. In other words, SWB or happiness may play a role in modifying temperament. Finally, the *spectrum* model

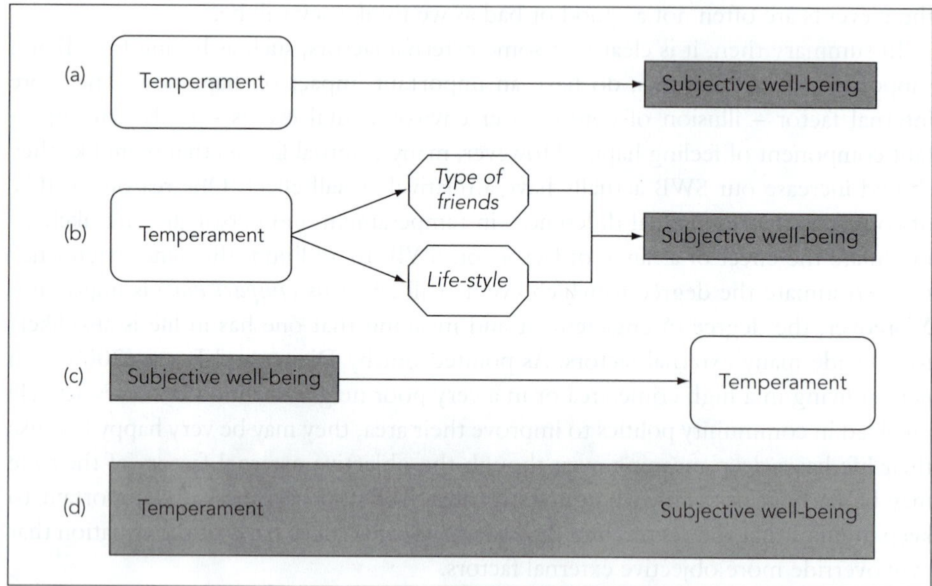

FIGURE 10.6 Four models of how temperament might be associated with the development of subjective well-being
(a) direct enhancement model
(b) indirect facilitation model
(c) consequence model
(d) continuity or spectrum model

(Figure 10.6(d)) assumes that SWB and E-PA form a continuum with SWB at the extreme end of the dimension.

It is clear that these four models are not mutually exclusive. For instance, it is likely that the experience of many positive life events in childhood may play an important role in the development of a sunny and outgoing temperament (i.e., high E-PA), which would support the *consequence* model. However, it is equally likely that energetic and happy children will attract both peers and adults and be more likely to experience positive events such as positive social interactions.This case would support the facilitation model. Thus, just as we discussed with regard to the relations between N-NA and emotional disorders, a positive cycle may be formed whereby high levels of E-PA can influence the type of events an individual might experience. This in turn, of course, can either increase or decrease the level of E-PA that is expressed. The direction of causality between E-PA and SWB can only be determined from longitudinal studies that measure both temperament and well-being over a long period of time.

We discussed a range of studies in Chapter 9 showing that the temperamental dimension of E-PA incorporates neurobiological systems such as the BAS (Gray, 1982) and the uninhibited behavioural temperament seen in children (Kagan, 1994) (see Figure 9.3). This higher-order dimension is also related to the general appetitive or approach systems within the brain. There are relatively few longitudinal studies examining the impact of E-PA and related personality traits on SWB. However, it has been shown that high levels of E-PA are related to reduced levels of depression (Clark and Watson, 1991), suggesting that temperament may be playing a causal role in SWB (assuming that low levels of depression are associated with higher levels of well-being). Further evidence was reported in a review of longitudinal studies which found that high E-PA actually seemed to provide a buffer against the onset of depression (Clark et al., 1994). However, these studies were in the context of emotional disorders and did not directly measure SWB or indicators of happiness. Studies that did directly measure SWB have found that people with high E-PA are more likely to experience positive events. This relationship seems to be indirect (i.e., facilitation model) in that extraverts were more likely to get the best out of the situations they experienced (Headey and Wearing, 1989; Magnus et al., 1993).

In terms of the Big Five personality traits – extraversion, neuroticism, openness to experience, agreeableness, conscientiousness – most of the evidence points to a link between happiness and extraversion. However, both *agreeableness* and *conscientiousness* have been found to make independent contributions to happiness over and above the contributions of the other factors (McCrae and Costa, 1991). It has been reported, however, that the relationship between the Big Five personality traits and happiness depends to a large extent upon how happiness or SWB is measured (DeNeve and Cooper, 1998). When the Satisfaction with Life scale is used, there appears to be a strong relationship between higher levels of SWB and *conscientiousness.* However, when happiness is measured in terms of the frequency of positive emotions experienced then the stronger relationship is with *extraversion.* This is understandable since the experience of positive emotions is, of course, a core component of extraversion. In terms of the model outlined by Seligman (2002) and shown in Figure 10.3, it is clear that extraversion might be associated most with the component of positive affect that is an important element of happiness. However, *engagement* is another core component of happiness that we might expect to be closely related to *conscientiousness*. People who are highly conscientious tend to set clear goals for themselves and to be very focused on achieving these goals. Thus, a conscientious person is likely to be far more engaged with their work and goals than somebody lower in this personality trait. Therefore, it is clear that this aspect of personality can have an important impact on a person's overall happiness. It is important to remember, however, that the way in which happiness is measured is an important factor to consider before drawing any strong conclusions.

The evidence in general, however, is consistent with the hypothesis that positive and negative emotions and moods have as much to do with our temperament as with external events (see Depue and Monroe, 1986, for review). As we have seen throughout this book, people with different temperaments and personality characteristics really do create different subjective environments for themselves. One thing that has consistently been found is that people with a high degree of E-PA tend to experience far more positive emotions and moods than those with low levels of E-PA. However, positive affectivity is just one component of happiness (Seligman, 2002) and other personality traits such as conscientiousness are likely to be influential in determining how engaged people are in various tasks.

COGNITIVE AND NEUROBIOLOGICAL FACTORS

Studies using the attentional probe task have found that positive moods are associated with a selective attentional bias towards reward-related words (Tamir and Robinson, 2007). This type of cognitive bias indicates that positive mood states do tend to sensitize people to rewards within their environment. Positive mood states are also associated with selective memory biases to recall more positive information. These persistent biases towards positively valenced material might help in understanding how the experience of positive emotions might contribute to overall happiness. They might also help to uncover at least one of the mechanisms underlying the relationship between temperament and SWB. In the following sections, we will also discuss evidence that the effects of positive emotions on cognitive functioning may occur primarily by means of activation of the dopamine (DA) and opioid systems in the brain (e.g., Ashby et al., 1999; Berridge, 2003, 2004).

The benefits of positive emotions

Much of the research within the SWB field has examined positive affect as a broad dimension or ongoing mood, but there have been some studies that specifically address discrete positive emotions such as joy, interest, gratitude and so on (Izard and Ackerman, 2000). We will briefly examine some of the evidence that these particular emotions have a range of effects on both cognition and behaviour, and will also consider whether these positive emotions have similar or dissimilar effects from each other.

Joy/Happiness

Happiness or joy is probably the commonest of the positive emotions that people experience on a fairly constant basis. It is considered by some researchers to be one of the basic emotions (e.g., Oatley and Johnson-Laird, 1987; Panksepp, 1998), and is associated with a clear facial expression – the smile – that seems to be universally recognized (Ekman, 1992). The eminent French neurologist Duchenne de Boulogne (1862/1990) discovered the critical difference between a genuine smile expressing joy and a fake smile. This is why a genuine smile is often called a 'Duchenne smile'. To illustrate, in a spontaneous or *Duchenne smile*, the muscle that surrounds the eye (orbicularis oculi) automatically contracts on both sides and this has the effect of raising the cheeks and gathering the skin inwards towards the nose. Paul Ekman's research has confirmed Duchenne's speculation that it is very difficult to control these eye muscles voluntarily, which is why it is very difficult to fake a genuine smile (Ekman et al., 1980). Thus, a genuine or Duchenne smile involves both the eyes and the lips. This type of smile is associated with a left-sided asymmetry in cerebral activity, which as we have seen is a neural marker of positive affect. Smiling with just the lips does not induce this type of neural asymmetry (Ekman et al., 1990).

The Duchenne smile does seem to be associated with genuine feelings of joy and happiness and those who smile more often have an enhanced SWB. As one illustration of this, an intriguing study has reported that women who demonstrated Duchenne smiles in their college yearbook reported higher levels of emotional and physical well-being over 30 years later than those whose smiles just involved the lips (Harker and Keltner, 2001). Thus, the experience of joy does appear to be associated with higher levels of SWB. It is difficult to determine how these results fit into the proposed relationships between positive emotions and SWB. If the spectrum model is correct, then of course we are measuring the same underlying concept at different extremes. However, it may be the case that experiences of happiness and joy are separable from SWB, and that the more frequent experience of joy causes a subsequent increase in overall SWB.

Several studies have shown that joy and happiness increase a person's openness to experience, and that, in turn, is associated with social interaction and the strengthening of social bonds (see Izard and Ackerman, 2000, for review). In particular, a person in whom mild positive affect has been induced tends to be more generous and helpful to others. For example, a series of studies in which happiness was induced by offering people a cookie or by praising them for their good performance on a task, found that the induction of happiness was associated with donating more money to a charity or being more helpful to a stranger who needed assistance (Isen, 1970; Isen and Levin, 1972).

The emotion of joy is strongly associated with the urge to play, which in turn is important in helping to develop lasting social bonds and attachments. Rough-and-tumble play is critical to many animal species because it enables individuals to learn the basic manoeuvres for hunting and other activities. Thus, play is essential for developing important survival skills as well providing the opportunity to learn how to interact with others successfully. Indeed, Panksepp has even suggested that 'youth may have evolved to give complex organisms time to play' (1998, p. 96).

The work of Alice Isen and her colleagues has also demonstrated that positive emotions such as joy have a beneficial effect on a variety of cognitive processes like creativity and problem solving (see Isen, 2000, for review). To illustrate, several experiments have shown that inducing a positive mood by asking people to watch a short comedy film or giving them a bag of candy leads to a significant increase in creativity on simple tasks such as finding word associates (Isen et al., 1985). Other research confirms that positive affect promotes creativity and innovation in a wide range of tasks, and also improves decision-making and negotiation skills. In general the induction of positive affect results in an increase in flexible thinking, which is also associated with improved problem-solving abilities (see Isen, 1999, 2000, for reviews). Most of these studies used some form of mood induction so it is difficult to know whether the specific discrete emotion of joy is critical or whether these effects are due to a more general positive affectivity. Nevertheless, it is clear that the emotion of joy and happiness and the general positive mood states are associated with enhanced social interactions and bonding, creativity and improved problem solving, all of which are associated with enhanced SWB.

Interest

Interest is a phenomenologically pleasant emotion – in other words, it feels good. We might question whether 'interest' is an emotion at all. Paul Ekman has argued that what he considers to be the crucial characteristics of emotions – automatic appraisal, commonalities in antecedent events, presence in other primates, quick onset, brief duration, unbidden occurrence, distinctive physiology, and distinctive signal – are likely to be present for a number of positive emotions including amusement, awe, contentment, interest and sensory pleasure. It should be noted, however, that he does not provide evidence for this, but rather suggests that the evidence will be found. Interest overlaps to a considerable extent with 'curiosity' 'wonder' and 'intrinsic motivation' (e.g., Deci, 1972) and plays an important role in generating the urge to explore the environment (Panksepp, 1998). This exploration is likely to ensure an individual's *engagement* with the environment and, as we have seen, engagement with one's surroundings is a key component of happiness (Seligman, 2002). Therefore, it is a reasonable hypothesis to assume that *interest* is associated with an enhancement in well-being and happiness by keeping the individual actively engaged with the environment.

Gratitude

Gratitude has been regarded for centuries as one of the most important manifestations of virtue. The teachings of most of the world's major religions are permeated with the concept of gratitude, usually encouraging their followers to be thankful to God and to demonstrate their thankfulness. Emotion scientists have also begun to turn their attention to the study of gratitude or the 'thankful state' (see Emmons, 2004). Following a comprehensive review of the psychological literature McCullough et al. (2001) concluded that the emotion of gratitude is experienced when people perceive themselves to be recipients of a benefit that was intentionally given to them. The emotional experience is most intense when people perceive that the benefit is valuable to the beneficiary and costly to the benefactor. Moreover, it was argued that the emotion of gratitude may be associated with an action tendency to contribute in the future to the welfare of the benefactor. Thus, an important function of gratitude might be to facilitate social cohesion by means of encouraging reciprocity. It should be noted that this aspect assumes that gratitude is an enduring state, closer to a mood state than an emotion. Some researchers have assumed that gratitude may also be an even more enduring personality trait. For example, a number of self-report instruments have been developed to measure gratitude as a personality trait. The Gratitude Questionnaire (GQ-6), shown in Table 10.2, has good psychometric properties (McCullough et al., 2002).

A number of studies have found evidence to suggest that gratitude as a temporary mood state may play an important role in facilitating pro-social behaviour. To illustrate, study participants were randomly assigned to one of two experimental conditions. In the gratitude condition they were led to believe that they had been helped by another person (who voluntarily shared winnings with them). However, in the other condition, even though they received the same amount of money, they were told that the reward was received by chance (Tsang, 2006). When study participants were later asked to share their money with other participants more winnings were donated to the perceived benefactor in the gratitude condition. One potential problem in interpreting these results, however, is that the study participants may simply have felt more indebted to the benefactor. This seems unlikely, however, as another study has found that gratitude effects are not only directed towards perceived benefactors.

TABLE 10.2 The Gratitude Questionnaire (GQ-6)

For each question the level of agreement is rated on a 1-7 scale with 1 being 'strongly disagree' and 7 being 'strongly agree' while 4 is 'neutral'.

Statement	*Rating*
I have so much in life to be thankful for right now	1 – 2 – 3 – 4 – 5 – 6 – 7
If I had to list everything that I felt grateful for at the moment, it would be a very long list	1 – 2 – 3 – 4 – 5 – 6 – 7
When I look at the world right now, I don't see much to be grateful for	1 – 2 – 3 – 4 – 5 – 6 – 7
As I get older I find myself more able to appreciate the people, events, and situations that have been part of my life history	1 – 2 – 3 – 4 – 5 – 6 – 7
Long amounts of time go by before I feel grateful to something or someone	1 – 2 – 3 – 4 – 5 – 6 – 7

Source: McCullough et al. (2002).

To illustrate, Bartlett and DeSteno (2006) induced gratitude by having a confederate of the experimenter help the participant to fix his/her computer, thus avoiding having to repeat a long and boring task. In the amusement condition, participants and the confederate watched and briefly discussed a funny video clip and in the neutral condition the confederate and participant engaged in a brief neutral conversation. In a different context, the confederate then asked each participant to help fill out a long and tedious questionnaire. Those in the gratitude condition were more likely to help relative to those in either the amusement or the neutral condition. A second experiment demonstrated that this extended to helping a complete stranger. Thus, the induction of gratitude seems to facilitate pro-social behaviour in the moment (Bartlett and DeSteno, 2006; Tsang, 2006). These findings indicate that an important function of gratitude is to aid in the ongoing construction of social relationships.

A particularly interesting finding in the study reported by Barlett and DeSteno (2006) was the demonstration that the induction of amusement, which is another positive emotion, did not have significant effects on pro-social behaviour. In other words, feeling good did not induce pro-social behaviour whereas feeling grateful did. It seems that receiving help from someone else makes us more likely to help others. This might be why, if someone lets you into a traffic queue, you are more likely to let another person enter. This may be due to the attributions associated with gratitude (e.g., attributing positive events to the intervention of others) and/or the modelling effect of others' generous behaviour influencing our own. Thus, the social nature of gratitude may be crucial to the effects on pro-social behaviour. If so, gratitude would be expected to differ from some other positive emotions such as pride in which the associated attributions are about one's own value and achievements.

Other studies have shown that the experience of gratitude is related to enhanced feelings of general well-being, For example, scores on the GQ-6 correlate highly with scores on the Satisfaction with Life Scale ($r = 0.53$, McCullough et al., 2002). Such correlations, however, do not tell us whether the relationship is causal, nor (if it is) in which direction. Some evidence for a causal relationship comes from findings that people who maintained a daily record of things they felt grateful for reported several positive effects, including an increased willingness to help those around them, enhanced levels of alertness, enthusiasm, determination, attentiveness and energy compared to those who wrote down lists of daily hassles (Emmons and McCullough, 2003). In addition, those who kept a weekly record of things to be grateful for reported that they took more regular exercise, were less prone to physical illness, displayed more optimism in relation to the coming week and generally reported a higher degree of SWB than participants in the control condition.

The experience of gratitude also has a range of cognitive effects. For example, it has been reported that when measured as a personality trait, gratitude was associated with a positive memory bias. Those who were higher on the grateful trait were more likely to recall positive life events than those who scored lower on this trait (see Watkins, 2004). Watkins (2004) has proposed that grateful individuals are more likely to count their blessings and that this leads to a greater accessibility of positive affective events in their memories. This ease of retrieval of positive information leads to a positive

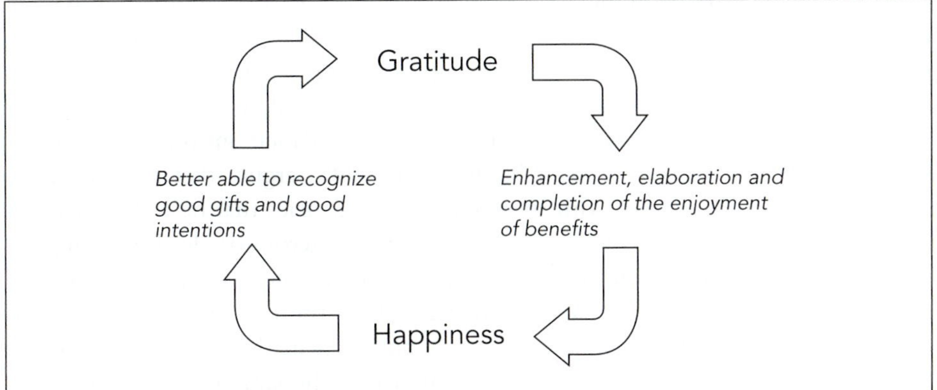

FIGURE 10.7 The adaptive cycle of gratitude and happiness

Source: Watkins (2004).

loop (Isen et al., 1978) or what might be called a 'cycle of virtue' (Watkins, 2004), which ensures that feelings of gratitude lead to feelings of happiness that in turn lead to feelings of gratitude. This cycle is illustrated in Figure 10.7 and demonstrates that the causal link between gratitude and SWB is likely to go in both directions.

It seems that gratitude has a number of positive effects on pro-social behaviour and feeling good, and may play an important role in strengthening social bonds and facilitating reciprocation of favours. As noted by Watkins (2004), it is important for researchers to try and establish more clearly whether the effects of gratitude act over and above the general effects of positive affect (or positive emotions). Typically, positive affect is induced by presenting study participants with an unexpected gift (e.g., Isen et al., 1978) and therefore it is not clear whether it is gratitude or positive emotions more generally that are associated with SWB. In terms of pro-social behaviour, however, it seems that gratitude does have effects over and above amusement (Bartlett and DeSteno, 2006).

Fredrickson's broaden-and-build hypothesis

Barbara Fredrickson has drawn upon a number of earlier theories (e.g., Tomkins, 1962; Izard, 1977) to define the functions of a range of positive emotions including joy, interest, contentment, and gratitude (e.g., Fredrickson, 1998, 2004). The overarching assumption is that positive emotions have been selected by evolutionary pressures to facilitate social interactions and cohesiveness, and there is growing evidence for this perspective. It is interesting to note that social interaction with friends and family is one of the most important determinants of happiness (Myers, 2000), and this might provide an important link between the experience of positive emotions and enhanced SWB.

Positive emotions have been shown to have a range of benefits for human health and well-being. Thus, people who express positive emotions are better able to cope with chronic stress (Folkman, 1997), are less likely to suffer from a stroke in older age (Ostir et al., 2001), and those who express the most positive emotions even seem to live longer (Danner et al., 2001). The broaden-and-build theory of positive emotions explains these correlations on the assumption that positive emotions *broaden* an individual's momentary thought-action repertoires, which allows them to then *build* a variety of personal resources that facilitate long-term adaptation to adverse circumstances (Fredrickson, 1998, 2001). Fredrickson (1998) argues that most negative emotions are tightly coupled with specific action tendencies that help the organism survive. However, positive emotions rarely occur in dangerous or life-threatening situations. Instead, they generally occur when people are in safe environments. In these situations, the narrow attentional focus that facilitates the fast and instant reactions that are characteristic of negative emotions is not particularly useful. On the other hand, positive emotions broaden a person's patterns of thinking so that the cognitive context is effectively enlarged (Isen, 1987). The proposal is that this broader mindset allows people to build personal resources for the future, ensuring that positive emotions have long-term adaptive benefits (Fredrickson, 1998).

Empirical evidence for the broaden hypothesis comes from numerous demonstrations that positive emotions have specific effects on cognitive processing, making people more open to new ideas and more flexible and creative in their thinking (see Isen, 2000, for review). More recent evidence, from a study in which a video clip producing positive emotions resulted in a more global perceptual bias than a neutral video clip, suggests that positive emotions do indeed broaden attentional focus (Fredrickson and Branigan, 2005). An important point is that all positive emotions are thought to produce comparable broadening effects relative to neutral states, even though several positive emotions are distinct at a subjective level (Fredrickson and Branigan, 2005).

Fredrickson (2004) has proposed that positive emotions generate an upward spiral that is opposite to the downward spiral that occurs in depression. In this way, the broaden-and-build theory of positive emotions provides a mechanism through which the experience of positive emotions can have a marked impact on improving subjective well-being. For example, in one study students were assessed at two time-points five weeks apart in terms of their experience of positive emotions and what was called 'broad-minded coping' (Fredrickson and Joiner, 2002). When the initial level of positive emotions was controlled statistically, higher initial levels of broad-minded coping were found to predict an increase in positive emotions from Time 1 to Time 2. The converse was also found. When the initial degree of broad-minded coping was controlled, the initial level of positive emotions predicted improvements in broad-minded coping from Time 1 to Time 2. These findings indicate that there is a reciprocal relationship between positive emotions and broad-minded coping in which they mutually build upon each other and result in an upward spiral towards enhanced subjective well-being (Fredrickson and Joiner, 2002).

Thus, the broaden-and-build theory explains how positive emotions play a vital role in transforming people, making them more effective and creative as well as more socially integrated and healthy. Positive emotions are assumed to boost well-being by the mechanism of broadening cognitive processes. Thus, this is very much a causal model suggesting that positive emotions can directly and indirectly lead to enhanced well-being. The pattern of results is, of course, also compatible with the spectrum model that assumes that positive emotions and SWB are at opposite ends of a continuum.

NEUROBIOLOGICAL MECHANISMS

The neurotransmitter dopamine (DA) seems to play an important role in the brain's reward system and, therefore, we would expect DA to be important for the experience of positive emotions. It has been found that those who report higher levels of E-PA have increased levels of DA activity compared to people with low levels of E-PA (Depue and Collins, 1999). It has also been argued that many of the effects of positive mood states on cognitive functioning may be attributed to the activation of the DA system (Ashby et al., 1999). To illustrate, it is known that DA is released into the parts of the ACC that are thought to play a role in flexible thinking skills. People with Parkinson's disease have reduced levels of DA in these areas and are also characterized by difficulties in shifting from one cognitive 'set' to another (e.g., Owen et al., 1993). In other words, low levels of DA are associated with a decrease in cognitive flexibility, while higher levels are associated with increased cognitive flexibility. Therefore, the release of DA that occurs during positive mood states might explain the increase in flexible thinking and general improvements in problem-solving abilities that are produced by such positive states (Ashby et al., 1999).

This is an area that requires a lot more work and it is likely that the links between positive affective states and neurotransmitter systems are complex. For example, we have already seen that DA does not seem to play a role in liking something, but is particularly important for wanting something (Berridge, 2003). Clearly, 'wanting' is an important component of positive affect, but 'liking' seems to be more similar to the feelings expressed when positive mood states are induced.

In addition to neurotransmitter systems that are likely to underlie positive affect, we have also discussed evidence throughout this book that a left-sided cortical asymmetry is also a neural marker of positive affect (e.g., Davidson, 1993, 1998a). In support of this, strong patterns of correlation have been reported between frontal EEG asymmetry and self-reported well-being. Specifically, base-line measures of a left-sided asymmetry were strong predictors of enhanced well-being in a group of adults (Urry et al., 2004). There is a growing body of evidence that specific patterns of neural activity are likely to be indicative of enhanced well-being. For example, the capacity to regulate negative emotions, that is often implemented in the brain by the suppression of subcortical structures (e.g., amygdala) by the PFC, is likely to provide a potential index of well-being. While much more work is required there is some evidence for this hypothesis (see Davidson, 2004, for discussion). For example, evidence for the hypothesis that well-being is related to more effective top-down regulation of the amygdala has been reported (van Reekum et al., 2007). As shown in Figure 10.8, when participants were required to evaluate negative (versus neutral) material people with a high degree of self-reported well-being were able to recruit areas of the ACC more effectively. This activation of the cortical areas was associated with a reduced

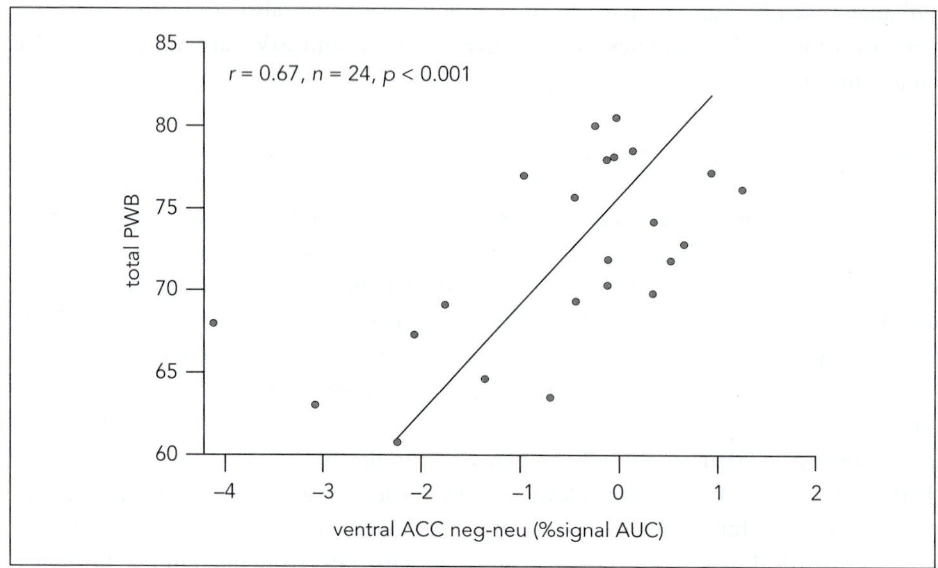

FIGURE 10.8 Activity in the ventral portion of the ACC in response to negative images is positively associated with total psychological well-being (PWB) scores

Source: van Reekum et al. (2007).

activation in the amygdala to aversive stimuli. There is a clear need for more detailed research on the neural correlates of positive emotions and moods. A reliable neural marker of well-being would be of great benefit to happiness research because neural indicators should not be subject to the problems of judgement biases that are always an issue with subjective assessment.

Are there interventions that can increase happiness?

One of the implications of hedonic adaptation theory is that it may be very difficult to permanently change a person's underlying level of happiness. If there really is a set-point to which people revert following even major life events, then perhaps it will not be possible to develop intervention strategies to help people achieve a better level of well-being. However, Lucas (2007a, b) has presented evidence that certain life events do seem to result in more enduring and fundamental shifts in happiness. Martin Seligman and his colleagues have also reported the results of a randomized double-blind placebo-controlled trial to assess whether specific interventions can lead to ongoing changes in self-reported happiness (Seligman et al., 2005). Using a sample recruited on the internet they randomly assigned people to do one of five exercises and then measured happiness and depression scores for up to three months following the intervention. The five exercises are listed in Table 10.3. The results showed that the gratitude exercise produced the largest changes in happiness and this effect lasted for up to one month. However, by three months these participants were no happier than the placebo controls. The 'using signature strengths' and 'three good things' conditions produced an increase in happiness and a decrease in depression scores for up to six

TABLE 10.3 Intervention exercises given by Seligman et al. (2005) in a randomized placebo-controlled trial to increase happiness

Exercise	*Description*
Placebo control: Early memories	Participants were asked to write about early memories every night for one week
Gratitude visit	During the week, participants had to write a letter of gratitude to someone who had been kind to them but had never been properly thanked. They then had to deliver the letter in person.
Three good things in life	Participants had to write down three things that went well each day for a week.
You at your best	Participants were asked to write about a time when they were at their best. They were also asked to reflect on the personal strengths displayed in the story.
Using signature strengths in a new way	Participants were asked to take an inventory of character strengths on-line and then to use one of their top strengths in a new way each day for one week.
Identifying signature strengths	This was a shortened version of the previous exercise. Participants were asked to take the inventory, to identify their top five strengths and to use them more often during the week.

Source: Seligman et al. (2005).

months when compared to placebo. Interestingly, many participants continued their exercises beyond the initial one-week period and this had a strong effect on keeping happiness scores high over the longer term. There are a number of potential problems with this intervention study, as acknowledged by the authors. One is the likelihood that many of the participants were mildly depressed and motivated to try and become happier. Thus, it is not clear whether these results would extend to the wider population. Nevertheless, this study provides an important first step in determining whether straightforward happiness interventions might be useful on a larger scale to enhance the level of general well-being.

In another interesting study, Richard Davidson and his colleagues addressed the question of whether repeated practice in the techniques of emotion regulation would lead to more enduring changes in patterns of neural activation (Davidson, Kabat-Zinn et al., 2003). Participants were randomly assigned to either a mindfulness-based mediation training programme that had been shown to be of benefit in emotion regulation or a wait-list control condition. Measures of prefrontal activation were measured by EEG both before the training programme began and then again 8 weeks later. The meditation group showed larger increases in left-sided prefrontal activation compared to the control participants, suggesting a higher degree of positive affect. More remarkably, following the 8-week study all participants were given an influenza vaccine and the number of antibodies produced was measured. A greater number of antibodies indicates better functioning of the immune system. The results clearly showed that those who had undergone meditation training had a stronger immune response than the control participants (see Figure 10.9). Thus, these findings demonstrate that training procedures designed to enhance subjective well-being and happiness resulted in strong changes in patterns of brain activity as well as improvement in immune functioning (Davidson, 2004; Davidson, Kabat-Zinn et al., 2003). These results are important in demonstrating a potential mechanism by which positive affect and well-being may play a role in improving both physical and mental health.

Transcendence and spirituality

A range of factors are clearly important in enhancing well-being and happiness. Having friends and social networks, expressing gratitude towards others are all ways that we can increase our happiness. However, philosophers and religious leaders have long argued that to experience a deeper level of well-being or self-actualization requires more than this. To be truly happy, we need to transcend the material and social world. For example, Karl Jaspers (1951) has argued that *wisdom* is different from *reason*, and that to be truly wise we need to be *transcendent*. Robert Cloninger (2004) explains Jaspers' view as follows (p. 25)

> we are transcendent when we allow ourselves to be spontaneously aware of the universal unity and freedom inherent in being in the world, thereby giving rise to love and faith in what transcends our transient material existence

In other words, an appreciation of the wider universe and a sense of spirituality or God are considered vital to true happiness.

Cloninger (2004) reviews a wide range of evidence from philosophy, psychology, psychiatry, neurobiology and theology to develop a more comprehensive science of well-being. He argues that three personal traits are essential for well-being: self-directedness, cooperativeness and self-transcendence. *Self-directedness* can be developed by learning to become calm, accepting one's limitations and letting go of everyday fears and conflict. *Cooperativeness* can be developed by increasing a sense of mindfulness and working in the service of others. Finally, people can learn to become *self-transcendent* by growing in self-awareness of the perspectives that produce negative emotions and limit their experience of them. By developing all three of these traits, it is argued that people can truly flourish and live the good life (Cloninger, 2004). Cloninger argues that psychology and psychiatry have been limited by focusing only on the psychological or neurological levels of analysis. Only by incorporating the biological, social, psychological and spiritual dimensions of life can people really experience an enhanced sense of well-being.

We do not have the space to do justice to Cloninger's views here, but his book *Feeling Good: The Science of Well-Being* provides a comprehensive introduction to the view that a science of well-being requires a new way of looking at ourselves and our relation to the world and other people. The central argument is that we need to cast off the dualistic notions that are characteristic of science and develop a more holistic approach to well-being and happiness. To achieve this, we need to develop a coherence of personality that only comes from developing a sense of self-awareness. As illustrated in Figure 10.10, the upward spiral of self-awareness leading to well-being, wisdom and creativity occurs when three conditions are met.

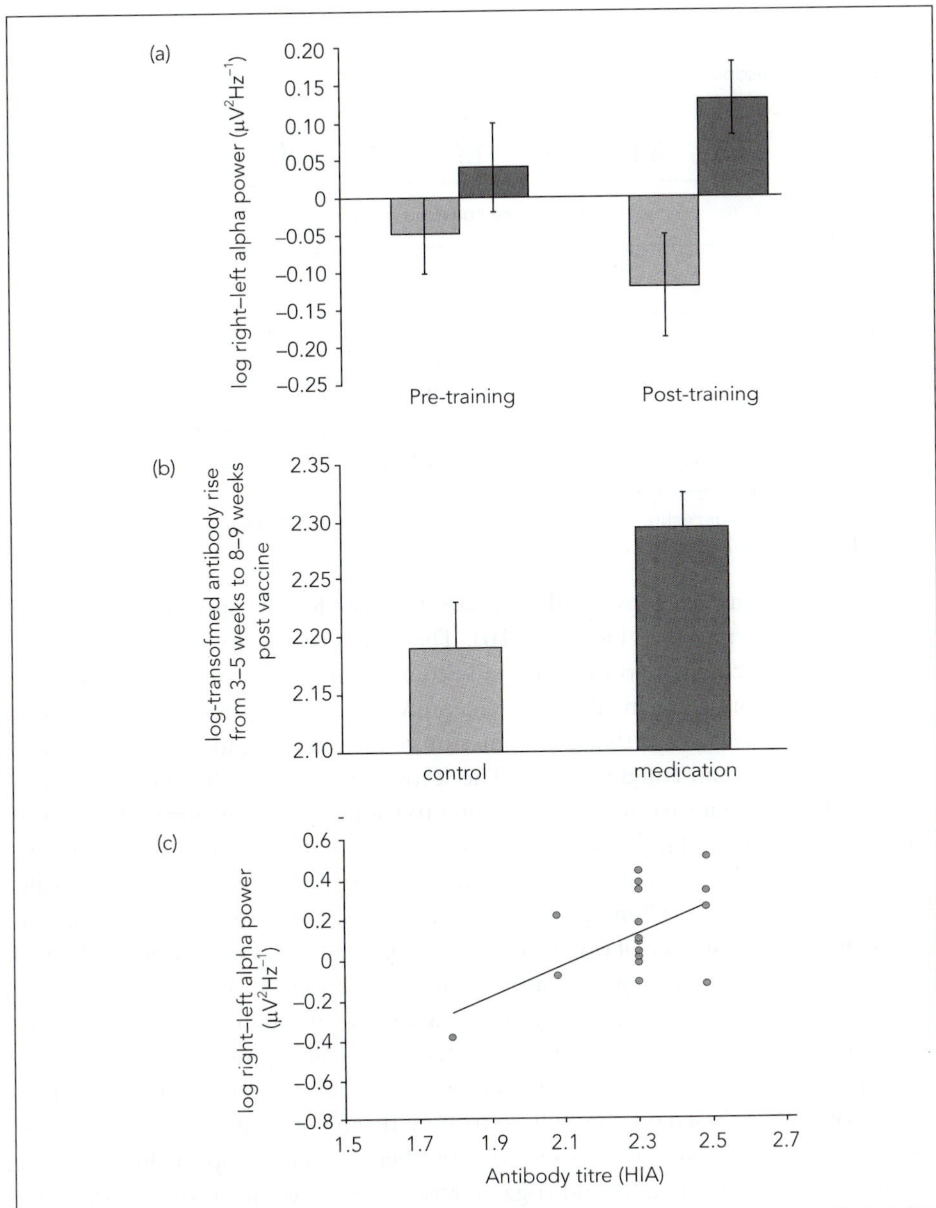

FIGURE 10.9 Changes in patterns of neural activation resulting from repeated practice of emotion regulation techniques

(a) Pre- and post-training brain asymmetry measures from participants in the meditation and control groups. Positive numbers denote greater left-sided activation and negative numbers denote greater right-sided activation.

(b) Differences between the meditation and control groups in antibody titres in response to influenza vaccine.

(c) The relation between pre- to post-test increases in left-sided activation and rise in antibody titres to influenza vaccine among participants in the meditation group only.

Source: Davidson, Kabat-Zinn et al. (2003).

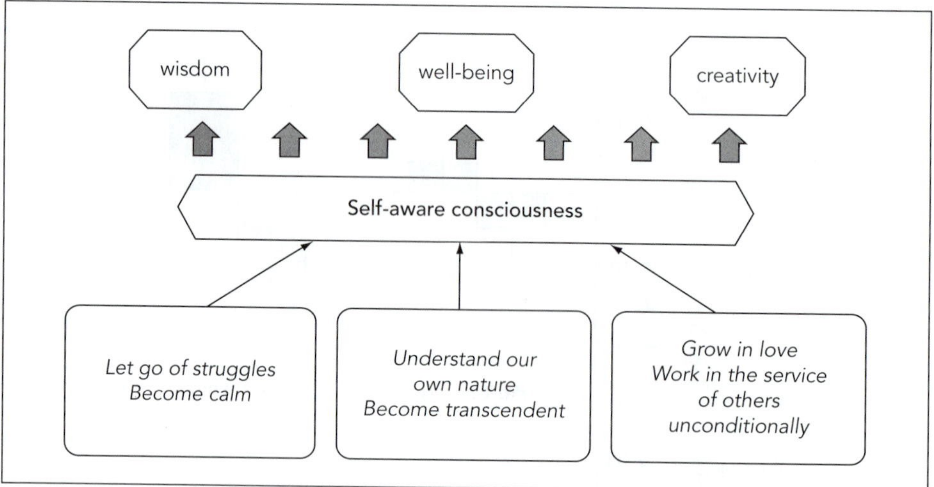

FIGURE 10.10 Cloninger's three necessary conditions for growth in self-awareness, leading spontaneously to well-being, wisdom and creativity

Three conditions are considered necessary to allow for the spontaneous upward spiral of self-awareness (see Figure 10.10). The first is the ability to let go of internal struggles and conflicts so that we can become calm and not resist the order and coherence that is inherent in all things (the unity of nature). When we let go of our struggles the valence of all things becomes more pleasurable and we become more open to new ideas and enlightenment. The second condition is the necessity of trying to understand our own nature. According to Cloninger, the dualistic elements of blaming, criticizing and judging are detrimental to growth in awareness. Instead, we need to become transcendent so that we can face the truth inherent in reality. Finally, in order to grow in love, Cloninger argues that we need to be free of prior conditioning and work in the service of others in an unconditional way. Only by unconditional service can we develop a deep compassion and unconditional love for others.

It is clear that Cloninger is setting out an ambitious programme to achieve well-being and wisdom that incorporates elements of spirituality, philosophy and science. Interestingly, many treatment strategies designed to treat depression and other emotional problems are based on mindfulness training that incorporates many of these notions. For example, mindfulness-based cognitive behavioural therapy includes a range of simple breathing techniques and yoga exercises to help people become more aware of the present moment by becoming more aware of moment-to-moment changes in their minds and bodies. This type of therapy has been successful in helping people to become more self-aware and transcendent (e.g., Teasdale et al., 2000). Creswell et al. (2007) have also reported that people differ in terms of 'dispositional mindfulness'. In an fMRI study they found that the more 'mindful' people were, the more effectively they were able to recruit areas of the PFC when categorizing affective stimuli. In particular, when mindful people were processing negative stimuli there was greater activation of the PFC and a reduced bilateral activation of the amygdala. This suggests that mindfulness and mindfulness meditation might be able to increase positive affect and well-being by strengthening the neural mechanisms underlying the regulation of negative affect. Mindfulness meditation especially in association with cognitive behavioural therapy holds promise as an intervention to help people to reach their full potential.

Robert Cloninger is also developing what he calls *coherence therapy*, which is based on the principles illustrated in Figure 10.10. While it is very difficult to operationalize many of the notions put forward in this system of coherence, it is clearly important to try and develop a more comprehensive understanding of how human beings can reach their full potential in a holistic way (i.e., spirituality, biology, psychology, social integration). By combining lessons learned from ancient spiritual systems such as Buddhism, with modern psychology and neuroscience perhaps we can begin to truly understand what makes us healthy and happy.

CHAPTER SUMMARY

In this chapter, a range of evidence looking at the determinants of both *resilience* and *well-being* was discussed. It is clear that both psychology and neuroscience have tended to focus almost exclusively on negative affect and disorders until relatively recently. However, there is now an acknowledgement that it is vitally important to understand the factors leading to wisdom, happiness, creativity, spirituality and the more positive side of human nature. Progress is being made in understanding the *subjective* aspects of human happiness and well-being, while a growing research literature is also examining the cognitive and neural correlates of happiness. The bringing together of spiritual, scientific and social views on human happiness is providing an exciting framework for future developments in this area.

RECOMMENDED READING

There are a number of excellent books now available that give an overview of the various developments within the scientific study of happiness and well-being. These include:

Robert Cloninger (2004) *Feeling Good: The Science of Well-being*. Oxford: Oxford University Press.

Daniel Gilbert (2006) *Stumbling on Happiness*. New York: Random House.

Richard Layard (2005) *Happiness: Lessons from a New Science*. New York: Penguin.

David Myers (1993) *The Pursuit of Happiness. Who is Happy and Why?*. New York: Harper Paperbacks.

Martin Seligman (2002) *Authentic Happiness*. New York: Free Press.

There are also a number of edited books that give a more academic overview of the research on well-being and happiness. These include:

Daniel Kahneman, Edward Diener and Norman Schwarz (1999) (eds) *Well-being: The Foundations of Hedonic Psychology*. New York: Russell Sage Foundation.

C. Keyes and J. Haidt (2003) (eds) *Flourishing: Positive Psychology and the Life Well Lived*. Washington, DC: American Psychological Association.

Finally, more detailed articles on the subjective aspects of well-being as well as the neural correlates of well-being are as follows:

Richard J. Davidson (2004) 'Well-being and affective style: Neural substrates and biobehavioural correlates', *Philosophical Transactions of the Royal Society*, 359, 1395–411.

Ed Diener, Shigehiro Oishi and Richard E. Lucas (2003) 'Personality, culture, and subjective well-being: Emotional and cognitive evaluations of life', *Annual Review of Psychology*, 54, 403–25.

Ed Diener, Richard E. Lucas and Christie Napa Scollon (2006) 'Beyond the hedonic treadmill: Revising the adaptation theory of well-being', *American Psychologist*, 61, 305–14.

11 THEORETICAL OVERVIEW AND SUMMARY

KEY ASPECTS OF EMOTION SCIENCE

Chapters 1 to 10 have considered empirical evidence and theory from a wide range of areas within emotion science. What are the salient features of the discipline and what conclusions can be drawn? Six key features have emerged from this overview, which has been drawn primarily from cognitive and neuroscientific approaches to emotion science.

- Affect is a pervasive part of our lives.
- Emotions, emotion schemas, moods, feelings and temperament are different aspects of affect.
- Affect can be studied at different levels of analysis.
- Affect recruits a wide range of both cortical and subcortical brain regions.
- Individual differences are important.
- The study of normal emotion and disordered emotion can inform each other

Affect is a pervasive part of our lives

It is clear that the affective life of human beings is rich and varied. It pervades every aspect of our lives. Most of our experiences and memories are marked by the *valence* of situations – we tend to remember the good times and the bad times – while the mundane often fades into insignificance. Thus, emotions, moods and especially conscious feelings are important markers of the main events of our lives. It is not surprising then that the inability to regulate these affective states, as occurs in emotional disorders, can have devastating consequences. Conversely, the capacity to regularly experience positive emotions and moods is an important component of our subjective well-being and happiness. The widespread role of affect in influencing a range of processes such as attention, memory and decision-making (see Davidson et al., 2003; Forgas, 2001, for reviews) suggests that mainstream cognitive psychology and cognitive neuroscience need to take affect into account. Indeed, in proposing a new paradigm for emotion science, Izard (2007) has argued that there is no such thing as an affectless mind – instead 'discrete emotions are always present in the human mind and always an influence in cognition and action' (p. 269). While the role of affect is increasingly being recognized in contemporary cognitive psychology and neuroscience there remain many who ignore the potential importance of emotions and mood states in cognition. The evidence reviewed in this book suggests that this is a mistake.

Emotions, emotion schemas, moods, feelings and temperament are different aspects of affect

The elements or components of affective life (e.g., emotions, emotion schemas, moods, feeling, and temperament) have often been conflated in emotion science. The use of different terms to refer to the same phenomenon or the same term to refer to different phenomena has led to confusion and misunderstandings in many parts of the discipline. Luckily, a consensus seems to be gradually emerging regarding the use of terminology (e.g., Humrichouse et al., 2007; Watson, 2000). I have tried to be consistent in the use of these terms throughout this book. Thus, the term *affect* is used as an overarching concept that incorporates both emotions and moods. While there is no general agreement on a definition of *emotion*, an emotion has been conceptualized as a rapid and short-lived response to a significant event that involves the coordination of a set of components such as bodily response; feeling state; cognitive appraisal (Scherer, 2001). For many emotion scientists, *basic emotions* are few in number and given to us by nature. They can be distinguished from *non-basic emotions*, which are sometimes referred to as *emotion schemas* (Izard, 1977, but see Feldman Barrett, 2006a, for an alternative view). These non-basic emotions are mental representations that combine affective and cognitive components. In other words, an emotion schema can integrate components of basic emotions with complex appraisals and cognitive biases. These complex emotion–cognitive interactions then form part of more general regulatory and motivational systems (Izard, 1977, 2007). Carol Izard (2007) has argued that much of the confusion in emotion science arises because many cognitive appraisal theorists have referred to emotion schemas as emotions (e.g., Ellsworth and Scherer, 2003).

Both basic emotions and emotion schemas can be distinguished from *moods*, which occur over a longer duration and can be seen as a type of *objectless core affect* (e.g., Russell, 2003) or as *an emotion that is extended over time* (Damasio, 1999; Izard, 1977). Many researchers argue that the function of moods is different from emotions in that they allow us to interpret how we are doing in life in a more general way (e.g., Lazarus, 1991; Morris, 1992; Prinz, 2004).

Feeling states are probably best seen as the conscious representations of emotions and moods. Many assume that basic emotions are associated with specific feeling states (e.g., Izard, 1977; Panksepp, 1998), while it has also been suggested that feelings form a core component of emotion schemas. Others argue that feelings are the conscious reflection of more general affective dimensions relating to valence and arousal (e.g., Feldman Barrett, 2006b; Russell, 1980). It is interesting that, while most people readily claim that feelings of *anger*, *sadness* and *fear* are easily distinguished, it seems that people find it difficult to get beyond general descriptions of valence (positive–negative) and arousal (low–high intensity). It may well be the case that language is not fine-tuned enough to make these subtle distinctions, which might nevertheless play an important role in affect. Since basic emotions evolved long before language it is possible that they are associated with specific feeling states but that language cannot provide an adequate description of these states. The evidence that direct brain stimulation can result in distinguishable feeling states supports this view (e.g., Shapira et al., 2006).

Finally, *temperament* refers to more enduring, perhaps life-long, dispositions to act in particular ways. While there are many views of temperament and personality traits there is reasonable consensus that there are a small set of broad temperamental dimensions relating to *Neuroticism-Negative Affectivity (N-NA)*, *Extraversion-Positive Affectivity (E-PA)*, and a third regulatory system (*disinhibition* versus *constraint*) that determines how both N-NA and E-PA are experienced and expressed (e.g., Clark, 2005). These broad dimensions are considered to be innate, and a number of different personality traits may emerge from their interactions with different environmental events. The overall affective tone of a person's life is likely to be the result of many complex interactions between temperamental dispositions, life experiences, experiences of different emotions, emotion schemas, and moods. While there may not be complete agreement on the definition of these components, it is important for emotion science to keep them apart in research studies, and for emotion scientists to take great care in defining exactly what they mean by the various terms. In particular, it would be useful if a common language could be implemented to avoid the type of confusions and misunderstandings that have happened in the past.

Affect can be studied at different levels of analysis

Emotion scientists have tended to focus primarily on a *single* level of analysis (e.g., activity of groups of neurons; expressive response; subjective experience) and then generalize findings from this level of analysis to all levels. These multiple levels undoubtedly relate to each other in complex ways and theories within emotion science are likely to progress more coherently if multiple levels of analysis are taken into account. Research focused on understanding the nature of the relationships between the different levels would seem to be particularly important for future progress. A number of multi-level theories of emotion–cognition interactions are now available (e.g., Teasdale and Barnard, 1993) and this issue will be examined in more detail in a later section (p. 366).

Affect recruits a wide range of both cortical and subcortical brain regions

A clear implication of the research discussed in this book is that emotions, moods and feelings recruit large and interconnected regions of the brain (and the body). It is almost certainly not the case that emotions are primarily subcortical (e.g., Panksepp, 1998). While subcortical regions are important, a number of cortical areas are also crucial (e.g., Rolls, 2005). In particular, the evidence suggests that neural circuits linking subcortical regions with cortical regions are especially important for the expression and experience of emotions and moods (Amaral and Price, 1990). This issue will be discussed in more detail in a later section.

Individual differences are important

The evidence discussed in this book demonstrates that there are strong individual differences in both emotional reactivity and emotion perception. People differ in consistent ways in terms of how they *react* to affective situations, and they also differ in terms of how they *attend* to, *interpret*, and *remember* different types of information. These cognitive biases and differences in reactivity are important determinants of affective experiences. While there is a large literature examining individual differences in both emotional response (Chapter 3) and emotion perception (Chapter 8), these differences are often ignored by cognitive psychologists and neuroscientists. However, the evidence indicates that individual differences are a fundamental component of emotion science, and should be taken into account in all studies examining emotion, mood and feelings.

The study of normal emotion and disordered emotion can inform each other

Traditionally, there has been a separation between studies of normal emotion and studies of emotional disorders, but this is changing to some extent. Hopefully, the growing evidence from basic science on the nature of both positive and negative emotional states may inform treatment strategies and clinical practice. In addition, a deeper understanding of the nature of emotional disorders is also likely to inform our understanding of normal emotional states. There have been a number of attempts to relate basic emotion science to psychopathology and clinical practice (see Craske et al., 2006; Rottenberg and Johnson, 2007, for overviews). It is hoped that future research and theoretical developments will allow closer links to be forged between the various disciplines. It is important to the development of emotion science for researchers in both clinical practice and basic science to be aware of each others' research, and for theoretical developments to provide more comprehensive frameworks to allow a closer bridging between the two endeavours.

It is obvious from the foregoing chapters that emotion science is a vibrant subject area. In this concluding chapter, I would like to re-assess Richard Davidson's 'seven sins' in the study of emotion Following this, I would like to highlight a number of important issues that would seem to be critical for the future development of emotion science. The first relates to the importance of acknowledging a *multiple levels of analysis approach.* The second relates to ways in which emotion scientists can *integrate* research at genetic, neurobiological, cognitive and social levels. Related to this, is the third issue of how we can provide better bridges or *translations* between theory in basic emotion science and clinical practice.

SEVEN SINS IN THE STUDY OF EMOTION

Davidson (2003) identified seven sins in the study of emotion and argued that developments in the emerging discipline of affective neuroscience could correct many of them. Following our overview of many different areas in the study of affect it is interesting to re-assess whether emotion scientists are still committing these sins and

TABLE 11.1 The seven sins in the study of emotion identified by Davidson (2003)

Sin 1	Affect and cognition are subserved by separate and independent neural circuits
Sin 2	Affect is subcortical
Sin 3	Emotions are in the head
Sin 4	Emotions can be studied from a purely psychological perspective
Sin 5	Emotions are similar in structure across both age and species
Sin 6	Specific emotions are instantiated in discrete locations in the brain
Sin 7	Emotions are conscious feeling states

whether new sins can be added to the list. The seven sins highlighted in 2003 are shown in Table 11.1.

Sin 1 is the assumption by some researchers that *affect* and *cognition* can be separated in the brain. While it is often easier to discuss affect and cognition as if they are separate systems, the evidence presented in this book shows that each of these domains is:

(a) made up of many subcomponents, and
(b) deeply integrated at neural levels.

In agreement with Davidson's original conclusion, there is now even more evidence that emotion is not a single system or process. Instead, it comprises many different processes and subcomponents that are instantiated in a widely distributed network of both subcortical and cortical neural circuits (e.g., Phelps, 2006, for review). These neuroanatomical facts cannot be ignored and indicate that affective and cognitive processes involve many different and overlapping brain regions.

This leads us on to the second sin: the assumption that affect is primarily subcortical. We have seen throughout this book that investigators examining emotions in rodents often adopt this view (e.g., Panksepp, 1998, 2007). There is no doubt that subcortical structures are critically important for a range of affective states. Nobody would argue, for example, that the amygdala is not important for a range of emotional behaviours, especially those relating to fear responses in both animals and humans (Phelps and LeDoux, 2005, for review). Damage to the amygdala in humans also leads to widespread deficits in the recognition of fear in others, as well as affecting the subjective experience of fear (Calder et al., 2001, for review). Thus, subcortical structures, such as the amygdala and nucleus accumbens, are clearly important for emotion.

Nevertheless, it is also important to acknowledge that there is abundant evidence that damage to *cortical* areas in humans and other primates can lead to profound deficits in the experience and expression of emotion (e.g., Damasio, 1999; Rolls, 2005). Likewise, many neuroimaging studies demonstrate that emotions activate a wide network of both subcortical and cortical areas (Berridge, 2003). Thus, the assumption that 'emotions are subcortical' clearly remains a sin. In addition, however, the view that 'emotions are cortical' should also be considered a sin. The range of evidence discussed in this book makes it clear that *both* subcortical and cortical areas are involved in affect. In particular, the evidence indicates that specific *subcortical-cortical circuits* are crucial for both the expression and the regulation of emotion. The notion that cognition and emotion are separate systems located in cortical and subcortical areas, respectively, is clearly wrong. Instead, cognitive and affective processes are implemented across a range of linked subcortical-cortical circuits.

While there is no doubt that we share many ancient emotional systems with all other species (e.g., Panksepp, 1998, 2007), it is also true that the rapid and extensive expansion of the cortical area in the human brain has resulted in profound changes in how emotions are implemented in the brain (e.g., Feldman Barrett et al., 2007; Berridge, 2003). The density and importance of subcortical-cortical circuits, for example, play a much stronger role in human affect when compared with rodents. The ability of cortical areas to inhibit subcortical activity gives far greater room for emotion regulation in higher primates, especially humans. It seems likely that these interconnections have changed the experience and the expressions of emotions, moods and feelings, as well as modifying the role of subcortical structures. A clearer understanding of how these circuits and connections develop and operate is likely to lead to a better understanding of affect, especially as it is implemented in the human brain.

The third sin is the assumption that emotions are entirely in the head. Many cognitive psychologists and neuroscientists have been guilty of ignoring the role of the body in emotions. Psychophysiological research, however, has shown that a range of peripheral processes is critical for the realization of emotions, moods and feelings. We act in the world by means of our bodies and a wide range of affective and behavioural processes involve both central (i.e., brain) processes as well as more peripheral physiological processes. There is little doubt that emotions are embodied phenomena. Research has shown, for example, that physiological arousal (Schachter and Singer, 1962) or 'somatic markers' (Damasio, 1999) are important determinants of feelings. Moreover, it is now clear that a number of physiological indicators may be markers or risk factors for psychopathology (e.g., Coan and Allen, 2003; Davidson, 1998a). Therefore, it is important to take bodily processes into account in emotion science.

Sin 4, the notion that neurobiology can be ignored totally, is also relatively common among cognitive psychologists, although this is changing (Smith and Kosslyn, 2006). While much has and can be learnt by focusing on cognitive processes, one of the messages in this book is that the understanding of cognitive and affective processes can be enhanced by taking brain processes into account. To illustrate, cognitive psychologists have established at a behavioural level that visual attention is oriented preferentially towards negatively valenced stimuli, especially if they are threat-related. The more recent discovery that neural responses (e.g., ERP responses) occur within a few hundred milliseconds of exposure to a threatening stimulus, and evidence from fMRI studies that amygdala–vmPFC circuits are activated in the presence of threatening stimuli surely deepen our understanding of these processes. Likewise, the discovery that different neural circuits are involved in *liking* something and *wanting* something (Berridge, 2003) deepens the understanding of *positive affect* that is often considered to be a single entity in psychological research (e.g., Isen, 2000). The fact that different neural circuits are involved in liking and wanting suggests that positive affect may be further decomposed into smaller subcomponents.

Cognitive psychology generally describes mental and affective processes in terms of how information is processed. In other words, how information comes in through the senses and is then transformed, stored and used. This *information-processing* level of analysis is important and is qualitatively different from a neural level of analysis that might provide a description of how physical brain processes give rise to certain behaviours. The cognitive and neural levels of analysis both provide important descriptions but it must be remembered that they can never replace each other. Each level might be important for the other, but we cannot reduce (or amplify) an explanation at one level to another. To illustrate this, let's take the example of someone waving when she sees a friend across a room. We can describe this action purely in terms of mechanics – the tensing of muscles gives rise to a lifting of the arm etc. In contrast, a description of the same event at a social level might be put in terms of how the person is welcoming her friend. Both of these levels of analysis are accurate and provide qualitatively different descriptions of the same phenomenon.

Sin 5 relates to the assumption that emotions are similar in structure across different age groups and different species. The development of emotions and emotion schemas across different age groups has not been examined in depth in this book. However, there is much evidence that emotions and especially emotion regulation changes significantly with aging (see Gross, 2007, for relevant reviews).

A range of evidence from both animal and human research has been discussed in this book. In my view, all of this evidence needs to be taken into account in emotion science. There are clearly cognitive processes and neural circuits that are very similar across different species. Therefore, studying a process (e.g., approaching a reward or avoiding a threat) in one species can tell us something about similar processes in other species. The issue of whether the investigation of the neural systems of emotions in rodents can inform our understanding of human emotion has, of course, long been a controversial issue. Jaak Panksepp (1998, 2007) has been at the forefront of the argument that studying basic emotional systems in rats is informative for the understanding of human emotion.

Much of the evidence discussed in this book supports the view that ancient emotional circuits do indeed play a powerful role in human emotion. A more controversial question is whether these circuits give rise to conscious feeling states that are similar across different species. Some neuroscientists are convinced that this is the case (e.g., Panksepp, 1998) while others are doubtful (e.g., Rolls, 2005). Panksepp tends to ignore the evidence that the basic anatomy of the prefrontal cortex, and especially the connectivity of the amygdala and other structures, is fundamentally different in humans compared to rodents (Amaral et al., 1992; Berridge, 2003; Rolls, 2005). This is a difficult, if not impossible, question to address. However, it does seem likely that conscious feeling states may be modified to a large extent by the expansion of the prefrontal cortex and the development of subcortical-cortical neural circuits. These facts suggest that study of the neural correlates of emotion in one species cannot replace investigation in the species of interest, even though they may be highly informative.

It also seems important not to ignore a species' capacity to assess self-reported experience, which is of course only possible when studying human emotion and mood.

Sin 6 relates to the assumption that different emotional systems are implemented in discrete locations in the brain. It has already been made clear that the evidence does not support this view. While there may be relatively differentiated neural systems underlying different emotions (Murphy et al., 2003; Panksepp, 1998) or affective dimensions (Murphy et al., 2003; Phan et al., 2002) the main message is that a large number of interconnected brain areas are activated across most affective states. Specific brain structures are generally involved in a variety of different processes. While broad regions of the brain may be specialized for specific tasks, each structure is also likely to be involved in a number of other circuits (e.g., amygdala–fusiform gyrus).

Finally, Davidson's seventh sin was the assumption that emotions are conscious feeling states. In this book, we have hopefully made it clear that emotions and moods can be distinguished from feeling states. As we have pointed out, feelings are the conscious mental representations of emotions and moods. What we feel is an important part of our conscious awareness. However, emotions can operate at different levels and may not necessarily be conscious. Therefore, to develop a comprehensive science of emotion we need to take emotions, moods and conscious feeling states into account.

The work reviewed in this book suggests that Davidson's seven sins are still very much in evidence in emotion science. However, there does seem to be an increasing awareness of the need to integrate research across information-processing and neural domains, as well as the importance of distinguishing different aspects of affect (e.g., emotions, moods, feelings, temperament). The ongoing development of neuroimaging technologies and genetic analysis has opened up new avenues of research that now allow us to address affect all the way from molecules to conscious experience. There is an extraordinary vitality to emotion science and research in this field is relevant to many areas of psychology and neuroscience. Moreover, fundamental research in emotion science is crucial for the understanding and the development of treatment strategies for a range of psychopathologies and is therefore also of relevance for much of psychiatry. As we discussed in Chapter 10, research in emotion science has more recently turned to the question of what really makes us happy and content, and the field of spirituality and well-being can also be informed by fundamental research in emotion science.

Before concluding this overview, I would like to discuss a number of important issues that seem to be critical for the future development of emotion science:

- Multiple-levels of analysis.
- Ways in which emotion scientists can integrate research at multiple levels with the emphasis on cognitive psychology and neurobiology. However, it is also clear that there is a need to integrate research at genetic and neural levels, as well as integrating these research domains with social and cultural levels of analysis.
- How emotion science can provide better bridges or translations between basic scientific research in emotion science and clinical practice.

MULTIPLE LEVELS OF ANALYSIS

Contemporary neuroscience is characterized by a move towards analysis on multiple levels (e.g., Albright et al., 2000). Human nature, including affect, can be studied at a number of levels, from an examination of individual molecules or cells, to analysis at the level of gross behaviour, as well as examination of how groups of neurons operate at a 'systems' level. Large social and cultural groups can also be used to assess aspects of human behaviour. Clearly all of these levels are important in themselves, and consideration of different levels of analysis leads to a highly dynamic and interactive view of how science should be conducted. This is because the influence of one level on another is almost always bidirectional. In terms of neuroscience, molecular and neural processes can have a strong impact on behavioural outcomes. In addition, behaviour and other social/cultural experiences can impact on the structure and functioning of the brain, as well as affecting gene expression (e.g., Dawson and Fischer, 1994; Kandel, 1998; Meaney et al., 1996).

It has been suggested that contemporary systems neuroscience developed from the convergence of five key subdisciplines: neuropsychology, neuroanatomy, neurophysiology, psychophysics, and computational modelling (Albright et al., 2000). The integration of evidence from across these five disciplines has resulted in a real improvement in our understanding of how neural systems operate. It has been argued that the field of developmental psychopathology has also benefited from adopting a similar multiple levels of analysis perspective (Cicchetti and Dawson, 2002). This area incorporates work on both normal and abnormal development and attempts to integrate research being conducted across a range of different scientific disciplines. Thus, research that examines development from biological, psychological, and social-contextual perspectives are all incorporated. Cicchetti and Dawson (2002) argue that, while much has been learned from studies at a single level of analysis, the development of psychopathology cannot be properly advanced unless all levels are understood and integrated.

Emotion science is an ideal candidate for such an integrated, multiple levels of analysis approach. In this book we have discussed a great deal of evidence that has been obtained from single levels of analysis, whether it be at the molecular level, the behavioural level, the neural level or the subjective level. One of the clear consequences of this single-level approach is the development of general theories that can provide a good explanation of data at one level of analysis but cannot explain data at other levels of analysis. Hence, evidence from the study of individual neural circuits and neurochemical systems has led to the view that there are a number of primary emotional systems located in subcortical brain structures (e.g., LeDoux, 1996; Panksepp, 1998). These models can explain a considerable amount of data, but cannot account for data that has been obtained from self-report (e.g., Russell, 2003). Evidence from self-report data suggests that affect is structured primarily around a small number of broad dimensions (e.g., valence, arousal), or from core affect and cognitive categorization processes, and that the evidence for separate and discrete emotions is actually quite weak (e.g., Feldman Barrett, 2006a; Feldman Barrett et al., 2007; Russell,

2003). Theories from the self-report perspective can explain much of what is known about the subjective experience of emotion (see Feldman Barrett et al., 2007, for review), but cannot explain much of what is known about the neural and neurochemical processes involved in emotion (e.g., Panksepp, 2007, for review). Indeed, neuroimaging studies of human emotion have produced roughly equal amounts of evidence for discrete emotions and dimensional approaches (Feldman Barrett and Wager, 2006; Murphy et al., 2003).

In my view, much of the debate between discrete emotions and dimensional approaches can be reduced to the fact that researchers in both camps usually focus on different levels of analysis. While each of these levels is important, it has to be remembered that they are describing *qualitatively different phenomena* and, therefore, theories derived from one level of analysis are highly unlikely to be useful in explaining another level of analysis. Both discrete emotions and dimensional approaches can be seen as complementary to each other (Diener and Iran-Nejad, 1986), even though they are frequently pitted against each other. As concluded by Izard (2007, p. 268):

> To advance emotion science and establish probabilistic relations between reliably measured affective variables, we probably will need both the dimensional and discrete approaches.

Izard goes on to suggest that these approaches may be equivalent at a theoretical level to the concepts of waves and particles used in physics. Both of these constructs are needed to explain the behaviour of electrons at the quantum level. In a similar way, perhaps both discrete and dimensional constructs are necessary to explain the totality of affective experience and expression.

A UNIFYING FRAMEWORK

An integrative framework of how dimensional and discrete approaches might be combined is shown in Figure 11.1. The framework assumes that there are a number of basic emotional systems, which are ancient in evolutionary terms, and operate in fairly similar ways across species. Panksepp's primary emotional systems have been incorporated into the diagram since there is extensive evidence for their existence in both animals and humans (e.g., Panksepp, 1998). These emotional systems are similar to basic emotions or affect programs (e.g., Ekman, 1994d; Izard, 1977; Tomkins, 1962, 1963), and are assumed to be activated rapidly and automatically upon the perception of an emotionally-competent stimulus. The basic emotional systems are highly adaptive and drive a narrowly focused and largely stereotypical range of responses which are activated rapidly and also tend to dissipate rapidly.

In Figure 11.1, the activation of these primary emotional systems leads to a disturbance in a general background core affective state, which is equivalent to notions of core affect (Feldman Barrett, 2006a, 2006b; Feldman Barrett et al., 2007; Russell, 2003), or mood (Davidson, 1994b; Lazarus, 1991; Morris, 1992; Prinz, 2004). The important point is that it is changes in this core background affect that are consciously perceived. A useful analogy might be to view the core affective system as a river and

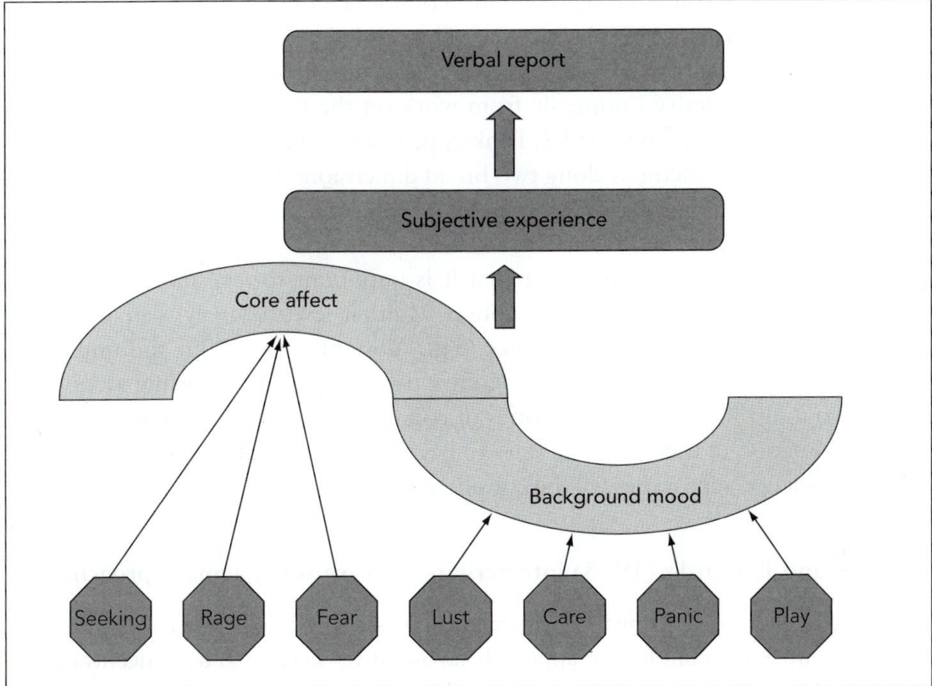

FIGURE 11.1 A schematic framework of how discrete emotion approaches and dimensional approaches may be integrated to explain human affect

the primary emotional systems as stones thrown into it when a significant event occurs. The stones cause ripples which can be observed as changes in intensity (e.g., the effects of a large stone versus a small pebble) or as gradual shifts in the overall flow of the river. The ripples can be interpreted as broad dimensions of valence (pleasure versus displeasure). This is why, when viewing the 'river' of subjective experience, people can really only report on arousal and valence, and not about discrete emotional systems that are submerged beneath the surface. In other words, discrete emotional systems may not reach conscious awareness in a direct way.

Perhaps more accurately, it may be the case that basic emotional systems are associated with specific feeling states, but that our linguistic abilities do not allow us to report these subtle distinctions adequately. Basic emotions evolved much earlier than language and therefore it is likely that our capacity to verbally report the subtle distinctions between primary emotional states may be limited. Instead, what we can report are the broader dimensions of how intense something feels (*arousal*) and how pleasant or unpleasant it feels (*valence*). In other words, what we consciously feel and can report are broad affective dimensions, but underlying these are separate and ancient discrete emotion systems. Davidson's (1994b) proposal is that these basic emotional systems cause perturbations or interruptions to the background mood or core affect, and these may or may not have direct consciously-felt feeling states. The evidence suggests, however, that when verbal self-report is required the mental representations that are accessible relate to the broader dimensions of valence and arousal.

In other words, the conscious representation of both emotions (primary systems) and mood (core affect) are accessible in terms of broad dimensions.

The framework shown in Figure 11.1 accounts for the evidence for separate and discrete emotions, derived primarily from work on the neural and facial expression level of analysis (e.g., Ekman, 1992; Panksepp, 1998), and also accounts for the evidence that affect is structured along two broad dimensions, which is derived primarily from work on the subjective and behavioural (approach-avoidance) level of analysis (e.g., Feldman Barrett, 2006b; Davidson, 1998a).

Figure 11.1 emphasizes the point that it is important to take different levels of analysis into account in the study of emotion. Multiple levels of analysis are now commonplace in contemporary neuroscience (e.g., Albright et al., 2000) and multi-level theories have also been developed in cognitive psychology. The following section discusses two multi-level cognitive theories of cognition–emotion interactions. Following a presentation of these models, ways to begin the process of integrating cognitive and neuroscience approaches will be considered.

Teasdale and Barnard's (1993) interacting cognitive subsystems approach

Most cognitive models emphasize information processing at just one *level* of the cognitive system. For example, the approach favoured by Beck (1976) concentrates on the thought processes involved in dysfunctional cognitions (e.g., 'I am a worthless person'). The approach favoured by Williams et al. (1988), in contrast, emphasizes the lower-level processes involved in the initial sensory registration of a stimulus. However, it is likely that lower-level sensory processes and higher-level conceptual processes are *both* important in the production, maintenance and regulation of normal emotion as well as emotional disorders. For these reasons, more recent theoretical developments have focused on 'multi-level approaches' to the interactions between affect and cognition. Many theories of emotion assume that many different components or subsystems are involved in emotion. An emotional response occurs when these different components are synchronized momentarily, perhaps due to an appraisal of a particular situation (e.g., Leventhal, 1979; Leventhal and Scherer, 1987; Scherer, 2001). Similarly, the *multiple-entry memory (MEM)* approach points out that many emotions can arise from low-level sensory processes (e.g., fear may arise upon processing the features of a snake) as well as from higher-level reflective processes such as imagining that you are trapped in an enclosure with a snake (Johnson and Multhaup, 1992). This is an important point as it suggests that, while some emotions may occur at *every* level in the system, other emotions may occur only at the more reflective levels. To illustrate, we can imagine that the traditional basic emotions – anger, fear, happiness, sadness, disgust – might occur at every level. Thus, if someone insults us we might become angry very quickly as a direct result of the sensory processing of the situation. We might also become angry by thinking in a more reflective way about someone who has regularly insulted us. However, there are some emotions, often referred to as *secondary emotions* or *emotion schemas* – jealousy, embarrassment, guilt etc – that generally arise from reflective processes and would not be expected to arise directly from sensory processing. An implication of this type of model is that different emotions can be generated at the same time at different levels within a system. This allows for the possibility that we may often experience 'mixed emotions'.

Perhaps the most comprehensive multi-level model is the *Interacting Cognitive Subsystems (ICS) framework* proposed by Philip Barnard and John Teasdale (Barnard, 1985; Teasdale and Barnard, 1993). This framework is derived from first principles and proposes nine different cognitive subsystems. While each cognitive subsystem is relatively simple in itself, the various subsystems interact with each other in highly complex ways. It is important to remember that ICS as a framework is supposed to simulate the cognitive system in a very general way. It was originally developed to account for performance on a wide range of attention and memory tasks involved with the processing of language. The framework has now been applied to a range of cognitive functions as well as to the understanding of cognition and affect (Teasdale and Barnard, 1993; Barnard et al., 2007).

An explicit assumption in ICS is that there are qualitatively different *kinds* of information that correspond to different types of experience. Each kind of information is processed by specialized subsystems that deal only with that kind of information. Three of these subsystems or mental codes are involved with the analysis of raw sensory input: the *acoustic*, *visual*, and *body-state* subsystems. At an intermediate structural level, the *morphonolexical* code represents regularities that have been detected by the acoustic code, such as the sounds of words. Likewise, the *object* code represents regularities detected by the visual code, such as spatial relations (above, below), and object properties (round, square etc). At a higher level of abstraction, the *propositional* and *implicational* codes represent meaning. An especially important aspect of ICS for emotion science is the proposal that meaning can be represented in two qualitatively distinct mental codes, *propositional* and *implicational*. Propositional meaning can be conveyed in a sentence (e.g., 'David is athletic'), whereas implicational meaning refers to a more intuitive or holistic schematic model of life experience. The final two codes proposed in the ICS framework relate to the production of an output, or what might be called the *effector* systems. They are the *articulatory* code that processes information necessary for speech output, and the *limb* code that encodes information required for the control of motor action and movement. These nine subsystems of the ICS framework are shown in a simplified form in Figure 11.2.

ICS also proposes that the specific processes occurring in each subsystem have similar internal structures, but operate completely independently of each other and can, therefore, occur in parallel. These processes can do two things:

(a) construct representations in a particular code;
(b) translate or transform information from one code (e.g., acoustic) into another (e.g., visual or morphonolexical).

It is the transformation processes that are considered to be the essential mechanisms underlying information processing in this framework.

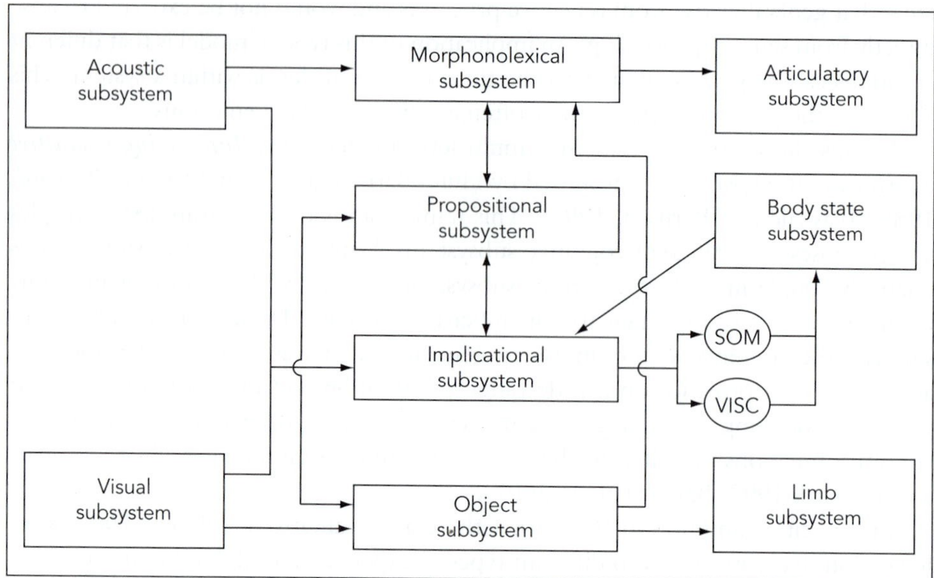

FIGURE 11.2 A simplified outline of the nine subsystems of the ICS
SOM and VISC are the *somatic* and *visceral* outputs of the implicational subsystem, respectively.
Source: Teasdale and Barnard (1993).

Propositional and implicational levels of meaning

One of the most important aspects of the ICS framework for emotion science is the distinction made between *propositional* and *implicational* levels of meaning. Propositional meaning can be expressed in language and leads to 'intellectual beliefs' that have a 'truth value'. For instance, the statement 'George Bush was president of the United States' becomes a proposition because it can be held to be either 'true' or 'false'. This type of information is not usually affected by information coming from things like the tone of voice or the particular body state a person is in when they hear such a proposition (e.g., state of arousal). For these reasons, propositional meaning is not thought to be involved *directly* in the production of emotion within the ICS framework.

In contrast, however, implicational meaning leads to 'emotional belief' or 'gut feelings' that are derived from actual emotional experiences. These beliefs reflect contributions from a variety of sources and do not have a specific truth-value. These are the intuitive feelings that we often have about situations, feelings that we find difficult to put into words. The abstract representations that are constructed at the implicational level in ICS are considered to be *schematic* models that combine information from a wide variety of sources. In other words, information from all of the other subsystems is drawn into the implicational subsystem.

The patterns of processing that occur on the implicational level represent schematic models that encode recurring themes extracted from the patterns detected in other codes (e.g., propositional, acoustic, visual), which have elicited emotions in similar situations. This is how implicational meaning gives rise to the intuitive *feeling* or *sense* one gets in a particular situation. Barnard and Teasdale illustrate implicational meaning by pointing out that a well-written poem can convey a 'holistic' meaning that often cannot be expressed, or is lost, by attempting to put it into propositional form. They give the example of the Keats poem entitled *La Belle Dame Sans Merci.* The first line of this poem reads 'O what can ail thee, knight-at-arms, Alone and palely loitering?' which they put into the following purely propositional form: 'What is the matter, armed old-fashioned soldier, Standing by yourself and doing nothing with a pallid expression?' Thus, by taking away the evocative sound and visual imagery (i.e., the sensory qualities) of the original poem, and leaving the same sequence of propositional meaning, the sense of emptiness and abandonment is largely lost. Thus, propositional meaning can be rather cold and factual, whereas implicational meaning tends to convey a deep sense of understanding that is often 'felt in the bones'.

A key proposal is that the implicational subsystem plays a fundamental role in the production of emotions as well as subjective experience, or feelings. The regularities in the patterns of information codes from other subsystems, that have previously been elicited in situations associated with a particular feeling, are extracted and integrated to produce implicational schematic models. When these affect-laden schematic models are activated by means of processing within the implicational subsystem, the corresponding emotion is produced. In agreement with the componential approach to emotion (Scherer, 2001), this emotional reaction is a coordinated phenomenon with subjective, physiological, motor, and expressive components. As can be seen in Figure 11.2, the physiological components of the emotional response depend upon the translation of codes within the implicational subsystem to the *somatic subsystem* (SOM), whereas the transformation of implicational codes into the *visceral subsystem* (VISC) allows for the production of motor components, including changes in facial expression and posture. A real benefit of the ICS framework is the emphasis it places upon the importance of bodily effects. The idea of embodiment and the importance of bodily states for emotions, moods and feelings can easily be lost in cognitive models of emotion that often focus exclusively on what Barnard and Teasdale would call the propositional level of meaning.

A particularly important aspect of ICS for the understanding of emotional disorders is the notion that only implicational levels of representation can *directly* induce emotions. The proposition that 'I am a failure' for example, will not necessarily make me feel depressed. However, if I process an *implicational* code that is typical of personal failure then the whole-body response, drawing upon all the other subsystems, would lead to an implicit and overwhelming feeling of failure. A common characteristic of emotional disorders is, of course, a split or dissociation between 'intellectual' beliefs and 'emotional' beliefs. A person with a phobic fear of spiders, for example, is generally well aware that most spiders are harmless and unlikely to pose any real danger. Nevertheless, the mere sight of a spider can elicit a strong fear reaction that is completely unaffected by the knowledge that there is nothing to fear. Likewise, a person who panics in a supermarket *knows* at an intellectual level that there is no real danger, but this knowledge cannot prevent the panic attack because the implicit or implicational level knowledge takes over.

In cognitive behavioural therapy it is common for depressed people to get to the point of accepting at an intellectual level that they are not 'complete failures'. Nevertheless, they may still *feel* like failures, even though they know at a logical level that this is not true. The ICS framework provides a clear explanation of how these dissociations between 'intellectual beliefs' and 'gut feelings' can occur. Thus, it provides a neat resolution to the problem of 'hot' and 'cold' cognitions that are very difficult to explain within associative network models (e.g., Bower, 1981) or general schema-based cognitive models (e.g., Beck and Clark, 1988). In those models, the activation of a proposition (e.g., I am a failure) leads in a fairly automatic way to the activation of related nodes (or the rest of the schema) so that a full-blown emotional response is experienced. This clearly does not happen, because it is quite possible to think about emotions and emotional situations without actually *feeling* the emotion. ICS can account for this phenomenon by proposing that meaning can be represented at both explicit (i.e., propositional) and implicit (i.e., implicational) levels, and these levels can operate in parallel without interfering with each other.

As we saw in Chapters 6 and 7 ongoing mood states can have profound effects on a range of cognitive processes such as attention, memory, and judgment. Typically, cognitive processes are biased in a mood-congruent way. ICS provides a principled account of how these biases emerge, as well as accounting for the negative thoughts and patterns of bias that are common in clinical depression (Barnard and Teasdale, 1993). Let us illustrate by looking at the example of how depressed mood states can bias evaluative judgments in a negative direction. ICS assumes that depressed mood states are generated and maintained by schematic models that have been created from a broad range of experiences involving disappointment, criticism, significant loss, and personal failure. It is likely, of course that, in addition to implicational processing, these type of situations will also have become associated with propositional processing (e.g., 'I am a failure', 'The world is a disappointing place', 'Others always let you down etc'). Within ICS the idea is that implicational codes can be translated into propositional codes and vice versa by extensive processing that transforms information from one code into another. All of the various co-occurrences and regularities that occur will be encoded in the system by means of these translational processes. Thus, when faced with a situation that activates implicational elements that were derived from both propositional and body-state sources, the coherence of the different aspects of the implicational code is sufficient to ensure a fusion of different schematic models that, in turn, ensures that evaluative judgments will be biased in a negative way.

The dynamic factors that can result in the maintenance of mood and emotional disorders are explained by ICS in a similar way. Once again, the recognition of two distinct forms of meaning is crucial, because only the implicational level is related directly to the production of emotion. In contrast, many cognitive approaches assume that propositional meaning is crucial for emotional disorders, and that these propositions should be the target of psychological therapies. ICS proposes that the processing of depression-related implicational schematic models is the immediate precursor to depressed mood. The negative automatic thoughts and other negative cognitive products that are typical of emotional disorders are not therefore considered to play

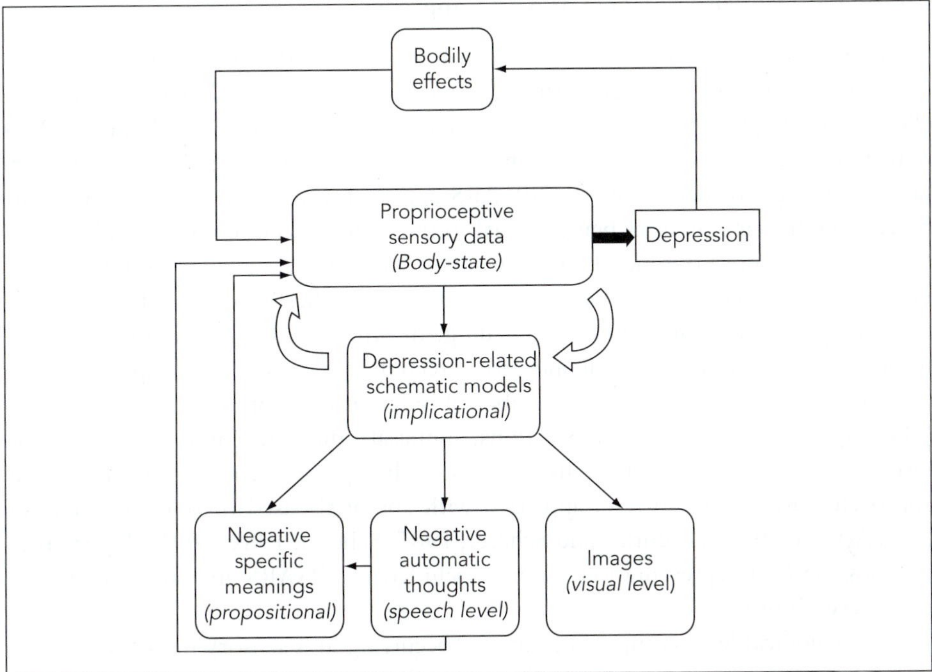

FIGURE 11.3 How ICS accounts for the maintenance of depression

Source: Based on Figures 12.6 and 16.1 in Teasdale and Barnard (1993).

a *direct* role in generating negative mood states like depression. They can, of course, play an indirect role by contributing to the synthesis of depression-related schematic models. The important point, however, is that the production of the mood state is only generated directly by the processing of depression-related schematic models as shown in Figure 11.3.

The upper part of Figure 11.3 can be seen as a *sensory loop*, while the lower part can be seen as a *cognitive loop*. Since processing involves the dynamic exchange and transformation of information among subsystems, different loops feeding into depression-related schematic models can become established or 'locked' into a self-perpetuating configuration that serves to maintain depression. Barnard and Teasdale call this the '*depressive interlock*' configuration and it represents the key means within the ICS framework by which dysfunctional mood states can become persistent. An important implication of the ICS framework in terms of therapeutic techniques is the assumption that intervention at many different points can lead to a change in the depression-related schematic model. For example, just as in Beck's model, directly changing negative automatic thoughts, as in cognitive behavioural therapy, will have an indirect effect on the depression-related schematic model. However, interventions that modify the bodily effects of depression will also modify the schematic model by feeding through the body-state subsystem (see Figure 11.3). A key therapeutic strategy within the ICS approach, therefore, is the ultimate replacement of depression-related schematic models by new, more adaptive schematic models that are related to the same topics.

Power and Dalgleish's (1997) SPAARS approach

Another multi-level model that is similar in some ways to ICS is the *Schematic, Propositional, Analogical and Associative Representation Systems (SPAARS)* approach (Power and Dalgleish, 1997). As can be seen from the terminology used, the SPAARS framework has a lot in common with ICS. However, there are also some important differences. In particular, the SPAARS approach puts great emphasis on goal-based cognitive appraisals as being crucial to the generation of emotion. In line with the cognitive theory outlined by Oatley and Johnson-Laird (1987) (see Chapter 4), Power and Dalgleish argue that human emotions are best understood in terms of the plans and goals that people are pursuing. In other words, the mind is conceived to be configured as a functional and goal-directed system. A key assumption is that, while emotions are made up of a number of different components (e.g., physiological changes, conscious awareness, actions, appraisal), different emotions can only be distinguished from each other on the basis of the appraisal component. Thus, this approach marries a multi-level approach with appraisal-based theories of emotions (e.g., Arnold, 1960; Leventhal and Scherer, 1987; Scherer, 1984, 2001). Figure 11.4 outlines the four representation systems included in SPAARS and shows how they relate to each other.

The analogical level comprises processes occurring at a sensory-motor level (e.g., the sight of a snake in the grass). The propositional level refers to representations (thoughts and beliefs) that can be expressed in language (e.g., 'the world is a safe place'). Thus, the proposition might be 'the snake might bite me'. The schematic level refers to more abstract representations about the state of the world and the self that cannot be expressed in language and is essentially the same as the implicational schematic models we discussed in the ICS account. These implicit models of the world,

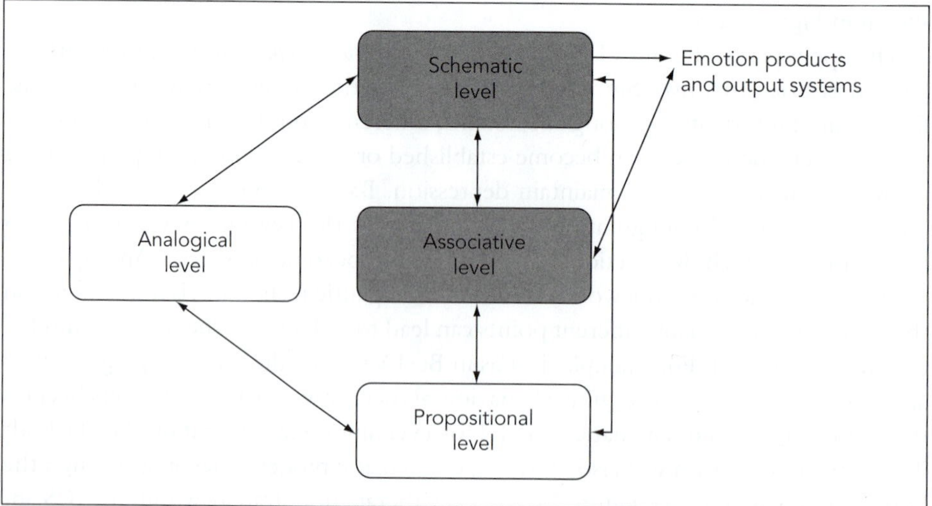

FIGURE 11.4 The SPAARS model of emotion, showing the proposed representational systems
Source: Based on Figure 5.7 in Power and Dalgleish (1997).

the self and others are of obvious importance to the understanding of emotional disorders. In the SPAARS approach, important goals and appraisals (e.g., 'my survival goal is threatened') are incorporated in an implicit way within the schematic level. In other words, the perception and interpretation of different situations are influenced within the schematic level by the person's active goals and plans, and it is this appraisal that is considered to generate emotion. Thus, as in the ICS framework, emotions are generated *directly* from the schematic level, while they can only be *indirectly* generated from the propositional level. The associative level in SPAARS, however, provides an additional level of processing that can directly generate emotion, as shown in Figure 11.4. Power and Dalgleish (1997) point out that with practice and experience all cognitive processes can become highly automatic, and there is no reason why this should be any different for emotion. Thus, well-established stimulus–response pairings (e.g., between snakes or spiders and a fear reaction, or between a particular taste and nausea) can become so tightly coupled with experience that they can generate an emotional response in a direct and automatic way. Thus, the associative level provides an alternative route to the generation of emotion without involving the schematic level.

To summarize then, the SPAARS framework assumes that emotions are represented at multiple levels with a cognitive architecture, just as with the ICS (Barnard and Teasdale, 1993) and MEMs (Johnson and Multhaup, 1992) approaches. However, there are some aspects of SPAARS that set it apart from other approaches. First, it is argued that emotions are primarily appraisal-based and, in turn, appraisals are determined to a large extent by goals. Thus, this model is consistent with cognitive appraisal theories of emotion in placing appraisals at centre stage in the generation and differentiation of emotions. Second, emotions can be elicited in SPAARS by two alternative routes: the schematic or implicational route well known from ICS and an associatively-driven automatic route. Third, it is proposed that the five basic emotions of anger, fear, sadness, disgust, and happiness are the fundamental building blocks of affective life. In a similar way to the theory of Oatley and Johnson-Laird (1987), it is proposed that the *function* of the basic emotions is to set the cognitive system within a particular framework. When a goal is blocked or disrupted in some way, an emotion (e.g., anger, fear) interrupts the system so that a readjustment can take place. Thus, a primary function of basic emotions is to reconfigure the cognitive system so that a new goal can be achieved (Oatley and Johnson-Laird, 1987; Power and Dalgleish, 1997). Finally, it is proposed that an understanding of both normal emotions and disorders of emotion can be derived from these basic components. Power and Dalgleish argue that most, if not all, emotional disorders originate from dysfunctions occurring in one of these five basic emotions. They summarize much evidence to support this view and an outline of how each basic emotion might relate to each emotional disorder is presented in Table 11.2.

Within the SPAARS approach, each basic emotion can reconfigure the entire system by highlighting the goals relevant to each emotion. Thus, the emotion of fear allows the individual to switch rapidly into a 'threatened survival' mode, while sadness switches the system into a mode where lost goals are reassessed and new priorities are

TABLE 11.2 A simplified outline of which emotional disorders are linked to which basic emotions, as proposed by the SPAARS approach

Basic emotion	*Emotional disorder*
Fear	Panic Specific phobias OCD GAD PTSD
Sadness	Pathological grief Depression
Anger	Pathological anger Morbid jealousy
Happiness	Polyannaism/pathological happiness Mania Love sickness
Disgust	Specific phobias OCD Suicide Eating disorders

Source: Based on Table 11.3 in Power and Dalgleish (1997).

assigned. All of these reconfigurations are highly functional and probably one of the reasons why emotions evolved in the first place (Oatley and Johnson-Laird, 1987). However, these emotions can become overactive and overgeneralize to a wide range of situations so that they become dysfunctional.

Overview of multi-level models

Multi-level approaches in cognitive psychology have a number of clear advantages in developing an overarching account that can help us to understand normal emotions as well as emotional disorders. This is especially advanced in the SPAARS approach in which the evolution of a small set of basic emotions is thought to underlie the development of normal human emotions (see Chapter 4), while a dysfunction in these primary emotional systems is thought to be at the core of many emotional disorders. The ICS approach also provides a principled account that can be applied equally to normal emotional reactions and experiences as well as providing a means by which emotional disorders can develop and be maintained. This potential to provide a coherent theoretical account of both normal and disordered emotions within a single framework is a real strength of multi-level approaches.

Moreover, the notion that information can be represented at many different levels is an intuitive one. We have all have been in situations where we have experienced a disconnection between our gut feeling and a more rationale analysis of the situation. This type of disconnection also captures the type of problem that can occur in emotional disorders when people may, for example, experience frequent panic attacks in places such as supermarkets even though they are fully aware at an intellectual level that there is no significant danger and that the panic attack is an over-reaction to the 'threat' imposed by the situation. Multi-level approaches explain these occurrences very easily by the assumption that information is processed by different subsystems in parallel within the cognitive system.

Multi-level approaches also make it easier to begin to understand how neural and cognitive levels of analysis may be combined. In terms of emotional responses, a variety of processes take place at the level of individual synapses and neuronal groups that relate in complex ways to processes occurring at psychological levels of analysis (e.g., attentional, memory and judgmental biases etc). Multi-level approaches incorporate these factors into their accounts, thus providing a more realistic framework to consider the complex interrelationships between different levels of processing. This is likely to be particularly important when we consider emotional disorders. These distressing conditions are complex. Genetic, neural, cognitive, and social elements all need to be taken into account in terms of understanding the essential nature of each disorder as well as developing more effective therapies.

INTEGRATING NEUROBIOLOGICAL AND COGNITIVE MODELS OF AFFECT

As we have seen throughout this book, there is an abundance of research within psychology (especially cognitive psychology) and neuroscience on the nature of affect. An important challenge is how to integrate research from across these domains. This is difficult since the different disciplines often use different approaches and different language, and frequently study different *levels* of the overall system. In addition, there is often confusion as to whether 'cognition' and 'affect' should be seen as separate systems or as parts of a unified whole (e.g., Lane et al., 2000). Even within psychology, it has proven difficult to agree on a consistent approach (e.g., debate on discrete emotions versus dimensions). What is required is a coherent framework that can incorporate data and theory from a wide range of levels. The framework outlined in Figure 11.1 demonstrates in a general way how all parts of the larger system play a role in determining affect. However, a more specific way of relating each of the levels to each other using a common language is now needed. The development of models that allow an analysis of how the various levels relate to each other in multiple ways would be especially useful. A number of proposed models capture the notion that cognitive and affective processes are likely to interact in complex and bi-directional ways (e.g., Lewis, 2005; Scherer, 2000a, 2001; Thayer and Lane, 2000). Marc Lewis (2005) in an extensive overview has argued that such *dynamic systems* (DS) approaches may provide an appropriate framework to enable a bridge between psychological theories of emotion and neurobiology.

A dynamic systems approach

There are a number of barriers to the development of collaborative research among psychologists and neuroscientists in the study of emotion (Lewis, 2005). While there are exceptions (e.g., Scherer, 2000a), cognitive approaches to emotion have traditionally tended to make rather simple linear assumptions about the nature of cause and effect. Thus, a cognitive process might be seen as causing an emotional response, or vice versa. In addition, psychological studies often focus on 'psychological wholes', such as 'attention', 'memory', 'judgment' or 'emotion', with few details about how these large wholes are derived from interacting parts. In contrast, neuroscience tends to emphasize the complexity of neural systems with a focus on how many different neural structures and circuits can influence each other in bi-directional ways. Thus, there is usually no assumption of linearity (e.g., A causes B causes C etc). Instead, the assumption is that there are multiple and bi-directional interactions between many components. There is much to be said for this approach according to Lewis, but what it lacks is a consideration of the properties and the functions of the whole. Thus:

> complex causal processes remain elusive for emotion theorists, psychologically meaningful wholes remain elusive for neuroscientists, and there is little common ground for truly integrative modelling. (Lewis, 2005, p. 169)

The dynamic systems approach allows for the development of computational models of how complex systems like the brain operate – models involving multiple reciprocal causal processes. Importantly, dynamic systems are characterized by the emergence of wholes out of interacting parts. This occurs by means of a number of processes related to *self-organization* and *circular causality* (see Haken, 1977). Self-organization is the spontaneous emergence of order from non-linear interactions among the components of a complex and dynamic system. Circular causality refers to the notion of bi-directional causality between the different levels of a system. Thus, from this perspective cognitive processes might be seen as reciprocal and characterized by multiple feedback cycles. This means that cause–effect relationships are bi-directional and not one-way. A second point is that effects occurring in dynamic systems are not viewed as linear functions of causes. This simply means that they may be exponential, subject to threshold effects, and are likely to be sensitive to either dampening or amplifying effects from other components of the system. To illustrate, imagine we have a drug that we know increases blood pressure. A linear relationship would be demonstrated if we found that every 10 mg of the drug led to a 10-unit increase in blood pressure. However, a non-linear relationship would be shown if we found that increasing levels of the drug had little or no effect up to 40 mg, and then there was a large effect. Moreover, each increase after 40 mg might lead to substantially larger effects on blood pressure. One implication of such a relationship is that it is very difficult to predict the future state of the system from its current state.

Dynamic systems approaches have important implications for how cognition is seen. For example, instead of making the linear assumption that information-processing systems process information from the outside world (e.g., sensory event) and translate it into an output (e.g., stored memory, motor response), the assumption is that information-processing systems reconfigure themselves in response to an ongoing stream of sensory events (Varela et al., 1991). The fact that dynamic systems approaches focus on bi-directional causal relationships among different levels of the system means that it may be possible to demonstrate how interactions between subcomponents (e.g., typical neural analysis) might be related to the emergence of higher order and coherent wholes (e.g., typical psychological analysis). Thus, dynamic systems modelling has the potential to integrate levels of description both for psychological studies of emotion as well as neurobiological studies of emotion (Lewis, 2005). A first question concerns whether multiple and bi-directional causal relationships are of relevance for the understanding of affect.

Are cognition–affect relations bi-directional?

Affect has been studied from a variety of perspectives within psychological science, with contributions from cognitive, clinical, physiological and social psychology as well as learning theory. However, cognitive psychology has been particularly interested in the nature of the relations between *affect* (often just called *emotion*) and *cognition*. In earlier chapters we discussed theoretical disputes concerning whether affect or cognition was primary (e.g., Lazarus, 1984; Zajonc, 1984). While this is not an ongoing debate, it still seems that the nature of the relations between affect and cognition is central to emotion theory. Lewis (2005) identified three main approaches to emotion–cognition relations within psychological research and theory.

First, *appraisal theory* has focused on how meaning is extracted from situations in order to help us to make sense of the world (e.g., Frijda, 1993). The general view is that appraisal sets the scene for an emotional response by producing meaning. Thus, the purpose of an appraisal is often considered to be the organization of cognitions and actions that are relevant to the situation at hand. As illustrated in Figure 11.5(a), most appraisal theorists view appraisal as occurring *prior* to an emotional response (e.g., Scherer, 1993), even though some now acknowledge that emotions must also influence appraisals in some way (Roseman and Smith, 2001; Scherer, 2000a). Thus,

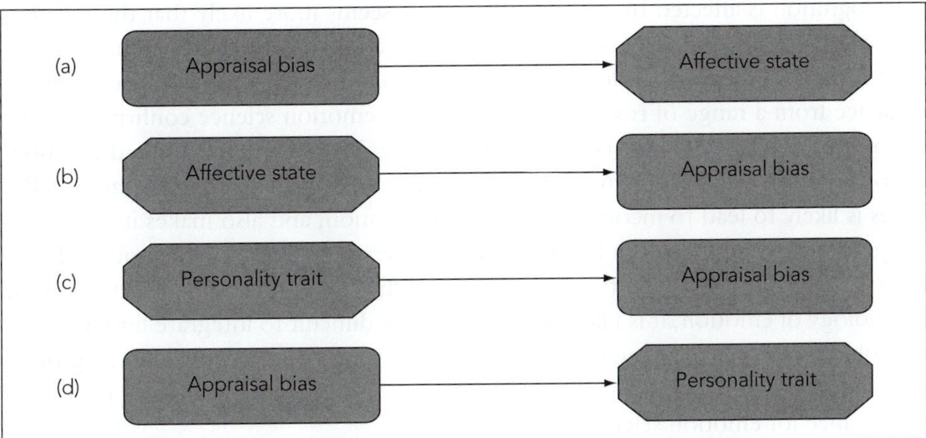

FIGURE 11.5 The nature of the relationship between cognitive processes (appraisals, biases) and affective states (moods, emotions)
(a) Appraisal theory approach
(b) Functions of emotions approach
(c) Trait influence approach
(d) Recent modelling from research on cognitive biases

there is a hint, even in appraisal theory, that the causal relations may be bi-directional (see also Frijda, 1993; Frijda and Zeelenberg, 2001).

A second approach identified by Lewis is research that focuses on the *functions of emotions.* One widely-held view is that a main function of emotions is to direct attention towards the momentarily most relevant aspects of the environment in order to facilitate the preparation of appropriate action tendencies. From this perspective, selectivity in attention is always *motivated* (Derryberry and Tucker, 1994). As discussed in Chapters 6 and 7, there is a large body of work demonstrating that affective states (especially moods) have profound effects on a number of cognitive processes such as attention, memory and judgment. From this perspective, the direction of influence is emotion to cognition as illustrated in Figure 11.5(b).

Lewis's third approach is the body of work suggesting that personality traits and clinical disorders influence cognitive biases. Empirical research discussed in Chapters 8 and 9 indicates that various personality dimensions (e.g., N-NA, E-PA) as well as lower-order traits (e.g., optimism, trait-anxiety etc) increase the probability, as well as the consistency, of trait-congruent cognitive biases. Thus, once again the assumption is of a linear relationship that goes from temperament to cognition (see Figure 11.5(c)). However, as discussed in Chapter 9 a more recent body of research examining techniques to modify cognitive biases has suggested that cognitive biases may play a causal role in the development of personality traits (Figure, 11.5(d)). Thus, the line of causality goes in the opposite direction.

An examination of Figure 11.5 suggests that the assumption of linear relations between the broad dimensions of cognition and affect is commonplace in psychological studies of emotion. However, what is also clear is that different research traditions conceptualize the direction of relationship as occurring in opposite directions: some view cognition as being an antecedent to an emotional state, while others consider that cognition is affected by emotional states. It seems more likely that the relations between these two constructs are actually bi-directional, with causal influences running in both directions. Indeed, as we concluded in earlier chapters, the empirical evidence from a range of research programmes in emotion science confirms that the nature of the relations between temperament, cognitive biases, moods and emotions is not one-way (see Figures 6.2 and 8.1). Ignoring such bi-directional causal influences is likely to lead to incomplete models of emotion, and also makes it difficult to integrate theory and research from across the different approaches to emotion theory (Lewis, 2005). If it is difficult to integrate research across different perspectives in the psychology of emotion, it is likely to be even more difficult to integrate findings from neurobiology into psychological models. Thus, it seems that an understanding of bi-directional causal relationships between affective and cognitive processes is of great importance for emotion science.

Characteristics of dynamic systems

While cognitive psychology has traditionally taken a rather linear approach, many cognitive scientists now highlight the dynamic nature of cognition , their assumption being that mental representations are distributed across a wide network of interconnecting parts. This non-linear approach to cognition also focuses on the emergent properties of cognitive systems. In other words, the investigation of how ordered structures emerge out of complex dynamic systems (see Kelso, 1995; Port and Van Gelder, 1995; Varela et al., 1991; Ward, 2002, for further details). From this perspective, cognition is essentially a form of self-organization that occurs in the context of a complex dynamic system. As we have seen, self-organization refers to the emergence of order from the apparent chaos of multiple and bi-directional interactions between many constituent parts of the system.

From the perspective of emotion science, Lewis (2005) argues that emotion–cognition amalgams can emerge from the dynamic cognitive system in the form of coherent states. These arise and stabilize by means of non-linear causal interactions among the various constituents of affect (e.g., action tendencies, feeling tone, attention). Figure 11.6 illustrates how such bi-directional causal relations can lead to a whole 'emotional interpretation', or what might be termed an *emotion schema* (c.f. Izard, 1977) The entire sequence begins with some trigger event that changes the dynamics of the cognitive system. Lewis presents an incident of road rage as an illustration. Thus, the trigger event might be a car cutting in in front of you, causing you to slam on the brakes. Following the trigger event, a phase of *self-amplification* begins, in which an emotional interpretation is formed. In the example, this might lead to interpretations that the driver in front is disrespectful leading to feelings of anger, in addition to the feelings of fear induced by the trigger event. Thus attention

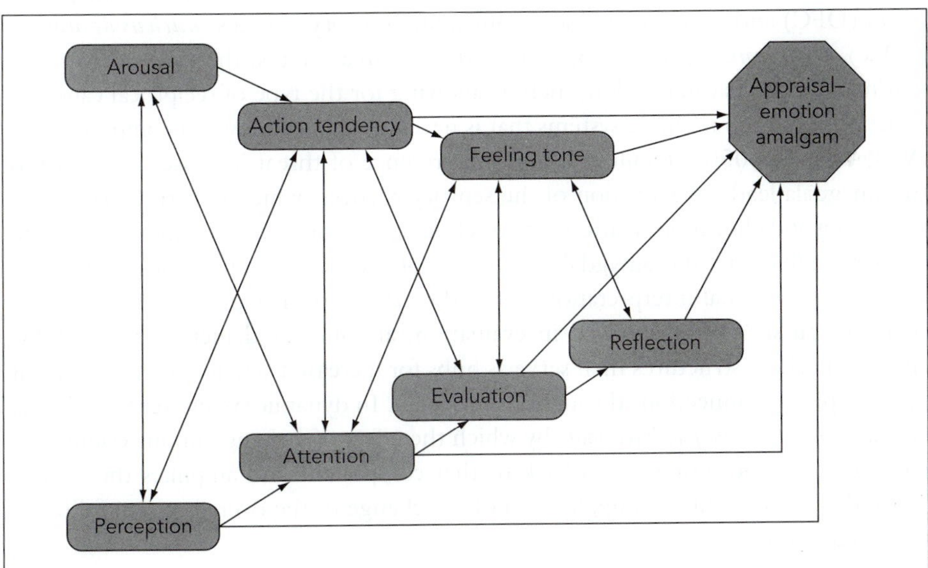

FIGURE 11.6 Schematic outline of how bi-directional causal relations between the constituents of emotion and appraisal can lead to a whole appraisal–emotion amalgam
This diagram captures the psychological level of description, but the components themselves have to be re-conceptualized at the neural level.

Source: Based on Figure 1 in Lewis (2005).

and arousal and many other components interact in a fast and dynamic way. The initial amplification phase gives way to a phase of *self-stabilization* in which a global coherence is established and higher levels of complexity appear. This might involve an angry-anxious affective state that becomes coupled with plans for revenge for the perceived act of disrespect. Any further signs of disrespect from the driver in front might now get easily interpreted as a further insult, possibly leading to a violent attack. Coherent states of the system that last for some time allow for learning to occur, and this extends the influence of the present appraisal to future events. It seems that there is evidence for all of these phases from emotion science as discussed next.

Trigger phase

In the biological sciences, living systems are commonly compared to taut springs, ready to respond to even very small perturbations that are of biological significance (Kaufman, 1993). In psychological studies, for example, it has been shown that attention is rapidly oriented towards stimuli that represent potential danger (e.g., Fox et al., 2000; Öhman, Flykt et al., 2001). In dynamic system terms, a trigger event marks a phase transition in which the order of the system is suddenly disrupted. Trigger events can occur at the beginning of an emotional episode, or at any point in the development of an emotional interpretation. A wide range of external events can act as trigger events, as well as internal events such as memories or images etc. At a neural level, the *amygdala* would seem to be a likely candidate for the rapid and initial detection of potential danger (e.g., Morris et al., 1998). As we have seen, the amygdala is richly interconnected to a range of other neural structures including the *orbitofrontal cortex* (OFC) and other cortical areas, including sensory cortices, *nucleus accumbens* (NAcc), *thalamus*, *hippocampus*, and *brain stem* areas. Thus, the evidence suggests that neural circuits can develop, thereby allowing for the type of reciprocal causal interactions between multiple systems that is necessary for stability in a complex system (Vuilleumier, 2005b). To illustrate, in the presence of threat increased activation of the amygdala leads to activation of the sensory cortices, which in turn enhances the processing and allocation of attention to relevant parts of the world, and this provides further feedback to the amygdala by means of reciprocal connections (see Figure 6.14). An emotional interpretation might then develop through the recruitment of other neural structures involved in evaluation, attention and memory: e.g., OFC, ACC etc). These structures then serve as hubs for increased activity due to their multiple reciprocal connections throughout the brain. In dynamic system terms, this is an example of a *positive feedback loop*, by which the effect of a change in one component (or circuit) of the system feeds back to that component and amplifies the change. Thus, there is a continual amplification of the change of the overall system following the trigger event.

Self-stabilization phase

Following the initial perturbation of the system a state of stabilization develops when *negative feedback* begins to dominate. Negative feedback is a process that leads to the *maintenance* of the current state of the system. In a negative feedback loop the effects of one component (or circuit) within the system are diminished by reciprocal effects in the opposite direction (e.g., inhibition). At a neural level, there is plenty of evidence for this type of negative feedback. For example, in the attempt to regulate emotion the increased activity of the amygdala is inhibited by increased activity within the OFC and the vmPFC. However, ongoing emotion regulation attempts lead to continual recruitment of OFC and vmPFC areas leading to a gradual reduction in amygdala activity. In this way the activity of both structures can become stabilized (e.g., Davidson, Putnam et al., 2000; Quirk, 2007). Moreover, as we discussed in Chapter 9, many emotional disorders are characterized by a difficulty in regulating emotion that correlates with problems in the relationship between the amygdala and regions of the PFC. For example, loss of the top-down inhibition of the amygdala by the vmPFC has been observed in both anxiety and depressive disorders (e.g., Drevets, 2001), while PTSD is associated with problems in the operation of a functional neural circuitry involving the ACC and the amygdala (e.g., Gilboa et al., 2004). Thus, as an emotional interpretation develops, stability can occur as attentional orientation and action tendencies lead to a narrowing of the focus of attention and behaviour to relevant material. The multiple interacting subcomponents ultimately lead to a stable system and a new emerging higher-order structure (emotional interpretation).

Learning phase

A dynamic systems perspective views the brain as a self-organizing system that shows increased connectivity among the various subcomponents that are reciprocally activated in real time. This can lead to the range of enduring cognitive biases and beliefs that have been well documented in emotion science. Stable emotional states are considered to be important for learning to occur (see Lewis, 2005, for further discussion). For instance, the increasing coherence and stabilization of neural interactions forms a whole, and this emerging whole may leave an enduring trace on some of its component parts. When similar events occur in the future, emerging configurations of the new system that include these components can be influenced by their previous encounter. The process, therefore, tends to be repeated. Thus, over time, enduring biases might develop that become very stable, as can be seen in the persistent cognitive biases apparent in clinical disorders.

A dynamic systems perspective, therefore, can explain the evidence suggesting that clinical conditions cause specific emotional interpretations, but can also explain the data indicating that changes in emotional interpretation play a causal role in the development of clinical traits (e.g., MacLeod et al., 2002).

To summarize then, a dynamic systems approach appears to provide a potential framework to integrate data and theory from cognitive and neurobiological studies of emotion. This approach emphasizes multiple and two-way interactions leading to bi-directional causality that results in the emergence and the stabilization of emotional interpretations. Affective and cognitive processes influence each other continuously across time in all directions. This perspective can account for much of the data in emotion science, which does seem to suggest multiple and bi-directional relationships

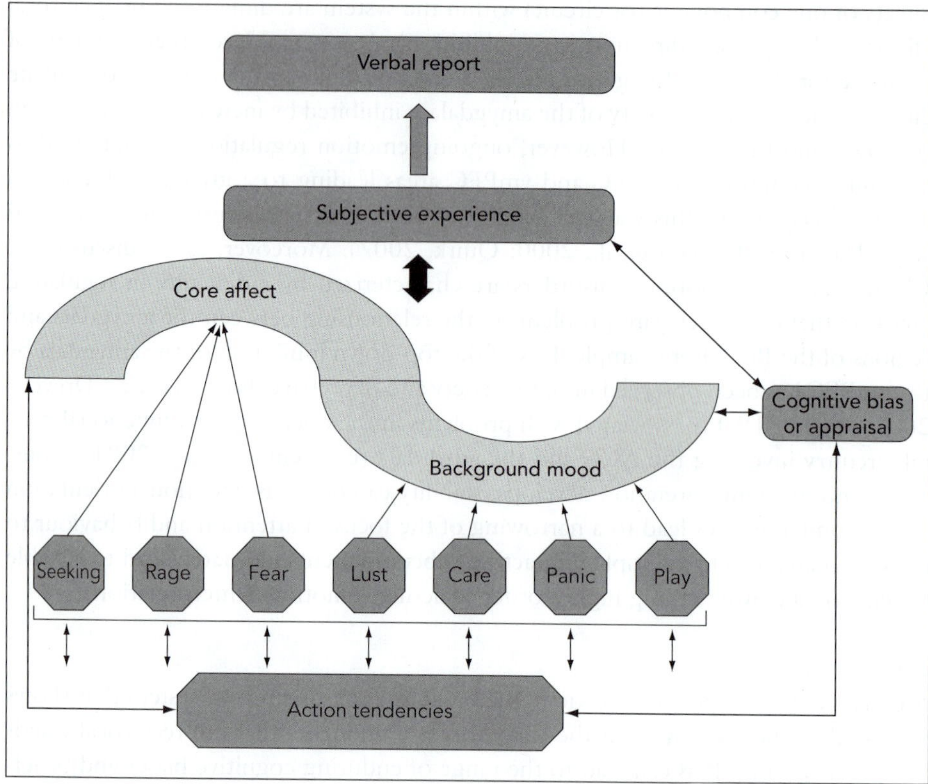

FIGURE 11.7 Extended framework of how discrete emotion and dimensional approaches may be integrated within a bi-directional dynamic systems framework

between temperament, emotions, moods and cognitive processes. This perspective also allows for greater detail to be incorporated into the framework in Figure 11.1. Figure 11.7 illustrates a more realistic framework in which causal relationships are likely to run in many directions. This model ultimately leads to a state of stable equilibrium: the system remains poised for change but also maintains a degree of stability. As shown in Figure 11.7, all the components involved in affect–cognition relations are connected with each other in both directions. This perspective allows us to frame the ways in which different levels of the system are connected, and how ancient neural circuits (e.g., fear) can perturb the system when activated by a triggering event. Likewise, the system can be perturbed by triggering events at higher levels of the system that could be related to background mood states, cognitive appraisals or subjective experiences. The important point is that a triggering event *at any level* can lead to a dynamic shift in the stable state of the entire system.

Dynamic systems approaches offer the potential to provide a realistic and comprehensive framework in which research in neurobiology can be more easily related to research on cognitive processes. The framework is the first important step, while the next and perhaps more difficult stage is formulating specific hypotheses that can be tested in the laboratory (Panksepp, 1998/2004). It is hoped that future research in emotion science will utilize dynamic systems perspectives (e.g., Lewis, 2005; Thayer and Lane, 2000) to help integrate neuroscientific and cognitive approaches. This broader framework with its emphasis on bi-directional causality may also be important in constructing bridges between basic scientific research (in both psychology and neuroscience) and clinical practice.

TRANSLATING BASIC EMOTION SCIENCE TO CLINICAL PRACTICE

The evidence reviewed in this book demonstrates that there has been an explosion of research and interest in emotion science since the mid-1990s. This has been characterized by rapid progress in our ability to develop better measures of all aspects of affect (see Coan and Allen, 2007, for extensive overview). However, in spite of extensive research programmes examining both normal and disordered emotions, there is still a large degree of separation between basic research on normal emotion and research and practice on emotional disorders.

There are a number of understandable reasons for this. First, the primary goals of basic scientists and clinicians are very different. For the basic emotion scientist, the goal is often to identify the causes as well as the consequences of a particular affective phenomenon (e.g., specific emotion, mood state, mood–memory congruence). This forces a somewhat reductionist approach in which a complex problem is broken down into smaller parts. In cognitive science, this approach has been highly successful (e.g., studies of specific components of attention, memory etc have led to progress in understanding a range of cognitive processes). It has also been successfully applied in emotion science, as we have seen throughout this book. However, a consequence of this approach is that few emotion scientists step back from their very specific and focused research programmes in order to consider the bigger picture. This has resulted in the proliferation of what have been called *micro-theories* (Barnard, 2004) that provide a good account of very specific aspects of mental life, but are not so good at providing a more general account of complex and dynamic mental processes.

Micro-theories and research programmes that focus on very specific aspects of affective–cognitive processes create a tension between basic science and clinical practice (Barnard, 2004). This is because the main goal of the clinician is to help people to feel better. Moreover, clinicians are dealing with highly complex situations and interactions between many levels, and it may not be possible to reduce these complex interactions to a simpler level (Strauman et al., 2007). Clinical practice, therefore, involves a degree of complexity and relatively uncontrolled experimental designs that are often unacceptable to basic emotion scientists. While it is possible under laboratory conditions to tightly control many variables (especially in animal research), this is almost impossible in a clinical trial of a psychotherapeutic intervention. To illustrate, imagine that we want to compare a particular treatment (e.g., cognitive behavioural therapy) with a placebo condition (e.g., general therapist–client interaction for the same amount of time). While it possible to randomly assign participants to the two treatment groups, there are still many factors that are very difficult to control. These include the personality of the individual therapist, the influence of the participant's family and friends and so on. This means that basic emotion scientists are often critical of the methodological aspects of psychotherapy outcome research (see Strauman et al., 2007).

Conversely, psychotherapists are often critical of studies in basic emotion science because many laboratory-based experiments can be seen as being rather artificial and largely irrelevant to complex human interactions. While therapists often deal with strong and raw human emotions, it is extremely difficult to recreate these emotions to the same degree of intensity in the laboratory. As we saw in Chapter 9, when emotions become dysregulated, as in the major affective disorders, there is a high degree of disruption not only to the individual concerned, but also to their family, friends, and work colleagues. In other words, emotional disorders have wide and complex implications for individuals, social groups and the larger society and culture. In this context, many of the research outcomes in emotion science are of little help to the clinician who is faced with a deeply distressed individual and family.

As we have seen throughout this book many aspects of emotion science concern behaviours and physiological responses that may not be available to conscious awareness. As noted by Arne Öhman and Christian Rück (2007) when discussing basic science approaches to the understanding of fear – 'In essence, evolution cares less for how we feel than for what we do' (p. 167). Thus, many emotion scientists are not concerned with the study of *feelings* per se. In contrast, while clinicians may be somewhat concerned with what people do, their primary focus is usually on how people *feel*. Likewise, many therapeutic intervention strategies are designed to make people *feel* better.

The different focus and research methods of basic and clinical scientists lead to some real difficulties in creating bridges between basic science and clinical practice. Nevertheless, while there is a gap between the goals of basic scientists and clinicians, there are also good grounds to encourage *translational research*. This is research in which the findings of basic studies of emotion can be translated into the development of better treatment approaches (see Craske et al., 2006; Rottenberg and Johnson, 2007). One strong reason for translational research is that almost all mental disorders involve a problem with some aspect of emotion or its regulation. As can be seen in

TABLE 11.3 Ten examples of emotional symptoms in psychopathology

Disorder	*Symptom*
Major depressive disorder	Sadness, guilt, anhedonia
Mania	Excessive euphoria, irritability
Schizophrenia	Flat affect, anhedonia
Panic disorder	Sudden unexplained bursts of fear
Specific phobia	Excessive fear of focal object
Obsessive-compulsive disorder	Repetitive anxious thoughts
Hypochondriasis	Persistent fear of serious disease
Pyromania	Pleasure from setting fires
Antisocial personality disorder	Irritability, aggressiveness, lack of guilt
Borderline personality disorder	Emotional instability, anger attacks

Source: Rottenberg and Johnson (2007).

Table 11.3, most of the diagnostic categories within DSM-IV involve severe disruption of some basic affective phenomenon. Thus, a good understanding of a basic affective phenomenon (e.g., sad mood state) is likely to facilitate the understanding of an extreme form of this phenomenon (e.g., major depressive disorders). Conversely, of course, a better understanding of emotional disorders also has the potential to illuminate the understanding of normal affective processes. This strategy has worked well in neuropsychology, for example, where studies of people with brain damage have led to important advances in the understanding of normal cognitive processes. The development of both dynamic systems approaches (Lewis, 2005) and multi-level approaches (Teasdale and Barnard, 1993) in emotion science is providing broader frameworks that can facilitate translational research and hopefully can provide clearer bridges between basic science and clinical intervention.

The application of basic science

Throughout the history of emotion science there have, of course, been many instances where basic scientific research has been useful for the development of clinical intervention. This has probably been most clear with the links between behavioural psychology, especially conditioning procedures, and the development of behavioural therapy. To illustrate, a large body of neuroscience has studied the fundamental mechanisms of fear in animals (e.g., Davis and Whalen, 2001; LeDoux, 2000; Phelps and LeDoux, 2005, for reviews). Using a variety of conditioning procedures it has been shown that when an innocuous stimulus (e.g., a tone) is associated with an aversive stimulus (e.g., an electric shock) the animal gradually learns to fear the tone (*acquisition of fear*). However, this fear response can be extinguished by presenting the tone a number of times without any shock. Eventually, the animal will stop responding to the tone with a fear response (*extinction of fear*). Research has shown that this process of extinction is not passive, but is an active learning experience that is dependent upon the amygdala (e.g., Davis and Whalen, 2001). In particular, during extinction it seems that the animal is actually learning to superimpose a memory of safety on top of a memory of fear.

From fear extinction to exposure therapy

This basic research programme has been translated into clinical practice in the form of *exposure therapy* that partly relies on extinction to be successful. Exposure therapy involves presenting a feared object (e.g., a spider to a person with a spider phobia) over and over again. Eventually, the fear dissipates, probably due to an active process of extinction. This fundamental research using behavioural psychology techniques has also been integrated with basic research in pharmacology. These developments are providing possibilities for fundamental research findings to be translated into clinical practice. For example, there is currently a great deal of excitement about the possibility that pharmacological compounds whose neurochemical mechanisms are well understood may be useful adjuncts to psychological therapies.

To illustrate, glutamate is one of the major excitatory neurotransmitters in the brain and operates by means of the N-methyl-D-aspartate (NMDA) receptor. NMDA receptor sites are abundant in the basolateral part of the amygdala which, as was discussed in Chapter 4, is known to be important for fear learning. Studies have shown that if NMDA receptor antagonists are infused directly into this part of the amygdala then extinction is prevented (Falls et al., 1992). In other words, the animal remains fearful even after many trials without aversive stimulation. In contrast, if d-cycloserine, which is an NMDA receptor agonist is infused into the same region of the amygdala then fear extinction is facilitated (Walker et al., 2002). In other words, administering d-cycloserine can facilitate the extent to which learned fears can be extinguished.

The potential of d-cycloserine to help eradicate some deeply embedded human fears is obvious and a number of clinical trials with human participants have now been conducted. In one study, the efficacy of d-cycloserine was tested in a randomized double-blind placebo controlled study with people who had a phobic fear of heights (Ressler et al., 2004). Using a simulated virtual reality system in which people were provided with exposure therapy using a high platform, patients who had received the drug demonstrated a larger reduction in their fear of heights two weeks after therapy than did those who had received the placebo. A number of other studies have also indicated that d-cycloserine can enhance fear reduction during exposure therapy in a range of human anxiety disorders (see Hofmann, 2007, for review).

Basic research with animals investigating the neural implications of acute and chronic stress have also provided useful models for studies of human PTSD (Miller and McEwen, 2006). While it is impossible to fully model the symptoms of human disorders in rodents, it is possible to learn about the neural mechanisms underlying the response to acute stress which is often quite similar across species. This research has now been applied to the development of potential treatment strategies for PTSD. For example, d-cycloserine has been tested in trials with PTSD patients because it is likely that an important part of the problem in PTSD is the failure to extinguish embedded fears. This research is unique in demonstrating that pharmacological compounds can be used to facilitate psychological therapies. Thus, d-cycolserine is not a direct treatment for specific phobias or PTSD. Rather, it can be used in conjunction with psychological treatment to facilitate the effects of the therapy. In other words, while exposure therapy is successful in treating specific phobias it may be even more effective when presented in conjunction with d-cycloserine. This is one example of how basic science research on the neurochemistry of fear responses in animals can provide hypotheses for plausible treatments for human mood disorders (see Barad, 2006; Hofmann, 2007, for further examples).

From cognitive bias to clinical intervention

The cognitive revolution in psychology has also resulted in the development of more cognitively focused therapies (e.g., cognitive behavioural therapy, CBT). In particular, the focus has moved from behavioural approaches such as exposure therapy to attempt to address the biases typical of depression and anxiety. However, while the foundations of behaviour therapy were clearly located in the laws of learning and psychophysiology, the development of cognitive therapies was not so clearly grounded in experimental cognitive psychology (see Brewin, 1988, for discussion). In contrast, cognitive approaches to therapy were often based on clinical experience and were surprisingly disconnected from basic research in mainstream cognitive psychology.

More recently, however, basic science research in cognitive psychology has been more closely linked to the development of potential new therapies and adjuncts to therapy. One example comes from the body of work demonstrating that increased levels of neuroticism (or trait-anxiety) are associated with fundamental biases in how people process affective information. This work essentially utilized a range of techniques developed from experimental cognitive psychology and applied them to clinical problems (e.g., Williams et al., 1988). The general finding is that higher levels of trait-anxiety are associated with a tendency to selectively attend towards threat-related information and to interpret ambiguous information in a more threatening way (see Mathews and MacLeod, 2005, for review). As discussed in Chapter 8, however, it is not entirely clear whether these cognitive biases are a cause or a consequence of emotional disorder. This uncertainty motivated the development of new paradigms in which fundamental biases in both attention (MacLeod et al., 2002) and interpretation (Mathews and Mackintosh, 2000) could be experimentally induced. These cognitive bias modification procedures (CBM) have now been shown to modify emotional vulnerability and early indications suggest that these simple computerized paradigms may play an important role in treating anxiety and depressive disorders (see Koster et al., 2008, for overview).

SUMMARY

To summarize, basic research in behavioural neuroscience and cognitive psychology have provided important data that have helped in the development of new therapeutic strategies for major emotional disorders. The current burgeoning research in affective neuroscience, especially with the increasing integration of neuroimaging, genetic and cognitive approaches to emotion, is also likely to lead to new developments in clinical interventions. Thus, while there are difficulties, there are also clear points of intersection between basic and clinical science.

In order to facilitate future integration, it is important to develop a common language as well as a comprehensive framework that can incorporate both basic science and clinical intervention. The emerging consensus with regard to the definition of different terms in emotion science is important in this regard. Thus, perhaps emotion scientists can agree to use the term *emotion* to refer to brief and intense reactions to significant situations and stimuli that involve the coordination of several subsystems. In contrast, the term *mood* can refer to more enduring and less intense states that can be related to emotions but can also represent a broader range of subjective states (e.g., Watson, 2000). *Feelings* refer to the conscious representation of both emotions and moods, while *affect* is a broader term that encompasses all affective reactions and experiences. If we adopt this terminology it becomes clear that 'emotional' disorders, such as anxiety and depression, are better thought of as disorders of mood, rather than disorders of emotion. Thus, basic research on mood states (rather than emotions) may provide clearer data that can help us to understand clinical problems.

Multi-level approaches such as ICS and dynamic systems approaches can also provide a common framework for models of both normal and abnormal emotions, moods and feeling states. While, up to now, the interaction between basic science and clinical practice has been rather one-way, it is to be hoped that research on the efficacy of clinical interventions as well as on the nature of serious mood disorders can begin to inform theories of normal emotions and mood states.

CHAPTER SUMMARY

This chapter has suggested a framework for facilitating the integration of neuro-biological, genetic and cognitive approaches in emotion science. A closer integration of these approaches is also likely to facilitate the links between basic science and clinical practice. Both aspects are clearly of importance to emotion science. It has been suggested that adopting a consistent terminology – agreeing on what we mean by *emotions*, *moods*, *feelings* and *affect* – is important for the development of more integrative approaches in emotion science. Developments such as *multi-level theories* and *dynamic systems approaches* are also crucial in laying the groundwork for the further integration of research data and theory across the different domains of emotion science.

RECOMMENDED READING

The following article along with the associated commentaries provides an excellent overview of a dynamic systems approach to affect–cognition interactions.

Marc Lewis (2005) 'Bridging emotion theory and neurobiology through dynamic systems modelling', *Behavioral and Brain Sciences*, 28, 169–245.

The following book provides an excellent introduction to multi-level approaches in cognitive psychology as applied to the study of emotion and emotional disorders:

John Teasdale and Philip Barnard (1993) *Affect, Cognition and Change: Re-modelling Depressive Thought*. Hove: Lawrence Erlbaum.

The following edited books provide many easy-to-read chapters examining different aspects of translational research.

M.G. Craske, D. Hermans and D. Vansteenwegen (eds) (2006) F*ear and Learning: From Basic Processes to Clinical Implications*. Washington, DC: American Psychological Association.

J. Rottenberg and S.L. Johnson (eds) (2007) *Emotion and Psychopathology: Bridging Affective and Clinical Science*. Washington, DC: American Psychological Association.

REFERENCES

Abercrombie, H.C., Schaefer, S.M., Larson, C.L., Oakes, T.R., Lindgren, K.A., Holden, J.E., Perlman, S.B., Turski, P.A., Krahn, D.D., Benca, R.M. and Davidson, R.J. (1998) 'Metabolic rate in the right amygdala predicts negative affect in depressed patients', *Neuroreport*, 9, 3301–7.

Abramson, L., Seligman Y. and Teasdale, M. (1978) 'Learned helplessness in humans: Critique and reformulation', *Abnormal Psychology*, 87, 49–74.

Adolphs, R. and Damasio, A.R. (2001) 'The interaction of affect and cognition: A neurobiological perspective', in J.P. Forgas (ed.), *Handbook of Affect and Social Cognition*. Mahwah, NJ: Lawrence Erlbaum.

Adolphs, R., Denburg, N.L. and Tranel, D. (2001) 'The amygdala's role in declarative memory for gist and detail', *Behavioural Neuroscience*, 115, 983–92.

Adolphs, R., Tranel, D. and Buchanan, T.W. (2005) 'Amygdala damage impairs emotional memory for the gist but not details of complex stimuli', *Nature Neuroscience*, 8, 512–19.

Adolphs, R., Tranel, D. and Damasio, A.R. (1998) 'The human amygdala in social judgment', *Nature*, 393, 470–4.

Adolphs, R., Tranel, D., Damasio, H. and Damasio, A.R. (1994) 'Impaired recognition of emotion in facial expressions following bilateral damage to the human amygdala', *Nature*, 372, 669–72.

Adolphs, R., Tranel, D., Damasio, H. and Damasio, A.R. (1995) 'Fear and the human amygdala', *Journal of Neuroscience*, 15, 5879–91.

Aggleton, J.P. (1992) *The Amygdala: Neurobiological Aspects of Emotion, Memory, and Mental Dysfunction*. New York: Wiley-Liss.

Albright, T.D., Jessell, T.M., Kandel, E.R. and Posner, M.I. (2000) 'Neural science: A century of progress and the mysteries that remain', *Neuron*, 25, S1–S55.

Alkire, M.T., Haier, R.J., Fallon, J. and Barker, S.J. (1996) 'PET imaging of conscious and unconscious memory', *Journal of Consciousness Studies*, 3, 338–462.

Alkire, M.T., Haier, R.J., Fallon, J.H. and Cahill, L. (1998) 'Hippocampal, but not amygdala, activity at encoding correlates with long-term, free recall of non-emotional information', *Proceedings of the National Academy of Sciences*, 95, 14506–10.

Alloy, L.B. and Abramson, L.Y. (1979) 'Judgment of contingency in depressed and non-depressed students: Sadder but wiser?', *Journal of Experimental Psychology*, 108, 441–85.

Allport, G. (1937) *Personality: A Psychological Interpretation*. New York: Rinehart & Winston.

Allport, G. (1961) *Pattern and Growth in Personality*. New York: Rinehart & Winston.

Amaral, D.G. and Price, J.L. (1990) 'Amygdalo-cortical projections in the monkey (Macaca fascicularis)', *Journal of Comparative Neurology*, 230, 465–96.

Amaral, D.G., Price, J.L., Pitkanen, A. and Carmichael, S.T. (1992) 'Anatomical organization of the primate amygdaloid complex', in J.P. Aggleton (ed.), *The Amygdala: Neurobiological Aspects of Emotion, Memory, and Mental Dysfunction*. New York: Wiley-Liss.

Amat, J., Paul, E., Zarza, C., Watkins, L.R. and Maier, S. F. (2006) 'Previous experience with behavioral control over stress blocks the behavioral and dorsal raphe activating effects of later uncontrollable stress: Role of the ventral medial prefrontal cortex', *Journal of Neuroscience*, 26, 13264–72.

Amies, P.L., Gelder, M.G. and Shaw, P.M. (1983) 'Social phobia: A comparative clinical study', *British Journal of Psychiatry*, 142, 174–9.

Anders, S., Lotze, M., Erb, M., Grodd, W. and Birbaumer, N. (2004) 'Brain activity underlying emotional valence and arousal: a response-related fMRI study', *Human Brain Mapping*, 23, 200–9.

Anderson, A.K. and Phelps, E.A. (2001) 'Lesions of the human amygdala impair enhanced perception of emotionally salient events', *Nature*, 411, 305–9.

Anderson, A.K., Christoff, K., Stappen, I., Panitz, D., Ghahremani, D.G., Glover, G., Gabrieli, J.D. and Sobel, N. (2003) 'Dissociated neural representations of intensity and valence in human olfaction', *Nature Neuroscience*, 6, 196–202.

Anderson, J. and Bower, G. (1973) *Human Associative Memory*. Washington: Winston.

Argyle, M. (1999) 'Causes and correlates of happiness', in D. Kahneman, E. Diener and N. Schwarz (eds), *Well-being: The Foundations of Hedonic Psychology*. New York: Russell Sage Foundation.

Armony, J.L. and LeDoux, J.E. (2000) 'How danger is encoded: Towards a systems, cellular, and computational understanding of cognitive-emotional interactions in fear circuits', in M.S. Gazzaniga (ed.), *The Cognitive Neurosciences*. Cambridge, MA: MIT Press.

Arnold, M.B. (1960) *Emotion and Personality*. New York: Columbia University Press.

Arnold, M.B. and Gasson, J.A. (1954) *The Human Person: An Approach to an Integral Theory of Personality*. New York: Ronald Press.

Ashby, F.G., Isen, A.M. and Turken, A.U. (1999) 'A neuropsychological theory of positive affect and its influence on cognition', *Psychological Review*, 106, 529–50.

Averill, J.R. (1980) *Anger and Aggression: An Essay on Emotion*. New York: Springer-Verlag.

Averill, J.R. (1985) 'The social construction of emotion: With special reference to love', in K. Gerken and K. Davis (eds), *The Social Construction of the Person*. New York: Springer-Verlag.

Averill, J.R. (1994) 'Emotions unbecoming and becoming', in P. Ekman and R.J. Davidson (eds), *The Nature of Emotion*. New York: Cambridge University Press.

Ax, A.F. (1953) 'The physiological differentiation between fear and anger in humans', *Psychosomatic Medicine*, 15, 433–42.

Banse, R. and Scherer, K.R. (1996) 'Acoustic profiles in vocal emotion expression', *Journal of Personality and Social Psychology*, 70, 614–36.

Barad, M. (2006) 'Anatomical, molecular, and cellular substrates of fear extinction', in M.G. Craske, D. Hermans and D. Vansteenwegen (eds), *Fear and Learning: From Basic Processes to Clinical Implications*. Washington, DC: American Psychological Association.

Bargh, J.A. and Williams, L.E. (2007) 'The nonconscious regulation of emotion', in J.J. Gross (ed.), *Handbook of Emotion Regulation*. New York: Guilford Press.

Bargh, J.A., Lombardi, W.J. and Higgins, E.T. (1988) 'Automaticity of chronically accessible constructs in person X situation effects on person perception: It's just a matter of time…', *Journal of Personality and Social Psychology*, 55, 599–605.

Bar-Haim, Y., Lamy, D., Pergamin, L., Bakermans-Kranenburg, M.J. and van Ijzendoorn, M.H. (2007) 'Threat-related attentional bias in anxious and nonanxious individuals: A metaanalytic study', *Psychological Bulletin*, 133, 1–24.

Barnard, P.J. (1985) 'Interacting cognitive subsystems: A psycholinguistic approach to short-term memory', in A. Ellis (ed.), *Progress in the Psychology of Language, Vol 2.* Hove: Lawrence Erlbaum.

Barnard, P.J. (2004) 'Bridging between basic theory and clinical practice', *Behaviour Research and Therapy*, 42, 977–1000.

Barnard, P.J., Duke, D.J. Byrne, R.W. and Davidson, I. (2007) 'Differentiation in cognitive and emotional meanings: An evolutionary analysis', *Cognition & Emotion*, 21, 1155–83.

Bartels, A. and Zeki, S. (2004) 'The neural correlates of maternal and romantic love', *NeuroImage*, 21, 1155–66.

Bartlett, M.Y. and DeSteno, D. (2006) 'Gratitude and prosocial behavior: Helping when it costs you', *Psychological Science*, 17, 319–25.

Baxter, M.G. and Murray, E.A. (2002) 'The amygdala and reward', *Nature Reviews Neuroscience*, 3(7), 563–73.

Bear, M.F., Connors, B.W. and Paradiso, M.A. (2001) *Neuroscience: Exploring the Brain.* Baltimore: Lippincott Williams & Wilkins.

Bechara, A., Damasio, A.R., Damasio, H. and Anderson, S.W. (1994) 'Insensitivity to future consequences following damage to human prefrontal cortex', *Cognition*, 50, 7–15.

Bechara, A., Damasio, H., Tranel, D. and Damasio, A.R. (1997) 'Deciding advantageously before knowing the advantageous strategy', *Science*, 275, 1293–4.

Bechara, A., Damasio, H., Tranel, D. and Damasio, A.R. (2005) 'The Iowa Gambling Task and the somatic marker hypothesis: Some questions and answers', *Trends in Cognitive Sciences*, 9, 159–62.

Bechara, A.,Tranel, D., Damasio, H., Adolphs, R., Rockland, C. and Damasio, A.R. (1995) 'Double dissociation of conditioning and declarative knowledge relative to the amygdala and hippocampus in humans', *Science*, 269, 1115–18.

Bechara, A., Tranel, D., Damasio, H. and Damasio, A.R. (1996) 'Failure to respond autonomically to anticipated future outcomes following damage to prefrontal cortex', *Cerebral Cortex*, 6, 215–25.

Beck, A.T. (1967) *Depression: Causes and Treatment.* Philadelphia: University of Pennsylvania Press.

Beck, A.T. (1976) *Cognitive Therapy and the Emotional Disorders.* New York: International Universities Press.

Beck, A.T. and Clark, D.A. (1988) 'Anxiety and depression: An information processing perspective', *Anxiety Research*, 1, 23–36.

Beck, A.T., Rush, A.J., Shaw, B.F. and Emery, G. (1979) *Cognitive Therapy of Depression.* New York: Guilford Press.

Beck, A.T., Steer, R., Kovacs, M. and Garrison, B. (1985) 'Hopelessness and eventual suicide: A 10-year prospective study of patients hospitalized with suicidal ideation', *American Journal of Psychiatry*, 142, 559–63.

Beck, A.T., Ward, C.H., Mendelson, M., Mock, J. and Erbaugh, J. (1961) 'An inventory for measuring depression', *Archives of General Psychiatry*, 4, 561–71.

Becker, E.S., Roth, W.T., Andrich, M. and Margraf, J. (1999) 'Explicit memory in anxiety disorders', *Journal of Abnormal Psychology*, 108, 153–63.

Beedie, C.J., Terry, P.C. and Lane, A.M. (2005) 'Distinguishing mood from emotion', *Cognition & Emotion*, 19, 847–78.

Bellew, M. and Hill, A.B. (1990) 'Negative recall bias as a predictor of susceptibility to induced depressive mood', *Personality and Individual Differences*, 11, 471–80.

Benjamin, J., Li, L. and Paterson, C. (1996) 'Population and familial association between the D4 dopamine receptor gene and measures of novelty seeking', *Nature Genetics*, 12(1), 81–4.

Berridge, K.C. (1999) 'Pleasure, pain, desire, and dread: Hidden core processes of emotion', in D. Kahneman, E. Diener and N. Schwarz (eds), *Well-being: The Foundations of Hedonic Psychology*. New York: Russell Sage Foundation.

Berridge, K.C. (2000) 'Measuring hedonic impact in animals and infants: Microstructure of affective taste reactivity patterns', *Neuroscience and Biobehavioural Reviews*, 24, 173–98.

Berridge, K.C. (2003) 'Pleasures of the brain', *Brain and Cognition*, 52, 106–28.

Berridge, K.C. (2004) 'Unfelt affect and irrational desire: A view from the brain', in A.S.R. Manstead, N.H. Frijda and A. Fischer (eds), *Feelings and Emotions: The Amsterdam Symposium*. Cambridge: Cambridge University Press.

Berridge, K.C. and Robinson, T.E. (1998) 'What is the role of dopamine in reward: Hedonic impact, reward learning, or incentive salience?', *Brain Research Review*, 28, 309–69.

Berridge, K.C. and Robinson, T.E. (2003) 'Parsing reward', *Trends in Neuroscience*, 26(9), 507–13.

Berridge, K.C. and Winkielman, P. (2003) 'What is an unconscious emotion: The case of unconscious "liking"', *Cognition & Emotion*, 17, 181–211.

Biederman J., Rosenbaum, J.F., Hirshfeld, D.R., Faraone, S.V., Bolduc, E.A., Gersten, M., Meminger, S.R., Snidman, N., Reznick, J.S. and Kagan, J. (1990) 'Psychiatric correlates of behavioral inhibition in young children of parents with and without psychiatric disorders', *Archives of General Psychiatry*, 47, 21–6.

Blanchard, R.J. and Blanchard, D.C. (1990) 'An ethoexperimental analysis of defense, fear and anxiety', in N. McNaughton and G. Andrews (eds), *Anxiety*. Dunedin: Otago University Press.

Blanchette, I. (2006) 'The effect of emotion on interpretation and logic in a conditional reasoning task', *Memory and Cognition*, 34, 1112–25.

Blaney, P.H. (1986) 'Affect and memory: A review', *Psychological Bulletin*, 99, 229–46.

Bless, H. (2000) 'The interplay of affect and cognition', in J.P. Forgas (ed.), *Feeling and Thinking: The Role of Affect in Social Cognition*. New York: Cambridge University Press.

Bless, H., Clore, G.L., Schwarz, N., Golisano, V., Rabe, C. and Wölk, M. (1996) 'Mood and the use of scripts: Does being in a happy mood really lead to mindlessness?', *Journal of Personality and Social Psychology*, 71, 665–79.

Blessing, W.W. (1997) 'Inadequate frameworks for understanding bodily homeostatis', *Trends in Neurosciences*, 20, 235–9

Block, J.H. and Block, J. (1980) 'The role of ego-control and ego-resiliency in the organization of behaviour', in W.A. Collins (ed.), *The Minnesota Symposia on Child Psychology*, Vol. 13. Hillsdale, NJ: Lawrence Erlbaum.

Blum, K., Sheridan, P.J. et al. (1996) 'The D2 dopamine receptor gene as a determinant of reward deficiency syndrome', *Journal of the Royal Society of Medicine*, 89(7), 396–400.

Bolger, N. and Zuckerman, A. (1995) 'A framework for studying personality in the stress process', *Journal of Personality and Social Psychology*, 69, 890–902.

Bolger, N., Davis, A. and Rafaeli, E. (2003) 'Diary methods: Capturing life as it is lived', *Annual Review of Psychology*, 54, 579–616.

Bonanno, G.A. (2004) 'Loss, trauma, and human resilience: Have we underestimated the human capacity to thrive after extremely aversive events?', *American Psychologist*, 59, 20–8.

Bonanno, G.A., Davis, P.J., Singer, J.L. and Schwartz, G.E. (1991) 'The repressor personality and avoidant information processing: A dichotic listening study', *Journal of Research in Personality*, 25, 386–401.

Bonanno, G.A., Keltner, D., Holen, A. and Horowitz, M.J. (1995) 'When avoiding unpleasant emotions might not be such a bad thing', *Journal of Personality and Social Psychology*, 69, 975–90.

Borkovec, T., Robinson, E., Pruzinsky, T. and Depree, J. (1983) 'Preliminary exploration of worry: Some characteristics and processes', *Behaviour Research and Therapy*, 21, 9–16.

Bornstein, R.F. and Pittman, T.S. (eds) (1992) *Perception without Awareness: Cognitive, Clinical, and Social Perspectives.* New York: Guilford Press.

Borod, J.C. (1992) 'Interhemispheric and intrahemispheric control of emotion: A focus on unilateral brain damage', *Journal of Consulting and Clinical Psychology*, 60, 339–48.

Bouchard, T. J. (1994) 'Genes, environment, and personality', *Science*, 264(5166), 1700–1.

Boucher, J.D. (1983) 'Antecedents to emotions across cultures', in S.H. Irvine and J.W. Berry (eds), *Human Assessment and Cultural Factors.* New York: Plenum.

Bower, G.H. (1981) 'Mood and memory', *American Psychologist*, 36, 129–48.

Bower, G.H. (1992) 'How emotions affect learning', in S. Christianson (ed.), *Handbook of Emotion and Memory: Research and Theory.* Hillsdale, NJ: Lawrence Erlbaum.

Bower, G.H. and Cohen, P.R. (1982) 'Emotion influences in memory and. thinking: Data and theory', in M.S. Clark and S.T. Fiske (eds), *Affect and Cognition.* Hillsdale, NJ: Lawrence Erlbaum.

Bower, G.H. and Forgas, J.P. (2001) 'Mood and social memory', in J.P. Forgas (ed.), *Handbook of Affect and Social Cognition.* Mahwah, NJ: Lawrence Erlbaum.

Bower, G.H. and Mayer, J.D. (1989) 'In search of mood-dependent retrieval', *Journal of Social Behaviour and Personality*, 4, 121–56.

Bower, G.H., Gilligan, S.G. and Monteiro, K. P. (1981) 'Selective learning caused by affective states', *Journal of Experimental Psychology: General*, 110, 451–73.

Bower, G.H., Monteiro, K.P. and Gilligan, S.G. (1978) 'Emotional mood as a context of learning and recall', *Journal of Verbal Learning and Verbal Behaviour*, 17, 573–85.

Bradley, B. and Mathews, A. (1988) 'Memory bias in recovered clinical depressives', *Cognition & Emotion*, 2, 235–45.

Bradley, B., Mogg, K., Galbraith, M. and Perrett, A. (1993) 'Negative recall bias and neuroticism: State vs trait effects', *Behaviour Research and Therapy*, 31(1), 125–7.

Bradley, B.P., Mogg, K., Falla, S.J. and Hamilton, L.R. (1998) 'Attentional bias for threatening facial expressions in anxiety: Manipulation of stimulus duration', *Cognition & Emotion*, 12, 737–53.

Bradley, B.P., Mogg, K. et al. (2000) 'Biases in overt and covert orienting to emotional facial expressions', *Cognition & Emotion*, 14, 789–808.

Bradley, B.P., Mogg, K. and Millar, N. (1996) 'Implicit memory bias in clinical and non-clinical depression', *Behaviour Research and Therapy*, 34, 865–79.

Bradley, B.P., Mogg, K., Millar, N. and White, J. (1995) 'Selective processing of negative information: Effects of clinical anxiety, concurrent depression and awareness', *Journal of Abnormal Psychology*, 104, 532–6.

Bradley, M.M. and Lang, P.J. (1994) 'Measuring emotion: The self-assessment manikin and the semantic differential', *Journal of Behavioural Therapy and Experimental Psychiatry*, 25, 49–59.

Bradley, M.M. and Lang, P.J. (1999a) *Affective Norms for English Words (ANEW): Instruction Manual and Affective Ratings. Technical Report no. C-1*, Center for Research in Psychophysiology, University of Florida, Gainesville.

Bradley, M.M. and Lang, P.J. (1999b) *International Affective Digitized Sounds (IADS): Stimuli, instruction manual and affective ratings. Technical report no. B-2*, Center for Research in Psychophysiology, University of Florida, Gainesville.

Bradley, M.M. and Lang, P.J. (2000a) 'Affective reactions to acoustic stimuli', *Psychophysiology*, 37, 204–15.

Bradley, M.M. and Lang, P.J. (2000b) 'Measuring emotion: Behavior, feeling and physiology', in R. Lane and L. Nadel (eds), *Cognitive Neuroscience of Emotion*. New York: Oxford University Press.

Bradley, M.M., Cuthbert, B.N. and Lang, P.J. (1990) 'Startle reflex. modification: Emotion or attention?', *Psychophysiology*, 27, 513–23.

Brauer, L.H., Cramblett, M.J., Paxton, D.A. and Rose, J.E. (2001) 'Haloperidol reduces smoking of both nicotine-containing and denicotinized cigarettes', *Psychopharmacology*, 159, 31–7.

Brefczynski, J.A. and DeYoe, E.A. (1999) 'A physiological correlate of the "spotlight" of visual attention', *Nature Neuroscience*, 2, 370–4.

Breiter, H.C., Etcoff, N.L., Whalen, P.J., Kennedy, W.A., Rauch, S.L., Buckner, R.L., Strauss, M.M., Hyman, S.E. and Rosen, B.R. (1996) 'Response and habituation of the human amygdale during visual processing of facial expression', *Neuron*, 17, 875–87.

Breiter, H.C., Rauch, S.L., Kwong, K.K., Baker, J.R., Weisskoff, R.M., Kennedy, D.N., Kendrick, A.D., Davis, T.L., Jiang, A., Cohen, M.S., Stern, C.E., Belliveau, J.W., Baer, L., O'Sullivan, R.L., Savage, C.R., Jenike, M.A.and Rosen, B.R. (1996) 'Functional magnetic resonance imaging of symptom provocation in obsessive-compulsive disorder', *Archives of General Psychiatry*, 53, 595–606.

Brewin, C.R. (1988) *Cognitive Foundations of Clinical Psychology*. Hove: Lawrence Erlbaum.

Brickman, P. and Campbell, D. T. (1971) 'Hedonic relativism and planning the good society', in M.H. Apley (ed.), *Adaptation-level Theory: A Symposium*. New York: Academic Press.

Brickman, P., Coates, D. and Janoff-Bulman, R. (1978) 'Lottery winners and accident victims: Is happiness relative?', *Journal of Personality and Social Psychology*, 37, 917–27.

Broadbent, D. and Broadbent, M. (1988) 'Anxiety and attentional bias: State and trait', *Cognition & Emotion*, 2, 165–83.

Brosch, T. and Sharma, D. (2005) 'The role of fear-relevant stimuli in visual search: A comparison of phylogenetic and ontogenetic stimuli', *Emotion*, 5, 360–4.

Brown, G.W. and Harris, T. (1978) *Social Origins of Depression: A Study of Psychiatric Disorder in Women*. London: Tavistock.

Brown, J.S., Kalish, H.I. and Farber, I.E. (1951) 'Conditioned fear as revealed by magnitude of startle response to an auditory stimulus', *Journal of Experimental Psychology*, 43, 317–28.

Brown, R. and Kulik, J. (1977) 'Flashbulb memories', *Cognition*, 5, 73–93.

Brown, S.M., Peet, E. et al. (2005) 'A regulatory variant of the human tryptophan hydroxylase 2 gene biases the amygdala reactivity', *Molecular Psychiatry*, 10, 884–8.

Brown, T.A. (2007) 'Temporal course and structural relationships among dimensions of temperament and DSM-IV anxiety and mood disorder constructs', *Journal of Abnormal Psychology*, 116, 313–28.

Brown, T.A., Chorpita, B.F. and Barlow, D.H. (1998) 'Structural relationships among dimensions of the *DSM-IV* anxiety and mood disorders and dimensions of negative affect, positive affect, and autonomic arousal', *Journal of Abnormal Psychology*, 107, 179–92.

Bruner, J.S. (1957) 'On perceptual readiness', *Psychological Review*, 80, 307–36.

Bruner, J.S. (1992) 'Another look at New Look 1', *American Psychologist*, 47, 780–3.

Bruner, J.S. (1994) *Acts of Meaning*. Cambridge, MA: Harvard University Press.

Bruner, J.S. and Postman, L. (1947) 'Tension and tension-release as organizing factors in perception', *Journal of Personality*, 15, 300–8.

Butler, G. and Mathews, A. (1983) 'Cognitive processes in anxiety', *Advances in Behaviour Research and Therapy*, 5, 51–62.

Butler, G. and Mathews, A. (1987) 'Anticipatory anxiety and risk estimation', *Cognitive Therapy and Research*, 5, 551–65.

Cacioppo, J.T. and Berntson, G.G. (1994) 'Relationship between attitudes and evaluative space: A critical review, with emphasis on the separability of positive and negative substrates', *Psychological Bulletin*, 115, 401–23.

Cacioppo, J.T., Berntson, G.G., Klein, D.J. and Poehlmann, K.M. (1997) 'The psychophysiology of emotion across the lifespan', *Annual Review of Gerontology and Geriatrics*, 17, 27–74.

Cacioppo, J.T., Berntson, G.G., Larsen, J.T., Poehlmann, K.M. and Ito, T.A. (2000) 'The psychophysiology of emotion', in R. Lewis and J.M. Haviland-Jones (eds), *The Handbook of Emotion*, 2nd edn. New York: Guilford Press.

Cahill, L. and Alkire, M. (2003) 'Epinephrine enhancement of human memory consolidation: Interaction with arousal at encoding', *Neurobiology of Learning and Memory*, 79, 194–8.

Cahill, L., Babinsky, R., Markowitsch, H.J. and McGaugh, J.L. (1995) 'The amygdala and emotional memory', *Nature*, 377, 295–6.

Cahill, L., Haier, R., Fallon, J., Alkire, M., Tang, C., Keator, D., Wu, J. and McGaugh, J.L. (1996) 'Amygdala activity at encoding correlated with long-term, free recall of emotional information', *Proceedings of the National Academy of Sciences*, 93, 8016–21.

Cahill, L., Prins, B., Weber, M. and McGaugh, J.L. (1994) 'Beta-adrenergic activation and memory for emotional events', *Nature*, 371, 702–4.

Calder, A.J., Keane, J., Lawrence, A.D. and Manes, F. (2004) 'Impaired recognition of anger following damage to the ventral striatum', *Brain*, 127, 1958–69.

Calder, A.J., Keane, J., Manes, F., Antoun, N. and Young, A.W. (2000) 'Impaired recognition and experience of disgust following brain injury', *Nature Neuroscience, 3,* 1077–8.

Calder, A.J., Lawrence, A.D. and Young, A.W. (2001) 'Neuropsychology of fear and loathing', *Nature Reviews Neuroscience*, 2, 352–63.

Calder, A.J., Young, A.W., Rowland, D., Perrett, D.I., Hodges, J.R. and Etcoff, N.L. (1996) 'Face perception after bilateral amygdala damage: Differentially severe impairment of fear', *Cognitive Neuropsychology*, 13, 699–745.

Calvo, M.G. and Castillo, M.D. (2001) 'Selective interpretation in anxiety: The role of uncertainty of threatening events', *Cognition & Emotion*, 15, 299–320.

Canli, T. (2006) *Biology of Personality and Individual Differences.* New York: Guilford Press.

Canli, T. and Lesch, K.-P. (2007) 'Long story short: The serotonin transporter in emotion regulation and social cognition', *Nature Neuroscience*, 10, 1103–9.

Canli, T., Congdon, E. et al. (2005) 'Amygdala responsiveness is modulated by tryptophan hydroxylase-2 gene variation', *Journal of Neural Transmission*, 112, 1479–85.

Canli, T., Amin, Z., Haas, B., Omura, K. and Constable, R.T. (2004) 'A double dissociation between mood states and personality traits in the anterior cingulate', *Behavioral Neuroscience*, 118(5), 897–904.

Canli, T., Omura, K., Haas, B., Constable, R.T., Lesch, K.P. (2005) 'Beyond affect: A role for genetic variation of the serotonin transporter in neural activation during a cognitive attention task', *Proceedings of the National Academy of Sciences USA*, 102, 12224–9.

Canli, T., Qiu, M., Omura, K., Congdon, B.W., Haas, B.W., Amin, Z., Herrmann, M.J., Constable, R.T. and Lesch, K.P. (2006) 'Neural correlates of epigenesis', *Proceedings of the National Academy of Sciences USA*, 103, 16033–8.

Canli, T., Sivers, H., Whitfield, S.L., Gotlib, I.H. and Gabrieli J.H. (2002) 'Amygdala response to happy faces as a function of extraversion', *Science*, 296, 2191.

Canli, T., Zhao, Z., Desmond, J.E., Kang, E.J., Gross, J. and Gabrieli, J.D.E. (2001) 'An fMRI study of personality influences on brain reactivity to emotional stimuli', *Behavioural Neuroscience*, 115, 33–42.

Cannon, W.B. (1927) 'The James–Lange theory of emotion: A critical examination and an alternative theory', *American Journal of Psychology*, 39, 10–124.

Carr, W.J., Martorano, R.D. and Krames, L. (1970) 'Responses of mice to odors associated with stress', *Journal of Comparative and Physiological Psychology*, 71, 223–8.

Carver, C.S. and White, T.L. (1994) 'Behavioral inhibition, behavioural activation, and affective responses to impending reward and punishment: The BIS/BAS scales', *Journal of Personality and Social Psychology*, 67, 319–33.

Caspi, A. (2000) 'The child is father of the man: Personality continuities from childhood to adulthood', *Journal of Personality and Social Psychology*, 78, 158–72.

Caspi, A. and Moffitt, T. (2006) 'Gene-environment interactions in psychiatry: Joining forces with neuroscience', *Nature Reviews Neuroscience*, 7, 583–90.

Caspi, A., McClay, J., Moffitt, T.E., Mill, J., Martin, J., Craig, I.W., Taylor, A. and Poulton, R. (2002) 'Role of genotype in the cycle of violence in maltreated children', *Science*, 297, 851.

Caspi, A., Sugden, K., Moffitt, T.E., Taylor, A., Craig, I.W., Harrington, H., McClay, J., Mill, J., Martin, J., Braithwaite, A. and Poulton, R. (2003) 'Influence of life stress on depression: Moderation by a polymorphism in the 5-HTT gene', *Science*, 301, 386–9.

Catalan, M.J., Honda, M., Weeks, R.A., Cohen, L.G. and Hallett, M. (1998) 'The functional neuroanatomy of simple and complex sequential finger movements: a PET study', *Brain*, 121, 253–64.

Cattell, R.B. (1957a) *Handbook for the IPAT anxiety scale questionnaire (self analysis form): Brief, verbal questionnaire, Q-form, as distinct from objective T-battery.* Savoy: Institute for Personality and Ability Testing.

Cattell, R.B. (1957b) *Personality and Motivation Structure and Measurement.* New York: World Book Company.

Cheung, F.M., and Leung, K. (1998) 'Indigenous personality measures: Chinese examples', *Journal of Cross-Cultural Psychology*, 29, 233–48.

Cho, M.M., DeVries, A.C., Williams, J.R. and Carter, C.S. (1999) 'The effects of oxytocin and vasopressin on partner preferences in male and female prairie voles (Microtus orchrogaster)', *Behavioral Neuroscience*, 113, 1071–9.

Christianson, S.-A. and Loftus, E.F. (1991) 'Remembering emotional events: The fate of detailed information', *Emotion and Cognition*, 5, 81–108.

Church, A.T. and Katigbak, M.S. (2000) 'Trait psychology in the Philippines', *American Behavioral Scientist, 44*, 73–94.

Cicchetti, D. and Dawson, G. (2002) 'Editorial: Multiple levels of analysis', *Development and Psychopathology*, 14, 417–420.

Clark, D.M. and Teasdale, J.D. (1982) 'Diurnal variations in clinical depression and accessibility of memories of positive and negative experiences', *Journal of Abnormal Psychology*, 91, 87–95.

Clark, L.A. (2005) 'Temperament as a unifying basis for personality and psychopathology', *Journal of Abnormal Psychology*, 114, 505–21.

Clark, L.A., Watson, D. and Leeka, J. (1989) 'Diurnal variation in the positive affects', *Motivation and Emotion*, 13, 205–34.

Clark, L.A., Watson, D. and Mineka, S. (1994) 'Temperament, personality, and the mood and anxiety disorders', *Journal of Abnormal Psychology*, 103, 103–16.

Clark, L.A. and Watson, D. (1991) 'Tripartite model of anxiety and depression: Psychometric evidence and taxonomic implications', *Journal of Abnormal Psychology*, 100, 316–36.

Clark, V.P. and Hillyard, S.A. (1996) 'Spatial selective attention affects early extrastriate but not striate components of the visual evoked potential', *Journal of Cognitive Neuroscience*, 8, 387–402.

Cloninger, C.R. (1983) 'Genetic and environmental factors in the development of alcoholism', *Journal of Psychiatric Treatment Evaluation*, 5, 487–96.

Cloninger, C.R. (1987) 'Neurogenetic adaptive mechanisms in alcoholism', *Science*, 236, 410–16.

Cloninger, C.R. (1994) *The Temperament and Character Inventory (TCI): A Guide to its Development and Use.* Washington University: Centre for Psychobiology of Personality.

Cloninger C.R. (2004) *Feeling Good: The Science of Well-being.* Oxford: Oxford University Press.

Cloninger, C.R. (2005) 'Antisocial personality disorder: A review', in M. Maj, H.S. Akiskal, J.E. Mezzich and A. Okasha (eds), *Personality Disorders.*

Cloninger, C.R. and Gilligan, S.B. (1987) 'Neurogenetic mechanisms of learning: A phylogenetic perspective', *Journal of Psychiatric Research*, 21, 457–72.

Cloninger, C.R., Svrakic, D.M. and Przybeck, T.R. (1993) 'A psychobiological model of temperament and character', *Archives of General Psychiatry*, 50, 975–89.

Clore, G.L. and Byrne, D. (1974) 'A reinforcement-affect model of attraction', in T.L. Huston (ed.), *Perspectives on Interpersonal Attraction.* New York: Academic Press.

Clore, G.L. and Gasper, K. (2000) 'Feeling is believing: Some affective influences on belief', in N.H. Frijda, A.S.R. Manstead and S. Bem (eds), *Emotions and Beliefs: How Feelings Influence Thoughts.* Paris: Cambridge University Press.

Clore, G.L., Gasper, K. and Garvin, E. (2001) 'Affect as information', in J.P. Forgas (ed.), *Handbook of Affect and Social Cognition.* Mahwah, NJ: Lawrence Erlbaum.

Clore, G.L., Schwarz, N. and Conway, M. (1994) 'Affective causes and consequences of social information processing', in R.S. Wyer and T.K. Srull (eds), *Handbook of Social Cognition: Volume 1 Basic Processes*, 2nd edn. Hillsdale, NJ: Lawrence Erlbaum.

Coan, J.A. and Allen, J.J.B. (2003) 'Frontal EEG asymmetry and the behavioural activation and inhibition systems', *Psychophysiology*, 40, 106–14.

Coan, J.A. and Allen, J.J.B. (2004) 'EEG asymmetry as a moderator and mediator of emotion', *Biological Psychology*, 67, 7–49.

Coan, J.A. and Allen, J.J.B. (2007) *The Handbook of Emotion Elicitation and Assessment.* New York: Oxford University Press.

Cohen, M.X., Young, J. et al. (2005) 'Individual differences in extraversion and dopamine genetics predict neural reward responses', *Cognitive Brain Research*, 25(3), 851–61.

Coifman, K.G., Bonanno, G.A., Ray, R.D. and Gross, J.J. (2007) 'Does repressive coping promote resilience? Affective-autonomic response discrepancy during bereavement', *Journal of Personality and Social Psychology*, 92, 745–58.

Cole, P.M., Martin, S.E. and Dennis, T.A. (2004) 'Emotion regulation as a scientific contrast: Methodological challenges and directions for child development research', *Child Development*, 75, 317–33.

Collishaw, S., Pickles, A., Messer, J., Rutter, M., Shearer, C. and Maughan, B. (2007) 'Resilience to adult psychopathology following childhood maltreatment: Evidence from a community sample', *Child Abuse and Neglect*, 31, 211–29.

Colman, A.M. (2001) *Oxford Dictionary of Psychology*. Oxford: Oxford University Press.

Comings, D.E., Rosenthal, R.J. et al. (1996) 'A study of the dopamine D2 receptor gene in pathological gambling', *Pharmacogenetics*, 6, 223–34.

Conn, S.R. and Rieke, M.L. (1994) *The 16PF Fifth Edition Technical Manual*. Champagne, IL: Institute for Personality and Ability Testing, Inc.

Cools, R., Calder, A.J. et al. (2005) 'Individual differences in threat sensitivity predict serotonergic modulation of amygdala response to fearful faces', *Neuropsychopharmacology*, 180(4), 670–9.

Corr, P.J. and Gray, J.A. (1996) 'Structure and validity of the attributional style questionnaire: A cross-sample comparison', *Journal of Psychology*, 130, 645–57.

Cosmides, L. and Tooby, J. (2000) 'Evolutionary psychology and the emotions', in M. Lewis and J.M. Haviland-Jones (eds), *Handbook of Emotions*, 2nd edn. New York: Guilford Press.

Costa, P.T. and McCrae, R.R. (1980) 'Influence of extraversion and neuroticism on subjective well-being: Happy and unhappy people', *Journal of Personality and Social Psychology*, 38, 668–78.

Costa, P.T. and McCrae, R.R. (1985) *The NEO Personality Inventory manual*. Odessa: Psychological Assessment Resources.

Costa, P.T., McCrae, R.R. et al. (1991) 'Facet scales for agreeableness and conscientiousness: A revision of the NEO Personality Inventory.' *Personality and Individual Differences*, 12, 887– 98.

Craske, M.G. (2003) *Origins of Phobias and Anxiety Disorders: Why More Women Than Men?*. Oxford: Elsevier.

Craske, M.G., Hermans, D. and Vansteenwegen, D. (eds) (2006) *Fear and Learning: From Basic Processes to Clinical Implications*. Washington, DC: American Psychological Association.

Creswell, J.D., Way, B.M., Eisenberger, N.I. and Lieberman, M.D. (2007) 'Neural correlates of mindfulness during affect behaviour', *Psychosomatic Medicine*, 69, 560–5.

Critchley, H.D., Mathias, C.J. and Dolan, R.J. (2001a) 'Neuroanatomical basis for first- and second-order representations of bodily states', *Nature Neuroscience*, 4, 207–12.

Critchley, H.D., Mathias C.J. and Dolan, R.J. (2001b) 'Neural activity relating to reward anticipation in the human brain', *Neuron*, 29, 537–45.

Critchley, H.D., Mathias, C.J. and Dolan, R.J. (2002) 'Fear-conditioning in humans: The influence of awareness and arousal on functional neuroanatomy', *Neuron*, 33, 653–63.

Csikszentmihalyi, M. (1990) *Flow: The Psychology of Otimal Experience*. New York: Harper & Row.

Cuthbert, B.N., Bradley, M.M. and Lang, P.J. (1996) 'Probing picture perception: Activation and emotion', *Psychophysiology*, 33, 103–11.

Cutler, S.E., Larsen, R.J. and Bunce, S.C. (1996) 'Repressive coping style and the experience and recall of emotion: A naturalistic study of daily affect', *Journal of Personality*, 64, 379–405.

Dalgleish, T. (2003) 'Information approaches to emotion', in R.J. Davidson, K. Scherer and H.H. Goldsmith (eds), *Handbook of Affective Sciences*. New York: Oxford University Press.

Dalgleish, T. (2004) 'The emotional brain', *Nature Reviews Neuroscience*, 5, 582–5.

Dalgleish, T. and Power, M.J. (1999) *Handbook of Cognition and Emotion.* Chichester, Wiley.

Damasio, A.R. (1994) 'Descartes' error and the future of human life', *Scientific American*, 271, 144.

Damasio, A.R. (1996) 'The somatic marker hypothesis and the possible functions of the prefrontal cortex', *Philosophical Transactions of the Royal Society of London B*, 351, 1413–20.

Damasio, A.R. (1999) *The Feeling of What Happens: Body and Emotion in the Making of Consciousness.* New York: Harcourt Brace.

Damasio, A.R. (2000) 'A second chance for emotion', in R.D. Lane and L. Nadel, *Cognitive Neuroscience of Emotion.* New York: Oxford University Press.

Damasio, A.R., Grabowski, T.J., Bechara, A., Damasio, H., Ponto, L.L.B., Parvizi, J. and Hichwa, R.D. (2000) 'Subcortical and cortical brain activity during the feeling of self-generated emotions', *Nature Neuroscience*, 3, 1049–56.

Damasio, H., Grabowski, T., Frank, R., Galaburda, A.M. and Damasio, A.R. (1994) 'The return of Phineas Gage: Clues about the brain from the skull of a famous patient', *Science*, 264, 1102–5.

Danner, D.D., Snowdon, D.A. and Friesen, W.V. (2001) 'Positive emotions in early life and longevity: Findings from the nun study', *Journal of Personality and Social Psychology*, 80, 804–13.

Darwin, C. (1872/1998) *The Expression of Emotions in Man and Animals*, 3rd edn, edited by P. Ekman. New York: Oxford University Press.

Davidson, R.J. (1984) 'Affect, cognition and hemispheric specialization', in C.E. Izard, J. Kagan and R. Zajonc (eds), *Emotion, Cognition and Behavior.* New York: Cambridge University Press.

Davidson, R.J. (1992a) 'Anterior cerebral asymmetry and the nature of emotion', *Brain and Cognition*, 20(1), 125–51.

Davidson, R.J. (1992b) 'Emotion and affective style: Hemispheric substrates', *Psychological Science*, 3, 39–43.

Davidson, R.J. (1993) 'Cerebral asymmetry and emotion: Conceptual and methodological conundrums', *Cognition & Emotion*, 7, 115–38.

Davidson, R.J. (1994a) 'Asymmetric brain function, affective style and psychopathology: The role of early experience and plasticity', *Development and Psychopathology*, 6, 741–58.

Davidson, R.J. (1994b) 'On emotion, mood and related affective constructs', in P. Ekman and R.J. Davidson (eds), *The Nature of Emotion: Fundamental Question.* New York: Oxford University Press.

Davidson, R.J. (1994c) 'Temperament, affective style and frontal lobe asymmetry', in G. Dawson and K. Fischer (eds), *Human Behavior and the Developing Brain.* New York: Guilford Press.

Davidson, R.J. (1995) 'Cerebral asymmetry, emotion, and affective style', in R.J. Davidson and K. Hugdahl (eds), *Brain Asymmetry.* Cambridge, MA: MIT Press.

Davidson, R.J. (1998a) 'Affective style and affective disorders: Perspectives from affective neuroscience', *Cognition & Emotion*, 12, 307–30.

Davidson, R.J. (1998b) 'Anterior electrophysiological asymmetries, emotion, and depression: Conceptual and methodological conundrums', *Psychophysiology*, 35, 607–14.

Davidson, R.J. (2000) 'Affective style, psychopathology, and resilience: Brain mechanisms and plasticity', *American Psychologist*, 55, 1196–214.

Davidson, R.J. (2003) 'Seven sins in the study of emotion: Correctives from affective neuroscience', *Brain and Cognition*, 52, 129–32.

Davidson, R.J. (2004) 'Well-being and affective style: neural substrates and biobehavioural correlates', *Philosophical Transactions of the Royal Society*, 359, 1395–411.

Davidson, R.J. and Fox, N.A. (1982) 'Asymmetrical brain activity discriminates between positive versus negative affect in human infants.' *Science*, 218, 1235–7.

Davidson, R.J. and Fox, N.A. (1989) 'Frontal brain asymmetry predicts infants' response to maternal separation', *Journal of Abnormal Psychology*, 98, 127–31.

Davidson, R.J. and Irwin, W. (1999) 'The functional neuroanatomy of emotion and affective style', *Trends in. Cognitive Sciences*, 3, 11–21.

Davidson, R.J. and Sutton, S.K. (1995) 'Affective neuroscience: The emergence of a discipline', *Current Opinion in Neurobiology*, 5, 217–24.

Davidson, R.J., Abercrombie, H., Nitschke, J.B. and Putnam, K. (1999) 'Regional brain function, emotion and disorders of emotion', *Current Opinion in Neurobiology*, 9(2), 228–34.

Davidson, R.J., Ekman, P., Saron, C.D., Senulis, J.A. and Friesen, W.V. (1990) 'Approach-withdrawal and cerebral asymmetry: Emotional expression and brain physiology', *Journal of Personality and Social Psychology*, 58, 330–41.

Davidson, R.J., Fox, A.S. and Kalin, N.H. (2006) 'Neural bases of emotion regulation in non-human primates and humans', in J.J. Gross (ed.), *Handbook of Emotion Regulation*. New York: Guilford Press.

Davidson, R.J., Kabat-Zinn, J., Schumacher, J., Rosenkrantz, M., Muller, D., Santorelli, S.F., Urbanowski, F., Harrington, A., Bonus, K. and Sheridan, J.F. (2003) 'Alterations in brain and immune function produced by mindfulness meditation', *Psychosomatic Medicine*, 65, 564–70.

Davidson, R.J., Marshall, J.R., Tomarken, A.J. and Henriques, J.B. (2000) 'While a phobic waits: Regional brain electrical and autonomic activity in social phobics during anticipation of public speaking', *Biological Psychiatry*, 47, 85–95.

Davidson, R.J., Putnam, K.M. and Larson, C. (2000) 'Dysfunction in the neural circuitry of emotion regulation: A possible prelude to violence', *Science*, 289, 591–4.

Davidson, R.J., Scherer, K.R. and Goldsmith, H.H. (2003) *Handbook of Affective Sciences*. New York: Oxford University Press.

Davis, M. (1986) 'Pharmacological and anatomical analysis of fear conditioning using the fear-potentiated startle paradigm', *Behavioural Neuroscience*, 100, 814–24.

Davis, M. (1989) 'Neural systems involved in fear-potentiated startle', *Annals of the New York Academy of Sciences*, 563, 165–83.

Davis, M. and Whalen, P.J. (2001) 'The amygdala: vigilance and emotion', *Molecular Psychiatry*, 6, 13–34.

Davis, M., Hitchcock, J.M. and Rosen, J.B. (1987) 'Anxiety and the amygdala: Pharmacological and anatomical analysis of fear-potentiated startle', in G.H. Bower (ed.), *The Psychology of Learning and Motivation: Advances in Research and Theory, Vol. 21*. New York: Academic Press.

Dawson, G. and Fischer, K. (eds) (1994) *Human Behavior and the Developing Brain*. New York: Guilford Press.

Deary, I.J., Battersby, S., Whiteman, M.C., Connor, J.M., Fowkes, F.G. and Harmar, A. (1999) 'Neuroticism and polymorphisms in the serotonin transporter gene', *Psychological Medicine*, 29, 735–9.

Deci, E.L. (1972) 'Intrinsic motivation, extrinsic reinforcement, and inequity', *Journal of Personality and Social Psychology*, 22, 113–20.

Delgado, P.L., Price, L.H., Miller, H.L., Salomon, R.M., Heninger, G.H. and Charney, D.S. (1994) 'Serotonin and the neurobiology of depression: effects of tryptophan depletion in drug-free depressed patients', *Archives of General Psychiatry*, 51, 865–74.

DeNeve, K.M. and Cooper, H. (1998) 'The happy personality: A meta-analysis of 137 personality traits and subjective well-being', *Psychological Bulletin*, 124, 197–229.

Denny, E.B. and Hunt, R.R. (1992) 'Affective valence and memory in depression: Dissociation of recall and fragment completion', *Journal of Abnormal Psychology*, 101, 575–80.

Depue, R.A. and Collins, P.F. (1999) 'Neurobiology of the structure of personality: Dopamine, facilitation of incentive motivation, and extraversion', *Behavioural Brain Science*, 22, 491–569.

Depue, R.A. and Monroe, S.M. (1986) 'Conceptualization and measurement of human disorder in life stress research: The problem of chronic disturbance', *Psychological Bulletin*, 99, 36–51.

Derakshan, N. and Eysenck, M.W. (1997) 'Interpretive biases for one's own behaviour and physiology in high trait anxious individuals and repressors', *Journal of Personality and Social Psychology*, 73, 816–25.

Derakshan, N. and Eysenck, M.W. (1999) 'Are repressors self-deceivers or other-deceivers?', *Cognition & Emotion*, 17, 1–13.

Derakshan, N., Eysenck, M.W. and Myers, L.B. (2007) 'Emotional information processing in repressors: The vigilance-avoidance theory', *Cognition & Emotion.*

Derakshan, N., Myers, L.B., Hansen, J. and O'Leary, M. (2004) 'Repressive-defensiveness and attempted thought suppression of negative material', *European Journal of Personality*, 18, 521–35.

Derryberry, D. and Reed, M.A. (1994) 'Temperament and attention: Orienting toward and away from positive and negative signals', *Journal of Personality and Social Psychology*, 66, 1128–39.

Derryberry, D. and Reed, M.A. (2002) 'Anxiety-related attentional biases and their regulation by attentional control', *Journal of Abnormal Psychology*, 111, 225–36.

Derryberry, D. and Reed, M.A. (2003) 'Information processing approaches to individual differences in emotional reactivity', in R.J. Davidson, K.R. Scherer and H.H. Goldsmith (eds), *Handbook of Affective Sciences.* New York: Oxford University Press.

Derryberry, D. and Rothbart, M.K. (1997) 'Reactive and effortful processes in the organization of temperament', *Development and Psychopathology*, 9, 633–52.

Derryberry, D. and Tucker, D.M. (1994) 'Motivating the focus of attention', in P.M. Niedenthal and S. Kitayama (eds), *The Heart's Eye: Emotional Influences in Perception and Attention.* San Diego: Academic Press.

di Pellegrino, G., Fadiga, L., Fogassi, L., Gallese, V. and Rizzolatti, G. (1992) 'Understanding motor events: A neurophysiological study', *Experimental Brain Research*, 91, 176–80.

Di Russo, F., Martinez, A. and Hillyard, S.A. (2003) 'Source analysis of event-related cortical activity during visuo-spatial attention', *Cerebral Cortex*, 13, 486–99.

Dickinson, A. and Dearing, M.F. (1979) 'Appetitive-aversive interactions and inhibitory processes', in A. Dickinson and R.A. Boakes (eds), *Mechanisms of Learning and Motivation.* Hillsdale, NJ: Erlbaum.

Diener, E. (1984) 'Subjective well-being', *Psychological Bulletin*, 95, 542–75.

Diener, E. (1994) 'Assessing subjective well-being: Progress and opportunities', *Social Indicators Research*, 31, 103–57.

Diener, E. and Diener, C. (1996) 'Most people are happy', *Psychological Science*, 7, 181–5.

Diener, E. and Emmons, R.A. (1985) 'The independence of positive and negative affect', *Journal of Personality and Social Psychology*, 47, 1105–17.

Diener, E. and Iran-Nejad, A. (1986) 'The relationship in experience between various types of affect', *Journal of Personality and Social Psychology*, 50, 1031–8.

Diener, E. and Larsen, R.J. (1984) 'Temporal stability and cross-situational consistency of affective, behavioural, and cognitive responses', *Journal of Personality and Social Psychology*, 47, 871–83.

Diener, E. and Lucas, R. (2000) 'Subjective emotional well-being', in M. Lewis and J.M. Haviland-Jones (eds), *Handbook of Emotions*, 2nd edn. New York: Guilford Press.

Diener, E. and Seligman, M.E. (2002) 'Very happy people', *Psychological Science*, 13, 81–4

Diener, E. and Seligman, M.E.P. (2004) 'Beyond money: Toward an economy of well-being', *Psychological Science in the Public Interest*, 5, 1–31.

Diener, E., Emmons, R.A., Larsen, R.J. and Griffin, S. (1985) 'The Satisfaction with Life Scale', *Journal of Personality Assessment*, 49, 71–5.

Diener, E., Lucas, R. and Scollon, C.N. (2006) 'Beyond the hedonic treadmill: Revising the adaptation theory of well-being', *American Psychologist*, 61, 305–14.

Diener, E., Oishi, S. and Lucas, R.E. (2003) 'Personality, culture, and subjective well-being: Emotional and cognitive evaluations of life', *Annual Review of Psychology, 2003*, 54, 403–25.

Diener, E., Sandvik, E. and Pavot, W. (1991) 'Happiness is the frequency, not the intensity, of positive versus negative affect', in F. Strack, M. Argyle and N. Schwarz (eds), *Subjective Well-being: An Interdisciplinary Perspective.* New York: Pergamon.

Diener, E., Suh, E.M., Lucas, R.E. and Smith, H.E. (1999) 'Subjective well-being: Three decades of progress', *Psychological Bulletin*, 125, 276–302.

Dillon, D.G. and LaBar, K.S. (2005) 'Startle modulation during conscious emotion regulation is arousal-dependent', *Behavioural Neuroscience*, 119, 1118–24.

Direnfeld, D.M. and Roberts, J.E. (2006) 'Mood congruent memory in dysphoria: The roles of state affect and cognitive style', *Behaviour Research and Therapy*, 44, 1275–85.

Dolan, R. (2002) 'Emotion, cognition and behaviour', *Science*, 298, 1191–4.

Dolan, R.J., Lane, R., Chua, P. and Fletcher, P. (2000) 'Dissociable temporal lobe activations during emotional episodic memory retrieval', *Neuroimage*, 11, 203–9.

Dolcos, F., LaBar, K.S. and Cabeza, R. (2004a) 'Dissociable effects of arousal and valence on prefrontal activity indexing emotional evaluation and subsequent memory: An event-related fMRI study', *NeuroImage*, 23, 64–74.

Dolcos, F., LaBar, K.S. and Cabeza, R. (2004b) 'Interaction between the amygdala and the medial temporal lobe memory system predicts better memory for emotional events', *Neuron*, 42, 855–63.

Drevets, W.C. (1999) 'Prefrontal cortical-amygdalar metabolism in major depression', *Annals of the New York Academy of Sciences*, 877, 614–37.

Drevets, W.C. (2001) 'Neuroimaging and neuropathological studies of depression: Implications for the cognitive-emotional features of mood disorders', *Current Opinion in Neurobiology*, 11, 240–9.

Drevets, W.C., Price, J., Simpson, J., Todd, R., Reich, T., Vannier, M. and Raichle, M. (1997) 'Subgenual prefrontal cortex abnormalities in mood disorders', *Nature*, 386, 824–7.

Duchenne de Boulogne, G.-B. (1862/1990) *The Mechanism of Human Facial Expression.* Cambridge: Cambridge University Press.

Dunn, B.D., Dalgleish, T. and Lawrence, A. (2006) 'The somatic marker hypothesis: A critical evaluation', *Neuroscience and Biobehavioural Reviews*, 30, 239–71.

Dunn, B.D., Dalgleish, T., Lawrence, A.D., Cusack, R. and Ogilvie, A.D. (2004) 'Categorical and dimensional reports of experienced affect to emotion-inducing pictures in depression', *Journal of Abnormal Psychology*, 113, 654–60.

Dunn, E.W., Wilson, T.D. and Gilbert, D.T. (2003) 'Location, location, location: The misprediction of satisfaction in housing lotteries', *Personality and Social Psychology Bulletin*, 29, 1421–32.

Dutton, D.G. and Aron, A.P. (1974) 'Some evidence for heightened sexual attraction under conditions of high anxiety', *Journal of Personality and Social Psychology*, 30, 510–17.

Easterbrook, J.A. (1959) 'The effect of emotion on cue utilization and the organization of behavior', *Psychological Review*, 66, 183–201.

Eastwood, J.D., Smilek, D. and Merikle, P.M. (2001) 'Differential attentional guidance by unattended faces expressing positive and negative emotion', *Perception and Psychophysics*, 63, 1004–13.

Ebstein, R.P., Novick, O. et al. (1996) 'Dopamine D4 receptor (D4DR) exon III polymorphism associated with the human personality trait of novelty seeking', *Nature Genetics*, 12(1), 78–80.

Edelman, G.M. and Tononi, G. (2000) *A Universe of Consciousness*. New York: Basic Books.

Eich, E. (1995) 'Searching for mood dependent memory', *Psychological Science*, 6, 67–75.

Eich, E. and Metcalfe, J. (1989) 'Mood dependent memory for internal versus external events', *Journal of Experimental Psychology: Learning Memory and Cognition*, 15, 443–55.

Eich, E., Macaulay, D. and Ryan, L. (1994) 'Mood dependent memory for events of the personal past', *Journal of Experimental Psychology: General*, 123, 201–15.

Eisenberg, N. (2007) 'Empathy-related responding and prosocial behaviour', *Novartis Foundation Symposium*, 278, 71–80.

Eisenberg, N., Hofer, C. and Vaughan, J. (2007) 'Effortful control and its socioemotional consequences', in J.J. Gross (ed.), *Handbook of Emotion Regulation*. New York: Guilford Press.

Eisenberg, N., Fabes, R.A., Nyman, M., Bernzweig, J. and Pinuelas, A. (1994) 'The relations of emotionality and regulation to children's anger-related reactions', *Child Development*, 65, 109–28.

Eisenberg, N., Hofer, C. and Vaughan, J. (2007) 'Effortful control and its socioemotional consequences', in J.J. Gross (ed.), *Handbook of Emotion Regulation*. New York: Guilford Press.

Eisenberg, N., Sadovsky, A., Spinrad, T.L., Fabes, R.A., Losoya, S.H., Valiente, C., Reiser, M., Cumberland, A. and Shepard, S.A. (2005) 'The relations of problem behaviour status to children's negative emotionality, effortful control, and impulsivity: Concurrent relations and prediction of change', *Developmental Psychology*, 41, 193–211.

Ekman, P. (1972) 'Universals and cultural differences in facial expressions of emotion', in J. Cole (ed.), *Nebraska Symposium on Motivation 1971, Vol. 19*. Lincoln: University of Nebraska Press.

Ekman, P. (1973) *Darwin and Facial Expression: A Century of Research in Review*. New York: Academic Press.

Ekman, P. (1992a) 'An argument for basic emotions', *Cognition & Emotion*, 6, 169–200.

Ekman, P. (1992b) 'Are there basic emotions?', *Psychological Review*, 99, 550–3.

Ekman, P. (1992c) 'Facial expression of emotion: New findings, new questions', *Psychological Science*, 3, 34–8.

Ekman, P. (1994a) 'All emotions are basic', in P. Ekman and R. Davidson (eds), *The Nature of Emotion: Fundamental Questions*. New York: Oxford University Press.

Ekman, P. (1994b) 'Antecedent events and emotion metaphors', in P. Ekman and R. Davidson (eds), *The Nature of Emotion: Fundamental Questions*. New York: Oxford University Press.

Ekman, P. (1994c) 'Moods, emotions and traits', in P. Ekman and R. Davidson (eds), *The Nature of Emotion: Fundamental Questions*. New York: Oxford University Press.

Ekman, P. (1994d) 'Strong evidence for universals in facial expressions: A reply to Russell's mistaken critique', *Psychological Bulletin*, 115, 268–87.

Ekman, P. (1999) 'Basic emotions', in T. Dalgleish and M.J. Power (eds), *Handbook of Cognition and Emotion*, Chichester: Wiley.

Ekman, P. (2004) 'Happy, sad, angry, disgusted', *New Scientist*, 184, A4–A5.

Ekman, P. and Davidson, R.J. (eds) (1994) *The Nature of Emotion*. New York: Oxford University Press.

Ekman, P. and Friesen, W.V. (1971) 'Constants across cultures in the face and emotion', *Journal of Personality and Social Psychology*, 17, 124–9.

Ekman, P. and Friesen, W.V. (1975) *Unmasking the Face: A Guide to Recognizing Emotions from Facial Clues*. Englewood Cliffs, NJ: Prentice-Hall.

Ekman, P. and Friesen, W.V. (1976a) *Pictures of Facial Affect*. Palo Alto: Consulting Psychologists Press.

Ekman, P. and Friesen, W.V. (1976b) 'Measuring facial movement', *Environmental Psychology and Nonverbal Behaviour*, 1(1), 56–75.

Ekman, P. and Friesen, W.V. (1986) 'A new pan cultural facial expression of emotion', *Motivation and Emotion*, 10, 19–168.

Ekman, P., Davidson, R.J. and Friesen, W.V. (1990) 'Duchenne's smile: Emotional expression and brain physiology II', *Journal of Personality and Social Psychology*, 58, 342–53.

Ekman, P., Levenson, R.W. and Friesen, W.V. (1983) 'Autonomic nervous system activity distinguishes between emotions', *Science*, 221, 1208–10.

Ekman, P., Roper, G. and Hager, J.C. (1980) 'Deliberate facial movement', *Child Development*, 51, 886–91.

Ekman, P., Sorenson, E.R. and Friesen, W.V. (1969) 'Pan-cultural elements in facial displays of emotions', *Science*, 164, 86–8.

Ellis, A. (1962) *Reason and Emotion in Psychotherapy*. New York: Lyle Stuart.

Ellis, G.F.R. and Toronchuk, J. A. (2005) 'Neural development: Affective and immune system influences', in N. Newton and R. Ellis (eds), *Consciousness and Emotions: Agency, Conscious Choice and Selective Perception*. Philadelphia: John Benjamins.

Ellis, H.C. and Moore, B.A. (1999) 'Mood and memory', in T. Dalgleish and M. Power (eds), *Handbook of Cognition and Emotion*. New York: Wiley.

Ellsworth, P. (1991) 'Some implications of cognitive appraisal theories of emotion', in K.T. Strongman (ed.), *International Review of Research on Emotion*. New York: Wiley.

Ellsworth, P.C. (1994a) 'Levels of thought and levels of emotion', in P. Ekman and R.J. Davidson (eds), *The Nature of Emotion: Fundamental Questions*. New York: Oxford University Press.

Ellsworth, P.C. (1994b) 'Sense, culture, and sensibility', in H. Markus and S. Kitayama (eds), *Emotion and Culture: Empirical studies of Mutual Influence*. Washington, DC: American Psychological Association.

Ellsworth, P.C. and Scherer, K.R. (2003) 'Appraisal processes in emotion', in R.J. Davidson, K. Scherer and H.H. Goldsmith (eds), *Handbook of Affective Sciences*. New York: Oxford University Press.

Emmons, R.A. (2004a) 'Gratitude', in M.E.P. Seligman and C. Peterson (eds), *The VIA Taxonomy of Human Strengths and Virtues*. New York: Oxford University Press.

Emmons, R.A. (2004b) 'The psychology of gratitude: An introduction', in R.A. Emmons and M.E. McCullough (eds), *The Psychology of Gratitude*. New York: Oxford University Press.

Emmons, R.A. and McCullough, M.E. (2003) 'Counting blessings versus burdens: An experimental investigation of gratitude and subjective well-being in daily life', *Journal of Personality and Social Psychology*, 84, 377–89.

Erdelyi, M.H. (1974) 'A new look at the New Look: Perceptual defense and vigilance', *Psychological Review*, 81, 1–25.

Erk, S., Kiefer, M., Grothe, J., Wunderlich, A.P., Spitzer, M. and Walter, H. (2003) 'Emotional context modulates subsequent memory effect', *Neuroimage*, 18, 439–47.

Evans, D. (2001) *Emotion: The Science of Sentiment.* Oxford: Oxford University Press.

Eysenck, H.J. (1953) *The Structure of Human Personality.* New York: Wiley.

Eysenck, H.J. (1959) *Manual of the Maudsley Personality Inventory.* London: University of London Press.

Eysenck, H.J. (1967) *The Biological Basis of Personality.* Springfield, IL: Charles C. Thomas.

Eysenck, H.J. (1976) *The Measurement of Personality.* Lancaster: Medical & Technical Publisher.

Eysenck, H.J. (1981) *A Model for Personality.* New York: Springer.

Eysenck, H.J. and Eysenck, S.B.G. (1975a) *Manual of the Eysenck Personality Questionnaire (Adult and Junior).* London: Hodder & Stoughton.

Eysenck, H.J. and Eysenck, S.B.G. (1975b) *The Eysenck Personality Questionnaire.* London: Hodder & Stoughton.

Eysenck, H.J., Eysenck, S.B.G. and Barrett, P. (1985) 'A revised version of the psychoticism scale', *Personality and Individual Differences*, 6, 21–9.

Eysenck, M.W. (1990) *Happiness: Facts and Myths.* Hove: Lawrence Erlbaum.

Eysenck, M.W. (1992a) *The Cognitive Perspective.* Hillsdale, NJ: Erlbaum.

Eysenck, M.W. (1992b) 'The nature of anxiety', in A. Gale and M.W. Eysenck (eds), *Handbook of Individual Differences: Biological Perspectives.* Chichester: Wiley.

Eysenck, M. and Keane, M.T. (1995) *Cognitive Psychology: A Student's Handbook*, 3rd edn. Hillsdale, NJ: Lawrence Erlbaum.

Eysenck, M.W., Derakshan, N., Santos, R. and Calvo, M. (2007) 'Anxiety and cognitive performance: Attentional control theory', *Emotion*, 7, 336–53.

Eysenck, M.W., MacLeod, C. and Mathews, A. (1987) 'Cognitive functioning and anxiety', *Psychological Research*, 49, 189–95.

Fahrenberg, J. (1992) 'Psychophysiology of neuroticism and anxiety', in A. Gale and M.W. Eysenck (eds), *Handbook of Individual Differences: Biological Perspectives.* Chichester: Wiley.

Falls, W.A., Miserendino, M.J. and Davis, M. (1992) 'Extinction of fear-potentiated startle: Blockage by infusion of an NMDA antagonist into the amygdala', *Journal of Neuroscience*, 12, 854–63.

Feldman Barrett, L. (1998) 'Discrete emotions or dimensions? The role of valence focus and arousal focus', *Cognition & Emotion*, 12, 579–99.

Feldman Barrett, L. (2004) 'Feelings or words? Understanding the content in self-report ratings of emotional experience', *Journal of Personality and Social Psychology*, 87, 266–81.

Feldman Barrett, L. (2006a) 'Emotions as natural kinds?', *Perspectives on Psychological Science*, 1, 28–58.

Feldman Barrett, L. (2006b) 'Solving the emotion paradox: Categorization and the experience of emotion', *Personality and Social Psychology Review*, 10, 20–46.

Feldman Barrett, L. (2006c) 'Valence as a basic building block of emotional life', *Journal of Research in Personality*, 40, 35–55.

Feldman Barrett, L. and Russell, J.A. (1998) 'Independence and bipolarity in the structure of current affect', *Journal of Personality and Social Psychology*, 74, 967–84.

Feldman Barrett, L. and Wager, T.D. (2006) 'The structure of emotion: Evidence from neuroimaging studies', *Current Directions in Psychological Science*, 15, 79–83.

Feldman Barrett, L., Lindquist, K.A., Bliss-Moreau, E., Duncan, S., Gendron, M., Mize, J. and Brennan, L. (2007) 'Of mice and men: Natural kinds of emotions in the mammalian brain? A response to Panksepp and Izard', *Perspectives in Psychological Science*, 2, 297–312.

Feldman Barrett, L., Mesquita, B., Ochsner, K.N. and Gross, J.J. (2007) 'The experience of emotion', *Annual Review of Psychology*, 58, 373–403.

Fiedler, K. (1990) 'Mood-dependent selectivity in social cognition', *European Review of Social Psychology*, 1, 1–32.

Fiedler, K. (1991) 'On the task, the measures and the mood in research on affect and social cognition', in J.P. Forgas (ed.), *Emotion and Social Judgments.* Elmsford, NY: Pergamon Press.

Fiedler, K. (2000) 'Towards an integrative account of affect and cognition phenomena using the BIAS computer algorithm', in J.P. Forgas (ed.), *Feeling and Thinking: The Role of Affect in Social Cognition.* New York: Cambridge University Press.

Fiedler, K. (2001) 'Affective states trigger processes of assimilation and accommodation', in L.L. Martin and G.L. Clore (eds), *Theories of Mood and Cognition: A User's Guidebook.* Mahwah, NJ: Erlbaum.

Fischer, H., Tillfors, M. et al. (2001) 'Dispositional pessimism and amygdala activity: A PET study in healthy volunteers', *NeuroReport*, 12, 1635–8.

Foa, E.B. and McNally, R.J. (1986) 'Sensitivity to feared stimuli in obsessive-compulsives: A dichotic listening analysis', *Cognitive Therapy and Research*, 10, 477–85.

Folkman, S. (1997) 'Positive psychological states and coping with severe stress', *Social Science and Medicine*, 45, 1207.

Forgas, J.P. (1995) 'Mood and judgment: The affect infusion model (AIM)', *Psychological Bulletin*, 11, 39–66.

Forgas, J.P. (2001) *Handbook of Affect and Social Cognition.* Mahwah, NJ: Lawrence Erlbaum.

Forgas, J.R. and Moylan, S. (1987) 'After the movies: Transient mood and social judgments', *Personality and Social Psychology Bulletin*, 13, 467–77.

Forgas, J.P., Bower, G.H. and Krantz, S. (1984) 'The influence of mood on perceptions of social interactions', *Journal of Experimental Social Psychology*, 20, 497–513.

Fowles, D. (2006) 'Jeffrey Gray's contributions to theories of anxiety, personality, and psychopathology', in T. Canli (ed.), *Biological Basis of Personality and Individual Differences.* New York: Guilford Press.

Fox, E. (1993) 'Allocation of visual attention and anxiety', *Cognition & Emotion*, 7, 207–15.

Fox, E. (2002) 'Processing emotional facial expressions: The role of anxiety and awareness', *Cognitive, Affective and Behavavioural Neuroscience*, 2, 52–63.

Fox, E. (2004) 'Maintenance or capture of attention in anxiety-related biases', in J. Yiend (ed.), *Emotion, Cognition, and Psychopathology.* Cambridge: Cambridge University Press.

Fox, E., Griggs, L. and Mouchlianitis, E. (2007) 'The detection of fear-relevant stimuli: Are guns noticed as quickly as snakes?', *Emotion*, 7, 691–6

Fox, E., Lester, V., Russo, R., Bowles, R.J., Pichler, A. and Dutton, K. (2000) 'Facial expressions of emotion: Are angry faces detected more efficiently?', *Cognition & Emotion*, 14, 61–92.

Fox, E., Mathews, A., Calder, A.J. and Yiend, J. (2007) 'Anxiety and sensitivity to gaze direction in emotionally expressive faces', *Emotion*, 4, 478–86.

Fox, E., Russo, R., Bowles, R. and Dutton, K. (2001) 'Do threatening stimuli draw or hold visual attention in sub-clinical anxiety?', *Journal of Experimental Psychology: General*, 130, 681–700.

Fox, E., Russo, R. and Dutton, K. (2002) 'Attentional bias for threat: Evidence for delayed disengagement from emotional faces', *Cognition & Emotion*, 16, 355–79.

Fox, E., Russo, R. and Georgiou, G.A. (2005) 'Anxiety modulates the degree of attentive resources required to process emotional faces', *Cognitive, Affective, & Behavioral Neuroscience*, 5, 396–404.

Fox, N.A., Rubin, K.H., Calkins, S.D., Marshall, T.R., Coplan, R.J., Porges, S.W. and Long, J.M. (1995) 'Frontal activation behaviour and social competence at four years of age', *Child Development*, 66, 1770–84.

Francis, D.D., Champagne, F. and Meaney, M.J. (2000) 'Variations in maternal behaviour are associated with differences in oxytocin receptor levels in the rat', *Journal of Neuroendocrinology*, 12, 1145–8.

Francis, D.D., Young, L.J., Meaney, M.J. and Insel, T.R. (2002) 'Naturally occurring differences in maternal care are associated with the expression of oxytocin and vasopressin receptors: Gender differences', *Journal of Neuroendocrinology*, 14, 349–53.

Frank, E., Kupfer, D.J., Jacob, M. and Jarrett, D. (1987) 'Personality features and response to acute treatment in recurrent depression', *Journal of Personality Disorders*, 1, 14–26.

Franzen, E.A. and Myers, R.E. (1973) 'Neural control of social behavior: Prefrontal and anterior temporal cortex', *Neuropsychologia*, 11, 141–57.

Fredrickson, B.L. (1998) 'What good are positive emotions?', *Review of General Psychology*, 2, 300–19.

Fredrickson, B.L. (2001) 'The role of positive emotions in positive psychology: The broaden-and-build theory of positive emotions', *American Psychologist*, 56, 218–26.

Fredrickson, B.L. (2004) 'The broaden-and-build theory of positive emotions', *Philosophical Transactions of the Royal Society of London: Biological Sciences*, 359, 1367–78.

Fredrickson, B.L. and Branigan, C. (2005) 'Positive emotions broaden the scope of attention and thought-action repertoires', *Cognition & Emotion*, 19, 313–32.

Fredrickson, B.L. and Joiner, T. (2002) 'Positive emotions trigger upward spirals toward emotional well-being', *Psychological Science*, 13, 172–5.

Fredrickson, B.L. and Kahneman, D. (2003) 'Duration neglect in retrospective evaluations of affective episodes', *Journal of Personality and Social Psychology*, 65(1993), 45–55.

Fredrickson, B.L. and Losada, M.F. (2005) 'Positive affect and the complex dynamics of human flourishing', *American Psychologist*, 60, 678–86.

Fredrickson, B.L., Tugade, M.M., Waugh, C.E. and Larkin, G. (2003) 'What good are positive emotions in crises?: A prospective study of resilience and emotions following the terrorist attacks on the United States on September 11th, 2001', *Journal of Personality and Social Psychology*, 84, 365–76.

Frick, R.W. (1985) 'Communicating emotion: The role of prosodic features', *Psychological Bulletin*, 97, 412–29.

Fridlund, A.J. and Izard, C.E. (1983) 'Electromyographic studies of facial expressions of emotions and patterns of emotions', in J.T. Cacioppo and R.E. Petty (eds), *Social Psychophysiology: A Sourcebook*. New York: Guilford Press.

Friesen, C.K. and Kingstone, A. (1998) 'The eyes have it!: Reflexive orienting is triggered by nonpredictive gaze', *Psychonomic Bulletin and Review*, 5(3), 490–5.

Frijda, N.H. (1986) *The Emotions*. Cambridge: Cambridge University Press.

Frijda, N.H. (1988) 'The laws of emotion', *American Psychologist*, 43, 349–58.

Frijda, N.H. (1993) 'The place of appraisal in emotion', *Cognition & Emotion*, 7, 357–87.

Frijda, N.H. (1994) 'Varieties of affect: Emotions and episodes, moods, and sentiments', in P. Ekman and R.J. Davidson (eds), *The Nature of Emotion*. Oxford: Oxford University Press.

Frijda, N.H. and Zeelenberg, M. (2001) 'Appraisal: What is the dependent?', in K.R. Scherer, A. Schorr and T. Johnstone (eds), *Appraisal Processes in Emotion: Theory, Methods, Research*. New York: Oxford University Press.

Friston, K.J. (2000) 'The Labile Brain I: Neuronal transients and nonlinear coupling', *Philosophical Transactions of the Royal Society*, 355, 215–36.

Fumagalli, F., Molteni, R., Racagni, G. and Riva, M.A. (2007) 'Stress during development: Impact on neuroplasticity and relevance to psychopathology', *Progress in Neurobiology*, 81, 197–217.

Funayama, E.S., Grillon, C., Davis, M. and Phelps, E.A. (2001) 'A double dissociation in the affective modulation of startle in humans: Effects of unilateral temporal lobectomy', *Journal of Cognitive Neuroscience*, 13, 721–9.

Gainotti, G. (1972) 'A qualitative study of the closing-in symptom in normal children and in brain-damaged patients', *Neuropsychologia*, 10, 429–36.

Gale, A. (1983) 'Electroencephalographic studies of extraversion-introversion: A case study in the psychophysiology of individual differences', *Personality and Individual Differences*, 4, 371–80.

Galynker, I.I., Cai, J., Ongseng, F., Finestone, H., Dutta, E. and Serseni, D. (1998) 'Hypofrontality and negative symptoms in major depressive disorder', *Journal of Nuclear Medicine*, 39, 608–12.

Ganster, D.C., Fox, M. and Dwyer, D. (2001) 'Explaining employee health care costs: A prospective examination of stressful job demands, personal control, and physiological reactivity', *Journal of Applied Psychology*, 86, 954–64.

Garlow, S.J. and Nemeroff, C.B. (2003) 'Neurobiology of depressive disorders', in R.J. Davidson, K.R. Scherer and H.H. Goldsmith (eds), *Handbook of Affective Sciences*. Oxford: Oxford University Press.

Garmezy, N. (1993) 'Children in poverty: Resiliency despite risk', *Psychiatry*, 56, 127–36.

Geertz, C. (1973) *The Interpretation of Cultures*. New York: Basic Books.

George, M.S., Ketter, T.A. and Post, R.M. (1994) 'Prefrontal cortex dysfunction in clinical depression', *Depression*, 2, 59–72.

George, M.S., Ketter, T.A., Parekh, P.I., Horwitz, B., Herscovitch, P. and Post, R.M. (1995) 'Brain activity during transient sadness and happiness in healthy women', *American Journal of Psychiatry*, 152, 341–51.

Gilbert, D.T. (2006) *Stumbling on Happiness*. New York: Random House.

Gilbert, D.T. and Wilson, T.D. (2007) 'Prospection: Experiencing the future', *Science*, 317, 1351–4.

Gilbert, D.T., Pinel, E.C., Wilson, T.D., Blumberg, S.J. and Wheatley, T.P. (1998) 'Immune neglect: A source of durability bias in affective forecasting', *Journal of Personality and Social Psychology*, 75, 617–38.

Gilboa, A., Shalev, A.Y., Laor, L., Lester, H., Louzoun, Y., Chisin, R. et al. (2004) 'Functional connectivity of the prefrontal cortex and the amygdala in posttraumatic stress disorder', *Biological Psychiatry*, 55, 263–72.

Gilboa, E. and Gotlib, I.H. (1997) 'Cognitive biases and affect persistence in previously dysphoric and never-dysphoric individuals', *Cognition & Emotion*, 11, 517–38.

Gilboa-Schechtman, E., Foa, E.B. and Amir, N. (1999) 'Attentional biases for facial expressions in social phobia: The face-in-the-crowd paradigm', *Cognition & Emotion*, 13, 305–18.

Gilboa-Schechtman, E., Revelle, W. and Gotlib, I.A. (2000) 'Stroop interference following mood induction: Emotionality, mood congruence, and concern relevance', *Cognitive Therapy Research*, 24, 491–502.

Gillespie, N.A., Cloninger, C.R., Heath, A.C. and Martin, N.G. (2003) 'The genetic and environmental relationship between Cloninger's dimensions of temperament and character', *Personality and Individual Differences*, 35, 1931–46.

Godden, D.R. and Baddeley, A.D. (1975) 'Context-dependent memory in two natural environments: On land and underwater' *British Journal of Psychology*, 66, 325–31.

Gomez, R., Gomez, A. and Cooper, A. (2002) 'Neuroticism and extraversion as predictors of negative and positive emotional information processing: Comparing Eysenck's, Gray's and Newman's theories', *European Journal of Personality*, 16, 333–50.

Gonzaga, G.C., Turner, R.A., Keltner, D., Campos, B.C. and Altemus, M. (2006) 'Romantic love and sexual desire in close bonds', *Emotion*, 6, 163–79.

Gorman, J.M. (1996) 'Comorbid depression and anxiety spectrum disorders', *Depression and Anxiety*, 4, 160–8.

Gotlib, I.H. and McCann, C.D. (1984) 'Construct accessibility and depression: An examination of cognitive and affective factors', *Journal of Personality and Social Psychology*, 47, 427–39.

Gotlib, I.H., Krasnoperova, E., Yue, D.N. and Joorman, J. (2004) 'Attentional biases for negative interpersonal stimuli in clinical depression', *Journal of Abnormal Psychology*, 113, 127–35.

Gotlib, I.H., McLachlan, A.L. and Katz, A.N. (1988) 'Biases in visual attention in depressed and nondepressed individuals', *Cognition & Emotion*, 2, 185–200.

Gottman, J.M. and Levenson, R.W. (1992) 'Marital processes predictive of later dissolution: Behaviour, physiology, and health', *Journal of Personality and Social Psychology*, 63, 221–33.

Gottman, J.M. and Levenson, R.W. (2000) 'The timing of divorce: Predicting when a couple will divorce over a 14-year period', *Journal of Marriage and the Family*, 62, 737–45.

Gouaux, C. (1971) 'Induced affective states and interpersonal attraction', *Journal of Personality and Social Psychology*, 20, 37–43.

Graf, P. and Mandler, G. (1984) 'Activation makes words more accessible, but not necessarily more retrievable', *Journal of Verbal Learning and Verbal Behavior*, 23, 553–68.

Graham, E.K. (1979) 'Distinguishing among orienting, defense, and startle reflexes', in H.D. Kimmel, E.H. van Olst and J.E. Odebeke (eds), *The Orienting Reflex in Humans*. New York: Erlbaum.

Grandjean, D., Sander, D., Pourtois, G., Schwartz, S., Seghier, M., Scherer, K.R. and Vuilleumier, P. (2005) 'The voices of wrath: Brain responses to angry prosody in meaningless speech', *Nature Neuroscience*, 8, 145–6.

Gray, J.A. (1970) 'The psychophysiological basis of introversion-extraversion', *Behaviour Research and Therapy*, 8, 249–66.

Gray, J.A. (1973) 'Causal theories of personality and how to test them', in J.R. Royce (ed.), *Multivariate Analysis and Psychological Theory*. London: Academic Press.

Gray, J.A. (1982) *The Neuropsychology of Anxiety*. New York: Oxford University Press.

Gray, J.A. (1987) *The Psychology of Fear and Stress*, 2nd edn. Cambridge: Cambridge University Press.

Gray, J.A. (1990) 'Brain systems that mediate both emotion and cognition', *Cognition & Emotion*, 4, 269–88.

Gray, J.A. (1994) 'Three fundamental emotion systems', in P. Ekman and R.J. Davidson (eds), *The Nature of Emotion*. New York: Oxford University Press.

Gray, J.A. and McNaughton, N. (2000) *The Neuropsychology of Anxiety*, 2nd edn. Oxford: Oxford University Press.

Greenberg, P.E., Sisitsky, T., Kessler, R.C., Finkelstein, S.N., Berndt, E.R., Davidson, J.R.T. et al. (1999) 'The economic burden of anxiety disorders in the 1990s', *Journal of Clinical Psychiatry*, 60, 427–35.

Greenberg, B.D., Tolliver, T.J. et al. (1999) 'Genetic variation in the serotonin transporter promoter region affects serotonin uptake in human blood platelets', *American Journal of Medical Genetics*, 88(1), 83–7.

Greenwald, A.G. (1992) 'New Look 3: Unconscious cognition reclaimed', *American Psychologist*, 47, 766–79.

Grey, S. and Mathews, A. (2000) 'Effects of training on interpretation of emotional ambiguity', *Quarterly Journal of Experimental Psychology*, 53, 1143–62.

Grimm, S., Schmidt, C.F., Bermpohl, F., Heinzel, A., Dahlem, Y., Wyss, M., Hell, D., Boesiger, P., Boeker, H. and Northoff, G. (2006) 'Segregated neural representation of distinct emotion dimensions in the prefrontal cortex – An fMRI study', *NeuroImage*, 30, 325–40.

Gross, J.J. (1998a) 'Antecedent- and response-focused emotion regulation: Divergent consequences for experience, expression, and physiology', *Journal of Personality and Social Psychology*, 74, 224–37.

Gross, J.J. (1998b) 'The emerging field of emotion regulation: An integrative review', *Review of General Psychology*, 2, 271–99.

Gross, J.J. (2007) *Handbook of Emotion Regulation*. New York: Guilford Press.

Gross, J.J. and John, O.P. (2003) 'Individual differences in two emotion regulation processes: Implications for affect, relationships, and well-being', *Journal of Personality and Social Psychology*, 85, 348–62.

Gross, J.J. and Levenson, R.W. (1993) 'Emotional suppression: Physiology, self-report, and expressive behaviour', *Journal of Personality and Social Psychology*, 64, 970–86.

Gross, J.J. and Munoz, R.F. (1995) 'Emotion regulation and mental health', *Clinical Psychology: Science and Practice*, 2, 151–64.

Gross, J.J. and Thompson, R.A. (2007) 'Emotion regulation: Conceptual foundations', in J.J. Gross (ed.), *Handbook of Emotion Regulation*. New York: Guilford Press.

Gross, J.J., Sutton, S.K. et al. (1998) 'Relations between affect and personality: Support for the affect-level and affective-reactivity views', *Personality and Social Psychology Bulletin*, 24, 279–88.

Gunderson, J.G., Triebwasser, J., Phillips, K.A. and Sullivan, C.N. (1999) 'Personality and vulnerability to affective disorders', in C.R. Cloninger (ed.), *Personality and Psychopathology*. Washington: American Psychiatric Press.

Haas, B.W., Omura, K., Constable, R.T. and Canli, T. (2007) 'Is automatic emotion regulation associated with agreeableness? A perspective using a social neuroscience approach', *Psychological Science*, 18, 130–2

Hagemann, D., Naumann, E. et al. (1998) 'Frontal brain asymmetry and affective style: A conceptual replication', *Psychophysiology*, 35, 372–88.

Haken, H. (1977) *Synergetics – An Introduction: Nonequilibrium Phase Transitions and Self-organization in Physics, Chemistry and Biology*. New York: Springer-Verlag.

Halgren, E. (1992) 'Emotional neurophysiology of the amygdala within the context of human cognition', in J.P. Aggleton (ed.), *The Amygdala: Neurobiological Aspects of Emotion, Memory and Mental Dysfunction*. New York: Wiley-Liss.

Hall, C.S. and Lindzey, G. (1970) *Theories of Personality*. New York: Wiley.

Hamann, S. (2001) 'Cognitive and neural mechanisms of emotional memory', *Trends in Cognitive Sciences*, 5, 394–400.

Hamann, S. and Harenski, C.L. (2004) 'Exploring the brain's interface between personality, mood, and emotion: Theoretical comment on Canli et al. (2004)', *Behavioral Neuroscience*, 118, 1134–6.

Hamann, S.B., Ely, T.D., Grafton, S.T. and Kilts, C.D. (1999) 'Amygdala activity related to enhanced memory for pleasant and aversive stimuli', *Nature Neuroscience*, 2, 289–93.

Hamm, A.O., Greenwald, M.K., Bradley, M.M., Cuthbert, B.N. and Lang, P.J. (1991) 'The fear potentiated startle effect', *Integrative Psychological and Behavioural Sciences*, 26, 119–26.

Hampton, C., Purcell, D.G., Bersine, L., Hansen, C.H. and Hansen, R.D. (1989) 'Probing "pop-out": Another look at the face-in-the crowd effect', *Bulletin of the Psychonomic Society*, 27, 563–6.

Hansen, C.H. and Hansen, R.D. (1988) 'Finding the face in the crowd: An anger superiority effect', *Journal of Personality and Social Psychology*, 54, 917–24.

Hariri, A.R. and Weinberger, D.R. (2003) 'Functional neuroimaging of genetic variation in serotonergic neurotransmission', *Genes, Brain and Behaviour*, 2, 341–9.

Hariri, A.R., Drabant, E.M. and Weinberger, D.R. (2006) 'Imaging genetics: Perspectives from studies of genetically driven variation in serotonin function and corticolimbic affective processing', *Biological Psychiatry*, 59, 888–97.

Hariri, A.R., Mattay, V.S., Tessitore, A., Kolachana, B.S., Fera, F., Goldman, D., Egan, M.F. and Weinberger, D.R. (2002) 'Serotonin transporter genetic variation and the response of the human amygdala', *Science*, 297, 400–3.

Harker, L. and Keltner, D. (2001) 'Expressions of positive emotions in women's college yearbook pictures and their relationship to personality and life outcomes across adulthood', *Journal of Personality and Social Psychology*, 80, 112–24.

Harlow, J.M. (1868) 'Recovery from a Passage of an Iron Bar through the Head', *Publications of the Massachusetts Medical Society*, 2, 327–47.

Harmon-Jones, E. and Allen, J.J.B. (1997) 'Behavioural activation sensitivity and resting frontal EEG asymmetry: Covariation of putative indicators related to risk for mood disorders', *Journal of Abnormal Psychology*, 106, 159–63.

Harré, R. (1986) *The Social Construction of Emotions.* Oxford: Blackwell.

Hayward, C., Killen. J.D., Kraemer, H.C. and Taylor, C.B. (2000) 'Predictors of panic attacks in adolescents', *Journal of the American Academy of Child and Adolescent Psychiatry*, 39, 207–14.

Headey, B. and Wearing, A. (1989) 'Personality, life events, and subjective well-being: Toward a dynamic equilibrium model', *Journal of Personality and Social Psychology*, 57, 731–9.

Heath, A.C. and Martin, N.G. (1994) 'Genetic influences on alcohol consumption patterns and problem drinking: Results from the Australian NH&MRC Twin Panel follow-up survey', *Annals of the New York Academy of Sciences*, 708, 72–85.

Heath, A.C., Cloninger, C.R. and Martin, N.G. (1994) 'Testing a model for the genetic structure of personality: A comparison of the personality systems of Cloninger and Eysenck', *Journal of Personality and Social Psychology*, 66, 762–75.

Hedlund, S. and Rude, S. (1995) 'Evidence of latent depressive schemas in formerly depressed individuals', *Journal of Abnormal Psychology*, 104, 517–25.

Heim, C. and Nemeroff, C.B. (1999) 'The impact of early adverse experiences on brain systems involved in anxiety and effective disorders', *Biological Psychiatry*, 46, 1509–22.

Heim, C., Plotsky, P.M. and Nemeroff, C.B. (2004) 'Importance of studying the contributions of early adverse experience to neurobiological findings in depression', *Neuropsychopharmacology*, 29, 641–8.

Heinz, A., Braus, D.F. et al. (2005) 'Amygdala-prefrontal coupling depends on a genetic variation of the serotonin transporter', *Nature Neuroscience*, 8(1), 20–1.

Heller, W. and Nitschke, J.B. (1998) 'The puzzle of regional brain activity in depression and anxiety: The importance of subtypes and comorbidity', *Cognition & Emotion*, 12, 421–44.

Heller, W., Nitschke, J.B. and Miller, G.A. (1998) 'Lateralization in emotion and emotional disorders', *Current Directions in Psychological Science*, 7, 26–32.

Hendersen, R.W. (1985) 'Fearful memories: The motivational significance of forgetting', in F.R. Brush and J.B. Overmier (eds), *Affect, Conditioning, and Cognition: Essays on the Determinants of Behaviour*. Hillsdale, NJ: Lawrence Erlbaum.

Henriques, J.B. and Davidson, R.J. (1991) 'Left frontal hypoactivation in depression', *Journal of Abnormal Psychology*, 100, 535–45.

Henriques, J.B., Glowacki, J.M. and Davidson, R.J. (1994) 'Reward fails to alter response bias in depression', *Journal of Abnormal Psychology*, 103, 460–6.

Hermans, D., Vansteenwegen, D. and Eelen, P. (1999) 'Eye movement registration as a continuous index of attention deployment: Data from a group of spider anxious students', *Cognition & Emotion*, 13, 419–34.

Hertel, P. (2004) *Emotion and Memory*. Oxford: Oxford University Press.

Heuser, I. (1998) 'The hypothalamic-pituitary-adrenal system in depression', *Pharmacopsychiatry*, 31, 10–13.

Hilgard, E.R. (1980) 'The trilogy of mind: Cognition, affection, and conation', *Journal of the History of the Behavioural Sciences*, 16, 107–17.

Hofmann, S.G. (2007) 'Enhancing exposure-based therapy from a translational research perspective', *Behavior Research and Therapy* (DOI:10.1016/j.brat.2007.06.006).

Hogan, R., Johnson, J.A. and Briggs, S.R. (1997) *Handbook of Personality Psychology*. San Diego: Academic Press.

Hoge, E.A., Austin, E.D. and Pollack, M.H. (2007) 'Resilience: Research evidence and conceptual considerations for posttraumatic stress disorder', *Depression and Anxiety*, 24, 139–52.

Hollon, S.D. and Garber, J. (1990) 'Cognitive therapy of depression: A social-cognitive perspective', *Personality and Social Psychology Bulletin*, 16, 58–73.

Holmes, T.H. and Rahe, R.H. (1967) 'The social readjustment rating scales', *Journal of Psychosomatic Research*, 11, 213–18.

Humrichouse, J., Chmielewski, M., McDade-Montez, E.A. and Watson, D. (2007) 'Affect assessment through self-report methods', in J. Rottenberg and S.L. Johnson (eds), *Emotion and Psychopathology: Bridging Affective and Clinical Science*. Washington: American Psychological Association.

Hurlburt, R.T. (1997) 'Randomly sampling thinking in the natural environment', *Journal of Consulting and Clinical Psychology*, 65, 941–9.

Hurlburt, R.T. and Heavey, C.L. (2001) 'Telling what we know: Describing inner experience', *Trends in Cognitive Sciences*, 5(9), 400–3.

Hurlburt, R.T and Heavey, C.L. (2002) 'Interobserver reliability of descriptive experience sampling', *Cognitive Therapy and Research*, 26, 135–42.

Inoue, T., Koyama, T. and Yamashita, I. (1993) 'Effect of conditioned fear stress on serotonin metabolism in the rat brain', *Pharmacology Biochemistry and Behavior*, 44, 371–4.

Inoue, T., Li, X.B. and Abekawa, T. et al. (2004) 'Selective serotonin reuptake inhibitor reduces conditioned fear through its effect in the amygdala', *European Journal of Pharmacology*, 497, 311–16.

Isen, A.M. (1970) 'Success, failure, attention and reaction to others: The warm glow of success', *Journal of Personality and Social Psychology*, 15, 294–301.

Isen, A.M. (1984) 'Toward understanding the role of affect in cognition', in R.S. Wyer and T.K. Srull (eds), *Handbook of Social Cognition*. Hillsdale, NJ: Lawrence Erlbaum.

Isen, A.M. (1985) 'The asymmetry of happiness and sadness in effects on memory in normal college students', *Journal of Experimental Psychology: General*, 114, 388–91.

Isen, A.M. (1987) 'Positive affect, cognitive processes and social behavior', in L. Berkowitz (ed.), *Advances in Experimental Social Psychology, Vol. 20*. San Diego, CA: Academic Press.

Isen, A.M. (1999) 'Positive affect', in T. Dalgleish and M. Powers (eds), *Handbook of Cognition and Emotion*. Hillsdale, NJ: Erlbaum.

Isen, A.M. (2000) 'Positive affect and decision making', in M. Lewis and J.M. Haviland-Jones (eds), *Handbook of Emotions*, 2nd edn. New York: Guilford Press.

Isen, A.M. and Levin, P.F. (1972) 'The effect of feeling good on helping: Cookies and kindness', *Journal of Personality and Social Psychology*, 21, 384–8.

Isen, A.M., Johnson, M.M.S., Mertz, E. and Robinson, G.F. (1985) 'The influence of positive affect on the unusualness of word associations', *Journal of Personality and Social Psychology*, 48, 1413–26.

Isen, A., Shalker, T., Clark, M. and Karp, L. (1978) 'Affect, accessibility of material in memory, and behaviour: A cognitive loop?', *Journal of Personality and Social Psychology*, 31, 1–12.

Ito, T.A. and Cacioppo, J.T. (2005) 'Variations on a human universal: Individual differences in positivity offset and negativity bias', *Cognition & Emotion*, 19, 1–26.

Izard, C.E. (1964) 'Personality similarity and friendship', in E.E. Sampson (ed.), *Approaches, Context, and Problems of Social Psychology*. Englewood Cliffs, NJ: Prentice Hall.

Izard, C.E. (1971) *The Face of Emotion*. New York: Appleton-Century-Crofts.

Izard, C.E. (1977) *Human Emotions*. New York: Plenum Press.

Izard, C.E. (1992) 'Basic emotions, relations among emotions, and emotion-cognition relations', *Psychological Review*, 99, 561–5.

Izard, C.E. (1993) 'Four systems for emotion activation: Cognitive and noncognitive processes', *Psychological Review*, 100, 68–90.

Izard, C.E. (2007) 'Basic emotions, natural kinds, emotion schemas, and a new paradigm', *Perspectives in Psychological Science*, 2, 260–80.

Izard, C.E. and Ackerman, B.P. (2000) 'Motivational, organizational, and regulatory functions of discrete emotions', in M. Lewis and J.M. Haviland-Jones (eds), *Handbook of Emotions*, 2nd edn. New York: Guilford Press.

Jack, A.I. and Roepstorff, A. (2002) 'Introspection and cognitive brain mapping: From stimulus-response to script-report', *Trends in Cognitive Sciences*, 6, 333–9.

Jaffee, S.R., Caspi, A., Moffitt, T.E., Polo-Tomas, M. and Taylor, A. (2007) 'Individual, family, and neighborhood factors distinguish resilient from non-resilient maltreated children: A cumulative stressors model', *Child Abuse & Neglect*, 31, 231–53.

James, W. (1884) 'What is an emotion?', *Mind*, 9, 188–205.

James, W. (1890/1950) *The Principles of Psychology*. New York: Henry Holt.

Jaspers, K. (1951) *Man in the Modern Age*. London: Routledge & Kegan Paul.

Jerison, H.J. (1977) 'The theory of encephalization', *Annals of the New York Academy of Sciences*, 299, 146–60.

John, O.P. (1990) 'The "Big Five" factor taxonomy: Dimensions of personality in the natural language and in questionnaires', in L.A. Pervin (ed.), *Handbook of Personality Theory and Research*. New York: Guilford Press.

John, O.P. and Gross, J.J. (2007) 'Individual differences in emotion regulation strategies: Links to global trait, dynamic, and social cognitive constructs', in J.J. Gross (ed.), *Handbook of Emotion Regulation*. New York: Guilford Press.

Johnson, E.J. and Tversky, A. (1983) 'Affect, generalization, and the perception of risk', *Journal of Personality and Social Psychology*, 45, 20–31.

Johnson, M.K. and Multhaup, K.S. (1992) 'Emotion and MEM', in S.-A. Christianson (ed.), *The Handbook of Emotion and Memory: Research and Theory*. Hillsdale, NJ: Lawrence Erlbaum.

Johnson, M.K., Kim, J.K. and Risse, G. (1985) 'Do alcoholic Korsakoff's syndrome patients acquire affective reactions?', *Journal of Experimental Psychology: Learning, Memory, and Cognition*, 11, 22–36.

Johnson-Laird, P.N. and Oatley, K. (1992) 'Basic emotions: A cognitive science approach to function, folk theory and empirical study', *Cognition & Emotion*, 6, 201–23.

Jonsson, E.G., Nothen, M.M. et al. (1999) 'Association between a promoter polymorphism in the dopamine D2 receptor gene and schizophrenia', *Schizophrenia Research*, 40, 31–6.

Joormann, J. and Gotlib, I.H. (2007) 'Selective attention to emotional faces following recovery from depression', *Journal of Abnormal Psychology*, 116, 80–5.

Josephson, B., Singer, J.A. and Salovey, P. (1996) 'Mood regulation and memory: Repairing sad moods with happy memories', *Cognition & Emotion*, 10, 437–44.

Kagan, J. (1994) *Galen's Prophecy: Temperament in Human Nature*. New York: Basic Books.

Kagan, J. (2003) 'Biology, context, and developmental inquiry', *Annual Review of Psychology*, 54, 1–23.

Kagan, J., Snidman, N., Zentner, M. and Peterson, E. (1999) 'Infant temperament and anxious symptoms in school age children', *Development and Psychopathology*, 11, 209–24.

Kagan, S., Resnick, J. and Snidman, M. (1987) 'The physiology and psychology of behavioural inhibition in children', *Child Development*, 58, 1459–73.

Kahneman, D. (1999) 'Objective happiness', in D. Kahneman, E. Diener and N. Schwarz (eds), *Well-being: The Foundations of Hedonic Psychology*. New York: Russell Sage Foundation.

Kahneman, D. and Tversky, A. (1973) 'On the psychology of prediction', *Psychological Review*, 80, 237–57.

Kahneman, D. and Tversky, A. (1982) 'The simulation heuristic', in D. Kahneman, P. Slovic and A. Tversky (eds), *Judgement under Uncertainty: Heuristics and Biases*. New York: Cambridge University Press.

Kahneman, D., Diener, E. and Schwarz, N. (1999) *Well-being: The Foundations of Hedonic Psychology*. New York: Russell Sage Foundation.

Kalin, N.H., Larson, C., Shelton, S.E. and Davidson, R.J. (1998) 'Asymmetric frontal brain activity, cortisol, and behavior associated with fearful temperament in Rhesus monkeys', *Behavioral Neuroscience*, 112, 286–92.

Kalin, N.H., Shelton, S.E., Davidson, R.J. and Kelley, A.E. (2001) 'The primate amygdala mediates acute fear but not the behavioural and physiological components of anxious temperament', *Journal of Neuroscience*, 21, 2067–74.

Kandel, E.R. (1998) 'A new intellectual framework for psychiatry', *American Journal of Psychiatry*, 155, 457–9.

Katigbak, M.S., Church, A.T., Guanzon-Lapeña, M.A., Carlota, A.J. and del Pilar, G.H. (2002) 'Are indigenous personality dimensions culture-specific? Philippine inventories and the five-factor model', *Journal of Personality and Social Psychology*, 82, 89–101.

Kauffman, S.A. (1993) *The Origin of Order. Self-organization and Selection in Evolution*. New York: Oxford University Press.

Kavanagh, D.J. and Bower, G.H. (1985) 'Mood and self-efficacy: Impact of joy and sadness on perceived capabilities', *Cognitive Therapy and Research*, 9, 507–25.

Kelso, J.A.S. (1995) *Dynamic Patterns: The Self-organization of Brain and Behavior*. Cambridge, MA: MIT Press.

Kensinger, E.A. and Corkin, S. (2004) 'Two routes to emotional memory: Distinct neural processes for valence and arousal', *Proceedings of the National Academy of Sciences*, 101, 3310–15.

Kensinger, E.A. and Schacter, D.L. (2006) 'Amygdala activity is associated with the successful encoding of item, but not source, information for positive and negative stimuli', *Journal of Neuroscience*, 26, 2564–70.

Kessler, R.C., Chiu, W.T., Demier, O. and Walters, E.E. (2005) 'Prevalence, severity and comorbidity of 12-month DSM-IV disorders in the national comorbidity survey replication', *Archives of General Psychiatry*, 62, 617–27.

Kessler, R.C., McGonagle, K.A., Zhao, S., Nelson, C.B., Hughes, M., Eshleman, S., Wittchen, H.-U. and Kendler, K.S. (1994) 'Lifetime and 12-month prevalence of DSM-III-R psychiatric disorders in the United States: Results from the National Comorbidity Survey', *Archives of General Psychiatry*, 51, 8–19.

Kessler, R.C., Sonnega, A., Bromet, E., Hughes, M. and Nelson, C.B. (1995) 'Posttraumatic stress disorder in the National Comorbidity Survey', *Archives of General Psychiatry*, 52, 1048–60

Ketter, T.A., Wang, P.W., Lembke, A. and Sachs, N. (2003) 'Physiological and pharmacological induction of affect', in R.J. Davidson, K.R. Scherer and H.H. Goldsmith (eds), *Handbook of Affective Sciences*. New York: Oxford University Press.

Keyes, C. and Haidt, J. (2003) *Flourishing: Positive Psychology and the life well lived*. Washington, DC: American Psychological Association.

Kilpatrick, D.G. and Resnick, H.S. (1993) 'PTSD associated with exposure to criminal victimization in clinical and community populations', in J.R.T. Davidson and E.B. Foa (eds), *PTSD in Review: Recent Research and Future Directions*. Washington, DC: American Psychiatric Press.

Kim, H., Somerville, L.H., Johnstone, T., Alexander, A.L. and Whalen, P.J. (2003) 'Inverse amygdala and medial prefrontal cortex responses to surprised faces', *Neuroreport*, 14, 2317–22.

King, D.W., King, L.A., Fairbank, J.A., Keane, T.M. and Adams, G. (1998) 'Resilience-recovery factors in posttraumatic stress disorder among female and male Vietnam veterans: Hardiness, postwar social support, and additional stressful life events', *Journal of Personality and Social Psychology*, 74, 420–34.

Kitayama, S. and Markus, H.R. (1994) *Emotion and Culture: Empirical Investigations of Mutual Influence*. Washington, DC: American Psychological Association.

Kitayama, S., Markus, H. R. and Kurokawa, M. (2000) 'Culture, emotion, and well-being: Good feelings in Japan and the United States', *Cognition & Emotion*, 14, 93–124.

Kluver, H. and Bucy, P.C. (1937) 'Psychic blindness and other symptoms following bilateral temporal lobectomy in rhesus monkeys', *American Journal of Physiology*, 119, 352–3.

Kobasa, S.C. (1979) 'Stressful life events, personality, and health: An inquiry into hardiness', *Journal of Personality and Social Psychology*, 37, 1–11.

Koepp, M.J., Gunn, R.N., Lawrence, A.D., Cunningham, V.J., Dagher, A., Jones, T., Brooks, D.J., Bench C.J. and Grasby, P.M. (1998) 'Evidence for striatal dopamine release during a video game', *Nature*, 393, 266–8.

Konorski, J. (1967) *Integrative Activity of the Brain. An Inter-disciplinary Approach.* Chicago: University of Chicago Press.

Kopp, C.B. (1982) 'Antecedents of self-regulation: A developmental perspective', *Developmental Psychology*, 18, 199–214.

Koster, E.H.W., Fox, E. and MacLeod, C. (2008) 'Cognitive bias modification in emotional disorders: A review', *Journal of Abnormal Psychology.*

Kringelbach, M.L. and Rolls, E.T. (2004) 'The functional neuroanatomy of the human orbitofrontal cortex: evidence from neuroimaging and neuropsychology', *Progress in Neurobiology*, 72, 341–72.

Kringelbach, M.L., O'Doherty, J., Rolls, E.T. and Andrews, C. (2003) 'Activation of the human orbitofrontal cortex to a liquid food stimulus is correlated with its subjective pleasantness', *Cerebral Cortex*, 13, 1064–71.

Krohne, H.W. (2003) 'Individual differences in emotional reactions and coping', in R.J. Davidson, K.R. Scherer and H.H. Goldsmith (eds), *Handbook of Affective Sciences.* New York: Oxford University Press.

Kunst-Wilson, W.R. and Zajonc, R.B. (1980) 'Affective discrimination of stimuli that can not be recognized', *Science*, 207, 557–8.

Lane, R.D. and Nadel, L. (2000) *Cognitive Neuroscience of Emotion.* New York: Oxford University Press.

Lane, R.D., Nadel, L., Allen, J.B. and Kaszniak, A.W. (2000) 'The study of emotion from the perspective of cognitive neuroscience', in R.D. Lane and L. Nadel (eds), *Cognitive Neuroscience of Emotion.* New York: Oxford University Press.

Lane, R.D., Reiman, E.M., Ahern, G.L., Schwartz, G.E. and Davidson, R.J. (1997) 'Neuroanatomical correlates of happiness, sadness, and disgust', *American Journal of Psychiatry*, 154, 926–33.

Lane, R.D., Reiman, E.M., Axelrod, B., Yun, L.-S., Holmes, A. and Schwartz, G.E. (1998) 'Neural correlates of levels of emotional awareness: Evidence of an interaction between emotion and attention in the anterior behavioural cortex', *Journal of Cognitive Neuroscience*, 10, 525–35.

Lang, P.J. (1980) 'Behavioral treatment and bio-behavioral assessment: computer applications', in J.B. Sidowski, J.H. Johnson and T.A. Williams (eds), *Technology in Mental Health Care Delivery Systems.* Norwood, NJ: Ablex.

Lang, P.J. (1995) 'The emotion probe: Studies of motivation and attention', *American Psychologist*, 50, 372–85.

Lang, P.J. (2000) 'Emotion and motivation: Attention, perception, and action', *Journal of Sport and Exercise Psychology*, 22, S122–S140.

Lang, P.J., Bradley, M.M. and Cuthbert, B.N. (1990) 'Emotion, attention, and the startle reflex', *Psychological Review*, 97, 377–95.

Lang, P.J., Bradley, M.M. and Cuthbert, B. N. (1997) 'Motivated attention: affect, activation and action', in P.J. Lang and R.F. Balaban (eds), *Attention and Orienting: Sensory and Motivational Processes.* Hillsdale, NJ: Lawrence Erlbaum.

Lang, P.J., Bradley, M.M., Fitzsimmons, J.R., Cuthbert, B.N., Scott, J.D., Moulder, B. and Nangia, V. (1998) 'Emotional arousal and activation of the visual cortex: An fMRI analysis', *Psychophysiology*, 35, 199–210.

Lang, P.J., Bradley, M.M. and Cuthbert, B.N. (2005) *International Affective Picture System (IAPS): Affective Ratings of Pictures and Instruction Manual.* Gainesville: University of Florida.

Lang, P.J., Greenwald, M., Bradley, M.M. and Hamm, A.O. (1993) 'Looking at pictures: Evaluative, facial, visceral, and behavioural responses', *Psychophysiology*, 30, 261–73.

Lange C.G. (1885/1922) 'The emotions', in E. Dunlap (ed.), *The Emotions*. Baltimore: Williams & Wilkins.

Langer, E.J. (1975) 'The illusion of control', *Journal of Personality and Social Psychology*, 32, 311–28.

Langer, E. and Rodin, J. (1976) 'The effects of choice and enhanced personal behaviourality for the aged: A field experiment in an institutional setting', *Journal of Personality and Social Psychology*, 34, 191–8.

Larsen, R.J. and Cutler, S. (1996) 'The complexity of individual emotional lives: A within-subject analysis of affect structure', *Journal of Social and Clinical Psychology*, 15, 206–30.

Larsen, R.J. and Ketelaar, T. (1989) 'Extraversion, neuroticism, and susceptibility to positive and negative mood induction procedures.' *Personality and Individual Differences*, 10, 1221–8.

Larsen, R.J. and Ketelaar, T. (1991) 'Personality and susceptibility to positive and negative emotional states', *Journal of Personality and Social Psychology*, 61, 132–40.

Lavie, N. and Tsal, Y. (1994) 'Perceptual load as a major determinant of the locus of selection in visual attention', *Perception & Psychophysics*, 56, 183–97.

Layard, R. (2005) *Happiness: Lessons from a New Science*. New York: Penguin.

Lazarus, R.S. (1966) *Psychological Stress and the Coping Process*. New York: McGraw-Hill.

Lazarus, R.S. (1982) 'Thoughts on relations between emotion and cognition', *American Psychologist*, 37, 1014–19.

Lazarus, R.S. (1984) 'On the primacy of cognition', *American Psychologist*, 39, 124–9.

Lazarus, R.S. (1991) *Emotion and Adaptation*. London: Oxford University Press.

Lazarus, R.S. (1994) 'The stable and the unstable in emotion', in P. Ekman and R.J. Davidson (eds), *The Nature of Emotion*. Oxford: Oxford University Press.

Lazarus, R.S. (1999) 'The cognition-emotion debate: A bit of history', in T. Dalgleish and M. Power (eds), *Handbook of Cognition and Emotion*. New York: Wiley.

LeDoux, J.E. (1987) 'Emotion', in F. Plum (ed.), *Handbook of Physiology. 1: The Nervous System. Vol. V. Higher functions of the brain*. Bethesda, MD: American Physiological Society.

LeDoux, J.E. (1996) *The Emotional Brain: The Mysterious Underpinnings of Emotional Life*. New York: Simon & Schuster.

LeDoux, J.E. (2000) 'Emotion circuits in the brain', *Annual Review of Neuroscience*, 23, 155–84.

LeDoux, J.E. and Phelps, E.A. (2004) 'Emotional networks in the brain', in M. Lewis and J.M. Haviland-Jones (eds), *Handbook of Emotions*, 2nd edn. New York: Guilford Press.

Lee, G.P., Loring, D.W., Meador, K.J. and Flanagan, H.F. (1987) 'Emotional reactions and behavioural complications following intracarotid sodium amytal injection', *Journal of Clinical and Experimental Neuropsychology*, 37, 565–610.

Lesch, K.P., Bengel, D., Heils, A., Sabol, S.Z., Greenberg, B.D., Petri, S., Benjamin, J., Müller, C.R., Hamer, D.H. and Murphy, D.L. (1996) 'Association of anxiety-related traits with a polymorphism in the serotonin transporter gene regulatory region', *Science*, 274, 1527–31.

Levenson, R.W. (1988) 'Emotion and the autonomic nervous system: A prospectus for research on autonomic specificity', in H. Wagner (ed.), *Social Psychophysiology and Emotion: Theory and Clinical Applications*. London: Wiley.

Levenson, R.W. (1994) 'Human emotion: A functional view', in P. Ekman and R.J. Davidson (eds), *The Nature of Emotion*. Oxford: Oxford University Press.

Levenson, R.W. (2003) 'Autonomic specificity and emotion', in R.J. Davidson, K.R. Scherer and H.H. Goldsmith (eds), *Handbook of Affective Sciences.* New York: Oxford University Press.

Levenson, R.W., Ekman, P., Heider, K. and Friesen, W.V. (1992) 'Emotion and autonomic nervous system activity in the Minangkabau of West Sumatra', *Journal of Personality and Social Psychology*, 62, 972–88.

Leventhal, H. (1979) 'A perceptual-motor processing model of emotion', in P. Pilner, K. Blankstein and I.M. Spiegel (eds), *Perception of Emotion in Self and Others, Vol 5.* New York: Plenum Press.

Leventhal, H. and Scherer, K.R. (1987) 'The relationship of emotion to cognition: A functional approach to a semantic controversy', *Cognition & Emotion*, 1, 3–28.

Lévesque, J., Eugene, F., Joanette, Y., Paquette, V., Mensour, B., Beaudoin, G., Leroux, J-M., Bourgouin, P. and Beauregard, M. (2003) 'Neural circuitry underlying voluntary suppression of sadness', *Biological Psychiatry*, 53, 502–10.

Levine, L.J. and Burgess, S.L. (1997) 'Beyond general arousal: Effects of specific emotions on memory', *Social Cognition*, 15, 157–81.

Levine, L.J. and Pizarro, D.A. (2004) 'Emotion and memory research: A grumpy overview', *Social Cognition*, 22, 530–54.

Levine, L.J. and Safer, M.A. (2002) 'Sources of bias in memory for emotions', *Current Directions in Psychological Science*, 11, 169–73.

Levitan, I.B. and Kaczmarek, L.K. (1997) *The Neuron: Cell and Molecular Biology.* New York: Oxford University Press.

Lewis, M. and Haviland-Jones, J.M. (2000) *Handbook of Emotions*, 2nd edn. New York: Guilford Press.

Lewis, M.D. (2005) 'Bridging emotion theory and neurobiology through dynamic systems modelling', *Behavioral and Brain Sciences*, 28, 169–245.

Lewis, P.A. and Critchley, H. (2003) 'Mood dependent memory', *Trends in Cognitive Neurosciences*, 7, 431–3.

Lewis, P.A., Critchley, H.D, Rotshtein, P. and Dolan, R.J. (2007) 'Neural correlates of valence and arousal in processing affective words', *Cerebral Cortex*, 17, 742–8.

Liberzon, I., Britton, J.C. and Phan, K.L. (2003) 'Neural correlates of traumatic recall in post-traumatic stress disorder', *Stress*, 6, 151–6.

Linley, P.A. and Joseph, S. (2004) 'Positive change following trauma and adversity: A review', *Journal of Traumatic Stress*, 17, 11–21.

Liu, D., Diorio, J., Tannenbaum, B., Cladji, C., Francis, D., Freedman, A., Sharma, S., Pearson, D., Plotsky, P.M. and Meaney, M.J. (1997) 'Maternal care, hippocampal glucocorticoid receptors, and hypothalamic–pituitary–adrenal responses to stress', *Science*, 277, 1659–62.

Loftus, E.F. (1975) 'Leading questions and the eyewitness report', *Cognitive Psychology*, 7, 560–72.

Loftus, E.F., Loftus, G.R. and Messo, J. (1987) 'Some facts about "weapon focus"', *Law and Human Behavior*, 11, 55–62.

London School of Economics (2006) 'The depression report: A new deal for depression anxiety disorders', London School of Economics Centre for Economic Performance Mental Health Policy Group.

Lucas, R.E. and Baird, B.M. (2004) 'Extraversion and emotional reactivity', *Journal of Personality and Social Psychology*, 86, 473–85.

Lucas, R.E. (2007a) 'Adaptation and the set-point model of subjective well-being: Does happiness change after major life events?', *Current Directions in Psychological Science*, 16, 75–9.

Lucas, R.E. (2007b) 'Long-term disability is associated with lasting changes in subjective well-being: Evidence from two nationally representative longitudinal studies', *Journal of Personality and Social Psychology*, 92, 717–30.

Luthar, S.S. (1991) 'Vulnerability and resilience: A study of high-risk adolescents', *Child Development*, 62, 600–16.

Lyons, W. (1999) 'The philosophy of cognition and emotion', in T. Dalgleish and M.J. Power (eds), *Handbook of Cognition and Emotion*. Chichester: Wiley.

Mackintosh, B., Mathews, A., Yiend, J., Ridgeway, V. and Cook, E. (2006) 'Induced biases in emotional interpretation influence stress vulnerability and endure despite changes in context', *Behaviour Therapy*, 37, 209–22.

MacLean, P.D. (1973) *A Triune Concept of Brain and Behaviour*. Toronto: University of Toronto Press.

MacLean, P.D. (1990) *The Triune Brain in Evolution: Role in Paleocerebral Functions*. New York: Plenum Press.

MacLeod, A.K. (1999) 'Prospective cognition', in T. Dalgleish and M.J. Power (eds), *Handbook of Cognition and Emotion*. New York: Wiley.

MacLeod, A.K. and Byrne, A. (1996) 'Anxiety, depression and the anticipation of future positive and negative experiences', *Journal of Abnormal Psychology*, 105, 286–9.

MacLeod, A.K., Tata, P., Kentish, J., Carroll, F. and Hunter, E. (1997) 'Anxiety, depression, and explanation-based pessimism for future positive and negative events', *Clinical Psychology and Psychotherapy*, 4, 15–24.

MacLeod, A.K., Williams, J.M.G. and Bekerian, D.A. (1991) 'Worry is reasonable: The role of explanations in pessimism about future personal events', *Journal of Abnormal Psychology*, 100, 478–86.

MacLeod, C.M. (1991) 'Half a century of research on the Stroop effect: An integrative review', *Psychological Bulletin*, 109, 163–203.

MacLeod, C. and Mathews, A. (1988) 'Anxiety and the allocation of attention to threat', *Quarterly Journal of Experimental Psychology. A, Human Experimental Psychology*, 40, 653–70.

MacLeod, C., Campbell, L., Rutherford, E. and Wilson, E. (2004) 'The causal status of anxiety-linked attentional and interpretive bias', in J. Yiend (ed.), *Cognition, Emotion, and Psychopathology: Theoretical, Empirical, and Clinical Directions*. Cambridge: Cambridge University Press.

MacLeod, C., Mathews, A. and Tata, P. (1986) 'Attentional bias in emotional disorders', *Journal of Abnormal Psychology*, 95, 15–20.

MacLeod, C., Rutherford, E., Campbell, L., Ebsworthy G and Holker, L. (2002) 'Selective attention and emotional vulnerability: Assessing the causal basis of their association through the experimental manipulation of attentional bias', *Journal of Abnormal Psychology*, 111, 107–23.

Magnus, K.B., Diener, E., Fujita, F. and Pavot, W. (1993) 'Extraversion and neuroticism as predictors of objective life events: A longitudinal analysis', *Journal of Personality and Social Psychology*, 65, 316–30.

Maia, T.V. and McClelland, J.L. (2005) 'The somatic marker hypothesis: Still many questions but no answers: Response to Bechara et al.', *Trends in Cognitive Sciences*, 9, 162–4.

Maier, S.F and Watkins, L.R. (2005) 'Stressor controllability and learned helplessness: The roles of the dorsal raphe nucleus, serotonin, and corticotropin-releasing factor', *Neuroscience and Biobehavioral Reviews*, 29, 829–41.

Mangun, G.R. and Hillyard, S.A. (1995) 'Mechanisms and models of selective attention', in M.D. Rugg and M.G.H. Coles (eds), *Electrophysiology of Mind: Event-related Brain Potentials and Cognition.* New York: Oxford University Press.

Markus, H.R. and Kitayama, S. (1991) 'Culture and the self: Implications for cognition, emotion, and motivation', *Psychological Review*, 98, 224–53.

Marshall, G.D. and Zimbardo, P.G. (1979) 'The affective consequences of inadequately explained physiological arousal', *Journal of Personality and Social Psychology*, 37, 970–88.

Martin, D., Abramson, L.Y. and Alloy, L.B. (1984) 'The illusion of control for self and others in depressed and nondepressed college students', *Journal of Personality and Social Psychology*, 46, 125–36.

Maslow, A. (1954) *Motivation and Personality.* New York: Harper.

Maslow, A. (1970) *Motivation and Personality*, 2nd edn. New York: Harper.

Mathews, A. (1990) 'Why worry? The cognitive function of anxiety', *Behaviour Research and Therapy*, 28, 455–68.

Mathews, A. and Mackintosh, B. (1998) 'A cognitive model of selective processing in anxiety', *Cognitive Therapy and Research*, 22, 539–60.

Mathews, A. and Mackintosh, B. (2000) 'Induced emotional interpretation bias and anxiety', *Journal of Abnormal Psychology*, 109, 602–15.

Mathews, A. and MacLeod, C. (1985) 'Selective processing of threat cues in anxiety states', *Behavioral Research Methods*, 23(5), 317–23.

Mathews, A. and MacLeod, C.M. (2002) 'Induced processing biases have causal effects on anxiety', *Cognition & Emotion*, 16, 310–15.

Mathews, A. and MacLeod, C.M. (2005) 'Cognitive vulnerability to emotional disorders', *Annual Review of Clinical Psychology*, 1, 167–95.

Mathews, A.M., Fox, E., Yiend, J. and Calder, A.J. (2003) 'The face of fear: Effects of eye gaze and emotion on visual attention', *Visual Cognition*, 10(7), 823–36.

Mathews, A., Mogg, K., Kentish, J. and Eysenck, M. (1995) 'Effects of psychological treatment on cognitive bias in generalised anxiety disorder', *Behaviour Research and Therapy*, 33, 293–303.

Mathews, A., Richards, A., and Eysenck, M. (1989) 'Interpretation of homophones related to threat in anxiety states', *Journal of Abnormal Psychology*, 98, 31–4.

Mathews, A., Ridgeway, V. and Williamson, D.A. (1996) 'Evidence for attention to threatening stimuli in depression', *Behaviour Research and Therapy*, 34, 695–705.

Mathews, A., Yiend, J. and Lawrence, A.D. (2004) 'Individual differences in the modulation of fear-related brain activation by attentional control', *Journal of Cognitive Neuroscience*, 16, 1683–94.

Matt, G.E., Vacquez, C. and Campbell, W.K. (1992) 'Mood-congruent recall of affectively toned stimuli – A meta-analytic review', *Clinical Psychology Review*, 12, 227–55.

Mattia, J.L, Heimberg, R.G. and Hope, D.A. (1993) 'The revised Stroop color-naming task in social phobics', *Behaviour Research and Therapy*, 31, 305–13.

Mauss, I.B., Levenson, R.W., McCarter, L., Wilhelm, F.H. and Gross, J.J. (2005) 'The tie that binds? Coherence among emotional experience, behavior, and autonomic physiology', *Emotion*, 5, 175–90.

Mayberg, H.S., Liotti, M., Brannan, S.K., McGinnis, S., Mahurin, R.K., Jerabek, P.A., Silva, J.A., Tekell, J.L., Martin, C.C., Lancaster, J.L. and Fox, P.T. (1999) 'Reciprocal limbic-cortical function and negative mood: Converging PET findings in depression and normal sadness', *American Journal of Psychiatry*, 156, 675–82.

McCauley, J., Kern, D.E., Kolodner, K., Schroeder, A.F., DeChant, H.K., Ryden, J., et al. (1997) 'Clinical characteristics of women with a history of childhood abuse: Unhealed wounds', *Journal of the American Medical Association*, 277, 1362–8.

McCrae, R.R. and Costa, P.T. (1985) 'Updating Norman's "Adequate Taxonomy": Intelligence and personality dimensions in natural language and in questionnaires', *Journal of Personality and Social Psychology*, 49, 710–21.

McCrae, R.R. and Costa, P.T. (1987) 'Validation of the five-factor model across instruments and observers', *Journal of Personality and Social Psychology*, 52, 81–90.

McCrae, R.R. and Costa, P.T. (1991) 'Adding liebe and arbeit: The full five-factor model and well-being', *Personality and Social Psychology Bulletin*, 17, 227–32.

McCullough, M.E., Emmons, R.A. and Tsang, J. (2002) 'The grateful disposition: A conceptual and empirical topography', *Journal of Personality and Social Psychology*, 82, 112–27.

McCullough, M.E., Kilpatrick, S.D., Emmons, R.A. and Larson, D.B. (2001) 'Is gratitude a moral affect?', *Psychological Bulletin*, 127, 249–66.

McEwen, B.S. (2000) 'The neurobiology of stress: From serendipity to clinical relevance', *Brain Research*, 886, 172–89.

McGaugh, J.L. (2000) 'Memory: A century of consolidation', *Science*, 287, 248–51.

McGaugh, J.L. (2004) 'The amygdala modulates the consolidation of memories of emotionally arousing experiences', *Annual Review of Neuroscience*, 27, 1–28.

McGaugh, J.L. and Petrinovich, L.F. (1965) 'Effects of drugs on learning and memory', *International Review of Neurobiology*, 8, 139–96.

McNair, D.M., Lorr, M. and Droppleman, L.F. (1992) *Manual for the Profile of Mood States*, revised edition. San Diego: Educational and Industrial Testing Service.

McNally, R.J. (1989) 'On stress-induced recovery of fears and phobias', *Psychological Review*, 96, 180–1.

McNally, R.J. (1990) 'Psychological approaches to panic disorder: A review', *Psychological Bulletin*, 108, 403–19.

Meaney, M.J., DiOrio, J., Francis, D., Widdowson, J., LaPlante, P., Caldji, C., Sharma, S., Seckl, J.R. and Plotsky, P.M. (1996) 'Early environmental regulation of forebrain glucocorticoid receptor gene expression: Implications for adrenocortical response to stress', *Developmental Neuroscience*, 18, 49–72.

Mesquita, B. (2003) 'Emotions as dynamic cultural phenomena', in R. Davidson, K.R. Scherer and H. Goldsmith (eds), *Handbook of Affective Sciences*. New York: Oxford University Press.

Mesquita, B., Frijda, N.H. and Scherer, K.R. (1997) 'Culture and emotion', in P. Dasen and T.S. Saraswathi (eds), *Handbook of Cross-cultural Psychology* (Vol. 2). Boston: Allyn & Bacon.

Miller, G.A. (2003) 'The cognitive revolution: a historical perspective', *Trends in Cognitive Sciences*, 7, 141–4.

Miller, M.M. and McEwen, B.S. (2006) 'Establishing an agenda for translational research on PTSD', *Annals of the New York Academy of Sciences*, 1071, 294–312.

Mineka, S. and Öhman, A. (2002) 'Phobias and preparedness: The selective, automatic and encapsulated nature of fear', *Biological Psychiatry*, 15, 927–37.

Mineka, S., Davidson, M., Cook, M. and Keir, R. (1984) 'Observational conditioning of snake fear in rhesus-monkeys', *Journal of Abnormal Psychology*, 93, 355–72.

Mineka, S., Rafaeli, E. and Yovel, I. (2003) 'Cognitive biases in anxiety and depression', in R.J. Davidson, K.R. Scherer and H.H. Goldsmith (eds), *Handbook of Affective Sciences*. New York: Oxford University Press.

Mineka, S., Watson, D.W. and Clark, L.A. (1998) 'Psychopathology: Comorbidity of anxiety and unipolar mood disorders', *Annual Review of Psychology*, 49, 377–412.

Mogg, K. and Bradley, B.P. (1998) 'A cognitive-motivational analysis of anxiety', *Behaviour Research and Therapy*, 36, 809–48.

Mogg, K. and Bradley, B.P. (2006) 'Time course of attentional bias for fear-relevant stimuli in spider-fearful individuals', *Behaviour Research & Therapy*, 44, 1241–50.

Mogg, K., Bradley, B.P., Dixon, C., Fisher, S., Twelftree, H. and McWilliams, A. (2000) 'Trait anxiety, defensiveness and selective processing of threat: An investigation using two measures of attentional bias', *Personality and Individual Differences*, 28, 1063–77.

Mogg, K., Bradley, B.P., Williams, R. and Mathews, A.M. (1993) 'Subliminal processing of emotional information in anxiety and depression', *Journal of Abnormal Psychology*, 102, 304–11.

Mogg, K., Bradley, B.P. and Williams, R. (1995) 'Attentional bias in anxiety and depression: The role of awareness', British Journal of Clinical Psychology, 34, 17–36.

Mogg, K., Mathews, A.and Weinman, J. (1989) 'Selective processing of threat cues in anxiety states: A replication', *Behaviour Research and Therapy*, 27(4), 317–23.

Mogg, K., McNamara, J., Powys, M., Rawlinson, H., Seiffer, A. and Bradley, B.P. (2000) 'Selective attention to threat: A test of two cognitive models of anxiety', *Cognition & Emotion*, 14, 375–99.

Morgan, M.A. and LeDoux, J.E. (1995) 'Differential contribution of dorsal and ventral medial prefrontal cortex to the acquisition and extinction of conditioned fear in rats', *Behavioural Neuroscience*, 109, 681–8.

Morris, J.S. (2002) 'How do you feel?', *Trends in Cognitive Sciences*, 6, 317–19.

Morris, J.S., DeGelder, B., Weiskrantz, L. and Dolan, R.J. (2001) 'Differential extrageniculostriate and amygdala responses to presentation of emotional faces in a cortically blind field', *Brain*, 124, 1241–52.

Morris, J.S., Friston, K.J., Buchel, C., Frith, C.D., Young, A.W., Calder, A.J. and Dolan, R.J. (1998) 'A neuromodulatory role for the human amygdale in processing emotional facial expressions', *Brain*, 121, 47–57.

Morris, J.S., Frith, C.D., Perrett, D.I., Rowland, D., Young, A.W., Calder, A.J. and Dolan, R.J. (1996) 'A differential neural response in the human amygdala to fearful and happy facial expressions', *Nature*, 383, 812–15.

Morris, J.S., Öhman, A. and Dolan, R.J. (1998) 'Conscious and unconscious emotional learning in the human amygdala', *Nature*, 393, 467–70.

Morris, J.S., Öhman, A. and Dolan, R.J. (1999) 'A sub-cortical pathway to the right amygdale mediating "unseen" fear', *Proceedings of the National Academy of Sciences, USA*, 96, 1680–5.

Morris, W.N. (1989) *Mood: The Frame of Mind*. New York: Springer-Verlag.

Morris, W.N. (1992) 'A functional analysis of the role of mood in affective systems', in M.S. Clark (ed.), *Emotion*. Newbury Park, CA: Sage.

Murphy, F.C., Nimmo-Smith, I. and Lawrence, A.D. (2003) 'Functional neuroanatomy of emotion: A meta-analysis', *Cognitive, Affective, and Behavioural Neuroscience*, 3, 207–33.

Myers, D.G. (1992) *The Pursuit of Happiness*. New York: Avon Books.

Myers, D.G. (1993) *The Pursuit of Happiness: Who is Happy and Why?*. New York: Harper Paperbacks.

Myers, D.G. (2000) 'The funds, friends, and faith of happy people', *American Psychologist*, 55, 56–67.

Myers, D.G. (2002) *Intuition: Its Powers and Perils*. New Haven, CT: Yale University Press.

Myers, D.G. and Diener, E. (1995) 'Who is happy?', *Psychological Science*, 6, 10–19.

Myers, L.B. and Derakshan, N. (2004) 'To forget or not to forget: What do repressors forget and when do they forget?', *Cognition & Emotion*, 18, 495–511.

Myers, L.B., Vetere, A. and Derakshan, N. (2004) 'Are suppression and repressive coping related?', *Personality and Individual Differences*, 36, 1009–13.

Neisser, U. (1967) *Cognitive Psychology*. Englewood Cliffs, NJ: Appleton-Century Crofts.

Neisser, U. and Harsch, N. (1992) 'Phantom flashbulbs: False recollections of hearing the news about Challenger', in E. Winograd and U. Neisser (eds), *Affect and Accuracy in Recall: Studies of 'Flashbulb' Memories*. New York: Cambridge University Press.

Nemeroff, C.B. (1998) 'The neurobiology of depression', *Scientific American*, 278, 42–7.

Nemeroff, C.B., Widerlov, E., Bissette, G., Walleus, W., Karlsson, I., Eklund, K., Kiltsc, C.D., Loosen, P.T. and Vale, W. (1984) 'Elevated concentrations of CSF corticotropin-releasing factor-like immunoreactivity in depressed patients', *Science*, 226, 1342–4.

Newman, P. (1964) '"Wild man" behaviour in a New Guinea highlands community', *American Anthropologist*, 66, 1–19.

Newmark, C., Frerking, R., Cook, L.K. and Newmark, L. (1973) 'Endorsement of Ellis' irrational beliefs as a function of psychopathology', *Journal of Clinical Psychology*, 29, 300–2.

Niedenthal, P.M. and Kitayama, S. (eds) (1994) *The Heart's Eye: Emotional Influences in Perception and Attention*. San Diego: Academic Press.

Niedenthal, P.M. and Setterlund, M.B. (1994) 'Emotion congruence in perception', *Personality and Social Psychology Bulletin*, 20, 401–11.

Niedenthal, P.M., Krauth-Gruber, S. and Ric, F. (2006) *Psychology of Emotion: Interpersonal, Experiential and Cognitive Approaches*. New York: Psychology Press.

Nisbett, R.E. and Wilson, T.D. (1977) 'Telling more than we can know: Verbal reports on mental processes', *Psychological Review*, 84, 231–59.

Nitschke, J.B., Heller, W., Palmieri, P.A. and Miller, G.A. (1999) 'Contrasting patterns of brain activity in anxious apprehension and anxious arousal', *Psychophysiology*, 36, 628–37.

Nixon, S.J. and Parsons, O.A. (1989) 'Cloninger's tridimensional theory of personality: Construct validity in a sample of college students', *Personality and Individual Differences*, 10, 1261–7.

Nolen-Hoeksema, S. (1991) 'Responses to depression and their effects on the duration of depressive episodes', *Journal of Abnormal Psychology*, 100, 569–82.

Nolen-Hoeksema, S. and Morrow, J. (1993) 'Effects of rumination and distraction on naturally occurring depressed mood', *Cognition & Emotion*, 7, 561–70.

Nolen-Hoeksema, S., Morrow, J. and Fredrickson, B.L. (1993) 'Response styles and the duration of episodes of depressed mood'. *Journal of Abnormal Psychology*, 102, 20–8.

Norman, W.T. (1963) 'Toward an adequate taxonomy of personality attributes: Replicated factor structure in peer nomination personality ratings', *Journal of Abnormal and Social Psychology*, 66, 574–83.

Norris, C.J., Larsen, J.T. et al. (2007) 'Neuroticism is associated with larger and more prolonged electrodermal responses to emotionally evocative pictures', *Psychophysiology*, 44, 823–6.

Nowlis, V. (1965) 'Research with the Mood Adjective Check List', in S.S. Tomkins and C.E. Izard (eds), *Affect, Cognition and Personality*. New York: Springer.

O'Doherty, J., Kringelbach, M.L., Rolls, E.T., Hornak, J. and Andrews, C. (2001) 'Abstract reward and punishment representations in the human orbitofrontal cortex', *Nature Neuroscience*, 4, 95–102.

Oatley, K. and Johnson-Laird, P. (1987) 'Towards a cognitive theory of emotions', *Cognition & Emotion*, 1, 29–50.

Oatley K., Keltner D. and Jenkins J.M. (2006) *Understanding Emotions*, 2nd edn. Malden, MA: Blackwell.

Ochsner, K.N. (2000) 'Are affective events richly recollected or simply familiar? The experience and process of recognizing feelings past', *Journal of Experimental Psychology: General*, 129, 242–61.

Ochsner, K. and Gross, J.J. (2005) 'The cognitive control of emotion', *Trends in Cognitive Sciences*, 9, 242–9.

Ochsner, K.N., Bunge, S.A., Gross, J.J. and Gabrieli, J.D. (2002) 'Rethinking feelings: An fMRI study of the cognitive regulation of emotion', *Journal of Cognitive Neuroscience*, 14, 1215–29.

Ochsner, K.N., Knierim, K., Ludlow, D.H., Hanelin, J., Ramachandran, T., Glover, G. and Mackey, S. (2004) 'Reflecting upon feelings: An fMRI study of neural systems supporting the attributions of emotion to self and other', *Journal of Cognitive Neuroscience*, 16, 1748–72.

Öhman, A. (1986) 'Face the beast and fear the face: Animal and social fears as prototypes for evolutionary analyses of emotion', *Psychophysiology*, 23, 123–45.

Öhman, A. (2000) 'Fear and anxiety: Clinical, evolutionary, and cognitive perspectives', in M. Lewis and J.M. Haviland (eds), *Handbook of Emotions*, 2nd edn. New York: Guilford Press.

Öhman, A. and Birbaumer, N. (1993) *The Structure of Emotion: Psychophysiological, Cognitive, and Clinical Aspects*. Seattle: Hogrefe & Huber.

Öhman, A. and Mineka, S. (2001) 'Fears, phobias, and preparedness: Toward an evolved module of fear and fear learning', *Psychological Review*, 108, 483–522.

Öhman, A. and Rück, C. (2007) 'Four principles of fear and their implications for phobias', in J. Rottenberg and S.L. Johnson (eds), *Emotion and Psychopathology: Bridging Affective and Clinical Science*. Washington, DC: American Psychological Association.

Öhman, A. and Soares, J.J. (1994) '"Unconscious anxiety": phobic responses to masked stimuli', *Journal of Abnormal Psychology*, 103, 231–40.

Öhman, A., Flykt, A. and Esteves, F. (2001) 'Emotion drives attention: Detecting the snake in the grass', *Journal of Experimental Psychology: General*, 130, 466–78.

Öhman, A., Lundqvist, D. and Esteves, F. (2001) 'The face in the crowd revisited: A threat advantage with schematic stimuli', *Journal of Personality and Social Psychology*, 80, 381–96.

Ong, A.D., Bergeman, C.S. and Bisconti, T.L. (2004) 'The role of daily positive emotions during conjugal bereavement', *Journal of Gerontology: Psychological Sciences*, 59B, 158–67.

Ong, A., Bergeman, C.S., Bisconti, T.L. and Wallace, K.A. (2006) 'The contours of resilience and the complexity of emotions in later life', *Journal of Personality and Social Psychology*, 91, 730–49.

Ortony, A. and Turner, T.J. (1990) 'What's basic about basic emotions?', *Psychological Review*, 97, 315–31.

Osgood, C.E., May, W.H. and Miron, M.S. (1975) *Cross-cultural Universals of Affective Meaning*. Urbana: University of Illinois Press.

Ostir, G.V., Markides, K.S., Peek, M.K. and Goodwin, J.S. (2001) 'The association between emotional well-being and the incidence of stroke in older adults', *Psychosomatic Medicine*, 63, 210–15.

Owen, A.M., Roberts, A.C., Hodges, J.R., Summers, B.A., Polkey, C.E. and Robbins, T.W. (1993) 'Contrasting mechanisms of impaired attentional set-shifting in patients with frontal lobe damage or Parkinson's disease', *Brain*, 116, 1159–75.

Panksepp, J. (1985) 'Mood changes', in P.J. Vinken, G.W. Bruyn and H.L. Klawans (eds), *Handbook of Clinical Neurology (Vol. 1)*. Amsterdam: Elsevier Science.

Panksepp, J. (1992) 'A critical role for "affective neuroscience" in resolving what is basic about basic emotions', *Psychological Review*, 99, 554–60.

Panksepp, J. (1998) *Affective Neuroscience: The Foundations of Human and Animal Emotions.* New York: Oxford University Press. Paperback edition 2004.

Panksepp, J. (2000) 'Emotions as natural kinds within the mammalian brain', in M. Lewis and J. Haviland (eds), *Handbook of Emotions*, 2nd edn. New York: Guilford Press.

Panksepp, J. (2004) 'Basic affects and the instinctual emotional systems of the brain: The primordial sources of sadness, joy, and seeking', in A.S.R. Manstead, N. Frijda and A. Fischer (eds), *Feelings and Emotions: The Amsterdam Symposium*. New York: Cambridge University Press.

Panksepp, J. (2006) 'Emotional phenotypes in evolutionary psychiatry', *Progress in Neuro-psychopharmacology & Biological Psychiatry*, 30, 774–84.

Panksepp, J. (2007) 'Neurologizing the psychology of affects', *Perspectives in Psychological Science*, 2, 281–96.

Panksepp, J., Normansell, L., Cox, J.F. and Siviy, S. M. (1994) 'Effects of neonatal decortication on the social play of juvenile rats', *Physiology and Behavior*, 56(3), 429–43.

Park, J. and Banaji, M.R. (2000) 'Mood and heuristics: The influence of happy and sad states on sensitivity and bias in stereotyping', *Journal of Personality and Social Psychology*, 78, 1005–23.

Parkinson, B. (1995) *Ideas and Realities of Emotion*. London: Routledge.

Parkinson, B., Fischer, A.H. and Manstead, A.S.R. (2005) *Emotion in Social Relations: Cultural, Group, and Interpersonal Processes.* New York: Psychology Press.

Parrott, W.G. and Hertel, P. (1999) 'Research methods in cognition and emotion', in T. Dalgleish and M.J. Power (eds), *Handbook of Cognition and Emotion*. Chichester: Wiley.

Parrott, W.G. and Sabini, J. (1990) 'Mood and memory under natural conditions: Evidence for mood incongruent recall', *Journal of Personality & Social Psychology*, 59, 321–36.

Parrott, W.G. and Spackman, M.P. (2000) 'Emotion and memory', in M. Lewis and J. Haviland-Jones (eds), *Handbook of Emotions*, 2nd edn. New York: Guilford Press.

Pashler, H. (1997) *The Psychology of Attention*. Cambridge, MA: MIT Press.

Paterson, A.D., Sunohara, G.A. and Kennedy, J.L. (1999) 'Dopamine D4 receptor gene: Novelty or nonsense?', *Neuropsychopharmacology*, 21, 3–16.

Pedersen, C.A., Caldwell, J.D., Walker, C., Ayers, G. and Mason, G.A. (1994) 'Oxytocin activates the postpartum onset of rat maternal behaviour in the ventral tegmental and medial preoptic areas', *Behavioural Neuroscience*, 108, 1163–71.

Penfield, W. and Faulk, M.E. (1955) 'The insula: Further observations on its function', *Brain*, 78, 445–70.

Pervin, L.A. (1976) 'A free-response description approach to the analysis of person-situation interaction', *Journal of Personality and Social Psychology*, 34, 465–74.

Peters, D.P. (1988) 'Eyewitness memory and arousal in a natural setting', in M.M. Gruneberg, P.E. Morris and R.N. Sykes (eds), *Practical Aspects of Memory: Current Research and Issues.* New York: Academic Press.

Peterson, C., Park, N. and Seligman, M.E.P. (2005) 'Orientations to happiness and life satisfaction: The full life versus the empty life', *Journal of Happiness Studies*, 6, 25–41.

Peterson, C., Semmel, A. et al. (1982) 'The Attributional Style Questionnaire', *Cognitive Therapy and Research*, 6, 287–9.

Pezawas, L., Meyer-Lindenberg, A., Drabant, E.M., Verchinski, B., Mattay, V.S., Hariri, A.R., Kolachana, B., Egan, M.F. and Weinberger, D.R. (2005) '5-HTTLPR polymorphism impacts human cingulate-amygdala interactions: A genetic susceptibility mechanism for depression', *Nature Neuroscience*, 8, 828–34.

Phan, K.L., Fitzgerald, D.A., Nathan, P.J., Moore, G.J., Uhde, T.W. and Tancer, M.E. (2005) 'Neural substrates for voluntary suppression of negative affect: A functional magnetic resonance imaging study', *Biological Psychiatry*, 57(3), 210–19.

Phan, K.L., Taylor, S.F., Welsh, R.C., Ho, S.H., Britton, J.C. and Liberzon, I. (2004) 'Neural correlates of individual ratings of emotional salience: A trial-related fMRI study', *NeuroImage*, 21, 768–80.

Phan, K.L., Wager, T.D., Taylor, S.F. and Liberzon, I. (2002) 'Functional neuroanatomy of emotion: A meta-analysis of emotion activation studies in PET and fMRI', *NeuroImage*, 16, 331–48.

Phelps, E.A. (2004) 'Human emotion and memory: Interactions of the amygdala and hippocampal complex', *Current Opinion in Neurobiology*, 14, 198–202.

Phelps, E. (2006) 'Emotion and cognition: Insights from studies of the human amygdala', *Annual Review of Psychology*, 57, 27–53.

Phelps, E.A. and LeDoux, J.E. (2005) 'Contributions of the amygdala to emotion processing: From animal models to human behavior', *Neuron*, 48, 175–87.

Phelps, E., Ling, S. and Carrasco, M. (2006) 'Emotion facilitates perception and potentiates the perceptual benefits of attention', *Psychological Science*, 17, 292–9.

Phillips, R.G. and LeDoux, J.E. (1992) 'Differential contribution of amygdala and hippocampus to cued and contextual fear conditioning', *Behavioural Neuroscience*, 106, 274–85.

Plomin, R., DeFries, J.C., McClearn, G.E. and Rutter, M. (1997) *Behavioural Genetics*, 3rd edn. New York: W.H. Freeman.

Plomin, R., Owen, M.J. and McGuffin, P. (1994) 'The genetic basis of complex human behaviors', *Science*, 264, 1733–9.

Plotsky, P.M., Owens, M.J. and Nemeroff, C.B. (1995) 'Neuropeptide alterations in affective disorders', in F.E. Bloom and D.J. Kupfer (eds), *Neuropsychopharmacology: The Fourth Generation of Progress*. New York: Raven Press.

Plutchik, R. (1962) *The Emotions: Facts, Theories and a New Model*. New York: Random House.

Plutchik, R. (1980) 'A general psychoevolutionary theory of emotion', in R. Plutchik and H. Kellerman (eds), *Emotion: Theory, Research, and Experience*. New York: Academic Press.

Port, R.F. and Van Gelder, T. (eds) (1995) *Explorations in the Dynamics of Cognition: Mind as Motion*. Cambridge, MA: MIT Press.

Posner, M.I. (1980) 'Orienting of attention', *Quarterly Journal of Experimental Psychology*, 32, 2–25.

Posner, M.I. and Petersen, S.E. (1990) 'The attention system of the human brain', *Annual Review of Neuroscience*, 13, 25–42.

Posner, M.I. and Raichle, M.E. (1994) *Images of Mind*. New York: Scientific American Library.

Posner, M.I. and Raichle, M.E. (1995) 'Precis of *Images of Mind*', *Behavioral and Brain Sciences*, 18(2), 327–83.

Posner, M.I. and Raichle, M.E. (1997) *Images of Mind*, paperback edition. New York: Scientific American Library.

Pourtois, G., Grandjean, D., Sander, D. and Vuilleumier, P. (2004) 'Electrophysiological correlates of rapid spatial orienting towards fearful faces', *Cerebral Cortex*, 14, 619–33.

Power, M.J. and Dalgleish, T. (1997) *Cognition and Emotion: From Order to Disorder*. Hove: Psychology Press.

Pratto, F. and John, O.P. (1991) 'Automatic vigilance: The attention-grabbing power of negative social information', *Journal of Personality & Social Psychology*, 61, 380–91.

Prinz, J.J. (2004) *Gut Reactions: A Perceptual Theory of Emotion*. New York: Oxford University Press.

Purcell, D.G., Stewart, A.L. and Skov, R.B. (1996) 'It takes a confounded face to pop out of a crowd', *Perception*, 25, 1091–108.

Putman, P., Hermans, E. and van Honk, J. (2006) 'Anxiety meets fear in perception of dynamic expressive gaze', *Emotion*, 6, 94–102.

Quirarte, G.L., Roozendaal, B. and McGaugh, J.L. (1997) 'Glucocorticoid enhancement of memory storage involves noradrenergic activation in the basolateral amygdale', *Proceedings of the National Academy of Sciences*, 94, 14048–53.

Quirk, G.J. (2007) 'Prefrontal-amygdala interactions in the regulation of fear', in J.J. Gross (ed.), *Handbook of Emotion Regulation*. New York: Guilford Press.

Rachman, S. (1981) 'Unwanted intrusive cognitions', *Advances in Behaviour Research and Therapy*, 3, 89–99.

Raleigh, M.I. and Brammer, G.L. (1993) 'Individual differences in serotonin-2 receptors and social behavior in monkeys', *Society of Neuroscience Abstracts*, 19, 592.

Rauch, S.L. (2003) 'Neuroimaging and neurocircuitry models pertaining to the neurosurgical treatment of psychiatric disorders', *Neurosurgery Clinics of North America*, 14, 213–23.

Rauch, S.L., Shin, L.M., Whalen, P.J., Pitman, R.K. (1998) 'Neuroimaging and the neuroanatomy of PTSD', *CNS Spectrums*, 3, 30–41.

Raymond, J.E., Shapiro, K.L. and Arnell, K.M. (1992) 'Temporary suppression of visual processing in an RSVP task: An attentional blink?', *Journal of Experimental Psychology: Human. Perception and Performance*, 18, 849–60.

Razran, G.H.S. (1940) 'Conditioned response changes in rating and appraising sociopolitical slogans', *Psychological Bulletin*, 37, 481.

Redelmeir, D. and Kahneman, D. (1996) 'Patients' memories of painful medical treatments: Real-time and retrospective evaluations of two minimally invasive procedures', *Pain*, 66, 3–8.

Regehr, C., Hill, J. and Glancy, G.D. (2000) 'Individual predictors of traumatic reactions in firefighters', *Journal of Nervous and Mental Disease*, 188, 333–9.

Reid, S.A., Duke, L.M. and Allen, J.J.B. (1998) 'Resting frontal electroencephalographic asymmetry in depression: Inconsistencies suggest the need to identify mediating factors', *Psychophysiology*, 35, 389–404.

Reif, A. and Lesch, K.P. (2003) 'Toward a molecular architecture of personality', *Behavioral Brain Research*, 139, 1–20.

Reisberg, D. and Heuer, F. (1992) 'Flashbulbs and memory for detail from emotional events', in E. Winograd and U. Neisser (eds), *Affect and Accuracy in Recall: The Problem of 'Flashbulb' Memories*. New York: Cambridge University Press.

Reisberg, D. and Heuer, F. (2004) 'Memory for emotional events', in D. Reisberg and P. Hertel (eds), *Memory and Emotion*. London: Oxford University Press.

Reisberg, D., Heuer, F., McLean, J. and O'Shaughnessy, M. (1988) 'The quantity, not the quality, of affect predicts memory vividness', *Bulletin of the Psychonomic Society*, 26, 100–3.

Reisenzein, R. (1983) 'The Schachter theory of emotion: Two decades later', *Psychological Bulletin*, 94, 239–64.

Reiss, S. (1991) 'Expectancy model of fear, anxiety, and panic', *Clinical Psychology Review*, 11, 141–53.

Ressler, K.J. and Mayberg, H.S. (2007) 'Targeting abnormal neural circuits in mood and anxiety disorders: from the laboratory to the clinic', *Nature Neuroscience*, 10, 1116–24.

Ressler, K.J., Rothbaum, B.O., Tannenbaum, L., Anderson, P., Graap, K., Zimand, E. et al. (2004) 'Cognitive enhancers are adjuncts to psychotherapy: Use of d-cycloserine in phobics to facilitate extinction of fear', *Archives of General Psychiatry*, 61, 1136–44.

Richards, A. and French, C.C. (1992) 'An anxiety-related bias in semantic activation when processing threat/neutral homographs', *Quarterly Journal of Experimental Psychology A: Human Experimental Psychology*, 45, 503–25.

Richards, A., French, C.C. et al. (1992) 'Effects of mood manipulation and anxiety on performance of an emotional Stroop task.' *British Journal of Psychology*, 83, 479–91.

Rinck, M., Glowalia, U. and Schneider, K. (1992) 'Mood-congruent and mood-incongruent learning', *Memory & Cognition*, 20, 29–39.

Rinck, M., Reinecke, A., Ellwart, T., Heuer, K. and Becker, E.S. (2005) 'Speeded detection and increased distraction in fear of spiders: Evidence from eye movements', *Journal of Abnormal Psychology*, 114, 235–48.

Rizzolatti, G., Fadiga, L., Fogassi, L. and Gallese, V. (1996) 'Premotor cortex and the recognition of motor actions', *Cognitive Brain Research*, 3, 131–41.

Robinson, R.G. and Downhill, J.E. (1995) 'Lateralization of psychopathology in response to focal brain injury', in R.J. Davidson and K. Hugdahl (eds), *Brain Asymmetry*. London: MIT Press.

Rodin, J. and Langer, E.J. (1977) 'Long-term effects of a control-relevant intervention with the institutionalized aged', *Journal of Personality and Social Psychology*, 35, 897–902.

Rogers, G. and Revelle, W. (1998) 'Personality, mood, and the evaluation of affective and neutral word pairs', *Journal of Personality and Social Psychology*, 74, 1592–605.

Rolls, E.T. (1999) *The Brain and Emotion*. Oxford: Oxford University Press.

Rolls, E.T. (2005) *Emotions Explained*, Oxford: Oxford University Press.

Roseman, I.J. and Smith, C.A. (2001) 'Appraisal theory: Overview, assumptions, varieties, controversies', in K.R. Scherer, A. Schorr and T. Johnstone (eds), *Appraisal Processes in Emotion: Theory, Methods, Research*. New York: Oxford University Press.

Rosen, J.B. and Schulkin, J. (1998) 'From normal fear to pathological anxiety', *Psychological Review*, 105, 325–50.

Rosenbaum, J.F., Biederman, J., Gersten, M., Meminger, S.R., Herman, J.B., Kagan, J., Reznick, J.S. and Snidman, N. (1988) 'Behavioral inhibition in children of parents with panic disorder and agoraphobia: A controlled study', *Archives of General Psychiatry*, 45, 463–70.

Rothbart, M.K. and Bates, J.E. (2006) 'Temperament', in W. Damon, R. Lerner, N. Eisenberg (eds), *Handbook of Child Psychology: Vol. 3. Social, Emotional, and Personality Development*, 6th edn. New York: Wiley.

Rothbart, M.K. and Derryberry, D. (1981) 'Development of individual differences in temperament', in M.E. Lamb and A.L. Brown (eds), *Advances in Developmental Psychology, Vol. 1*. Hillsdale, NJ: Lawrence Erlbaum Associates.

Rothbart, M.K. and Rueda, M.R. (2005) 'The development of effortful control', in U. Mayr, E. Awh and S.W. Keele (eds), *Developing Individuality in the Human Brain: A Festschrift Honoring Michael I. Posner*. Washington, DC: American Psychological Association.

Rothbart, M.K. and Sheese, B.E. (2007) 'Temperament and emotion regulation', in J.J. Gross (ed.), *Handbook of Emotion Regulation*. New York: Guilford Press.

Rothbart, M.K., Derryberry, D. and Posner, M.I. (1994) 'A psychobiological approach to the development of temperament', in J.E. Bates and T.D. Wachs (eds), *Temperament: In-*

dividual Differences at the Interface of Biology and Behavior. Washington, DC: American Psychological Association.

Rothbaum, B.O., Foa, E.B., Murdock, T., Riggs, D. and Walsh, W. (1992) 'A prospective examination of post-traumatic stress disorder in rape victims', *Journal of Traumatic Stress*, 5, 455–75.

Rottenberg, J. and Johnson, S.L. (2007) *Emotion and Psychopathology: Bridging Affective and Clinical Science*. Washington, DC: American Psychological Association.

Rottenberg, J., Kasch, K.L., Gross, J.J. and Gotlib, I.H. (2002) 'Sadness and amusement reactivity differentially predict concurrent and prospective functioning in major depressive disorder', *Emotion*, 2, 135–46.

Rubin, D.C. and Kozin, M. (1984) 'Vivid memories', *Cognition*, 16, 81–95.

Russell, J.A. (1980) 'A circumplex model of affect', *Journal of Personality and Social Psychology*, 39, 1161–78.

Russell, J.A. (1983) 'Pancultural aspects of the human conceptual organization of emotions', *Journal of Personality and Social Psychology*, 45, 1281–8.

Russell, J.A. (1991) 'Culture and the categorization of emotion', *Psychological Bulletin*, 110, 426–450.

Russell, J.A. (1994) 'Is there universal recognition of emotion from facial expressions? A review of cross-cultural studies', *Psychological Bulletin*, 115, 102–41.

Russell, J.A. (1995) 'Facial expressions of emotion: What lies beyond minimal universality?', *Psychological Bulletin*, 118, 379–99.

Russell, J.A. (2003) 'Core affect and the psychological construction of emotion', *Psychological Review*, 110, 145–72.

Russell, J.A. and Feldman Barrett, L. (1999) 'Core affect, prototypical emotional episodes, and other things called emotion: Dissecting the elephant', *Journal of Personality and Social Psychology*, 76, 805–19.

Russell, J.A. and Lemay, G. (2000) 'Emotion concepts', in M. Lewis and J.M. Haviland-Jones (eds), *Handbook of Emotions*, 2nd edn. New York: Guilford Press.

Russo, R., Fox, E., Bellinger, L. and Nguyen-Van-Tam, D.P. (2001) 'Mood congruent free recall bias in anxiety', *Cognition & Emotion*, 15, 419–34.

Russo, R., Whittuck, D., Roberson, D., Dutton, K., Georgiou, G. and Fox, E. (2006) 'Mood-congruent free recall bias in anxious individuals is not a consequence of response bias', *Memory*, 4, 393–9.

Rusting, C.L. (1999) 'Interactive effects of personality and mood on emotion-congruent memory and judgement', *Journal of Personality and Social Psychology*, 777, 1073–86.

Rusting, C.L. (2001) 'Personality as a moderator of affective influences on cognition', in J.P. Forgas, *Handbook of Affect and Social Cognition*. Hillsdale, NJ: Erlbaum.

Rusting, C.L. and DeHart, T. (2000) 'Retrieving positive memories to regulate negative mood: Consequences for mood-congruent memory', *Journal of Personality and Social Psychology*, 78, 737–52.

Rusting, C.L. and Larsen, R.J. (1998) 'Personality and cognitive processing of affective information', *Personality and Social Psychology Bulletin*, 24, 200–13.

Rusting, C.L. and Nolen-Hoeksema, S. (1998) 'Regulating responses to anger: Effects of rumination and distraction on angry mood', *Journal of Personality and Social Psychology*, 74, 790–803.

Rutter, M. (1987a) 'Psychosocial resilience and protective mechanisms', *American Journal of Orthopsychiatry*, 57, 316–31.

Rutter, M. (1987b) 'Resilience in the face of adversity: protective factors and resistance to psychiatric disorders', *British Journal of Psychiatry*, 147, 598–611.

Rutter, M. (2006) 'Implications of resilience concepts for scientific understanding', *Annals of the New York Academy of Sciences*, 1094, 1–12.

Rutter, M. (2007) 'Resilience, competence and coping', *Child Abuse and Neglect*, 31, 205–9.

Rutter, M., Tizard, J. and Whitmore, K. (1970) 'Appendix 6: A children's behaviour questionnaire for completion by parents', *Education, Health and Behaviour*. London: Longmans.

Ryff, C.D. and Singer, B. (2003) 'The role of emotion on pathways to positive health', in R.J. Davidson, K.R. Scherer and H.H. Goldsmith (eds), *Handbook of Affective Sciences*. New York: Oxford University Press.

Safer, M.A., Christianson, S.-Å., Autry, M.W. and Österlund, K. (1998) 'Tunnel memory for traumatic events', *Applied Cognitive Psychology*, 12, 99–117.

Safer, M.A., Levine, L.J. and Drapalski, A. (2002) 'Distortion in memory for emotions: The contributions of personality and post-event knowledge', *Personality and Social Psychology Bulletin*, 28, 1495–507.

Sander, D., Grafman, J. and Zalla, T. (2003) 'The human amygdala: an evolved system for relevance detection', *Reviews in the Neurosciences*, 14, 303–16.

Sander, D., Grandjean, D. and Scherer, K.R. (2005) 'A systems approach to appraisal mechanisms in emotion', *Neural Networks*, 18, 317–52.

Sanderson, W.C. and Barlow, D.H. (1990) 'A description of patients diagnosed with DSM-III-Revised generalized anxiety disorder', *Journal of Nervous and Mental Disease*, 178, 588–91.

Sanghera, M.K., Rolls, E.T. and Roper-Hall, A. (1979) 'Visual responses of neurons in the dorsolateral amygdala of the alert monkey', *Exploratory Neurololgy*, 63, 610–26.

Savitz, J.B. and Ramesar, R.S. (2004a) 'Genetic variants implicated in personality: A review of the more promising candidates', *American Journal of Medical Genetics*, 131, 20–32.

Savitz, J.B. and Ramesar, R.S. (2004b) 'Review: The genetics of personality: an update', *American Journal of Medical Genetics*, 15, 20–32.

Schachter, S.S. and Singer, J.E. (1962) 'Cognitive, social and physiological determinant of emotional state', *Psychological Review*, 69, 379–99.

Schacter, D.L. (1987) 'Implicit memory: History and current status', *Journal of Experimental Psychology: Learning, Memory and Cognition*, 13, 501–18.

Schafe, G. and LeDoux, J.E. (2000) 'Memory consolidation of auditory Pavlovian fear conditioning requires protein synthesis and PKA in the amygdala', *Journal of Neuroscience*, 20, 8177–87.

Schaffer, C.E., Davidson, R.J. and Saron, C. (1983) 'Frontal and parietal electroencephalogram asymmetry in depressed and nondepressed subjects', *Biological Psychiatry*, 18, 753–62.

Scherer, K.R. (1979) 'Non-linguistic indicators of emotion and psychopathology', in C.E. Izard (ed.), *Emotions in Personality and Psychopathology*. New York: Plenum.

Scherer, K.R. (1984) 'On the nature and function of emotion: A component process approach', in K.R. Scherer and P. Ekman (eds), *Approaches to Emotion*. Hillsdale, NJ: Erlbaum.

Scherer, K.R. (1986) 'Vocal affect expression: A review and a model for future research', *Psychological Bulletin*, 99, 143–65.

Scherer, K.R. (1989) 'Vocal measurement of emotion', in R. Plutchik and H. Kellerman (eds), *Emotion: Theory, Research, and Experience. Vol. 4: The Measurement of Emotion*. New York: Academic Press.

Scherer, K.R. (1994) 'Toward a concept of "modal emotions"', in P. Ekman and R.J. Davidson (eds), *The Nature of Emotion: Fundamental Questions*. New York: Oxford University Press.

Scherer, K.R. (2000a) 'Emotions as episodes of subsystem synchronization driven by nonlinear appraisal processes', in M.D. Lewis and I. Granic (eds), *Emotion, Development, and Self-organization: Dynamic Systems Approaches to Emotional Development*. Cambridge: Cambridge University Press.

Scherer, K.R. (2000b) 'Psychological models of emotion', in J. Borod (ed.), *The Neuropsychology of Emotion*. New York: Oxford University Press.

Scherer, K.R. (2001) 'Appraisal considered as a process of multi-level sequential checking', in K.R. Scherer, A. Schorr and T. Johnstone (eds), *Appraisal Processes in Emotion: Theory, Methods, Research*. New York: Oxford University Press.

Scherer, K.R. (2003) 'Vocal communication of emotion: A review of research paradigms', *Speech Communication*, 40, 227–56.

Scherer, K.R. (2004) 'Feelings integrate the central representation of appraisal-driven response organization in emotion', in A.S.R. Manstead, N.H. Frijda and A.H. Fischer (eds), *Feelings and Emotions: The Amsterdam Symposium*. Cambridge: Cambridge University Press.

Scherer, K.R. (2005) 'What are emotions? And how can they be measured?', *Social Science Information*, 44, 693–727.

Scherer, K.R., Banse, R. and Wallbott, H.G. (2001) 'Emotion inferences from vocal expression correlate across languages and cultures', *Journal of Cross-Cultural Psychology*, 32, 76–92.

Scherer, K.R., Johnstone, T. and Klasmeyer, G. (2003) 'Vocal expression of emotion', in R.J. Davidson, K.R. Scherer and H. Goldsmith (eds), *Handbook of Affective Sciences*. New York: Oxford University Press.

Schildkraut, J.J. and Kety, S.S. (1967) 'Biogenic amines and emotion', *Science*, 156, 21–30.

Schmidt, L.A. (1999) 'Frontal brain electrical activity in shyness and sociability', *Psychological Science*, 10, 316–20.

Schneider, F., Gur, R.E., Mozley, L.H., Smith, R.J., Mozley, P.D., Censits, D.M., Alavi, A. and Gur, R.C. (1995) 'Mood effects on limbic blood flow correlate with emotional self-rating: A PET study with oxygen-15 labelled water', *Psychiatry Research: Neuroimaging*, 61, 265–83.

Schneirla, T.C. (1959) 'An evolutionary and developmental theory of biphasic processes underlying approach and withdrawal', in M.R. Jones (ed.), *Nebraska Symposium on Motivation*. Lincoln: University of Nebraska Press.

Schulz, R. and Hanusa, B.H. (1978) 'Long-term effects of predictability and control enhancing interventions: Findings and ethical issues', *Journal of Personality and Social Psychology*, 36, 1194–201.

Schwartz, C.E., Snidman, N. and Kagan, J. (1999) 'Adolescent social anxiety as an outcome of inhibited temperament in childhood', *Journal of the American Academy of Child and Adolescent Psychiatry*, 38, 1008–15.

Schwartz, C.E., Wright, C.I., Shin, L.M., Kagan, J. and Rauch, S.L. (2003) 'Inhibited and uninhibited infants "grown up": Adult amygdalar response to novelty', *Science*, 300, 1952–3.

Schwartz, G.E., Brown, S.L. and Ahern, L. (1980) 'Facial muscle patterning and subjective experience during affective imagery: Sex differences', *Psychophysiology*, 17, 75–82.

Schwarz, N. and Clore, G. (1983) 'Mood, misattribution, and judgments of well-being: Informative and directive functions of affective states', *Journal of Personality and Social Psychology*, 45, 513–23.

Schwarz, N. and Clore, G.L. (1988) 'How do I feel about it?: The informative function of affective states', in K. Fielder and J. Forgas (eds), *Affect, Cognition and Social Behavior: New Evidence and Integrative Attempt*. Toronto: Hogrefe.

Sedikides, C. (1995) 'Central and peripheral self-conceptions are differentially influenced by mood: Tests of the differential sensitivity hypothesis', *Journal of Personality and Social Psychology*, 69, 759–77.

Sedikides, C. and Green, J.D. (2000) 'On the self-protective nature of inconsistency-negativity management: Using the person memory paradigm to examine self-referent memory', *Journal of Personality and Social Psychology*, 79, 906–22.

Sedikides, C. and Gregg, A.P. (2003) 'Portraits of the self', in M.A. Hogg and J. Cooper (eds), *Sage Handbook of Social Psychology*. London: Sage.

Seligman, M.E.P. (1972) 'Learned helplessness', *Annual Review of Medicine*, 23, 407–12.

Seligman, M.E.P (2002) *Authentic Happiness*. New York: Free Press.

Seligman, M.E.P. and Csikszentmihalyi, M. (2000) 'Positive psychology: An introduction', *American Psychologist*, 55, 5–14.

Seligman, M.E.P., Steen, T., Park, N. and Peterson, C. (2005) 'Positive psychology progress: Empirical validation of interventions', *American Psychologist*, 60, 410–21.

Seyfarth, R.M., Cheney, D.L. and Marler, P. (1980a) 'Monkey responses to three different alarm calls: Evidence for predator classification and semantic communication', *Science*, 210, 801–3.

Shankman, S.A., Klein, D.N., Tenke, C.E. and Bruder, G.E. (2007) 'Reward sensitivity in depression: A biobehavioral study', *Journal of Abnormal Psychology*, 116, 95–104.

Shapira, N.A., Okun, M.S., Wint, D., Foote, K.D., Byars, J.A. and Bowers, D. (2006) 'Panic and fear induced by deep brain stimulation', *Journal of Neurology, Neurosurgery, and Psychiatry*, 77, 410–12.

Shapiro, K.L., Arnell, K.M. and Raymond, J.E. (1997) 'The attentional blink', *Trends in Cognitive Sciences*, 1, 291–6.

Shapiro, K.L., Caldwell, J. and Sorenson, R.E. (1997) 'Personal names and the attentional blink: A visual "cocktail party" effect', *Journal of Experimental Psychology: Human Perception & Performance*, 23, 504–14.

Sharot, T., Delgado, M.R. and Phelps, E.A. (2004) 'How emotion enhances the feeling of remembering', *Nature Neuroscience*, 7, 1376–80.

Shin, L.M., Rauch S.L. and Pitman, R.K. (2006) 'Amygdala, medial prefrontal cortex, and hippocampal function in PTSD', *Psychobiology of Posttraumatic Stress Disorder*, 1071, 67–79.

Silver, R.L. (1982) 'Coping with an undesirable life event: A study of early reactions to physical disability'. Unpublished doctoral dissertation, Northwestern University, Evanston, IL.

Simon, H.A. (1967) 'Motivational and emotional controls of cognition', *Psychological Review*, 74, 29–39.

Singer, J.A. and Salovey, P. (1988) 'Mood and memory: Evaluating the network theory of affect', *Clinical Psychology Review*, 8, 211–51.

Singer, J.A. and Salovey, P. (1996) 'Motivated memory: Self-defining memories, goals, and affect regulation', in L. Martin and A. Tesser, *Striving and Feeling*. New York: Erlbaum.

Skinner, E.A. and Zimmer-Gembeck, M.J. (2007) 'The development of coping', *Annual Review of Psychology*, 58, 119–44.

Small, D.M., Gregory, M.D., Mak, Y.E., Gitelman, D., Mesulam, M.M. and Parrish, T. (2003) 'Dissociation of neural representation of intensity and affective valuation in human gustation', *Neuron*, 39, 701–11.

Smith, A.P.R., Henson, R.N., Dolan, R.J. and Rugg, M.D. (2004) 'fMRI correlates of the episodic retrieval of emotional contexts', *Neuroimage*, 22, 868–78.

Smith, C.A. and Ellsworth, P.C. (1985) 'Patterns of cognitive appraisal in emotion', *Journal of Personality and Social Psychology*, 48, 813–38.

Smith, C.A., and Ellsworth, P.C. (1987) 'Patterns of appraisal and emotion related to taking an exam', *Journal of Personality and Social Psychology*, 52, 475–88.

Smith, C.A. and Kirby, L.D. (2000) 'Consequences require antecedents: Toward a process model of emotion elicitation', in J. Forgas (ed.), *Feeling and Thinking: The Role of Affect in Social Cognition*. New York: Cambridge University Press.

Smith, C.A. and Kirby, L.D. (2001) 'Affect and cognitive appraisal: From content to process models', in J. Forgas (ed.), *Handbook of Affect and Social Cognition*. Hillsdale, NJ: Lawrence Erlbaum.

Smith, E.E. and Kosslyn, S.M. (2006) *Cognitive Psychology: Mind and Brain*. New Jersey: Prentice Hall.

Smith, K.S. and Berridge, K.C. (2005) 'The ventral pallidum and food reward: neurochemical maps of "liking" and food intake', *Journal of Neuroscience*, 25, 8637–49.

Smith, N.K., Cacioppo, J.T., Larsen, J.T. and Chartrand, T.L. (2003) 'May I have your attention, please: Electrocortical responses to positive and negative stimuli', *Neuropsychologia*, 41, 171–83.

Snowdon, C.T. (2003) 'Expression of emotion in nonhuman animals', in R.J. Davidson, K.R. Scherer and H. Goldsmith (eds), *Handbook of Affective Sciences*. New York: Oxford University Press.

Soetens, E., Casaer, S., D'Hooge, R. and Hueting, J. (1995) 'Effect of amphetamine on long-term retention of verbal material', *Psychopharmacology*, 119, 155.

Spector, P.E. (2002) '24 nation/territory study of work locus of control in relation to well-being at work: How generalizable are Western work findings?', *Academy of Management Journal*, 45, 453–66.

Spielberger, C. (1966) *Anxiety and Behavior*. Orlando: Academic Press.

Spielberger, C.D., Gorsuch, R.L. and Lushene, R.E. (1970) *The State-Trait Anxiety Inventory*. Palo Alto: Consulting Psychologists Press.

Spielberger, C.D., Gorsuch, R.L. et al. (1983) *Manual for the State Trait Anxiety Inventory*. Palo Alto, Consulting Psychologists Press.

Sprengelmeyer, R., Young, A.W., Calder, A.J., Karnat, A., Lange, H.W., Homberg, V., Perrett, D.I. and Rowland, D. (1996) 'Loss of disgust: Perception of faces and emotions in Huntington's disease', *Brain*, 119, 1647–65.

Sprengelmeyer, R., Young, A.W., Sprengelmeyer, A., Calder, A.J., Rowland, D., Perrett, D.I, Homberg, V. and Lange, H.W. (1997) 'Recognition of facial expressions: Selective impairment of specific emotions in Huntington's disease', *Cognitive Neuropsychology*, 14, 839–79.

Stallings, M.C., Hewitt, J.K., Cloninger, C.R., Heath, A.C. and Eaves, L.J. (1996) 'Genetic and environmental structure of the Tridimensional Personality Questionnaire: Three or four temperament dimensions?', *Journal of Personality Social Psychology*, 70, 127–40.

Stein, N.L. and Trabasso, T. (1992) 'The organization of emotional experience: Creating links among emotion, thinking and intentional action', *Cognition & Emotion*, 6, 225–44.

Stewart, J. and Vezina, P. (1988) 'A comparison of the effects of intra-accumbens injections of amphetamine and morphine on reinstatement of heroin intravenous self-administration behavior', *Brain Research*, 457, 287–94.

Still, A.W. and Costall, A.P. (1991) *Against Cognitivism: Alternative Foundations for Cognitive Psychology*. London: Harvester Wheatsheaf.

Stolarova, M., Keil, A. and Moratti, S. (2006) 'Modulation of the C1 visual event-related component by conditioned stimuli: evidence for sensory plasticity in early affective perception', *Cerebral Cortex*, 16, 876–87.

Strauman, T.J., Eddington, K.M. and McCrudden, M.C. (2007) 'Affective science and psychotherapy: In search of synergy', in J. Rottenberg and S.L. Johnson (eds), *Emotion and Psychopathology: Bridging Affective and Clinical Science.* Washington, DC: American Psychological Association.

Stroop, J. (1935) 'Studies in interference in serial verbal reactions', *Journal of Experimental Psychology*, 18, 643–61.

Stroop, J.R. (1935) 'Studies of interference in serial verbal reactions', *Journal of Experimental Psychology*, 18, 643–62.

Stutzmann, G.E. and LeDoux, J.E. (1999) 'GABAergic antagonists block the inhibitory effects of serotonin in the lateral amygdala: a mechanism for modulation of sensory inputs related to fear conditioning', *Journal of Neuroscience*, 19(11), RC8.

Styles, E.A. (1997) *The Psychology of Attention.* Hove: Psychology Press.

Suh, E.M., Diener, E. and Fujita, F. (1996) 'Events and subjective well-being: Only recent events matter', *Journal of Personality and Social Psychology*, 70, 1091–102.

Suls, J. and Martin, R. (2005) 'The daily life of the garden-variety neurotic: Reactivity, stressor exposure, mood spillover, and maladaptive coping', *Journal of Personality*, 73(6), 1485–509.

Surguladze, A., Brammer, M.J., Young, A.W., Andrew, C., Travis, M.J., Williams, S.C.R. and Phillips, M.L. (2003) 'A preferential increase in the extrastriate response to signals of danger', *Neuroimage*, 19, 1317–28.

Surguladze, S., Russell, T., Kucharska-Pietura, K., Travis, M., Giampietro, V., David, A. and Phillips, M. (2003) 'A reversal of the normal pattern of parahippocampal response to neutral and fearful faces is associated with reality distortion in schizophrenia', *Biological Psychiatry*, 60, 423–31.

Sutton, S.K. and Davidson, R.J. (1997) 'Prefrontal brain asymmetry: A biological substrate of the behavioral approach and inhibition systems', *Psychological Science*, 8, 204–10.

Tackett, J.L. (2006) 'Evaluating models of the personality-psychopathology relationship in children and adolescents', *Clinical Psychology Review*, 26, 584–99.

Talarico, J. and Rubin, D.C. (2003) 'Confidence, not consistency, characterizes flashbulb memories', *Psychological Science*, 14, 455–61.

Tamir, M. and Robinson, M.D. (2007) 'The happy spotlight: Positive mood and selective attention to rewarding information', *Personality and Social Psychology Bulletin*, 33, 1124–36.

Taylor, S.E. (1983) 'Adjustment to threatening events: A theory of cognitive adaptation', *American Psychologist*, 38, 1161–73.

Taylor, S.E. and Brown, J.D. (1988) 'Illusion and well-being: A social psychological perspective on mental health', *Psychological Bulletin*, 103, 193–210.

Teasdale, J.D. and Barnard, P.J. (1993) *Affect, Cognition and Change: Re-modelling Depressive Thought.* Hove: Lawrence Erlbaum.

Teasdale, J.D. and Russell, M.L. (1983) 'Differential effects of induced mood on the recall of positive, negative and neutral words', *British Journal of Clinical Psychology*, 22, 163–71.

Teasdale, J.D., Segal, Z.V., Williams J.M.G., Ridgeway, V.A., Soulsby, J.M. and Lau, M.A. (2000) 'Prevention of relapse/recurrence in major depression by mindfulness-based cognitive therapy', *Journal of Consulting and Clinical Psychology*, 68, 615–23.

Thayer, J.F. and Lane, R.D. (2000) 'A model of neurovisceral integration in emotion regulation and dysregulation', *Journal of Affective Disorders*, 61, 201–16.

Thayer, R.E. (1989) *The Biopsychology of Mood and Arousal.* New York: Oxford University Press.

Thayer, R.E. (1996) *The Origin of Everyday Moods.* New York: Oxford University Press.

Thayer, R.E., Newman, J.R. and McClain, T.M. (1994) 'Self-regulation of mood: Strategies for changing a bad mood, raising energy, and reducing tension', *Journal of Personality and Social Psychology*, 67, 910–25.

Thomas, A. and Chess, S. (1977) *Temperament and Development.* New York: Brunner.

Thompson, C.P., Skowronski, J.J., Larsen, S. and Betz, A. (1996) *Autobiographical Memory: Remembering What and Remembering When.* New York: Erlbaum.

Thompson, R.A. (1990) 'Emotion and self-regulation', in R.A. Thompson (ed.), *Socioemotional Development.* Lincoln: University of Nebraska Press.

Thompson, R.A. (1994) 'Emotion regulation: A theme in search of definition', *Monographs of the Society for Research in Child Development*, 59, 25.

Tipples, J. (2006) 'Fear and fearfulness potentiate automatic orienting to eye gaze', *Cognition & Emotion*, 20, 309–20.

Tomarken, A.J., Davidson, R.J., Wheeler, R.E. and Doss, R.C. (1992) 'Individual differences in anterior brain asymmetry and fundamental dimensions of emotion', *Journal of Personality and Social Psychology*, 62, 676–87.

Tomkins, S.S. (1962) *Affect, Imagery, and Consciousness: Vol 1. The Positive Affects.* New York: Springer.

Tomkins, S.S. (1963) *Affect, Imagery, and Consciousness: Vol 2. The Negative Affects.* New York: Springer.

Tomkins, S.S. (1984) 'Affect theory', in K.R. Scherer and P. Ekman (eds), *Approaches to Emotion.* Hilldale, NJ: Erlbaum.

Tomkins, S.S. and McCarter, R. (1964) 'What and where are the primary affects: Some evidence for a theory', *Perceptual and Motor Skills*, 18, 119–58.

Tooby, J. and Cosmides, L. (1990) 'The past explains the present: Emotional adaptations and the structure of ancestral environments', *Ethology and Sociobiology*, 11(4–5), 375–424.

Tooby, J. and Cosmides, L. (2000) 'Toward mapping the evolved functional organization of mind and brain', in M.S. Gazzaniga (ed.), *The New Cognitive Neurosciences*, 2nd edn. Cambridge, MA: MIT Press.

Toronchuk, J.A. and Ellis, G.F.R. (2007) 'Disgust: Sensory affect or primary emotion', *Cognition & Emotion*, 21, 1799–1818.

Treisman, A. (1988) 'Features and objects: The Fourteenth Bartlett Memorial Lecture', *Quarterly Journal of Experimental Psychology*, 40A, 201–37.

Triandis, H.C. (1989) 'The self and social behavior in differing cultural contexts', *Psychological Review*, 96, 506–20.

Tsang, J. (2006) 'Gratitude and prosocial behavior: An experimental test of gratitude', *Cognition & Emotion*, 20, 138–48.

Tugade, M.M. and Fredrickson, B.L. (2004) 'Positive emotions and health', in N. Anderson (ed.), *Encyclopedia of Health and Behavior.* Thousand Oaks, CA: Sage.

Tugade, M.M., Fredrickson, B.L. and Feldman Barrett, L. (2004) 'Psychological resilience and emotional granularity: Examining the benefits of positive emotions on coping and health', *Journal of Personality*, 72, 1161–90.

Turner, S.M., Beidel, D.C. and Wolff, P.L. (1996) 'Is behavioral inhibition related to the anxiety disorders?', *Clinical Psychology Review*, 16, 57–172.

Turner, S.W., Bowie, C., Dunn, G., Shapo, L. and Yule, W. (2003) 'Mental health of Kosovan Albanian refugees in the UK', *British Journal of Psychiatry*, 182, 444–8.

Turner, T. and Ortony, A. (1992) 'Basic emotions: Can conflicting criteria converge?', *Psychological Review*, 99, 566–71.

Ucros, C.G. (1989) 'Mood state-dependent memory: A meta-analysis', *Cognition & Emotion*, 3, 139–67.

Urry, H.L., Nitschke, J.B., Dolski, I., Jackson, D.C., Dalton, K.M., Mueller, C.J., Rosenkranz, M.A., Ryff, C.D., Singer, B.H. and Davidson, R.J. (2004) 'Making a life worth living: Neural correlates of well-being', *Psychological Science*, 15, 367–72.

Urry, H.L., van Reekum, C.M., Johnstone, T., Kalin, N.H., Thurow, M.E., Schaefer, H.S. et al. (2006) 'Amygdala and ventromedial prefrontal cortex are inversely coupled during regulation of negative affect and predict the diurnal pattern of cortisol secretion among older adults', *Journal of Neuroscience*, 26, 4415– 25.

van Reekum, C.M., Urry, H.L., Johnstone, T., Thurow, M.E., Frye, C.J., Jackson, C.A., Schaefer, H.S., Alexander, A.L. and Davidson, R.J. (2007) 'Individual differences in amygdala and ventromedial prefrontal cortex activity are associated with evaluation speed and psychological well-being', *Journal of Cognitive Neuroscience*, 19, 237–48.

Varela, F.J., Thompson, E. and Rosch, E. (1991) *The Embodied Mind: Cognitive Science and Human Experience*. Cambridge, MA: MIT Press.

Velten, E. (1968) 'A laboratory task for induction of mood states', *Behaviour Research and Therapy*, 6, 473–82.

Vuilleumier, P. (2005a) 'How brains beware: Neural mechanisms of emotional attention', *Trends in Cognitive Sciences*, 9, 585–94.

Vuilleumier, P. (2005b) 'Staring fear in the face', *Nature*, 433, 22–3.

Vuilleumier, P. and Pourtois, G. (2007) 'Distributed and interactive brain mechanisms during emotion face perception: Evidence from functional neuroimaging', *Neuropsychologia*, 45, 174–94.

Vuilleumier, P. and Schwartz, S. (2001) 'Emotional facial expressions capture attention', *Neurology*, 56(2), 153–8.

Vuilleumier, P., Armony, J.L., Clarke, K., Husain, M., Driver, J. and Dolan, R.J. (2002) 'Neural response to emotional faces with and without awareness: Event-related fMRI in a parietal patient with visual extinction and spatial neglect', *Neuropsychologia*, 40, 2156–66.

Vuilleumier, P., Armony, J.L., Driver, J. and Dolan, R.J. (2001) 'Effects of attention and emotion on face processing in the human brain: an event-related fMRI study', *Neuron*, 30, 829–41.

Vuilleumier, P., Richardson, M.P., Armony, J.L., Driver, J. and Dolan, R.J. (2004) 'Distant influences of amygdala lesion on visual cortical activation during emotional face processing', *Nature Neuroscience*, 7, 1271–8.

Wachtel, S.R., Ortengren, A. and de Wit, H. (2002) 'The effects of acute haloperidol or risperidone on subjective responses to methamphetamine in healthy volunteers', *Drug Alcohol Depend*, 68, 23–33.

Wager, T.D., Phan, K.L., Liberzon, I. and Taylor, S.F. (2003) 'Valence, gender, and lateralization of functional brain anatomy in emotion: A meta-analysis of findings from neuroimaging', *NeuroImage*, 19, 513–31.

Walker, D.L., Ressler, K.L., Lu, K.T. and Davis, M. (2002) 'Facilitation of conditioned fear extinction by systemic administration or intra-amygdala infusions of d-cycloserine as assessed with fear-potentiated startle in rats', *Journal of Neuroscience*, 22, 2343–51.

Walker, W.R., Vogl, R.J. and Thompson, C.P. (1997) 'Autobiographical memory: Unpleasantness fades faster than pleasantness over time', *Applied Cognitive Psychology*, 11, 399–413.

Walker, W.R., Skowronski, J.J. and Thompson, C.P. (2003) 'Life is good – and memory helps to keep it that way', *Review of General Psychology*, 7, 203–10.

Ward, L.M. (2002) *Dynamical Cognitive Science*. Cambridge, MA: MIT Press.

Watkins, P.C. (2004) 'Gratitude and subjective well-being', in R.A. Emmons and M.E. McCullough (eds), *The Psychology of Gratitude*. New York: Oxford University Press.

Watkins, P.C., Mathews, A., Williamson, D.A. and Fuller, R.D. (1992) 'Mood-congruent memory in depression: Emotional priming or elaboration?', *Journal of Abnormal Psychology*, 101, 581–6.

Watkins, P.C., Vache, K., Verney, S.P., Muller, S. and Mathews, A. (1996) 'Unconscious mood-congruent memory bias in depression', *Journal of Abnormal Psychology*, 105, 34–41.

Watson, D. (1988) 'Intraindividual and interindividual analyses of positive and negative affect: Their relation to health complaints, perceived stress, and daily activities', *Journal of Personality and Social Psychology*, 54, 1020–30.

Watson, D. (2000) *Mood and Temperament*. New York: Guilford Press.

Watson, D. and Clark, L.A. (1984a) 'Negative affectivity: The disposition to experience negative emotional states', *Journal of Personality and Social Psychology*, 60, 927–40.

Watson, D. and Clark, L.A. (1984b) 'Negative affectivity: The disposition to experience unpleasant emotional states', *Psychological Bulletin*, 95, 465–90.

Watson, D. and Clark, L.A. (1994) 'Emotions, moods, traits, and temperaments: Conceptual distinctions and empirical findings', in P. Ekman and R.J. Davidson (eds), *The Nature of Emotion*. New York: Oxford University Press.

Watson, D. and Clark, L.A. (1995) 'Depression and the melancholic temperament', *European Journal of Personality*, 9, 351–66.

Watson, D. and Tellegen, A. (1985) 'Toward a consensual structure of mood', *Psychological Bulletin*, 98, 219–35.

Watson, D., Clark, L.A. and Tellegen, A. (1988) 'Development and validation of brief measures of positive and negative affect: The PANAS Scales', *Journal of Personality and Social Psychology*, 54, 1063–70.

Watson, J.B. (1919) 'A schematic outline of emotions', *Psychological Review*, 26, 165–96.

Watts, F.N., McKenna, F.P. et al. (1986) 'Colour naming of phobia-related words', *British Journal of Psychology*, 77, 97–108.

Weiskrantz, L. (1956) 'Behavioural changes associated with ablation of the amygdaloid complex in monkeys', *Journal of Comparative Physiology and Psychology*, 49, 381–91.

Weisz, J.R., Rothbaum, F.M. and Blackburn, T.C. (1984) 'Standing out and standing in – the psychology of control in America and Japan', *American Psychologist*, 39, 955–69.

Wells, A. and Matthews, G. (1994) *Attention and Emotion: A Clinical Perspective*. Hove: Lawrence Erlbaum.

Wessel, I., Meeren, M., Peeters, F., Arntz, A. and Merckelbach, H. (2001) 'Correlates of autobiographical memory specificity: The role of depression, anxiety and childhood trauma', *Behaviour Research and Therapy*, 39, 409–21.

Whalen, P.J., Rauch, S.L. et al. (1998) 'Masked presentations of emotional facial expressions modulate amygdala activity without explicit knowledge', *Journal of Neuroscience*, 18, 411–18.

Wheeler, R.E., Davidson, R.J. et al. (1993) 'Frontal brain asymmetry and emotional reactivity: A biological substrate of affective style', *Psychophysiology*, 30(1), 82–9.

Whittle, S., Allen, N.B., Lubman, D. and Yucel, M. (2006) 'The neuroanatomical basis of affective temperament: Towards a better understanding of psychopathology', *Neuroscience and Biobehavioural Reviews*, 30, 511–25.

Wierzbicka, A. (1994) 'Emotion, language, and cultural scripts', in S. Kitayama and H.R. Markus (eds), *Emotion and Culture: Empirical Studies of Mutual Influence*. Washington, DC: American Psychological Association.

Wierzbicka, A. (1995) *Emotions across Languages and Cultures: Diversity and Universals.* Cambridge: Cambridge University Press.

Williams, J.M.G. (2004) 'Experimental cognitive psychology and clinical practice: Autobiographical memory as a paradigm case', in J. Yiend (ed.), *Cognition, Emotion and Psychopathology.* Cambridge: Cambridge University Press.

Williams, J.M.G. and Broadbent, K. (1986) 'Autobiographical memory in suicide attempters', *Journal of Abnormal Psychology*, 95, 144–9.

Williams, J.M.G., Watts, F.N., MacLeod, C.M. and Mathews, A. (1988) *Cognitive Psychology and Emotional Disorders.* Chichester: Wiley.

Williams, J.M.G., Watts, F.N., MacLeod, C.M. and Mathews, A. (1997) *Cognitive Psychology and Emotional Disorders*, 2nd edn. Chichester: Wiley.

Williams, J.M.G., Mathews, A. and MacLeod, C.M. (1996) 'The emotional Stroop task and psychopathology', *Psychological Bulletin*, 120(1), 3–24.

Williams, L.M., Phillips, M.L., Brammer, M.J., Skerrett, D., Lagopoulos, J., Rennie, C., Bahramali, H., Olivieri, G., David, A.S, Peduto, A. and Gordon, E. (2001) 'Arousal dissociates amygdala and hippocampal fear responses: Evidence from simultaneous fMRI and skin conductance recording', *NeuroImage*, 14, 1070–9.

Williams, R.B., Marchuk, D.A. et al. (2003) 'Serotonin-related gene polymorphisms and central nervous system serotonin function', *Neuropsychopharmacology*, 28(3), 533–41.

Williams, W.A., Shoaf, S.E., Hommer, D., Rawlings, R, and Linnoila, M. (1999) 'Effects of acute tryptophan depletion on plasma and cerebrospinal fluid tryptophan and 5-hydroxyindoleacetic acid in normal volunteers', *Journal of Neurochemistry*, 72, 1641–7.

Wilson, E. and MacLeod, C. (2003) 'Contrasting two accounts of anxiety-linked attentional bias: Selective attention to varying levels of stimulus threat intensity', *Journal of Abnormal Psychology*, 112, 212–18.

Wilson, E.J., MacLeod, C., Mathews, A. and Rutherford, E.M. (2006) 'The causal role of interpretive bias in anxiety reactivity', *Journal of Abnormal Psychology*, 115, 103–11.

Wilson, T.D. and Gilbert, D.T. (2003) 'Affective forecasting', in M.P. Zanna (ed.), *Advances in Experimental Social Psychology*, vol. 35. San Diego: Academic Press.

Wilson, T.D. and Gilbert, D.T. (2005) 'Affective forecasting: Knowing what to want', *Current Directions in Psychological Science*, 14, 131–4.

Winston, J.S. and Dolan, R.J. (2004) 'Feeling states in emotion: Functional imaging evidence', in A.S.R. Manstead, N.H. Frijda and A.H. Fischer (eds), *Feelings and Emotions: The Amsterdam Symposium.* New York: Cambridge University Press.

Winston, J.S., Gottfried, J.A., Kilner, J.M. and Dolan, R.J. (2005) 'Integrated neural representations of odor intensity and affective valence in human amygdala', *Journal of Neuroscience*, 25, 8903–7.

Winston, J.S., O'Doherty, J. and Dolan, R.J. (2003) 'Common and distinct neural responses during direct and incidental processing of multiple facial emotions', *NeuroImage*, 20, 84–97.

Wright, J. and Mischel, W. (1982) 'Influence of affect on cognitive social learning variables', *Journal of Personality and Social Psychology*, 43, 901–14.

Wundt, W. (1874/1905) *Principles of Physiological Psychology*, 5th edn. Leipzig: Engelmann.

Yiend, J. (2004) *Cognition, Emotion and Psychopathology: Theoretical, Empirical and Clinical Approaches.* Cambridge: Cambridge University Press.

Yiend, J. and Mathews, A. (2001) 'Anxiety and attention to threatening pictures', *Quarterly Journal of Experimental Psychology. A, Human Experimental Psychology*, 54(3), 665–81.

Yiend, J. and Mathews, A. (2002) 'Induced biases in the processing of emotional information', in S.P. Shohov (ed.), *Advances in Psychology Research*, Vol. 13. New York: Nova Science Publishers.

Yik, M.S.M., Russell, J.A. and Feldman Barrett, L. (1999) 'Integrating four structures of current mood into a circumplex: Integration and beyond', *Journal of Personality and Social Psychology*, 77, 600–19.

Yonelinas, A.P. (2002) 'The nature of recollection and familiarity: A review of 30 years of research', *Journal of Memory and Language*, 46, 441–517.

Zajonc, R.B. (1968) 'Attitudinal effects of mere exposure', *Journal of Personality and Social Psychology*, 9, 1–29.

Zajonc, R.B. (1980) 'Feeling and thinking: Preferences need no inferences', *American Psychologist*, 2, 151–76.

Zajonc, R. (1984) 'On the primacy of affect', *American Psychologist*, 39, 117–24.

Zajonc, R.B. (1998) 'Emotion', in D.T. Gilbert, S.T. Fiske and G. Lindzey (eds), *The Handbook of Social Psychology*. Boston: McGraw-Hill.

Zajonc, R.B. (2000) 'Feeling and thinking: Closing the debate over the independence of affect', in J.P. Forgas (ed.), *Feeling and Thinking: The Role of Affect in Social Cognition*. New York: Cambridge University Press.

Zautra, A.J., Affleck, G. et al. (2005) 'Dynamic approaches to emotion and stress in everyday life: Bolger and Zuckerman reloaded with positive as well as negative affects', *Journal of Personality*, 73, 1511–38.

Zautra, A.J., Smith, B., Affleck, G.G. and Tennen, H. (2001) 'Examinations of chronic pain and affect relationships: Applications of a dynamic model of affect', *Journal of Consulting and Clinical Psychology*, 69, 786–95.

Zelenski, J.M. and Larsen, R.J. (2002) 'Predicting the future: How affect-related personality traits influence likelihood judgments of future events', *Personality and Social Psychology Bulletin*, 28(7), 1000–10.

Zillmann, D. (1979) *Hostility and Aggression*. Hillsdale, NJ: Erlbaum.

NAME INDEX

SUBJECT INDEX